HEGEMONIC GLOBALISATION

In loving memory of my Grandparents

Hegemonic Globalisation
U.S. centrality and global strategy in the emerging world order

THANH DUONG

LONDON AND NEW YORK

First published 2002 by Ashgate Publishing

Reissued 2018 by Routledge
2 Park Square, Milton Park, Abingdon, Oxon OX14 4RN
711 Third Avenue, New York, NY 10017, USA

Routledge is an imprint of the Taylor & Francis Group, an informa business

Copyright © Thanh Duong 2002

The author has asserted his moral right under the Copyright, Designs and Patents Act, 1988, to be identified as the author of this work.

All rights reserved. No part of this book may be reprinted or reproduced or utilised in any form or by any electronic, mechanical, or other means, now known or hereafter invented, including photocopying and recording, or in any information storage or retrieval system, without permission in writing from the publishers.

Notice:
Product or corporate names may be trademarks or registered trademarks, and are used only for identification and explanation without intent to infringe.

Publisher's Note
The publisher has gone to great lengths to ensure the quality of this reprint but points out that some imperfections in the original copies may be apparent.

Disclaimer
The publisher has made every effort to trace copyright holders and welcomes correspondence from those they have been unable to contact.

A Library of Congress record exists under LC control number: 2001099955

ISBN 13: 978-1-138-71981-1 (hbk)
ISBN 13: 978-1-138-71978-1 (pbk)
ISBN 13: 978-1-315-19527-8 (ebk)

Contents

List of Tables and Appendices   ix
Abstract   xi
Acknowledgements   xiii

INTRODUCTION

An Analysis of the United States' Global Strategy in the Emerging World Order   3

PART I: THEORY AND METHODOLOGY

1   A Conceptual Framework and Principles of Inquiry   17
Problems for Inquiry: The Limits of 'Theory'   17
Mode of Analysis   20
Theory and Practice   23
Conclusion   31

2   An Inquiry into Power   34
The Four Spheres of Power   37
The 'Realist' Tradition   40
Realism: First Image   42
Realism: Second Image   45
'Liberalism' and Power   47
'Marxism' and Power   50
Other Definitions of Power and Conflicting Interests   55

3   An Inquiry into Hegemony   57
Introduction   57
Definitions and Theories of Hegemony   57
(Neo)-Gramscian Hegemony   59
The Long-Cycle Approach to World Power   62
Hegemonic Stability Theory   64
The 'Final Word' on Hegemony?   66

PART II: THE DEBATE AND THE CHALLENGE

4 The 'Design' of the International System and 'the U.S. Hegemony' After the Collapse of the Bretton Woods' Fixed Exchange Rate System — 71
Introduction — 71
Section I: The U.S. as 'Chief Architect' of the International Political and Economic System — 71
Section II: The Declinist-Renewal Debate — 75
Geopolitical Decline — 75
Economic Decline — 76
Section III: The 'Realists' Rejection of the Declinist School — 78
The 'Liberals' Rejection of the Declinist School — 82
The Neo-Gramscian/Marxist Rejection of the Declinist School — 84
Section IV: The End of the Cold War and the Emergence of 'Global Hegemony' — 85
Conclusion — 87

5 Balance of Power or Hegemony? — 89
Introduction — 89
The Balance of Power Strategy and the Return to Multipolarity — 90
Eight Arguments for the Balance of Power — 92
Responses to the Balance of Power Strategy — 95
The Liberal Response to Balance of Power, and Their Idea of 'Liberal Hegemony' — 103
Marxist Critique of Balance of Power and Liberal Hegemony — 106
Conclusion — 107

6 Hegemonic Globalisation: The United States and the Integration of the Great Powers — 110
Introduction — 110
The Determinates of Hegemonic Globalisation — 111
The United States as the 'Centre' — 120
Conclusion — 125

PART III: THE CONTENDERS IN THE EMERGING WORLD ORDER

7 Russia: 'Political Backlash Without Economic Conversion?' — 129
Introduction — 129
Historical Political Background Following the Collapse of the Soviet Union — 130
Liberal Economics: The Collapse of Egalitarianism — 132

	The Problems of Crime and Corruption	134
	Leadership Failures	137
	Nationalistic Economic Policy	138
	Nationalistic Foreign Policy	139
	The 'West's' Perception of Russia	148
	Conclusion	153
8	**The PRC and the U.S. in the 21st Century: 'Preventing the Clash of Civilisations'**	**158**
	Introduction	158
	Part I: From 'Celestial Kingdom' to 'Third World' Country	161
	Historical Background of Sino-U.S Relations	163
	The Communist Split and the Convenient Alignment	166
	Part II: Sino-U.S. Relations in the Post-Cold War	171
	The New Seers of Doom	172
	Perceptions of 'International' Law and the 'International' System	174
	Re-evaluating the Seers of Doom	176
	Chinese Military Power	180
	'Greater' China?	183
	Taiwan: Back to Sarajevo, 1914?	184
	The China Challenge: Has the Cycles of Great Powers Finally Broken?	187
	A 'Democratic Peace'?	191
	Historic Development Settings for Democracy	194
	Conclusion	197
9	**The European Union: The 'Grand Plan' or Just 'Hanging Together'?**	**200**
	Introduction	200
	Section I: U.S. Strategy and European Integration	201
	Section II: Post-Cold War Relations Between the EU and the USA	205
	The EU as a Challenger	206
	Why the EU is Not a Challenger	209
	Section III: U.S-EU-NATO and Russia	212
	Section IV: Joint Condominium?	215
	Conclusion	225
10	**U.S-Japan Relations: 'The Anchor in the East'**	**228**
	Introduction	228
	Section I: The 'Making' of Post-1945 Japan: 'Compromised Sovereignty'	229
	The Emerging Economic Power and the Emerging Tensions	231
	The 'Collapse' of the Japanese Challenge	235
	Why Japan is Not a Challenger	236
	The 'Re-designing' of Japan, Again	238

Section II 243
The Changing Security Regime 243
Is Japan a (U.S.) Economic System Supporter? 249
Is Japan a 'Liberal Democratic' Promoter? 251
Unfinished Business 254
Conclusion 255

11 **U.S. Grand Strategy in the Emerging World Order:
'The Sun and Its Planets'** 257
Aspects of U.S. Foreign Policy Preferences in the Post-Cold War Era 265
The 'Neo-Gramscian' Strategy of Hegemonic Globalisation 268
Conclusion 270

PART IV: CONCLUSION

Hegemonic Globalisation: 'The Highest Stage of Capitalism'? 275
The Complexity of U.S. Centrality 277
Conclusion 285

Appendices 289
Bibliography 307
Index 359

List of Tables and Appendices

Tables

1.1	A 'Simple' View of the Mainstream Theories in International Relations	29
1.2	A 'Complex' View of the Multiple Theories in International Relations	30
5.1	The Great Powers, 1700-2000	102
6.1	The Diplomatic, Political and Military Relations of the Five Leading Powers	116
6.2	The Economic and Trade Relations / Cultural and Educational Exchanges	117
6.3	The Relations Among the Five Major Powers	118
8.1	The PRC v the U.S.A: A Comparison	181-182

Appendices

1A	A Comparison of Capabilities Amongst the Five Leading Powers in the World in 2000	290
1B	U.S. Troops Deployed Overseas	291
2A	Arms Trade (Value of Arms Deliveries 1996)	293
2B	Arms Trade (Value of Arms Deliveries 1996)	294
3A	Purchasing Power Parity (PPP) Exchange Rate GNP ($U.S. bn) in 1996	295
3B	Market Exchange Rate GNP ($U.S. bn) in 1996	296
3C	GDP ($U.S. bn) in 1999	297
3D	GDP ($U.S. bn) in 1999	298
4A	World Defence Expenditure, 1985 by Proportion ($U.S. m) (percentage)	299
4B	World Defence Expenditure, 1996 by Proportion ($U.S. m) (percentage)	300
Russia, 7A	Exchange Rate, 1998	301
Russia, 7B	Inflation Trends (% Change) and Unemployment Rate	302
Russia, 7C	External Sovereign Debt (mid-1998)	303
Russia, 7D	Ethnic Russians Outside Russia	304
Russia, 7E	Russian Forces Abroad	305
9A	Membership of European Security Organisations	306

Abstract

This book is organised into three main sections. The first section investigates strategies of research and methods of inquiry to understanding theory and practice. The thesis contends that instead of dogmatically following any one theory, the thesis utilises the insights of several theories to explain the 'specific' and the 'general' of international affairs. The thesis examines the concepts of power and hegemony in relation to the U.S. position in the international system in the contemporary period.

Part two interrogates the U.S. strategy during the Cold War in laying the foundations for global power, i.e., via the development of global political/military alliances, international economic regimes and institutions. With theories, concepts and empirical evidence developed, the thesis refutes the positions proposed by the 'declinists' from the 1970s and the promoters of 'balance of power' theories. Instead of decline and drifting towards global balance of power, the thesis demonstrates how the U.S. is the 'centre' power that is attempting to 'hegemonically globalise' the entire international system.

To evaluate hegemonic globalisation, part three analyses four major powers/regions: Russia, the PRC, the EU, and Japan, as case studies in their respective historical, political, economic, cultural and geopolitical relations with the United States. Each case study examines the tangible and intangible sources of their relationship and inquires into the tensions and potential resistance to U.S. hegemonic globalisation. In evaluating the power relations of the 'great powers', the section illustrates how the 'great powers' are *not* actually challenging the 'hegemonic globalisation' strategy of the United States per se, but are themselves engaged in it for their own power interests. Therewithal by increasing their power interests by incorporating within the hegemonic globalisation, they inadvertently reinforce the U.S.-led hegemonic globalisation even further.

The conclusion draws on the arguments developed and evaluates the validity of the mode of analysis as an explanation and understanding of the contemporary U.S. power position and U.S. relations with its main contenders in world politics.

Acknowledgements

This book began in 1995-6 with my MA dissertation, and later developed into my PhD thesis, which was completed in 2000. Many of the events that have happened since, in itself, would probably deserve another book. Keeping abreast of events has not only been challenging to the journalists and commentators – but, now increasingly to the 'academic' arena, as well. This book was, however, never meant to be journalistic. It is a deep and a careful study of the United States' foreign policy strategy in the emerging world order, and its relations with the five leading powers in the world. The events of September 11, and the war with the Taleban and al-Qaida that ensued, may, at first glance, seem to over-shadow issues. This, however, is not the case. Instead, it reinforces the contours of the arguments developed in this book on the nature of the United States power and global strategy in the emerging world order. My hope is that the significance of this power has been brought into sharper relief.

In the years, I have been most fortunate to be under the supervision of Dr. Barry K. Gills, a premier thinker in the field of international relations, international political economy, and history. I am greatly indebted to him for his analytical depth, wealth of knowledge, unreserved time, and guidance in academia and in life in general.

I would like to thank my family for generously supporting me in completing this work. To my parents, who put total belief in me and have never faltered in confidence, I thank them. To my grandparents (who both passed away whilst I was completing this book), who, like my parents have put total faith and conviction in me. I dedicate this book in their memory. To my uncle Toan and his family in Canada, who have financed me most generously throughout my academic years, I thank them. To my brother, Sam, and sisters, Binh and Diana. I am deeply grateful to them, for their patience and understanding. To my auntie Quynh and her husband Cuong for generously funding my fieldwork in China. I thank them. Finally to Michelle, whose delightful wit, keen editing, and loving patience and care helped me tremendously. Thank you.

I would also like to extend my appreciation and gratitude to the following individuals.

Anna Watson for proofreading large parts of my dissertation. She has been unreserved with her time and kindness. Thank you.

The Department of Politics at the University of Newcastle has been helpful with advice and criticism. For this, I would like to thank Professor Tim Gray, Dr. Anthony Zito, Dr. Randall Germain, Professor Reinhard Drifte, Dr. James Babb, to the politics department's secretaries Margaret Hill and Catherine Aitkin, and finally to Roderick Hague, who suggested that my thesis should be published.

Professor Michael Cox, in directing me to some valuable sources in the United States. His suggestions opened new doors for me whilst I was there.

Professors Henry Nau and G. John Ikenberry for their valuable time and patience when I was in Washington, D.C.

Dr. Erik Peterson of the CSIS, who also helped open doors in the United States. I thank him for introducing me to Dr. Hans Bennindijk and anonymous persons in the State Department, the Treasury, and the Pentagon. I thank all the persons for their valuable time and patience. In addition, I would like to thank all the internees in Washington, from whom I gained valuable and interesting insights into the 'grass-root' operations of the United States power base.

The Hoang family in China for showing me some fascinating insights into the Chinese people and country. I would also like to thank the La family for providing generous accommodation and friendship during my stay in New York.

Ashgate Publishing Ltd for the professionalism and guidance in getting this book published.

To my friends, associates and colleagues for their friendship and support throughout the years, obviously, there are too many to mention here.

Finally, I thank all my previous teachers and the books I read throughout my life. There are obviously too many to mention here, but, I would like to give special credit to all the citations that are made in this book. The bibliography should be seen as a thank note to all the authors, and also be seen as a source for further reading. However, the full responsibility or shortfall of what follows are mine alone.

Thanh Duong

INTRODUCTION

An Analysis of the United States' Global Strategy in the Emerging World Order

For, if Fortune ordains that a powerful and enlightened people should form a republic, – which by its very nature is inclined to perpetual peace – this would serve as a centre of federal union for other states wishing to join, and thus secure conditions of freedom among the states in accordance with the idea of the law of nations. Gradually, through different unions of this kind, the federation would extend further and further.
Immanual Kant, 1795, *Perpetual Peace* (translated by M. Campbell Smith, 1903: 135).

Despite all the difficulties, the United States is at the most fortunate juncture in all its favoured history. As the sole global superpower, it has an unprecedented opportunity. For those with parts to play in the saga of 21st century American statecraft, not to infuse our power with farsighted purpose, not to think and act strategically because of its difficulty, would be a moral abdication of the worst sort. All that is necessary for evil to triumph is that good men and women do nothing.
Fundamentals of Statecraft, obtained from The U.S. National War College, Academic Year 1998-9.

The need of a constantly expanding market for its products chases the bourgeoisie over the whole surface of the globe. It must nestle everywhere, settle everywhere, establish connections everywhere. . . . The bourgeoisie, by rapid improvement of all instruments of production, by the immensely facilitated means of communication, draws all, even the most barbarian, nations into civilisation. . . . It compels all [nations] to introduce what it calls civilisation into their midst.
Karl Marx and Friedrich Engels, *The Communist Manifesto* (translated by A.J.P. Taylor, 1967: 83-4).

Capitalism and democracy are forces for peace . . . the further capitalism and democracy develop, the more imperialism will disappear.
Joseph A. Schumpeter cited in M.W. Doyle, 1997: 245.

The objective of U.S. government . . . in the international sphere has, quite simply been attainment of universal power by the United States over every capitalist country.
Michael Hudson, 1968: ix.

It was never the Soviet Union but the United States itself that is the true revolutionary power. We believe that our institutions must confine all others to the ash heap of history. We lead an economic system that has effectively buried every other form of production and distribution – leaving great wealth and sometimes great ruin in its wake. The cultural messages we transmit through Hollywood and

McDonald's go out across the world to capture and also undermine other societies. Unlike more traditional conquerors, we are not content merely to subdue others: we insist that they be like us. And of course for their own good. We are the world's most relentless proselytisers. The world must be democratic. It must be capitalistic. It must be tied into the subversive messages of the World Wide Web. No wonder many feel threatened by what we represent.
Ronald Steel cited in Thomas Friedman, 1999: 310-11.

Introduction

When the Soviet empire became exhausted in 1989-91, the United States was left as the lone superpower. What has developed since is what some analysts have envisioned as the 'unipolar moment'.[1] Not since the times of Imperial Rome, ancient China and the Mongol empire has one power towered over others in such a manner. Krauthammer argued that 'the true geopolitical structure of the post-Cold War world . . . *is* a single pole of world power that consists of the United States at the apex of the industrial West' (1990/1: 24). Yet, within two years, Kenneth Waltz (1993), Robert Jervis (1993), Christopher Layne (1993), Henry Kissinger (1994) and others argue that the unipolar moment was an illusion; that the United States should not seek international primacy, but should instead prepare itself for a world of multipolarity and the mechanics of balance of power in military and economic affairs.[2] In 1996, John Ruggie queried the assumptions of primacy in American power and raised the question: 'does the current preponderance of American military power define an unipolar world, or, rather, does the rapid and vast economic growth of nations such as Japan and Germany indicate that we are at the beginning of a new multipolar balance of power?' (1996: ix; see also J. Scott, ed.,

---

[1] Charles Krauthammer (1990/91), 'The Unipolar Moment', *Foreign Affairs*, Vol. 70, No. 1, pp. 23-33, also in G. Allison and G. Treverton (Eds.) *Rethinking America's Security: Beyond Cold War to New World Order* (W.W. Norton); Alfredo Valladao (1993/96), *The Twenty-First Century Will be American* (Verso); Joshua Muravchik (1991), *Exporting Democracy: Fulfilling America's Destiny* (The AEI Press); Joshua Muravchik (1996) *The Imperative of American Leadership: A Challenge to Neo-Isolationism* (The AEI Press).
[2] The advocates of a balance of power scenario include, Robert Jervis (1993), 'International Primacy: Is the Game Worth the Candle?' *International Security*, Vol. 17, No. 4, pp. 52-67; Christopher Layne (1993), 'The Unipolar Illusion: Why New Great Powers Will Rise', *International Security*, Vol. 17, No. 4, pp. 5-51; Fred Halliday and Justin Rosenberg (1998), 'Interview with Kenneth Waltz', *Review of International Studies*, Vol. 24, No. 3, pp. 371-86; Henry Kissinger (1994) *Diplomacy* (Simon and Schuster); John J. Mearsheimer (1994/95), 'The False Promise of International Institutions', *International Security*, Vol. 19, No. 3, pp. 5-49; Christopher Layne (1997), 'From Preponderance to Offshore Balancing: America's Future Grand Strategy', *International Security*, Vol. 22, No. 1, pp. 86-124; Christopher Layne (1998), 'Rethinking American Grand Strategy: Hegemony or Balance of Power in the Twenty-First Century?' *World Policy Journal*, summer, pp. 8-41.

1998: 15). This is a fascinating question, because it addresses the conundrum of the transformation of the international system from one of bipolarity (between the Soviet Union and the United States), into a conjuncture of both unipolarity and multipolarity. This thesis attempts to analyse the prevailing position of the United States in the international system today. It inquires into the issue as to whether the U.S. power position has become 'hegemonic' (or 'unipolar'), or is the U.S. just one amongst many great powers in a multipolar world order (even if/or primus inter pares).[3]

In seeking to evaluate the conflicting views, this thesis asks: if the world is militarily unipolar, can we speak of an economically multipolar balance of power? Moreover, if such is the case what are the significance of international economic interdependence and the phenomenon of 'globalisation'? What are the connection and significance of a militarily unipolar world and an economically multipolar world? In addition, why was it that with the existence of the Soviet Union and the conflict of the international system in a bipolar system, scholars[4] often asserted the existence of a hegemonic power, i.e., the United States? Why is it that with the collapse of the Cold War bipolar system, the United States is not considered a hegemonic state?[5]

Instead, 'There is now a global hegemony shared by three principle core

---

[3] Josef Joffe (1995), '"Bismarck or Britain"?: Towards an American Grand Strategy after Bipolarity', *International Security*, Vol. 19, No. 4, p. 101, cites Samuel Huntington for the term 'uni-multipolarity' to describe the current international order as neither 'multipolar' nor truly 'unipolar'.

[4] For example, Ronald Steel (1967/68), *Pax Americana* (Hamish Hamilton); Michael Hudson (1968), *Super Imperialism: The Economic Strategy of American Empire* (Holt, Rinehart and Winston); J. Kolko and G. Kolko (1972), *The Limits of Power: The World and the United States Foreign Policy* (Harper & Row); V.G. Kiernan (1978), *America: The New Imperialism, From White Settlement to World Hegemony* (Zed Press); Robert W. Cox (1981), 'Social Forces, States and World Order: Beyond International Relations Theory', *Millennium*, Vol. 10, No. 2, pp. 126-55; Susan Strange (1982), 'Still an Extraordinary Power: American Role in a Global Monetary System', in Raymond Lombra and Willar Witte (Eds.) *Political Economy of International and Domestic Monetary Relations* (Iowa University Press); Robert W. Cox (1983), 'Gramsci, Hegemony and International Relations: An Essay in Method', *Millennium*, Vol. 12, No. 2, pp. 162-75; Bruce Russett (1985), 'The Mysterious Case of Vanishing Hegemony; or, Is Mark Twain Really Dead?' *International Organisation*, Vol. 39, No. 2, pp. 207-31; Susan Strange (1987), 'The persistent myth of lost hegemony', *International Organisation*, Vol. 41, No. 4, pp. 551-74; Joseph S. Nye Jr. (1988), 'Underestimating U.S. Strength', *Foreign Policy*, Vol. 72, (fall); Henry Nau (1990), *Myth of America's Decline: Leading the World Economy into the 1990s* (Oxford University Press); Joseph S. Nye Jr. (1990), *Bound to Lead: The Changing Nature of American Power* (Basic Books).

[5] James Chace (1992) *The Consequence of the Peace: The New Internationalism and American Foreign Policy* (Oxford University Press); Phil Cerny (1993) *Finance and World Politics: Markets, Regimes and States in the Post-Hegemonic Era* (Edward Elgar); T. Akaha and F. Langdon (Eds.) (1993) *Japan in the Posthegemonic World* (Lynne Reinner); James Chace (1997), 'An Empty Hegemony', *World Policy Journal*, summer, pp. 97-8.

zones of the world economy. This trilateral, or G-3/7 hegemony puts an end to the temporary and somewhat abnormal unipolarism of the Pax Americana and returns the global political economy to a situation of tripolarism similar to that which characterised it at the end of the nineteenth century and in the early twentieth century, with new institutional forms' (Gills in Gill, 1993: 188). The world economy may appear to be trilateral, but at the apex of this nexus of the world economic system is the United States. It lies at the centre of the economic triangle, between the Pacific and Atlantic oceans.

In fact, the United States is by far the most powerful state both militarily and economically in the international system. Further, it commands an extremely favourable position in geopolitical terms, military and diplomatic leverage, financial assets and capital, production capabilities, hi-tech information and 'structural' cultural influences, as well as the increasingly influential use of the American-English language as the primary language for international communication. In addition to this, there is an increasing appearance of a corporate 'transnational class' (K.V. der Pijl, 1984; 1998; S. Gill, 1990; S. Strange, 1988; 1992) intertwining and webbing of ideas and beliefs to other sections of the international community to maintain and expand a U.S.-led capitalist-democratic ideal. This may stand in conflict with the idea of a single state hegemony. However, what this thesis assumes is that the 'transnational class' is comprised of mainly U.S. elites and that others are 'co-opted' allied elites. Basically, the U.S. is the centre that drives or pulls others into this regime.

Moreover, I will contend that the United States is presently the closest to a hegemonic power the modern state system has ever experienced and that, in the main, its influence is being used to enforce more liberal principles for operating the international political/economic system. This is, in part, the geopolitical reality and set of evolving economic arrangements which are also being described as 'globalisation'. This is not to say that the United States does not resort to traditional geo-strategic behaviour if the occasion demands (see Z. Brzezinski, 1997; B. Catley, 1997: 377-99). Yet, some scholars (M. Horsman and A. Marshall, 1994; M. Water, 1995) have contended that the 'forces' of globalisation have set about the decline of the state, thus making geopolitics irrelevant. However, if the state is in decline, where has its power and authority gone to? Has it just 'evaporated'? (S. Strange, 1995: 56). Or, are there other forces in contention? Many scholars have identified multinational corporations (MNCs) and other non-state actors as being responsible for the 'retreat of the state' (S. Strange, 1996). This may appear so in some quarters, but it is not necessarily the whole case, in fact the most proliferating operation in the international system has been the predominance of the United States 'over' others – both state and non-state actors. The U.S. has managed to 'lock' both (most) states and non-state actors into its complex system of intertwining and inter-locking institutions and regimes.

Although the study of 'globalisation' has seen many different variants, and has been well documented elsewhere (see for example, M. Featherstone, 1990; P. Hirst and G. Thompson, 1996; E. Kofman and G. Young, 1996; Baylis and

Smith, 1997; R.J. Holton, 1998; and many others). The interest of this thesis is not in the 'process' of globalisation as such, but the inherent policies that have guided its operation. This is especially evident in the end of the Cold War, where U.S. foreign economic policy has 'guided' the phenomenon of globalisation. Samuel Berger, the Assistant to the U.S. President for National Security Affairs, states: '... I believe President Clinton's most fundamental achievement is that he steered America from the Cold War era to the era of globalization in a way that enhanced not only our power but also our authority' (2000: 39).

Initially, however, the United States may have followed a more nationalistic economic practice to 'reviving' the United States economy. Certainly, in the Bush administration and early stages of the Clinton administration there were (and there still are signs inside the U.S. body politic, such as the billionaire Ross Perot in the Reform Party; labour union interests behind Senator Richard Gephardt; and conservative nationalistic leaders such as Patrick Buchanan) forces that aimed to flirt with the nationalistic economic policies to 'restoring U.S. economic dynamism' (see J. Garten, 1992; L. Thurow, 1992; L. Tyson, 1992). In fact, Clinton had argued that 'U.S. business had not received the support needed or deserved ... in a cut-throat world economy where governments in other countries were actively promoting business' (quoted in M. Cox, 1995: 24). In addition, other major economic powers of the G7, according to David Mulford, the U.S. Treasury under-secretary for international affairs in the Bush administration, 'at this point ... really began to diverge' (in R. Roberts, 1998: 16). This fear was reinforced by the formation of NAFTA by the U.S., Canada, and Mexico, which was believed to formalise a Western Hemispheric regional bloc with countries in Latin America as affiliates. Already in Western Europe, the EU had been endeavouring to become a single political and economic entity. In East Asia, Japan was focusing on developing ties with the region's booming 'tigers' and co-ordinating closer ties with the Association of South East Asian Nations (ASEAN). It was speculated that in regionalising trade, each major power would protect its own needs and interests rather than construct the truly 'global' free market.

Had the United States taken a 'bloc' or neo-mercantilist course, this would have meant a break from post-1945 U.S. economic strategy. It would almost certainly have meant the U.S. losing its central position amongst the 'allies' in Western Europe and East Asia, thus returning it to being another 'great power'. In this perspective, the chain of events that may emerge from the nationalistic economic strategy would probably lead to neo-mercantilistic economic practices emerging from other major capitalist countries as well. The scenario of the 1920s to 1930s, which had seen the 'age of extremes' (E. Hobsbawm, 1995) of revolution, political and economic instability, the Great Depression, and ultimately global war, was speculated to be the most likely outcome. Faced with such a scenario, a nationalistic economic strategy was not a viable option. The alternative was how to promote 'free trade' to best serve U.S. interests (R. Reich, 1991). Therefore, the U.S. strategy not to adopt nationalistic economic policies was designed to help enhance globalisation. The Clinton administration, like the Bush administration earlier, felt that to 'expand' economic liberalism, thence intensifying globalisation, was not just to serve U.S. interests, but to avert neo-mercantilist regional trade practices and their adverse consequences. Michael Cox states,

> ... it would ensure continued U.S. leadership of the world economic system; it would prevent any move by these regions towards self-sufficiency; and it would facilitate the movement towards a more open world economy upon which future U.S. prosperity and influence depended – one idea central to this was globalisation (1995: 24).

The strategy was well orchestrated, and it raised the dilemma that either the U.S. Congress and/or other major powers' decision-makers were to support and legitimise 'globalisation', or alternatively, return to neo-mercantilist bloc formation, thence in probability leading to another great depression and general war. Since no one wants this, the United States was able to create a situation whereby the United States' interest was also a universal interest.[6] The message was to defend the U.S.-led economic liberal order. Any serious challenge from Japan or the EU/Germany would have meant reversion to regional trading blocs, which would have led to a repeat of the 1920s and 30s, with the Great Depression, and then general war. For Japan, this dilemma coincided with a 'decade of recession'. Japan has been unwilling to take a radically different approach – in fear that the consequences will be even worse for Japan. Given the 'Pacific War' episode, the option to 'break out' of the 'U.S.-led system' is unthinkable. The East Asian crisis (1997-9) shows the U.S. significance of U.S. power. The U.S. has demanded conformity from East Asian states to liberalise economics and political practices (M. Mastanduno, 1998; P. Gowan, 1999; B. Gills, 2000). In fact, 'America in many ways is a gatekeeper ... over the choices nations make'. It is not just because of 'globalisation', but because 'we chose to [influence the developments]' (S. Berger, 2000: 24, emphasis added).

In conjunction with this 'globalisation' climate, the United States, despite various claims otherwise, is the sole global military power, being more powerful than the ten next major powers combined in terms of military expenditure (see Appendixes 1A and 4B). Following the dismantlement of the Warsaw Pact and the Soviet Union, there is now no significant military force to balance U.S. supremacy. Although the United States knows it is the most powerful state, it is also aware of the intrigue of power-political diplomacy in the international system. Indeed, Martin Wight had warned, '"[d]ominant power" is not an accepted phrase of diplomacy. The other states in the states-system recognise a dominant power ... either by collaborating with it or by uniting in resistance to it; but hegemony has never been accepted' (1946: 41). Therefore, following the collapse of the Soviet Union and in the wake of the Iraqi-UN/U.S. war, U.S. decision-makers and

---

[6] See E. H. Carr (1939/46/64) *The Twenty Years' Crisis, 1919-1939* (New York: Harper & Row), pp. 75-88, for a parallel of British global strategy in the 19th and early 20th centuries.

academics were extremely reluctant to acknowledge or call for a unipolar world order. Instead, they called for international collaboration and a 'new world order' based on co-operation and consensus.[7] Yet, it was well known that the U.S. was by far the most influential and powerful partner in any collaboration or consensus. What appears to be happening is that the United States has been trying to formulate a new consensus in the international system and even 'cloud over' previous international agreements, whereby it was to become 'legitimate' (L. Brilmayer, 1994) for the United States to act or intervene 'anywhere' in the world when the interest(s) of the United States are/were at stake.

In terms of economic strength, the United States is the largest economy in terms of GDP/GNP (see Appendixes 3A to 3D). Contrary to classical understanding of power politics, where secondary powers often align with each other to balance the dominant power; other powers (i.e., Britain, France, Germany, Japan, countries of the OECD, and even Russia) are in fact themselves involved in an arrangement that is multidimensional and multi-layered, in interdependence with the United States. That is, they co-operate to dominate and determine the direction of 'world peace and prosperity'.

In addition, the United States under Bush,[8] then Clinton, has attempted to reconcile some fundamentals from Cold War strategy, such as the maintenance of international regimes and institutions – e.g., NATO, WB, IMF, GATT (replaced by WTO), and readjusted strategies, such as containment and the policy of deterrence. In place of containment and deterrence policies, the U.S. emphasis on 'selective engagement' in areas of interest. The Bush administration's Defense Strategy for the 1990s: The Regional Defense Strategy was to be the forerunner in Clinton's *A National Security Strategy for Engagement and Enlargement*. This new strategy means that the U.S. does not necessarily have to involve in open-ended commitment to military intervention, as pledged by John Kennedy's 'to bear any burden, pay any cost' against communism. The new directive driving the United States' global strategy, which Evans and Newnham (1998: 68-70) have termed as the 'Clinton Doctrine', essentially involves four fundamental strategies. First, the retention of global military predominance. Second, the quest for economic prosperity. Third, the promotion of free market and democracy (this is especially captured by the (neo)Kantian idea that 'democracies do not go to war with each other' (W. Christopher, 1995: 15; 1998)). Finally, it is asking allies to 'burden share' with it to maintain 'global' stability.

Therefore, the international political economic system is neither multipolar

---

[7] See Tyler, P.E. (1992a) 'US Strategy Plans Calls for Insuring no Rivals Develop: A One-Superpower World', *The New York Times*, 8 March 1992, pp. 1, 14; and Tyler, P.E. (1992b) 'Pentagon Drops Goal of Blocking New Superpowers', *The New York Times*, 24 May 1992, pp. 2, 14.
[8] See Dick Cheney (U.S. Secretary of Defense, February 1992) *Annual Report to the President and the Congress* (U.S. Government Printing Office); Dick Cheney (January 1993) *Defense Strategy for the 1990s: The Regional Defense Strategy* (U.S. Government Printing Office).

nor a balance of power in economic affairs (elaborated in chapter five). Perhaps what we are witnessing is what some scholars have identified as a phase of the 'transnationalisation of liberalism' amongst the leading elite of the (secular) state system (H. Nau, 1990; M. Doyle, 1997). But why has the international system arrived at such a destination now? Who are the actors (public and private) involved in this phenomenon? What strategy and resources have they adopted to conjure the world into this 'new order'? (for 'order' see H. Bull, 1977; B. Roberts, 1995). Has 'history' really come to an end? (F. Fukayuma, 1992). Or, is this the advent of an international system never witnessed before?

According to both classical realism and neo-realism, if international relations history and theory abhors primacy (see for example, M. Wight, 1978; K. Waltz, 1979), the United States should have become the object of mistrust, fear and containment. Why then have other powers not aligned together to balance US military primacy? Why has the '(neo)-realist' theory of balance of power been unable to comprehend this changing nature of international relations? What is even more puzzling is that instead of being challenged, the U.S. military alliance is actually expanding. For example, at the July 1997 NATO summit in Madrid, three new members, the Czech Republic, Poland and Hungary were admitted, whilst leaving half a dozen others waiting in frustration. Moreover, despite calls from Russia and China for a multipolar world order, and their strange efforts at rapprochement to balance U.S. military might, both are increasing their willingness to join the U.S.-led club of capitalist states for further economic integration into the 'hegemonic globalisation'. Why has this phenomenon after the Cold War been so paradoxical in relation to the classical theories (and real history) of world politics?

In fact, the 'theories' (of International Relations) based on Eurasian experience, expect balance of power and power politics, but may not equate reality when the U.S. is added into the puzzle. In fact, when the U.S. is added, world power politics fundamentally changes the situation. The reason for this fundamental difference has been demonstrated by the United States' entering of World War I and II. With the demise of communism and the disappearance of the Soviet Union, the United States global strategy is entering a phase in world history never witnessed before by any 'great power'. This development may render the theories of cycles of great powers inappropriate today. The theories developed by Wallerstein (1974; 1980a; 1980b), Gilpin (1981; 1987), Modelski (1987a; 1987b), Goldstein (1988) and others, in the expectation of or in the prediction of regular war in the 'cycle of hegemony', may not hold. The major problem with these theories seems to be one fatal similarity, in that they set too narrow confinement of understanding, and thus unnecessarily trap themselves, thus preventing new understandings of wider implications and developments. This dissertation stresses that the more formal the theory, the more it must be based on abstractions. Thence the basis renders such theories remote from 'reality', and therefore unable to understand 'reality' properly.

By trying to comprehend the 'reality' and change, the dissertation demonstrates how the United States' power strategy has the special ability to innovate, adapt, and sustain its centrality in world politics. This 'art of politics' and strategy has its coherence within the politics invoked by Machiavelli. In adhering to the 'art of politics' and the ability to adapt and to learn from history, the United States has (so far) succeeded in avoiding major mistakes. Moreover, perhaps because of its history as a nation of immigrants, the United States has managed thus far also to avoid the ossification of the ruling elite. However, this same flexibility and adaptability in U.S. strategy makes it extremely difficult to pin-down, both for practitioners and theorists alike (this is elaborated in chapter eleven).

In uncovering the nature of U.S. power, the thesis shows how traditional theories 'failed' to recognise major changes. First, they faltered in their understanding of the end of the Bretton Woods fixed exchange rate system which they took to mean an end to U.S. economic prowess (this is explored in chapter four). Secondly, there is their inability to comprehend the decline and eventual collapse of the USSR and communist ideology (M. Cox, 1998). Thirdly, they overestimated Japanese power as a means to 'challenge' the U.S. power position. The miscomprehension of these three events/issues are by no means small in analysing the direction of relations of states and the international trading system. The central question which emerges from this is simply: 'why did scholars fail to read properly these unfolding events?' Is the diagnosis simply difficulties of observation of the power relations of the contending powers, or were the theoretical methods which they used at fault, which prevented them from seeing what was 'really' happening?

I argue that U.S. hegemony has helped and is continuing to shape and facilitate economic globalisation, particularly in the dimension where the promotion of transnational class interests and liberal democratisation in the core and periphery states are concerned. This aetiology will be the main driving force in understanding U.S. and capitalist intentions for the core and periphery states in the international system. Under U.S. hegemony, I will argue, the capitalist class aims to advocate its 'own style' of democracy to different regions in the world to enable them to have better links, influence and control over the reigning local elite (see S. Smith, 1999). The thesis also assumes that promoting the elite 'polyarchy' class (W. Robinson, 1996) in these countries is a means for U.S. hegemony to attempt to globalise, democratise and legitimise its economic and political position in the world system, hence bringing forth a 'new' consensus of liberal democratic states.

Any rising power attempting to break the consensus will find it extremely difficult as well as costly. The difficulty in breaking this system is so costly that the power in question will be isolated and its economic base for competitiveness and well-being of its nation and people will be greatly restrained. The thesis assumes that most if not all national economies are becoming increasingly integrated into the world system to construct and mould a 'hegemonic globalisation' order under U.S. leadership. This creation of the superstructure is the 'transnationalisation' of political processes and systems, involving changes and shifting structures in world politics, political economy, ideology, and power relationships.

With the collapse of the Soviet challenge, the dissertation shows that the United States and the world is entering a new phase in history where one power is *primus inter pares* in the nation-state system. The thesis will examine and analyse the power relations and analyse the different theoretical approaches that offer their respective paths to explaining the emerging world order. The thesis contends that the United States has the power to substantially alter the international environment to suit its needs and to its advantage when necessary. The emergence, difficulties, and controversies involved will be explored in detail in the thesis, with the main emphasis to examine and analyse the power relationship between the U.S. and the four major powers: Russia, China, the EU, and Japan. The individual chapters will tailor each case individually, by its history, strategic concerns, interests, economic relations and power relations with the United States. The thesis argues that there are mutual relations within this set of great powers in what appears to be a structure in which they are to run the world together. Actually, however, because the U.S. is more powerful than any other state and very active in diplomatic, economic and security relations with all of them, it is the U.S. that is actually running the system. What I want to show is that none of the four main powers have come together, and examine why have they not come together. I will demonstrate why the U.S. strategy in the emerging world order has been essentially anti-balance of power, by which the U.S. has manipulated the balance of power idea to serve as a warning to others.

In order to unveil the complexity of the nature of the prevailing power predominance of the U.S. with regard to the contemporary international order, numerous concepts need to be established to give the research sufficient tools necessary to tackle the complexity of that order. The thesis examines how the U.S. strategy of 'engagement and enlargement', which I have termed as 'hegemonic globalisation', is aimed at the possible integration and the removal of not just economic barriers for international trade and economic activities, but also at the removal of different cultural barriers. For many in the U.S. and elsewhere this is seen as 'a vital step toward both a more stable world and better lives for the people in it' (D. Rothkopf, 1997: 39). At the same time however, these advocates recognise that there will always be a diversity in cultures, races, belief, and other distinctive differences of humanity. Nevertheless, what is of interest is the U.S. strategy for the promotion (and attempt to understand in greater depth) of other cultures, the toleration of racial differences, and other belief systems. The U.S. strategy aims to comprehend these differences and possible conflicts and frictions between them, and to resolve the differences in the interest of U.S. global hegemonism.

This perspective of world order stands in contrast to that of the learned Professor Samuel Huntington: In 'Clash of Civilisations' and 'The West Unique, Not Universal' (1993b; 1996a and b). Professor Huntington states:

> The great divisions among humankind and the dominating source of conflict will be cultural. Nation states will remain the most powerful actors in world affairs, but the principal conflicts of global politics will occur between nations and groups of different civilisations. The clash of civilisation will be the battle line of the future (1993b: 22).

Huntington's thesis examines how diversity inflames people because of their differences.[9] He explores the 'natural' differences and explains why these differences are reinforced by the perception of different people's history. Because of the different perception of race, culture and belief system, Huntington draws upon and manipulates these differences and establishes cultural, religious, and racial fault-lines which he believes are the emerging politics of contemporary international affairs. The U.S. government and its academic circles have not dismissed these comments lightly. However, there is nothing that can really be said to be 'new' in the Huntington thesis; it is trying to emphasise what has happened in the past in the conflicts between different races, cultures and belief systems. Yet, what significantly sets the U.S. strategy apart from Huntington's analysis is prescribing to 'rule' over separate cultures by attracting as many diverse traits as possible to the benefit to the U.S. system of hegemony, rather than to Huntington's 'Atlanticism'. A second weakness in Huntington's argument is identified by pointing out that throughout human history, clashes and conflicts have not only occurred between civilisations, cultures, societies, religions, races, tribes and so on, but, also *within* the civilisation, culture, society, religion, race, and family. In fact, the clashes of the *near* have been more frequent and more devastating than the conflict of the *far*.

Because of the tensions and conflictual nature seen in Huntington's analytical framework, a subtle study is deserved, and Huntington's words should give us a reasonable clue as to the type of scenario that 'could' occur in international affairs. However, the complexity of world politics (even at the domestic level) leaves any analysis unlikely to comprehend reality completely. Although Huntington's analysis attempts to build a framework for explaining the whole, what he ended up with is an array of simplicity that barely explains a part rather than explain the whole.

The U.S. government, and the majority of governments, recognise the ghosts in Huntington's thesis. It is recognisable that reinforcing conflict between cultures, religions, and races would decrease the U.S. power position rather than increase it. This however, does not mean that the U.S. and Western countries are worried about being overwhelmed by the countries on their periphery, but the U.S. strategy is more subtle than simply one of being worried. The U.S. recognises that

---

[9] Professor Peter Taylor has rejected this by stating that: 'Thus whereas the opponents of socialism are anti-socialists, the opponents of liberalism are anti-liberalism, and so on, the opponents of nationalists are typically other nationalists'. Peter J. Taylor (1996) 'The Modern Multiplicity of States', in Eleonore Kofman and Gillian Young (eds) (1996) *Globalisation* (London: Pinter).

at least at the moment (G. Kennan, 1995; U.S. National Defense College, 1998-9), there is an opportunity for them to have 'followers' rather than having 'enemies'. The U.S. strategy aims to make the entire set of nation-states 'followers' of U.S. hegemonic globalisation. It aims to maintain and sustain U.S. pre-eminence not by creating or emphasising differences, but to have pre-eminence over differences, and to ultimately dilute and defuse differences. It talks of multiculturalism and cosmopolitanism; embracing 'them' to rule 'them'!

Yet, how the U.S. aims to achieve this is still controversial. The U.S. universalism strategy has often seen it engaged in a simplified scenario of 'them' versus 'us', and especially 'good' versus 'evil', as seen in the Reaganite phrase 'evil empire' for the Soviet Union and 'free world' for the U.S. and allies. However, the use of the scenario 'good' versus 'evil' remains highly dubious, especially given the U.S. tactics and strategies deployed. Many would argue that it is anything but 'good'. Essentially, the U.S. may have liberal ends, but the means to achieving these ends are not necessary 'good'. To the Americans, however, those that do not conform or follow are either 'strange', are not 'rational', or are dubbed 'renegades' for confronting the American 'gospel' of 'goodness'. This emphasis is easily identified in the U.S. assuming a position of absolute 'moral' rectitude, whatever its actions. The U.S. has often portrayed itself as 'we are the good guys!' Therefore, by definition, the U.S. can do no wrong, i.e., no immoral action is conceivable – only a 'mistake' in execution, not in intent, because the U.S. always has 'Good' intentions. Madeleine Albright captures this American imagination by stating: 'I truly believe in the goodness of U.S. power ... [W]e are the organising principle' (*New Internationalist*, October 2000: 29).

Thus, to many Americans the spreading of the 'American revolution' is the spreading of the 'gospel of goodness', those that counter this Puritan belief are regarded with suspicion of being associated with 'evil' (see for example H. Brogan, 1985). In this way, the 'American revolution' needs 'total victory' over evil, but to have this would mean to also have 'total security' for 'liberal' style democracy and 'free trade', and ultimately the global hegemony of the 'American way'!

PART I

THEORY AND METHODOLOGY

Chapter 1

A Conceptual Framework and Principles of Inquiry

Do not believe what you have heard.
Do not believe in tradition because it is handed down
   many generations.
Do not believe in anything that has been spoken of many times.
Do not believe because the written statements come from
   some old sage.
Do not believe in conjecture.
Do not believe in authority or teachers or elders.
But after careful observation and analysis, when it agrees
with reason and it will benefit one and all, then accept it and live by it.
The Buddha (563 BC-483 BC)

. . . have courage to use your own reason.
What is Enlightenment? Immanuel Kant

Each master has his own footstep(s).
Anonymous proverb.

Problems for Inquiry: The Limits of 'Theory'

Before this work may commence, there are several inherent issues and problems in the International Relations' tradition which need brief clarification. Firstly, the interactions and tensions between theory and practice. For instance, in what order should these two concepts come; should practice determine theory, or does theory determine practice, or are they both completely separate from each other, and/or should they both be in a condominium of importance?

A second problem is what Chas W. Freeman, a career officer in the U.S. Foreign Service, wrote, 'Scholarships . . . are often narrowly focused within a single discipline and intent on proving a thesis, theory, or methodology. Their perspectives and the subject they research are therefore seldom congruent with the practical issues and decisions before policy makers' (1997: 24). This left Susan Strange to argue that 'a lot of "theoretical work" . . . is not really theory at all' (1988: 11). This may be so, but Strange goes on to state that 'policy-making . . . involves value judgements and risk assessment that are exogenous to theory that are better made by practical policy-makers . . . Whilst [the] academic that follow[s] how policy-makers proceed with their prescript risk becoming [an] "irresponsible academic theorist"' (1988: 12, emphasis added). This opens a conflict between the academic and the practitioner on what constitutes the 'responsible' and what is congruent with the actual practice of politics. However, the roles of the academic and the decision-maker are different, because 'the academic' is in the job of 'investigating', 'analysing', and 'explaining' the role of states and their agents. How can academic work thus be deemed 'responsible', let alone adequate or accurate for/with the policies outlined by the decision-makers, if it is not in parallel or in recognition of what practitioners are doing? Attempting to neutralise these difficulties, John Ikenberry commented,

> . . . what academics and what decision-makers do are very different. . . Policy-makers are trying to pursue interests and sometimes respond to different kinds of pressure. Whilst academics try to develop theories that explain something that they find puzzling, but not necessarily everything.[1]

Thirdly, what (and/or in whose) interests are involved in determining the theory and the mode of inquiry, especially on who decides what constitutes an appropriate approach or method of inquiry? Michael Cox states that:

> [Academic disciplines are] discouraged, or not inclined, to ask big questions. They are deterred from doing so. . . Those who stray outside the narrow channel do so at some professional risk (1998: 16; see also T. Kuhn, 1962/1996 3rd edit.).

He continues:

> . . . [L]arge-scale problems about the dynamics or contradictions of this or that social system . . . are simply pushed off the agenda. . . . [First] the very nature of conventional social sciences would [make] it extraordinarily difficult for the student. . . In fact, they are literally invoked not to, with the result that most academics were almost incapable of examining the large picture historically. Indeed, in terms of training, the large picture was precisely what they were not supposed to look at (1998: 16).

Again:

> The proper object of study was the very specific and the highly detailed; parts of the whole but not the whole itself . . . Large issues [were ignored or] were best left to the speculator or the journalist; [or] to the Toynbee or the Marx, neither of whom would have felt very much at home in an academic department in the post-war period . . . [Second] It is quite extraordinary, in fact, how much effort seems to have gone into educating otherwise intelligent people into believing that prediction was for fools and crystal-ball gazers and not serious intellectuals – . . . Accurate prediction, it was argued, could only take place under conditions of perfect knowledge: and because that was impossible to achieve, prediction in any form was clearly a waste of time (1998: 16-17, emphasis added).

---

[1] Interview with G. John Ikenberry, Washington D.C., 16 July 1998.

Finally, Reinhard Drifte states that, 'What has failed is not social sciences but rather our application of social science approaches and the damage of focusing too narrowly on one single academic discipline' (1996: 6). The snare and application of narrowness in the discipline has not only seen failure to anticipate change, such as the 'systemic' collapse of the entire Soviet empire, but also failed to analyse why that 'great' power did not respond to preventing its total collapse. The scholarship of rise and decline of great powers, thus needs serious re-evaluation if it is to escape the 'ambush' set by the methods and application used by academics. Moreover, the so-called 'declinist-renewal' debate (such as the U.S. failure in Vietnam, the collapse of the Bretton Woods fixed exchange system, and the 'new hegemonic' challengers of Japan, and the European Union) have failed to understand the extent and continuity of U.S. power position and its relationship with the international community. These failures are by no means 'small', the inability to 'understand' let alone 'explain', if one is to be honest, has been abysmal. If the discipline is to continue its value and relevance to anticipate change and continuity, we need to have to study history properly, and not to be confined by a 'self-imposed prison' set by 'Cold War' scholars, where restrictions and the creation of 'mythical', 'scientific', myopic methods were set to cloud our ability to see the 'real' events of international affairs.

What I am arguing here is that analysts must reconsider their position in the context of current international climate. This can be done without abandoning core principles, but by recapturing traditional axioms, which 'have been sacrificed over the past several decades in a futile endeavour to construct [ultra-parsimonious theories]' (R.L. Schweller in E.B. Kapstein and M. Mastanduno, 1999: 32; emphasis added).

Fourthly, precisely because of the inherent problems outlined in point three, a mode of inquiry immediately faces difficulties in analysing the division of interpretation of historical facts and empirical evidence, especially when espousing questions of legitimacy, morality, value, and change, in a practical and theoretical framework. This problem involves the nature and technique of inquiry into the search for knowledge (and possibly truth). Christopher Norris wrote: 'Modes and categories inherited from the past no longer seem to fit the reality experienced by a new generation' (1982/1991 rev. edit: vii). In this perspective, it is important to recall an old proverb, 'in war as it is in politics, the first casualty is truth' (Vietnamese proverb). As such, can an analyst reflect history from a value-free perspective or is s/he entrapped by the society of which s/he is part? Furthermore, 'How can history have truth if truth has a history? Truth is not something external to social settings, but is instead part of them' (M. Foucault in J. Baylis and S. Smith, 1997: 181).

Mode of Analysis

In the complexity and diversity of world affairs, the above questions, problems and warnings may not hold any definitive answers, nor would an immediate analysis be able to command the sufficient layers involved to answer the questions and problems. In addition:

> ... the concept of absolute truth[2] is also not appropriate to the world of history. ... At a more sophisticated level, the historian who contests, say, the verdict of one of his predecessors will normally condemn it, not as absolutely false, but as inadequate or one-sided or misleading, or the product of a point of view which has been rendered obsolete or irrelevant by later evidence (E.H. Carr, 1961/1986 2nd edit: 114).

This complexity leads my inquiry of international relations (to follow) with a set of simple assertions. First, there is no self-evident reading of any theory (M. Wight, in H. Butterfield and M. Wight, 1966: 17-34), whether scientific or otherwise, that can claim to or give a complete picture of the complexity of the dynamics of society. There are conflicting interpretations and concepts, and my work is another interpretation, which attempts to add a grain of sand in the search for the 'truth'. It attempts to plant another seed of knowledge into the rich garden of international relations.

Second, this book is not an attempt to create a new axiom or as argued to deny other theories their 'rightful' places in the discipline. My inquiry is a seed that has been germinated from the lessons of knowledge. Thence, since some of my knowledge is based around some of the scholarly works, to condemn them would be just like condemning my own work. In another old proverb: 'when drinking water one should always remember the source'. For this very important reason, scholarly works of the past offer us a particular compass for our mode of inquiry. It might be inappropriate for a specific configuration, but it does give the analyser a basic understanding. E.H. Carr correctly reminds us that:

> [First] ... you cannot fully understand or appreciate the work of the historian unless you have first grasped the standpoint from which he himself approaches it; secondly, that that standpoint is itself rooted in a social and historical background ... The historian, before he begins to write history, is the product of history (1961/1986 2nd edit: 34).

Moreover, 'if everything is a social construction and nothing is permanently

---

[2] Note: The I Ching, texts in Hinduism and Buddhism, Western religions of Judaism, Christianity, Islam, all offer different versions of absolute truth. In addition, natural science, such as physics, claims and attempts to understand the universe with a 'grand unifying theory'. Finally, mathematics, especially the work of John Von Neuman, has attempted to understand human society, the weather system, stock markets, and the universe by applying mathematical equations for estimation, forecast and mathematical prediction.

true, then how can *a* view of the world and history as a set of social constructions be anything but a social construction?' (J.A. Vasquez, 1998: 224, *emphasis added*). From this perspective, our understanding of inquiry into knowledge is likely to be reflected in our experiences, beliefs, and interpretations. It is as Michael Doyle correctly argued: 'Understanding history requires an epistemological foundation, for without a teleology . . . the complexity of history would overwhelm human understanding' (1997: 278). What I am offering is a reconsideration of the known techniques and methods used to understand history.

Notwithstanding these reflective modes of epistemic complexity, the interest of this inquiry is to attempt to analyse the way in which scholars have used certain data, conceptual tools, and empirical evidence to frame certain theoretical approaches that help to explain certain conditions in time and space. My inquiry attempts to ask whether some of them are applicable to the conceptualisation of realities of contemporary international affairs and actions taken by states and their agents. Obviously, the difficulties in framing any theory to the 'real' world stem from the fact that the 'actual reality' does not always correspond to any theory perfectly. Barry Gills points out that 'no one has ever been able to come up with an analytical framework that can claim to be truly encompassing of all social reality'.[3] No one mind (or even a great number of minds) can possibly conceive of a way to solve this (see also T. Kuhn, 1962/1996 3rd edit: 145). The first difficulty is that the world is full of contradictory and 'irrational' forces and the human mind is infinite in thought and nature (see also S. Strange, 1988: 11). It would be false to claim that the world can be conceptualised or conformed (summarised or contained) in a simple set of axioms.[4] Because human behaviour, unlike objects of physics 'interpret their own behaviour' (M. Nicholson and P. Bennett in A.J.R. Groom and M. Light, 1994: 199), it constantly shifts with different time and circumstance (contrast this with Waltz, 1979). This set of analysis leaves Thomas Kuhn to state that, 'no theory ever solves all the puzzles with which it is confronted at a given time; nor are the solutions already achieved often perfect' (T. Kuhn, 1962/1996 3rd edit: 146). He argues that: 'a theory must seem better than its competitors, but it need not, and in fact never does, explain all the facts with which it can be confronted' (1962/1996 3rd edit: 17-18). The danger of trying to do so would leave serious contentious questions from surrounding theories and disciplines. According to E.H. Carr, 'to give one priority over the other, you fall into one of two heresies. Either you write scissors-and-paste history without meaning or significance; or you write propaganda or historical fiction, and merely use facts of the past to embroider a kind of writing which has nothing to do with history' (1961, 1986 2nd edit: 23). Finally, Robert Cox emphasised that 'theory [*the structuration of knowledge*] is always for someone and for some purpose. All theories [*structuration of knowledge*] have a perspective. Perspective(s) derives from a position in time and space' (1981: 128, *emphasis added*).

---

[3] I am grateful to Barry Gills for this valuable citation.
[4] In physics, there is a formation of a 'grand theory' that claims to encompass all theories that can explain the operation(s) of the universe!

Absorbing these warnings, what I attempt to do is to carefully select case studies on important questions which are appropriate for a certain time and space. Unlike Waltz (1979), this analysis is not an attempt to understand the entire history of the global system through time and space (see below) in a single formal theory. My book attempts to investigate theory(ies) and their concepts which I believe to offer the ability to provide a succinct and a logical picture of understanding contemporary events, and possibly to guide practice. Thus, this study follows the criteria to appraise 'the adequacy of . . . theories, explanations, and prescriptions: empirical accuracy, theoretical fertility (progressive vs. degenerating research programs), empirical soundness, explanatory power, and relevance (J.A. Vasquez, 1998: 9) to explain contemporary international relations.

The methodological approach that I aim to apply attempts to offer a more accurate picture for understanding international affairs (i.e., the 'large scale problem' of the whole rather than part of the whole (M. Cox, 1998: 16) following partly what Richard Higgot calls 'large-scale historical change' (in A.J.R. Groom and M. Light, 1994: 9-26) in my systemic analysis of the United States, its hegemonic position in the relations with the four major powers/regions in the world (i.e., Russia, the EU, Japan, and the PRC). This approach aims to look at the five major powers in international affairs that I believe are and will be the determining factor in global hegemonic power distribution. The focus on these major powers does not mean that I will lose sight of lesser ones or of non-state actors. However, I contend that the fate of the latter requires attention on the former. Although I disagree with Waltz's theoretical approach on the understanding of the 'international system', I agree with Waltz on what he called 'the states that make the most difference in the international system' (1979: 73) which must be analysed with great care and attention. Thus, the book will analyse the four major powers in relation to the United States (the hegemonic power) and question the possibility of any one of them attempting to challenge the position of the hegemonic structure of the United States and possibly move away from the current system. If there is no such challenge, then this book can safely suggest that there is indeed 'globalisation' directed by the hegemonic power, the United States.

The 'large-scale historical change approach' has, however, been attacked especially by Karl Popper (1957/1960) in his *Poverty of Historicism* on the ground that the big system builders in history (such as Marx) seek to predict grand patterns of the system rather than offering more limited explanation (M. Nicholson, and P. Bennett in A.J.R. Groom and M. Light, 1994: 200). With Sir Karl Popper's warning, my work offers case studies of five parts (or jigsaw pieces) that attempt to offer a framework to build a greater systemic picture. In defence of my systemic approach, I contend that if the whole framework is not clear, it is reasonable to suggest therefore that the parts in the whole used for analysis would not be accurate either. Obviously, large-scale analysis cannot cover every aspect of societal behaviour. To alleviate the 'Popperian problem' (for a critique on Popper see B.T. Wilkins, 1978), this book tries to cover large-scale contemporary events and change, and to dig deep into each country as case studies. My work aims to give accuracy in historical accounts, precision, and scope. It is thus very crucial to have a large framework before the analyses of the smaller parts are possible. Metaphorically speaking, a builder cannot begin to build a house without a certain framework or plan; to do so would leave his/her house having serious problems in the future. This mode of analysis aims at an inquiry of the whole, as well as to investigate the nature of the 'brick(s)' that make up the whole. It inquires into the anatomy of the structure(s) and agents within each case study and their relationship within the prevailing hegemonic power. It follows what Kenneth Waltz correctly points out in comparing the affairs of nations to chess, that the '*game cannot* be successfully played unless the chessboard is accurately described' (Waltz, 1979: 160). Thus, if the chessboard of international affairs is not clearly seen as a whole, the smaller parts, even if they are analysed in great depth, would not fit to or allow us to comprehend world politics.

The third mode of interest in this book is the interaction and the manipulation of 'theories' by decision-makers, individuals, groups and others – sometimes without realising or really defining themselves as realists, liberals, Marxists, and/or any other contemporary theory.[5] In my understanding, 'people' very often apply a range, if not a combination of approaches and concepts that are identifiable within different perspectives as possible 'guides' to behaviour and perception. The question of whether they are realists, liberals and/or other contemporaries, and/or whether an approach is absolutely 'better' or 'truer' than its competitor is the wrong question (this is elaborated in more detail below). What is important is how they use those concepts and approaches.

Theory and Practice

In this section, I attempt to offer some answers to the problems of inquiry as raised above. I will inquire into the extent which practice can be reflected in theory, and ask whether theory is itself reflected in practice. Dr. Sun Yat-Sen in *The Three Principles of the People* emphasised: 'universal principles are all based first upon fact and then upon theory, theory does not precede fact' (translated by Frank W. Prince, 1985: 61). Arnold Wolfers recorded:

> ... all fields of human activity ... cannot be bridged by any theorising operation. ... Theorising about almost any feature of international politics soon becomes entangled in a web of controversy. Even the identity of the 'actor' – those who properly can be said to perform on the international stage – is a matter of dispute (1962: xiii, 3).

---

[5] These theories have been discussed at great length elsewhere, for example (R.O. Keohane, 1986; D.A. Baldwin, 1993; A.J.R. Groom and M. Light, 1994; F. Halliday, 1994; M.W. Doyle and G.J. Ikenberry, 1997; M.W. Doyle, 1997), it is only recapitulation of them here briefly.

In addition, even the usage of language and terminology in phrasing certain conditions becomes an abstraction, for example to claim that a certain actor, let's say the United States, has applied such and such theory/strategy is itself very abstract. For a start, who or what is the United States? Is it the President, the Secretary of State, the Pentagon, Wall Street, the Council on Foreign Relations, or Congress? Different people have different motives and different strategies. Take for example, Robert Rubin – (former) Secretary for the Treasury; who does he represent? Does he represent capitalism or does he represent the American State?[6]

It is, therefore, no great surprise to find that there does not exist a comprehensive theory or literature on how 'states' and statesmen practice their political techniques. It obviously depends on the political framework from which scholars define how politicians and their subordinates pursue their interests.[7]

This returns to the problem as posed by C.W. Freeman, that academic research is 'seldom congruent' with practical issues and policy-making (1997: 24). I would add here that seldom (if ever) does any theory claim to encompass the whole. Policies implemented by individuals, groups and states may be interpreted more clearly under certain theories, whilst at different modes of inquiry it is understood clearer in others (see Tables 1.1 and 1.2 on pages 29 and 30). Therefore, the fundamental purpose of theory is to 'explain, comprehend and interpret "reality"' (D. Marsh and G. Stoker, 1995: 16). Vasquez observes that '[d]iplomats may make poor decisions either because they have no theory and hence do not know what they are doing or because they have a bad theory and make choices that are worse than doing nothing' (1998: 291). Marsh and Stoker argue that, 'it is possible to go further and argue that without theory of some sort it is impossible to understand "reality"' (1995: 16). But one thing that is recognisable in the 'art of politics': seldom does a practitioner allow him/herself to be trapped in any one axiom – to do so would leave the practitioner easily exposed to opponents. In the art of politics, 'wise' practitioners have often found it necessary to discriminately select an 'appropriate' approach that s/he feels may comprehend the situation more clearly than others. Hence, the actor will use different approaches differently for different needs, different situations and different times. For,

> . . . [w]ithout some idea of what is important, we cannot cut into the seamless web of our world. Theory, in crude terms, helps us to see the wood for the tree. Good theories select out certain factors as the most important or relevant if one is interested in providing an explanation of an event. Without such a sifting process, no effective can take place. The observer would be buried under a pile of detail and be unable to weigh the influence of different factors in explaining an event. Theories are of value precisely because they structure all observation (D. Marsh and G. Stoker, 1995: 16-17).

---

[6] Interview with G. John Ikenberry, Washington D.C., 16 July 1998.
[7] See for example works by Plato; Machiavelli; the Guanzi; Francis Bacon; Adam Smith; Fredrick Hegel; Karl Marx/Frederick Engels; Kautilaya; Fredrick List, and many others that attempt to admonish 'states-persons' with 'guidelines' for political practice and governance.

Joshua Muravchik comments:

> ... international politics is something like chess, with statesmen constantly seeking to gauge the effect of the loss of a pawn here, the movement of a rook there. The problem is that in chess the number of permutations is virtually infinite, and so is the number of strategies. This is all the more true in international politics, which has more pieces than a chess game, a board that is unbounded, and no fixed rules governing how each piece may move. Each statesman has an infinite choice of moves and a vast menu of strategies for advancing a nation's interests. Therefore to discover a law of politics saying that states will behave according to their interests is to discover almost nothing about how any state will actually behave (1991: 29).

In such circumstances, I have decided not to follow a single theory, as such, but to take a broad 'agnostic' (theoretically speaking) hermeneutic approach (this is elaborated below) to understand the affairs of states and statesmen, because the different broad ontological and epistemological positions inform different methodological orientations and preferences (D. Marsh and G. Stoker, 1995: 14).

Although I have found theories of certain strands of 'realism', 'liberalism', 'Marxism' and/or other theories to have great 'usefulness' in approaching certain conditions of space and time. Each group will use certain measures (or even re-invent itself) to defend their paradigm and to explain human interaction. This hermeneutic premise does not make the theory wrong or ineffectual, because each practices their theories for different reasons. Even the Buddhist classic, the *A Ch'an*, emphasised that, 'When you meet a swordsman draw your sword: Do not recite poetry to one who is not a poet'. That is why none of the theories may overlord the other competing theories if that theory is to compete in that specific realm of knowledge (see Table 1.1).

Nevertheless, there are obviously some fundamental 'flaws' in theories that may not explain certain conditions in certain situations of time and space; especially the chimerical nature of the decision-makers in politics, and the struggle for power that *is* inherent in human society (discussed in chapter two). In attempts to avoid 'flaws' in the theories, my approach aims to be clear of biased dogmatic and static tenets, or the belief that scientific formulae and/or parsimonious elegance are ideally suitable for the understanding of the enormous complexity (and often very messy) affairs of human kind (contrast this to Waltz, 1979). From such a basis, I argue that the international system is dynamic, transformatory, and continuously contested with different sets of values and interpretations.

In the inquiry into politics, especially politics in the contemporary period, the terminology such as 'them and us' is becoming increasingly difficult to deliberate without invoking contentious debates. My inquiry does not identify the world via the dictum of 'oil and water', nor to identify it in terms of 'black and white', although, the temptation for such an approach would make things easier and more consistent. However, as argued above, my analysis is intended to understand the behaviour of states and their agents, and not to be trapped within a certain theory or as Kuhn called 'inflexible boxes', which would in any case be incapable of fully understanding the dynamics of human society. Thence, the complexity of the affairs of mankind cannot be understood under one theory, but probably are better understood under a combination of theories. This approach can similarly be found in Marvin Minsky's *The Society of Mind*, where Minsky emphasised that 'The power of intelligence stems from our vast diversity, not from any single, perfect principle' (cited in H.C. Dyer, 1997: 134).

Because politics (whether domestic or international) is never straightforward and is full of controversies, this book deems it necessary to cut across theories and utilise their concepts and integrate some of them to create a framework that tries to comprehend the realities or behaviour of states and their agents. It will manipulate established theories to compare and utilise what is useful, accurate, and isolate those tenets within the theories that fail to analyse the contemporary period effectively.

This deliberation besieges the set standard of mainstream international relations paradigm and mode of inquiry, and is seen by some critics as a violation of theoretical and methodological 'rules' (see M. Cox, 1998: 16 warning above). Wendt has warned that to 'subscribe to such a discourse, will probably please no one' (A. Wendt, 1992: 425). Or simply because the approach(es) that 'do not fit the box are not seen at all' (T. Kuhn, 1962/1996 3rd edit: 24), they are condemned and restricted! Baylis and Smith also warned:

> At first sight each seems to be particularly good at explaining some aspects of world better than the others, and an obvious temptation would be to try and combine them (the theoretical approaches) into some overall account. But we need to warn you that this is not as easy an option as it may seem . . . [the] approaches are really in competition with one another; and, whilst you certainly choose between them it is not so easy to add bits from one to the others (1997: 6, emphasis added).

Perhaps the most dangerous outcome of such an approach would be to create a monster: 'it is as though an artist were to gather the hands, feet, head and other members for his image from diverse models, each part excellently drawn, but not related to a single body, and since they in no way match each other, the result would be monster rather than man' (quoted in T. Kuhn, 1957, *The Copernican Revolution*, p. 138). However, perhaps the most serious problem of such an approach, metaphorically speaking, is: fire does not mix with water. Zuckerman refers to this to the 'deep conflict over appropriate assumptions, foci and methods of analysis, and they offer hypothesis and theories that directly contradict one another. They frequently describe the same phenomenon, but offer different analysis of it. They observe the world in different ways' (1991: 7). I recognise the fundamental opposing views of the theories and their incompatible mode of inquiry, and to fit them together would indeed create uneasiness. Yet, 'to reject certain questions because their answers cannot conform to the standard classical is to fall into the trap of method driven rather than question-driven science' (A. Wendt, 1992: 425). The discipline of international relations itself is heavily influenced by the categorisation of paradigms, which therewithal was heavily influenced by the European age of 'Enlightenment' from the late 17th century,[8] and Cold War scholarships. It raises a difficult question as to whether to proceed with research within these boxes or resist them (T. Kuhn, 1962, 1996 3rd edit: 5).

Perhaps it is not my collection of the different theories that has created a monster, but the competing theories are themselves monsters, and the techniques used by scholars to anticipate change and continuity – what I do is to 'dilute' them to explain what I perceive to fit with the behaviour, change and continuity of states and agents. In such circumstances, I follow what Richard Little argues as to how IR scholars [for example, R. Cox, 1981; 1987; A. Linklater, 1986; 1990], '[endeavour] to demonstrate how realism in IR and the Marxist strand of HS [Historical Sociology] can be woven together to produce a more effective [understanding of world politics]' (in A.J.R. Groom and M. Light, 1994: 19, emphasis added). Similarly, Wendt suggested that 'proponents of [*each theory*] can and should join forces . . . Each group has characteristic weaknesses that are complemented by the other's strength. . . . [Separate theories] have much to learn from each other if they can come to see this through the smoke and heat of epistemology' (1992: 425, emphasis added). To Keohane, labels are 'uncomfortable', he suggests that liberal institutionalism 'borrows as much from realism as from liberalism' (in D. Baldwin, 1993: 11). From this 'array of light', I have found it necessary to incorporate much of the vocabulary and apparatus, both conceptual and manipulative, of the competing theories to give a more balanced and accurate picture of international affairs. This position follows from *The Prince*, where Machiavelli wrote: 'a Prince . . . [must keep his mind] ready to shift as the winds and tides of fortune turn and the varying circumstances of life may dictate . . . he should not depart from the good [courses] if he can hold to it, but he should be ready to enter on evil if he has to' (Ch. XVIII, translated by R. Adams, 1977/92: 49, emphasis added).

The determination of my approach is to cling to historical events – and to understand and possibly explain the actors and agents that operate using different 'theories' and variables to comprehend historical events and power relations. Hence, my research makes great use of concepts within theories, but is sceptical of 'formal' theory (see E.P. Thompson, 1978; K. Popper, 1945/66 2 editions, *Open Society and Its Enemies*, but compare this to Popper's *The Poverty of Historicism*, 1957, the second book shows the two faces of Popper's 'scientific' study of history). From this caution of theories, my research is to use concepts to build frameworks of analysis based on the 'real' structure of power. The development of this involves an 'understanding' via the empirical and flexibility in interpretation, where essentially the philosophy being that having 'no theory means having no trap' for mode of analysis. The approach of this book, as such, is based on a set of concepts, explained via analysis of behaviour and pattern of states and statesmen.

---

[8] Obviously this is opening a large 'Pandora's' box and it is not in the interest of my book to descend fully into this debate. I am also aware of the debate over legitimate method, problems, and standards of solution for the mode of inquiry. I shall leave this epistemological and ontological debate for a moment in the future that is more appropriate.

This book is not to fall back into the trap of formal theory which itself is not grounded on classical realist approach. The study attempts to allow more flexibility and nuance in interpretation but to stay close to empirical reality.

This pragmatic position does not mean that my research does not have principles. In fact, this logic is the core principle[9] (see Tables 1.1 and 1.2 below). In Table 1.1, I have illustrated that the three paradigms all have a mixture of reality and unreality (for an excellent analysis, see J.R. Searle, 1995; P. Berger and T. Luckmann, 1966). For example, my illustration of unreality with some 'realists' is their assumption of the international system as permanently anarchic and the separation between domestic and foreign politics as a means to understand International Relations. In disagreement with Marxists, I contend with their assumption of the continual and inevitable class conflict in society and across societies and the idea of class unity across different cultures and races. With liberals (especially neo-classical liberals, such as David Ricardo and his followers), I disagree with their assumption that non-intervention in society creates optimum utility for individuals, larger entities, and the state. I further disagree with the prophecy that individuals are 'rational' actors, in that the behaviour of individuals and larger entities can be 'mechanised' to explain the nature of human beings and larger entities.

To alleviate some of these problems, Table 1.1 illustrates how the centre shifts according to the dynamics of the power distribution within each theory and its assumption abilities to comprehend reality. If, for example, the Marxist assumption of class unity were to hold across different cultures and races, then the centre of impermanence would move closer to the Marxist box. On the other hand, if that assumption does not hold, the centre of impermanence would push that Marxist assumption more towards unreality. This rule applies to all theories. The line of impermanence also shows how unreality can become reality[10] – just as ideas can be translated into practice – therefore depending on time, circumstance and space each theory will have its zenith and nadir in explanatory and analytical power (this is elaborated in Table 1.2). This shows that each theory acting within the reality realm does comprehend to a certain view of human affairs. These views are then structured and developed into new theories – such as neo-liberalism, neo-Marxism, neo-realism, and so on which tries to cover greater scope by adding and refining established variables of other theories. This process would through time bring theory closer to the point of origin and reality.

---

[9] See Miyamoto Musashi *The Book of the Five Rings* for the logic of this approach.
[10] I am talking here of 'institutional facts' and not 'brute facts'. See especially John R. Searle (1995) *The Construction of Social Reality* (London: Penguin).

A Conceptual Framework and Principles of Inquiry 29

Table 1.1   A 'Simple' View of the Mainstream Theories in International Relations

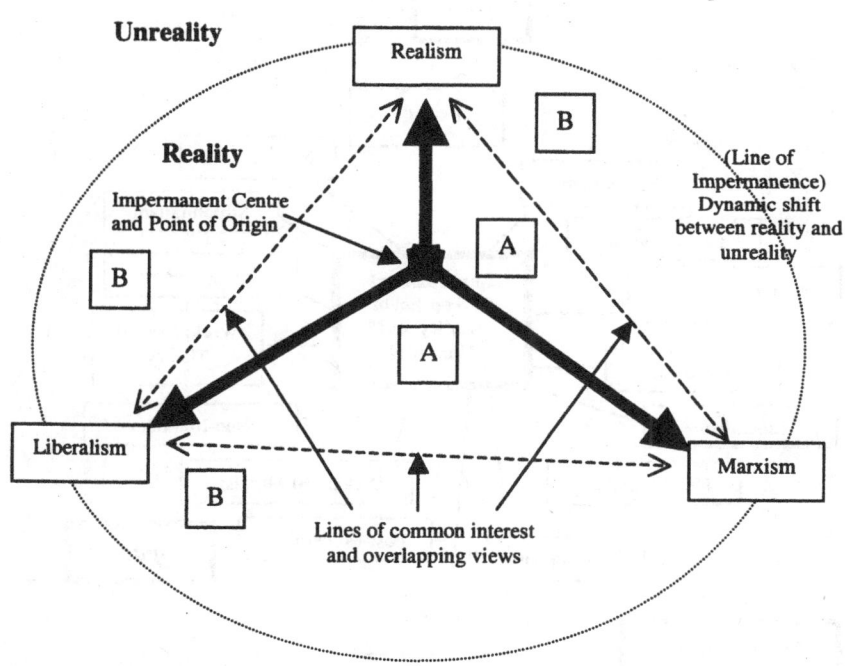

Note:
A = Brute facts
B = Historical facts

Table 1.2 A 'Complex' View of the Multiple Theories in International Relations

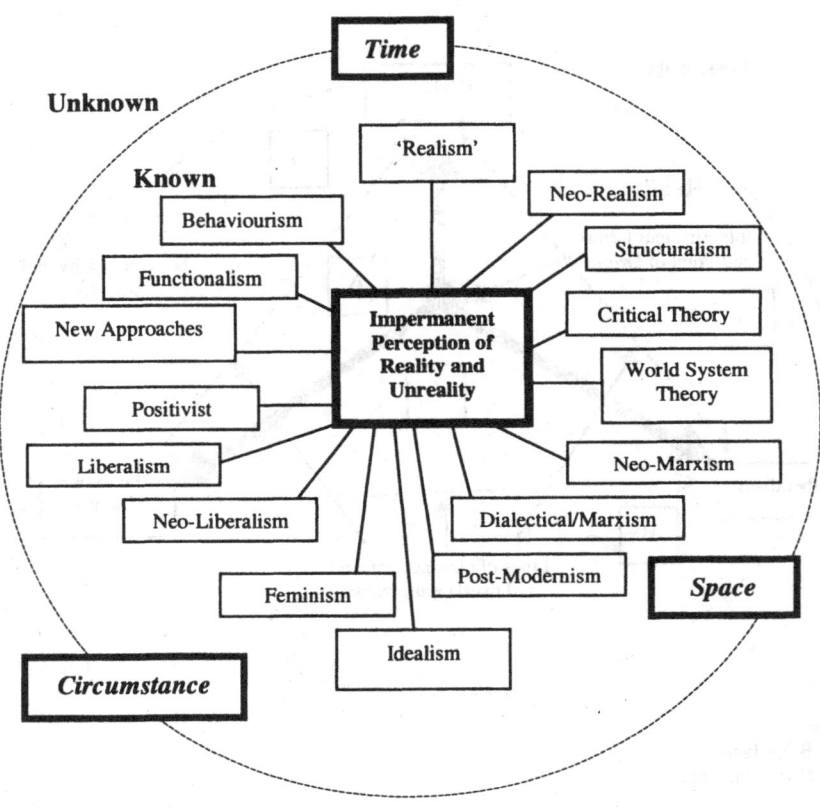

In Table 1.2, the complexity of theories and structures and paradigms in international relations are multiplied. In this table, all the paradigms fall within the realm of the 'known' – as the idea already exists: it is both real and unreal. In the realm of the 'unknown', it is ideas that do not exist, not what is unreal. Unreality becomes reality when assumptions and hypothesis are accepted and tested. Moreover, reality becomes unreality (or myth) if its assumptions and hypotheses are disproved or falsified (see K. Popper 1957). Within the realm of virtual reality, what is unknown is tested as unreality. It struggles for existence out of non-existence. As the line of impermanence to determine shifts from the unknown to the known, it enlarges the realm of existence from non-existence. Unknown thus becomes known. As illustrated in Table 1.1, known reality and known unreality are in continuous shift and struggle, they are dependent on the perception of the individual and the make up of society. The impermanence of perception ascertains how s/he perceives the reality and unreality. These perceptions change and shift according to time, space, and circumstance. The powers that determine these changes are the forces within the power structure, power relationship that compete continuously for the make up of reality (this is discussed in greater depth in chapter two). The tendency for struggle determines how theories and paradigms peak or decline in reality and unreality, according to the power influence of the determinate user in the dynamics of time, space and circumstance. In this sense, the 'validity' and usefulness of a theory, depends upon specific factors of 'position' in time, space, and circumstance both of the theorist and the theory itself.

From these propositions and position, my analysis argues that states, groups, statesmen, and individuals in one time or another use *certain* means to maintain or further their power position. Obviously the form, the content, and the means, which are used and applied, have changed and will change as the world does, but in essence they are very recognisable if not the same. As such, I follow the assumption that human nature is possessed by an inherent lust for power, glory (A. Wendt, 1992: 409), continuous calculation of gain and loss, and is constantly 'reinventing itself' according to changes in circumstance, time and space. Man-made laws change, power positions change, great people of prominence come and go, and nation's rise and decline; what remains is the 'human beings' that continue to contest (in various conditions and circumstances) for the helm of power (see also E. Carr, 1939/1946/1964; K. Polanyi, 1957: 45-6).

Conclusion

In conclusion, because of the failure of scholars to anticipate change and continuity in international affairs by using 'self-imposed' methods, the reader is, thus, forewarned that there are areas where my methodology intends to readjust the lenses within which the different theories perceive the world in their respective time and conditions, just as the practitioner will shift his/her or their position to relate to changing times and conditions in the search for power. Machiavelli wrote: 'in the political affairs of man, try to imitate both the fox and the lion in order to be wary of traps and to overawe the wolves' (*The Prince*, Ch. XVIII). I appeal here that 'reality' is never tidy, and to mechanise or categorise it into some form of boxes is not only not real, it distorts severely our understanding of human affairs and its change. Understanding the strategy of a single entity, let alone multiple entities, is never straightforward. The statecraft of contemporary powers and their agents encompasses policy instruments often beyond one set of paradigmatic inquiry of theories (see R. Drifte, 1996: 6). Peter Gowan understood this clearly when he pointed out that the 'the external policies of the . . . powers are not transparent, and that their operational goals are rarely captured by their public presentation' (1999: x). In such difficulties of inquiry, he found it necessary to 'stray across disciplinary boundaries even where [he] felt ill-equipped to do so' (P. Gowan, 1999: xi, emphasis added). I sympathise with this, and although I admit to shifting positions in the complex and dynamic realities of international affairs, I aim to keep this at a minimum, to keep the book coherent, clear and balanced.

The operation and framework of my analysis and evaluation, therefore, can be seen in an analogy with (metaphorically speaking) something like the weather: it shines, it rains, and sometimes there might even be violent storms – but what is crucial is that it is acting/interacting within a weather system. In such a circumstance, a person not prepared for these conditions will either have to adapt or will perish. For survival, that person will build necessary shelter to protect him/herself from the often not so amicable environment. In addition, a person cannot wear thick winter clothing when the weather is boiling hot, or reciprocally wear summer clothing when it is freezing cold. This is not double standard; it is just simply plain 'common sense' to suit human needs in changing environments. Basically, what it means is that individuals, groups and even states will have to have a multiple 'utility' belt (or utility of theories and experiences) that can help it survive and comprehend more clearly in different conditions. For example, strategic issues concerning the United States, e.g. over Iraq, Bosnia, Serbia, the near clash with China over Taiwanese independence in 1996, and the stationing of military personnel in East Asia and Western Europe, are much better explained in the realist and geostrategist tradition than under liberal or class theories. Whereas, where the increased interdependence in global communication, finance, trade and movement of people are concerned, some 'realists' and geostrategists often fail, liberal and class theories offer better explanations. Overall, however, what is important is that the U.S., as an actor, has a strategy that falls within each theory (see also R. Haass, 1995). *The Guanzi* emphasised: 'The clever will have a superabundance of things while the stupid never have enough' (*The Guanzi*, translated by Allyn Ricket 1985: 85). The more (quantity and quality; reflective and rational; tangible and intangible) sophisticated utilities there are in the utility belt the more likely the chances of providing a clearer picture (this is analysed in more detail in the next chapter). As such, successful analysis, evaluation, and implementation of the person's/group's, or state's policy (obviously it depends on what type of policy and how and to whom it is to be implemented) to have a successful outcome and understanding of the situation is dependent on the level of knowledge. The objective, thus, is 'to increase man's understanding of, and mastery over, his environment' (E.H. Carr, 1961/1986 2nd edit: 108).

In this way, this study attempts to rectify 'realism', not the realism that is static and unable to comprehend change and transform. This study challenges the balance of power theories; the separation of domestic and foreign policy making; the use of econometrics as 'primary' mode of inquiry; state-centricism; the billiard-ball scenario; and timeless anarchy. Many would argue that these concepts and theories are the 'heart and soul' of realism. This is not true. Traditional realists (such as Thucydides and Machiavelli) never said anything about the formalisation of these concepts and theories as the basis for understanding human interaction. Waltz and neo-realists have thus made the study of international relations 'unreal', and have made it into a study of 'what ought to be', rather than of 'what is'. Traditional *real* realism was essentially based on 'actor-centric', anti-structure, ability to adapt and change, and placing enormous complexity of actors in history. It is certainly not parsimonious and/or ahistorical. In addition, it invokes qualitative understanding over quantitative line of inquiry. Most formal theories that have evolved since 1945 have essentially been quantitative orientated, this is due to the emphasis on mathematics formulas (see H.R. Alker, 1996). However, can we really understand history using only formal mathematical models? No. My book is an attempt to carry out a study of contemporary American global power using *real* realism as an approach.

Given this approach, my emphasis in this study is to uncover what may be appropriate from theory to fit with past and contemporary world affairs; to analyse what has happened, not analyse what theory(ies) say(s) ought to happen. As such, my approach is highly sensitive to the historical events. 'Those who should question the present should investigate the past. Those who do not understand what is to come should look at what has gone before' (*The Guanzi*, translated by Allyn Ricket 1985: 83, contrast however with Popper, 1957/60). Thence, 'if the gaze of history hides its evils from us; we must rebuild society for ourselves, learning from the past lessons and what warnings we are capable of learning. Perhaps by doing so we might also bear in mind that the causation of human affairs [is] too deeply tangled to be wholly unravelled by the wisest minds' (R. MacIver in K. Polyani, 1957).

Chapter 2

An Inquiry into Power

Never Outshine the Master
Baltasar Gracian in R. Greene and J. Elffers (1998) *The 48 Laws of Power.*

Perhaps one concept that is recognisable, but which has ultimately eluded all, whether early or contemporary theory and practice, in the east, the south, the west, or the north, is the concept of power. Power has such a complicated and slippery meaning that scholars have found it a 'portmanteau concept . . . [and] impossible to define with any precision' (G. Evans and J. Newnham, 1998: 446). Robert Gilpin describes the 'concept of power as one of the most troublesome in the field of international politics' (1981: 13). To Robert O. Keohane and Joseph Nye, 'power has always been an elusive concept for statesmen and analysts of international politics; now it is even more slippery' (1977/1989 2nd edit: 11). Because of its centrality for the understanding of U.S. power relations, it is thus helpful here to analyse the perception of this concept before entering further into the argument of the book.

According to Joseph Nye, power in international politics is something like the weather system. Everyone talks about it, but few understand it (1990: 25). To Akaha and Langdon, the dynamics of the weather appears to have more agreement 'than about the dynamics of power among nations' (1993: 18). Why is a concept which is 'central' (S. Strange, 1988: 23; R. Drifte, 1996: 8) and the 'ultimate aphrodisiac' (H. Kissinger in C. Freeman, 1994: 223) in deciding the nature of the affairs of humanity and the study of politics been so difficult to define?[1] (Morgenthau, 1948/93: 29).

To begin, in a general definition of the concept power, the *Chambers 20th Century Dictionary* defines power as the 'ability to do anything – physical, mental, spiritual, legal, etc.: capacity for producing an effect: strength: energy: faculty of the mind: moving force of anything: right to command, authority: rule: influence: control: governing office . . .' (E.M. Kirkpatrick, 1983/1985/1986: 1007). The *Oxford Concise Dictionary of Politics* defines power as the 'ability to make people (or things) do what they would not otherwise have done' (I. Mclean, 1996: 396). Adaptively, power is argued to be relative between the interaction of individuals (or things). If only one actor existed, there would be no opportunity to (or need to) exercise power over the other. As John Rothgeb has put it: 'power is found only

---

[1] Given that there are so many possible interpretations of power, and because of limited space and time, I can only venture into a small part of the subject.

when members of the international system interact with one another'.[2]

In Chas W. Freeman's *Arts of Power*, power is defined as the ability to 'control events, including the decisions and actions of others' (1997: 20 and 33). In these events, the ability of the power-wielder to direct the course of events and to affect outcomes *is* power. Thus, the basis for power is the controlling of available resources, 'military, economic, political, or cultural strength and potential with will' (1997: 33). What is interesting here is the interpretation of 'will' to power. According to Freeman, 'will' is perhaps the most crucial power base (1997: 33), without which political pursuits would be of little direction (see also H. Kissinger, 1957). 'Will' enables an actor to exercise power, make decisions, and pursue objectives with precision (R. Greene and Elffers, 1998), yet without being too precise and public about the objective in pursuit. The ability to concentrate wilfully to power may secure compliance without losing track of the actor's intentions. That is to have total commitment to a certain policy. Indeed, the will to power, Freeman argues, creates the perception of power capabilities. For in power relationships, the 'power . . . lies . . . in the mind of the opponent [and the power wielder]' (1997: 15, emphasis added). The psychological reality of this is so important that Freeman argues that 'perceived power is real power' (1997: 20). He emphasises that no matter how immense the military, economic, or political capabilities of an actor, it is of no use 'if adversaries disbelieve it' (1997: 15, and 1994: 228). An actor's history, reputation, and will are major analytical assessment determinates that may be used by opponents or friends to perceive the power reality or unreality of that actor.[3] On the other hand, this invokes the question of reality and unreality of power base and the capacity or ability to make that perceived power base credible to others. Henry Kissinger remarked: 'To rely on the efficacy of diplomacy [creation of perceptions] . . . may lead to disaster, but to rely on power with insufficient means is suicide' (1964).

In such a case, the reputation and the 'solid' aggregate foundations of power capabilities (discussed below), as well as the creation of image (or in others creating that image (this is analysed later in the nature of how 'others' perceived the United States power base) is seen as the 'cornerstone of power' (R. Greene and J. Elffers, 1998: 15). Thus, the ability to manipulate others' perceptions of power potential, capabilities, and the will to carry it out, creates an elusive assessment of 'real' power. Niccolo Machiavelli (in C. Freeman, 1994: 227) wrote:

> Among the many . . . indications by which the power of a republic may be recognised is the relation in which they live with their neighbours; if these are

---

[2] J.M. Rothgeb (1993) *Defining Power – Force and Influence in the Contemporary International System* (New York: St. Martin's), p. 17, quoted in K. Aldred and M.A. Smith, (1999: 1).

[3] Similarly, Evans and Newnham stated: 'Power relations exist over time and perceptions of the past can influence reactions in the present or anticipate for the future. Moreover this mixing of past, present, and future will be multidimensional in the power structure and capability of actors' (1998: 448).

tributary to her by way of securing her friendship and protection, then it is a sure sign that that republic is powerful. But if these neighbouring states, though they may be more feeble than herself, draw money from her, then it is a sure sign of great weakness on the part of the republic.

In these circumstances, accurate assessment of both what an actor's own power may be and what power the opponent perceives the actor to have entwines into the age old dictum of Sun Tzu (*The Art of War*): 'to know thyself, know thy enemy: forever victorious'. However, the attainment of complete accuracy of this has not always been possible in any given circumstance. To do so, would mean ultimate power. Even if a clear picture of the assessment of power capabilities of self and opponent were possible, the 17th century author Miyamoto Musashi (*The Book of the Five Rings*) argues: 'Even if your opponent knows a hundred stances and you know a hundred stances, the ultimate point is solely in the perception of ability and intention . . . Because this is not transmitted secretly, it is not written in the real way, but in homophonic words' (1645?/1993: 86). Accordingly, timing and the availability of capabilities in the exercise of a power relationship is of essence in deciding outcomes. Another problem is that people are never 100 per cent certain about each other's intentions because they 'cannot read minds and minds can always change' (A. Wendt, 1999: 107) and are 'infinite' in thought and nature (S. Strange, 1988: 11).

In enabling images and credibility for power contestation, Freeman argues that effort should be made to 'persevere in the face of setbacks and sacrifices' (1997: 15-16), otherwise the actor would lose credibility in the power perception of others. In fortitude 'statesmen [should not rush to compromise] when faced with [a] disadvantageous position' (1997: 16, emphasis added). Thus, in diplomatic negotiations, the ability to convert a disadvantageous position into an advantageous position requires delicate manipulation of limited means without displaying them. This positional power shift enables the actor to move out of moments of difficulties.

The ability to move out of difficult situations is in turn dependent on the power variables and experience available to actors. In the end, power is to have things your way. On the other hand, can it be argued that power is an end rather than a means to controlling (to some extent) outcomes? In the next section of this chapter, I will examine whether or if power is assessed as a means or an end to political practice, or alternatively could it be viewed as both an end and a means for the discourses of politics? In attempting to answer this question, I will commence to analyse the structures of power involved and assess how it is exercised. In the final section, I analyse the three mainstream theories for final assessment in understanding power as a means to an end or an end to a means. It is only from a clear understanding of these difficulties, that I can commence my analysis of U.S. hegemonic globalisation.

The Four Spheres of Power

This section analyses the power base/structures that enable actors in exercising relational power contestation. Many scholars (M. Mann, S. Strange, C. Freeman, R. Gilpin, and others) have identified *four* power structures that are inherent in the makeup of power in the strength of actors (individual, group, and/or state). The importance of each structure will be analysed below in turn of the power perception and definition in contending theories of international relations. That section will analyse how the selection of methods by the theories determines their differences in perception and analysis of power relationship(s). The inquiry here is to analyse briefly the four power structures: political, cultural/ideological/symbolic attributes, economic resources and capabilities, and military strength and capabilities (compare to or refer to M. Mann, 1993, and C. Freeman, 1997, for more details). This analysis helps to give a clearer understanding for the study of 'hegemonic globalisation' in the following chapters.

- *Political power*, according to Hans Morgenthau, is 'the most immediate aim in politics' (1948/1993: 29). In this sense, politics depends on power, as fire requires fuel to burn. Without power, the capacity to influence, persuade or even to determine the course of events would be empty. Power enables the power wielder legitimacy to regulate, gives him/her authority to employ action and to set the action of others (to some extent). Ultimately, political power stems from the authority to organise the activities of individuals, groups, and organisations and to control and command (to some extent) social activities. As such, it is perhaps the most subtle power base and the central power structure to unite the other three power structures (discussed below) in the pursuit of a particular objective.
- *Cultural/ideological/symbolic power* is the activity that inspires and persuades others to emulate ideas from an actor. This type of power shows to others the achievements of a particular actor. Its attributes to setting 'consensual' norms, values, rituals, standards of practice and language, through accruing past and present prestige. The power determinates in this sense are closely related to political power and influence.
- *Economic power* is based on the ownership or control of resources. This power sphere enables the power bearer to possess the ability to transform human, material, and financial resources into goods and services, for sale or exchange in a market, in order to generate a means of subsistence. Economic power is often expressed by 'other nations' reliance on the nation's capital, output, and market . . . [to] influence depends on the presence of banks, business, and business people abroad and a comparable foreign presence at home' (C. Freeman, 1997: 17). In addition, economic power can be used as a coercive measure, such as through economic sanctions and embargoes. However, the ability of the targeted group or country to substitute goods, services and capital, means that the threats to employ these measures are

- *Military/coercive power* is perhaps the most visible element of power. Military power is also the most costly in national treasure and in blood. Military power revolves around institutions such as the army, the police, or other groups or organisations – the first two constitute legitimate coercive power, whilst the latter less so. This form of power is perhaps the most immediate and brutal means by which national power may be brought to bear on other states in pursuit of their compliance. The state, which often has political legitimacy, has monopoly over this form of power to protect and coerce internal rebellion or external conflict. It is perhaps most effective when it is self-sufficient and can be brought to bear unilaterally. The augmentation by alliances and other auxiliaries, however, reduces its capacity to intimidate.

In addition to this four power sphere, some would contend that 'knowledge' (see S. Strange, 1988, and especially important in the Gramscian understanding of power – discussed below) should be added to the four part list of power structure, because it is argued that 'knowledge is power' and who ever has most knowledge has most power. Although I do not disagree with this assertion, I contend that knowledge without wisdom or focus is not power, it is a mere collection of facts – and without purpose it is of little relevance. Further, without the ability to interpret that knowledge into reality is barely to be in the shadow of knowledge – not the controller of knowledge. The ability to control, interpret and implement knowledge for circumstance, time and place, is real power.

Withholding these weaknesses, however, it is well known that throughout human history, having knowledge has often also meant having more sophisticated technology than opposing forces. The knowledge of sophisticated technology has supplied vital sources of advantage to actors as a means to control other people and/or to 'dispose' of their opponents, and as a measure to 'counter' the 'harsh' natural environment as well. Unlike the four power spheres above, knowledge in the guise of technology is visible and less subjective (theoretically) than other power variables. The benignity or malignity of use depends on the actor's intention and preference to use that knowledge or technology. In contemporary society, the rapid advances and changes in technology such as biotechnology, nano-technology (see for example K.E. Rexler, 1990) and information technology (whereby mass communication is strengthening) are enhancing societies, but this also has a high potential for unleashing challenges to traditional understandings of the power structure and its relational bases. *If* the focus of technological structure is determined in such way, it may allow the power-wielder to move beyond 'normal' practices of daily life. It gives the power-wielder the ability to do 'good' as well as 'bad', depending on the 'preference' and motive(s) of that power-wielder with regard to that technology.

Like my analysis of theories earlier, these spheres of power may often overlap and at times are in a mutual supportive relationship with the overall power structure of social interaction. No power sphere exists in isolation; they are entwined with each other (although, I contend that political power with an objective gives the others a purpose for action). What is different is how to exercise a power resource (or a combination of them) with will and focus to bring into being an advantageous position for the power-wielder. The ability to discern the right time under the circumstance, and to apply a method that is effective to that situation is foremost in power relationships. Obviously, application of power will also depend upon to whom and at what distance that action is to be directed!

In another guise of power, Susan Strange talked of how 'structural power', as compared to relational power, actually sets the shape of global affairs, where states, institutions, enterprises, and individuals operate (1988: 24-5). According to Strange the significance of this power 'decide[s] how things shall be done, the power to shape frameworks within which states relate to each other, relate to people or relate to corporate enterprise' (1994: 25). The structure of power, which influences the operation of world affairs, according to Strange, consists of: security, knowledge, production and finance. Each structure is equal in weight, and each is interconnected with others. Like the power spheres outlined on pages 37-8, Strange's power pyramid is said to be in continuous interaction and the significance of each will shift according to how actors place emphasis on each structure (1988: 31). This in turn will affect and probably shift the structure of the international system (1988: 232). Later, she suggested that there is another layer of secondary structure (transport systems, trade, energy and welfare), which are all linked to shape the framework of power spheres.

In addition to the four spheres of power, three relational characteristics determine the 'movement' of power structure and the structure of international affairs. According to Mann (1993: 6) these are:

- Distributive and collective power. Distributive power is the power of *a* over *b* (for *a* to acquire more distributive power, *b* must lose some). Collective power is the joint power of actors (where *a* and *b* co-operate to exploit nature or another actor *c*).
- Power may be intensive or extensive. Extensive power can organise large numbers of people over far-flung territories. Intensive power mobilises a high level of commitment from participants.
- Power may be authoritative or diffused. Authoritative power comprises will commanded by an actor and conscious obedience by subordinates. It is to be found most typically in military and political organisations. Diffused power is not directly commanded; it spreads in a relatively spontaneous, unconscious, and de-centred way. People are constrained to act in different ways, but not by command of any particular person or organisation. Diffused power is found most typically in ideological and economic power organisations.

Further to the characteristics of power, to incorporate others' strengths and capabilities into one's own power base is significant for increasing power credibility and capabilities. The ability to manipulate (or charm) the strengths and capabilities of others to incorporate it into one's own gives the power-wielder a multiplier effect in the exercise of power (the significance of this ability is discussed in greater depth in the later chapter with regard to U.S. hegemonic manipulation of international regimes, institutions and allies). However, the incorporation of the others' power base without mastery of intentions is likely to create vulnerabilities and the impact of power implemented would most likely be curtailed (chapter eleven shows how the United States, more so than any other power, has understood this strategy and has applied measures to counter possible short-falls). Finally, the exercise of a power relationship is likely to be determined by the distance, time, mutual connection, credibility of capabilities and resources, and experiences of the power-wielder *vis-à-vis* the power relations of actors. The seeking of objectives is to ensure that all elements of power are integrated in a coherent nature so as to ensure the determined outcome.

With some basis for understanding the power spheres and the exercise of power, it is the aim here to analyse briefly the three mainstream ('Realism', 'Liberalism', and 'Marxism') theories of power and their definition and structuration of the power sphere. The interpretations of power invoke changes under different lenses of analysis. As such, I have found it necessary to incorporate the work of Lao Tzu's *Tao Te Ching* into the three mainstream ideologies. In my reading, I have found Lao Tzu to cover the realms of all three theories with regard to power. From this perspective, I contend that the nature of humanity and the affairs of governance cannot be subdivided into separate boxes when trying to comprehend the nature of power which involves inherently the interactions of the affairs of man.

The 'Realist' Tradition

As in any general theory or approach that attempts to analyse the affairs of humanity, 'realism' appears in many forms (see for example J. Baylis and S. Smith, 1997; M. Doyle, 1997; A. Wendt, 1999). For most realists the above definitions and exercise of power would be compatible, depending on circumstance and understanding of power capabilities and exercise, with the view of 'reality'. It is compatible because 'the main signpost [of political realism] is the concept of interest defined in terms of power' (H. Morgenthau, 1948/993: 5).

On the other hand, because of its many facets, realism is probably a term/theory which has often been misunderstood. Scholars, whether explicitly or unknowingly, have sometimes misinterpreted it[4] and even dogmatised it to such an

---

[4] During the Cold War there was a deliberate attempt by modern realists to separate domestic and international politics (i.e., Waltz, 1979) as an appropriate axiom in understanding the complexity of world affairs. I do not subscribe to the deliberate separation between domestic and international politics set out by modern realists. I contend that the modern 'realists' that have laid claim in separating this have not only made a serious mistake in judgement; they are by nature very vulgar; to so simplify the complexities of international affairs into some boxes and formulas. By placing domestic politics into a form of black box, and ignoring it from contention in international events, they placed the reputed name of 'realism' into a corner which 'traditional realists' would find misleading and

extent as to simplify its operations into a mechanical structural dogma (for argument against this see R. Keohane, 1986 (especially the chapter by Richard Ashley); J. A. Vasquez, 1997: 899-912; Schroeder, 1994: 108-48). The fabrication of mechanical tenets into realist philosophy has not only imprisoned the theory into a set of 'abysmal' assumptions (S. Strange, 1988: 11), it also raises the question as to whether the modern interpretation of realism has anything in common with 'reality', let alone the classical realism of Thucycides, Sun Tzu, and Machiavelli (R. Keohane, 1986; S. Guzzini, 1998; J.A. Vasquez, 1998; E. Kapstein and M. Mastanduno, 1999; F. Wayman and P. Diehl, 1994; J. Baylis and S. Smith, 1997; M. Doyle, 1997; and many others). Hugh Dryer, for example, critically notes, in 'attempting to provide a general theory of international politics, the realists have lost sight of their goal ("reality"; a kind of truth claim) in search for rigor, simplicity and means of political "control". . .' (1997: 43). Schroeder showed how 'a normal, standard understanding of neo-realist theory, applied precisely to historical era where it should fit best, gets the motives, the process, the patterns, and the broad outcomes of international history wrong . . . it prescribes and predicts a determinate order for history without having adequately checked this against historical evidence' (1994: 147). The misunderstanding has become so contagious that Vasquez claims that 'the realist paradigm is a fundamentally flawed and empirically inaccurate view of the world' (1998: 1). He charges that 'realists' 'ransack history', and 'would support their case by going through history to collect examples that buttress their point' (1998: 293).

There are certainly many serious accusations levelled against 'realism', and it would be an arduous affair to vigorously define all realist attributes. Given these circumstances, the only viable way which I believe can 'demystify' some of the attributes of what is and what is not realism in its relation to power is to try to understand the nature of the 'classical realists' position and their explanation of history and human affairs.

From my understanding, the realism of the classics is based upon the ability of the power-wielder to understand how to permutate (or change) into different formations and be ready for the dynamics of the given environment, and if necessary to use (or utilise) all (or some) means or resources to move from a disadvantageous position to an advantageous one (Sun Tzu; Thucydides; Machiavelli; *The I Ching*,[5] *The Guanzi*; Kautilya). The source is to anticipate

---

'unreal'. 'Traditional realists' believe that the nature of politics is the 'art of politics', and one of the basic principles of that art is not to be 'trapped into a dark pit'. It is by this art that the understanding of the contemporary framework of world affairs, both the domestic and the international agendas are necessary and relevant to understand the dynamic nature of power that operates in that environment.

[5] A 'book' which many have 'condemned' as a book for divination, fortune tellers and even being associated with 'new age' cults. There are obviously many reasons for condemning and distorting (some honest, others not so) this major work, but one thing that must be made strictly clear, *The I Ching* was never meant to be interpreted into such mannerisms! It is interesting, however, to see why and how certain people have decided to do so.

change (and/or to understand what is appearing) and how to 'govern' or even to control that change without losing balance of reality. A second connotation of this 'realism' (and some neo-realism) is to look at the world as it really is. This follows from E.H. Carr's analysis of realism as compared to idealism. Carr stated that realism is 'what was and what is' (1946: 11), in contrast to what could and what should be. These two levels of analysis are what could be interpreted as what really differentiates 'realism' from the 'rest'. Power is central to politics (in theory and practice). Idealism forgot this, so it was a mistake. Power is always transmuting.

The misinterpretation of realism by modern scholars by incorporating 'unreality' and ahistorical mechanical assumptions (especially Waltz, 1979 over emphasis on neo-classical economic theory as a way forward for political science) has narrowed the fluidity of 'realism'. From this distortion, the definition of power, which is at the centre of realist ideology, has been turned into something rather vulgar and illusionary. Finally, connected to the first understanding of the nature of classical realism, many scholars have criticised the 'simplification' of 'realism' as rendering it unable to comprehend change and/or to have sufficient ability to understand and anticipate change (this is especially directed to 'realist' scholars who were unable to 'forecast' the fall of the Soviet Union and systemic collapse of communism – see M. Cox, 1998). I do not intend to invite a major debate here at this moment (because it would move beyond this chapter and not the focus of this book), however, I can indicate that given how 'realism' has been understood and interpreted, it is not surprising that these (major and systemic) anticipations were not foreseen (please refer back to chapter one on M. Cox, 1998, comments) by modern 'realists' and others.

My aim here is to give a brief analysis of the elements of realism's interpretation of power, and try to dethrone some of the 'myths' created by scholars concerning what realism is or is not (A. James, 1989: 215-29) in their understanding of power.

Realism: First Image

The most common claim made by scholars about realism is the assumption that realists place military power and coercive force above all other power resources, and that force is therefore the final arbiter. Michael Howard, for example, argued that military capabilities constitute the main defining characteristic of power (cited in K. Aldred and M.A. Smith, 1999: 7). This may be so in a very strict sense, but unless military power is used in a brutal and annihilating manner, military power does not necessarily mean political control – in the medium or the long-term. The politics of the affairs of mankind are far subtler than the naked use of force as a final arbiter as a means of pursuing interests. What the critics appear to have missed out are the scenarios by which actors may manipulate power spheres without falling into such a path. In itself, force is impotent. Blaise Pascal stated: 'force without justice is tyranny. Justice without force is a myth because there are always bad men; force without justice stands convicted of itself' (cited in C. Freeman, 1994: 151). Kenneth Waltz identified that: 'Possession of power should not be identified with the use of force, and the usefulness of force should not be confused with its usability' (1979: 185).

Yet, there is another side to this, because of the multiple meaning of realism, critics may have legitimacy in portraying realists as followers of the brute concept, suggesting that most realists believe that military variables determine the legitimacy for the use of force – meaning that 'might is right'. Critics argue that most, if not all, realists would agree that power without strength and will is merely an aimless exercise. Critics argue that the ultimate source for a realist is strength, and to deny this is an attempt to create illusion and to mislead. Critics use the example of Oliver Cromwell's statement, 'A man-of-war is the best ambassador', (in C. Freeman, 1994: 228), and Mao Zedong's reputed saying, 'power issues from the barrel of a gun'. Furthermore, a state/kingdom was legitimate if it had the ability to defend itself or to wage war. Even E.H. Carr in *The Twenty Years' Crisis* wrote, 'The supreme importance of the military instrument lies in the fact that the *ultima ratio* of power in international relations is war' (1939/46/64: 110). In this strict sense, military power defines the determinates of war and peace, and the life and death of a nation. Sovereigns reigned because of military power, and war was seen as the 'sport of kings'. Whether it is in the intention to create confusion or to mislead opponents, most realists would, however, argue that 'Force is cheap' (Waltz, 1979: 186).

This Waltzian position sounds very much like a laissez faire approach to governance and power relations. Yet there is more subtlety here than merely prescribing a policy of minimum intervention. For stability to have any reverence in society, power is needed to maintain order, because 'the use of force signals a possible break down' (Waltz, 1979: 185). Interestingly, Lao Tzu in number 36 of the *Tao Te Ching*, wrote:

> He who is to be made to dwindle [in power]
> Must first be caused to expand.
> He who is to be weakened
> Must first be made strong,
> He who is to be laid low
> Must first be exalted to power.
> He who is to be taken away from
> Must first be given,
> This is the Subtle Light.
> Gentleness overcomes strength:
> Fish should be left in the deep pool,
> And sharp weapons of the state should be left where none can see them.

Again, Waltz says, 'Force is most useful, or best serves the interests of such a state when it need not be used in actual conduct of warfare' (1979: 186). Therefore, can the 'realists' (even the Waltzian approach) be criticised for being mere followers of 'raw' power?

However, ardent military power (or hard power) has often been visible in 'paving' the way for legitimacy that allowed and determined the makeup of national and international law on the right to govern in certain territorial entities and peoples. Jean-Jacque Rousseau wrote: 'The strong party is never strong enough to remain the master forever, unless he transforms his strength into right and obedience into duty' (*The Social Contract* translated by Christopher Betts, 1994: 48). In these circumstances, kings such as Louis XIV of France even claimed to be the state, meaning that without the King there would be no state and thus no legitimacy. Similarly, others were just or even more exuberant, for example laying claim to be mandated by God or Heaven[6] (as in the case of Britain, China, and Russia) and/or even claiming to be descendants of god(s) (as in the case of the Roman, French and Japanese emperors) than just purely basing their reign on military power. The mandate to rule from God gave the aristocracies (the ruling class) a mythical romantic legitimacy over the brutal original foundation of military victory of their forefathers. Barry Gills states that, 'Conquerors throughout the ages have been quick and astute to invoke divine sanction or absorb the existing tradition to this end'.[7]

Depending on how well military strength is maintained, economic resources and economic power are not far behind, sometimes being the determining factor in the survival of the state. However, many strands of realism assert that economic power 'has always been an instrument of political power' (E.H. Carr, 1939/1946/1964: 113), and was always subordinated to a supporting role in the capacity to wage war successfully rather than a determinate factor of military power. However, the extent to which military power can prevail over other power forms and variables, especially without accumulated economic power as a source for that power, is sometimes questionable. For example, recall the legend of the descendant of Aeneas. When the thirteenth King of Alba died, he left two sons, whose names were Amulius and Numitor. It could not be decided which of the two should be King. So Amulius said to Numitor:

> Let us divide what we have. Here, on the one hand, is the city and the land; and here, on the other, is all the treasure that Aeneas brought to Italy from Troy, hundreds of years ago. Which will you have, Numitor – the treasure or the land?"
> "I will choose the land," said Numitor, "and you shall keep the treasure. You will be a richer man than I, but I will be the King of the land.[8]

Amulius agreed to this, and the division was made. However, Amulius longed for land as well as the treasure, and he was now a rich man, while Numitor was only a

---

[6] Religion became a powerful tool for sovereigns to lay claim to legitimacy. The 'creation' of God, mysticism, prophets, and their descendants gave unchallenged authority over people and to treat non-believers as heretics or 'treacherous infidels'.

[7] I am grateful to Barry Gills for this valuable citation.

[8] Eleanor Farjeon (1924) *Mighty Men: Book 1, From Achilles to Julius Caesar* (Oxford: Basil Blackwell), pp. 72-3.

poor King. Therefore, with his money, Amulius paid the soldiers to fight for him, and he turned Numitor out of the city and became the King of Alba. In this way, he had the money and the land as well. From this perspective, and according to Jacob Viner, 'trade is the source of finance, and finance is the vital nerve of war' (cited in M. Doyle, 1997; see also P. Kennedy, 1989).

In most other cases, however, political power also meant military strength and political legitimacy. Political legitimacy enables leaders to make or amend laws in their favour. Take for example, contrary to the Amulius-Numitor legend, the case of the Chinese in Southeast Asia, i.e., in Malaysia and Indonesia (compare to the Jews in pre-1933 Europe). It is often reported that this small grouping control some 60 to 80 percent of the wealth of these nations. Yet, on many occasions they have been unable to transform it into military power or even political power to make their economic power effective. Partially due to disunity and greed amongst the richest Chinese, the mass Chinese minorities remain treated as near second class citizens in what many of them claim to be their homes. Wealth alone, without clear manipulation and unity of that force, would never be able to influence and control the political sphere. Political power is the ability to make or change laws. Laws can be used to make the wealth of the Chinese illegitimate. In this sense, many realists would agree that political power is supreme, because a 'wise ruler' or group can use this power to define or design the way we interpret historical evidence and make up laws and legislation that would help their cause.

Yet, contrary to the abuse of political power, 'Force is least visible where power is most fully and most adequately present' (E.H. Carr, 1946: 103, 129-32). This is different to authority or influence. It is the power of confidence, high morale, and will. The concentration of these variables is significant for potential power increase. Waltz states:

> [P]ower maintains order. The better ordered a society and the more competent and respected its government, the less force its policemen are required to employ. ... Similarly in international politics states supreme in their power have to use force less often ... Powerful states need to use force less often than their weaker neighbours because the strong can more often protect their interests or work their wills in other ways – by persuasion and cajolery, by economic bargaining and bribery, by the extension of aid, and finally by posing deterrent threats (1979: 185).

Realism: Second Image

The second image that realism has been associated with is its close relationship to power-politic and the negative connotations associated with it. In this interpretation power is seen as some 'evil dark force', that aims at domination and arbitrary control (E.H. Carr, 1939/46/64: 103). Nevertheless, this subjective 'evil' force may be seen reflectively in most states, organisations, and individuals that are in areas of importance (subjectively). Thucydides stated: 'Into . . . human affairs the question of justice only enters when there is equal power to enforce it, and . . . the powerful exact what they can, and the weak grant what they must' (in C. Freeman, 1994: 152). Ironically, and subjectively, power in this sense can sometimes be seen as a 'good light force'. This is often associated with churches, or status quo powers that are content with their position and are powerful enough to create positive images that suit their needs (this is examined in greater length in the following chapters). Kenneth Thompson noted, 'Politics are means and ethics are ends. Means may be evil, but good ends, to which means are subordinated, can endow means with good ethical content. The dictum that "the end justifies the means" seems in the realm of politics, to furnish a simple clue to the problem. Yet for men and for nations, the universal practice is to justify every evil measure by claiming it serves an ethical goal' (Kenneth W. Thompson, 1960, *Political Realism and the Crisis of World Politics*, p. 137; compare to Machiavelli, *The Prince*). From such a perspective, it is difficult to comprehend objectively what is good and what is evil particularly when the values defining different interests are in conflict (elaborated in chapter five). However, the question is not whether power can be used for good or evil, but to understand that 'the only good use of power is the power to do good'.[9]

Nevertheless, subjectively, because of the 'dark' nature associated with power-politics, many practitioners have been careful to deliberately try to disguise and distance themselves from it. Why not, since only fools would openly identify themselves with evil. This emphasis is easily identified in the U.S. assuming a position of absolute 'moral' rectitude of whatever its action. The U.S. has often portrayed itself as 'we are the good guys!' Therefore by definition the U.S. can do no wrong (i.e. no immoral action is conceivable – only a 'mistake' in execution, not in intent, because the U.S. always has *Good* intention. Madeleine Albright captures this American imagination by stating: 'I truly believe in the goodness of U.S. power.' . . . '[W]e are the organising principle.'[10]

Philosophically, however, and as outlined above, sometimes identifying what is good and what is evil is very difficult in politics.[11] Furthermore, '[d]espite the bad odour that clings to the very notion of power because of the misuses to which [it] has been put, power in itself is neither good nor bad. It is an inescapable aspect of every human relationship . . . To a greater degree than most imagine, we are the products of power.'[12] In an informative study of Japan, Reinhard Drifte

---

[9] This epigram is Barry Gills'. See also F. Bacon (1601) *The Essays* – 'Of Great Place – ' . . . power to do good, is the true and lawful end of aspiring.' Note also the 'Fundamentals of Statecraft' (U.S. National War College) citation on p. 1.
[10] *New Internationalist* (October 2000), p. 29.
[11] This is a little caption of what the 'Devil' stated: 'I AM EVIL; the only created being that *should* be evil . . . Evil is doing that which one *shouldn't* do . . . I *shouldn't* do GOOD, so for ME, GOOD is EVIL . . . But I *should* do EVIL. So I *should* do GOOD . . . . Hmm.' *Philosophy Now*, issue 26, April/May 2000: 20.
[12] Alvin Toffler (1990) *Powershift* quoted in Stephen Dando-Collins (1998) *Business Wisdom*, p. 225.

suggests that Japan aims to avoid being seen as 'powerful'. It has 'real' power but does not want others to perceive it as being 'powerful' (1996: 8-9). In this sense, to have power does not necessarily mean that one has to continuously show it. This lesson is vitally important in the art of politics and diplomatic relations. Metternich counselled, 'Diplomacy is the art of avoiding the appearance of victory' (Metternich, *Memoirs of Prince Metternich*, 1880). In a similar fashion, former German Chancellor Helmut Kohl stated: 'We know we are number one in Europe . . .We don't have to say and show it everyday.'[13] Thus, the ultimate art of politics is to have what you want, whilst others feel it is in their interest to get it for you. That is the true power of power politics (J.A. Vasquez, 1999) and why power is the 'ultimate aphrodisiac' (H. Kissinger, 1964) for the practitioner of power.

'Liberalism' and Power

Traditionally liberalism has not been the opposite of realism. The usual opposite to liberalism is conservatism and mercantilism. Like realism, the theory of liberalism has assumed many forms – classical, neo-classical, Keynesian, monetarist, Austrian, rational expectation, commercial liberalism, republican liberalism, sociological liberalism, neo-liberalism, etc (R. Gilpin, 1987: 27). However, in a basic definition, most liberals would adhere to the principle that for an actor to achieve maximum efficiency, growth, liberty, and happiness: there must be a laissez faire approach in general.

Most liberals do not deny realism's thesis of anarchy and the struggle for power in the international system, however there is disagreement as to what this means and why it matters with respect to the nature and consequences of international interaction (D. Baldwin, 1993: 4). Consequently, unlike vulgar realist (or mercantilist) emphasis on military power, zero-sum game, and prestige, ultra-liberals argue that the enhancement of laissez faire activities will in actuality enhance the power of the individual and society. Lao Tzu, for example, perhaps the first liberal writer, stated in lesson number 57 of the *Tao Te Ching*[14] that sovereigns should:

> Rule a kingdom by the Normal.
> Fight a battle by [abnormal] tactics of surprise.
> Win the world by doing nothing.
> How do I know it is so?
> Through this:–
> The more prohibitions there are, the poorer the people become.
> The more sharp weapons there are,

---

[13] Cited in *Financial Times* (1999, 25 May) 'The rebirth of confidence', p. 19.
[14] Note: *The Far Eastern Economic Review* traced Adam Smith's brand of liberalism, via the physiocrat Francios Quesnay (1694-1774), whose 'laissez faire' was influenced by the *Tao Te Ching*.

> The greater the chaos in the state.
> The more cunning things are produced.
> The greater the number of statutes,
> The greater the number of thieves and brigands.
> Therefore the Sage says:
> I do nothing and the people are reformed of themselves.
> I love quietude and the people are righteous of themselves.
> I deal in no business and the people grow rich by themselves.
> I have no desires and the people are simple and honest by themselves.

In these principles, many liberals, in one way or another, would follow Lao Tzu's brief definition of non-interference ('wu-wei': i.e., 'to do by not doing' or 'non-action'). In economic liberalism, for example, the utility of society and individual are maximised when individuals are 'free' to choose to (re)allocate resources according to the point of expected optimum. Smithian liberals would argue that excessive government interference in society is seen as 'retrogressive' to society, whilst a 'non-interference' approach would be seen as 'progressive' (Gilpin, 1987: 30).

Robert Gilpin following a neo-classical interpretation of liberalism, states that economic and military/political powers are separate spheres of power. Secondly, he argues that liberals assume that individuals are rational actors, have 'complete knowledge', and are, moreover, 'able to select the most efficient course of action' (1987: 28).[15] Thirdly, Gilpin maintains that 'economic intercourses are the source of peaceful relations' among actors because of mutual benefits gained through trade, whereas politics, he argues, tends to 'divide' (1987: 31).

In the works of Adam Smith (especially *Wealth of Nations*), the connection between wealth and security does not appear to be strikingly 'delinked', as in the 'neo-classical' (such as David Ricardo, Paul Samuelson, and many others, especially those in the monetarist school) liberals would argue. The difference between the neo-classical economists and Adam Smith is significant. Neo-classical liberals would agree with Gilpin's almost ahistorical assumptions of human behaviour and the make-up of society. In the *Wealth of Nations*, however, Smith explicitly indicated three *'and only three'* duties for states and other externalities involved in a not so 'perfect' world. First, 'protecting the society from violence and invasion of other independent societies, [which] can only be performed by means of military force' (Book 5, Ch. 1, p. 393). He continues, 'An industrious, and upon the account a wealthy nation, is of all nations the most likely to be attacked; and unless the people render them altogether incapable of defending themselves' (Book 5, Ch. 1, p. 400). Secondly, Smith outlined that the duty of the sovereign is 'protecting, as far as possible every other member of it, or the duty of establishing an exact administration of justice' (Book, 5, Ch. 1: 407). Finally, he states that 'the duty of the sovereign or commonwealth is erecting and maintaining

---

[15] Interestingly this position is also followed by 'neo-realists' on the assumption that individuals and state are rational actors, and both seek to maximise their position.

those public institutions and those public works, which, though they may be in the highest degree advantageous to a great society, are, however, of such a nature, that the profit could never repay the expense to any individual or small number of individuals should erect or maintain' (Book 5, Ch. 1: 413).

The work of Adam Smith was a direct attack on the mercantilist practices (which flourished in Western Europe in the centuries between the Renaissance and the Industrial Revolution), which was state-centred and self-regarding in their approach to other nations. Protectionism and the hoarding of precious metals or bullion were important to the country's balance of payments. This is best described as 'beggar-thy-neighbour' policy. This accretion of wealth, mercantilists argue, was the necessary condition for increasing capabilities and putative power to protect against foreign aggression. Smith and other liberals, however, argued that through trade and cooperation in international political economy actors may benefit mutually. To mercantilists, on the other hand, both wealth and power are seen in terms of a zero-sum game – that is, one country's gain is another's loss. The mercantilists' ultimate analysis of the relations among nations was that it is the priority for the state to be in a condition (or preparation) for war against all. Relative gain by others, especially in bullion, was dangerous to the survival of the state and sovereignty.

Although, Smithian liberals, neo-liberals, realists and neo-realists, would agree on national security, the anarchic nature of the international system (to some extent), and economic welfare, they differ in relative emphasis on goals and arrangements of governance. Secondly, 'liberals' and 'realists' would disagree on the relative importance of non-state actors, although both treat states as primary actors (D. Baldwin, 1993: 9). While not denying the anarchic character of the international system, 'liberals' argue that 'realists' and neo-realists place too high a priority on the state and underestimate the power base of other actors, such as multinational corporations, quasi-governmental organisations, and non-government organisations. Neo-liberals, such as Robert Axelrod and Robert Keohane argue that 'not only can actors in world politics pursue different strategies within an established context of interaction they may seek to alter that context through building institutions embodying particular principles, norms, rules, or procedures for the conduct of international relations' (in D. Baldwin, 1993: 87).

Whereas most realists would argue that the state is the highest place of sovereignty, liberals would contend that power is more diffused (and that includes the U.S.) in the international system. Liberals defend their position by arguing that relations between nations (as with individuals) are never equal, and that the neo-realists' emphasis on the equality of state sovereignty is nothing more than a misperceived assumption. Unlike neo-realists, the realists, from Thucydidian to Machiavellian perspective, never argued the equality of sovereignty for all nations. The power differential between them is significant in deciding whether a state is a great power or a minor power that has to act as a vassal to the greater. Secondly, liberals emphasise that international regimes and institutions are building and moulding principles, norms, rules and procedures to conduct international affairs which limits the 'sovereign' manoeuvre of state. Although not disagreeing with all realists, especially regarding the 'art of politics' that is involved inside and between regimes, liberals do not see the state as 'totally' sovereign or can simply isolate themselves. Liberals argue that power is being diffused increasingly into international affairs especially with the increased number and importance of regimes and other international bodies. Some realists would accept this to be true, but they emphasise that most if not all international regimes and international institutions are derived from the state entity. Furthermore, realists contest that the most dominant international regimes and organisations are actually dominated by powerful countries pursuing their own needs and benefits by this means.

The power strategy of interest in the liberal approach is its emphasis on toleration and avoidance of extremes. This toleration, however, unlike the almost intolerant of Kantian liberalism against non-liberals, emphasises the embracing of all into a cosmopolitan world – that is the acceptance of non-liberals also. Yet, the 'embracing of all' is seen from the 'realist' perspective as 'power maximisation', in the sense that it would increase the power of the actor further.

How 'power' is viewed and 'implemented', the following chapters will investigate the 'liberal' strategy of toleration and acceptance in light of the realist strategy of power maximisation. I will elaborate on the question: If world politics today is understood in terms of the (U.S.) 'liberal' hegemony at the level of 'superstructure', what is the power base or capabilities necessary to uphold that 'superstructure'?

'Marxism' and Power

Whereas 'liberalism' attempted to offer a diagnosis to mercantilist beliefs of 'self-interest' and zero-sum game analysis, Marxism attempted to offer diagnoses for the 'unfair' nature of established ideas of liberalism and mercantilism. Like realism and liberalism, however, and because of the difficulties in analysis of the concept of power (N. Poulantzas, 1973: 99), Marxism has also taken many forms since the original writings of Karl Marx and Fredreich Engels. The strands of Marxism have been seen to operate across, permeate into, and overlap into some of the basic assumptions of realism and liberalism.

Firstly, Marx and Engels in *The Communist Manifesto* are diametrically opposed to the liberal philosophy of classical economics.[16] However, many Marxists now adhere to evolutionary Marxism or social democracy, while the egalitarian form of liberalism is not so distinctively different from the Marxist approach. Secondly, whilst Marxists and liberals (especially ultra liberals) may disagree on economic distribution and welfare, somehow both believe that the utility of human society is best when, for Marxists, the 'withering away' of the

---

[16] Most Marxists would adhere to an idea of communism, where an efficient and equitable society would eventually be achieved through a central command economic system where goods and resources are allocated according to the central command's goals.

state occurs, and for ultra-liberals, when there is no state at all. Thirdly, many Marxists are seen as operating in a realist epistemological framework (e.g., R. Cox and T. Sinclair, 1996; R. Cox, 1997), in both theory and practice. The former Soviet Union, for example, acted and behaved in a distinctively realist fashion from its foundation in 1917 to its demise in 1991. One of the prime objectives of that country was to build a powerful army and industry to 'withstand' the 'anarchical' pressure of capitalist countries and their bourgeois agents' intention of undermining that new state. The second example is that the politics of many communist leaders are recognisable, if not identical, to the politics practised by non-communists leaders. Henry Kissinger (a conservative capitalist), for example, described Zhou Enlai, the former Chinese Foreign Minister and Prime Minister under Mao Zedong, as someone who understood his (Kissinger's) politics. Both operated under a similar theoretical lens of realism, and both were thus compatible, although their dispute followed from different ideologies of political economy.

The infusion of other theories into the 'purity' of Marxism, concludes Doyle, was precisely why socialists 'fail to behave as they seemed to have said they would, when in fact socialists joined the capitalists – that is, when both behave like nationalists' (1997: 316). The failure of Marxism was not the collapse of the Soviet Union or the communist states in Eastern Europe in 1989-1991. It happened much earlier. It was the failure of the Marxists to have a 'united front' against the bourgeois imperialists in 1914 that undermined international proletarian solidarity. Observers saw that 'the bond of brotherhood between nations had been broken and the spirit of international solidarity of the working class superseded by a spirit of national solidarity between proletariat and the ruling classes'.[17]

Having failed the decisive test in 1914, the Marxist movement has never managed to fully recover. It failed to break humanity's age-old curse of 'them and us' via nationalism, race, culture, religion, history, and ultimately the struggle for power. All these latter forms remain locked (and maybe un-lockable) doors for a revolutionary theory. So, what then is there left in Marxism to warrant a separate theory for analysis?

Despite 'grand plan failure' (in Eastern Europe and the USSR at least), and the overlapping with other theories, Marxism does have its own distinctive conception of power and politics. Although many countries have rejected it as the official ideology, Marxism still has significant ideological and intellectual prowess in the operation of domestic issues of class, race, structure, and social construction. So whereas most realists and liberals are 'horizontal' (relations between states), the Marxist view is 'vertical' (relations between classes) (G. Evans and J. Newnham, 1998: 317). In the sense that there is no separation between the international and the domestic policy; the international policy is just an extension of the domestic, in order to gain advantages.

---

[17] Julius Brauthal, 1967, *History of the International*, vol. 1, 1864-1914, trans. Henry Collins and Kenneth Mitchell (New York: Praeger), p. 355 in M. Doyle, 1997: 317.

Perhaps most central to the Marxist conception of power is the control of economics, politics, communication, military power forms, and structures by the dominant class in order to subordinate and cajole the lower classes. According to Marx, it is in the interest of the lower classes, especially the proletariat, to unite in concerted effort to break the chain of control of the dominant classes. To Marx and his followers, no social harmony may exist until the control of wealth and power are more evenly and fairly re-distributed.

As such, Poulantzas (1978/80: 44) advances the following propositions in a Marxist reading of power structure and relationship:

- Class power is the cornerstone of power in class divided social formations, whose motive force is the class struggle;
- Although grounded on economic power and the relations of production, political power is primordial in that changes in its character condition every essential transformation in the other fields of power (even if they are not themselves a sufficient condition);
- In the capitalist mode of production, political power occupies a field and a place that are distinct from the other fields of power, however much they may intersect one another;
- This power is pre-eminently concentrated and materialised by the State, which is thus the central site of the exercise of power.

Marx and his followers, thus, argue that power rests in the hands of those who control the means of production and the means to manipulate vast pools of wage labour. This Marxist (and neo-Marxist) approach outlines that those who own and control economic capital are at the heart and brain of society. They are at the heart because by disguising and manipulating the maintenance of 'tradition', 'social' values, 'virtuous' norms, 'codes' of practice, and other subjective morals, they are in fact, sustaining their own power position *vis-à-vis* the lower classes. They are at the brain because by the ownership and control of economic capital, activities, and production, this allows the privileged classes greater opportunity to be able to gain access to knowledge, and to understand how knowledge is assembled, utilised, and manipulated. Because of the privileged position of many dominant class members via their access to knowledge (largely because of the vast pool of wealth), the source of power-knowledge is inherently controlled or 'institutionalised' in such a manner that it protects and even determines the framework for interpreting and commencing of messages. In this sense, Michel Foucault argues that power produces knowledge and knowledge is necessary for power. 'All power requires knowledge and all knowledge relies on and reinforces existing power relations. Thus there is no such thing as "truth", existing outside of power' (in J. Baylis and S. Smith, 1997: 181).

In this way, the control of knowledge enables the ruling class to determine the framework for interpreting messages, which encourage it further to construct readings that are consistent with the interests of the dominant class. Many established institutions, such as churches, education institutions, communication agencies, and the state are inherently status quo establishments of the dominant classes, which issue ideas that are consistent in protecting and reinforcing the interests of the dominant classes. Poulantzas argued that these institutions and the state are 'the strategic site of organisation of the dominant class in its relationship to the dominated classes' (1978/1980: 147-48).

To discourage rebels, the institutions, norms and values, persuade and cajole lower classes or rebellious people into believing that to work within and for the system is in their best interest. This reinforcement and encouragement are to construct readings that continue to be consistent with the interests of the dominant classes' culture/ideology and practice. Breaking out, for Marxians, would need a revolutionary new mode of thinking and perception.

Fearing possible rebellion by the lower classes, the dominant classes cajole and 'educate' (to a certain extent) some sections of the lower classes, and allow them to 'move up' the economic and social ladder (but only in wealth and not blood, although through wealth, the lower classes may obtain titles). The dominant classes reinforce and defend their position and increase it further as the new lower classes move into social activities of 'respectability'. This class was what Marx termed a class that betrayed the proletarian origin. It was this class that Marx termed the bourgeoisie, whose slippery and unloyal allegiance except to itself, dismantled the aristocracy. According to Marx, in due course, the proletariat would challenge and overthrow the bourgeoisie.

In other (neo-)Marxist works (especially the philosophy developed by Antonio Gramsci and his followers), the ideational realm of power, that is knowledge, influence and propaganda, were seen as key elements of how to change the behaviour of individuals and the make-up of society (in what Joseph Nye 1990, latter termed 'soft power'). Instead of the revolutionary approach emphasised by Marxist-Leninists, Gramscians argued that by exposing increasing numbers of people to knowledge of social principles and virtues, society may eventually organically grow out of the capitalistic mode. It may appear that Gramsci and neo-Gramscians are a divergence from the revolutionary approaches of Marx and Engels. In *The Communist Manifesto*, Marx and Engels indicated that: 'The weapons with which the bourgeoisie felled feudalism to the ground are now turned against the bourgeoisie itself . . . But not only has the bourgeoisie forged the weapons that bring death to itself; it has also called into existence the men who are to wield those weapons – the modern working class' (translated by A.J.R. Taylor, 1967: 87). Those weapons were of course knowledge for the masses. The obvious danger is that once the proletariat has access to knowledge, will the proletariat remain loyal to the proletarian cause – or ironically, just become enchanted by bourgeois lifestyle and nationalistic sentiments?

Interestingly, Lao Tzu, in lesson 61 of the *Tao Te Ching*, wrote on the shifting power position from the weak to the strong and on relations between the hegemonic power and the weaker actors.

> A big country [should be like] the delta region,
> Being the concourse of the world,
> [And] the Female of the World.
> The Female overcomes the Male by quietude,
> And achieves the lowly position by quietude.
> Therefore if a big country places itself below a small country,
> It absorbs the small country;
> [And] if a small country places itself below a big country,
> It absorbs the big country.
> Therefore some place themselves low to absorb [others],
> Some are [naturally] low and absorb [others].
> What a big country wants is but to shelter others,
> And what a small country wants is but to be able to come in and be sheltered.
> Thus (considering) that both may have what they want,
> A big country ought to place itself low.

Lao Tzu's work, rather than being altogether 'counter-hegemonic', does show that the hegemonic power/class cannot afford to act malignantly towards the lower classes/states. This lesson also offers some insights into the intentions of the lower groups to 'overthrow' the powerful and wealthy. It is like saying that if the foundation is insecure even the footing of a giant has a very strong likelihood of being tumbled. That is, the ruler should not rule over the people, but rather should be the (greatest) servant of the people, and as Barry Gills states, '[i]n order to lead, one must be the servant of all'.[18]

Thus, power relationship in the Marxian perspective are perhaps most problematic. 'Pure' Marxian analysis would largely follow the belief of an equitable and 'equal' society amongst fellow men. Nevertheless, having power and the lust for power and its distribution remains almost insoluble in human affairs. Moreover, by emphasising power, even overthrow the capitalist system, the Marxist power-wielder has become the arbiter of power. In this sense, s/he has become the controller. Yet, the abolition of the means of control was the original intention of Marxism. By breaking away from the proletarian cause, however, the controller sets the goal for what society should be.

Another problem concerns human nature, and its inherent blindness to material gain and self-regarding betterment. Even if society were to become enlightened by the desire for a fairer and equitable environment, a deviant would appear (inadvertently) trying to better him/herself from the rest. In another scenario, a person becomes enlightened, but the surrounding environment is full of misery and materialist greed, with the envious desire to enhance oneself through any means. In this environment, what is enlightenment is seen as 'irrational' because it means that the enlightened person would not contend for material gain or loss. In this sense and in such environment, to be enlightened and 'rational' would be to those that have material wealth or power. How to break out of this

---

[18] This epigram is Barry Gills'. See also Robert K. Greenleaf (1998) (edited by Larry C. Spears), *The Power of Servant Leadership* (San Francisco: Berret-Koehler).

'realist-liberal' environment of human nature/society, and to offer a paradigmatic shift for how society is to be based is beyond the realisation of this book. However, before a revolution of a Marxist nature may be initiated, a simple question is raised – what happens after? Amongst the considerations would be, what condition of laws are necessary to 'govern' humanity? Moreover, is humanity 'perfectable'? What is the moral requirement for 'true' 'socialist man'? Is it realistically socially attainable? Or will 'power' always corrupt man and society?

Because of the scarcity and finiteness of resources, human beings would find it extremely difficult to live in peace with one another. Geographically, if one area has an abundance of resources whilst the others have few resources (this also applies to areas with suitable climate for habitation and vegetation), in such circumstances to prevent 'malpractice' and the accumulation of scarce resources, laws would be needed and agreed upon to govern. On the one hand, by enforcing laws, would it not mean some form of manipulation by the inhabitants and the employment of a law enforcer? Paradoxically, would not by having laws mean that this 'new society' would have just another form of control, although it might be different, but still there are inherent laws and rules. Can human society ever disperse with the necessity of power?

Again, power in the Marxian perspective is perhaps the most problematic, because Marxism largely believes in equality. Thence, having power and its distribution are perhaps insoluble, for as long as human nature remains imperfect. The means to control is difficult for the Marxist approach. By actually 'breaking out' of bourgeois control, what type of organisation would be involved without 'reverting' to the 'failed' lessons of the Soviet Union and allies. Human nature has the tendency to often be blinded by material gain. Even when the enlightened person desires a fair and equitable society, the surrounding environment of opportunists may not allow a new 'nature' to flourish. To the enlightened person, the world is indeed full of misery and greed, but to the opportunist this is what the world is – to do otherwise would be seen as 'irrational' because it would mean a minimum gain materially.

Other Definitions of Power and Conflicting Interests

Largely due to these different frameworks of analysis, it becomes consistent to argue that no agreement of the theory of power or the theory of international relations exists in a comprehensive or unitary form. All these ideologies fundamentally disagree about both the causes and consequences of the distribution or the uneven distribution of power among contemporary nation-states, groups, and individuals.

The concept of power overlaps across various bases and theories. A strict confinement of the definition of the concept 'power' thus cannot be achieved. What develops from this analysis is that rather than being inconsistent with one approach, the concept of power exists in almost 'all comprehensible' forms as interpreted by all contemporary theories of analysis.

Adding to the 'slippery' and complicated meaning of the concept power, there are in addition differences of culture, religion, race, gender, age, and other distinct differences, as well as the situational positioning and timing of strategy. This adds multidimensional pinnacles and multiple layers to the already complex concept of power. In addition, the cause and control of events, whether through timing, situational positioning (i.e., the war of positioning), and application of different methods to power (as a means to an end or a set of means to an end objective) is under analysed. Whilst increasing the means (or utility) of achieving the objective, other actors are, at the same time, in a constant struggle to either move into a position of power or to move out of a position of being controlled.

As indicated in the realist definition, power is often portrayed as a negative aspect in the affairs of humanity. Other power variables that are often not present in the analysis, but highly critical in the affairs of humanity include terms such as love, kindness, virtue,[19] will, and charisma – that are often labelled as intangible or immeasurable forms of power. It is in fact these intangible variables that I contend are the actual main engines behind the basis for the structure of economic, military, political and ideological spheres of power. With the intangible operations, moreover, the workings of power relations and structural change become highly subjective and emotional. The will or the focus of the subject of these intangible power variables has a greater significance than the four spheres of power base. I contend that, sometimes, to have vast power does not necessarily mean controlling all outcomes. If power is not used with cooperation in the intangible variables, it is wasted. Unless power is to be understood, the actor will remain powerless and its influence for good, limited.

---

[19] These three variables are especially powerful messages from 'religious institutions' – the 'power' of Jesus, Mohammed, Buddha and other religious icons is beyond what 'normal' conceptions of 'power' would illustrate. Yet, if power is to influence the behaviour of people and actors, these three religious icons are by far the most powerful beings to walk on the face of the earth.

Chapter 3

An Inquiry into Hegemony

Introduction

Having established a basic understanding of power, the priority of this chapter is to explore the theoretical basis for understanding the nature of U.S. power in the prevailing international order. U.S. power is so significant that many contemporary scholars have termed the U.S. as hegemonic. What do we understand by this term, the nature of the U.S. power, and its operation in the international system? To assist our understanding of U.S. power position, I have drawn upon three lines of thoughts that have offered insights into that nature. These lines of thoughts are reflected in the three main theories of hegemony. The first is the neo-Gramscian school of hegemony and transnational class relations. The second is associated with world-system analysis of the great powers' rise and decline, cycles and transition. The third is the neo-realist/neo-liberal (Kindleberger-Gilpin-Keohane) understanding of hegemony as a regime of stability for order.

Although these theories will provide useful premises for the way hegemony is used, the emphasis of the book will be to try to offer a *sui generis* consideration of the U.S. power position. This reconsideration assumes that the models for explanation of power relationship needs modification, especially with regard to the power relationship and structure of U.S. strategy in the emerging world order.

Definitions and Theories of Hegemony

The term 'hegemony' derives its origin from the Greek word, *hegemon*, meaning 'chief', 'leader', or 'ruler'. Following this, the *Oxford Dictionary* defines hegemony as 'leadership or dominance, especially by one state or social group over others', and hegemonic as 'ruling or dominant in a political or social context' (J. Pearson, 1998: 851). One of the earliest analyses of hegemony in western historical records can be traced to the writing of Thucydides, the fifth century BC Greek historian/soldier, who wrote the *History of the Peloponnesian War* on the contestation between Athens and Sparta for 'hegemony' in the Greek city-states. In Thucydides' writing the importance of power projections and the assets and attributes that were required for exercising power were crucial for understanding power and hegemony. In the *History of the Peloponnesian War*, four identifiable power attributes were essential for hegemony. First was naval power. This was particularly important given the geography of the ancient Greek world. Thucydides wrote 'they [naval forces] were the means by which the islands were reached and reduced, those of the smallest area falling the easiest prey' (translated by R. Crawley, 1997: Book 1, p. 11, para. 15). A second factor that was of significance was the stability and legitimacy of governance. Thucydides wrote of how the Lacedaemon, the city-state around which Sparta was founded, 'at a very early period obtained good laws, and enjoyed a freedom from tyrants which was unbroken for more than four hundred years, reckoning to the end of the late war, and has thus been in a position to arrange the affairs of the other states' (translated by R. Crawley, 1997: Book 1, p. 11, para. 18). Thirdly, economic grants and subsidies to allies and client states were also important for hegemonic power position. Thucycides wrote of how the Corinthian allies of Sparta informed the latter that 'supremacy has its duties . . . leaders are required to show special care for the common welfare in return for the special honours accorded to them by all in other ways' (translated by R. Crawley, 1997: Book 1, p. 60, para. 120). Finally, Thucydides and other Greek leaders were aware of the close connection between economic resources and military capability. He quotes one Spartan leader as stating that 'For unless we can beat them [Athenians] at sea, or deprive them [Athenians] of the revenues which feed their navy, we shall meet with little but disaster' (translated by R. Crawley, 1997: Book 1, p. 43, para. 81).

Following this tradition, Martin Wight identified three similar natures of hegemony in contemporary world affairs.[1] The first condition of hegemony is what he describes as the provision of an international public good. The second condition for hegemony is the existence of free riders (and the unequal distribution of costs for the provision) and/or a loss of legitimacy that undermines the relative power position of the hegemon. Finally, the declining hegemonic power presages a declining provision of the international public good (M. Wight, 1978: 289).

Amongst contemporary international affairs scholars who have also taken on the term with great interest is Robert Keohane. Keohane synthesised the word 'hegemony' and used it to refer to a:

> . . . state that has the possession of preponderant attributes and must have access to crucial raw materials, control major resources of capital, maintain a large market for imports, and hold comparative advantages in goods with high value added, yielding relatively high wages and profits. It must also be stronger, on these dimensions taken as a whole, than any other country (1984: 33-34).

---

[1] 'We have seen that the international anarchy is restrained and to some extent systematized in practice by two opposing kinds of common interest, pulling alternatively to and fro. The first is the common interest of all powers in their freedom, of which they are faintly conscious in peace, and assert at the eleventh hour in war by an armed coalition against a common danger. The second is the kind of common interest represented by successive dominant powers. For their predominance has generally safeguarded real values, and offered real benefits for other nations, and sometimes they have wielded an international ideology as their most potent weapon – as the Hapsburg powers were the protagonists of the Counter-Reformation, as Napoleonic France was the carrier of the French Revolution throughout feudal Europe, as Britain in the 19th century was the champion of liberalism' (Martin Wight, 1978, *Power Politics*, p. 289).

Similarly, although from a different strand of political thinking, Immanuel Wallerstein interpreted an hegemonic power as being in:

> ... that situation in which the ongoing rivalry between the so-called 'great powers' is so unbalanced that one power is truly *primus inter pares*; that is, one power can largely impose its rules and its wishes (at the very least by effective veto power) in the economic, political, military, diplomatic and even cultural arena [and that]... all allied powers are *de facto* client states and opposed major powers feel relatively frustrated and highly defensive vis-à-vis the hegemonic power (1974: 405).

The chapters on Russia, China, Japan, and the EU which follows will elaborate on great power relations in conjunction with the hegemonic power. These chapters will question and analyse the validity of the claim that the current international system is a hegemonic global system. In addition, these chapters will ask whether the major powers feel frustrated *vis-à-vis* the hegemonic power. The interest here is to establish a foundation for that argument.

(Neo)-Gramscian Hegemony

Drawing upon Thucydides, an important and significant cogitation of hegemony derives from the Italian Marxist Antonio Gramsci (1891-1937) in his contemplation of the leading elite and their control and management of civil society and institutions in fascist Italy in the 1920s to 1930s. Hegemony, in the Gramscian approach, does not mean the predominance of a 'state entity' as defined by Keohane or Wallerstein, but rather a group or a class that have abundance of resources and means to control and cajole other groups to support that structure. In this sense, Gramsci observed how the dominant class (largely the bourgeois class) was able to create and manipulate organs and institutions of state that were responsible for controlling society. According to Gramsci, hegemony is achieved when a provisional alliance of certain social groups exerts a consensus, which makes the power of the dominant group appear both natural and legitimate. Institutions such as the mass media, the education system, religious groups, and even the family (inadvertently) play a key role in the shaping of people's awareness and consciousness, and are, thus, agents through which hegemony is constructed, exercised and maintained.

Although Gramsci's analysis of hegemony was mainly based around domestic politics of interests, its usage was amplified when adapted and applied to the international system especially with regard to the 'business civilisation' (S. Strange, 1988). Robert Cox (1981), in an analysis of the general principles of production and control of civil society of leading classes and states over semi- and peripheral classes and countries, elaborated much of Gramsci's work into the international system and synthesised that this does not necessarily mean 'the dominance of a single world power'. Instead, it is understood as:

> ... dominance of a particular kind where the dominant state creates an order based ideologically on a broad measure of consent, functioning according to general principles that in fact ensure the continuing supremacy of the leading state or states and leading social classes but at the same time offer some measure or prospect of satisfaction to the less powerful (R. Cox, 1987: 7).

In this argument, hegemony is not simply a political order among states, but:

> It is an order within a world economy with a dominant mode of production which penetrates into all countries and links a dominant mode of production. It is also a complex of international social relationships which connect the social classes of different countries (R. Cox, 1983: 171).

According to this view, world hegemony is the intertwining of social, economic, political structures, and of the classes, all of which are rooted in a particular mode of production. From this, the hegemon co-opts other agents and actors to support the hegemonic system. Any functions that fall outside the hegemonic 'universal' structure would be seen as 'counter-hegemonic'. Counter-hegemonic forces often consist of labour unions, nationalistic groups, religious groups, environmentalists, some academics, Marxists, and some third world countries that are 'unhappy' with the current international political and economic order. This is a very wide group with very little in common, the only common agenda that is identifiable being their opposition to the liberal/hegemonic system. Obviously changing the current system would be desirable for some, but how 'they' are intending to replace the prevailing system, or what should happen to those that do not wish to change the current system remains difficult questions. The status quo forces have abundant resources and influence; the replacement of the current system will not be an easy task, as many would anticipate.

An important aspect of Gramscian thought is the emphasis on 'war of position' and 'war of manoeuvre'. What this entitles is the penetration of the hegemonic regimes and institutions by 'counter-hegemonic' agents that disguise themselves in order to influence, change and possibly undermine the nature of the politics prevailing and the structure of these regimes and institutions, from within. The fifth column technique being applied by some modern day Gramscian scholars is quite interesting, with its capability to 'undermine' not just one state, but intentionally the entire international state system. The difficulties for this counter-hegemonic technique, are that the reigning hegemonic forces also understand this technique and have even greater abundance of resources to counter the counter-hegemonic forces; with the hegemonic institutions managing to absorb many so-called 'counter-hegemonic' forces into their wing to actually work against the same principles which the 'counter-hegemonic' agents had intended.

Another aspect that the hegemon has utilised to permeate the counter-hegemonic forces is what Nye denotes as 'soft' cooptive power (J. Nye, 1990; R. Drifte, 1996). However 'soft power' is a tool that is used by both the hegemony and the counter-hegemonic forces. The 'soft' power of the hegemony is a strategy, whereby the hegemon makes its power legitimate in the eyes of others. The counter hegemonic forces will try to deter these perceptions by organically installing into the brains of people the nature of the hegemonic institutions. The obvious agenda for the dominant class is to propagate ideas of the dominant class in order to create a 'false consciousness' by which to subjugate the rest. The manipulation of the mass media has become a powerful tool by which the elite class can control the isolated citizens of society. This has worked so effectively that Cox argues that 'it will encounter less resistance to its wishes'.[2]

In addition, soft power has the penetrative force whereby 'hard' power cannot sufficiently manage without seriously erasing the foundations of societies and culture. Simply, the 'soft' power of the hegemony enables it to magnify its 'splendid' culture and ideology for others to (psychologically) believe that it is an attractive posture from which to follow. In achieving this posture, Cox and neo-Gramscians argue that the leading state establishes international norms, rules, and regulations, international regimes and institutions that are consistent with its society, to magnify these on a universal level. With the existence of these 'extra-state' regimes, other states' powers are limited or channelled in ways the hegemonic order prefers. Therefore, the hegemon may not need to exercise coercive or hard power in bargaining situations because everyone behaves in essentially the same level of mode of conduct. According to Russett and Gill, the U.S. used its hegemonic power (as Gramsci and Cox described) to promote liberal democracy as a political model after World War II, making U.S. style liberal democracy the cultural norm in the world (Russett, 1985: 230-1; Gill, 1990: 53; see also Pigman, 1992: 15).

The neo-Gramscian approach would, thereby, highlight issues of global class-consciousness and behaviour, not such matters as the rise and decline of hegemonic states. It also depends on how other actors perceive the hegemon's capability (as opposed to actual possession) and the willingness to use that capability.

However, what the cognition of this analysis fails to perceive is the inherent 'continuation' of the dominant to remain preponderant. Firstly, it fails to understand the cognitive reason as to why the rich and the powerful remain rich and powerful, whilst the poor and uneducated usually, through time and space, remain at the bottom. Secondly, it fails to foresee the agenda of the state to set its own interests. For example, what does it mean to the workers that are predominantly controlled by foreigners? Does the mode of production throughout the world necessarily mean that the workers or managers share the same interests? With the increasing importance of flexible means of production, the class interest has often been giving way to the interest of the individual, where the good of the group does not necessary mean the good of the individual. Thirdly, it failed to identify the uniformity of technology and subsequent emphasis on efficiency by the hegemony and hegemonic group. This process has created the standardisation and

---

[2] The author thanks Robert Cox for this valuable comment (December 1999).

commodificaton of social-cultural behaviour. Finally, as regard to the counter hegemonic proposition and position, Gramscians and neo-Gramscians failed to perceive the survival strategy of the hegemon – whether it be the class or the nation-state. I contend that the survival of the hegemony results from its flexible ideology to satisfy the demand of the masses. Todd Gitlin has described that, '[i]n satisfying the consumers' utility, the hegemon has also identified itself to giving the consumer the ultimate goal to happiness. In this consumer capitalist ideology, the ideas of liberty, equality or fraternities are conformed into the commodity forms, with a heavy (if not benign) eye of the national security state' (in Horace Newcomb, 1994, *Television: the Critical View*).

The Long-Cycle Approach to World Power

A second analysis of hegemony is long-cycle or transition theory. The most popular amongst the long-cycle theories is perhaps the work of George Modelski.[3] In adapting the Kondratieff wave theory, Modelski assumes the basic principle of synchronised movement and activities in the economy which can be systematically related to the role of political activities in society and in the world system as a whole. Modelski argues that the activities of economics are closely linked with and dominate the role of political activities (1987: 62). Therefore, Modelski argues that a down swing in economic activities tends to lead to political upheaval. In Modelski's long cycle theory, two distinctive modes are separated, the systemic mode and the learning mode. In the systemic cycle, a further four-phase schema is depicted as: Global War; World Power; Delegitimation; and Deconcentration. These phases are the descriptive events that occur at the global level of world politics. In the learning cycle, a four-phase sequence is identified: Clarification, Coalition, Macrodecision, and Implementation. Following these events of assessment, mobilisation, and development, a world power emerges. This is, however, only cumulated through a general war, usually a global-war that often follows economic decline and political tension. On this tenet, a proposed hundred year cyclical view of change in world leadership and great power is established. The theory contends that a long cycle begins with a major war. A single state then emerges as the new world power and legitimises its preponderance with post-war peace treaties. According to Modelski, the new leader supplies order for the international system. Through time, the leader loses legitimacy, and deconcentration of power leads to another global war. In Modelski's narrative analysis of world power, he identifies four distinctive world powers that have led the world system (in succession) since 1500; these were: Portugal, the Netherlands, Great Britain, and the United States.

---

[3] George Modelski (1987) *Long Cycles and World Politics* (Seattle: Washington University Press), refrains from using the term hegemony to explain his theoretical framework of world powers' rise and decline. Instead, he refers to the dominant power as a 'great power' or world leader.

Modelski's model of rise and decline of great powers has, however, come under criticism for its 'parsimony'. Political scientist and former assistant U.S. Defense Secretary Joseph Nye (1990) is extremely sceptical of the empirical evidence applied by Modelski on long cycle waves and change. Nye argues that the theory fails in its attempt to predict the future of U.S. hegemony, or evaluate the risk and consequences of nuclear war. Nye contends that Modelski's models are very heavily influenced by naval power (although this is to follow the Thucydidian emphasis of the importance of naval power) and are heavily Western orientated, i.e., Portugal, Netherlands, Britain and the United States, as a *sine qua non* of global power. Empires and powers such as the Mongol empire in the twelfth and thirteenth century that dominated virtually all of the Eurasia landmass are left out. China, with its long and often brilliant history, is explored by Modelski, but again it does not qualify as a global hegemon. The Ottoman empire, despite it being larger and more powerful than both Portugal and the Netherlands during its peak does not appear to appeal to Modelski, in fact the Ottoman empire had at its peak a greater and larger navy than Portugal and the Netherlands, its sailors and ships dominated much of the Mediterranean Sea, Red Sea, the Persian Gulf, the Indian Ocean and even entered the South China Sea in both trade and as a crusade for Islam. Technologically and ideationally the Ottoman empire was not in any sense inferior to those of the two powers mentioned above (for example see Barraclough, 1978/87; J.M. Roberts, 1995). The Russian empire, with its vast expansion into Asia from the 17th century, and how it played the most significant part in defeating Napoleon's hegemonic ambitions, again does not qualify. The Hapsburg empire, despite its jigsaw shape territory, had a far superior military force than both Portugal and the Netherlands, yet Modelski claims that the Hapsburgs suffered economic inefficiency and technological backwardness. Modelski's theory generally underrated these powers and empires despite their having a relatively superior military, geographic, and in some cases even technological scale. In Modelski's model, none of the great powers (with the exception of the U.S.) really had a great land army. In addition, the theory fails to comprehend the importance of the increasing interdependence of economics, ecological situations and the growing importance of mass telecommunication and its military usage – such as cyber-warfare – that has emerged with the development of computers. Failure to understand these situations leaves many to question the validity of professor Modelski's claim that hegemonic power such as that of the United States can decline and a period of discord and conflict will inevitably (re)occur.

Despite the 'heavy-handed' critics, the Modelski model does offer some fruitful scope for further study. It allows scholars to assess possibilities of rising powers and declining ones in the international systems in the traditional sense of sea power (in which sense this is consistent with Thucycides' argument as outlined above) and the domination of west Europe via the utilising of this particular power resource to eventually 'punish' other land orientated powers. Professor Modelski's work offers sources of enquiry to possibly answer why global conflicts occur and how they could be averted, or at least for potential rising powers and status quo powers to relatively analyse their power position before setting about a potential clash.

Hegemonic Stability Theory

The third school to use the term hegemony takes its characteristic in the form of hegemonic stability theory. Hegemonic Stability Theory (HST) was a research program developed by neo-liberal/Marxist economist Charles Kindleberger in 1973 and later advanced by neo-realists/liberals.[4] In an effort to revive the realist tradition of IR, HST combines various tenets of the above theories to assert similar definitions of hegemony. However, the main difference is that it argues for a stable and liberal world economic system under the reign of the United States. Its main reasoning is that there must be a hegemonic distribution of power; that is, one state must exercise preponderant power and influence over other states and actors in the political, economic and social structures of the world system for that system to be stable. In addition, the hegemon must be a state that is 'powerful enough to maintain the essential rules governing interstate relations, and willing to do so' (R. Keohane and J. Nye, 1977, 1989 2nd edit: 44).

The theory of hegemonic stability is often quoted as being associated with the era of British hegemony in the 19th century and the U.S. hegemonic dominance since 1945 and its assumed collapse after the breakdown of the Bretton Woods system (Calleo, 1987). The fundamental point of the theory is based on the relative stability of the global economic system during periods of hegemony and the alleged relative instability in the world economic system when there exists no hegemony to maintain and sustain that system. As Kindleberger proposed:

> . . . there has to be a stabiliser, one stabiliser . . . a country which is prepared, consciously or unconsciously, under some system of rules that it has internalised, to set standards of conduct for other countries and to seek to get others to follow them, to take on an undue share of the burdens (1973: 28, 305).

The second argument of HST follows from the neo-Gramscian deployment of regimes and institutions to arrange or at least to institute sets of rules, procedures, norms, and principles to maintain international order and stability. A third stems from the Thucydidian and Wightian emphasis on providing (international) public goods to followers. This strategy, however, has a reverse psychology to the literature of power-politics, especially in the distribution of power resources: hegemony is, thus, said to be the source of public goods that benefit all countries, regardless of their size differentials and whether or not they contribute. Indeed, following Kindleberger's work, the hegemon may benefit from the system also, but it must do so only whilst others benefit as well. To benefit at

---

[4] [Krasner (1976); Gilpin (1981, 1987) and popularised and criticised by Keohane (1982, 1984)].

the expense of others, Kindleberger argues, 'is exploitation' (1981: 242). In the power maximisation thesis, the likelihood of the power to allow others benefit without something in return is questionable. Economic theory would argue that although the intention of the hegemon is not to provide security for others, i.e., NATO to Switzerland and Ireland, but because of the size and geographical location of Switzerland and Ireland, the Swiss and Irish can benefit from the externalities without having to pay for it.

In this predicament, as the hegemonic power erodes because it is no longer able to support that system; rising states that occupy a disadvantageous position, whether an ally or an enemy, in the system inevitably challenge both the hegemon and the order with which it is associated. According to Kindleberger, the blame for the decline of the hegemony rests solely on the abundance of free riding, especially by allied powers and the inability of the hegemonic power to maintain control. As the problem of free-riding and declining hegemony increases, Kindleberger claims that 'the public good is under-produced, and that there is neither domination nor self-abnegation in the interest of responsibility' (1981: 249). In this respect, Kindleberger, describes that 'too much free riding makes the leader grow weary under burdens, which grow as more and more free riders seek more free rides that are luxurious' (1981: 251). Kindleberger's theory suggests that the hegemon may grow weary and become coercive because of its relative decline in the world economy.

According to HST, the danger in the world economy without a sole power leader would be serious. Kindleberger argues that for the world economy to operate without a stabiliser would inevitably lead to the world economy being run to a scenario of 'out of control' (Z. Brzezinski, 1993), as experienced during the late 1920s and the 1930s. In addition, HST argues that without a hegemonic country setting liberal goals and standards, all states would return to neo-mercantilistic trading policies. Gilpin reiterated this by arguing that 'in the absence of a dominant liberal power, international economic co-operation has been extremely difficult to attain or sustain and conflict has been the norm' (1987: 88).

As a critique of the hegemonic literature, it is reasonable to argue that hegemonic theories align themselves more closely with aspects of international economics than to international politics/security. HST, for example, failed to evaluate the direct challenge that the leading power, the United States, was having from the Soviet Union. To write about 'hegemony' in a period of bipolarity is interesting, but it must be clarified that the U.S. certainly never had hegemony over the USSR and its affiliate (including China).

Secondly, the United States was, during the larger part of the Cold War, prepared to allow allied powers in East Asia and Europe to free ride against its economic strategy in basically a 'zero-sum' game to defend the 'free world' from communism. To suggest that there were no benefits to the hegemon in co-opting these areas into the hegemonic system is questionable. Had the U.S. not secured compliance and influence over European and some East Asian countries, and had just allowed them to 'stray' into the communist camp, it would undoubtedly have brought serious consequences for U.S. global strategy against communism.

Thirdly, and perhaps most damaging, is that hegemonic stability theory has not been consistent with historical facts. For example, in the widely acknowledged period of British hegemony during the 19th century, Britain was, however, itself 'balanced' by the Concert of Europe. Britain did have the largest empire amongst the European powers, and it had the largest naval fleet amongst them. Nevertheless, Britain certainly never had 'hegemony' over France, Prussia/Germany, Russia, or the Austro-Hungarian empire. Its role in Europe from the 18th to early 20th centuries was that of a 'balancer' in the geo-political affairs of Europe and it was careful to detach itself and manipulate the balance of power system in Europe (M. Wight in H. Butterfield and M. Wight, 1966). Similarly, as outlined in points one and two, even the much-emphasised 'hegemonic' period of the U.S. from 1945 to 1973 was itself 'balanced' by the Warsaw Pact under Soviet predominance. The former is an example of 'oligopolistic hegemony', whilst the latter is an example of 'bipolar hegemony'. In both cases, the models of hegemony illustrated that hegemonic power is geographically restricted and global power had to be shared (or divided) with others.

Fourthly, during their periods as 'hegemons' Britain and the United States were not unmitigated sponsors of free trade. Free trade was, rather, a part of their strategy to gain advantages in trading high-value goods with certain partners. The benefits of hegemony accrued overwhelmingly to the hegemon. Calleo (1987) has shown how both the 'Pax Britannica' and the 'Pax Americana' were characterised by self-serving behaviour on the part of the respective hegemons at the expense of the system as a whole.

Finally, and in regard to the U.S. hegemony, the hypothetical analogy would be to suggest that had there been no Soviet Union, a general U.S. hegemony might have existed. However, the real characteristic of the world from 1945 to the demise of the Soviet Union in 1991 meant that U.S. preponderance was in fact limited in economic resources and preponderance over capitalist states and large areas of the Third World. Now that the Soviet Union no longer exists and the Warsaw Pact is buried away with most parts of the communist ideology, does this mean that in the coming decades the world will experience for the *first* time in human history a truly global hegemony, a proper Pax Americana?

The 'Final Word' on Hegemony?

Aside from the three theories of hegemony, the hegemonic concept, because of its close relations with the concept power, is used in as diverse and confused ways as the power concept, which depends on the perception of scholars and their definition of power and outcome. Scholars, such as Joseph Nye, acknowledge that:

> ... part of the problem is that unequal distribution of power is a matter of degree, and there is no general agreement on how much inequality and what types of power constitute hegemony (1990: 38).

He argues that all too often, hegemony is used to refer to different behaviours and degrees of control, which obscures rather than clarifies the analysis. Alan Cafruny reinforces this and asserts that the concept 'has generated more confusion than clarity' (1990: 97), especially when applied to U.S. hegemony and its alleged decline. Furthermore, the ambiguity of the term makes any clear empirical assessment difficult. Some writers have even gone to the length of complicating the term by closely relating or often associating it with leadership (J. Weinner, 1994). Hegemony is, however, of little theoretical or descriptive value if it does not imply something considerably stronger than leadership.

These problems would suggest that understanding the term 'hegemon' is often derived from agreement or disagreement over how evidence and power distribution are to be interpreted. As yet, no consensus has been established as to whether there can be either a simple hegemonic power in the world system, or a multiple hegemonic system where several hegemonies[5] co-exist as interlinking hegemonic powers (A.G. Frank and B.K. Gills, 1993: chap. 4).

As a compromise, but in no way breaking the confusion, Christopher Chase-Dunn outlines that in the modern world-system, 'the core of the interstate system is sometimes dominated by a single hegemon (a unicentric situation), and at other times power is more evenly distributed (multicentric)' (1990: 217). Even if there does exist a single hegemon or an existence of several hegemonies, how relevant is it to our understanding of international political economy and how does 'it', relate to empirical facts? Certainly, the idea of various great powers, i.e., the U.S., the EU, Japan, China, and Russia, dominating different regions in the world system is highly tempting. However, this book contends and explains that the international system after the Cold War does not appear to be heading down this path. The following chapters will examine this argument and the power relations between the major powers. It will show how these major powers are co-operating and collaborating for their own benefit and inadvertently consolidating the hegemonic globalisation as pursued by the central power, the United States.

---

[5] There is in this sense more than one hegemon; hegemony can be relative to one particular subgroup of states.

PART II

THE DEBATE AND THE CHALLENGE

Chapter 4

The 'Design' of the International System and 'the U.S. Hegemony' After the Collapse of the Bretton Woods' Fixed Exchange Rate System

Introduction

This chapter is organised into five sections. The first section tries to give a historic account of U.S. interests after 1945, to structure an international system that can best serve U.S. and allies' interests and needs. The second section examines the alleged 'decline' of that system and American power following the breakdown of the Bretton Woods system and the U.S. failure in Vietnam. It assesses the geopolitical and economic 'declinist' argument of U.S. power position. Section three evaluates the validity of the declinists' position with regard to the three main IR theories (Realist, Liberal, and Marxist/Gramscian). Section four briefly gives accounts of the perceived nature of U.S. power and strategy since the collapse of the Soviet Union. The conclusion draws on the arguments developed and it attempts to disclose emerging debates in the post-Cold War era.

Section I: The U.S. as 'Chief Architect' of the International Political and Economic System

It is widely acknowledged that World War II, instead of weakening U.S. power, left the United States as the world's foremost economic superpower, accounting for an amazing one-half of the world's total production (S. Chan, 1990). The international economic order and to some extent, the international political order was virtually under the hierarchical tutelage of the United States, though opposed by the Soviet Union.

Yet, the idea that the United States only became hegemonic after World War II (and after the Cold War) is an oversimplification of both history and theory. There was a desire in the United States from the end of the First World War to become a great or global power (H. Brogan, 1985). How it was to become a great power without getting too involved with other world powers, especially with the affairs of Europe, was important for its eventual emergence as global hegemon. The 'hegemonic' design advanced by political leaders in Washington during and after World War II was significant (see for example see N.J. Spykman, 1942/1970 reprint; R. Steel, 1967; M. Hudson, 1968). U.S. officials believed that they could not allow the U.S. 'merely to be a buffer state between the mighty empires of Germany and Japan' (N.J. Spykman, 1942/1970 reprint: 195). The U.S. must seek openness, access, and balance in Europe and Asia (G.J. Ikenberry, 1997: 11). It became in Washington's national strategic interest to expand from its hemispheric area in the Americas and the Pacific Ocean, to cover virtually the entire globe. For the United States, the initial goal was essentially to 'restructure the world so that American business could trade, operate and profit without restriction everywhere' (J. Kolko and G. Kolko, 1972: 2). In order to achieve this, the international system had to be redesigned and restructured to the benefit and needs of America. However, because of the predominance of the USSR's power position on the Eurasian landmass, Washington officials followed, but modified the ideas outlined by the British imperialist geographer Halford Mackinder (1904) concerning the Rim-Heartland theory (see also Z. Brzezinski, 1997a). U.S. strategists, like their British forebears, believed that it was in the United States' vital interest not to allow one or several hostile powers to dominate the Eurasia landmass. In Washington's prospectus, access to Asian and European markets and resources was vital for ensuring the U.S. position of global pre-eminence. Defense officials began to see that America's security interests required the building of an elaborate system of forward bases in Asia and Europe (see G.J. Ikenberry, 1997: 12) as part of the containment plan against communism (G. Kennan, 1947). In this sense, the United States was not strictly speaking a global 'hegemony' during the Cold War.

On the economic management of the global system, the U.S. along with Great Britain agreed to form the Bretton Woods system. This 'system' consisted of the International Monetary Fund (IMF), the World Bank,[1] a system of fixed exchange rates,[2] and later the General Agreement on Tariff and Trade (GATT), to maintain a liberal world trade system. Some scholars have argued that by creating these institutions and regimes, the United States could gel, consolidate, and extend its international economic leadership (Keohane and Nye, 1977; Krasner, 1983; Keohane 1984). They believe (via the 'hegemonic stability theory') that under U.S. leadership, international trade, investment, and monetary policy would be more stable (C. Kindleberger, 1973; R. Gilpin, 1981; 1987). The 'blood-line' for these institutions to operate effectively was the use of the U.S. dollar. The international exchange rate for gold was linked directly to the dollar at the par value of 35 dollars per ounce.

Whilst the international economic system was being redesigned, the empires of the imperialist powers (especially Britain and France) proved to be more difficult. Firstly, most colonial powers were important allies to the United States. Secondly, decolonisation proved to be highly difficult without former colonies falling under Soviet influence. Although there were conflicting interests and

---

[1] Formally known as the International Bank for Reconstruction and Development (IBRD).
[2] Known as the Gold Exchange Standard of the Bretton Woods system. Its main purpose was to stabilise currencies amongst major capitalist trading nations.

objectives of how to 'handle' these delicate affairs, the U.S. policy-makers recognised that before these empires could be dissolved, the United States and its allies must prevent the international system from descending into anarchy and prevent these countries from falling to communism. The aim of the U.S., after World War II, was to minimise conflict amongst the 'Western' alliance's major powers and stop them going to war with each other over these newly independent states.

The United States, along with its allies, recreated the international system. They agreed to replace the League of Nations with the United Nations. It was agreed that emphasis on great power interests should be catered for with the power of the veto as an important factor to minimise conflict of interests amongst the great powers. However, given the 'inevitable break' with the communist USSR and the threat perceived from it, the U.S. and its allies in Western Europe, Asia, and other parts of the world deemed it necessary to create security alliances. The United States established a 'balance' against Soviet conventional forces' superiority using nuclear deterrence and the stationing of American troops in Western Europe and Asia (G. Kennan, 1947, see also chapters on EU and Japan). In response to the economic weakness of Europe and Asia, and the growing 'menace' that communism posed to these economically weakened states, the United States initiated the Marshall Plan to rejuvenate the West and provide aid to allied Asian governments.

Despite Cold War hostilities, the new institutions, such as the UN, IMF, World Bank, BIS, NATO and others, have had more power installed in them than any other international institutions that were ever formed.[3] Stephen Krasner (1983) conceived the new regimes as being 'quasi-legal' in character. States have, according to Krasner, come to adopt a set of rules, norms, principles, and/or fixed sets of collective decision-making process. Robert Keohane argues that,

> . . . world politics lacks authoritative governmental institutions, and is characterised by pervasive uncertainty. Within this setting, a major function of international regimes is to facilitate the making of mutually beneficial agreements among governments, so that the structural condition of anarchy does not lead to a complete 'war of all against all' (in Krasner, 1983: 148).

To a large extent many of the countries of the world, despite gaining independence

---

[3] However, 'rarely if ever has it been American policy to endow multilateral institutions with significant independent power. Thus, the United States insisted on a veto in the UN Security Council every bit as much as the Soviets did. Voting in the International Monetary Fund and World Bank was and remains weighted, with the United States still having the largest single share. At American insistence, the General Agreement on Tariff and Trade barely existed as a formal organisation, though it has now been folded into an institutionally stronger World Trade Organisation. And the 'O' in NATO refers to a policy forum, secretariat, and largely American-dominated military command structure, not an autonomous body providing security to its members' (in John Gerald Ruggie (1996) *Winning the Peace: America and World Order in the New Era*, p. 21).

from their European colonial masters, have had their sovereign power curtailed by these international institutions, especially by the IMF and the World Bank. The anarchic international system was not truly anarchic.[4] The constraints on the ambitions of statesmen were further exacerbated by the bipolar system of the United States and the Soviet Union. Instead of anarchy, the world was locked into a bipolar system – a contestation with rules and regulations in which the U.S. and USSR were the main determinates of that order.

The organisations, institutions, and regimes were, as Arrighi pointed out, 'instruments for the transformation of the capitalist world into the U.S. image, the scaffolding for the substantive elements of hegemony' (in G. Amin, G. Arrighi, A.G. Frank and I Wallerstein, 1982: 57). Arrighi emphasised that these 'elements' were three: the reconstruction of the world market, the transnational expansion of capital, and the spread of Taylorist and Fordist modes of production and management. It was also through these institutions that the U.S. kept the defeated Axis powers of Japan and (western) Germany, and other allied powers, under the paternalistic wing of its liberal capitalist democracy. The establishment of these international institutions and/or regimes had the effect of 'influencing' 'the way other states pursued their interests, but also how they understand their own behaviour and define their national interests' (J. Nye, 1990a: 192). Indeed, by creating regimes, institutions, and organisations the U.S. had effectively created the rules, norms, and values that were parallel to its core interests and strategy (S. Gill, 1990; W. Robinson, 1996). These institutions would eventually become recognised universally through some form of mediation or pressure. Thenceforth, these institutions and/or regimes would enhance U.S. tangible and intangible operations by assigning to itself the legitimacy to lead the international system.

The promotion of economic prosperity and security guarantees for allies (and even non-allies) was not in any sense of the word 'free riding'. Instead, these were, as Hudson pointed out, 'the first among many disguises that the United States has applied to dominate the world' (1968: 18). They were manipulated by the United States in its quest for dominance of the capitalist system (M. Hudson, 1968; J. Kolko and G. Kolko, 1972). In its quest to subordinate secondary powers, the United States has had to cooperate, cajole, initiate, and even directly form a consensus (for example, the Trilateral Commission, G-3, G-7, NATO, OECD and other institutions), in order to stabilise aggressive competition amongst industrialised states (W. Robinson, 1996). In this Amero-centric 'consensus' the U.S. has often initiated, reared, and directed the main agenda for modifying the

---

[4] This is a direct rejection of Hobbsian realist assumptions that the international system is anarchic. In addition, these regimes acted as useful means for the United States and core countries of the capitalist system to minimise and cushion disruptive reactive Third World leaders from attempting to overthrow the *ancien regime*. Furthermore, when these regimes, institutions, and organisations were working in favour of U.S. interests, they would be maintained or consolidated. Those that were not, like the fixed gold exchange standard of the Bretton Woods system, or the WHO, and at times the UN, the U.S. would either abolish or abandon, e.g., by not funding its operations.

international order. With the collapse of the Soviet Union and communism that quest for global mastery is very close to finally being accomplished. If this being the case, was the discussion on the decline of American power wrong? The next section examines some of the debates that led to the basis of the declinist argument and the responses to that thesis.

Section II: The Declinist-Renewal Debate

In hindsight, it would seem that the declinist theories had their calculations wrong. However, what was more serious was that they had emphasised the fall of the *wrong* hegemon, and miscalculated U.S. strategy towards the USSR and Japan.

Before, we can question the validity of the declinist theories, we must first try to understand their position(s). The declinist school based their arguments on a number of events in American foreign, military and economic policy credibility. For clarity I have divided their arguments into two sections. The first deals with geopolitics, which, if we discount the fall of China in 1949, four major problems may be identified by the declinist argument in U.S. national security policy setbacks. The second was economics, which seven notable factors were considered to have led to the U.S. in, or heading for, decline. I will first discuss the four aspects of geopolitical decline, and then review the seven aspects of U.S. economic decline.

Geopolitical Decline

According to the declinist perception of U.S. and Western alliance geopolitical credibility, the first crack in the American leadership was the French decision in 1966 to withdraw from the American-led NATO military organisation. The French withdrawal from the alliance openly questioned the reliability of the North Atlantic alliance structure as a defence mechanism against possible Soviet attack. The French, under President Charles de Gaulle, were especially concerned about the American ability as leader of the 'western' capitalist world. The French decision-makers at that time were concerned as to whether American leaders would sacrifice the mutual assured destruction (MAD) doctrine in the event of war occurring on the European landmass.

Second, and more severe, was the long, costly and tragic war in Vietnam (from the early 1960s to 1975) and the American failure to understand the situation,[5] which eventually led to the United States' humiliating withdrawal

---

[5] Interestingly former U.S. president, Theodore Roosevelt had stated, 'A really great people, proud and high-spirited, would face all the disasters of war rather than purchase that base prosperity which is brought at the price of national honour' (Theodore Roosevelt, 1907 cited in C.W. Freeman, 1994: 131). If this perspective is understood in the U.S., how does it reflect on the people in Vietnam?

between 1972-1975. The Vietnam War was the first major defeat for the United States. The inability to gain victory or even stalemate produced severe setbacks to American confidence, in terms of both military strategy and history. The lessons (and/or even non-lessons) from Vietnam have become a psychological 'syndrome' in the consciousness of both the U.S. public and U.S. administrations, when considering intervening into the affairs of other nations.

Third, strategically, following the Strategic Arms Limitation Talks (SALT) in 1972, it became popular knowledge that the Soviet Union had actually 'caught up' with the United States in terms of military capability. President Nixon and Secretary of State Henry Kissinger prescribed a multipolar world consisting of five major powers/regions: U.S., USSR, China, Japan, and the Western European countries.

> As we look ahead 5 years, 10 years, perhaps it is 15 . . . we see five great economic powers . . . these are the five that will determine the economic future and, because economic power will be the key to other kinds of power, the future of the world in other ways in the last third of this century . . . we face a situation where four other potential economic powers have the capacity [to] challenge us on every front.[6]

In this sense, the United States was perceived as no longer the leader in the alliance, and Japan and Western Europe were perceived as challengers. Thence, the 'democratic' capitalist union between them would almost certainly seem irrelevant.

Fourth, blows to the American position were further dented following two spontaneous events in 1979. Firstly, the *fall* of Iran to Islamic fundamentalism, and the American failure to resolve the problem. Secondly, the Soviet Union's invasion of Afghanistan, later that year, triggered fears that the USSR was attempting to roll into the Indian Ocean and Persian Gulf. These two events challenged U.S. and Western interests in the area and control over vital energy resources.

Economic Decline

First, according to declinists, the Vietnam War was sustained and manipulated by the dollar's status and seignorage in the international monetary system. This manipulation, along with the unwillingness of U.S. political leaders to tax their people to cover the costs meant the U.S. budget deficit began to balloon. As the U.S. deficit increased, financial speculators and major countries (especially France) began to raise serious doubts about the ability of the United States government to be able to sustain its promise on the ability to maintain the amount of gold necessary to finance the inflationary monetary supply of dollars.

Because of the monetary speculation on the inability of the U.S. to have

---

[6] Richard Nixon (1971, 6 June) 'Remarks to Midwestern News Media Executives Attending a Briefing on Domestic Policy in Kansas City, Missouri', *Public Papers of the Presidents*, pp. 806-7.

sufficient credibility to support the fixed exchange rate, the collapse of the system was inevitable. President Nixon's decision to devalue the dollar in August 1971 allowed declinist scholars (i.e., J.A. Frieden and D.A. Lake, 1991 2nd edit.) an opportunity to announce that international capitalism was having its last breath. They openly argued that the collapse of the fixed gold exchange standard system would also mean 'the end of American hegemony' (K. Oye, R. Rothchild, and R. Leiber, 1979: 4-5). It was assumed that the international economic system had the potential for a return to a neo-mercantilistic trading system in which the major capitalist countries create their own 'trading areas'. Robert Gilpin purported that 'protectionism and economic nationalism are once again threatening the liberal international economic order' (1987: 88), whilst Kindleberger stated that, 'Part of the world's economic problem today is that the United States has resigned (or been discharged) as leader of the world economy' (1981: 248). Rosecrance said the American 'role as maintainer of the system *was* at an end' (1976: 1).

Second, it would appear that one failure often leads to another, just as the U.S announced its decision on the devaluation of the dollar, thus ending the gold exchange standard, the OPEC oil crisis ensued. Oil prices were quadrupled in early 1974, causing widespread economic panic across the world (see J. Spero, 1990 4th edit.).

Third, inter-related to the rise in oil prices, the investment policies implemented by OPEC from the mid-1970s and early 1980s caused (directly or indirectly) the so-called, 'lost decade' for most developing countries in the 1980s, as many of them were unable to repay their debts. As surplus oil producers suddenly found themselves unable to find sensible investment projects, and since many lacked good returns on investing in their own country, they began to deposit their oil money in developed countries' commercial banks. The banks, with masses of oil dollars, in turn had no better place for increasing their returns, lent them to other developing countries in an unmanaged spree. The banks failed to foresee any problems in repayment by less developed countries, and the less developed countries failed to foresee the increases in interest rates in the core states. The 'third world debt crisis' as it became known was escalated by Mexico's call for default in 1982. A crisis in the financial markets was only averted by direct U.S. intervention into the Mexican economy (R. Gilpin, 1987). With sporadic monetary crises in the 1980s and the world recession in the late 1980s and early 1990s (R. Gilpin, 1987; P. Cerny, 1993), the U.S. position as leader of world capitalism was seriously questioned (Pigman, 1992: 7-8).

Fourth, during the Reagan administration(s), the American balance of trade and balance of payments spiralled heavily into deficit, turning the U.S. from the largest creditor to the largest debtor nation in less than four years. To overcome credibility problems of the United States economy, the United States' real interest rates were raised to ward off financial speculative attacks. Inadvertently, however, the raising of U.S. interest rates had the direct effect of adding further problems to the debt crisis in most developing countries. Confidence in the United States, economy and the confidence of the United States to lead were low.

Fifth, the declinists' argued that the central element of a nation's strength is its economic power (P. Kennedy, 1989). It was claimed that a decline in economic power directly leads to a decline in other power dimensions. It was argued that the U.S. was declining economically compared to other market economies, especially Japan, Germany/EU, and the NICs of East Asia. It was contended that the East Asians/Japanese and Germans/Europeans were not only becoming increasingly important poles of world power, but also able to challenge U.S. preponderance. To override the potential challenge, Robert Keohane discussed co-operation with these areas in *After Hegemony* (1984).

Sixth, it was argued that the United States had become so entangled and fallen so far behind that it 'no longer has the power to "govern" the system as it did in the past' (R. Gilpin, 1981: 231-232). In the classic, *The Rise and Decline of the Great Powers*, Paul Kennedy based the assessment of the hegemonic collapse of the United States on its military 'overstretch'. He suggested that the United States should withdraw some of its commitments and concentrate on reorganising its internal market. Kennedy contended that the relative decline of U.S. economic performance rests on the fact that it spends too heavily on defense and the United States ought to redirect its resources more to domestic issues. He emphasised that the U.S. should concentrate on scientific research, technological innovation, and educational progress, which he claimed were necessary to revive American competitiveness.

Seventh, Immanuel Wallerstein, in studying the cycle of hegemonic power, bluntly stressed that, 'as soon as a state becomes truly hegemonic, it begins to decline; for a state ceases to be hegemonic not because it loses strength . . . but because others gain at the same time that the 'cost of political imperium' becomes too high (1980: 38).

These assertions were, however, rejected by many scholars, who ranged across the political spectrum. I have classified them into three main schools: The neo-'realist', 'liberal', and Gramscian/Marxist schools.

Section III: The 'Realists' Rejection of the Declinist School

Although many of the proponents of U.S. decline were 'realists' or 'neo-realists', there were elements inside the 'realist' tenet that rejected the declinist schools' argument. Firstly, conservative 'neo-realists', such as Samuel Huntington (1988), argue that, if '"hegemony" means having 40 percent or more of the world economic activity (a percentage Britain never remotely approximated during its "hegemonic" years), American hegemony would have disappeared a long time ago. If hegemony means producing 20 to 25 percent of the world's products and twice as much as any other individual country, American hegemony looks quite secure' (1988: 84). The U.S. position in the industrial world of the 1950s and 1960s accounted for more than half the world's industrial output. However, this was largely because European and East Asian economies were heavily devastated during World War II. The American economy was among the lucky few that did not suffer. It is, therefore, not surprising that as these areas redeveloped, it was inevitable that the U.S. share and domination in most economic sectors, and especially manufacturing, should decline relatively. Therefore, the United States,

> ... has not experienced an absolute decline, and relative decline is in large part an artefact of the extraordinary base line of the 1950s. The United States is not being challenged by a rising military power. Nor are external commitments sapping America's internal strength ... the United States [is] better placed than most societies to adapt to new dimensions of power (J. Nye, 1990: 106).

Second, with regard to the Bretton Woods system, the breaking away from the fixed exchange system, as Joseph Nye argues, was the ability to:

> ... change the rules of the game when it felt pinched and that other nations chose to hold dollars after the gold window was closed indicated that the United States still possessed unparalleled economic strength (1990: 94).

If hegemony means the ability to 'change the rules' of the international economic game, then the 1970s certainly did not mark the end of U.S. economic hegemony. Alan Cafruny supports this judgement and states that:

> ... as a result of President Nixon's decision to remove the dollar from its gold standard, U.S. influence in global financial markets has actually increased, rendering the analogy between the processes of U.S. decline misleading. Precisely because the dollar's power is largely structural, and not always evident in bargaining over international monetary policies, it has been underestimated, at least in the United States (1990: 102-3).

Fred Lawson summed up the U.S. position and stated that, '[a] truly hegemonic power is one that is able to manipulate both the structure and the agenda of international relations in such a way that serious challenges to its predominance do not arise' (1983: 335).

Third, realists argue that the gathering of oil producing nations in an effort to form a cartel controlling the price of oil (but still operating within the capitalist system) did not initiate an end to capitalism. The OPEC decision to increase oil prices was no accident. Neither was it an enactment of a New International Economic Order. The OPEC countries were not just targeting the rich countries in the West, but also targeting third world countries. In fact, the policies implemented by OPEC had a more devastating impact on many third world countries reliant on oil for their industries than on the richer countries, who were able to access energy substitutes. Peter Gowan argues that the oil crisis of the 1970s was in fact 'masterminded by the Nixon administration, with the OPEC countries to deal a crippling blow to the Japanese and European countries' (1999: 21), and not, as it was widely believed a plan of Gulf states against Israel or an anti-U.S. policy following the Yom Kippur War in 1973. According to Gowan, Nixon had planned to get OPEC to raise its oil price two years prior to the outcome of the Yom Kippur War in 1973 (1999: 21).

Fourth, concerning military expenditure, Paul Kennedy's thesis (1987; reprint Fontana 1989) of 'imperial over-stretch' which assumes that heavy defence spending is bad for the economy, is suspect. Kennedy emphasised that the U.S. should cut its military expenditure to a level comparable to Japanese defence spending (about 1 percent of GNP) to rejuvenate economic growth. It was contended that,

> ... military commitments tend to increase over time and eventually undermine that country's rate of economic growth. Other states without extensive military commitments can invest more in their economies and thus overtake the hegemon in terms of economic capabilities (J. Agnew and S. Corbridge, 1995: 109).

Such co-relations are, however, extremely debatable. South Korea, Taiwan, and the PRC, for example, have much higher defence expenditure than Japan; yet have higher economic growth rates than Japan. Moreover to balance the economics of defence expenditure is very complex and the net effect is difficult to assess. In fact, contrary to the theory of over-stretch, the U.S. defence burden is lighter today than it was in the 1950s (J. Nye, 1990; J. Muravchik, 1996). In addition, some sectors of the economy depend on the military as a basis for employment and industrial production. Therefore, as Nye notes, 'cutting defence expenditure and withdrawing from global commitments might do little to resolve U.S. economic problems, but it may very likely exacerbate America's international situation' (1990: 115). Joseph Nye argues that by providing the defence for other countries, America actually increased its influence and helped maintain regional stability. Curtailing international commitments, he argues, 'would leave the United States less able to influence other governments . . . [and] would reduce U.S. influence without necessarily strengthening the domestic economy' (1988: 115, 129). In arguing for a sustained or even an increase in U.S. security expenditure, Muravchik, Nye, and Krauthammer have taken the position that the danger in the post-cold war would actually be imperial *'understretch'* rather than imperial over-stretch. Muravchik argues that rather than demand a reduction in America's national security expenditure, the 'economic imperatives' require a greater defence spending to forestall future disputes (J. Muravchik, 1996).

Fifth, realists contend that the declinist school was heavily influence by the short-term United States economic performance. Realists assert that the declinists had largely ignored the importance of geo-politics, which were manipulated by the U.S. administrations from Nixon onward. Perhaps the most significant in the power politics manoeuvre was the recognition of the PRC as a 'normal' state. This opened the way to the understanding that communism was not one coherent challenger. Playing the 'China card' gave the United States an important strategic leverage over the Soviet Union. For China, it no longer had to worry about two formidable superpowers (for more details see chapter eight on Sino-U.S. relations). China was able to concentrate on the Soviet Union. This suited the United States.

Hence the realist dictum: 'my enemy's enemy is my friend'. The Soviet invasion of Afghanistan reinforced this view. Just as the Soviets and the Chinese supported the Vietnamese against the Americans; so the Chinese and the Americans supported the Afghans against the Soviets.

Sixth, the revolution in Iran; in proclaiming an Islamic state, it had the real potential of spreading radical Islamic ideas across the Muslim world and challenging the international status quo. The Iranian revolution was, however, offset by another Middle Eastern state. The Iraqi's decision to go to war with Iran was a 'blessing' in disguise for U.S. geopolitical strategy.

Geopolitically, the 1980s saw most of the U.S.'s fundamental enemies and powers that were hostile, checking or fighting one another. Was the U.S. to take advantage of this? This 'advantage' was not clear to some, especially when most analysts were 'hijacked' by short-term economic concerns against the allies, whilst others, with validity, suggested that the U.S. was on the verge of creating an apocalyptic scenario by luring the Soviet Union into a final decisive war. Indeed, President Reagan's strategy to force the Soviet Union into a final decisive arms race, within which either the United States or the Soviet Union was to collapse, was highly contentious for many. The Reagan 'gamble' was risky and highly dangerous, but it was a gamble in which the United States knew it had a more favourable position, and more allies to support it in its quest. The Soviet Union's inability to resolve the war in Afghanistan drained it of resources, and the allies in East Europe were in no state to support the Soviet economy in a decisive arms race with the U.S.

Second, the unwillingness and inability to manipulate the economic and financial crisis in the third world during the late 1970s and 1980s were serious miscalculations by the communists if their goal was to undermine the capitalist system. Had the Soviet Union and its allies manipulated and allured the economic crisis stricken countries into their sphere of influence and offered them an alternative form of development (or even just to 'de-legitimise' Western loans), the outcome of the cold war might have been different. Instead, the Soviet Union continued to play the 'international game' according to the rules, which were set by the capitalist countries, and, hypocritically, was even more demanding on its ally countries than Western countries were to the debt stricken countries.[7] It is only inevitable, one way or another, that, if a player cannot 'create' its own rules and has to follow those set by others, the limited room for manoeuvre would eventually doom it. Finally, the heightened arms race with the United States, with its rich allies in support, meant the internal bankruptcy of the Soviet Union and Eastern Europe. For the Reagan administration, the Cold War with the USSR was like a game of chicken; but it would not be the United States who would blink first; a desperate and hungry Soviet Union would be first to go. The United States' victory over the USSR would not have been so decisive and peaceful had not the visionary Mikhail Gorbachev been in control of the Soviet Union. Had the Soviet

---

[7] i.e., Vietnam.

Union's leadership been replaced with someone of the character of Joseph Stalin, the American game of chicken would not have been so easy or ended so peacefully.

Nevertheless, the fate of the Soviet Union was sealed. The USSR was asphyxiated internally and externally – the Reagan strategy proved to be one of the most perfect and sophisticated strategies in human history (M. Cox, 1995). How to win over the enemy, without fighting the enemy: the ultimate feat for the grand strategist!

The Reagan era was successful in restoring some pride and prestige in U.S. foreign policy. However, its aims were expensive and dangerous, and this did not quench the declinist and alarmist attack on the continuing decline of American economic power, especially *vis-à-vis* its allies in Western Europe and East Asia. Calleo depicts that 'thanks to economic strain and mismanagement, relative decline has begun to turn absolute' (1988: 32). He then blames the weakening of American hegemony on the partially coercive actions that were manifest in American unilateralist reassertion. In this perspective, the United States was manipulating the world economy during the 1970s and 1980s in order to compensate for its own internal economic disorder and decline. It is, as Susan Strange argued, that the international disorder has been the result of the U.S. exploiting its position 'for its own particular ends rather than for the general welfare' (1988: 96).

The 'Liberals' Rejection of the Declinist School

Like their realist counterpart, many liberal scholars also belonged to the 'declinist' school. And like the realist diversity, there were many liberals that rejected the declinist assumptions. First, they contend that even with the collapse of the Bretton Wood system, the United States had still by far the largest economic power resources than any other country, and it continues to possess such capabilities. In fact, the end of the fixed exchange rate system was 'a world restored – with the U.S. still pre-eminent if not pre-dominant' (C. Wolf, 12 May 1988: 22). Liberals argue that the U.S. had freed itself from obligations that were of no benefit to the United States. By breaking out of the fixed exchange rate system in 1971, the United States has had greater freedom to manoeuvre in a market oriented world, rather than being burdened by the controls of the Bretton Woods system. By breaking away from the fixed exchange rate system, the United States returned to its principle economic goals of minimal intervention and economic efficiency.

Peter Gowan (1999), in an insightful study of U.S. power, argue that the break up of the Bretton Wood system 'was part of a strategy for restoring the dominance of U.S . . . the liberation was, over the longer term, an illusion. It was more like a trap [*for other states*]' (1999: 19, 23 emphasis added). The new international monetary arrangement gave the United States government far more influence over the international monetary and financial relations of the world than it had enjoyed under the Bretton Woods rules. It was increasing its power via unregulated world finance and by making other states increasingly 'powerless to resist such dominance' (P. Gowan, 1999: 31).

In efforts to reduce the trade deficit and yet uphold the notion of free trade, and in order to deflect domestic protest against Japan, East Asia, and Europe, the then Secretary of the Treasury, James Baker, started a campaign to open-up markets for U.S. products world-wide (S.D. Cohen, 1988: 215). The Trade Act of 1988 gave the U.S. administration tools to retaliate against foreign discrimination. Section 301 of the 1988 Trade Act created a 'crowbar' that could, with the aid of threatened tariff retaliation, pry open foreign markets determined by the United States to be closed to its exports (J. Bhagwati, 1989: 440). The exposure and 'interconnectedness' of the economies of East Asia and Western Europe to the United States meant that the Trade Act of 1988: Section 301 was used as a bargaining weapon against the countries in these regions.[8] This bargaining weapon acted with such great effectiveness that Scherrer notes:

> The economies of Japan and Western Europe have become addicted to exporting to the United States. An exclusion from this market would cause severe domestic problems (1995: 17).

The tightening in U.S. policies, thence produced, in the early 1990s a world economic recession – a recession which Japan is still figuring out how to recover from (see chapter ten on Japan). Both the European Union and Japanese economies have slowed behind the growth rate of the United States. By the mid-1990s to late 1990s, the United States' economy was performing better and more competitively than both European and Japanese economies largely because it had freed itself from excessive or traditional 'state' regulations. Since the beginning of the operation of the WTO in 1995, there have been public concerns in Japan not only over economic stagnation but on the sustainability of the traditional Japanese economy. With financial and banking instability rife in the Japanese economy, the Japanese economic bubble has burst, causing widespread uncertainty, both at home and abroad. The so-called Japanese challenge has all but subsided. The economic turmoil in East Asia in 1997 to 1998 can be argued to have been a phase in the re-alignment of 'un-normality' of the economic 'miracle' in that region. The economic chaos there is just an indication to leaders[9] in that region that the United States is the hub around which these countries heavily rely. If the Asian economies believe that they can 'break away' from the U.S. led world economy they are very much mistaken.

---

[8] See 105th Congress 1st Session, Committee on Ways and Means U.S. House of Representatives, *Overview and Compilation of U.S. Trade Statutes* 1997 Edition., pp. 80-94 and 522-7.
[9] i.e., Prime Minister Mahatir of Malaysia and former Singaporean Prime Minister Lee Kuan Yew, have bluntly asserted, (although deep inside they would like to challenge Western dominance), the 'unfairness' of the Western dominated international political economic system.

The Neo-Gramscian/Marxist Rejection of the Declinist School

The rejection of U.S. hegemonic decline from the neo-Gramscian perspective is as follows: First, neo-Gramscians argue that the process of hegemony does not relate alone to the United States' political economic system (S. Gill, 1990; 1992). Instead, the importance of capital mobility and the objective of the United States and core industrial powers was to form a class. Their class would be transnational, to legitimise the U.S. position around the world. From this transnational class structure, neo-Gramscian analysis, such as Mark Rupert's *Producing Hegemony* (1995), illustrates how American global power was moulded by the ways in which mass production, division of labour, i.e. Fordism and Taylorism, were institutionalised in the U.S. He argues that these processes have reconstructed and influenced the world economy since World War II, creating what Mark Rupert describes as 'productivity-oriented political consensus . . . that was to be generalised around the globe' (1995).

Second, although not a self-confessed Gramscian, but arguing on similar lines, Susan Strange argued that the internationalisation of production and finance created, what she believes is, a 'global business civilisation' (1990: 260ff), an international business class that spreads the idea of American liberal business and culture throughout the world. Strange believed that the hegemony of America *is* based on its control of this global business civilisation. She pointed out that the 'location of production is less crucial than where the decisions are made on what is to be produced, where and how it is designed, and who directs sales successfully on the world market'. Thus, all the statistics 'so commonly trotted out about the U.S. share of world manufacturing capacity, or the declining U.S. share of world exports of manufacturing is so misleading – because they are territorially based' (cited in C.W. May, 1996: 187).

Third, neo-Gramscians accused the declinist writers of 'underestimat[ing] the structural continuities in U.S. power and hegemony, as well as failing to take account of certain aspects of the post-war institutional order, which facilitate the exercise of U.S. power and influence' (S. Gill, 1986: 311). Gill suggests that the United States has acquired a larger degree of cultural hegemony at a time when the increased interdependence of the international economy has given unprecedented importance to co-optive or 'soft' power. According to neo-Gramscians, the central problem in the declinist argument has been its inability to distinguish between various forms and applications of power, and even more importantly how to explain how the resources were measured or translated into effective power.

Section IV: The End of the Cold War and the Emergence of 'Global Hegemony'

Strategically, U.S. power and influence in world affairs during and after the Cold War has not declined to the level anticipated by theories of the declinist school. U.S. power has been readjusted and since the demise of the Soviet Union in 1991, and the successful 1991 Gulf crisis and war against Iraq, U.S. power has even increased, to the extent that American officials openly spoke of creating a 'New World Order' (see J. Hippler, 1994). In transforming that New World Order, the U.S. Pentagon almost admitted that 'the key to US foreign policy after the demise of the Soviet Union should be preventing the emergence of a rival superpower in Western Europe, Asia, or the Soviet republics. The goal was to ensure continued American dominance' (in P. Tyler, 8 March 1992: 14). Although the idea of preventing emergence of rivals was later dropped, (i.e., P. Tyler, 24 May 1992: 2, 14), it however does not escape the nature of U.S. intentions. Indeed, President Clinton in 1993 reinstated America's interests to lead in an effort to build a world order shaped by U.S. values. Such a way, he states, is 'between unstable, highly nationalistic states with centralised and potentially oppressive governments, on the one hand, and democratic states...on the other'. If America fails in its responsibilities, President Clinton warns, 'we will miss an opportunity to create a more democratic and stable world' (quoted in C. Layne and B. Schwartz, 1993: 7). Accordingly, U.S. Secretary of State Warren Christopher stated, 'the United States had three goals in the post-cold war era. These were to strengthen the American economy, modernise the American military and extend democracy and human rights around the world' (quoted in M. Cox, 1994: 643).

Therefore, any suggestion that the U.S. has lost its number one position is highly exaggerated, both economically and militarily. The idea that the contenders – Japan, Germany, and others, are going to take over the role as the world's principal economic power or become the provider of the world's reserve currency is wrong. Any militarisation of Japan and Germany would reduce, rather than increase, Japan's or Germany's ability to achieve their political purposes abroad. For Japan, the suspicion aroused from her neighbours may cause more concern than benefits. The same applies to Germany, although Germany has integrated itself successfully into the European Union. It is most unlikely that Germany would want to develop a nuclear programme and upset its European partners, or alarm Russia and the United States. In fact, Japan and the EU, are themselves involved in co-operation with the United States in what scholars have termed partners in the 'zone of democratic peace and prosperity'.

For the development of this, it is not simply a matter of dominance by the United States over others, but it may involve something which is more sophisticated from which the leading powers in the international community actually control the direction of international affairs. As argued earlier, the United States' strategy after World War II was to establish the international structure based around U.S. interests. This development served to 'gel' other major industrial powers to U.S. ideas and interests. One of the most important developments from this was to make the 'group' (civil society) of international capitalists feel that they have a common interest to uphold the ideas. From this, a common network had to be established with former elites of both former imperial colonial powers and of new 'third world' states (B. Gills et al, 1993; William Robinson, 1996). This group was essentially 'global' capitalists, anti-communists, and sought to reducing the 'breaking of rank' within the group. The transnational class analysis identified by Kees van der Pijl's *The Making of the Atlantic Ruling Class*, and Stephen Gill's *The Trilateral Commission* shows the significance of power play by these groups.

In the development of this 'transnational' class, the U.S. strategy has tried to overlap into every forum. This 'imbricated' (see Gills in M. Cox et al, 2000) strategy makes it extremely difficult for the U.S to lose its control. On regionalism the U.S. has its interests well covered in APEC, the Atlantic Council, NATO, and the North Atlantic Free Trade Area. On great power relations, they co-ordinate it via the UNSC, and bilateral security alliance with Japan. On global economics, the U.S. is the leading nation in the OECD, G3, G7(8), IMF, WB, BIS. In fact, the United States has left no stone unturned, President Clinton for example showed interests in the Sub-Sahara African economic development; he also visited the Indian sub-continent.

In addition, to setting up the basis of centrality and to continue its reign, the U.S. has added, adapted and innovated new institutions, especially WTO in the 1990s, and NATO expansion and PfP. This implements the 'intensification' and 'expansion' of U.S. power. What is even more intriguing in the continuity and intensification of U.S. power is that it is not just the United States that is carrying out this strategy, but also by allies and countries that are within that system.

Why have challenge(s) to the United States-led system not been forthcoming? First, there is no substitute to existing international institutions. Second, to substitute would be too costly (viz USSR). Third, the U.S. has taken measures to prevent challengers from within them (e.g., multilateral and regional regimes and institutions). Fourth, the counter hegemonic challenges from 'below', the disadvantaged and dissidents have 'failed' to materialise into 'co-ordinated action'. Despite protests witnessed in Seattle and elsewhere, the prospects of this 'group' overwhelming the 'hegemon' remains very limited, partially because of the lack of coherence and insufficiencies in the 'war of position'. Moreover, the transnational elite are closing ranks, rather than breaking ranks, when it see its position challenged by so called 'anarchists'. Any success for the 'counter-hegemonic' movement would (and can only) come when the forces of 'hegemony' break rank. Therefore, any really significant challenge to topple the 'hegemonic system' stems from potential great powers that may offer substantial 'backing' for challenge. These potential challenges are explored in the Case Study chapters that follow.

Conclusion

In conclusion, there remains substantial disagreement over whether the period of U.S. hegemony is definitively at an end and if so, what will happen next.[10] There is also disagreement over who benefited from the hegemonic system, the United States or the nations that are subordinated into that system.[11] All the talk of 'imperial over-stretch' in the military arena, or the decline in areas of economics, finance, and production, and the idea that America should retreat behind the Oceans of the Atlantic and Pacific was essentially misguided. The collapse of the Soviet Union and the failure and unwillingness of other potential hegemons, such as Japan and the European Union, to become leaders on 'global' level, have encouraged a view of the United States as a singular superpower untroubled by a serious challenge to its global hegemonic status.

In addition, it remains debatable as to whether Japan or Germany/Europe have become the new challengers to American hegemony in global politics, certainly in the Gilpin sense of 'hegemonic war'. I argue that the 'challengers' are not the EU/Germany or Japan. These states are, themselves, trying to resolve difficulties and maintain U.S. dominance, in order to have world economic stability and growth, as well as maintain their position in the U.S.-led international system.

Thus, the aim of this chapter was to investigate and question the relevance of the 'declinist-renewal' debates to understanding and analysing theories surrounding the issue of continuing U.S. power predominance. It inquired into how that debate evolved with the demise of the Soviet Union and into the current supremacy of U.S. power. I have contended that that debate appears to have asked the wrong questions, and the methods used by analysts to understand emerging international order are limited. It was a debate that concentrated too heavily on (or more correctly underestimated) the U.S. power projection, whilst largely ignoring (or over-emphasising) other contenders in the international system. Although the thesis shares some ground with the renewalist position, I reject the renewalist notion that the U.S. *ever* declined, because why speak of renewal when the U.S. has not declined? It is not a matter of decline or renewal. What is relevant is the central power relationship of the U.S. in the international system with other powers.

Moreover, the chapter has argued that the United States 'reconfigured' itself, rather than having to 'renew' or reconcile its power position(s) with either allies or enemies. The chapter showed how the U.S. actually freed itself from the restricting gold standard, and set about a decisive manoeuvre against both allies and enemies. By freeing itself from the rigidity of that system, the U.S. was able to

---

[10] Compare, in particular, Nye (1990) *Bound to Lead* with Kennedy (1989) *Rise and Fall of the Great Powers*.

[11] Bruce Russett (1985), for example, argues that the United States received substantial private benefit from running the international order. 'The Mysterious Case of Vanishing Hegemony; or, is Mark Twain Really Dead?' whilst Mark Boyer (1993), *International Co-operation and Public Goods: Opportunities for the Western Alliance* argues the reverse.

influence how its allies' monies were to be forwarded to serve U.S. interests in the final stage of the Cold War. Once the fight with the USSR was over, the U.S. used this same reconfiguration to recapture U.S. global competitiveness and further increase the U.S. power position.

This reconfiguration has, today, become popularly acknowledged as 'globalisation'. Although it can be argued that 'globalisation' has been operating for a substantial period in world history (M. Water, 1995), it is its intensification following the collapse of the Bretton Woods system that signifies it has really taken off. Within the globalisation context, the U.S. is extending its prowess into areas not witnessed by any single power in modern history. It is the intentions of the use and deployment (and even non-deployment) of that power by the U.S. that the thesis is most interested in, not the absolute or relative decline of the U.S. hegemonic position. In essence, the continuing and changing nature of power reveals the ability of the U.S. hegemony to transform itself. The U.S., with its affiliates, aims to globalise the world and intends to form a global 'consensus' that enables the U.S. to further enhance the globalisation process and legitimise the U.S. power position. In essence, it is not simply just hegemony in the traditional sense, but a 'hegemonic globalisation' process that is attempting to eventually globalise the entire planet, with America as the hub around which other centres revolve.

The grip on global predominance of the U.S. is so overwhelming that it has been suggested that it is the only and possibly even the last hegemonic power (A. Valladao, 1996). The U.S. has incorporated the idea of globalisation to the extent of universalising it in order to legitimise and serve U.S. power position and interests. In this strategy of seeking universal legitimacy, the U.S. has placed itself in a most favourable position to overcome any possible challenger to the U.S. power position. Any challenge to the U.S. would be seen as a challenge to the international system itself!

Chapter 5

Balance of Power or Hegemony?

Some indeed still hold to the now somewhat obvious delusion that we of the United States can safely permit the United States to become a lone island, a lone island in a world dominated by the philosophy of force. Such an island may be the dream of those who still talk and vote as isolationists. Such an island represented to me and to the overwhelming majority of Americans today a helpless nightmare, the helpless nightmare of a people without freedom. Yes, the nightmare of a people lodged in prison, handcuffed, hungry and fed through the bars from day to day by the contemptuous, unpitying masters of other continents.
Franklin D. Roosevelt, Charlottesville Address, 10 June 1940 (cited in Hugh Brogan, 1985/90: 568).

Introduction

When the Soviet empire became exhausted in 1989-91, the United States was left as the lone superpower. What has developed since is what some analysts have envisioned as the 'unipolar moment' (C. Krauthammer 1990/91; A. Valladao, 1996; J. Muravchik, 1996; E. Lefever, 1999). Not since the times of Imperial Rome, ancient China and the Mongol empire has one power towered over others in such a manner. Krauthammer argued that 'the true geopolitical structure of the post-Cold War world . . . *is* a single pole of world power that consists of the United States at the apex of the industrial West' (1990/91: 24). Yet, within two years, Kenneth Waltz (1993), Robert Jervis (1993), Christopher Layne (1993), Henry Kissinger (1994) and others argued that the unipolar moment was an illusion; that the United States should not seek international primacy, but should instead prepare itself for a world of multipolarity and the mechanics of balance of power in military and economic affairs.[1] In 1996, John Ruggie queried the assumptions of

---

[1] The advocates of a balance of power scenario include, Robert Jervis (1993) 'International Primacy: Is the Game Worth the Candle?' *International Security,* Vol. 17, No. 4 (spring) pp. 52-67; Christopher Layne (1993) 'The Unipolar Illusion: Why New Great Powers Will Rise', *International Security,* Vol. 17, No. 4 (spring), pp. 5-51; Fred Halliday and Justin Rosenberg (1998) 'Interview with Kenneth Waltz', *Review of International Studies,* Vol. 24, No. 3, pp. 371-86; Henry Kissinger (1994) *'Diplomacy.'* (London: Simon and Schuster); John J. Mearsheimer (1994/95) 'The False Promise of International Institutions', *International Security,* Vol. 19, No. 3, winter, pp. 5-49; Christopher Layne (1997) 'From Preponderance to Offshore Balancing: America's Future Grand Strategy' International Security, Vol. 22, No. 1, summer, pp. 86-124; Christopher Layne (1998) 'Rethinking American Grand Strategy: Hegemony or Balance of Power in the Twenty-First Century?' *World Policy Journal,* summer, pp. 8-41.

primacy in American power and raised the question: 'does the current preponderance of American military power define a unipolar world, or, rather, does the rapid and vast economic growth of nations such as Japan and Germany indicate that we are at the beginning of a new multipolar balance of power?' (1996: ix; see also J. Scott, 1998: 15). This is a fascinating question, because it addresses the conundrum of the transformation of the international system from one of bipolarity (between the Soviet Union and the United States), into a conjuncture of both unipolarity and multipolarity. This chapter attempts to analyse the prevailing position of the United States in the international system today. It inquires into the issue as to whether the U.S. power position has become 'hegemonic' (or 'unipolar'), or is the U.S. just one amongst many great powers in a multipolar world order (even if/or *primus inter pares*).

To begin this analysis, I will investigate the advocates of multipolarity and the strategy of balance of power. The second objective is to look at the question of why two almost contradictory concepts, i.e., balance of power and hegemony, both applicable to the 'realist' paradigm, and are being applied to the current international order. This chapter assesses the espousers of balance of power and the responses to that argument. The third section will inquire briefly into liberal and Marxist understandings of multipolar politics and the question of hegemony. The conclusion draws on the arguments developed.

The Balance of Power Strategy and the Return to Multipolarity

Before investigating the balance of power, it is important to remember that the 'balance of power is the very heart of Realist strategy in world politics' (M. Doyle, 1997: 161). Not to all, however. Because 'Realism' has many perspectives, the balance of power concept thus 'involves a [high] degree of abstraction . . . [and] the notion of the balance of power is full of confusion' (M. Wight in H. Butterfield and M. Wight, 1966: 149, emphasis added).

According to Martin Wight (1966: 151), the multiple 'laws' and principles in the balance of power concept are as follows:

- An even distribution of power.
- The principle that power *ought* to be evenly distributed.
- The existing distribution of power. Hence any possible distribution of power.
- The principle of equal aggrandisement of the Great Power at the expense of the weak.
- The principle that our side *ought* to have a margin in strength in order to avert the danger of power becoming unevenly distributed.
- (when governed by the verb 'to hold') A special role in maintaining an even distribution of power.
- (Ditto): A special advantage in the existing distribution of power.
- Predominance.
- An inherent tendency of international politics to produce an uneven distribution of power.

Amongst these 'laws' and 'principles', the most frequent conceptualisation of the balance of power theory is that, in the interaction of states, all states abhor the condition of a single state or coalition of states becoming hegemonic. In this framework, it follows that relations between nations and states are anarchic, suggesting that the international system is self-serving and that the foremost policy for a state is its survival and sovereignty. On the assumption that the international system is anarchic, states must 'first and foremost' provide their own security as they may face many real or apparent threats, where even the closest ally may not come to the rescue or may come too late to be rescued once others have taken over.[2] Under this condition, the first priority for the statesperson is the old Roman motto 'to have peace, prepare for war'. The belief in peace through strength' is more than a mere slogan however. Even George Washington, in his first State of the Union Address, emphasised, 'To be prepared for war is one of the most effectual means of preserving peace' (cited in E. Lefever, 1999: 137).

Secondly, in the event of a single state or coalition of states becoming predominant, balance of power theorists expect that a league of minor or weaker powers will align with each other in order to counter the predominance of the hegemonic power and thus ensure their political survival. Kenneth Waltz argues that it does not matter what the intentions of the hegemonic power may be, but if it means the survival of the state, the weaker powers will align together to ensure their survival (1979: 126-27).

A third aspect of the argument that balance of power theorists put forward is that, although the idea of global society (see for example, Bruce Russett, 1993; M. Brown et al, 1993) put forward by scholars critical of power politics may be attractive, the nature and tensions of power politics between and within nations, religions, and people of different (and same) racial groups and class groups will make the universal cosmopolitan society impractical because the enduring reality is one of differences, and, difference means conflicts (S. Huntington, 1993b, 1996). Because of this, balance of power theorists emphasise that we must understand the reasons behind great power challenges and their attendant diplomatic 'games' before leading to a clearer understanding of the practicalities of a global society. Given this logic, it is reasonable to suggest that hegemony can only be a good thing for the hegemonic power alone, since after all, hegemony is a situation where the hegemonic state can maximise its power position. Balance of power theorists do not disagree with this, but they argue that any unipolar system tends to be short-lived and that hegemons invariably fail to achieve lasting dominance or even peace because power in the international system is unevenly distributed. Robert Gilpin reminds us that over time, 'the differential growth in the power of various states in the system causes a fundamental redistribution of power in the system' (1981: 13). This pattern therefore inevitably leads to the rise of other competitors. Paul Kennedy has shown that in time, relative 'economic shifts heralded the rise of new

---

[2] Although this perspective is heavily contested, the advocates are Kenneth N. Waltz (1979) *Theory of International Politics* (Reading, Mass: Addison-Wesley); Henry Kissinger (1994) *Diplomacy* (London: Simon & Schuster).

Great Powers which one day would have a decisive impact on the military/territorial order' (1989: xxii).

The fourth scenario that balance of power scholars have raised since the decline-renewal debate (elaborated in chapter three and in point two) has been the relative economic gain of other powers in relation to the hegemonic power. Because the power distribution in the domestic and the international system is unequal, states and statesmen, they argue, will become highly attentive to changes in their relative power position. A relative power shift can have serious political/security implications. In such conditions, states are stimulated, and may be compelled, to increase their power: 'at least, it necessitates that the prudent state prevent relative increase in the powers of competitor states' (R. Gilpin, 1981: 87-8).

With these propositions, scholars of this school argue that the United States *should* seek some form of strategy whereby the United States *could* prepare itself for a scenario of balance of power in the twenty-first century. These scholars claim that because the international system abhors hegemony, it is thus 'counterproductive [for the United States] to pursue a strategy of preponderance' (C. Layne, 1993: 45 emphasis added). The United States, Layne claims, 'needs to design a strategy that will: 1) safeguard its interests during the difficult transition from unipolarity to multipolarity; and 2) enable the United States to do as well as possible in a multipolar world' (1993: 45).

I have compiled below eight propositions which balance of power theorists have advocated concerning the U.S. power position in the emerging world order.

Eight Arguments for the Balance of Power

- Balance of power theorists complain that despite the end of the Cold War the United States has not chosen a different strategy in a system where there is 'no real' external threat. Layne (1993) contends that the United States is essentially pursuing the same goals and using the same means to achieve ends, which no longer exist. As such, the 'international system', i.e., the economic system and the military alliance system, that the U.S. constructed and preserved since World War II as counter-balance against Soviet expansionism, is giving way to the weight of its own success. Moreover, because the threat from communism is no longer credible, can the existence of such 'expensive' alliance structures still have validity for the United States?
- In regard to point one, balance of power theorists (such as, L. Thurow, 1992; C. Layne, 1993, 1996, 1997; F. Friedman and M. Lebard, 1991 and others) contend that U.S. allies are paying next to nothing or 'free-riding' on the security structure and, yet, are 'deliberately eating' on the largesse of 'generous' U.S. economic policies, deploying restrictive trade practices of their own. Why should the United States be compelled to bear the high costs

of providing security for these states when clearly they (i.e., Japan and Western Europe) have the means (economic, technological and manpower) and capabilities to defend themselves?

- As such, and contrary to the strategy of preponderance, the security/interdependence nexus posited in the economic openness of the United States has adverse strategic consequences. Layne claims that economic openness 'contributes to, and accelerates, a redistribution of relative power among states in the international system, allowing rising competitors to catch up to the United States more quickly than they otherwise would' (1997a: 109-10). In order to prevent the potential 'catch up' to the U.S. power position, Layne has proposed that the United States should become less 'interdependent' with the international community.
- Balance of power theorists (i.e., Kissinger, 1994) state that the geopolitics of great powers (such as Russia, China, India and even allies, i.e., France) implies that the well being of the international system is not guaranteed, if one power is hegemonic. It thus becomes meaningless for the United States to take such a position. Balance of power theorists show that the leaders of China[3] (see chapter eight), Russia (see chapter seven), Iran, France,[4] and the non-aligned countries[5] have all expressed their opposition to a hegemonic world order, be that of the United States or of any other sole power. These countries' policy-makers all continuously verify that the international system cannot be dominated by one power or a group of powers, dominating or controlling the affairs of the system of states. One of the strongest protests to the unipolar system was delivered during the April 1996 and 1997 meetings between Presidents Boris Yeltsin and Jiang Zemin. Both Presidents denounced hegemonism in the post-Cold War world. These two countries (Russia and China) were no doubt complaining about U.S. supremacy and were trying to find ways to contain that power. At the EU and East Asian summits in 1997 and 1998, although nothing significant was achieved other than mere diplomatic 'hand shakes' among statesmen, it was a summit that indicated that

---

[3] David Shambaugh (1992) 'China's Security Policy in the Post-Cold War Era' *Survival*, Vol. 34, No. 2 (summer), p. 92, argued that, 'Chinese analysts reacted with great alarm to President George Bush's "New World Order" proclamations, and maintained that this was a ruse for extending U.S. hegemony throughout the globe. From China's perspective, unipolarity was a far worse state of affairs than bipolarity.'

[4] Former French Foreign Minister Roland Dumas warned that America 'might reign without balancing weight', and he and former European Union Commission President Jacques Delors called for the EU to counterbalance the United States. 'Europe is now threatened mainly by an unchallenged American ascendancy in world politics', quoted in 'France to U.S.: Don't Rule', *New York Times*, 3 September 1991, p. A8.

[5] At the September 1992 Non-aligned Movement Meeting, (former) Indonesian President Suharto warned that the 'New World Order' cannot be allowed to become 'a new version of the same old pattern of domination of the strong over the weak and the rich over the poor'. Whilst Malaysian Prime Minister Mahatir Mohammed pointed out that a 'unipolar world is every bit as threatening as a bipolar world'.

the EU and East Asian countries may work together to stem the unilateralist position of the United States. Thus, balance of power theorists argue that any attempts to maintain U.S. hegemony are self-defeating because this provokes other states to 'balance' against the United States, and, therefore, results in depletion of American (relative) power. The hegemon's 'unbalanced' power threatens others and spurs the emergence of new powers.

- According to M. Singer and A. Wildavsky (1993), the core and periphery are interdependent strategically; however, while the core remains constant, the turbulent frontier in the periphery is constantly expanding. Balance of power theorists believe that the risk factor for the United States' involvement in 'non-vital' areas would be too great. They thus remind the U.S. public of unnecessary over-extension and over-commitment into areas where the U.S. has no real strategic interest, such as the United States' involvements in Vietnam or Somalia. In the context of the obligations of military alliances and commitment to international treaties, balance of power theorists argue that because the United States has to honour its security commitments: 'The credibility of U.S. alliance can be undermined if key allies, such as Germany and Japan, believe that the current arrangements do not deal adequately with threats to their security. It could also be undermined if, over an extended period, the United States is perceived as lacking the will or capability to lead in protecting their interests' (C. Layne, 1997a: 103). This leads the United States to continue to have to defend some areas merely to preserve U.S. commitment and credibility.

- Following the thesis developed by Gilpin (1981) and Kennedy (1989), balance of power theorists are convinced that the relative economic rise of Germany/EU, Japan, and increasingly China and India will inevitably lead to a new multipolar balance of power.

- As great powers' *inevitably* emerge, they will seek a sphere of influence over neighbouring smaller states – i.e., those that are in its 'backyard' or 'near abroad'. Balance of power theorists argue that this is true in most cases of past emerging great powers. Even the United States itself created such a sphere in the Caribbean, Central America, South America and the Pacific. Thus, balance of power theorists suggest that China, Russia, and the EU, should or will have their own 'backyard' (see Huntington, 1996; J. Kurth, 1996). According to Huntington, (four or) five great powers with the potential capabilities to upset the international system are now intent upon restoring some version of their own spheres of influence. These are: Germany (and EU), Russia, China, Japan, and (possibly) India. For Germany/EU, the desire to have a sphere of influence stems back to its early history; the areas of Central and Eastern Europe are obvious candidates for the expansion of German/EU interests. For Russia, a cultural basis for a traditional sphere of influence has rested in Christian Orthodoxy. Huntington termed this the 'Slavic-Orthodox civilisation'. Strategically, Russia has both anxiety and vital interest in its 'underbelly' to the south, i.e., Transcaucasia, and Central Asia. Historically,

Russia has systematically annexed these territories. For China, the cultural basis for its traditional sphere has been 'the Chinese world order' or Confucian tributary system. During most of Chinese history, the areas considered to be under Chinese influence were: Korea, Vietnam, Central Asia, and the South China Sea (S. Huntington, 1993a and 1996).

- In the multipolar balance of power system, some theorists, such as Layne (1993; 1997), Waltz (1993), and Kissinger (1994), contend that the United States would operate within the dynamics of alliance relationships. Whereas the strategy of preponderance assumes that the multipolar system is unstable, these American balance of power theorists contend that instability does not affect all states equally. They argue that advocates of American preponderance have failed to consider geography's differential effects. Because America is an insular power, it is substantially less likely to be affected by instability faced by states that are geographically proximate to each other. In its insularity, the United States can 'stand aloof' from other security competitions and capitalise on the hemispheric insular position of the United States. They suggest that the United States might try to mimic the former British role of an offshore 'balancer' during the 19th century in Europe, where the United States and other great powers could both compete and co-operate to avoid hegemonism and global war.

Responses to the Balance of Power Strategy

The arguments developed by balance of power theorists outlined above are reasonable as precautionary visions. But why does the United States need to prepare for such a scenario when clearly other powers such as Japan, the EU, and probably China and Russia do not want to 'balance' it or at least do not have the capabilities to challenge it militarily? None of the major powers in the world is giving any solid signals that may suggest that they wish to see the United States 'balanced' (see the chapters on China, Russia, the EU, and Japan). Europe is not saying to Japan, China or Russia, we should all come together to balance American supremacy, because if we fail to do so the United States will use its might to make a claim on our rights. Nor is Japan giving any signs to China, Russia, or EU of wanting to 'balance' the United States. Instead, it is the U.S. that has been most active in improving and 'sustaining' its diplomatic, strategic, cultural and economic relations with all the major powers. The attempts by China and Russia at 'new strategic partnership' forged in 1997 appear at least as anachronistic, because both need the United States more than they need each other. Russia is in such an economic 'mess' that without IMF and World Bank loans, it would probably not survive (and that will not be a nice state of affairs); it is not going to Beijing to ask for help, but to the West and America. Beijing on the other hand is not going to Moscow for market access and technological abundance; it is going to Washington.

Balance of power theorists have a tendency to advocate that former allies should go their separate ways because their 'interests' inevitably lead them to do so. This prophecy has not happened, however, because their interests lay not in their going their separate ways but in co-operating with each other. These powers have found working together more beneficial. Today, this is even the case with China and Russia *vis-à-vis* the U.S. and the 'West'. China and Russia does not perceive working with the Americans as endangering their 'national-security'. Both Russia and China now believe that their interests are and can be maximised by co-operating with the U.S., as well as with each other, rather than opting to 'balance' each other.

Thus, balance of power theorists may have misinterpreted and over-simplified the nature of the immediate power relations amongst the major powers in relation to the U.S. In such circumstances, it is important first to distinguish between the balance against a power, as opposed to a balance against a threat (see S. Walt, 1987). The significance of this difference is better illustrated by the old Arab dictum: 'The friend of my friend is my friend, the enemy of my friend is my enemy, the enemy of my enemy is my friend.' In this scenario, it is not a balance of power but a balance of threat doctrine. The hypothesis here, is that when a power faces grave danger to itself, it will take allies that it believes can help avert that danger no matter the shade of their political belief. Winston Churchill captured this in his famous statement: 'If Hitler invaded Hell, I should at least make a favourable reference to the Devil in the House of Commons' (quoted in S. Walt, 1987: 38).

Following this position, I have assembled ten points, which I believe theorists of the balance of power have missed in their analysis of the contemporary international system with regard to the United States. These are as follows:

- In the post-Cold War era, the United States is in a unique position, unlike any previous power relationship, which makes other powers follow the U.S. rather than the U.S. having to have to expand out to them. The power of the U.S. is such that it acts almost like a magnet which compels others to join with that power. Josef Joffe described this type of power as '[radiating] outwards and a market that draws inwards – rest on pull, not on push; on acceptance, not on conquest' (J. Joffe, 1998: 40; see also T. Friedman, 1999). It is like in the old dictum, 'nothing succeeds like success', and as Scott Thompson showed, '[m]omentum accrues to the gainer and accelerates his movement. The appearance of irreversibility in his gains enfeebles one side and stimulates the other all the more. The bandwagon collects those on the sidelines' (in S. Walt, 1987: 19).
- Balance of power theorists claim that U.S. interventionism around the world is imprudent and blindly heading into areas for the sake of humanitarianism where the U.S. has minimum interests. This policy risks undermining a finite U.S. power position, and more importantly, damaging relations with others. I argue, however, that the U.S. has been selective in its engagement and enlargement policies. The 'humanitarian' intervention in Somalia in 1993

taught the United States an important lesson in determining the nature of interventionism in world affairs. Instead of identifying enemies via differences in ideology, religion, or race, the U.S. has essentially concentrated on its traditional areas of interests, i.e., Europe, East Asia, Latin America, and the Middle East (see Appendix 1B).

In defence of its selectivity and even contradictory policies, the United States has manipulated the media for support, guarding American values and interests (J. Scott, 1998). For example, the U.S. has pursued issues such as human rights and free trade with countries such as China, Israel, Saudi Arabia, and others, whilst imposing stiff sanctions against regimes with similar humanitarian abuses, like Burma (Myanmar), Cuba, Serbia, Libya, Iran, Iraq, and others. In the case of selecting China (see chapter eight), American officials believe that China can evolve from its one party system into a pluralistic democratic system through deep engagement via trade and open exchanges, and toleration of ideas and differences (and it is too big a market and too big a power to be left out or to be isolated). Yet, the same idea applied to China cannot be applied to Cuba, a country barely 90 miles from the U.S. mainland.

The United States government has also learned to be selective over its strategic involvement; for example, it initially allowed its allies in the EU to take the lead in Bosnia. Although the EU *failed* to solve the problem, the United States had indicated to Europe, 'you are a mature democracy, you are the main pillar in Europe, and closest ally to us, it is your backyard, you should take some responsibility to solve that problem'.[6] However, in the end the problem was only solved with American military might and Russian agreement and co-operation.

Thirdly, the U.S. has been selective on the question of credibility. Despite balance of power theorists' claims to the contrary, the United States has been consistent in its policy of deterrence. Take, for example, the Taiwanese move to call for independence (see chapter eight). The Taiwanese case placed Washington in a serious dilemma, i.e., whether to challenge China and risk setting off a time bomb for World War III, or to let the Taiwanese decide their own fate. Despite the unease in (the mainstream) American policy-making circles over Taiwanese behaviour, and Chinese reactions, the Clinton administration sent two aircraft carrier squadrons to maintain the United States' commitment to its ally and to impose some order so as to stabilise the region. This action deterred China, but the U.S. also warned Taiwan not to declare independence, hence President Clinton's 'three no's'.[7]

- Balance of power theorists contend that international history abhors hegemony, thus the advocacy of hegemony is set to fail. However, hegemony, in the current international order, is unlike that of any other period in history.

---

[6] Interview with Henry Nau, 16 July 1998, Washington, D.C.
[7] Interview with Hans Binnendijk, 10 July 1998, Washington, D.C.

It is 'not a hierarchical pyramid. Rather, America stands at the centre of an interlocking universe, one in which power is exercised through continuous bargaining, dialogue, diffusion, and quest for formal consensus' (Z. Brzezinski, 1997: 28). As I have indicated in the previous chapters, the United States has managed its power-play extraordinarily well with other powers and peoples, so much so as to make it appear that it is in a fortunate and favourable position – for fortune is for those that make it, seldom does fortune come to those that sit by idly. The accumulation of power, the skills levied in the power game, and the power relationship with others have all been 'immense', and effective to 'interlock' others into the U.S. led system. Josef Joffe may assert: 'The ideal is to maintain better relations with all possible contenders than they do among each other' (1995: 113). However, this is not the 'divide and conquer' dictum used in the past by Europeans against most 'Third World' countries. The U.S. has accumulated so much power that it is not 'afraid' to conceal it or the need to make the U.S. 'indispensable'. The 'indispensable' notion is the ultimate aphrodisiac of control and influence, the way to make others depend on you for their happiness and prosperity, and you have nothing to fear (see R. Greene and J. Elffers, 1999: 37).

- Traditional power-politics often predicts that military power soon follows economic power, and that very soon countries like Japan and Germany will return to the traditional power balancing game. This assumption, though perhaps true in some sense, does not really apply to the understanding of contemporary relations between the United States and its main allies, Japan and Western Europe. Although there is no denying that a sound economic base is important for the development of military power, it is not necessarily always the case for aggressive military manoeuvres. Other power variables, such as the structure and restraints of domestic culture and politics, and international political 'norms' may often deny powerful economic powers from becoming powerful military players (this point is elaborated below).
- Prestige remains one of the most important factors in international relations. Realists (of whatever colour or perspective) often agree that a relative increase in economic power inevitably leads to an increase in political influence and power, and thus ultimately to prestige. However, competition among states, especially in economics, has changed significantly and relative gains of the economic kind does not automatically lead to military conflict or similar sanctions. The lessons of history have an important role in this behaviour. Josef Joffe recalls Winston Churchill's famous phrase, 'No matter how nasty their quarrels, the nations of the West managed by "jaw-jaw" and not "by war-war"' (1998: 46). Hans Binnendijk points out that one of the 'big breakthroughs in current thinking in international affairs is we no longer see the world as in zero sum terms, but rather we see it as much more as a place where working together benefits all parties.'[8]

---

[8] Interview with Hans Binnendijk, 10 July 1998, Washington, D.C.

- Reinforcing point five, the balance of power and the notion of the distribution of power ignores completely the democratic peace phenomenon that has taken place since the end of World War II. According to Henry Nau, 'it has to do not just with the culture of the hegemon, but it also has to do with the culture of its allies . . . all of these countries, now, for the first time ever in the history of Europe, in the history of the world . . . are all mature, stable democracies'. The second essential criterion of the 'democratic peace' Nau argues is the 'accountability of institutions', 'that is all of the government institutions are accountable to elected officials'. He argues that 'it is absolutely critical that the military bureaucracy gets accountable to elected officials who in turn are rotated in office by opposing parties, competing openly, freely with the protection of basic political and civil rights'. The third element of the democratic peace is the protection of basic civil liberties. Nau suggests that it does not really matter 'whether this is done by custom, as in the case of Great Britain, or it is done by the constitution, as in the case of the United States, Germany, and other countries. But the idea that there are basic rights that . . . are not granted by the government, they are granted outside the context of government . . . therefore the government cannot interfere with those rights, freedom of speech, freedom of assembly, freedom of religion. The government's responsibility should be to protect those rights.' Fourthly, Nau points out, '[n]ow if countries have these features, and maybe as a consequence of trading with each other, then we find that they do not go to war with each other, or they don't even militarise disputes with one another. That is they solve their disputes long before they become military disputes, and they do it by peaceful, legal procedures. International organisations play a role in this.' Thus, 'there is no real incentive for countries to "counterbalance" each other. They don't worry that much about differences in relative power, because in some sense none of them fear what the other is going to use its relative power to do the first country any substantial harm.'[9]
- Balance of power theorists contend that because the United States is insular, it should take advantage of its social geography. Again, the balance of power theorists have misconceived the nature and revolutionary change in technology and power relations. Although geography remains important it is not as significant as it once was (see for example, C.S. Gray, 1996; M. Libicki, 1996; Z. Brzezinski, 1997). Increasingly, ideas matter more. Even back in 1942 Nicholas Spykman warned: 'With air power supplementing sea power and mobility . . . the essence of warfare, no region in the globe is too distant to be without strategic significance, too remote to be neglected in the calculation of power politics . . . any war that affects the power relations between great powers in one zone inevitably affects the power relations in all others' (N.J. Spykman, 1942, 1970: 165). In the 'information age', with the sophistication of 'cyber' warfare, where billions of dollars of stocks, shares

---

[9] Interview with Henry Nau, 16 July 1998, Washington, D.C.

and credit can be wiped out of stock markets in a matter of seconds (this is even before the use of nuclear weapons) makes the argument that because the United States is insular geographically and cannot be affected is a geographic myth. In addition, the danger of attacks from information warfare are not necessarily from state to state; groups and/or even individuals can attack communication and command centres without even having to send in armies or missiles across the oceans (see also B. Graham, 8 July 1998). Therefore, the balance of power theorists claim that the United States can just 'de-link' from the international environment is ludicrous. Ever since European settlements on the North American continent, America has never been 'isolated'. Rather, it has acted more like a magnet for millions of migrants from Europe, and later from the rest of the world. Not only is the United States closely interlocked with the international community, the United States is also the most important player in that environment. For the U.S. to be delinked from international affairs would be like the hub cutting off from its spokes.

- Balance of power theorists claim that there is no inherent reason why the United States should be compelled to bear the high cost of providing security for others. In this argument, the burden of NATO would gradually decline in relative importance and 'be replaced (or in effect be taken over) by the Western European Union (WEU) (the military arm of the European Union) or by an individual great power in Europe. The United States' leadership in NATO would disappear' (Z.M. Khalizad, 1995: 17-18). The military power of either Germany or the EU as a whole would have to be deepened and increased. The eventual need for U.S. troops in Europe would evaporate and U.S. forces would be withdrawn. In East Asia, because of a lack of multilateral security arrangements (compared to Europe's OSCE, NATO and WEU), balance of power theorists contend that it is meaningless for the United States to even try to become hegemonic in that region. Layne (1997a) proposes that the U.S. ought to play an 'off-shore' strategy to prevent any major power from seeking hegemonism. In this strategy, Layne views it as 'necessary' to allow these powers to balance one another, thus lowering the burden of U.S. military presence and expenditure.

    The flaw in this argument, however, is that by undermining the security structure, the economic structure would almost certainly revert to nationalistic tendencies (as seen before World War II). Each power will pursue its own economic interests more vigorously, and would believe in 'self-help' rather than co-operation for the advantage of both or all parties. Under this Hobbesian world order, the liberal international economic institutions, such as the WTO, NAFTA, APEC, IMF and World Bank and others, would eventually cease to exist. Contrary to advocates of balance of power, the undermining of both security and economic structures would not only dislodge the U.S. from its 'hegemonic position', but would almost certainly mean greater political uncertainty in the actions of the major powers.

- In 1996, James Kurth advocates: 'The task of the United States is to guide

China and Russia into shaping their spheres in ways similar to those that the United States followed in its own sphere . . . the U.S. objective in regard to the Chinese and the Russian sphere . . . is to motor and monitor for the international order and the model and mentor for the spheres of influence. In short, it is to be the global hegemon of regional hegemons, the boss of all the bosses' (1996: 18). The intention here is interesting. However, what would it mean if China or Russia were not democratic liberal states or share the common principles of free trade such as those of the U.S. and the 'Western' alliance? Certainly, it is interesting to ask how the U.S. can 'guide' China (or Russia) to having its own spheres of interests. The power to influence here is just not applicable. The scenario advocated by Kurth *can* only be stabilising *if* China and Russia become mature democracies, free market economies, and do not exhibit nationalist tendencies and the aim to regain past histo-geographic (imperial) glories.

- Hans Binnendijk points out that, 'the concept of balance of power scenario that they envision may not be the right model for the 21st Century'.[10] He observes that, '[h]istorically the world has tended to operate in a balance of power basis'. Since 1789, he argues, there have been five international systems that can be argued to be balance of power: 1) the Napoleonic system; 2) the Congress of Vienna system with Britain being the balancer; 3) the rise of Germany and the period between the Crimean War and the First World War; 4) the inter-war period; 5) and the Cold War (see Table 5.1 below).

---

[10] Interview with Hans Binnendijk on 10th July 1998. Washington, D.C.

Table 5.1   The Great Powers, 1700-2000

	1700	1800	1875	1910	1935	1945	1975	1991	2000
China	*	*?					*	S?	S
Turkey (Ottoman)	*								
Spain+	*								
Sweden+	*?								
Netherlands	*?								
Austria (Austria-Hungray)	*	*	*	*?					
France+	*	S?	*	*	*				
England+	*?	S?	S	S	*				
Prussia (Germany)+		*?	*	S?					
Russia (USSR)	*?	*	S?	*	*	S	S	S?	*
Italy+			*?	*?					
Japan				*	*		*?	*	*
U.S.			*?	*	*	S	S	H	H
EU							*?	S?	S?
India									*?

Notes:
* = Great power status
S = Super power
H = Hegemonic power
? = Great power (or super power) status suspected or in question
+ + Later integrating to becoming the E.U.

Source : Adapted and modified from Quincy Wright (1965) *A Study of War: Second Edition, with a commentary on War since 1942* (Chciago: University of Chicago), Appendix 20, Table 43.

Over these periods, 'there have been elements of balance of power and traditional conflict between "realists" who think that balance of power is the way to stabilise the world, and on the other hand the Wilsonian approach that talked about values. However, the point is, in these five international systems, there is a historic trend, which is a sort of a life cycle in each of these systems. Each system tends to start with a fairly flexible, fluid system that is often manipulated by a Napoleon or a Bismarck, or a flexible system that is created flexibly like the Congress of Vienna system or the League of Nations. In the life cycle of that system, they tend to get more rigid and rely more on traditional balance of power, certainly rely on alliance systems; they become very bipolar in nature. And it seems to me that the new trick in the international system that we are living now is to avoid that cycle.'[11]

From the points developed above, the chapter will now analyse the response by 'liberals' and 'Marxists' in respect to balance of power and the idea of U.S. preponderance in the contemporary international system. Obviously, to investigate all the critiques from 'liberalism' and 'Marxism' against balance of power theorists and hegemony would be beyond the scope of this chapter, and some of their aspects are to be explored elsewhere in this book. It is the aim here to look very briefly only at their main arguments and to continue with these points in the following chapters.

The Liberal Response to Balance of Power, and Their Idea of 'Liberal Hegemony'

In liberal perception of international affairs, threat is defined in terms of institutional, economic, and ideological factors (liberals versus non-liberals) rather than in terms of the realists' assumptions of power (i.e., capabilities versus rival capabilities). In liberal philosophy, a liberal would not expect to 'balance' against a fellow liberal. They would, however, expect to balance against non-liberals (M. Doyle, 1997: 168). In regard to hegemony, liberals believe fellow liberals are not hegemonic with each other since each party co-operates with each other (as noted in point five and six in the response to balance of power) for pursuit of a common interest.

Second, liberals reject the balance of power 'mechanism' and imperial hegemonic preponderance for world order and peace. Liberal critique of the theory of balance of power can be traced back to Immanuel Kant. Kant stated:

> The maintenance of universal peace by means of the so-called balance of power in Europe is – like swift's house, which a master-builder constructed in such perfect accord with all the laws of equilibrium, that when a sparrow alighted upon it, it immediately collapsed – a mere figment of imagination (in H. Butterfield and M. Wight, 1966: 170-1).

---

[11] Ibid.

In such a case, the concept of balance of power, liberals would argue, has too many variables and is 'too slippery' to be the mechanism of maintaining world peace and stability. Cobden, for example, argued that the 'balance of power is a mere chimera – a creation of the politician's existence – a mere conjunction of syllables, forming words which convey sound without meaning' (in H. Butterfield and M. Wight, 1966: 171). On hegemony, on the other hand, liberals advocate (although not in terms of power and control as realists and neo-realists would) a world liberal 'hegemonic' order based on 'peace-loving' states and peoples co-operating and trading for the benefit of human society in general. The liberal hegemony was not only of the world becoming a federation of 'liberal' republican states, but according to Kant, for the realisation of a cosmopolitan constitution to cover the world. Kant argued, '[f]or only by endeavouring to fulfil the conditions laid down by this cosmopolitan law can we flatter ourselves that we are gradually approaching that ideal' (I. Kant, 1795, translated by M.C. Smith, 1903: 142).

Third, and as argued in chapter two, liberals do not deny that the international system is anarchic (in the sense that there is no world government). However, the condition of their anarchy is different to the Hobbesian proposition of anarchy. Liberals contend that world affairs are not relatively about a state of war, but a heterogeneous state of war and peace, and to the Kantian liberals, it might become a state of global peace. Rather than being overwhelmingly captured in the Hobbesian framework of endless contestation and zero-sum games, liberals believe in positive or negative games, in the sense that they can win or lose together.

This distinction between the 'realists' and liberals does not apply to all realists, however. As developed in chapter two, 'pragmatic' realists would argue that in pursuing general interests, skilful negotiations are necessary for general advantage for all or none. Like the liberal counter-part, failure to co-ordinate in seeking compatible goals may undermine the general interest. Thus, the inability to 'trust' may also undermine co-operation. Unlike liberals, who view other liberals as constituting no threat, pragmatic realists do not view others (whether liberals or otherwise) in such distinctive manner. To the pragmatic realist, the level of assessment is more sophisticated. To pragmatic realists, if benefits are open and trust is guaranteed with obligations, the opportunity for co-operation is high. On the other hand, if the trust were not guaranteed with obligation, the opportunity to co-operate would sink to a lower level, and if inconsistency continues, the trust of the opposite is discarded. In the 'trust' scenario, pragmatic realists would be prudent in trading with others, in such manner that they will assess the opportunities and benefits of the co-operation involved, and question the benefits to act collectively.

Fourth, contrary to pacifists, liberalism is not inherently 'peace-loving', nor is it consistently restrained or peaceful in intent, especially to non-liberal states. To liberals, alignment with similar states may be viewed as a way of defending one's own political principles. In this Kantian philosophy, '[c]onquest for the sake of reforming an unjust enemy state is permitted' (M. Doyle, 1997: 255). Further

Kantian liberals would 'force' non-liberals 'to accept a new constitution if that is unlikely to encourage their warlike inclination' (Kant in M. Doyle, 1997: 255). In this regard, the Kantian liberal states' idea of peace is one extending gradually to encompass all states and leading to 'liberal' perpetual peace (I. Kant, 1795, Perpetual Peace, translated by M.C. Smith, 1903: 134). Kant's logic of 'perpetual peace' amongst nations is as follows,

> For, if Fortune ordains that a powerful and enlightened people should form a republic, – which is by nature inclined to seek peace – this would serve as a centre of federal union for other states wishing to join, and thus secure conditions of freedom among the states in accordance with the idea of the law of nations. Gradually, through different unions of this kind, the federation would extend further and further (I. Kant, 1795, Perpetual Peace, translated by M.C. Smith, 1903: 134-5).

In this sense, to liberals, if statesmen believe their own system of government is inherently 'good', then protecting states with similar systems must be considered 'good'. Secondly, states with similar traits are likely to fear one another less, because they find it harder to imagine an inherently 'good' state deciding to attack them. Third, alignment with similar states may enhance the legitimacy of a weak regime by demonstrating that it is part of a large, popular movement.

From this simple logic of 'good' and 'bad', Walt sarcastically stressed, 'if ideology is in fact an important determinant of alliance choices, then identifying friends and foes will be relatively easy' (S. Walt, 1987: 37). Thence, states with similar domestic systems are one's natural allies, and those with different political systems or beliefs should be viewed with suspicion. The international system unfortunately has never been this 'simple'. In addition, this belief has other implications as well. 'Liberal' states have a tendency to intervene in the internal affairs of other countries simply because they are not 'liberal'.

This inherent strategy and its implications are explored in the developing chapters, when I will analyse the United States' policy of engagement and enlargement, and the idea of liberal democracy and free-trade in light of the Kantian philosophy of 'extend[ing] further and further'. The chapters will show (and as indicated in the responses to the balance of power theories) how the U.S., although involved in this Kantian philosophy, does not entirely distinguish 'enemies' in terms of 'liberals' and 'non-liberals'. This 'inconsistency' is illustrated when I explore how the U.S. administrations sees other complex realities and puts these views into consideration as well, thus making U.S. external policies sometimes appear to be contradictory or even incoherent. As the 'liberal hegemony' will be analysed in greater depth later, I will not repeat them here, I will instead commence to the Marxist response to balance of power and the idea 'liberal hegemony'.

Marxist Critique of Balance of Power and Liberal Hegemony

The Marxist approach to international order is, perhaps, the most critical to balance of power theory, the liberal alternative, and the hegemony of the U.S. and their affiliates. Before moving into the Marxist critique, I will briefly recount the Marxist understanding of the 'international system'. According to Karl Marx and Friedrich Engels' *The Communist Manifesto*, capitalism has to spread and develop around the globe and move into a social development. In this mode, the creation of a balance of power 'mechanism' is a superficial creation of the leading classes to separate the unity of the international proletariat. For Marx and Engels, the ultimate goal was the 'withering away' of the bourgeois state, which would also ultimately mean the abolition of the theory of balance of power amongst states. In this sense however, Marx's advocacy of the abolition of the state is actually rather similar to the liberal's (see chapter two) viewpoint.

However, unlike the liberal contention, Marxists fundamentally question the existing distribution of wealth, especially the gap between the rich and poor, whereas liberals and some realists generally ignore (or even encourage) this issue and see it as a necessary condition of laissez-faire economics. Marxists thus question the liberal and realist position on the policies of the hegemonic principles concerning the creation of the (growing) gap in wealth both within society and between nations.

In another sense, despite advocacy of the abolition of the state, Marx and Engels are in some sense similar to balance of power theorists, although for different reasons. Both Marxists (i.e., S. Amin, 1997) and balance of power theorists question the policies and intentions of migration and the so-called 'liberal' policy of 'mingling' of different cultures into a Kantian cosmopolitan 'melting-pot'. Marxists would advocate the international proletariat to 'balance against' and 'challenging' the bourgeois, balance of power theorists on the other hand would suggest it in terms of power and quantifiable capabilities. Unlike balance of power theorists, however, who aim to uphold barriers, or, to build up barriers and to keep an 'unequal balance' between the 'haves' and 'have nots'. Marxists would advocate a breaking down of these barriers to all people and to allow them 'fair' distribution and access to wealth. Whereas Kantian liberal advocate a cosmopolitan 'melting pot', Marxists desire to create a 'melting pot' for all with regard to wealth and property.

The reality of the 'liberal' globalisation thesis concerning the 'melting pot of cultures' is, however, severely questioned by Marxists and their affiliates. Marxists, socialists, and others (such as the critical theorists, and 'submerged forces' i.e., the groups in Seattle 1999) criticise liberals on the grounds that despite the 'humanitarian' interventions in areas (such as Yugoslavia, Iraq, and others), the so-called 'liberal' governments continue to exercise restraints on international migration of the poor (from developing countries into the rich countries) in the 'zone of liberal peace'. As such, Marxists argue that the liberal governments are really not liberals, but rather hypocritical, and are acting out of self-interest rather than really intending to advocate a 'melting pot' amongst different cultures and people. Marxists and others maintain that despite the government of the 'liberal democratic' area jawing on about the promotion of prosperity and 'liberal democracy', these governments have really had no intention of promoting the 'melting pot' of cosmopolitan society. For example, the United Kingdom's policy and public response on the issue of asylum seekers from Kosovo once the war against Yugoslavia was over. What appears instead is that the governments, the institutions, and most of the general public in the 'zone of democratic peace and prosperity' are intent on maintaining an unequal balance of power in terms of wealth (see S. Amin, 1997).

As such, Marxists called for a balance of class, and/or as world system analysts would like to see, 'a balance between the developing countries (as the main source of primary products) against developed countries (the exploiters of the third world)'. This has been explored elsewhere (see B. Gills, 2000). The resistance to 'liberal hegemony' (see Ikenberry, 1997; 1998) order has, however, had only very limited success and has failed to materialise into 'substantial' political resistance against the 'hegemonic' position of the developed countries. Moreover, the collapse of the communist ideology in Eastern Europe and the USSR has undermined the Marxist ideological 'resistance' to the 'liberal' world order. What remains in resistance to the 'hegemonic order' of liberalism is what can be described as 'submerged' forces. However, this counter-hegemonic force, as yet, remains disunited and undermined by hegemonic agents and the regimes and institutions of civil society.[12] In addition, the techniques applied by the counter-hegemonic globalisation forces have been unattractive to the mass population and media. They are often portrayed as hooligans and being a nuisance rather than seen as promoting peace or prosperity. These forces will need serious reorganisation, if they are to have any impact on promoting their cause of a fairer international system.

Conclusion

In conclusion, how an international order emerges (H. Bull, 1977), remains an intensely debated issue. Some scholars have argued that the 'immediate' international system is 'abnormal' by 'international history standards' (K. Waltz,

---

[12] For possible 'campaign' against the 'hegemonic forces', see T.E. Lawrence (1997 edn.) *Seven Pillars of Wisdom* (London: Wordsworth). Lawrence wrote: 'The decision of what was critical would always be ours. Most wars were wars of contact, both forces striving to staying in touch to avoid tactical surprise. Ours should be a war of detachment. We were to contain the enemy by the silent threat of a vast unknown desert, not disclosing ourselves until we attacked. The attack might be nominal, directed not against him, but against his stuff; so it would seek neither his strength nor his weakness, but his most accessible material', quoted in D. Krause (1998) *The Book of Five Rings for Executives* (London: Nicholas Brealey), pp. 146-7.

1993). In politics, as in history, however, a central query that has, as yet, eluded both practitioner and scholar is what constitutes 'normality' and 'abnormality' (P. Berger and T. Luckman, 1966). This is especially so, when the concept of power is involved. 'History' has shown that those who have the power are the ones that create 'normality' or 'abnormality'. Those that do not have power will either resist that power or be overwhelmed by it, and may even eventually follow it. How the 'other' forces follow, blindly, or by having an agenda of their own (including to undermine that order) remains at the heart of the vitality of politics and the quest for power. By 'international history standards', the U.S. has never been a 'normal' country. Its creation and its quest for power and glory have not by any means been 'normal' in 'historical terms'.

In this chapter, I have outlined the advocates of balance of power and responses to that theory from 'realism', 'liberalism', and Marxist critiques. The way each theory 'views' the contemporary world will no doubt intensify the debate further. However, if the 'lessons' of international history can be offered as a map to possible outcomes in future dimensions of international military and economic affairs, the enticement of balance of power thinking demands a more subtle approach. The experience of international history makes any multipolar system very unattractive. Most importantly, there are several reasons why an 'offshore' balance strategy would increase – not lower – the risk of U.S. involvement in a major war, and why the strategy of preponderance should not be abandoned. Despite criticism of U.S. 'heavy-handedness' on many issues, these remain bearing if the scenario was to turn into a multipolar system, where world war looms just around the corner. What is disappointing is that advocates of multipolarity are fixated on the notion that the United States must become a 'balancer'. It is not only illusionary to believe that the United States can be disengaged from the international community, it is also extremely dangerous. The early twentieth century can remind us that an American policy of 'drift' inevitably led to major wars on the Eurasian landmass. In the current world order, it is certainly 'cheaper' for the U.S. to continue its security commitment to Europe and East Asia as a form of insurance rather than to stand on the sidelines only to be compelled to intervene later under what presumably would be much more dangerous conditions.

Such is the awesome capacity of the weapons of mass destruction that the world cannot possibly face a situation where one fatal error by any of the great powers would lead to the end of human civilisation as we know it. Furthermore, the principle weakness associated with the balance of power system is that some countries are likely to be deficient in significant power resources. Thus, the analogy of a classical military, multipolar balance of power is highly misleading. With the bipolar system just evicted, the world certainly does not want a return to that 'similar' situation.

So what of the future? Currently Russia is a threat in abeyance. The three rising powers – China, Japan and Europe – are far from ready to challenge the United States (these countries/region will be examined individually in relation to the United States in their respective chapters that follows). With these three areas performing quite well economically and their people prospering, the need for rivalry with the United States is quite minimal, at least when it comes to military disputes. Even when security issues come to the fore, the U.S. has been extremely careful in its dealings with China, Russia, Europe, and Japan. Gilpin warns us that, '[e]ven if modern science and technology have given mankind a new consciousness of shared values and common problems, this situation is no guarantee to common interest or of a willingness to subordinate selfish concerns to the larger good' (Gilpin, 1981: 225). This is in contrast to the politics of nation-states, especially to the mercantilist era of centuries past where trade disputes often led to war and war unsheathed trade weapons like embargoes and blockages. Although the strategic control over main trade routes, resources and markets remains vital, the likelihood of the great powers going to war over these issues, although not obsolete, has decreased significantly. In fact, as 'democratic peace' theorists have advocated, it might not necessarily mean conflict between them. Instead, it could be one of co-operation between the major powers (especially the 'liberal-democratic' countries), and even 'closing ranks' against challengers of either groups or nation-states.

Whatever the theoretical approach to the 'realities' of the 'direction' of the 'international order', one thing that cannot be denied is the power base of the U.S. (see Appendix 1A) compared to others. In this 'hegemonic globalisation order', and despite the contending forces in the form of major powers and/or submerged groups, the U.S. has become so powerful that it may not need to play by the rules of balance of power. Instead, the U.S. has been intent on power maximising, rather than 'balancing' its power, to further serve its interests. This is evident in its reversal of the nuclear test ban treaties, and the issues surrounding the United States 'homeland' missile defence system.

In regard to 'submerged' and discontent fringe forces, the U.S. and its allies are prepared, equipped, and fully aware of the intentions of these groups to undermine the hegemonic order. Accordingly, the development of institutions, regimes, and other civil society groups (old and new) have acted and operated as counters to the 'submerged' forces. These emergent and overlapping regimes and civil society groups have made it difficult for the 'submerged' groups to potentially 'emerge' into a tangible challenge to the 'hegemonic globalisation order' without being seen as deviants. Unless there is a breaking of ranks amongst the major industrialised countries and their 'elite class', the possibility for replacing the United States-led order is remote. For this the next chapter will analyse the strategy(ies) that the United States has deployed to maintain support amongst allies for sustaining its central position in the emerging world order.

Chapter 6

Hegemonic Globalisation: The United States and the Integration of the Great Powers

> The present moment is marked, most happily, by the fact that there are no great conflicts among the great powers. This situation is without precedent in recent centuries, and it is essential that it be cherished, nurtured, and preserved. Such is the destructive potential of advanced modern weapons that another great conflict between any of the leading powers could well do irreparable damage to the entire structure of modern civilisation.
> G. Kennan, 1995: 125-6.

> The shortest and best way to make your fortune is to let people see clearly that it is in their interests to promote yours.
> Jean de la Bruyere in R. Greene and J. Elffers, 1999: 47.

Introduction

How the international system is taking shape in the post-cold war era has been of great interest and concern to scholars in international affairs.[1] The above statement by George Kennan is by no means an idealistic dream or a scientific standard for peace in a 'realistic' and unscientific world when considering the relations amongst the leading powers in world affairs. Unlike idealistic desires or scientific equations, Kennan represents a realist (who participated in the Second World War and Cold War intrigues) who aims to offer a realist solution to the highly competitive and sometimes 'irrational' nature of politics. His vision is to offer a prudent opportunity to leaders of the leading powers to value and nurture the

---

[1] See for example, Philip Allott (1990) *Eunomia – New Order for a New World* (Oxford: Oxford University Press); Paul Kennedy (1993) *Preparing for the Twenty-First Century*. (London: HarperCollins Publishers); Hamish McRae (1994) *The World in 2020: Power, Culture and Prosperity: A Vision of the Future* (London: HarperCollins Publishers); Robert Heilbroner (1995) *Visions of the Future* (Oxford: Oxford University Press); Samuel P. Huntington (1996) *The Clash of Civilisations and the Remaking of World Order* (New York: Simon and Schuster); Zbigniew Brzezinski (1997) *The Grand Chessboard: American Primacy and Its Geostrategic Imperatives* (New York: Basic Books); Ken Booth (1998) (Ed.) *Statecraft and Security: The Cold War and Beyond* (Cambridge: Cambridge University Press).

'present moment', rather than to return to the 'destructive' power politics of the past.

This chapter inquires into this political discourse and questions the validity of Kennan's argument that the 'present moment' should be 'cherished, nurtured, and preserved'. It examines the intensification of this order following the end of the Cold War. In itself, this 'order' can be seen in the light of the United States and its allies maximising their capitalist mode of development and profit, as well as integrating others into their quest for markets and capital. Chapter three had illustrated how the United States' foreign policy and the advancement of capitalism are intertwined. The chapter showed how with the collapse of the Soviet Union and the demise of communism as a possible alternative, the capitalist system (alias globalisation) is attempting to expand and deepen. Chapter four investigated how the theories of balance of power, which were central to the maintenance of peace and stability (or more accurately non-peace and instability) in previous international systems does not apply to the immediate international system, and it certainly does not apply to the United States global strategy of preponderance. The United States global objective as this chapter will unveil shows how the United States aims to 'break' with the theories of the rise and fall of great powers, and by using its massive power base to change 'norms' and 'standards' in order to sustain its central position in world affairs.

With this realisation, the 'globalisation process', as the chapter uncovers, is in actuality the 'grand' strategy of the United States and its allies to integrating competing powers into that system, and maintaining their position at the apex. It is a grand design to make geopolitical conflict amongst 'rising' great powers less likely, and thus maintaining and securing global capitalism as the way the United States and allies desire.

The Determinates of Hegemonic Globalisation

To begin this realisation of 'peace', we must first comprehend the nature of this political reality – which is what George Kennan and other practitioners of power politics have experienced – that is, the political nature of intrigue, conflicts and struggles. A political analysis of this nature is not about unrealistic ideals, or to attempt to predict scenarios without sufficient concrete variables of historical events. As outlined in Chapter One, I argue that the interpretation of the past, through careful evaluation, analysis, and assessment, may actually help actors avoid the mistakes of the past in the future – at least it gives actors valuable lessons and sets of variables from which to assess and analyse unpredictable events and to avoid similar errors. Recall the old dictum 'the best way to avoid mistake(s) is to learn from (other people's or one's own) mistakes'. Whether one accepts this argument or not will entirely depend on one's view of 'reality'.

If this argument can be falsified – let *it* be so! On the other hand, if we are to accept that there are lessons to be learned from the past, this book will address the historical relations between the major powers and analyse the possible power relations between them in the future. 'For the future knows no guide and it is from history that we may gather specks of evidence to formulate present action' (D.J. Hill cited in C.W. Freeman, 1994: 129).

In order to better understand 'our' history, it is likely that we should better understand the history of others. A primary source for understanding human nature is Hobbes' *Leviathan* on the nature of realism, which expresses itself through a pessimistic mode of inquiry as the primary standard for the understanding of human nature and the behaviour of man. Reflectively, however, such a position is not always the case. Human nature, the human condition, and political activities are more often seen in multiple combinations of pessimism, optimism, and neutrality, that are drawn from the practitioners' past ancestors and their own experiences. From this perspective, the progression and revisionism of society and the interaction of human beings are set by continuous struggles between neutral, optimist, and pessimist forces. In the (multiple) linear movement of human society, one force does not necessarily overwhelm the other. Often, they are balanced. If the pessimistic mode is in operation, the most likely event is that the world would be seen to be a hostile and cold place (as well as zero-sum) and any co-operation would be deemed to be unrealistic, and there would be a perpetual state of war. On the other hand, if the optimistic variables become prominent, any failure in co-operation would prompt a revision of the optimistic variables. Whilst neutrality does not follow either case to the extreme, it is in itself often stagnated between its lack of both pessimism and optimism for change. In this perspective, history is a continuous cycle of struggles between pessimism and optimism; it does not 'end' in optimism, nor is it perpetually damned in pessimism.

However, the practice of international politics and diplomacy has often been shaped by experiences seen in the lenses of 'power politics' and via intrigues involved in shaping the nature of world affairs (see H. Nau, 1990; J. Nye, 1990; C.W. Chase, 1993; H. Kissinger, 1994; Z. Brzezinski, 1997; W. Christopher, 1998). In this sense, international politics is shaped in terms of 'realist' power struggles. Yet, the 'failure' in the practice of power politics in the past has been so catastrophic that it becomes highly suspect if world leaders do not recognise its past failures. The primary aim for the realisation of peace is, therefore, to modify and/or refine power politics as the first approach to political practices in international political/economic affairs. In this way, it is important to follow the proposal not on 'about what may happen ... [but] about what must not be allowed to happen' (Z. Brzezinski, 1993: ix, emphasis added). On the other hand, however, this remark would invoke the question, 'what must not be allowed to happen, to whom, and why?' In addition, it is prescriptive and thus endangers a subjective perspective. As argued previously, this book is not a crusade against anyone, it is not an attempt to dogmatise or idealise a view of any specific power or contender in world politics.

It is, rather, an *honest* attempt to face political facts and to get to a realisation that there are measures by which conditions of peace may prevail or not prevail. Historically, wars and cycles of power struggles are persistent in the political reality.

An idealist prescription would perhaps often lead to 'unrealistic' ends, as Machiavelli wrote, 'A man who wishes to make a profession of goodness in everything must necessarily come to grief among so many who are not good' (1977: 42). Moreover, since the politics of man is endless, 'the solution of one problem usually leads to another' (J. Reston, 1967 in C.W. Freeman, 1997: 119). This observation does not mean that the opportunity to avert future wars, especially hegemonic ones, should not be open to analysis. For any reasonable person, averting wars and preventing them from occurring should be amongst the prime concerns. It may sound idealistic that we can stop wars or alarmist to suggest that humanity is doomed with the persistence of armed conflict. However, this is neither an alarmist warning nor an idealist desire.[2] My priority is to understand the relationships of complex international interactions and to offer a 'realistic' vigilance to avoid tension becoming inflamed into major conflict. As E.H. Carr knew well, the weapons of idealism are more dangerous to itself than the weapons of realism.

From this framework, the intention of this chapter is to capture the historical relationships among the leading powers: the U.S., China, the EU, Russia, and Japan in the international arena today. The aim of this chapter is to construct a framework around which the basis for the following chapters may operate. I have chosen to study (as argued in chapter one) the five main powers because I believe they are the 'main' actors in the international system that set the primary course of contemporary world affairs. Obviously, other powers, such as India, South Africa, some Islamic countries (such as Pakistan, Saudi Arabia, Indonesia), and others may be mentioned to make a 'fuller' understanding of the operation of the international system. Unfortunately, because of limitations of time and space, my immediate analysis is to concentrate on the five powers/regions that I perceive to be the major players (at least the main determinants) directing world political, economic, military, and cultural affairs. Other factors such as social classes, religious groups, environmental groups, multinational corporations, the flow of international finance, communication, and non-governmental agencies, may be significant, but again I contend that the main and ultimate agenda remains the secular relation between states (S. Krasner, 1983). International affairs, without states, would certainly be set and entertained at a different framework – certainly the 'high' politics ('security', politics and diplomacy) would be seen differently. Without the structural barriers of 'high' politics – the territorial nation-state, the national anthem, the national flag, the nation (not to mention the ethnicity, language and religion) and so forth – we would live in a world 'without borders', and the study of international affairs would take a new turn and a new meaning. However, this is

---

[2] Given E.H. Carr's (1939/46) devastating critique of 'Idealism' as an epithet for naivete and utopianism, I naturally want to avoid this pitfall of analysis.

not yet the case, and although non-state actors are significant in influencing state behaviour, the world continues to be determined by states and their agents. Until the nation-state tradition evaporates, or the world comes to be in a situation, or circumstance of 'statelessness', the emphasis remains on the role of the state in the operation and progress of international affairs.

It could be argued that this view is biased towards state-centrism. However, this is not the case. The level of analysis and evaluation depends on the type of questions being asked, and different questions need different answers. In this inquiry, I intend to examine the present international system. It is an attempt to look at the 'entire' jigsaw puzzle, rather than looking at one jigsaw piece (see chapter one). If we were to use an analogy, we might say we are studying the 'forest'. At what level would we begin our study? Different people studying this subject will have different answers as to what constitutes the 'forest'. Some would want to study the leaves, others the type of plants and fruits and vegetation and so on. Others simply see trees. Now, if we were to apply this same analogy to the study of international politics, some people are studying groups, whilst others specialise in specific areas of the world, and others study the state(s). In the end, they all have a certain perspective in understanding their view of the world. In my attempt to analyse the international political system, I will try to analyse or evaluate every level of the political structure. However, the main focus in my analysis is the inter-relations between 'states', because the state is the sovereign entity. Again, this might be criticised for being a 'state-centric' conception of international politics, but to do so, is just like claiming that to study forests one is blamed for being 'tree-centric' (A. Wendt, 1999: 9).

Unlike trees, however, states interact, and sometimes these interactions lead to conflict. From this realisation, the foundation for this study is to inquire into the nature and reason for power conflicts. Obviously, there are too many reasons to be listed. The object here is, therefore, to analyse the power relationship between the leading states/regions in the international system. Wars and squabbles between smaller nations are persistent and probably inevitable. However, what are the alternatives to avert major wars, especially hegemonic ones?

The basis for this realisation is to inquire into the nature of the power of the United States and its attempts to act as the centre of the power relationship between all the leading powers in the world. Obviously, other powers will have their own sphere of influence, and may act to counter U.S. interests. However, when it comes down to the global scale structure of operations, only the United States has the capabilities to interact in nearly every corner of the power structure – directly and indirectly. That is, the U.S. is now in a position of global centrality.

In analysing the power relationship of the United States and the other four leading powers/regions, my book contends that the U.S. is attempting to manage or even lead the other four main powers in order to gain a 'trickle-down' effect, which the U.S. believes would be to the benefit of the entire international system and, thus, the United States. This is different to the concert of powers in that it is the U.S. that is dominant and it does not act in the concerted manner of traditional power politics (as R. Rosescrance, 1992 points out). Furthermore, this book argues that unlike Brzezinski (1993; 1997), who proposed that three major powers – Japan, the EU, and China act as anchors for the United States on the Eurasian landmass, and as containment partners against the Russian Federation. Brzezinski even proposed the fragmentation of the Russian Federation altogether. Although interesting in theory, the implications of this are highly contentious and the perceived dangers involved in the fragmentation of the Russian Federation would bring more ambiguities than benefits (see chapter seven on U.S.-Russia relations). In the Russian chapter, I analyse how the Russian Federation too is part of the U.S. grand strategy of hegemonic globalisation. In this perspective, the U.S. strategy is aiming to encompass all these main powers, and hold them close to the United States, which the U.S. believes would offer it a 'golden opportunity' to expand the idea of the 'liberal democratic peace' (R. Russett, 1993; M. Brown et al, 1997; L. Diamond, 1997) into areas which otherwise might have challenged those ideals. In addition, by engaging and expanding liberal democratic ideals to the four powers/regions, these powers at the same time are indirectly influencing other countries which otherwise 'might' not be friendly to U.S. policies of liberal engagement and enlargement. Via the exertion of these ideals to the major powers and minor ones, the ideals inadvertently gravitate towards the agenda of hegemonic globalisation. The analogue of this agenda can be seen as the United States acting like the Sun, whilst other powers are as the planets with their own lunar satellite systems, all connected and revolving around the Sun's gravity (this is discussed and elaborated in chapter eleven).

Using this framework, I assess how the U.S. intends to sustain its leading position by applying a multi-layered, multi-dimensional, strategy in its relations with the other four powers and the international system. In elaborating on that investigation I have found it necessary to deploy a set of assumptions on the power relations of these 'big five' powers based on their depth (i.e., from 'cordial' power relationship to 'indifference' in power relationship to 'hostile' power relationship) and historical patterns that shape their relationships. However, power relations may shift and change over time and circumstances, partially due to the perception and interpretation of information by the decision-making of states, statesmen, and other subordinates. In the present day (1996-99) scenario the relationships of the five leading powers are sketched as follows:–

Table 6.1 The Diplomatic, Political and Military Relation of the Five Leading Powers

	Diplomatic/Political Relations				**Military Relations**	
	U.S.	**China**	**Russia**	**Japan**	**EU**	
U.S.		Mutual-hostile military relationship	PfP with NATO, but mutual-hostile military relationship	Japan-U.S. Strategic Security Alliance	Allies (NATO), North Atlantic Council	**EU**
China	Mutual-hostile diplomatic/political relationship		Mutual-hostile military relationship	Mutual-hostile military relationship	Mutual-hostile military relationship	**Japan**
Russia	Cordial diplomatic and political relationship	Mutual-hostile diplomatic/political relationship		Mutual-hostile military relationship	PfP with NATO, but mutual-hostile military relationship	**Russia**
Japan	Cordial diplomatic and political relationship	Mutual-hostile diplomatic/political relationship	Mutual-hostile diplomatic/political relationship		Cordial military relationship, but no military alliance	**China**
EU	Mutual-hostile diplomatic/political relationship	Mutual-hostile diplomatic/political relationship	Mutual diplomatic/political relations	Cordial diplomatic and political relationship		**U.S.**

Table 6.2 The Economic and Trade Relations/Cultural and Educational Exchanges

	Trade and Economic Relations				
Cultural/Economic Relations	EU	Japan	Russia	China	U.S.
EU		Area of democratic peace (competitive/co-operative trade relations)	Mutual economic/trade relations	Mutual economic/trade relations	Area of democratic peace (competitive/co-operative trade relations)
Japan	Area of democratic peace and co-operative/competitive prosperity		Mutual-hostile trading/economic relations	Mutual economic/trade relations	Area of democratic peace (competitive/co-operative trade relations)
Russia	Mutual cultural/educational relations	Mutual-hostile cultural/educational relations		Mutual economic/trade relations	Mutual economic/trade relations
China	Mutual-hostile cultural/educational relations	Mutual-hostile cultural/educational relations	Mutual-hostile cultural/educational relations		Mutual-hostile economic/trade relations
U.S.	Area of democratic peace and co-operative/competitive prosperity	Area of democratic peace and co-operative/competitive prosperity	Mutual cultural/educational relations	Mutual cultural/educational relations	

Table 6.3 The Relations Among the Five Major Powers

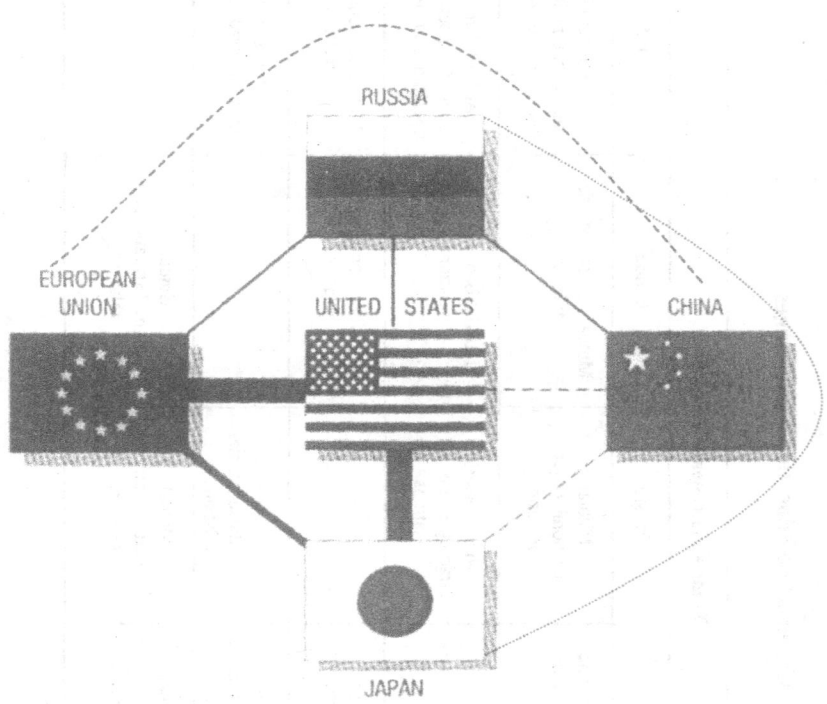

The thicker the line, the closer the ties

Source: Adopted and modified from Institute for National Strategic Studies (1997) *Strategic Assessment 1997: Flashpoints and Force Structure* (Washington D.C: National Defense University), p. xii.[3]

Obviously these are some sweeping generalisations that could (and should) be challenged. There is the difficulty of validating the meaning of such a grand project, for example to speak of an entire nation-state (not to mention an entire region – the EU) in terms of presumed characteristic values and the behaviour traits of its inhabitants is questionable. There is the problem that the notion of the nation-

---

[3] Other countries/groups of countries may be added to the graph showing their assumed relationship with each other. In the framework of this analysis, however, I have only concentrated on the five major powers. The author would like to thank Hans Bennindijk for this source.

state/region pre-supposes that there is an actual topology or range of values that make the nation and people, in the sense that the 'nation' acts as a collective personality. Moreover, are the power relations describing any 'real' people? There are also the observer's own biases and idiosyncrasies, which is in itself hostage to prior assumptions and perceptions, thus making the notion of neutrality and impartiality in analysis and evaluation problematic. Often, individuals naturally tend to ascribe 'good' values to friends and 'bad' values to enemies (R. Whitcomb, 1998: 1).

Yet, no matter what the observer's own prejudices, the point remains: if there is no such thing as a national/regional character then there are no real clear-cut distinctions that differentiate nations and regions. Thence, Freeman argues that 'Nations interpret the present by reference to their past. If that past includes traumatic events, their interpretation of the present will often diverge radically from objectively verifiable reality' (1994: 130). As I have argued in chapter one, the history of a respective actor is often moulded by its conception of the world, and its role in that world is manifested by the characteristics of its conduct. These characteristics are expressed by ideas and ideals, and by action and reaction that actor may have with others. Traits that epitomise behaviour – at least in a reflective manner of the power's habitual conduct and behaviour in its relationship with others – are moulded by the perception or misperception of itself and/or of others (J. Scott, 1998: 3). Obviously, members of a particular power differ in their individualistic outlooks. However, very often, but not always, people of certain states share common denominator values and traits which often comprise a sort of basic 'personality structure', formed as they mature with their cultural environment and reinforced by civil society and the state. Although not all of its inhabitants can be measured and because of the absence of well-tested data, or even of widely accepted agreement, the commentary that follows is designed to help to elucidate the void image and the reality. I emphasise again that a nation's conduct of its foreign relations will be largely conditioned by its experience, such as war, economic depression, educational change and level of education, colonisation, revolution, migratory pattern – whether they are external immigration or internal migration. More importantly, and again following Wendt,

> Contemporary states have been interacting for dozens, even hundreds of years, during which they have accumulated considerable knowledge about each other's interests. They know something about each other's grievances and ambitions, and thus about whether they are status quo or revisionist states. They know something about each other's styles of dispute resolution . . . they even know something about the conditions under which these conditions might change. None of this knowledge is perfect or complete, but neither is it wholly unreliable or irrelevant. Part of what makes it reliable: over the course of their interactions states have made policies on the basis of inferences about each other's intentions (pessimistic or optimistic), which were then tested and revised against the reality of what those intentions really were. Through this interacting with reality, states have learned a great deal about each other, and today can often assign reasonably confident probabilities of inferences about what others want . . . History matters. And since that history is

based in part on what others' interests really are, the distribution of interests must have an independent role in constituting the meaning of anarchy and distribution of power (1999: 108-9).

In these experiences, the impact of the values gives individuals a subjective guide to future paths, for better or for worse. I use the term 'subjective guide' because values and traditions are not fixed firmly in the characteristics of nations. In many or even all cases, values and characteristics are evolving, gradually adapting according to changing conditions and at other times manipulated by civil society and the state for a certain means or an end. On the other hand, with the accelerating pace of globalisation (especially telecommunication and cultural interaction) the changing conditions become even more difficult to pinpoint with accuracy in order to define a specific national character. Nevertheless, some traits still remain, and until 'full-scale' 'hegemonic globalisation' is realised, national traits will persist.

Thus, the study of world politics remains relative rather than absolute. This confusion of debate is no doubt continuous and will not end here, and because 'we cannot study everything at once' (A. Wendt, 1999: 14), I will now leave this debate and return to the main argument of the book. In due course my exploration will clarify what is at stake here.

The United States as the 'Centre'

From Figure 6.3, the intention of the United States in the Cold War and in the post-Cold War era has been quite clear.[4] It has been to make sure that no one country

---

[4] Halford J. Mackinder (1904) 'The Geographical Pivot of History' *The Geographical Journal*, Vol. 23, No. 4, April. pp. 421-44, and later refined in *Democratic Ideals and Reality* (1919) asserted that the state that could control the Eurasian landmass between Germany and central Siberia would be able to control the world. Mackinder expressed that 'Who rules East Europe commands the Heartland, Who rules the Heartland command the World Island, Who rules the World Island command the World'. This theory was widely interpreted as a rationalisation and justification for British policy of maintaining a European balance of power and of preventing heartland hegemony by either Germany or Russia. In 1942, John N. Spykman in *America's Strategy in World Politics*, took this up and argued that the key area was the 'inner crescent', which was called the 'Rimland', control of which could neutralise the power of the Heartland. The conceptual Heartland-Rimland thesis became the basis for U.S. policies of containment, being an effort to seal up the Rimland in order to hem in the Heartland (Soviet Union). U.S. sea and air power and alliances, NATO in Europe, CENTO in West Asia and SEATO in East Asia were specific attempts to do this. Z. Brzezinski (1997) *The Grand Chessboard: American Primacy and Its Geostrategic Imperatives*, proposed that the U.S. post-Cold War strategy should press further into the Heartland (into Eastern Europe and into the former Soviet Republics) and neutralise efforts by Iran and Afghanistan to export Islamic fundamentalism to the region; see also Paul Starobin (1999) 'The New Great Game', *National Journal* (13 March), citing U.S. Sen. Brownback: 'After years of fighting communism in this part of the world, the doors are open

controls the Eurasian landmass and that a *balance* be maintained so as to prevent a power that is strong enough or aims to align with other powers to challenge or overthrow the United States as the current hegemon.[5] The aim is that 'no state or combination of states gains the ability to expel the United States or even diminish its decisive role' (Z. Brzezinski, 1997b: 52) on the Eurasian landmass. The promotion of a stable transcontinental balance, however, was not an end in itself, only a means toward shaping genuine strategic partnerships in the key regions of Eurasia. Josef Joffe has suggested that in order to achieve this and prevent any rising aspirant from challenging the existing system,

> ... the United States should act as regional protector, by providing security to those potential rivals – Japan, China, Western Europe – who would otherwise have to produce security on their own by converting economic strength into military assets (1995: 117).

This view has been systematically deployed by the United States since the collapse of the Soviet Union, where the United States does not wish to see any one power or a coalition of powers on the Eurasian landmass dominating either the East, the West and/or the Middle. Basically, the U.S. aims are 'preventing the emergence of hostile regional coalition or hegemons'.[6] However, three questions remain unsolved from this strategy. First, how and why the United States has been able to 'manage' the international system without much resistance, at least in the most dynamic regions of the world, i.e., Latin America, Western Europe and East Asia? Second, what are the policies that the United States is trying to convey to the world? Finally, what are the speciality and motive behind U.S. power manoeuvres and organisation that has made these regions follow the United States' lead? Is it its ideals of free trade, human rights, and democratic liberalism or something else

---

to promote institutions of democratic government and to create the conditions for the growth of pluralistic societies'. p. 671.

[5] See Tyler, P.E. (1992, 8 March) 'US Strategy Plans Calls for Insuring no Rivals Develop: A One-Superpower world' *The New York Times*, p. 1, p. 14; (1992, 24 May) 'Pentagon Drops Goal of Blocking New Superpowers' *The New York Times*, p. 2, p. 14; Dick Cheney (Secretary of Defense) (1992, February) *Annual Report to the President and Congress*, (U.S. Government Printing Office, Washington D.C.); Dick Cheney (Secretary of Defense) (1993, January) *Defense Strategy for the 1990s: The Regional Defense Strategy* (U.S. Government Printing Office, Washington D.C.); The White House (1996, February) *A National Security Strategy of Engagement and Enlargement*, www.fas.org/spp/military/docops/national/1996stra.html; The White House (1997, May) *A National Security Strategy for A New Century*, www.whitehouse.gov/wh/eop/nsc/strategy/; Warren Christopher (1998) *In the Stream of History: Shaping Foreign Policy for a New Era* (Stanford: Stanford University Press); William S. Cohen (U.S. Secretary of Defense) (1999) *Annual Report to the President and the Congress*, www.dtic.mil/execsec/adr1999/toc.html.

[6] Dick Cheney (Secretary of Defense) (1993, January) *Defense Strategy for the 1990s: The Regional Defense Strategy* (U.S. Government Printing Office, Washington D.C.); William S. Cohen (U.S. Secretary of Defense) (1999) *Annual Report to the President and the Congress*, www.dtic.mil/execsec/adr1999/toc.html.

that are appealing to the rest of the world?

In order to make (the imperative of) this grand strategy appear attractive to others, the U.S. has positioned itself as the main pillar (of power) around which other powers, such as the EU, China, Japan, Russia, India and others must revolve. This strategy does not involve balancing but involves a strategy of 'bandwagoning' (see S. Walt, 1987). If necessary, the U.S. takes 'preventive' measures against possible upstarts.[7] It is a strategy that implies that without U.S. involvement at strategic levels and taking preventive measure against potential rivals that do not share similar values on international order (especially with countries in the liberal zone of peace and competitive prosperity), the U.S.-led international state system would become highly volatile. The United States has used and manipulated this scenario as an advantageous tool to warn both internal groups and external powers, in Europe, East Asia and elsewhere, of the serious consequences of systemic collapse and anarchy if the United States were to disengage itself.[8]

In this environment, the United States has tried to portray itself as being the supporter for a global environment that is more secure, receptive to democracy, free trade, and the rule of law. The U.S. government has argued that such a world would have a better chance of dealing co-operatively with its major problems, such as nuclear proliferation, threat of regional hegemony by renegade states, low level conflicts, and international crime and terrorism.

In this highly delicate and complex strategy, the U.S. has tried to maintain its position at the apex. The U.S. strategy has been to make sure that other powers do not align with each other, so as to challenge U.S. supremacy. The stationing of troops in Western Europe, East Asia, and the Middle East are no coincidence in this strategy (see Appendix 1B), whilst it has maintained a military cap on the 'strategic' areas around the world – namely North and South America, Europe, the Middle East, East Asia, and all the major sea lines and oceans. The U.S. has managed to stay 'closer' to Europe, Japan, China, Russia, and India, whilst these powers have, for reasons of historical, geographical, or/and racial or religious tensions, been quite reluctant and mistrustful of each other to align or to rely on each other. Most of these rising contenders, e.g., China, Russia, Japan, the EU, and India do not trust each other historically. Hence, India feels China is its greatest national security, more so than its bitter enemy, Pakistan. China, on the other hand, feels that Russia, rather than the United States, is its major national security

---

[7] The economic turbulence in Japan and East Asia in 1997-9 is an example of economic preventive measures, whilst the war against Iraq, Serbia, and the military brinkmanship against China over the Taiwan straits are examples of military preventive measures. See Edward Luttwak (1976) *The Grand Strategy of the Roman Empire*, which gives a similar analogy to the preventive measures taken by the Roman Empire against upstarts. Robert Gilpin (1981) *War and Change in World Politics* also follows this argument.

[8] This strategy has its origins in the hegemonic stabilising theory, see Chapter One. Brzezinski has even stated that, '[s]hort of American abdication, the only real alternative to American leadership is international anarchy', (1997b: pp. 51-52). See also Joseph S. Nye (1990) *Bound to Lead*.

threat (historically and geographically). Russia, throughout most of its history continues to feel that it is being engulfed on all its flanks; in the east by China, in the west by the dynamic western European states and the U.S., and in the south by rising Islamic insurgence. In traditional Russian strategy, 'there can be no security until there is total security' – that is for Russia to have control of the entire Eurasian landmass and beyond.[9] Henry Kissinger lambasted this strategy in the grounds that by advocating 'absolute security for one power means absolute insecurity for all others' (1964). For the Japanese, both China and Russia are historical national security concerns and threats that needed to be cushioned or countered. In Western Europe, the main threat stems largely from Russia, and possibly by its Islamic southern neighbours, however, the worst threat of all is the threat from within the nation-states of the EU itself (this is discussed in more detail in that respective chapter). The classic balance of power applies to each and every one of these powers, as they try to continue to increase their wealth and secure military balance with each other. They are indeed, to use Huntington's phrase, divided by deep civilisational fault lines and the system of multipolar balance of power exists between them both openly and discreetly (S. Huntington, 1993; 1996). When the U.S. is added to this puzzle, however, reassessment of the classical balance of power regimes and civilisation fault lines need deeper contemplation. America's world role is entirely different from that of the other powers. Without the United States' engagement, deep resentments and great apathy will emerge in the Eurasian landmass and the cycle of great power wars more apparent.

This U.S. strategy can be argued to have analogues to a combination of Bismarckian alliance configuration of late 19th century Europe,[10] the preventive strategy of the Julian-Claudian Roman Empire, the vassal state and cosmopolitan cultural assimilation strategies of the Han and T'ang dynasties of China, and the diplomatic and commercial strategy of the United Kingdom during the 19th

---

[9] This perspective is drawn from conversations with Turkish friends. This view is also elaborated in conversation with Professor Trevor Taylor.

[10] The Bismarckian alliance strategy has similarity to the wheel of hub and spokes. The hub was Germany, and the spokes were the alliances that radiated outward into Europe. 'The twin purpose of the cartwright was to draw Austria, Russia, et al, into the German orbit and to make sure that their association with the hub were more important to them than their ties to one another. That way they would look to the centre rather than to each other, bandwagoning with, rather than balancing against, the leading power', Josef Joffe (1995: 111). It can be argued that during the Cold War, the United States also applied the Bismarckian strategy of isolating the Soviet Union from the international system. However, in the post-cold war, from its actions and intentions, the United States is operating a more sophisticated strategy than the Bismarckian realpolitics scenario. The main difference is that the United States does not face a known mortal enemy (with perhaps the exception of the 'weaker' 'rogue' states such as Iraq, Cuba, North Korea, Libya and Iran), whereas Germany had to face France which was relatively more equal in 'power' projection. The United States has that significant advantage where it can reign over the globe without seriously being challenged by another major power that wishes to see its total destruction.

century. However, one advantage that the Americans have in the post-Cold War era over that of Otto Von Bismarck, Julian-Claudian Rome, Han and T'ang China, and Victorian Britain, is that the United States does not have to get involved in the classic strategy of trying to be closer to any of the powers than they are already among themselves. In this position, the United States needs neither to create an enemy nor to develop a global balance of power scenario. Unlike Bismarckian Germany (J. Joffe, 1995), that feared encirclement by France and Russia, the United States' officials and military leaders manifest that there is no major country that they now see as an enemy (save the so-called 'renegade' countries like Iraq, Libya, the Sudan, Cuba, and North Korea), and they see no major power or group of powers capable of encircling the U.S. The United States establishment (at the moment) does not consider (at least diplomatically) any of the major powers (China, Russia, the EU, and Japan) to be enemies or enemies in waiting and does not (as yet) foresee any one of them aligning with each other to balance the United States' supremacy. Unlike Britain, the United States does not have an empire where local inhabitants may rebel against its imperial rule. It is not involved in open and deliberate humiliation of other major powers, i.e., as Britain was with China, Russia, the Ottoman empire, and others. Instead, the United States has built security alliances with two of the four main power regions (NATO with most Western European states, and the Japan-U.S. security alliance). In addition, Russia and China are members of the U.S.-led trade organisation, APEC. Finally, Russia, Japan, and the larger EU members (Britain, France, Germany, and Italy) are in the G8 (this is examined and elaborated in greater detail in chapter eleven).

In addition to maintenance of high level politics of the 'great' nation-states power relationship, the United States is the leading nation and leading promoter of global regimes and institutions, such as the G7/8, the OECD, the IMF, the World Bank, and the WTO. On regional arrangements, the United States is a member and leader of NAFTA, AFTA, NATO, and APEC. In all these international regimes the United States is the main power where major decisions are made. It is often only with U.S. approval that policies can be approved. The significance of these institutions is so enormous that Khalilzad states that it '. . . may in the long-run be a greater achievement than the victory against the Soviet Union' (Z.M. Khalilzad, 1995: 6). Finally, the United States has more bilateral agreements with other countries across the globe, i.e., with Canada, Israel, Egypt, Saudi Arabia, South Korea, Japan, Singapore, Taiwan, South Africa, Chile and many others, on areas of mutual economic and military interests, than any other country (see Appendix 1B). In some of these states, the reliance on the bilateral agreement with the United States has often meant their own geopolitical survival (Israel, Kuwait, South Korea and Taiwan are classic examples). All of these states heavily rely on the United States, not only for their economic survival, but also at times for their very existence. No one power on earth has such an extensive range of combination of complex associations and alliances than the United States. Moreover, U.S. diplomatic ties, connections, influence, and 'culture' is so overwhelming it is probably no exaggeration to say that it is the 'exceptional' power in influencing the direction of the policies developed by some of these countries.

Conclusion

In conclusion, the United States, the remaining superpower, is really the only power in the international system that does not have serious grudges against or grudges from any of the other major powers/civilisations of China, Europe, Russia, and Japan. With regard to other countries, the U.S. has tried to reconcile old wounds and reconfigure the devastation left over by European colonialism. The U.S. has attempted to alleviate the problem of the 'West' and the 'Rest' by building regimes, norms for standardising practices, institutions, and by bringing better understanding within and without societies. The intention here is the establishment of toleration and the 'socialisation of norms' as a means and buffer to breaking down mistrust and misunderstanding and lowering national sentiments of past grievances (see G.J. Ikenberry, 1998: section M). This, whether it is denied or otherwise, is the U.S. search for global hegemony. It has been a strategy of building its power on the idea of both legitimacy and universality.

In relation to the major powers, the United States has been extremely active in developing and maintaining good relations with all the powers to the advantage of the United States. By politics and via the international institutions and regimes developed, the United States effectively controls the differences, and refines the differences, between these powers. In the post-Cold War era, despite critics from America, Russia, China, and others arguing that the world should be defined as multi-polar (this was discussed in previous chapters), the U.S. has moved beyond this strategy. Moreover, if history can show to scholars and practitioners that an emphasis on balance of power has fatal consequences for such a system, then it is only reasonable to suggest that it would be logical to avoid that situation reoccurring again. Obviously, the United States should be prudent of being too arrogant (B. Catley, 1999) when dealing with powers that are 'unhappy' with the status quo. Being the most dominant state in the international system, there is a great temptation by the United States to dictate and impose its will on others (R. Steel, 1995). A strategy of imprudence and domineering would place the United States into a power trap that would only make the U.S. into another 'normal' great power trapped in the traditional system of power politics.

Given this scenario and the 'opportunities' following the collapse of the communist ideology as an alternative to U.S. hegemony, the United States' preponderant position is more visible than it has ever been. The premature talk of American decline is clearly wrong. To avoid complacency (although the arrogance of American power is difficult to hide), the United States has applied and is adopting a multiple strategy of configuration that may bring the major and minor states, and non-states actors together for the (final) globalisation/harmonisation of interstate relations. It is likely that the United States and its allies in this community would like to expand into yet other areas as well.[11] Perhaps the optimal option for the United States, to minimise military conflict with the major powers, especially China and/or Russia, and to ultimately gain hegemonic globalisation, is to find a way to move these two countries into the zone of democratic peace and prosperity. By locking these states into the U.S.-led system, the United States would be in an even stronger position to direct international affairs, and maintain and expand hegemonic globalisation. The activating of this strategy is discussed and examined in greater depth in the following chapters.

---

[11] The strategy of expansion has been careful and selective. It involves both security and economic aspects of conduct. Whilst not all areas of the world are treated equally, certainly Sub-Saharan Africa has been left on the side-line in America's 'grand-strategy' for hegemonic globalisation (despite Clinton's diplomatic gestures in 1998, the United States remains rather aloof from the political development of that continent as a whole). See also The White House (1999, 16 March) *'President Clinton: The U.S.-Africa Ministerial – A Partnership for the 21st Century'*, www2.whithouse.gov/wh/work/031699.html. The areas that the U.S. has placed significant interest in are the countries of the OECD, East Asia, the Middle East and the traditional American 'backyard' countries.

PART III

THE CONTENDERS IN THE EMERGING WORLD ORDER

Chapter 7

Russia: 'Political Backlash Without Economic Conversion?'[1]

The moment of victory is often the moment of greatest peril. In the heat of victory, arrogance and overconfidence can push you past the goal you had aimed for, and by going too far, you make more enemies than you defeat.
R. Greene and J. Elffers, 1998: 175.

Introduction

Perhaps, the most under-rated, under-valued, and nervous power in the post-Cold War era is Russia. Being stunningly neutralised in the quest for global dominance, Russia, today, faces humiliation, not only from the richer West, but also from former allies in Eastern Europe and the Third World.[2] Many Russians accuse the 'liberal' and 'democratic' reforms of Mikhail Gorbachev as, '. . . *gutting* the nation's legitimating ideology, its economic integrity and its international status'.[3] Russia's trade share in the world economy has slumped drastically to merely one percent from the once 15 percent it had represented, whilst Russian share of world GDP is merely two-thirds of one percent (see Appendix 1A). The Red Army, once respected and feared all over the world, is now so deficient that it does not have enough resources to maintain the simplest tasks. Commentators summed this up with reference to the Chechen fiasco: 'Russia . . . can no longer even invade itself' (in K. Aldred and M. Smith, 1999: 106). Russia's diplomatic power is so low that it is seen as going around the world as a power that 'begs' international regimes

---

[1] This title is taken from the Institute for National Strategic Studies, *Strategic Assessment, 1997: Flashpoints and Force Structure*, p. 13.
[2] It is obviously beyond the limits of this book to examine the causes and reasons behind the collapse of the Soviet Union. However to leave out such an important country in the analysis of the hegemonic globalisation thesis is not possible. I will attempt to give an overview of the relationship that has developed between the United States and Russia since the collapse of communism.
[3] Kurginian et al (1990) *Post Perestroika*. To Kurginian the accelerating technological backwardness and its increasing political uncertainty are products of the seductiveness of foreign, liberal, and democratic ideas. He argued that 'the leadership in the Kremlin had allowed the exemplary intellectual and political resources of the nation to decay', cited in A. James Gregor (1998) (emphasis added).

and foreign powers to bail it out of its economic difficulties.[4] Russia is caught between its past legacy and the realities of its immediate situation. Even George Soros, a long-time critic of the command economy system in Eastern Europe has argued that the situation in Russia has 'swung from one extreme of a rigid society to the other extreme of lawless capitalism' (G. Soros, 1998: 152). This fragility of Russia's socio-economic structure makes it more difficult for the Russian government and people to come to terms with the decay of state control and destructiveness of liberal capitalism.

This chapter attempts to analyse the problems and issues in Russia and relate it to the relations that have evolved with the U.S. and 'the West', since the collapse of communism. It aims to understand the relationship in their respective perceptions (of strategic interests) in the unfolding events of the post-Cold War scenario. The question that is under investigation in this chapter is, 'is Russia a supporter or a revisionist challenger of the U.S.-led international system'? Alternatively, is Russia a supporter and a revisionist state that *will* support the system, if its interests are involved and it can benefit from it, but which will not if its interests are challenged?

Before these problems and issues can be addressed, an internal understanding of Russian domestic affairs is required to establish a picture of the perceptions created. This involves an examination and analysis of the historical background of Russia's political, economic and military situation since the end of the Cold War. By the analysis and examination of these factors the chapter inquires into the contributing factors that have caused the debacle in Russian society, and its shifting perceptions towards external powers, in particular its relations with the United States.

Historical Political Background Following the Collapse of the Soviet Union

When Communist hard-liners launched a coup against Gorbachev in August 1991, the world watched nervously. *Fortunately,* the Russian President Boris Yeltsin and the Russian people quickly defeated the coup. Out of the chaos, 11 of the 15 republics of the Soviet Union quickly declared their independence from the Union, and the political authority of Gorbachev was swept aside. On 25 December 1991, the Soviet Union ceased to exist as a political entity. A Commonwealth of

---

[4] See David Hoffman (1997, 20 June) 'Denver Spotlight: The U.S. Boom and Yeltsin: Down but Never Out, Russian Rebounds', Washington Post Service in *International Herald Tribune,* http://www.iht.com/iht/today/fri/fpage/yeltsin.html; *The Washington Post* (1999, 2 April) 'Bailing Out Moscow', in *International Herald Tribune,* http://www.iht.com/iht/today/fri/ed/edrussia.2.html; *International Herald Tribune* (1999, 16 April) 'World Bank has New Loan for Russia', http://www.iht.com/iht/today/fri/fin/ruble.2.html; UofT G8 Information Centre: *Financial Post* (1998, 19 June) 'G7 playing "a very dangerous game" in Russia', http://www.library.utoronto.ca/www/g7/fp/fp980609.html.

Independent States was formed, with many of the republics and the world acknowledging that Russia should take over the diplomatic (UNSC) and military (nuclear weapons) responsibilities of the old Soviet Union.[5]

Even before Yeltsin could consolidate his position, however, a power struggle began between the presidency and the 'conservative' Russian parliament. In March 1993, the parliament voted to curtail Yeltsin's power. Yeltsin retaliated by invoking presidential rule and calling for a special referendum. In this referendum, the Russian people voted in support of Yeltsin and his economic reform programme. Unmoved by the result, Vice-President Aleksander Rutskoi and Parliamentary Speaker Ruslan Khasbulatov led an armed rebellion from their headquarters in the Russian Duma (Parliament) in October 1993 to try to reverse the economic/political reforms. Yeltsin responded by ordering loyal troops to storm the building and arrest the rebels. Elections followed in December to restructure the Parliament with a new upper house called the Federal Assembly. However, the voters elected many independents and nationalist extremists. The most notorious of the new deputies was Vladimir Zhirinovsky, whose open racism and calls for a restoration of the Soviet Empire have conveyed the perception of fascism harvesting the misery of Russian society. Although the legislature's power was weakened by the referendum in favour of a stronger presidential system of government, the parliament continuously defied Yeltsin by calling for an end to economic reform and denouncing the break-up of the Soviet Union.

In the 1995 parliamentary elections, the communists reminded the capitalist world that Marxism was far from totally defeated. The Communists gained a majority of the seats in the Duma, soundly defeating Yeltsin's 'Our Home' party. Yeltsin, however, 'bounced back' with a convincing (aided heavily by Western media and other organisations) presidential election victory in 1996, defeating the Communist challenger Gennady Zyuganov (see G. Yavlinsky, 1998).

In March 1998, President Yeltsin, after recovering from a series of major illnesses, sacked all his chief advisors, and brought in a new team of young economic reformers. Within months of their appointment, they too were removed, thus placing serious doubt over the political stability of Russian politics and society. At the time of writing, the incumbent Prime Minister Primakov was dismissed. Is post-cold war Russia cursed with political instability, until authoritarianism again takes control? Certainly, 'It is hard to see how Russian democracy can be stabilised on the basis of persisting poverty and falling standards of living' (E. Weede, 1995: 4). I have analysed three factors, which I believe may have contributed most severely to this Russian debacle:–

---

[5] According to Aldred and Smith (1999: 98), President Yeltsin believed that the Russian state could and should effectively slip into the defunct USSR's shoes to the maximum extent possible in terms of assuming the latter's international status and rights. M. Weber (1996) found that Russia is a 'continuing state' rather than a successor state. Most Russian government officials have, however, preferred to avoid using the term continuing state. The obvious diplomatic game is to reassure the U.S. that Russia has no aspiration to be the Soviet Union under a different name.

Liberal Economics: The Collapse of Egalitarianism

First, perhaps, the most critical factor that has been blamed for the economic depression in Russia has been the 'blind' embracing of laissez faire capitalism, without seriously debating the consequences of its destructiveness and/or questioning whether the Soviet style of production and management was capable of coping with such draconian changes. For an economy and a population that has lived under a communist system all their lives (professing to its greatness and virtues) to be suddenly uprooted overnight, claiming the old system to be derelict and moving into a system that virtually reverses their understanding of the past would be, by any measure, extremely difficult to swallow. The sudden change not only meant the removal of the flag and national anthem of the USSR to the traditional Russian one, but it also meant undermining and challenging the social, industrial/agricultural, economic/financial, military/political, and educational structure and foundation of Russian society. The rapidity of change in the former Soviet Union/Russia was not gradual – it was revolutionary. If revolution means the jettisoning of an old system for a new system, the collapse of the Soviet system in Russia was a revolution (or more correctly the reversing of a revolution). As in all revolutions, the beginning was bright and naively optimistic. However, suddenly replacing the old regime without adequately planned new regimes or infrastructural institutions with the checks and balances to restrain the externalities of society and economic forces has led to serious paradoxes and crises. Brzezinski warned:

> Haste will not only make waste but is likely to plunge Russia into *another* revolutionary situation. . . . Until – and unless – a structure of laws, a system of political parties, and stable parliamentary procedures are effectively established, the pursuit simultaneously of the goals of democracy and of the free market can prove to be mutually self-defeating (1993: 172).

In these tumultuous political events, economic reforms have brought hardship to many Russian people. Instead of witnessing economic success and prosperity, many ordinary Russians are facing a gloomy prospect in the 'free' market economy. The 'trickle-down effect' of economic liberalism and success that were promised to them by politicians and the media has not happened. Instead, the Russian economy is more vulnerable than ever, as shown by the financial collapse in August 1998. Real GDP has slumped severely, now predicted to be just above half its 1989 value by the year 2000 (*The EIU Country Report 4th Quarter 1998, Russia*, p. 10); unemployment is about 11% (see Appendix Russia 7B), and workers are paid infrequently. Households have tended not to bank their savings, and banks have lent relatively little to industry. Most industrial turnover increasingly relies on barter, mutual offsets, and money surrogates.

Although the stores are 'better' filled with 'consumer' products and the dazzling sight of shiny buildings developed around the city centres, the price of these products and the decay of rural/suburban areas have stark contrasts. Increasingly, perceptions of two worlds in one city, between the well-to-do and corrupt, and the poor, are becoming more abundant. As Yavlinsky portrayed, 'the current Russian market economy has created a handful of super-wealthy individuals while leaving the rest behind to struggle' (1998: 71). 'Mass-consumerism' has emerged in Russia, but with persistent economic instability, financial crisis (with devaluation and default in August 1998) and hyperinflation, mass-consumerism has only happened to the few that can afford it, whilst leaving many bleakly looking on. Even the financier-philanthropist George Soros, well known for his shrewd exploits, has expressed his concern by stating:

> Although I have made a fortune in the financial markets, I now fear that the untrammelled intensification of laissez-faire capitalism and the spread of market values into all areas of life is endangering our open and democratic society. The main enemy of the open society, I believe, is no longer the communist but the capitalist threat (cited in J. Gates, 1998: 249).

Adding to these worries, Russia (1998-1999) is suffering its worst harvest for 40 years, with the total grain harvest down to 49m tonnes, from 88.6m tonnes in 1997, and below even the very poor harvests of 1995 and 1996 of 63.4m tonnes and 69.3m tonnes respectively. Were it not for the financial collapse (summer 1998), food supplies would probably not become a problem, despite the disastrous harvest. Without sufficient economic aid and food supplies, there is a real danger that famine may grip the lives of many ordinary Russians. At the time of writing, the geostrategic manoeuvre by Primakov with regard to NATO intervention in Kosovo is intriguing. Kosovo, in my opinion, has been used by the Russians as a bargaining chip for increased Western economic aid and food supplies.

Despite these dilemmas, liberal minded reformers persevere, believing that by continuing the progress of liberal economic reform and working with Western societies, Russia's economic crisis will one day bear fruit (see S. Ashwin, 1998; V. Shlapentokh, 1998). To many ordinary Russian people, that fruit may soon grow out of their graves! Stringent liberal-minded reformers continuously emphasise 'patience' and Western assistance. According to Ashwin, the failure of economic reform has been partly due to the internal structure left over by the Soviet command system, so a return to the old Soviet system would only make matters worse, not better. Ashwin claims that Russian liberals believe that the economic system engraved during the communist era has left Russia inadequately placed to cope with the shifting patterns of information technology, mass-consumerism and competitive world capitalism – that is why Russia has to face so many difficulties in its initial take-off stage.[6] Once these initial problems are out of

---

[6] Brzezinski (1993) *Out of Control*, p. 173, states that: 'Communism has ravaged both the Russian soul and the Russian body to such an extent that any recovery will be prolonged, painful, with the outcome more than uncertain. The near-term prospects are especially grim, with growing evidence that Russia is beginning to experience socio-economically a decline

the way, they stressed, Russia could readjust from the dislocations of the closed market economy to a market system similar to those in Western Europe, North America and/or East Asia, and begin to prosper (see also D. Johnston, 1996).

To the nationalists and communists, however, the uncontrolled free market economy is the main source of the economic problems (see A.G. Frank in B.K. Gills and S. Qadir, 1995). They argue that the sooner Russia abandons or at least modifies the brutal capitalist destruction (see K. Polanyi, 1957), the better it is for Russian society (K. Aldred and M. Smith, 1999: 120). Many Russians are reconsidering the possibilities of a return to the old command system, with emphasis placed on the re-development of the old CMEA (Council of Mutual Economic Assistance). However, despite this rhetoric, even the former communist trade unions have been unable to transform themselves into organisations representing worker interests. The reasons for this are also related to the structure of the traditional Soviet enterprise. The unions themselves were part of the patronage system. Rather than channelling the conflict, they usually attempt to contain it (S. Ashwin, 1998: 195).

The Problems of Crime and Corruption

The second problem that has been persistent (and even to the point of endemic) in Russian society, since the fall of communism, has been the rise of crime, anti-social behaviour, extortion and corruption.[7] Reports from the western media often portray Russia as a 'super-criminal' state[8] and a haven for the mafia. According to the U.S. Institute for National Strategic Studies, the relations between organised crime and the state can be traced back to the 1960s, where the relationship was

---

in many ways comparable to the American Great Depression of the early 1930s: a dramatic drop in production and consumption, hyperinflation, and increasing unemployment. The country also faces the prospect of intensifying class conflict – with the increasingly poor masses tempted to vent their jealousy of the few newly rich – and deepening political hatreds. In that setting, the Russian people are not likely to absorb either the entrepreneurial spirit or the political culture of compromise needed for a successful transformation into a democratic and economically pluralistic system. The resulting casualties might well be both the free market and the incipient Russian democracy.'

[7] The demise of communism and weakening of state power in Russia have diminished the resources available to law enforcement and the criminal judicial system. As a result of such trends, organised crime in its various guises – drug trafficking, counterfeiting, dealing in stolen cars and art objects, arms smuggling and commerce in illegal aliens and human body parts – is flourishing in many post-Communist states. Organised crime – like many modern organisations- has developed new strategies and structural arrangements to compete effectively in the international market. This includes corrupt relations with government officials and political leaders, like the multinational corporation, criminal organisations seeking partners to maximise market opportunities, improve logistics and reduce business exposure.

[8] *BBC2* Newsnight *Special Correspondence on Russia's Religion*, 13 March 1999.

based upon a mutual understanding of the ability of the criminals to provide Soviet officials with consumer goods and services unavailable under the Communist system (*Strategic Assessment, 1997*: 205). As capitalism evolved in the early 1990s, and as the state apparatus of law enforcement broke down, the Russian criminals were well-positioned to take advantage of this chaos, and grew rich accordingly. As the law enforcement weakened, the power relationship of criminals and officials shifted in favour of the criminals. There are prevailing reports that criminals actually control most of Russian officials by either bribes or extortion. In this self-regarding system, many ex-Communists were forced from or chose to leave the police, security and intelligence services due to minimising respect and dwindling levels of income and resources, they began to seek their livelihood elsewhere. These forces with the knowledge and skill, have, thus, been natural for the mafia to entice them into these criminal gangs for better fortune.

What is even more disturbing is that the 'legitimate' economic elites, such as national banks, in Russia find that the mafia fills an important vacuum in society (A. Aslund, 1999). In the absence of functioning commercial and legal codes and a viable judicial system, mobsters provide protection to business and regulation of disputes (including helping businesses avoid taxes, stave off unfriendly creditors and collect bills).[9] Nevertheless, a compelling international security concern in the 1990s, has been the soaring illegal traffic in radioactive isotopes and other nuclear materials. For instance, the capture by the German authorities of 363 grams of plutonium-239 in Munich in August 1994 was a case in point. A catastrophic scenario is not beyond imagination, had these dangerous weapons of mass destruction fallen into the hands of terrorist groups or extreme religious groups.

The level of corruption extends deeply into the political reality of Russian life. The Russian government's inability to deal with corruption has allowed it to become an even greater aspect of Russian life.[10] For example, government

---

[9] National Defense University *Strategic Assessment, 1997: Flashpoints and Force Structure*, pp. 205-6.
[10] This is not only chronic in Russia, but also in other countries, from my understanding of most countries that have had fixed incomes in the communist world, such as China and Vietnam. Corruption is not necessarily a bad thing for early capitalist development and transition. Official government posts are disproportionately under-paid compared to the private sector. I hypothesise that when the public sector can reach a similar level as the private sector in pay, the levels of corruption should decline. When the prestige of working for the government sector returns to its former prestigious level, government officials will be less prone to bribes, corruption, and are even keen to tackle corruption because of the rewards involved in bringing corruption to justice. Even if bribes were made, the likelihood that officials can be corrupted are minimal, since if caught the bureaucrats would lose their job and reputation. The differentiation in wage levels means that most officials are corrupt, because if he/she is not corrupt he/she will be hungry: a man/woman has to earn a living to feed his/her family. With the low wage level of official government wages, these people need to find different avenues to earn their living. This is a real problem, however, once laws on the practice of bribes are in place. Officials will have to declare their source of income., i.e. similar to British MPs. See also Vito Tanzi (1998) 'Corruption around the

properties, including government-owned facilities have been illegally converted for private use on a large scale; tax evasion has been estimated to deny the Russian government almost 50 percent of its expected revenue; and it is reported that high-level officials routinely accept (or expect) bribes that divert more money from the government's accounts (*Strategic Assessment, 1997*: 14-15). Even the Russian Orthodox Church is believed to be involved. It is often argued that the privatisation of monopolies is a natural way to reduce corruption because it eliminates political corruption. Unfortunately, the processes of privatising public or state enterprises has created situations, whereby some individuals (ministers, high political officials) have the discretion to make basic decisions, while others (managers and other insiders) have information not available to outsiders, so that they can use privatisation to benefit themselves (D. Kaufman and P. Siegelbaum, 1996; M. Goodman, 1997; G. Soros, 1998: 152-68). Some individuals have become enormously rich because of these abuses. For example, in the privatisation of large monopolies, such as Russia's RAO Gazprom, 'many close to the corridors of power received highly valued shares at very low prices' (V. Tanzi, 1998: 564) and the 'loans-for-shares' scheme made some bank(s) shareholders of enterprises by extending loans to the firms. Gazprom produces one-fifth of the world's natural gas; with one-third of the world's known gas reserves and supplier of 21 per cent of Western Europe's natural gas. When Gazprom sold just over 1 percent of its shares in October 1996, investors found that several non-Russian investors, reportedly in cahoots with Gazprom managers, had already acquired a stake, paying one-twentieth the issue price. Their $16 million investment bought them shares that were quickly worth more than $300 million.[11]

These developments have made many Russian citizens highly sceptical about the virtues of a market economy. Western correspondents claim that corruption in Russia has reached such high levels (V. Tanzi, 1998: 579-80) that even the Russian auditors have suggested that no more money be lent to Russia without some form of Western supervision. The media claims that 'what Russia needs is external help on organising internal regimes and institutions that can control the corruption, rather than to leave Russia to run its own affairs'.[12] In addition, reports of the Russian government and the central bank shifting the money abroad rather than putting it into the ailing economy have been blamed for the extent of Russian elite corruption (G. Yavlinsky, 1998: 70).

Whilst the level of crime, anti-social behaviour, extortion and corruption in Russian society have increased significantly since the collapse of the Soviet Union,

---

world: Causes, Consequences, Scope, and Cures' *IMF Staff Paper*, Vol. 45, No. 4, (December), pp. 559-94, Caroline Van Rijkehem and Beatrice Weder (1997) 'Corruption and the Rate of Temptation: Do low wages in the Civil Service cause corruption?' *IMF Working Paper*. 97/73 (Washington, D.C: International Monetary Fund).

[11] 'How Western Investors Won a Coveted Stake in Russian Gas Concern' *The Wall Street Journal*, 16 January 1997, p. 1, cited in Jeff Gates (1998) *The Ownership Solution: Toward a Shared Capitalism for the Twenty First Century* (London: Penguin Books), pp. 247-48.

[12] BBC2 Newsnight, 14 October 1998.

the methods to tackle it differ significantly. Liberals argue that democratic regimes and the rule of law should be institutionalised inside Russia to solve the persistence of crime, anti-social behaviour, extortion and corruption (see G. Yavlinsky, 1998). For nationalists and communists, the best way to solve the problem is to return to some form of central system of control (see A.J. Gregor, 1998).

Leadership Failures

The third factor that has contributed to undermining Russian efforts to re-organise and develop into an affluent society (at least for the majority of the population) has been the slow, inconsistent and uncoordinated reform policies from the Russian government. Liberals may blame the Communist forces in the Duma for blocking vital reform bills of economic liberalisation. However, I contend that the major factor behind the failure of reform in Russia has been the 'uncoordinated' policies adopted by the authoritarian nature of President Boris Yeltsin's rule towards his beleaguered government(s) and Russian parliament (see also J. Lowehardt et al, 1998; J.T. Ishiyama and M. Velten, 1998). For example, in 1993, he threatened to oust the parliament if it did not grant him further presidential powers. Moreover, President Yeltsin appears to be indifferent, or unable and/or even unwilling to tackle corruption (perhaps because he is already heavily influenced by it). For example, during the 1996 presidential elections,

> ... the seven largest capitalists, who also controlled the media, decided to cooperate to ensure the reelection of President Yeltsin. It was a remarkable feat of political engineering. Subsequently the newly established oligarchy proceeded to divide up the remaining assets of the state among themselves (G. Soros, 1998: 154).

Although Russian law set a maximum of $2.5 million on campaign spending, members of the Yeltsin campaign conceded that its leaders spent $100 million (opponents put the figure at about $500 million) (J. Gates, 1998: 372). In addition, the activities of these oligarchs and their influence are so immense that any rule of law, that is, any policy implemented by the Russian Duma to regulate their activities, would come into conflict with the Russian government if it endangered the activities of the oligarchs. For example one of the oligarchs, 'Boris Berezovsky, threatened to pull down the tent around him, if he was not given the spoils that he had been promised. The vicious quarrel damaged Anatoly Chubias, who had acted as campaign manager for Yeltsin and had received illegal payments from the oligarchs' (G. Soros, 1998: 154). Many others were also exposed in covering possible embarrassing links and the contagion of the East Asian economic crisis. Yeltsin, just out of hospital, sacked the entire Russian cabinet including Prime Minister Viktor Chernomyrdin in March 1998. In a give-and-take struggle that followed, he bullied the Russian parliament into approving the appointment of Sergei Kiriyenko as Chernomyrdin's replacement. Within less than six months of Kiriyenko's appointment he was, himself, dismissed by Yeltsin. Yeltsin again tried to bully the parliament to renominate Chernomyrdin but the Russian parliament refused. In this struggle, Yeltsin failed to have his way. The compromise candidate, was Yevgeny Primakov (former foreign minister), whose appointment was confirmed by the State Duma on 11 September 1998, to tackle the worsening economic crisis, exacerbated by the events ensuing in East Asia and the debt default in August, as well as to bring compromise between the Russian Duma and the Russian business oligarchy. At the time of writing this book, Primakov was himself sacked (12 May 1999) in the mist of the Kosovo crisis and economic turmoil. Russia again found itself in political instability and turmoil. With NATO threatening the traditional structure of Russian influences in Eastern Europe, Yeltsin's decision to dismiss Primakov in a sensitive situation has created an unorthodox power unbalance in the internal and external power relations. It is too early to speculate on the power intrigues of Yeltsin's strategy. Despite Yeltsin blaming the Primakov cabinet for its inconsistency to restore economic credibility to the economic situations, unlike his predecessors, Primakov did succeed in slowing down the bad economic situation. With the presidential elections due in 2000, a disassociated political manoeuvre from Primakov of the unpopularity of Yeltsin cannot be ruled out, Primakov, unlike his previous predecessors, is more popular amongst the Russian Duma and the Russian people and according to *The EIU Country Report: Russia 1998 4th quarter*, Primakov may well have his eye on the presidency and a power struggle may emerge.

The second problem with the credibility of the Russian President has been his state of health and his irregular efforts to mind the affairs of state. His chronic and persistent health problems have created speculation that the President could die or become disabled in office (*The EIU Country Report: Russia 1998 4th quarter*, p. 12-13). In time of economic, financial and social instability and crisis, Russia cannot do without a credible/fit leader. Yeltsin appears to be cut off from day-to-day decision-making, spending more time worrying about his health than effectively tackling the problems of the economy and society. He also appears to be increasingly incapable of performing even ceremonial duties. The Kremlin, itself, acknowledged the situation in late October 1998 when a presidential aide announced that Mr Yeltsin was withdrawing from day-to-day governance of Russia, but would remain in office until his term ends in mid-2000, concentrating on reviewing the constitution and ensuring a smooth succession.

With these failures, unsurprisingly Russians are progressively looking for alternatives for their social and economic development. There have been three responses to Russia's problems.

Nationalistic Economic Policy

First, many Russians believe that instead of following the neo-liberal style of economic development, Russia should develop its own nationalistic system of economic growth and development. These nationalistic sentiments are growing.

Even President Boris Yeltsin, often cited as a Western-orientated leader and sympathiser with Western liberalism, declared that: 'the country's continuing problems have been caused by the blind embrace of the Western-style capitalist ideology and the disregard for traditional social values' (in V. Shlapentokh, 1998: 203). However, the fragile political bases, after 1993, have made such nationalistic economic reforms more difficult. They fear that structural reforms would threaten the survival of much of industry and inflict further hardship on the population. In the indecisiveness, the Russian government is deeply divided over the direction of economic policy. Following the August 1998 default, the government of Mr Primakov has delayed adopting a clear and coherent anti-crisis programme. There are stark cabinet contradictions in the current Primakov government – e.g., Yuri Maslyukov, First Deputy Prime Minister, and Mikhail Zadornov, Finance Minister, have rarely expressed the same views with respect to any major economic policy issue. In times of economic crisis, political instability and diplomatic humiliation, Mr Primakov's government appears to be trying to 'muddle' its way through, rather than adopting a consistent nationalistic economic strategy. (*The EIU Country Report: Russia 1998 4th quarter*, p. 8).

Nationalistic Foreign Policy

Second, the economic failures, political corruption, and intrigues have convinced many Russians that the prosperous West and the Russian leadership have betrayed them. This scenario is painted by some analysts as disturbingly similar to the distresses of the Weimar Republic in Germany after World War I. Obviously, the differences between Germany's defeat in 1918 and the Soviet Union's collapse in 1991 are enormous. First, Russia was not defeated on the battlefield, but collapsed internally. Second, there has been no reparation payment to the victors. Nevertheless, there are parallels between the 'shock' defeat of Germany in 1918 and the 'shock' collapse of the Soviet Union in 1991. The German people and its military, like its Russian counterparts, did/do not know exactly why they were suddenly 'defeated' or collapsed. As during the Weimar Republic, nationalist Germans felt humiliation, similarly '[t]oday, the Russian elite feel not dignity, but national humiliation' (V. Shlapentokh, 1998: 206).[13] As regard to the reparation

---

[13] Even Vietnam, once a poor client country for the Soviet Union, today does not consider Russia to be any better than they are. In fact, many in Vietnam believe that Vietnam has a better prospect of economic development than Russia. Russia has demanded the loans lent to Vietnam during the Soviet era to be repaid immediately. Russia insists that Vietnam pay in $US. Vietnam rejected this demand and said that whatever monetary unit they borrowed, they will repay in that currency. Because of the current weakness of the rouble, Vietnam has benefited from Russia's troubles. Had Vietnam taken such action during the Cold War period, Vietnam would have been severely punished or totally isolated. However, Russia is unable to influence Vietnam, today. It has lost so much power that even one of its poorest former clients laughs at Russia's woes. (Personal experience and perception of Vietnamese

payment by the Germans to the victorious powers after 1918, the debt payment to the IMF and World Bank and its draconian structural adjustment programmes has its similarities. Whilst the Germans were caught in the reparation trap, the Russians are caught in the economic debt trap.

If the economic crisis of 1998 (to 1999) is comparable to the economic meltdown of the late 1920s to early 1930s, the analogy would be extremely alarming, given that the rise of Nazism in Germany was a direct consequence of political indecisiveness, economic instability and corruption of the oligarchs. For a country that still commands an equal par in military power as the United States, at least on the nuclear front, thus, the most immediate warning from Russia should not be taken lightly – one mistake and there will (I am not being apocalyptic, but being very realistic about the consequences of nuclear war or even nuclear meltdown) be catastrophe.

With economic difficulties, political corruption and dwindling national pride, Russian nationalism is trying to find scapegoats for their failures. The most obvious has been to express resentment towards the West. The accusations are, however, not without warranty. From the Russian perspective the stances taken by the United States and its allies on foreign, economic and military actions are regarded with suspicion. In many respects, the actions taken by the U.S. and allies have led indirectly to the ill feeling that is evolving in Russian society against the West. Many Russians continue to suspect that the United States and others are trying to undermine Russian integrity because of its current political and economic weakness.[14] I have compiled eight points which highlight the problems.

- Russians learned that Western financial aid (from 1992 to 1999) was limited and that Western private corporations 'were more interested in the profit margins than in pulling Russia out of its economic morass' (V. Shlapentokh, 1998: 205). This has left many Russians feeling extremely disgruntled at being treated as nothing more than a mere 'Third World' country. For a power that had enjoyed 'superpower' status for the past fifty years and great power status for even longer, the sudden collapse and treatment of Russia by 'foreigners' as a 'third world' country is like salt being rubbed into the wound. In despair of their desperate economic situation, Russians are wavering in the belief that the Western countries do not want Russia to prosper. Noam Chomsky has attacked the extent to which, in his view, 'U.S. "aid" programmes in Russia are actually geared more towards opening doors for U.S. business to make money there than providing genuine assistance to Russian businesses and workers' (cited in K. Aldred and M. Smith, 1999: 120). This, however, is an unfair argument

---

attitudes towards Russians and Russia; Hanoi and Haiphong, Vietnam 1998.) During the Soviet era, the Soviets were deemed as 'poor Yankees', now they are mocked for their lack of common sense, entrepreneurial skills in business and their stupidity to earn profits.

[14] N.B. Russian communists have always suspected and regarded the United States as the number one enemy to Russia and communism. To them the United States and West have no initiatives to help Russia, instead their mission has always been to destroy them.

against the Western governments, since the relationship between firms and state are not always co-operative but sometimes conflictual (see J. Stopford and S. Strange, 1991). Certainly, the United States government and Congress sometimes have differing perceptions about profit and public equity as compared to private multinational companies. Without realising the intrigues of businesses and government relations, many Russian citizens suspect that Europeans and Americans continue to believe that if Russia begins to prosper, Russia may return to pose a direct threat to Western Europe, its periphery, and eventually to the United States.

- Russians have accused the West of exaggerating the extent of Russia's criminality, for example *The Financial Times* in November 1996 claimed that Russia is effectively ruled by a corrupt oligarchy that controls more than half of the Russian economy (cited in G. Yavlinsky, 1998: 69), in order to discredit their country's businesses and deter foreign investors from strengthening the Russian economy. Some Russians have accused the U.S. of 'supporting the myth about Russia as a super-criminal state' (V. Shlapentokh, 1998: 205) which threatens the world.
- Russians have accused the West of undermining the rapprochement efforts between Moscow, Kiev,[15] and other former Soviet and communist capitals (V. Tsepkalo, 1998). Russian nationalists charged the West with inciting nationalism against Russians, and they indict the United States of trying to curb Russian influence in the Baltic states, the Caucasus and Central Asian republics. Most significant of their accusations towards the United States concerns the military agreements signed by the U.S. with Ukraine (July 1993), Azerbaijan (July 1997), Kazakstan (November 1997), and Georgia (March 1998). Former deputy Prime Minister Mikoyan complained that: '[s]ince all these countries participate in NATO's partnership for Peace (PfP) programme, it is not clear why these special bilateral agreements were also necessary' (S.A. Mikoyan, 1998: 119).

---

[15] John Vinocur (1997) 'NATO Embraces Ukraine as Partner.' *International Herald Tribune*, 10 July 1997, http://www.iht.com/IHT/TODAY/THU/FPAG/nato.html; 'Soon after the Soviet Union collapsed, U.S. diplomats started to play "the Ukrainian card". Joint NATO-Ukraine military manoeuvres took place in early 1997 in Crimea's Kerch region, a few miles from Russian territory. In August 1997, Sea Breeze-97 joint U.S.-Ukraine military exercises were in Simferopol, capital of the Crimean Autonomous Republic. Selecting this site for the exercise provoked Russians in the Crimea and elsewhere. The exercise's initial mission, as officials declared, was to resist a hypothetical Russian-backed secessionist movement in the Crimea. Only strong protest by Primakov convinced the Americans to redefine the exercise as safeguarding humanitarian aid to the population. Such episodes can only be viewed as provocative and cause resentment and anger within Russia. If Russian and Mexican forces were carrying out military exercises in the Gulf of Mexico, close to the Texan border, the American public would not be amused', Sergo A. Mikoyan (1998) 'Russia, the U.S. and Regional Conflict in Eurasia' *Survival*, Vol. 40, No. 3 (Autumn), p. 122-3; See also 'Russian, Ukrainian MPs Protest Sea Breeze '97 Exercises' *FBIS-UMA-97-116*, 26 April 1997; and www.robust-east.net/Net/usa/breeze.html.

- Despite the West claiming to be the champions of democracy and human rights, Russians complain that the West has remained indifferent to the fate of Russians in the Baltic republics and its near abroad, where they argue overseas Russians have been transformed into second class citizens.[16] Gorbachev, speaking to the U.S. Congress in May 1992, warned:

  > No Russian government would allow the problems of discrimination of a Russian-speaking population . . . because it leads to military conflict and . . . thousands of refugees. If democrats fail to solve this problem, nationalists of a totalitarian nature will solve it. It is doubtful that U.S. interests demand not to take into account that circumstance when dealing with Russia and other states of the CIS (cited in S.A. Mikoyan, 1998: 123).

  There is, however, no evidence that Moscow may use force to defend its citizens in the near abroad, or even attempt to use force to minimise the 'ill treatment' of overseas Russians (*Strategic Assessment*, 1997: 17; see also Appendix Russia 7D).

- Russians are critical of American foreign policy, especially NATO air strikes against Bosnian Serbs, and treatment of, and air strikes against the Serbians over the Kosovo issue without UN consultation let alone Russian affirmation.[17] Ostensibly, the Western government perceptions of the intervention in Yugoslavia was to deter the abuse of human rights and ethic cleansing in the republic. However, some Western strategists had conceived that such an attack on the Russian periphery was necessary to damage Russia's claim to great power status (Staar, 1996; Brzezinski, 1997a; Pipes, 1997; Starorbin, 1999). Historically and 'culturally', Serbia has been like a suzerain state in Russia's sphere of influence. Russian analysts perceive that because Russia is currently weak, others took advantage of that situation by 'bullying' a 'fellow Slav' and humiliating Russia in the process. NATO intervention in Kosovo (Serbia) has, therefore, not gone down well in Russia. In Russian perceptions, the Kosovo Albanian separatist movement has uncomfortable parallels in some of Russia's ethnically based federal units, most notably Chechnya. This situation, if not handled carefully, could rupture Russian-Western relations, as Russia may demand that the status quo and stability be maintained in the Balkans by sending troops and military equipment to support its ally. As mentioned earlier, the geo-strategic manoeuvre of Russia to ensnare the United States and NATO

---

[16] Approximately 20-25 million are thought to reside outside the Russian Federation: 12 million live in the Ukraine, Kazakhstan, Kyrgyzstan, Latvia and Estonia, where they form large minorities (22-40 percent of the population). – See *Strategic Assessment, 1997*, p. 17. 'While the Russians residing in the Slavic republics (Ukraine, Belarus) suffer no ethnic discrimination, the opposite is true of Estonia, Latvia, as well as some Muslim republics', in Oles M. Smolansky (1998) 'Can Russia Escape from its Past' in Ken Booth (1998) (Ed.) *Statecraft and Security*, p.149.

[17] *International Herald Tribune* (1999, 20 July) 'Beware of Preemptive Aggression'.

allies into the issue cannot be ruled out.[18] On the other hand, the economic situation in Russia is so weak that the Russian elite may use the Kosovo crisis to gain concessions from Western economic programmes to prevent potential famine occurring in Russia.[19]

- Russia is particularly concerned over the clash of interests with the United States over air strikes against Iraq and the alleged involvement of CIA (Central Intelligence Agency) sources posing as UN arms inspectors in Iraq. Russia, China and others have on countless occasions complained of the United States being 'hegemonic' in the handling of the situation in Iraq – this is particularly the case over non-consultation with permanent members of the UNSC (United Nations Security Council) over air strikes against Baghdad.
- Perhaps the most controversial items in U.S.-Russian relations, has been the United States and Western European countries' strategy to allow NATO expansion into three countries of the former Warsaw Pact – Poland, Hungary, and Czech Republic – full membership was formalised in March 1999. Whilst Western European analysts argued NATO expansion was: 'the best way to keep the United States bound to Europe, to give NATO responsibility to engage in out-of-area operations and to spread democracy to the former Soviet satellites' (A.Z. Rubinstein, 1997: 35).

However, according to David Hoffman of the *Washington Post*, the eastward expansion of NATO with its intervention in Serbia was a direct challenge and a threat to Russian political and strategic integrity and influence.[20] Russian strategists complained that the envisaged PfP (Partnership for Peace), which the Russian leadership thought was a strategic partnership was nothing more than a trick by Washington and that the NATO-Russia Founding Act[21] of May 1997 in Paris was a diplomatic smokescreen to further 'Western' interests. Washington denied that there was any 'trickery' in the enlargement plans, and propagates the idea that it is non-threatening, certainly non-aggressive, and 'that we are not promoting just our own interest or power engrandisement'.[22] Washington's plans have, however, not convinced even its own Russian backers. For example, liberal reformers, such as Grigory

---

[18] *International Herald Tribune* (1999, 14 April) 'U.S-Russia "Narrow Differences" or a Common Approach to Kosovo'.
[19] *International Herald Tribune* (1999, 6 April) 'World Bank has New Loan for Russia'.
[20] *Washington Post* (1999, 12 June) 'Russia Laments Lost Power', p. A1.
[21] 'Founding Act on Mutual Relations, Cooperation and Security between the North Atlantic Treaty Organisation and the Russian Federation', Paris, 27 May 1997, available in *NATO Review*, Vol. 45, No. 4, (July-August).
[22] Madeleine Albright (1997) 'Enlarging NATO: Why bigger is better' *The Economist* (15-21 February), pp. 21-3; John P. White (1997) *'Transforming the NATO Alliance for the 21st Century'* U.S. Department of Defense, Washington D.C., http://www.usis.usemb.se/speeches/jpwhite/nato.htm; Christopher L. Ball (1998) 'Nattering NATO negativism? Reasons why expansion may be a good thing' *Review of International Studies*, Vol. 24, No. 1, (January), pp. 43-67.

Yavlinsky, who is supported by the West, warned:

> If a military alliance moves closer to a country's borders without incorporating that country, it means that the country's foreign policy has dismally failed. Talk that this is a different NATO, a NATO that is no longer a military alliance, is ridiculous. It is like saying that the hulking thing advancing toward your garden is not a tank because it is painted pink, carries flowers, and plays cheerful music. It does not matter how you dress it up; a pink tank is still a tank . . . [W]hen the West says to Russia: 'Russian democracy is fine, and therefore NATO is expanding to Russia's borders', the logic does not work, leaving the Russian people and their leaders bewildered and bitter (1998: 77).

The NATO air strikes in Serbia did not bring any confidence or any reason why Russia should trust the West. It is concerned that as NATO plans to expand further east, where else will Western governments stop to intensify ethnic tension, to then send military warning, followed by military action? With regard to NATO expansionism, Alexei Mitrofanov, chairman of the Russian State Duma's Geopolitics Committee, stressed in mid-September 1997 that:

> It is now abundantly clear . . . that Russia is heading for isolation from the rest of Europe, that the country is in danger of being quarantined by hostile states, united by systems of military blocs with the United States of America and its closest allies, the weakening of our country, the growth of centrifugal tendencies and subsequent demise with the formation on its [Russian] ruins of some 10 to 15 satellite countries feuding with each other and depending entirely on the external suzerains (1998: 8).

Even prominent, Western diplomatic historians, such as John Gaddis (1998) and George Kennan (1997), have stated that NATO expansion is an unnecessarily provocative step by Europe and America. They have argued that NATO expansion is a serious miscalculation of American foreign/security policy. Gaddis, for example, expressed his dismay because NATO expansion has broken the most fundamental rules of diplomacy. Kennan explains why current U.S. policy must be viewed in Russia as directed against Russian prestige and security, and characterised NATO expansion as 'the most fateful error of American policy in the entire post-cold war era' (7 February, 1997).

However, the 'fateful error' *could have* been avoided. Washington decision-makers in 1994 initially planned that Russia should become a member of NATO (see C. Bell, 1990/91), which would have been the 'fateful' move in American policy in the post-Cold War era (see M. Cox, 1994). The United States was unable to add Russia into the NATO framework, because the U.S.'s two most powerful allies in NATO, Germany and France[23], seriously disagreed

---

[23] For example Hubert Vedrine (French Foreign Minister from June 1997) expressed that Russian membership would upset existing patterns of influence in the Alliance, and might subordinate the Europeans to a U.S.-Russian tandem. He even contends that the NATO-Russian Founding Act could lead to a U.S.-Russian condominium harmful to European

with NATO expansion that would include Russia. For example, in September 1994, German Defence Minister Volker Ruhe stated bluntly that 'Russia cannot be integrated, neither into the European Union nor into NATO'.[24] He added, 'if Russia were to become a member of NATO it would blow NATO apart ... It would be like the United Nations of Europe – it wouldn't work'[25] (see also A. Stent, 1999: 217-22). William Perry (then U.S. Secretary of Defense) disagreed with Ruhe saying that the U.S. 'is not prepared to close the door on that issue'.[26] In May 1997, Ruhe reiterated the issue by stating that:

> ... the sheer size of Russia, covering eleven time-zones on the Eurasian continent, prohibits full integration into the Euro-Atlantic structure. And Europe does not want to be dragged into and be burdened by defence commitments reaching far into Asia.[27]

According to Yost, many Europeans hold Ruhe's view (D. Yost, 1998). In Ruhe's perception, Russia's relations with its near abroad (i.e., Chechnya and Tajikistan) and its vast geopolitical position, as well as its historical disputes with China and other countries, would mean that Russia's inclusion into NATO would unnecessarily bring these disputes into Europe's decision-making. Therefore, it was not prudent in the framework or in the interest of Western European NATO members to get involved in areas that were not of interest to the European members. Ruhe argued that an alliance with Russia would undermine NATO's collective security alliance structure into a loose organisation like the OSCE (Organisation for Security and Cooperation in Europe), which would be weak and feeble because of the Kantian and Wilsonian natures in which it would operate in a 'realist' world order. It would mean that the alliance would lose its real tenure. In addition, the Europeans perceived that had Russia joined, Russia would deliberately weaken the alliance. However, I believe that there were geopolitical strategic implications on the part of France and Germany for not including Russia into the alliance. An alliance with Russia would push them both further on the sidelines with the U.S. and Russia dominating. Moreover, with Russia's chronically weak

---

defence autonomy. Hubert Vedrine (1997, 12 April) 'Defense: l'Europe sous tutelle', *Le Point*, p. 12.

[24] Volker Ruhe cited in Thom Shanker (1994, 10 September) 'Bonn Rebuffs U.S. over NATO for Russia' *Chicago Tribune*, p. 2.

[25] Volker Ruhe cited in Rick Atkinson (1994, 10 September) 'Allies Seek New Ties to Bind NATO; German and U.S. Defense Ministers Differ on Russian Membership', *Washington Post*, p. A16.

[26] William Perry cited in Thom Shanker (1994, 10 September) 'Bonn Rebuffs U.S. over NATO for Russia' *Chicago Tribune*, p. 2.

[27] Volker Ruhe, speech to the Yomiuri International Economic Society, Tokyo, 28 May 1997, p. 15. Text supplied by the German Ministry of Defence, Bonn, cited in David S. Yost (1998) 'The New NATO and Collective Security' *Survival*, Vol. 40, No. 2 (Summer), p. 140.

economic situation, the United States would increase its power even more.

However, allowing Eastern European countries membership and not including Russia has created potential strategic errors that may not be repairable. The United States, instead of pursuing its strategy of enlargement and engagement was pressured by the Western Europeans, certainly by the two most powerful states, France and Germany, into not including Russia in NATO membership. If NATO is to expand further east (at the time of writing this book, NATO is celebrating its fiftieth birthday), its leaders, especially America, should seriously consider bringing Russia in. Some sections in France[28] and Germany[29] do not seem to want a vision of democratic peace and prosperity for Russia. Recognising that the United States might fall into a trap set by European Union interests, President Clinton in March 1997 restated the U.S. interests in eventual positioning of Russia in the NATO apparatus:

> . . . one of my dreams for the twenty-first century world is a Europe that for the first time is united, democratic and free . . . The final capstone of that . . . is working out a security with NATO, a European Union that is expanding, and still tied . . . to the United States and Canada . . . not only economically and politically but also in terms of our security alliance, but also has a special relationship with Russia, and does not rule out even Russian membership in a common security alliance (*Washington Post*, 8 March 1997, p. A11).

Despite the vagueness of the phrase 'common security alliance' and some other U.S. statements, official U.S. openness to the principle of eventual Russian membership remains evident.[30] In my view, this is conceivable, since NATO and Russia do not consider each other as adversaries. Moreover, since Russia is 'democratic' and moving towards a liberal economy, Russia outside NATO is not politically, economically and diplomatically sound, and would almost certainly turn out to be a system challenger. A Russia inside NATO, on the other hand, would enhance the strength of the zone of democratic peace and economic prosperity.

However, a Russia in the zone of democratic peace and economic prosperity, as outlined earlier, would automatically pose a strategic reconsideration towards China and other countries. China would feel extremely

---

[28] The French have been especially hostile vocally to an idea of America global hegemony. Cohen, Richard (1997, 28 November) 'What Sort of Friend Is a Resentful France?' *International Herald Tribune*, http://www.iht.com/iht/today/fri/ed/cohen.html.

[29] In September 1994, German Defence Minister Volker Ruhe stated, 'Russia cannot be integrated, neither into the European Union nor into NATO', cited in 'Bonn Rebuffs U.S. over NATO for Russia', *Chicago Tribune*, p. 2.

[30] According to James Goldgeier's interview with Clinton administration officials, President Clinton told President Yeltsin during his September 1994 visit to Washington that 'NATO was potentially open to all of Europe's new democracies, including Russia'. James M. Goldgeier, (1998) 'NATO Expansion: The Anatomy of a Decision' *Washington Quarterly*, Vol. 21, (winter), p. 97.

uneasy at being pincered by NATO in the North and the American bilateral alliances with Japan and other East Asian countries in its East, whilst also facing an increasingly hostile India and resurgent Islamic force(s). The odds are heavily stacked against China. It is very unlikely that China can resist (see S. Walt, 1987, for balancing and bandwagoning theories). A compromise or even joining the alliance would be a possibility for China – perhaps even with Japan. It may mean the dilution of NATO, turning into something like the OSCE or an OSCE in Eurasia and North America. This organisation would cover almost the entire northern Hemisphere. Under this one organisation, the security of three of the most powerful countries/region on the Eurasia landmass and Japan would be under a security axis of the United States. The structure for such an organisation would be more powerful than the UNSC or UN peace keeping forces. The objective of this strategy would mean that any rogue countries defying the international order would be dealt with, not only by the United States, but also by the other four main powers as well. Such a framework of 'great power concert' (see H. Bull, 1977/95) or more appropriately with the five major powers in the zone of democratic peace and prosperity would ensure greater security of Eurasian landmass and beyond (see also M. Cox, 1994: 645). The establishment of this security framework would almost ensure the political stability of this large region and beyond for prosperity to develop, globalisation to grow, and for pluralistic democratic participation to take stronger roots.

- The United States' attempts to reverse the ABM Treaty of 1972 to develop an anti-ballistic missile system that would allow Washington to counter aggression by 'rogue' missile states, such as the growing threat from North Korea and other nations, is giving Russia grievances.[31] Arguing in defence of the United States' aim to develop the system because of the threat posed by 'rogue' states and possible terrorists, U.S. Defense Secretary William Cohen stated in January 1999:

> We are affirming that there is a threat, and the threat is growing, and that it will pose a danger not only to our troops overseas but also to Americans here at home. . . . The limited national missile defense capability we are developing is focused primarily on countering rogue nation threats and will not be capable of countering Russia's nuclear deterrent.[32]

To the Russian parliament and government, this is yet another sign of America's unfaithfulness towards Russia. The proposal to move ahead with a U.S. national ballistic missile defence system, (although still needs to be confirmed as of writing), from the U.S. decision-making bodies. However, the development of such a system without seriously considering the security interests

---

[31] *International Herald Tribune* (1999, 22 January) 'U.S. Plan Threatens Moscow Arms Pact', and (1999, 23 January) 'Russia Rejects Any Changes in ABM Treaty'.
[32] David Hoffman (1999, 22 January) 'U.S. Plans Threatens Moscow Arms Pact' *International Herald Tribune*, http://www.iht.com/iht/today/fri.fpage/miss.html.

of others, i.e., the security dilemma would probably cost the U.S. more in terms of diplomatic and political manoeuvres than the proposal development of the defence system (estimated at about $60 billion). The psychological insecurity of others, especially Russia and China, would pitch these countries into a dilemma of whether to allow the U.S. to develop alone or to increase military expenditure or use other diplomatic means to hinder U.S. interests.

The alternative strategy is outlined throughout the book, where the objective is to embrace the four (and where possible more) powers into the U.S. hub. Unless the U.S. can find diplomatic and political manoeuvres to persuade China and Russia that the ABM system does not pose to them serious security considerations, a system of that type would create unnecessary signals against U.S. (open) power.

Whereas the objective of engagement and enlargement, via globalisation has been its ability to absorb other powers into that direction, the development of the ABM defence system is likely to repel others (especially China and Russia) into feeling that the U.S. despite its overwhelming superiority in military power posits it necessary to 'push' these powers to reconsider their security alternatives.

Unsurprisingly, Russian strategists have insisted that the development of the ABM system would 'violate strategic stability'.[33] The development of the ABM system poses serious deterrence problems, for China also – since the United States is planning to extend that system into East Asia, from Japan, Korea to Taiwan.

The above analysis has indicated the problems and opportunities opened to the U.S. and Western alliance by the perceived nature of Russian economic development and political discourse. The section below will turn the other side of the coin and analyse the West's perception of Russia. First, the view taken by the U.S. towards Russia since the collapse of communism.

The 'West's' Perception of Russia

Initially, the collapse of communism in December 1991 was viewed as both an opportunity and a serious reconsideration for strategic analysts in the West (M. Cox, 1994). As highlighted in the analysis above, that opportunity appears to be wavering in light of U.S. perceptions of Russian internal politics. In this perspective, instead of seeing Russia as an opportunity to furthering the goals of liberalism, capitalism, and democracy, the U.S. has increasingly treated Russia as a problem that needed to be 'contained' and its power base that needed curtailing (Z. Brzezinski, 1997; P. Starobin, 1999; P. Stone, 1999; J. Kitfield, 1999). Russians view this U.S. position as attempting to humiliate it further. Former Russian deputy Prime Minister Mikoyan states: 'Most U.S. foreign policy decision-makers do not seem concerned with humiliation or insults directed at

---

[33] Daniel Williams (1999, 23 January) 'Russia Rejects Any Changes in ABM Treaty' *International Herald Tribune*, http://www.iht.com/iht/today/sat/in/moscow.html.

Russia' (cited in S. Mikoyan, 1998: 114).

It is not just the 'Russians' who are suspicious of the policies applied by the Clinton administration, but also U.S. Congressional Republicans.[34] Republican Senator Richard Lugar, for example, accused the Clinton administration of a 'failed' opportunity for 'a strategic partnership . . . to one that is lurching toward malign neglect'.[35] Lugar contends that, rather than as a 'strategic partnership' for opportunities, the Clinton administration views Russia as a 'strategic patience and persistence'.[36]

From this perspective, an analogue can be drawn from the Austrian-Prussian relationship in the 1860s to the current U.S.-Russian relationship. In defeating the Austrian Empire in 1866, the Prussian Chancellor Otto von Bismarck taught his Kaiser the importance of exercising caution in not humiliating a defeated adversary that may be needed as a friend. The growing misunderstanding of U.S. policy towards Russia appears to indicate that the U.S. has not heeded Bismarck's words. It is curious to ponder why an opportunity that was open to the U.S. with regard to Russia seemed to be squandered. Is it that the U.S. is activating a greater strategy that even Bismarck would find complex to solve?

To explain this phenomenon, this section attempts to understand the nature of the relations of the two powers, their practices, and the international relations theories that may help explain the reason for the behaviour towards each other as such.

The first scenario is to question the optimism that soared following the collapse of communism in Eastern Europe and then the Soviet Union. Had the optimism over communist collapse prematurely swollen? Did the media and other communication means prematurely advocate that because communism was dead, old enemies can just forget their history and become friends overnight? In politics, as it is in history, this is not necessarily always the case, sometimes a careful analysis of history would not reflect what is seen through the lenses of optimism. History can remind us of the past grievances, but the present reality and the action and words initiated by Russian and U.S. decision-makers are significant in deciding whether there is really a break from the Cold War hostilities to a new dawn of open politics between the two old rivals. On the other hand, they could be just playing the old game in different grounds?

The perception created by the media following the collapse of communism and the Soviet Union was one in which U.S. and Russian relations was dubbed as a 'honeymoon'. Whether this can be taken for granted needs to be carefully analysed

---

[34] *International Herald Tribune* (1999, 16 September) 'Republicans Accuse Clinton of Failure in Russia Policy'.
[35] Richard Lugar cited in Fred Hiatt (1999, 8 March) 'Russia Matters, So "Strategic Patience" Isn't Enough' *International Herald Tribune*, http://www.iht.com/iht/today/mon/ed/edfred.html.
[36] Strobe Talbott (Deputy Security of States) stated this, cited in Fred Hiatt (1999, 8 March) 'Russia Matters, So "Strategic Patience" Isn't enough' *International Herald Tribune*. http://www.iht.com/iht/today/mon/ed/edfred.html.

in the diplomatic and political relations that ensued between the two powers. Another interpretation depends on what is looked at, and how the word 'honeymoon' is interpreted. If it was a 'honeymoon', then surely there must be a great deal of amiability between the political operations in Moscow and Washington. This was never the case, it was a media perception, not the perception of the U.S. policy-makers or their Russian counterparts. The U.S. and Russians still view each other with caution. Yet, for the U.S. there was a choice, as to whether to embrace the 'new' Russia as a 'born again Christian' (theologically speaking) or to view it with reservations – meaning that the leopard does not change its spots overnight. For the United States, this dilemma would be 'huge' and catastrophic, if it was to 'slip up'.[37] The United States government recognised the problems and, according to Strobe Talbot (U.S. Deputy Secretary of States): 'The stakes, for us, are huge.'[38] The problem, however, is that the United States does *not* appear to know how to handle this delicate matter. Michael Cox indicated that:

> . . . if the United States did not play a more active economic role in the ex-communist countries, there was a good chance that, having won the Cold War, it would now lose the peace (1994: 640).

From the government policies implemented and the academic research planning available in the United States, there appears to be conflicting interests with regards to Russian democracy and Russian prosperity and its huge military capabilities. Many analysts in Washington regard the building and consolidating of Russian prosperity and democracy as important – these, I will term 'realist pragmatists', whilst others perceive that it should: '*prevent* Russian obstructionism of U.S. and Western policies in the UN and elsewhere' (D. Johnson, 1996: 84). This latter policy I will term as 'realist antagonists'. Russians have unsurprisingly openly condemned the antagonists' position:

> As long as the U.S. could effectively press its interests with Russia's support or quiescence, the Russians were 'partners'. However, as Moscow began to pursue its national interests in a more determined way, the relationship became increasingly adversarial (S.A. Mikoyan, 1998: 113).

This adversarial view of Russia is most evident in the American perception of the Russian Duma. From the United States' perspective, the Russian Duma is no more than a domain of communists and nationalists,[39] and from that perception, Cold

---

[37] Strobe Talbot (Deputy Security of States) stated this, cited in Fred Hiatt (1999, 8 March) 'Russia Matters, So "Strategic Patience" Isn't enough' *International Herald Tribune*, http://www.iht.com/iht/today/mon/ed/edfred.html.
[38] Ibid.
[39] After the state election in 1995, the 450 seat of the State Duma consisted of 250 communists and 50 ultra-nationalists.

War hostilities towards the U.S. still linger.[40] For example, the Americans complained that in previous negotiated arms control agreements – such as the START II agreement in 1993 – whilst formalised and agreed by the Russian government, the Russian Duma lambasted these as being 'unequal' treaties that needed revising. They complain also of the recent development of the ABM strategy by the United States; the U.S.-British air-strikes against Iraq; and NATO air-strikes against Serbia (Yugoslavia). It is not difficult to see why the Russian Duma does not believe that it can trust the United States enough to pass the START II treaty into law.[41] On the other hand, how can the United States or the West share principles or values if Russia constantly challenges those values and principles that the United States aims to promote?

Regarding Russia's policy on its 'near abroad', U.S. hawks continue to believe that Russia's historical imperialistic expansion tendencies – the age old Russian military doctrine's fixation of insecurity, and its aim to have 'total' security around all its frontiers – have not convinced American hawks that Russia can ever be a country that can live in peace, despite the fact that the Russian military no longer has such a perspective in its military doctrine. According to American hawks, the geographic size and position of Russia will always make Russia formidable whether it is economically weak or strong.[42] In their opinion, Russia is a country that spans eleven time zones, making it by far the largest and most important geopolitical state on the Eurasian landmass. It is an area that shares borders with nations in Europe, the Middle East, Central and East Asia, and North America. Its geo-political importance is considerable. U.S. hawks argue that America's post-cold war strategy should be based on the synthesis of the old Mackinder theory of Heart-land-Rim-land, which argues that whoever controls the heartland controls the world.[43] In the 1993 *Defense Strategy for the 1990s: The Regional Defense Strategy* follows almost precisely this notion:

---

[40] Oles M. Smolansky (1998) 'Can Russia Escape Its Past?' in Ken Booth (1998) (Ed.) *Statecraft and Security*, p. 156, stated: 'even after the dissolution of the USSR, many former communists . . . continue to occupy prominent positions in the high echelons of the military and secret police establishment, as well as the administrative and managerial bureaucracy. The influence which they continue to wield is bound to hamper the efforts to restructure Russian society.'

[41] Recently there have been concerns in Russia about the United States abandoning the Anti-Ballistic Missile Treaty that was signed in 1972. Daniel Williams (1999, 23 January) 'Russia Rejects Any Changes in ABM Treaty' *International Herald Tribune*, http://www.iht.com/iht/today/sat/in/moscow.html.

[42] Also, Western European, Turkish, Iranian, Chinese and Japanese, share similar views to the Americas. (My perception from informal conversations with German, Swedish, Turkish, Iranian, Chinese and Japanese friends and colleagues, and reading.)

[43] Alfred Mackinder (1904) 'The Geographical Pivot of History' *The Geographical Journal*, Vol. 23, No. 4, (April), pp. 421-44; Zbigniew Brzezinski (1997) *The Grand Chessboard: American Primacy and Its Geostrategic Imperatives* is the modern version.

> *. . . it is our (the United States') goal* to preclude any hostile power from dominating a region critical to our interests . . . These regions include Europe, East Asia, the Middle East/Persian Gulf, and Latin America (D. Cheney, 1993).

A further weakening of Russia's position in order to preclude it from dominating such a vast area, is, therefore, needed, so as not to pose a threat to U.S. interests. Brzezinski (1997a) has suggested that Russia *should* be fragmented into three zones. The problem with this argument is the problem of determining how far a weakened Russia's position needs to be before that country collapses into chaos?

The 'slow' pace, level and depth of liberal economic reform in Russia has been accused by some in Washington, (such as the IMF, the World Bank Group, the Brookings Institute, the CSIS, Council for Foreign Relations), as being not liberal enough and being very inconsistent.[44] They contend that structural reforms have proceeded slowly throughout the 1990s, with powerful vested interests generally opposing them. These vested interests include industrial managers, regional elites and (for most of the period), the leaders of the rail, gas and electric monopolies. They have hindered quick Russian recovery or the beginning of economic growth – and the increasing re-nationalisation economic programmes have done no more than endanger economic liberalism. Russia's measures to implement IMF and World Bank guidelines on Structural Adjustment programmes have been slow. Instead of being directed at innovative companies, the IMF and others have accused the Russian government of wasting its money in rescuing inefficient industries.

These arguments, however, miss the whole point of establishing the roots of democracy and prosperity in societies. The major re-structuring reform would involve inflicting considerable economic pain on the population in the form of unemployment and reduced social subsidies – thus, causing social instability or worse. The immediate priority for the Russian government is to restore political calm and stability, and to avert mass disorder, principally by regaining its grip on the economy.

With the conflicting difficulties and overriding contradictions, the paramount question that has been posed by Western strategic planners and decision-makers is this: is Russia a friend, or an enemy, or a bit of both? (R. Pipes, 1997). The same question may be reversed to Russia: is America and/or Western Europe an enemy or a friend? And/or are both Washington and Moscow viewing each other with mutual distrust? Officials from Washington, London, Paris and Bonn have maintained that Moscow is no longer the enemy (see A. Stent, 1999). Moscow also elaborates that America and the West are no longer enemies. Yet, despite these reassuring words, the analysis above on the conflicting difficulties show that 'screen-play' diplomatic discourse is not convincing. The practices of political and diplomatic intrigue remain. Even though governments recognise that the stakes involved have changed, nevertheless, some in the American public and some in the U.S. Congress and the U.S. Defense department, have been rather

---

[44] L. Aaron (1998, 12 June) 'What Stalled Russian Reform', *The Washington Post*, p. A27.

reluctant to draw this conclusion. A similarly static view of the United States is taken by the Russian communists and nationalists (who together command a majority in the Russian Duma and some in the Russian military).[45] 'Old habits die hard', as Grant T. Hammond (1998) has correctly noted, or as Sergo Mikoyan puts it:

> American Russophobes seem to be suffering from an 'enemy-deprivation syndrome' and do not seem interested in seeing – or do not believe it is possible to imagine – a predictable, reliable, democratic Russia . . . It has been easier for the U.S. to view Russia as having inherited its predecessor's imperial aspirations than to adjust to the changes that have occurred in Russian civil and political society since 1989 (1998: 112-13).

These suppositions of perception/misperception of an enemy syndrome remain a major obstacle for Russia to become a fully 'trustworthy' partner with the United States and the West. On the other hand, why has Russia been unable to realign itself with others (even with China) to balance U.S. power?[46] In the 1950s, the U.S. was fearful of the alliance of the USSR and China. From this evidence, ever since the collapse of that alliance, the U.S. has manoeuvred to prevent this appearing again. Although prudent realism is necessary, a grand strategy for continued American preponderance cannot continue,

> . . . unless old suppositions about Russia are jettisoned and new approaches considered, unless Russia is welcomed as a partner and afforded the same opportunities others enjoy thanks to the unprecedented collapse of the Soviet Empire, the United States will be the worse off for the oversight (F.C. Ikle, 1996: 126-7).

Conclusion

Whatever the 'real' intentions of the United States[47] over the Russian Federation, or the 'real' intentions of the Russian Federation over the United States, good relations between Russia and the United States remain pivotal for world peace and stability. It is common knowledge that Russia has dual parity in weapons of mass destruction with those of the United States. Economic and political stability in

---

[45] Colonel General Valerii Mironov, a former deputy defence minister and former principal military advisor to Russia's premier, stated in 1996 that the 'Cold War still goes on and only one definite period of it is over', cited in Richard F. Staar (1996) 'Moscow's Plans to Restore Its Power', *Orbis*, Vol. 40, No. 3, (summer) p. 375.
[46] This is discussed in greater length in chapter eight, I do not want to duplicate that argument here.
[47] There are elements within the United States Congress and academia that wants to destabilise Russia, and even suggestions by Brzezinski that Russia be split into three independent regions.

Russia is not only crucial for Russia, but also for the United States and its allies. The American ideal of the enlargement of democratic peace and liberal free trade cannot expand and become peaceful if a vital area in world geopolitics is in constant fluctuation. A stable economic/political regime that is friendly towards democratic peace and free trade is vital. An unstable Russia would not only have the risk of unleashing a combination of extreme nationalist sentiments and communist zealots that are inward looking, but it may also have dire consequences for the surrounding regions. As former Secretary of State Warren Christopher has warned: '. . . if Russia falls into anarchy or lurches back to despotism, the price that we pay could be frightening' (1998: 45).

Indeed, the consequences would be another Cold War. This time Russia will be hungrier than the Soviet Union, because its power and prestige have been damaged and it wants to regain that power and prestige (see R. Gilpin, 1981). Under combination of strenuous pressure from financial and agricultural crisis, and potentially isolated from the rest of Europe, where Russia is neither accepted as part of the EU or NATO, the desire to reverse the 'imbalance' of power is gaining ground. Politically isolating Russia gives Russia very little room to manoeuvre except to become a direct threat to the West and the United States.

The United States can play with the patterns of history and find ways to further weaken and even make Russia disintegrate. And indeed the pattern of history *will* emerge. However, if it does so, the old prophecy of war will resurface. The alternative, however, is for the United States and the West to offer Russia a real path of peace, prosperity, and co-operation that can for once in human history bring the cycle of great power struggle to an end.[48]

The quest for the United States is to find ways to avoid or stop a combination of Russian 'red'-nationalism turning into extremism or flirting with other extreme groups and countries (see A.J. Gregory, 1998). The recommended proposition here is for the United States to increase its economic and political assistance to sectors in the Russian elite and groups that are favourable to American ideals/interests – that is towards democracy, free trade, individualism and human rights – and aim to web and expand this group in Russian society; perhaps even a Marshall Plan, especially designed for Russia, not to build the Russian arms industry or to help the oligarchs, but to act as a means to stabilise the economic situation in Russia and influence their military industries, and to develop checks and balances in Russian society. By fostering and moulding these groups, the United States *can* effectively influence their behaviour and thoughts that are more tolerant and favourable to the United States and towards democratic peace and prosperity. By establishing and ingrowing into these areas, the United States' influence *will* increase as its ideals of democracy, human rights and free trade will be cemented and flourish in Russian society. This in turn may expand into other areas.

---

[48] See counter-argument by Robert Gilpin (1994) 'The Cycle of Great Powers: Has it Finally Been Broken?' in Geir Lundestad (1994) (ed.) *The Fall of Great Powers: Peace, Stability, and Legitimacy* (Oxford: Oxford University Press).

Without finding solutions to the Russian dilemma, we may be drawn closer to Sergo Mikoyan's warning:

> When those problems (Russian) are resolved, people who try to intimidate Russia will regret their mistakes or, more accurately, those who will deal with Russia in the future will regret their predecessors' errors. The U.S. should start working to prevent such errors today in order to avoid disaster in the next millennium (1998: 124).

The success of democratic and economic reforms in Russia and other former Soviet republics represents the best long-term answer to Sergo Mikoyan's aggressive nationalistic view asserting itself, helping business transparency, and countering tyrannical power structures. The success of the democratic bodies can only grow indigenously, moderating elite power struggles, with or without Western guidance. By nurturing and organically increasing the basis for a stronger democratic liberal tolerant society in Russia, extreme elements of nationalism and communism could be submerged or banished from decision-making in Russian society. In return, American and other businesses can gain fair access to business opportunities, without being accused of neo-imperialism. American and other business access to these regions are crucial, both for economic development in these regions and political influence for the United States, and the eventual development and encompassing of Russia into the zone of democratic peace and prosperity.

On the other hand, the U.S. thinks it is (hypothetically) enhancing its own security by proceeding with the way it has, by reassuring Eastern European states about their position in the inter-state system, coaxing them into the Western security system; offering Russia the Partnership for Peace in NATO, but not offering Russia a substantively new role of co-ordinating international (and regional) peace and stability. The U.S. views this as very innocent, it is benign and so on. These very moves, however, alarm Russian strategists and policy-makers. Those that are not alarmed are undermined in confidence about Western intentions. In other words, the West is mirroring its perception in saying that it is logical and non-threatening and certainly not aggressive and so on. Russia, on the other hand, perceives these moves as actually working towards isolating it, and relapses into the age-old game of intrigue.

As a final analysis, I have four propositions to make to balance conflicting interests in the U.S.-NATO-EU and Russia relations:

(1) The United States *should* encourage Russia in pursuing stable aspects of a modern society – a democratic government, a market economy, demilitarisation of the economy, reduction of conventional and nuclear forces, and enhancement of the security surrounding nuclear weapons and materials. Although the United States has been the main supporter of IMF loan programmes to Russia – in terms of aid, Russia lags far behind what its power projection status allows it to be.[49] The United States *should*, with Western aid, concentrate on helping the Russian

---

[49] For example Israel, Egypt, South Korea get more aid than Russia.

people.

(2) Whilst the politics of powers is not dead, it *should not* be in the interest of the United States to pursue these deadly games or antagonise others to resort to that game – and *not to be snared* by others *to play that game*. Although, idealistic vision(s) are often unrealistic and dangerous, a return to the power politics scenario is also a self-fulfilling prophesy and potentially catastrophic. If:

> ... *the United States* exercises its leadership/*position* wisely, this strategic environment ought to conduce to a prolonged peace (that is, no major war on the European continent) and the promotion of vital U.S. national interests (A.Z. Rubinstein, 1997: 31 emphasis added).

Realistically, it will be difficult for the West to persuade Russian security specialists to accept NATO expansion – with Poland, Czech Republic, and Hungary being formal members in April 1999. There are also prospects during the second round of expansion due in April 1999 of taking in Romania, Slovenia, and some Baltic republics. The United States and its allies continually preach that NATO expansion and NATO air strikes against traditional Russian allies, or the expansion of the EU, pose no threat to Russia. This can only happen, if Russia is invited into the NATO apparatus as a full member of NATO. Russia is a young and struggling democracy, it needs sincere western help and aid. A Marshall Plan to help the Russian ailing economy is urgently needed – it is not much to ask to avoid intimidating Russia and causing it to slide back into its old Cold War practices. The United States *should* attempt to bring Russia into the zone of peace and prosperity – the acceptance of Russia into the G7/8 is a welcome sign.

(3) The United States' policy makers, *if* they intend to remain the predominant world power, must be aware of the historical sources of conflict in Europe and move beyond the interests of the Western Europeans, by devising their own strategy towards Russia rather than being pressured by Europeans to accept their perception of Russia. Russia at the end of the millennium and at the beginning of a next one is in an extremely fragile situation. The collapse of Russian democracy is real. The gap between the rich and poor has grown so disproportionately, that a revolt against democratic liberalism cannot be ruled out. In addition, corruption has led many to have access to easy money, others not playing by that game are tempted in. The task for Russians and their government is monumental. There is a real danger that the weight may become unbearable to many Russians. The objective of the U.S. is to try to sustain and build the fragile economic and political structure of Russia. The United States *should* deal with Russia with great care and delicacy. The economic and political trouble in Russia can escalate, as shown by the rise in fascism and economic corruption. If these problems are not resolved it would certainly soon turn into a huge area 'out of control' (Z. Brzezinski, 1993). Russia, for all its economic and social troubles, remains a nuclear superpower. Russia retains the capability to inflict unacceptable damage on the U.S. and the world through use of its nuclear weapons if it is continuously humiliated and isolated. The primary interest for the United States,

therefore, is for a secure and unthreatening Russia. If history acts as a guide for pinpointing a country's/society's behaviour in international affairs, Russia demonstrated vis-à-vis Napoleon,[50] and Hitler's campaigns against it, and, as an old dictum of Russia goes: 'beware of the bear when it is wounded, as it is at its most dangerous state when it has been hurt'.

(4) Russia now faces a chronic disorder of dislocation of natural and human resources, and wealth distribution. The United States *can* influence and *should* help the Russians develop a better redistributive allocative economic system that minimises the risk of poverty turning towards extreme nationalism.

By helping Russia through its vulnerable stage, the United States *can* gain better and deeper understanding of the Russian perception of the West and the United States in particular. The integration of Russia into the zone of peace and prosperity is a desirable goal that would lend an extra spoke for American manoeuvres and strategy to integrate the global system into the American hub, and for that reason the American hegemonic globalisation would be more secure.

---

[50] See Leo Tolstoy (1997) *War and Peace* (London: Penguin Edition).

Chapter 8

The PRC and the U.S. in the 21st Century: 'Preventing the Clash of Civilisations'[1]

Do not do unto others what you would not like them to do unto you.
Roman Herzog, 1999: ix, 40, 43.

Henry Kissinger: 'The white area of the egg always surrounds the yellow part.'
Zhou Enlai: 'We will scramble the egg.'[2]

Differing cultural traditions are surely among the sources of international conflict today; by themselves, however, they rarely lead to major conflicts between states. It is their interactions with scarcities of resources, rival claims on territory, conflicting agendas on trade and historic memories of ethnic or religious enmity that make cultural differences a source of war. Thinking of international conflicts as clashes of civilisations involves a grand and dangerous simplification of these complicated and often obscure interactions.
(J. Gray, 1998b: 151).

The men who have change the universe never gotten there by working on leaders, but rather by moving the masses. Working on leaders is method of intrigue and only lead to secondary results. Working on the masses, however, is the stroke of genius that changes the face of the world.
Napoleon Bonaparte quoted in R. Greene and J. Elffers, 1998: 161.

Introduction

Perhaps the most sensitive relation in the post-Cold War era is that of the United States and China. With the Soviet Union, all but, in the pages of history, and Russia in economic tatters, the suggestion that Japan may challenge American economic superiority currently looks unconvincing. The European Union (EU) challenge is still on paper and ripe only for speculation. The EU still has to define its political/military intentions. In addition, both the EU and Japan are supporters or like outposts of U.S. hegemonic order, rather than challengers to that system

---

[1] Title borrowed from Roman Herzog (1999) *Preventing the Clash of Civilisations: A Peace Strategy for the Twenty-First Century* (New York: St. Martin's).
[2] During the 1972 meeting, told to the author by an anonymous source.

(see the respective chapters on Japan and the EU). China stands out as the most obvious candidate to challenge the United States-led system. Unlike the EU, Japan, and Russia to some extent, China is still not democratic and does not (politically) view the U.S. hegemonic order as legitimate. Many analysts argue that China, for all the good things said about it, remains a police state controlled by 'a self-perpetuating communist dictatorship, a regime for which lawless coercion remains very much fundamental tool of politics' (A. Waldron, 1998: 40). The Tiananmen Square massacre should not be forgotten when dealing with the communist regime in China. Dick Wilson (1996), and R. Berstein and R.H Ross (1997a and 1997b) speculate that it is most likely that China will pose both a military and economic threat to the United States and to international security and economic order more generally. However, how far and how realistic are Chinese challenges to the United States? More importantly, is China potentially dangerous to liberal-democracy or is liberal-democracy dangerous to China?

This chapter does not submit to the view that we will be in an ideal world where peace prevails and/or where the people will live together in perpetual peace, nor does this chapter argue that the world will be plagued by continuous war cycles. These are two extreme scenarios. It must be noted that both the U.S. and China policy-making is not in a perfect universe of single interests, but of multiple, societal forces and conflicting interests struggling to force their way into 'national' policy (see J. Scott, 1998: 1-21). Thence, it is shades of contesting forces, and nuances of interpretations and perceptions between states and their agents that one of two scenarios will either be made or broken.

This chapter attempts to investigate the continuity of Chinese foreign policy through China's accumulation of experience in diplomatic practices. The chapter inquires into the long-term Chinese interests and the long-term accumulation of diplomatic practices and experiences. This is not easy to study. Questions that are raised would probably involve: 'who or which experience' of the political culture? Moreover, there are the diplomatic failures, such as those experienced during the 19th and early 20th centuries. This chapter assesses the tension in Chinese domestic politics following its shift from traditionally being the centre of the East Asian universe to one of equality amongst the surrounding countries. This chapter questions whether the Chinese actually follow this modern policy.

From this psychological background, the chapter examines the shift in Chinese diplomatic relations after 1949. The chapter analyses the characteristics in these relations where there have been a mixture of personal involvement by the elite and then evolving into the operation and practice of flexible and pragmatic diplomatic relations. In answering this question, a brief discussion of the cold war is required. It examines the (shifting) relations and power alignment with the USSR, the U.S., and its relations with its neighbours.

The nature of Chinese diplomatic practice has seen a combination of war, peace, and intrigue. The chapter shows how and why China takes advantages of others, especially where other great powers are in decline or in demise in a specific region on the one hand, whilst on the other, it plays by the rules with the 'hegemonic' power when it serves Chinese interests and where it feels it cannot gain from challenging existing rules. This is examined in the Taiwan sub-study.

However, in this chameleon practice of diplomatic relations, this chapter shows that not for one moment does China view itself as a 'puppet' to U.S. hegemonic globalisation aspirations. In the Cold War, China rejected hegemonism from both the Soviet Union and the United States. After the Cold War, it has also rejected hegemonism. The term, U.S. hegemonic globalisation, is intensely suspect in Chinese political circles. This chapter shows how both the Chinese authorities and U.S. have been extremely careful to (re)-interpret the words and terms to suit the perception held by ordinary Chinese with regard to the idea that globalisation was associated with American hegemonism. The term 'economic engagement' has been used instead, these are important concepts that coax the Chinese people into believing that there are benefits for all to gain (and maybe there are mutual gains for all), but not for one moment should we lose sight of group(s) that are influencing the spheres of interests. The contestation and promotion of ideas and the interest of power positioning is deeply struggled for, both in China and in the United States.

Given these contending interests in operation, the chapter shows how China is especially watchful over its macro-economic stability and economic sovereignty. The chapter explains why China has been careful to guard itself against the liberalisation of finance, as China is wary of overseas finance coming into the country and taking over which many Chinese fear would create serious internal instability for the Chinese economy, and even ultimately the survival of the communist state. However, at the same time these policy-makers recognise that without openness to international trade and the liberalisation of finance, Chinese economic growth would not meet the required levels necessary for China to prosper. This is a serious dilemma for the current ruling group in the communist regime.

For the U.S., Chinese economic development offers both opportunity and wariness. On the one hand, Chinese economic development and prosperity falls directly into the U.S. policy of economic engagement (a la globalisation and thus increasing U.S. hegemonic power). Whilst on the other, Chinese economic growth would inevitably make Chinese power increase, therefore, has the eventual ability to challenge U.S. interests (not only of economics, but if the economic engagement strategy does not 'change' the Chinese regime into a more pluralistic democratic society – that very policy of economic engagement would foster the Chinese military to becoming more powerful, which the U.S. fear would challenge U.S. security interests in East Asia).

Finally, the chapter attempts to evaluate the lessons to be learned from history, (this is not to say that it is repeating itself, but it can offer us an analytical tool or act as guidance to see the similarity in historical trends) of how relatively the greatest challenge to liberal-democracy will be to guide the rise of Chinese power into the path of supporting international order and stability – that is, to do what Britain failed to do with Germany in the first decades of this century – rather than directly challenging or containing it. For China on the other hand, it is to understand that the liberal-democracy is not an enemy to the Chinese people, because if liberal-democracy means getting rid of despots and corrupt politicians, then only tyrants will view liberal democracy as a threat.

Part I: From 'Celestial Kingdom' to 'Third World' Country

The Chinese refract their history through 5000+ years of civilisation (see G. Barraclough, 1978/87; P. Buckley, 1996). With one of the oldest,[3] continuous civilisations in world history, the legacy of this monumental past is both a source of inspiration and a source for blind pride.

In the 'West', Chinese are both patronised and humiliated in extreme manners. They were once placed as people of the Celestial kingdom – heaven on earth. Later, during the late 19th and early 20th centuries they were treated almost on the same par as animals. The underscoring of China goes deep; even the learned Fernand Braudel conveys the Sinic culture as:

> ... [to be frank] China's economic achievement were modest and ... backward compared with those of the West ... Her inferiority lay in her economic structure, her market outlets and her merchant middle class [which was] less developed than that of Islam or the West ... Nor were their entrepreneurs eager to make profits ... [T]hey only half-heartedly shared the capitalist mentality of the West ... [The large population] made machines unnecessary ... in China they come so cheap ... China had no need to devise machines to spare human labour (F. Braudel, 1987, 1993: 194-8; see A.G. Frank, 1998: 19-20 for a critique of Braudel).

The humiliation endured and experienced at the hands of the European powers have hardly healed. With these psychological obstacles, many Chinese are asking how they were allowed to be subdued or ridiculed.

Whilst the psychological impact of European exploits and the masterful cunning exploits of Europeans remain deep in the back of many Chinese minds, the fear of potential foreign subjugation, and the degradation of national dignity are perhaps the most important concern to Beijing and its people – for both mainland and overseas. There is a danger that what may be regarded as 'suggestions' for 'good' governance by 'Western' governments, may be interpreted as outright interference and imperialism.[4]

---

[3] However, an English mockery: 'as far back as the Chinese', referring to someone who is ignorant of technical progress, or not abreast of modern times. (The author would like to thank Anna Watson for this source).

[4] Gary Klintworth and Murray Mclean (1996) 'China and the United States: Neither Friends nor Enemies', in Stuart Harris and Gary Klintworth (1995) (Eds.) *China as a Great Power: Myths, Realities and Challenges in the Asia-Pacific Region* (Longman: Melbourne), Klintworth notes that 'this has left China hypersensitive to anything that smacks of interference in its internal affairs', p. 71.

To many Chinese, the 'Western' countries, and increasingly the United States' criticisms of China's internal affairs are often interpreted as outright interference (G. Xu, 1998). To the Chinese observers, the United States (or Western European countries) has no right to lecture on human rights, since throughout most of the United States history, human rights abuses (slavery and the genocidal destruction of the original American inhabitants) were a standard way of life.[5] But what is significant is their interpretation of human rights. On the onset most Chinese elites talk of a societal human rights over individualistic human rights (some would argue that the 'west' praises hedonistic individual rights rather than the right for the well being of the individual).

Reflectively many Chinese strongly believe that 'China . . . needs no lessons in moral philosophy from nations which in the past have treated it with contempt' (M. Cox, 1998b: 236). Yet, this attitude was precisely why China descended into defeat and semi-colonialism. Despite being critical of certain 'Western' lifestyles and the way 'Westerners' would regard acceptable societal behaviour, China and Chinese need to learn why 'Westerners', as the way they are, their histories, their religions, their cultures (high, middle, low, and under-class of their society), their sufferings, their perception of themselves and of others, and their symptoms, were able to manipulate the peoples around the world so effectively.

Chinese manipulation by the 'West' was not only due to the fact that the Chinese were technologically more backward than Europe (latter exploited to the maximum by the Japanese). The determining factor, more often than any foreign intellectual superiority or military fire-power, was the Chinese mentality towards themselves, their inability to understand themselves and others. This has proven to be fatal to China, that even today Chinese continue to have symptoms of this cancerous disease.[6] Their short-sightedness, without any regard for dignity of their own kind, will trap China and will forever humiliate it. To overturn the scars of European exploits would probably mean a synthesis of Chinese traditional perceptions concerning themselves, the family, society, and others. Mao, his followers and the current regime have tried this, but with limited success. The *true*

---

[5] There are numerous examples of American abuse of its power. These are just a short-list of U.S. misdeeds and atrocities that have gone unpunished or have gone unwarranted. First, the genocidal destruction of the original American inhabitants for the 'advancement of Western civilisation'. Second was the most inhumane treatment of and enslavement of black people. Third, the United States used neo-colonial practices in Central, South America and the Pacific converting into what was to be viewed from the American perspective as America's backyard and its lake. Fourth, in its imperialist expansion the United States indiscriminately massacred Filipinos for its colonisation of the islands. Fifth was the United States' indiscriminate carpet bombing and use of chemical and biological weapons in the Vietnam War. During that war more TNT was used than the whole of the First and Second World Wars combined, including also the two atomic bombs.

[6] This mentality is captured and illustrated by Lu Xun (1983) 'The True Story of Ah Q' in Lu Xun et al *Masterpiece of Modern Chinese Fiction, 1919-1939* (Beijing: Foreign Language Press).

discovery is to rediscover the classical Chinese texts, and to analyse and evaluate them to explain, and to come to terms with the source of Chinese psychology, not on a collection of foreign 'texts' or an ideology that has treated the Chinese civilisation with contempt and even barbarity.

It is not the aim here, to analyse the historical contacts between the 'Western' countries and the Chinese people; yet historical accounts do make perceptions and misperceptions vital to the development of painful and fruitful relations between 'Western' countries and China. Since the United States has often been heralded the 'leader' of the Western world, this section of the chapter analyses historical relations between China and the U.S. as a guide to the developing relationship.

Historical Background of Sino-U.S. Relations

As outlined in the previous chapters, the United States explicitly does not want to face a single dominant power or a group of powers hostile to its values and beliefs in any region of the world. From very early in its history, the United States has been concerned with the possibility of one single power dominating in Europe and East Asia. In Asia, it was the fear of Japan and other imperialist European powers' intentions towards China that initiated the United States to conceive the 'Open Door' policy in 1899 under Secretary of State Hays and President McKinley. The principle of the 'open door' policy was, however, meant for commercial purposes and not designed to 'help' China against foreign exploitation. However, when Europeans and Japanese 'threatened to close the door to China not only commercially, but also militarily and politically, the open door policy was interpreted to cover territorial integrity and political independence of China' (H.J. Morgenthau, 1952: 6). It was always assumed that the domination of China by another state would lead to so great an accumulation of power as to threaten the security of the United States.

Unlike the Europeans that aimed to 'carve up' China, the United States had an unusual romanticisation of China, believing that one day China could become the United States of the East, an area that would keep a lid on the 'mischievous' Japanese and to keep at bay the 'shrewd and greedy' Europeans. The U.S. sought for the Chinese what the U.S. already established in Central and South America, that is, the U.S. had desired China to become a democratic country that would influence and control the troubles in East Asia.

Despite being ravaged by civil war and the corruption of the Kuomingtang that ruled China, President Franklin Roosevelt continued to believe and was eager to allow China a seat in the United Nations Security Council to act as the stabiliser for the security of the East Asian world, a China that could, in the end, act as a spoke for the United States' led system that would keep other powers from moving out of control in that gravitational system.[7]

The communist victory over the Kuomintang (KMT) nationalists in 1949 brought the United States dream to a premature end.[8] For China, the communist victory finally ended an unstable, bloody and most humiliating period in the history of China.[9] China and the Chinese people could at last say to themselves: 'we can stand up and walk straight again'.[10]

The communist consolidation and Chinese jubilation were, however, short lived. The communists quickly issued a series of draconian reforms that were even 'more' brutal than those endeavoured either during foreign occupation or the preceding 'warlord' and civil war era. However, to the 'proud' Chinese, and in principle, it was 'at least done by Chinese and not by foreigners against Chinese'.[11]. This psychology remains puzzling, as one commentator has noted:

> ... there is considerable acceptance among the Chinese public for the notions that the Chinese Communist Party (CCP), despite some serious mistakes along the way, has brought great overall social and economic improvements and enhanced China's international political standing (D. Roy, 1998: 226-7).

The communist draconian reforms brushed aside and destroyed much of traditional Chinese order/philosophy and values. Its draconian measures attacked anything that was viewed as feudalistic and ideas that were associated with the 'exploitative capitalist' 'West' and the old elite.

The Chinese 'revolutionary' position at home was also to be transferred abroad, and unlike the Soviet Union, which had been cautionary about world revolution, especially following Stalin's statement of 'socialism in one country' (D. Townsend, 1994: 813), the PRC was ideologically revolutionary – it wanted the colonised countries, the workers, the 'peasants' and the oppressed people of the world to rise up and initiate a world wide communist revolution.

Although novel in its cause, the strategy was dangerous and naïve. It led many senior U.S. policymakers (such as Dean Rusk) into conceiving Beijing rather than Moscow as being 'the more serious political threat to global order' (M. Cox, 1998b: 225). Certainly in statements during the 1950s and 1960s,[12] the PRC rather

---

[7] Certainly to this day, the situation between the United States and China is critical, and according to Brzezinski, 'there will be no stable equilibrium of power in Eurasia without a deepening strategic understanding between America and China', Z. Brzezinski (1997) 'A Geostrategy for Eurasia', *Foreign Affairs*, Vol. 76, No. 5, (September/October), p. 58.

[8] Many Americans (especially in the U.S. Congress) continue to feel that they had 'lost' China.

[9] For over three hundred years, 1644 to 1911, China was under foreign rule, the Manchu subjugation; semi-colonialism by 'Western' powers and Japan; the self-imposed submission and denuding to the self-inflicting feudal system; and to natural disasters and famine.

[10] Quote from speech given by Mao Tse Tung on the Declaration of the People's Republic of China, 1 October 1949.

[11] Told to author by an anonymous source.

[12] Peter Calvocoressi (1991, 6th edit.) argued that 'what China achieved in these years of

than the Soviet Union was more explicit in its support for armed struggle in the Third World, and indifferent towards the consequences of nuclear war with the U.S.[13]

With more than half of Europe (geographically speaking) under communist rule, and Asia and other parts of the Third World swerving and/or falling into the communist ideology, many policymakers in the United States and Western European countries seriously perceived that capitalism was being undermined by a 'red menace'. The American Congress and the American public became hysterical about the forthcoming 'red peril'. The Soviet Union's explosion of the atomic bomb in 1949 made the traditional view that the United States can be safe from Eurasian geopolitics obsolete. The communist victory over the U.S. backed KMT in China, and Kim Il Sung's invasion of South Korea, reinforced the hysteria. McCarthyism (1950-1954) exploited the American mood and embarked on a witch-hunt against anyone suspected of having the slightest 'socialistic' views. The communist threat had become personal, it was a cancerous disease that needed to be removed or contained.

The Vietminh's success over the French in Dien Bien Phu in northern Vietnam in spring 1954 confirmed America's fears over communist expansion. In an attempt to contain the spread of communism ('X' (G. Kennan), 1947; T.H. Etzold and J.L. Gaddis, 1978), a strategy of counter-revolution under the guise of the NSC-68 policy of what became know as the domino theory[14] was initiated to prevent the expanding communist threat. Communism had to be contained wherever and whenever, and where possible had to be pushed back[15] (for details

---

travail was to project so menacing an image of its future power as to make the world take it very seriously in the present and even to be more afraid of China than of any other country in the world. This fear was not merely a consequence of adept Chinese diplomacy; it was also a product of the mysteriousness with which China was cloaked by the outside world's own determination to treat it as not just different but out of this world', *World Politics since 1945* (London: Longman), p. 110.

[13] For example, during the Korean War, the United States' threat to use nuclear bombs against China went unheeded. Mao is reported to have said that the mass Chinese people will fight the United States whether it dropped the atomic bombs or not. In addition, during the Cuban missile crisis in 1962, Mao said to Moscow that the communist world must stand firm against the U.S. bluff. However, the Chinese were well aware that a nuclear war would be a universal disaster and that China and the Chinese Communist Party would be among the victims. Although they clung to the not implausible thesis that wars were inevitable, they did not apparently regard nuclear war as inevitable. Like others, they hoped to prevent a nuclear war by a policy of deterrence but, unlike others, they could not in the 1950s and 1960s do the deterring themselves. China in this period was exposed to nuclear threats or preventive war in the same way as the USSR had been exposed between 1945 and 1949.

[14] The term of domino theory was given by President Eisenhower, he believed that the states of Southeast Asia were like a row of dominoes that might fall to communism if communists managed to 'knock one down'.

[15] Unfortunately, President Eisenhower's aim at 'pushing back' communism had the adverse effect that led to the Hungarian uprising of 1956.

see P. Calvocoressi, 1991 6th edit.; T.E. Vadney, 1992). The conflict scenario between capitalism and communism was to be a zero-sum game – there was no other alternative, not even for countries in the non-alignment movement.

The rigid political manoeuvre of containment led to the fixation that Soviet communism was the same as the communist nationalism in East Asia. On close analysis, however, the Communism of the USSR and China were distinctively different[16] – communists in the PRC and the Vietnamese in particular, (despite their world revolutionary rhetoric), were more nationalistic than international revolutionary Marxists. According to Michael Oksenberg:

> ... the wars fought between China and the United States in Korea, and for China indirectly, in Vietnam were avoidable contests that flowed in large part from a United States failure to appreciate China's insecurity and engage in a constructive relationship.[17]

Before analysing the American perception of the PRC politics, it is necessary here to have an overview of the Soviet Union's (Russia) relations with PRC (China), which would help explain the shifting of U.S.-Sino relations, and U.S. power position with regard to the major powers in international affairs.

The Communist Split and the Convenient Alignment

Chinese and Russian[18] history have been plagued with mistrust and conflict ever since the two civilisations encountered each other (G.F. Hudson, 1931; R.K.I. Quested, 1984). Both (civilisation/country) were 'leaders' in their own right and operated with their own laws and sphere of influence/interests. The rift between the PRC (China) and the Soviet Union (Russia) was not unpredicted.[19]

---

[16] The British had warned the Americans of the differences (the author wishes to thank Dr. B.K Gills, for pointing this out). – Alas however the mixed signals that the British were giving did not help the United States – certainly Churchill who had warned of Soviet atrocities and intentions, but then suggesting that Chinese communism was different, despite Chinese statements and threats. Because of the zero-sum nature of containment, the United States was not flexible enough (or unwilling to distinguish between them) to be able to pursue pragmatic policies against all communist forces.

[17] Michael Oksenberg, President of East-West Center, address to the Asia Society, Washington, 21 September 1993, USIS Wireless File, 23 September 1993, cited in Gary Klintworth and Murray Mclean (1996) 'China and the United States: Neither Friends nor Enemies' in Stuart Harris and Gary Klintworth (1995) (Eds.) *China as a Great Power: Myths, Realities and Challenges in the Asia-Pacific Region* (Longman: Melbourne), p. 76; Note: contrary to the suspect belief of 'realist' paradigms in the enhancement of power, Hans Morganthau was critical of the American involvement in Vietnam.

[18] The Union of Soviet Socialist Republics (USSR) from 1917 to 1991.

[19] According to R.K.I. Quested (1984) and G.F. Hudson (1931), China-Russian history is plagued with distrust and misunderstandings. Since the two civilisations encountered each

Even the communist victory in mainland China took the Soviet Union by surprise. It had already been agreed at the Yalta conference (4-11 February 1945), between Roosevelt, Stalin and Churchill, that China should fall under the United States' sphere of influence – just as Eastern Europe was to be under the Soviet Union's influence and Western Europe under U.S. influence. With these settlements already decided, Stalin and other communist cadres in Moscow were half-hearted about the ability of the communist forces in China and had even initially supported the KMT against the communists. For Stalin and his generals, China strategically under the U.S. made more historical and geopolitical sense. A communist success in China was seen more of as a burden for the Soviet Union than an emancipation of the proletariat from the exploiting nature of the capitalists and bourgeoisie. Certainly, China in Soviet eyes was not an industrialised country, and it had a much weaker proletariat base relative to farmers. It could not be transformed into a communist state/society without forgoing the historical stages proposed by Marx and Engels.

Geographically for the Soviet Union, China under communism would mean that the territories gained by the Soviet Union during the latter part of World War II against Japan in North East Asia had to be returned to China. Yet, despite the 'unwanted' success of communism in China, the Soviet Union was, nevertheless, in a 'better' strategic position to continuously overthrow the 'capitalist' states. It did initially try to improve Chinese industrialisation and committed to a policy of international communist 'brotherhood'.

During Stalin's last years, the PRC was regarded as a smaller socialist brother. The law of equal sovereigns did not apply to Mao in his visits to Moscow. Instead, Mao found himself having to pay homage to Generalissimo Stalin in the tsarist tradition. Stalin's death in 1953 and the PRC's military 'success' in withholding the U.S./UN counter-offensive on the Korean peninsula, showed that the PRC could not be conceived of as a 'smaller' socialist brother. What is more, with no 'heavy-weight' leader visible in Moscow, in the PRC's view the new leaders in Moscow did not have the psychological clout of the traditional 'emperor' of imperial Russia or of imperial China, so tensions inevitably mounted as to who would lead international communism. To the Chinese the new Russian leaders were not worthy to lead the communist movement. The communist cadres in the Soviet Union on the other hand had always believed that 'they' were the centre and heart of world communism, any revolution or programmes to start revolution should be coherent and stem from Moscow. It was assumed that whoever reigned in Moscow – should de facto be the supremo of the communist world. Mao without disrespect to Lenin or Stalin felt he should be the new supremo of the communism movement. To the Soviets, Mao was disrespectful.

Unable to solve the personal symbolism or prestige, the relations between the Soviet Union and the PRC during the post-Stalin era were embroiled in elite personality differences and conflict. Adding salt to the wound, national historical

---

other *vis-à-vis* Russia expansionist policy, an uneasy sense of distrust remains.

accounts between the two countries re-emerged and 'needed to be settled'. The relations between Beijing and Moscow turned from international communist comradeship into a cold war within another cold war. This geopolitical divide is often ignored by the declinist school, and would help the U.S. in strengthening its position against the Soviet Union for global preponderance.

The denunciation of the dictatorship of the proletariat, and pronouncement of 'peaceful coexistence with capitalism' – thus, modifying Lenin's idea of the dictatorship of the proletariat and tampering with the idea of class struggle thesis of Marx – by Khrushchev in the late 1950s and the early 1960s cracked open an irreparable ideological and psychological dispute between the PRC and the Soviet Union. In the PRC's psychological perspective, Stalin's achievements (despite his disrespect towards the Chinese communists) were: First, the almost single-handed defeating of Hitler – where three quarters of the German army confronted the Soviet Union and failed – was an extraordinary historical strategic triumph. Second, in the Chinese perception, the 'romantic' transformation and the accelerated development of the Soviet Union from a fairly 'backward' European and devastated country (the First World War, counter-Bolshevik war, and the Second World War) into superpower status was monumental. To Mao, these 'successes' were 'worth the price to pay' to bring a poor and humiliated power and people on par with the 'West'.

The second issue that inflamed PRC and USSR relations was Khrushchev's shifting support for India (Bulganin and Khrushchev visited India in 1955) with massive economic aid, and agreement with India on its claims in the disputed areas against the PRC. This severely re-opened a geostrategic game between the two countries. The PRC responded by developing and framing a friendship treaty and delineating the boundary line with Mongolia (then a Soviet satellite) and Albania (making it China's first European satellite). The Soviet response was swift and austere; in July 1960, it withdrew all Soviet scientists and specialists in the PRC, leaving many projects incomplete and inefficient. The Soviet Union then supported Muslim separatists in Xinjiang in 1962. These moves by the USSR made the PRC hysterical, and it claimed that its communist neighbour had 'betrayed it to the lowest' position (not only directly interfering in the internal affairs of the PRC, but also masterminding its attempted break-up). The PRC retaliated by closing all Soviet consulates in the PRC. The Soviet Union responded with freezing all economic aid. In January 1963, the PRC for the first time openly attacked Khrushchev on his 'heretical' views with regard to world communism. Two months later, Beijing launched the 'Three Spheres of World Theory', whereby it was to challenge Moscow for influence in the Third World (R.K.I Quested, 1984: 129). By spring of 1964, the ideological dispute was full-blown as the two camps were in competition with each other regarding the alternative interpretations of Marxism-Leninism.

As the Soviet Union shifted more towards 'peaceful coexistence' with the 'West' and détente with the 'capitalist' Americans, the PRC became even more revolutionary. It initiated the 'Great Proletarian Cultural Revolution' in the mid-

1960s to 'cleanse', humiliate, attack, and/or re-educate people associated with traditional family values, hierarchy, bureaucracy, bourgeois capitalist ideology and capitalist 'western foreigners'. The rift between the two communist states was severe. Following the Warsaw Pact troops invasion of Czechoslovakia in spring 1968,[20] Beijing felt that it might be the next target of Brezhnev's limited sovereignty doctrine! The fear was not baseless. Soviet troops had dramatically increased along the PRC-Soviet border and the Soviets increased the number of troops stationed in Mongolia.[21] In March and August 1969 respectively, the tense PRC-Soviet relations resulted in clashes. The cold war between PRC and the Soviet Union was on the verge of becoming a 'hot war'. To the Kremlin, Mao was a thorn in the side of Soviet communism, and had to be overthrown. Rumours of assassination and coup attempts against Mao in the late 1960s to early 1970s stemming from Moscow fuelled the Chinese mistrust of the Soviet Union even further.[22]

Initially, the United States' desire to exploit the division between the PRC and the Soviets, deferred to the American public and Congress' fixation of anything that was 'red' was evil, and its commitment to the KMT in Taiwan. U.S. Presidents Kennedy and Johnson wanted[23] to develop relations with the PRC to strategically out-manoeuvre the Soviets and the Vietnamese, but were unsure of the response from the American public and Congress. It was only following Republican President Nixon (whose staunch critic of communism made him less suspect in the eyes of the Congress and American people, that the White House was not 'selling out to the reds') coming to power in 1969 that a rapprochement with the PRC become less difficult to 'sell' to the American public and Congress.[24]

America's desire to readjust its stance on 'China' was partly designed to disentangle its rigid policy of containment in Southeast Asia and to 'find a way

---

[20] Brezhnev justified the action by declaring a doctrine (later known as the Brezhnev doctrine) of limited sovereignty, whereby a socialist state was justified in interfering in the affairs of another in order to uphold socialism.

[21] The Soviet Union encroached the PRC territory of Zhenbai Island (which is on the Wusuli River in the eastern side section of the PRC-Soviet border) and the Tiehliekti region (in the Xinjiang Uygur autonomous region in the western section of the PRC-Soviet border).

[22] Those rumours brought mass crackdown and purges in the Chinese communism party to mass imprisonment and execution. Lin Biao who had been thought to be behind the plot fled to Russia but his aeroplane crashed under 'mysterious circumstance' in 1971.

[23] See James Chace for a contrast. Chace argues that 'by ignoring the rift between Moscow and Beijing in the 1960s, the Kennedy and Johnson administrations may have actually contributed to Sino-Soviet solidarity' (1992) *The Consequences of the Peace: The New Internationalism and American Foreign Policy* (Oxford: Oxford University Press), p. 86. In this author's opinion, this was never the case.

[24] In April 1971 the U.S. table tennis team was invited to the PRC (it was actually a stepping stone for rapprochement and a desire to readjust relations). Just months later on 9 July Henry Kissinger, Advisor on National Security Affairs to the U.S. President secretly visited the PRC for the first time, during which the two sides concentrated on the question of Taiwan and paved ways for an official presidential visit in 1972.

out' of its involvement in Vietnam 'without losing face'. For the PRC, improving relations with America and other the 'Western' countries were important steps. It was a turning point away from regarding the PRC as being treated as a revolutionary country – a country that was portrayed as aiming to destabilise the internal affairs of others, and a country that throughout its foundation in 1949 had lambasted the United States as imperialists and the cradle of capitalism and the head of exploiters – the PRC was keen to move from an ideologically based policy to a flexible (realpolitics) foreign policy approach. Readjusting the PRC's position with the rich capitalist countries also opened avenues for technological exchanges necessary to improve the PRC's technological 'backwardness' sectors, since before the break-up of the PRC-Soviet relations, the PRC had relied heavily on Soviet and Eastern European technical expertise.

Finally, for the PRC and the U.S., readjusting and reconfiguring relations was a significant strategy to balance the perceived threat coming from the Soviet Union, especially after the defeat of the U.S. in Vietnam, and then the Soviet involvement in Afghanistan in 1979. Ignoring the fundamental differences in political systems, Nixon and Mao used the old realist dictum: 'The enemy of my enemy is my friend.' Both sides saw the benefits of rapprochement with each other. Both had a common interest in countering the power of the Soviet Union.[25]

However, following the Tiananmen Square massacre in spring 1989, the systemic collapse of communism across Eastern Europe by the end of 1989 and finally the Soviet Union itself in 1991, the China-American 'strategic' relations no longer seem to fit the dictum. Instead, China is '[n]o longer . . . perceived as a "card" to be played, but in a sense the card has become the new game' (R.E. Zoellick, 1996/7: 15).

If China is to be the game, what are the rules involved? Are the rules applicable to the players in the game? Should the U.S. and others treat China merely as a 'game' to be played with?[26] Finally, if China is to be the game, what type of game is it likely to be? Is the game likely to be a zero-sum game or a game of mutual gain for all parties? These are serious and difficult questions. The sections below attempt to open the debate that has emerged in the U.S. concerning the relative growth of Chinese power and the shifting relations it has with the U.S. It also looks at the Chinese perceptions.

---

[25] In the word of Michael Cox: President Nixon and Chairman Mao saw 'the strategic necessity of tilting towards the United States in order to balance the power of the Soviet Union', in Ken Booth (ed.) (1998) *Statecraft and Security: The Cold War and Beyond* (Cambridge: Cambridge University Press), p. 226.
[26] Note: China in the late 19th and early 20th century was a 'play-ground' for the Western powers and Japan.

Part II: Sino-U.S. Relations in the Post-Cold War

The post-Cold War analysis of Sino-U.S. relations has re-opened grave areas of concern (i.e., the Cox Report in 1999; B. Gertz, 1999). It is as though having barely escaped the battle tantrums of the cold war; the international system is again entering another dangerous geopolitical confrontation (*Far Eastern Economic Review*, 17 June 1999: 10-14). Michael Cox analyses that: 'there is a danger that having escaped from the twisted logic of one Cold War with the Soviet Union, the United States . . . could easily get sucked into planning another one with China.' (in K. Booth, ed. 1998: 227). The volatile perceptions between Beijing and Washington had ebbed from the romanticisation of China in the late 19th and early/middle 20th centuries, to a zero-sum game on the aftermath of the foundation of the PRC, to a strategic partnership during the 1970s and 1980s, and to the recent development of power relations. The present scenario has spine-chilling analogies of the British-German power struggle before the onset of World War I (the analogies of Sino-U.S. and British-German struggle is discussed below).

In these circumstances, 'neo-realists' in the United States are quick to revamp traditional real-politics. The 'neo-realists' argue the growing Chinese power could only produce an intractable security dilemma. Christopher Layne in his parody of 'neo-realism' stressed:

> Short of preventive war, there is nothing the United States can do to prevent China from eventually emerging as a great power . . . *Because the* [u]nfettered free trade . . . will simply accelerate the pace of China's great power emergence: the more China becomes linked to the global economy, the more rapidly it is to grow in both absolute and relative economic power (1997b: 89, emphasis added).

To the 'neo-realists', the expanding Chinese economy will inevitably impinge on prevailing regional and global security arrangements (D. Johnston, 1996). They fear that as China's economy grows and it becomes confident militarily, China may set out its 'traditional' territorial claims in the Yellow and South China seas, and territories in central Asia and Northeast Asia.

These contentious security concerns would not only bring new dimensions in the foreign policy perception of not just the United States, but of the ASEAN states, India, Japan, Russia and other surrounding countries. In an already fragile security environment, the unease over China's rise could easily spiral into direct military conflict. In addition, the uncertainty of political reform in China *vis-à-vis* the sheer size and geographic proximity of China has been sufficient to produce fear of Chinese power and migration[27] in other countries of the region.[28] Given this

---

[27] For example, Russians fear Chinese moving into their territory – for more details see chapter seven on Russian nationalism.
[28] There is a Cantonese saying, 'When China sneezes, Hong Kong catches pneumonia' cited in Adeline Yen Mah (1997) *Fallen Leaves Return to Their Roots: The true story of an unwanted Chinese daughter* (London: Penguin Books), p. 244.

fear, the following pages analyse the development of paranoia and show how this perception may become reality.

The New Seers of Doom

To predict the direction of any living organism is still beyond any modern science (J.L. Casti, 1989), to predict the course of nations would be more than daunting, it would also be dangerous and would probably end up in disappointment. This was exactly what happened in the intellectual predictions of the decline of U.S. power propagated in the 1980s and early 1990s and the so-called Japan challenge. Presently, many seers are sending a fresh warning of the rise of the People's Republic of China (PRC) and the potential difficulties and conflict arising from its ascendance. President John Kennedy had stated '[t]he great enemy of truth is very often not the lie – deliberate, contrived and dishonest – but myth – persistent, pervasive and unrealistic' (cited in A.G. Frank, 1998: 7). Are we to be in danger of following foul of another myth?

In the much publicised book, *The Clash of Civilisations*, Samuel Huntington stressed that 'Western' civilisation should guard against and prepare war against the potential of an Islamic-Sinic collaboration.[29] In *China: The Coming Conflict with America*,[30] Richard Berstein and Ross Munro argue that the PRC 'is bound to be no longer a strategic friend of the United States, but a long-term adversary' (1997: 22).[31] Berstein and Munro consider that the most likely outcome of present Chinese political evolution to be 'a kind of corporatist, militarised, nationalist state, one with some similarity to the fascist states of Mussolini or Francisco Franco' (1997: 29).[32] The William Casey Institute in Washington, D.C., asserted that '[t]he nature of the threat posed by China is in key respects of a greater magnitude and vastly greater complexity than that mounted by the Soviet Union at the height of the Cold War' (K. Zinsmeister, 1998: 5). Patrick Buchanan warns, 'China is not only a trade problem, it is a national-security problem' (1998: 31). In Bill Gertz's book *Betrayal*, Gertz asserts that: 'America must treat China as a rival for power

---

[29] For debate on the Clash of Civilisation see *Foreign Affairs* (1996) The Clash of Civilisations? The Debate (New York: Foreign Affairs); *Far Eastern Economic Review* (1997, 6 February) 'Collision Course', pp. 39-40; *Far Eastern Economic Review* (1997, 1 May), 'The Coming Battle', pp. 36-9; R. Herzog, (1999) *Preventing the Clash of Civilisation* (New York: St. Martin's Press).

[30] See also their book (1997), *The Coming Conflict with China* (New York: Alfred A. Knopf).

[31] Also printed in A Foreign Affairs Reader (1998) *The Rise of China* (New York: Foreign Affairs), p. 70

[32] Compare this to Henry Kissinger's forecast on Russia: 'Early in the new century, after many ups and downs, Russia is likely to have restored its central authority. It may well be closer to the political structures favoured by Pinochet or Salazar than to a Western pluralistic system – though it will be freer than Communism.' 'A World We Have Not Known', *Newsweek*, 27 January 1997.

and not as a strategic partner. Dismissing current and future threats by China is dangerous and could lead to devastating miscalculation and war' (1999: 214). Whilst David Shambaugh et al (1995) emphasised a 'Greater China', with the PRC, Taiwan, and other Chinese overseas communities poising a conspiratorial attempt of economic, political and cultural assimilation of others.

The accusations of the PRC's potential emergence as a 'great power' have set in motion a call for preventive measures against the PRC and possibly against the 'Chinese' race in general. The 1999 Congressional 'Cox Report' on China, condemned the Chinese for espionage and fifth column activities in American industry and society.[33] The report and the scholarship documents set in motion a xenophobic (re)call of wariness against the Chinese.[34]

Whilst to the seers in Beijing, the United States is viewed as the main source for 'weakening', 'dividing' and 'Westernising' the PRC. They believe that without the political/military balance of the Soviet Union, the United States is enjoying greater political freedom to manoeuvre on a spectrum of issues, including direct military intervention. The firepower displayed in Desert Storm in 1991 and the Serbian conflict in 1999 has caused alarm amongst the Chinese communists,[35] who perceive the United States as becoming 'pushier and more arrogant'.[36]

Other issues that have also unsettled relations and have fallen directly into the Chinese 'neo-realists' perceptions have been the U.S. State Department's and U.S. Congressional annual condemnation of the Chinese Government's human rights record and political dissidents; expressing stringent and embittering remarks about Beijing's bid to host the 2000 Olympic Games in 1993; 'meddling' in the

---

[33] *USA Today* 'U.S. National Security and Military/Commercial Concepts with the People's Republic of China', www.usatoday.com/news/special/corept/report.html; John Maggs (1999, 29 May) 'Secrets Shanghaied' *National Journal*, pp. 1454-62; Sydney J. Freedberg Jr. (1999, 29 May) 'Misdirected Energy', *National Journal*, pp. 1463-6; Carl M. Cannon (1999, 29 May) 'First Denials, Then Spin', *National Journal*, pp. 1467-8; James A. Barnes (1999, 29 May) Republican Issue for 2000?' *National Journal*, pp. 1469-70; Richard E. Cohen (1999, 29 May) 'Hot Trade Winds' *National Journal*, pp. 1471-2; Bruce Stokes (1999, 29 May) 'Lethal Exports', *National Journal*, pp. 1473-5. For a counter argument see *Beijing Review* (1999, 14 June)' U.S. Congress Anti-China Resolution Slammed', p. 6; Zhao Qizheng (1999, 14 June) 'Cox Report Undermines Sino-U.S. Relations', *Beijing Review*, pp. 9-11.

[34] Although hypothetical, there are already motions of an 'invisible' containment policy directed against China and the Chinese people.

[35] China shares Russia's dismay at U.S./NATO action against the Yugoslavia republic. China as well as Russia has interests to limit and to even curb America's global power. For now, however, Chinese analysts reject the idea that shared interests could bring about a rapprochement between Beijing and Moscow, saying 'Beijing's alliance with its Soviet "big brother" in the 1950s left both sides bitter' (*Far Eastern Economic Review* (1999, 8 April) 'Behind the Lines', p. 19).

[36] Informal talk to an anonymous source (spring 1998); See also Lee Hockstader (1997, 24 April) 'Russia and China Agree: Washington Is Too Bossy', *Washington Post Service* in *International Herald Tribune*, www.iht.com/iht/today/thu/fpage/moscow.html; *Beijing Review* (1999, 14 June) 'Paper Comments on U.S. Hegemonism', p. 7.

Taiwan and Tibet issues; deliberately increasing difficult economic conditions necessary for China to enter the World Trade Organisation; the unauthorised air strikes against Iraq, and the unlawful (unauthorised by the UN Charter or UN Security Council) bombing of Yugoslavia; the alleged 'mistaken' missiles attack on the Chinese embassy in Belgrade; allegations of Chinese 5th column operating in American society; and attempts by American scholars and populist journalism to portray the Beijing government as a 'threat' to international security and vilifying China as a 'new evil empire' (Si Cheng, 21-27 Oct. 1996: 13); and the possible development of the ABM defence system that would cover not only the United States territory but also Japan and Taiwan.

Many analysts have argued that the United States' hostility towards the PRC stems from the pathological need for an enemy in the post-Soviet age – the PRC is still communist and has a tendency to support countries that are regarded in the U.S. perception as 'rogue' states. The PRC and these 'rogue' states are often the most critical of Washington policies. Others have however detected a more sinister element in American strategy. Professor Michael Cox, for example, identified that some in the United States would view:

> ... the deeper cause of U.S. anger is a refusal on its part to accept that this non-white nation has not only succeeded in the short and medium term, but might – over the longer term – challenge what many in the U.S. assume is their right to dominate world politics (1998b: 243).

He suggests that the reason for the U.S. concern is 'less fear of China and more a worry about its own capacity to shape international relations into the twenty-first century' (1998b: 243).

Perceptions of 'International' Law and the 'International' System

The perception of China challenging the U.S. position has called into question the position of the structure of international law and international system as viewed by the PRC and by the United States. The PRC has complained that the U.S. is routinely breaking the laws of national sovereignty enshrined in the United Nations Convention by flaunting with the banners of 'freedom', 'democracy' and 'human rights' to act as universal criteria of modern state to interfere in the internal affairs of developing countries (see *Beijing Review*, 14 June 1999: 7). Without referring to the United States, the PRC President Jiang Zemin stated in his visit to the UN in October 1995:

> ... certain big powers, often under the cover of freedom, democracy and human rights, set out to encroach upon the sovereignty of other countries, interfere in their internal affairs and undermine their national unity and ethnic harmony (quoted in A. Mitchell, 25 Oct. 1995).

Similarly from a neo-realist position, Professor Kenneth Waltz argues that:

> The powerful state may, and the United States does, think of itself as acting for the sake of peace, justice, and well-being in the world. But these terms will be defined to the liking of the powerful, which may conflict with the preferences and the interests of others. In international politics, overwhelming power repels and leads others to try to balance against it. With benign intent, the United States has behaved, and until its power is brought into a semblance of balance, will continue to behave in ways that annoy and threaten others (1991: 669).

The United States and allies, on the other hand, deny flatly that they have any intention of implementing a 'neo-colonial' strategy under any guise. The United States and its allies firmly believe that the engine for a 'humane' world order lies in the formation of democratic government and a liberal trading system for all states (M.E. Brown, S.M. Lynn-Jones and S.E. Miller, 1997 2nd edit.).

For PRC leaders, as it is with neo-realists, the idea of a privileged position of the United States as the 'keeper' of the 'New World Order' or an 'unchallenged superpower' (D. Shambaugh, 1992; H.L. Huo, 1992; S.S. Zhao, 1992; J.W. Wang and Z.M. Lin, 1992) is unacceptable. To the PRC leaders, the root of China's aspirations is to participate in world affairs and international problem solving on equal footing with the United States – possibly, this also applies to Russia, Japan and EU.

This contradiction between the perception of the U.S. and the PRC risks a direct collision for scholarship and policy-making in Washington and Beijing. Theoretically, this contradiction would lead to an uneasy relationship and would almost certainly spiral into what may be called a 'hegemonic war' (see, for example, R. Gilpin, 1981; I. Wallerstein, 1974, 1980, 1988; G. Modelski, 1987; P. Kennedy, 1989; A.G. Frank and B.K. Gills, 1993; G. Lundestad, 1994; C. Chase-Dunn, 1998, updated edit.).

However, the type of analysis offered above is not only erroneously inappropriate to understanding the power relations between the U.S. and other powers; it is also a self-prophesying thesis. It is based on the assumption that great powers should fall and decline, and that this inevitably leads to conflict between the present hegemon, the United States and the rising power, the PRC. No one else is in a better position to talk about balance of power and multipolarity than former U.S. Secretary of State and former National Security Advisor Professor Henry Kissinger, who reminds us that: 'The rejection of history extols the image of a universal man living by universal maxims, regardless of the past, of geography, or of other immutable circumstances . . . those who ignore history are condemned to repeat it' (1994: 833).[37] It is precisely those that ignore history are more likely to repeat past mistakes. Without being circumstantial, the history of multipolarity and balance of power has led to many great miseries for human kind. By suggesting

---

[37] Despite these words, H. Kissinger continues to emphasis the logic of balance of power and multipolarity. Has he forgotten the lessons of previous balance of power systems?

that a world would be more stable and peaceful under such a system, are we not forgetting a very critical lesson of history?

Re-evaluating the Seers of Doom

This section contests the validity of the assumptions underlying certain realist views of world politics, and likewise challenges the assumptive frameworks of Chinese leaders. Their views are not only inapplicable to the multiple historical dimensions of current affairs, but has the danger of sliding into old practices. They recognise these dangers. Yet, collectively both neo-realists and Chinese leaders are setting frameworks that aim to do exactly that. Their framework merely helps condemn humanity to the cauldron of war and disaster with multipolarity and balance of power. To reiterate Brzezinski's maxim it is not 'about what may happen, [but] what must not be allowed to happen' (1997: ix).

The framework of this analysis aims to argue how, amidst the tantrums of cold war rhetoric against the PRC, analysts have *failed* to see the main and crucial concerns in Chinese historical/political/economic domestic and international relations and the vulnerabilities of PRC.

Before setting out to unveil the empirical and theoretical frameworks behind the allegations and the suggestion that the PRC poses a 'great threat', there is no escape from the fact that the communist regime has changed significantly since the PRC undertook the 'four modernisation' programmes initiated in the mid-1970s.

First, analysts generally grossly overestimate current PRC power capabilities, with the fixation that as the PRC becomes economically developed, its military force will develop and the PRC will become more assertive internationally. Chinese scholars and leaders on the other hand use this as an opportunity to stress that the PRC is an important player, and does not need to become part of an American led system or any 'western' orientated system. However, by incorporating and interlocking with the international economic system, China is conforming to international laws and standards. In this sense, the Chinese foreign, diplomatic and military relations are a mixed combination, as the PRC is both a system supporter and a system challenger.

Second, as was outlined during the declinist-renewalist debate in chapter four, analysts grossly underestimate U.S. power and the ability of the U.S. to respond and initiate policy objectives to counter threat, or to assimilate challenges or challenger(s). However, Chinese nationalists refuse to accept that the international order can be assimilated. They view their history and culture as distinctively superior by right and that in due time they will prevail. On the other hand, the cosmopolitan life style that is emerging in China refutes the argument that the Chinese, let alone its 'culture', can be viewed as distinct.

Third, analysts fail to realise that the PRC will only become potent economically, if it allows itself to become free and decentralised politically – in which case its potency would aid international prosperity and peace, not threaten the system which brings with it benefits. Yet, to Chinese hard-liners this perspective is a conspiracy to overthrow communism in China.

Fourth, analysts often overlook a very important factor that has transcended contemporary PRC's political-societal behaviour. Many Chinese citizens are questioning the truth behind the Great Leap Forward,[38] the Cultural Revolution,[39] and even the taboo on the mass crackdown after the Tiananmen Square massacre and what it might have meant had the 'student' demonstrators succeeded in bringing down the communist party. Reference has been made to Russia and the terrible consequences it has had to pay in its draconian reform policies, the idea of capitalism with Chinese socialist characteristic, different forms of democracy (from multiparty pluralistic systems to the people's democracy), individual rights and collective interests, and religious freedom and the implications of religious fundamentalism taking advantage of that freedom especially the intolerance of religions alongside each other,[40] and the 'moral crusade' of the United States, and its 'inability to stay out of other people's business'.

Fifth, 'Western' popular media groups often fail to perceive China's historical concern about its independence (Li Xiguang, 21-27 Oct. 1996: 12). Chinese popular media, on the other hand, portray the West as being hegemonic and imperialistic. According to McCormick (1998), for the United States decision-makers and their Chinese counterparts to be unable to go beyond the media's vision of world affairs is dangerous. Reporters in both the West and China have a mission to report what is there immediately; the public (in both China and the West) digests this information often without clear understanding, and sometimes reinforces the reporter's bias (see C.F. Freeman, 1997).

Sixth, and perhaps most importantly analysts underrate the intrigues of elite politics in both the PRC and the 'West'. They generally mis-comprehend with the assumption that the PRC and the communist party are all one single entity, and

---

[38] I interviewed various party cadres, with one member having served the communist party for 44 years. In our informal conversations, he and others accepted that the Great Leap Forward was an economic disaster by trying to increase industrial production, where Mao and his henchmen completely neglected the agricultural sector – thus bringing mass famine. (My grandparents and parents also witnessed the disasters of the Great Leap Forward.)

[39] According to the many Chinese that I talked with, the 'Cultural Revolution' between 1966 to the mid-1970s, was set to wipe out and destroy the bourgeois societal and economic modes of control and production, but created side-effects which have severely distorted the 'Trust' factor for many PRC Chinese, towards foreigners and amongst themselves. The trust that Mao envisioned for the PRC Chinese people was orientated towards the state and the communist party rather than to the local community, friends and even family. The psychological effects of the Cultural Revolution is still felt today, especially on the fear that the 'state' would suddenly about-change and take everything away again. This has made many Chinese citizens wary of the 'states' intentions. Thence, many Chinese would desire the 'short-term' benefits and enjoyment rather than prudently wait for the future. For them the future cannot wait, because the government might change face and take it all away again.

[40] Note: see chapter two on the discussion on naked power, control, and compare it with the laissez-faire approach of power and control.

have a single interest. This is also reflected in the Chinese perception of the U.S., which many Chinese perceive as the cradle of capitalism and imperialism. This type of analysis grossly misunderstands the nuances of political activities inside and outside China and the United States.

In addition to the six points outlined, neo-realists argue that one of the dangerous legends of contemporary development policies is the belief that rapid economic growth promotes social and political stability, and eventually enables some form of liberal democracy to take hold. They argue that the experience of European history during the 19th to early 20th centuries has shown that rapid growth produced extremely acute economic, social and political problems. Germany was an illuminating example. Instead of being satisfied with economic development, Germany was not content with its status and power. In its dissatisfaction of the existing system, it set out to revise that system to accommodate its power. Does the Germany of the late 19th to early 20th centuries show a similar resemblance to the rapid Chinese economic development in the late 20th century? Bismarckian Germany directly challenged the European balance of power system once it became industrialised (N. Porter, 1970; C. Layne, 1997b). Would rapid economic growth in China correspond with the way the post-Bismarckian Germany turned out to be? How can the United States or the international system avoid the present China from turning into something of a post-Bismarckian Germany?

Just as rapid economic and industrial development in Germany did not bring about democracy, so, neo-realists argue that democracy appears to be progressing slowly relative to economic development in China. In post-Bismarckian Germany, imperial glory was epidemic. Is the increasing Chinese economic growth and confidence going down a similar road? Certainly as China becomes more affluent, the Chinese have re-emerged as becoming again proud, even to the point of being xenophobic of their achievements. Many Chinese remain bitter at the humiliation endured during the reigns of European, Japanese, and American imperialism in the 19th and early 20th centuries. There is a real danger that as the 'cycle of control' progresses in the Chinese favour, that that position may be used as a means to 'settle scores' with the Japanese and Europeans – which ultimately would mean the involvement of the United States.

In one sense, to evaluate the Chinese position by reference to the German position is unfair. For a start the imperial powers, Great Britain, France, Russia, and even America were certainly not in the same mode of democracy as in today's society; they were the powers that practised imperialism and colonisation. Nevertheless, the analogy of Germany's rise and China's rise is there, and we must pause to examine it further. First, what are the lessons (if any) to be learnt from the post-Bismarckian German system in relation to the PRC's political system transforming into a liberal democracy? What happens if America fails? Would the Hobbesian realist notion revitalise itself into the pre-1914 scenario? These are all daunting questions, and the answers offered may not turn out as expected.

Given the thesis that the relative strength of major powers is in constant flux, by the changes in different rates of technological, military, economic, political, and other material bases of national power, such as population and resources (R. Gilpin, 1981: 15), differential rates of growth will vary in a constant or sometimes discontinuous process (K.R. Dark, 1998: 16). According to Wallerstein (1974), Modelski (1987), Paul Kennedy (1989) and Robert Gilpin (1981) that flux is often associated with hegemonic wars.

For a rising state, neo-realists argue, the distribution of benefits associated with the existing system is unacceptable because it does not take into account the new distribution of power in that state. Following the analogy of the German rise in the late 19th and early 20th centuries, China is believed to be that rising state in the late 20th century and early 21st century. How can the existing system, with the United States being the hegemonic power in that system, avert the cycle of hegemonic war?

Neo-realist theory suggests that the 'emerging powers insist that international practices be modified to accommodate their interests by conferring a distribution of benefits more consonant with the new realities of power' (W.J. Murphy, 1994: 62). Robert Gilpin using rational choice theory and economic cost-benefit analysis, describes 'an international system *to be* stable (i.e., in a state of equilibrium) if no state believes it profitable to attempt to change the system. A state will attempt to change the international system if the expected benefits exceed the expected costs (i.e., if there is an expected net gain)' (1981: 10, emphasis added). Is China a hungry power? And/or for that matter, is the U.S. a satisfied power?

Diplomatically China rejects claims that it wants to become hegemonic, globally or regionally, and lambasts those that are hegemonic and acting hegemonically.[41] Officials, both senior and junior, active and retired, in Beijing continually deny any intention of becoming a hegemonic state or a challenger to the international system.[42] They claim, 'China will never be a "hegemon" in the region' (Fu Ying, 10 June 1999: 29). Chinese leaders responded to the charges as an 'absurd argument, to the effect that a strong China will pose a threat to other countries by seeing it as either an utterly groundless rumour reflecting a lack of understanding or an attempt to sow discord' (S.G. Liu, 1993: 4). Obviously, this could be a diplomatic screen for their true intentions. The following section will examine the most likely scenario whereby the PRC may poise as challenger to the current international system. I will assess the military power of the PRC, the so called 'Greater China' scenario, and the dangers lurking

---

[41] For example the Chinese accuse the Soviet Union following its invasion of Czechoslovakia and Afghanistan of acting hegemonically and there is increasing sense of resentment about the current hegemonic position of the United States.

[42] Although there are certain parts of the Chinese populace that would like to see the United States and its imperialist allies defeated, there are no clear methods and techniques that indicate that they may succeed, and even if their Marxist techniques and Marxist allies around the world do grow or defeat capitalism, there are only the slimmest indications that Western societies, especially the United States will adopt to Marxist ideology. See various *Beijing Review* articles.

behind PRC-U.S.-Taiwan relationship.

Chinese Military Power

The most obvious and immediate problem that the 'China threat' may pose to the international order and the U.S. is its military forces. Militarily, the PRC has about 17 ICBMs compared to the thousands belonging to the United States. To suggest that the PRC has the capabilities and resources to pose a greater military threat than the Soviet Union (see p. 255) during the cold war is 'preposterous'. During the Cold War, the Soviet Union had parity in military might with that of the U.S. and its allies (see Table 8.1 below and Appendix 1A). The PRC (according to the British IISS Military Balance 1997/98, U.S. intelligence (CIA) and State Department sources) has a share of only about 4.5% of the total world defence expenditure, and logistically it has to rely heavily on imports of basic foodstuffs. By contrast, the U.S. has about a third of the total of world defence expenditure and it is also a major supplier of foodstuffs. If we add ally NATO countries, allies in Europe, in the Middle East, in East Asia, in South America, and in other parts of the world that total would account to more than 80% of total world defence expenditure (see Appendix 1A). A hegemonic challenge, let alone a hegemonic war, would be most unfavourable to the PRC.

Critics may argue that defence expenditure does not tell the whole truth. Yet, if we are to look at the percentage of persons under arms, the PRC has less than half of that of the United States and Western European countries; in fact, the 'peace loving' Europeans have one of the highest percentage of persons under arms in the world (see Appendix 1A). In addition, according to the IISS, CIA and Pentagon sources, a large part of the PRC's armament dates back to the 1950s and 1960s.[43] Cynics may argue that the revelation of the PRC's espionage concerning advanced nuclear technologies indicates that the PRC's nuclear expertise could be equal to that of the United States. This is unconvincing. The most significant fact behind the espionage revelation was its timing. The U.S. intelligence had known the activities of the PRC for some time; the release of the espionage issue/drama was revealed only following the 'mistaken' bombing of the PRC's embassy in Belgrade (C. Johnson, 6 June 1999).

From the data in Table 8.1 and Appendix 1A, the PRC is far from being a serious challenger to U.S.'s hegemonic position. Even taking account of the fact that the data differs significantly depending on the method with which the calculations are applied, [Peter Berstein has argued that [i]f you torture the data long enough, the numbers will prove anything you want' (1998: 161)] the PRC is not spending disproportionately on defence (T.J. Hirschfield, 1999). The U.S. Department of Defense states that the PRC is 'carefully being watched', and the

---

[43] See IISS 1997/98 Military Balance; William S. Cohen, Secretary of Defense (1999) *Annual Report to the President and Congress*, http://www.dtic.mil/execsec/adr1999.html.

PRC's defense budget is 'basically very moderate' (F. Wisner, 1993: 169). Former U.S. Assistant Secretary for Defense Joseph Nye stated that the PRC, 'had a long way to go to match the kind of precision firepower and battlefield dominance that had been displayed by the U.S. in Desert Storm'. Nye outlined that Operation Desert Storm during the Gulf War in 1991 demonstrated that the PLA's level of military technology 'was not just obsolete – it was hopelessly obsolete'. With the 'accuracy', 'positioning' and demonic nature of weapons displayed in the NATO-Serbian conflict, PRC strategists are deeply concerned about PRC's ability to counter a worst-case scenario in the event that the PRC and the U.S. should come to blows (for Taiwan see below). With this and the technological backwardness of PRC's defence weaponry, the U.S. enjoys superior military capability in terms of both quality and quantity.

Table 8.1 The PRC v the U.S.A.: A Comparison

	PRC	U.S.A
GDP (US$bn)	616bn	7,6tr.
GDP (US$bn in 1999)*	978.3bn	8,848.4bn
GDP (US$bn in 1999)**	3,5tr	
GDP (US$bn in 1999)***	2,9tr	7,247.7bn 7,3tr
GDP per capita (US$)	3,100	27,600
GDP per capita (US$ in 1999)*	779	32,616
GDP per capita (US$ in 1999)**	2,895	27,336
Population	1.221bn	268.1m
Population*	1.25bn	272.3m
Population**	1.234bn	270.m
Land Area (000 sq. km)	9,597	9,373
Land Area (000 sq. km) **	9,557	9,809
Grain deficit or surplus (metric million tons)***	-26.0m	+95.7m
Crude oil production (barrel/day)***	3.0m	6.6m
Coal production (short tons/yr.)***	1.5bn	1.0bn
Personal computer in use	3.5m	121m
Defence expenditure (US$bn)	34.7bn	265.8bn
Defence expenditure (US$bn)***	38-78bn (est.)	262bn
Defence expenditure as % of GDP	5.7	3.6
Defence expenditure as % of GDP*	3.5	3.0
Defence expenditure as % of GDP**	1	3.7
Defence expenditure as % of GDP***	1.3-2.7 (est.)	3.6
Defence expenditure US$ per capita	29	1,001
Defence expenditure US$ per capita*	28	976
Defence expenditure US$ per capita**	28	984
Armed forces (000)	2,935.0	1,483.8
Armed forces***	2.9m	1.5m

% of population under arms*	0.23	0.54
% of population under arms***	0.24	0.55
Estimated Reserves (000)	1,275.0	1,880.6
Paramilitary (000)	1,200.0	88.3
Troops deployed overseas	0 (40 +UN peacekeeping)	200,000+ See below
Principal surface combatants	54	143
Carriers	0	12
Submarines	61	95
Submarines***	61	78
SSBN	1	18
SSBN***	1	17
Strategic nuclear warheads***	300	11,000
ICBMs	17+	1000+
Long-range bombers***	0	178
Combat aircraft	4,970	3,485
Modern tactical aircraft***	697	4,450
Arms Trade (US$m in 1995)	584	17,000

Notes

* Using *The Economist* – The World in 1999 figures.
** Using *World Facts and Maps* (1999 Edn.) Rand McNally figures.
*** Using U.S. Bureau of the Census; International Institute for Strategic Studies; U.S. Central Intelligence Agency; U.S. Energy Information Administration; U.N. Food and Agriculture Organisation; Chinese Business Review; office of Rep. Lee Hamilton; U.S. Arms Control and Disarmament Agency; Internet Industry Almanac.[44]

Sources: Secretary of Defense, *Annual Report to the President and the Congress 1995* (Washington, D.C.: Defense Department); Secretary of Defense, *Annual Report to the President and the Congress 1999* (Washington, D.C.: Defense Department); Country Profile: China (Washington, D.C.: State Department); *1998 Annual Report of the United States of America* (Washington, D.C.: McGraw-Hill); World Bank, *World Development Report 1996*; *World Facts and Maps (1999 Edn.)*, Rand McNally; *The Economist* – The World in 1999; Institute for National Strategic Studies, *1997 Strategic Assessment: Flashpoints and Force Structure* (Washington, D.C.: National Defense University); International Institute for Strategic Studies, *The Military Balance 1997/98*, IISS, London, for all other.

Obviously, if the PRC becomes rich it may develop a more sophisticated weaponry inventory, but, even then, the PLA will not emerge as a 'formidable player in the global balance of power over the next decade or even a number of decades'.[45]

---

[44] Quoted in Arthur Waldron (1998) 'Why China Could Be Dangerous', *The American Enterprise*, July/August, p. 42.
[45] See remarks by Joseph Nye, former Assistant Secretary of Defense for International Security, and Winston Lord, Assistant Secretary of State for East Asian and Pacific Affairs, hearings, Senate Foreign Relations Subcommittee on East Asia and Pacific Affairs, Washington, 11 October 1995, quoted in USIS Wireless File 12 October 1995; And according to Klintworth and Mclean, 'The U.S. is at least technologically 20-30 years ahead

Without underestimating the PRC's abilities, therefore the PRC cannot compete in an arms race with the United States. An arms race would almost certainly jeopardise the PRC's economy and the chances for affluence amongst its people. From Table 8.1, the PRC is simply no match for the U.S. outside its own area.

Furthermore, the PRC has serious shortages of scientific, technical and managerial personnel. Its command, control, communications, computer, and surveillance systems (C4S)[46] are backward and out-numbered in comparison to the United States.[47] Technically and numerically, the PRC's navy, airforce, and space technology are no match for the United States. The PRC does not have the capabilities, strategic prerequisites for power projection, and/or sophisticated technology to envisage a hegemonic military challenge to the U.S., and to actually attempt such a challenge would be suicide.

Even before heading for the worst-case scenario or contemplating a cold war style conflict with U.S., the PRC logistically would be starved of food supplies (see Table 8.1), isolated from the international community and its internal strife would become easier to be manipulated by the U.S. and its allies. A PRC challenge would almost automatically set off the U.S. alliance trip wire around the world. The reaction from the U.S. and neighbours would be to restrict and even isolate the PRC. And even if East Asian neighbours do not yield to U.S. restrictions on technology and trade to PRC, the U.S. has the ability to isolate East Asia totally!

'Greater' China?

This section examines the scenario that has been developed by scholars suggesting that 'China' is becoming a 'Greater' China. What does 'greater' China mean? The sphere of influence of the PRC is far 'lesser' or relatively 'smaller' in geographical scale than any since or during the pre-1911 and/or the pre-1949 period. If we are to look at imperial China since the Sui-Tang-Yuan-Ming-Ching dynasties, the Chinese sphere of influence has 'sunk' from a high position of the 'celestial empire' to the humble position of a 'backward third world country'. It is more than a decline; it is a civilisational 'plunge'.

---

in areas such as electronics, aircraft engine design, missile propulsion, metallurgy, communications, space technology, fire control, automated systems, lasers and infrared technology', in Stuart Harris and Gary Klintworth (1995) (Eds.) *China as a Great Power: Myths, Realities and Challenges in the Asia-Pacific Region* (Longman: Melbourne), p. 69.

[46] See William S. Cohen, Secretary of Defense (1999) *Annual Report to the President and Congress* www.dtic.mil/execsec/adr1999.html.

[47] Even with allegations of espionage of U.S. nuclear (which apparently was available on the Internet), the PRC still significantly lacks the means/will to develop (that is if the PRC does have the blueprint to develop, the W88, as the allegation suggests, testing it for data is another thing) such weapons – to develop and test the weapons would mean the PRC abandoning its obligation to the NPT. Analysts have suggested that the U.S. is no more at threat now than before the alleged espionage. (See Maggie Farley (1999, 1 June) 'China's Military Power Lags Behind U.S. Despite Spy Fears', *Los Angeles Times*.

However, the complexity of Chinese intentions are mixed. On the one hand, in its dispute and relationship with Vietnam and the countries in Southeast Asia, China's intentions should be viewed as suspect. On the other hand, it does not necessarily mean that China is in the same mode of revolutionary expansionist rhetoric of the 1950s and 1960s. It is no longer supporting revolutionary moments around the world to overthrow capitalist regimes as it did during the Mao era. Contrary to its actions in Vietnam and the South China Sea, the PRC, more so than the United States, insists that the internal affairs of sovereign states should not suffer interference by foreign powers. Whilst the Americans are incensed by the allegation that sources stemming from the People's Liberation Army (PLA) were used to fund the Democratic presidential campaign and the recent spying allegations,[48] the Chinese, on the other hand, are accusing the United States of supporting groups intent on overthrowing its structure of government and geopolitical structure. In particular, it has named the United States as the main perpetrator behind the Tiananmen Square incident in 1989. Moreover, the bombing by NATO forces against Yugoslavia in the name of humanitarian intervention was condemned by the PRC as setting new standards in international law, and over the bombing of the PRC's embassy in Belgrade, the PRC showed mixed emotions and even restraint, despite claims from Western media (Luo Tongsong, 7 June 1999: 12-14). The PRC did not respond more vociferously on these issues because it anticipated that the United States and allies might use a similar case against North Korea or even one of the provinces within and without the PRC. The move by the United States to initiate a Missile Defense Theatre System in Japan, possibly covering Taiwan, has alarmed the PRC's military strategists (Xu Zhixian and Yang Bojiang, 14 June 1999: 12-14).

Taiwan: Back to Sarajevo, 1914?

However, what is, perhaps, the most significant issue that has the potential of souring Sino-U.S. relations into real conflict is Taiwan. Handled badly, 'the Taiwan issue might trigger an explosive crisis in Sino-American relations'.[49] The issue of that island on the East shore of China has caused considerable concern that it could potentially turn into an analogy of the pre-1914 scenario, where the great powers were so obsessed by power gain and loss, that they sacrificed all for the sake of these sentiments. It is that lesson that this part of the book would like to address briefly.

---

[48] *New York Times* (1999, 25 May) 'Text of House Committee Report' www.nytimes.com/library/world/asia/052699china-spy-report.html.

[49] Colonel Xu Xiaojun (1994) 'China's Grand Strategy for the 21st Century', paper for the 1994 Pacific Symposium, Asia in the 21st Century: Evolving Strategic Priorities, Washington, 15-16 February, cited in Gary Klintworth and Murray Mclean (1996) 'China and the United States: Neither Friends nor Enemies' in Stuart Harris and Gary Klintworth (1995) (Eds.) *China as a Great Power: Myths, Realities and Challenges in the Asia-Pacific Region* (Longman: Melbourne), p. 72.

Before 1972, the Republic of China (Taiwan) was the official representative of China at the UN. The PRC was then seen as a renegade and an outcast. That relationship changed as the U.S. began rapprochement with the PRC and conceded that the PRC was the legitimate ruler of all China. Chiang Kei-shek gave up the UN seat and the UNSC under U.S. pressure, with the aspiration of one day reunifying all of China under his control. This recognition, which was a major wind change in PRC-U.S. relations, the importance of which is such to the PRC that it continuously refers to it, if the U.S. dubiously strays to support its long term ally in Taiwan. To the PRC, the communiqués issued between 1972, 1979, and 1982 by the U.S. and Chinese governments are the formal recognition of the U.S. to 'acknowledge' Beijing's position that 'there is but one China and Taiwan is part of China'.

The developments in Taiwan in the late 1980s and the move to becoming more democratic and the declining power of the KMT has caused complications in that acknowledgement.

In a more affluent and democratic state, many Taiwanese are becoming vocal about their 'true' identity – are they 'Chinese' or are they 'Taiwanese'? However, the tension became conflictual when in 1996 Taiwanese President Lee announced that Taiwan would redefine the issue regarding the possible reunification with the PRC. This move was further exacerbated by Lee's unofficial visit to the United States. From the PRC position, Lee's intentions were seen as a reinforcement of the U.S. support on the issue of Taiwanese independence. Lee's announcement and visit to the U.S. caused a serious diplomatic row which almost led to military clashes between the PRC and Taiwan. The PRC responded by massing troops[50] around the island, and firing missiles towards Taiwan, (in what the PRC described as military exercises). The tension was only cooled when the U.S. reassured the PRC that it does not recognise Taiwanese claims for independence. Fearing, also, that the PRC would not yield to its assurances, and reassuring the Taiwanese that they had not been abandoned, the U.S. dispatched two carrier squadrons to the area as a symbolic strategic move against the PRC and a political gesture to Taiwan.

China's behaviour in the Taiwan Strait and the South China Sea, led analyst Gerald Segal to point out that, 'it is not constrained by fears that its muscular foreign policy will adversely affect its overseas trade' (G. Segal, 1996). Hans Binnendijk on a 'more strategic' perspective however argues:

> ... if Taiwan is smart they can avoid Chinese use of power against them ... If war developed between China and Taiwan, the U.S. would probably get involved, and China will be a loser. Yet, Taiwan has to be smart enough not to declare

---

[50] There were indications that the Chinese might have used the exercise to see the US. response following the Russian internal war in Chechnya. However, Hans Binnendijk states: 'Chechnya is totally different ... we never had a treaty with them. We have a security alliance with Taiwan and the Taiwan Relations Act; there is an obligation towards Taiwan as a result of that. So if China read it that way, they were wrong', interview with Hans Binnendijk on 10th July 1998, Washington, D.C.

independence. That would trigger this whole set of events and some in the U.S. who would say to Taiwan, 'OK, you have followed policy that we advised against and we are going to abandon you if you are going to do that' . . . it was a clear signal to Taiwan 'don't do that again' . . . If they [Taiwanese] think they have a blank check from the U.S. for independence they're wrong. That's what the 'three No's' are about. I think the right policy is to protect Taiwan . . . in order to do that, as long as Taiwan doesn't abuse that security relationship. If Taiwan is smart enough not to abuse it, then I think China is going to be deterred from doing anything'.[51]

In Shanghai, on 30 June 1998, Clinton reinforced the communiqués and publicly stated that: 'we don't support independence for Taiwan' and 'we don't believe that Taiwan should be a member of any organisation for which statehood is a requirement' (*The Washington Post*, 25 June 1998). On the other hand, Roy argues that '[w]hile the Taiwanese may feel that they have lost ground as a result of Clinton's China trip, the heart of the policy remains: Washington will still intervene if the PRC moves unilaterally to attempt to incorporate Taiwan by means of military conquest or coercion' (1998: 232).

Given the delicate diplomatic relations between PRC-U.S.-Taiwan, I have developed a scenario, whereby tensions between Taiwan and the PRC may get out of hand and the implications involved. First, Taiwan (by stealth) develops a nuclear deterrent[52] and a system capable of deterring PRC aggression in event of declaring itself 'independent' from Beijing. The PRC (might) shift its strategic relations with Russia, whereby an axis would develop between the two powers. The PRC puts a naval blockage around Taiwan. The PRC warns Taipei that Taiwanese investment and monies in China would be confiscated if Taipei does not back down. China further intimidates Taiwan by firing large numbers of missiles off the coasts of Taiwan. Taiwan warns China that if the intimidation does not stop, it will not be responsible for the use of nuclear weapons! U.S. reassures China that it does not support Taiwanese independence. The U.S. sends stern warning to Taiwan that it does not support Taiwan declaration of independence and would not support Taiwan in an event of military conflict. Taiwan is unmoved. U.S. nevertheless sends an armada to the East Sea. Japan is under heavy pressure from U.S. to support the U.S. armada. China warns Japan and U.S. to stay out of what it believes to be an internal affair. Russia gives full backing to China for an invasion of Taiwan. North Korea views an opportunity in the confusion to initiate an invasion of South Korea. Japan opens its nuclear weapons options . . .!

From the defence data above, the feasibility of the PRC sustaining its military attack on Taiwan would not be credible. The PRC does not have the capabilities to launch a serious and sustained attack against Taiwan. The PLA is deficient in air, sea and amphibious forces. Most of China's submarine boats are based on 1960s Soviet design, which means they are technologically backward,

---

[51] Interview with Hans Binnendijk on 10th July 1998, Washington, D.C.
[52] *The Japan Times* (1999, 30 July) 'Taiwan denies recent missile, A-bomb development program', p. 4.

noisy and costly to maintain. However, if the Taiwanese should declare independence, a civil war, or acts of terrorism on that island may well follow, given the PRC's determination to reclaim that island.

From the PRC's perspective, the U.S. military presence in East Asia is seen from Beijing as a direct obstacle to the reunification of Taiwan. China believes that:

> ... if America is prepared to risk its forces for Kosovar Albanians, what might it be willing to do for democratic, middle-class Taiwanese in the event China tries to assert its long-time claim to Taiwan? Or, in the case of unrest in Tibet, for the West's favourite oppressed minority, the Tibetans? (*Far Eastern Economic Review*, 8 April 1999: 18).

In addition, China argues that if the U.S. brings Taiwan under a missile defence theatre system which the U.S. plans to have with Japan, the U.S. would effectively be resuming the joint military relationship with Taiwan that it dropped as a condition of establishing diplomatic relations with Beijing in the 1970s.

U.S. strategists argue:

> The challenge for Beijing is to accept the U.S. military presence and still feel secure. In similar fashion, for Washington the challenge is to accept Beijing's rising military capabilities while also feeling that it does not seek to exclude it or to marginalise its regional position, while the United States must convince China that it does not seek to contain, or otherwise threaten it (H. Binnendijk and R. Montaperto, 1998: 12).

Taiwan is important to the PRC as a symbolic sign. To the PRC, Taiwan must not be allowed to break away in any circumstance, with a referendum or otherwise. If Taiwan declares independence, China will not only challenge that decision, it will most probably invade that island. The obvious danger here is that Taiwan can turn out to be another version of Sarajevo in the summer of 1914.

The China Challenge: Has the Cycles of Great Powers Finally Broken?[53]

Besides the Taiwanese issue turning into a potential 1914 scenario, I believe that the greatest challenge to liberal-democracy will be the inability to guide the rise of PRC power into the path of supporting international order and stability – that is, to do what Britain failed to do with Germany in the first decades of this century, and what Germany failed to do itself – rather than directly challenging or containing. In the following pages, I attempt to assess the prospect for the PRC's economic development, democratic reform and stability and to argue why 'China',[54] too,

---

[53] This sub-title paraphrases Robert Gilpin (1994) 'The Cycle of Great Powers: Has it Finally Been Broken?' in Geir Lundestad (ed.) *The Fall of Great Powers: Peace, Stability, and Legitimacy* (Oxford: Oxford University Press), pp. 313-30.
[54] That is the PRC, The Republic of China (Taiwan), Mongolia, Hong Kong, and Macau.

could become an extra spoke in the U.S. hegemonic globalisation system.

If militarily the threat from the PRC is minimal, can we speak of the PRC being an economic threat? A cultural threat and/or even a racial threat?[55] Economically, the PRC does not appear to fit the category as a threat. Observers have asserted that as China becomes richer, it will increasingly become dependent on the region and beyond for its economic growth and prosperity. This in turn will reinforce the diplomatic and economic constraints shaping China's regional behaviour. For example, APEC takes 75 percent of China's exports and provides 70 percent of its imports. APEC provides most of China's foreign investment capital, and it is also the most important market for China's food imports. The booming foreign investment has brought with it improved technology and management practices that have raised productivity in manufacturing industries.

In addition, amidst the 1997-1999 financial/economic crisis in East Asia that suggested impending dangers of undermining the global capitalist system, the PRC was determined not to allow the worsening economic situation to spiral out of control. It refrained from devaluing its currency amidst heavy market attacks on its stock markets (the Hong Kong, Shenchen, and Shanghai stock markets fell drastically). The PRC could easily have devalued its currency and played a 'beggar-thy-neighbour' policy against the world (thus, releasing the financial time bomb and initiating widespread panic that could have had serious consequences for the world economy), instead the PRC was prudent not to further strain an already stressed financial/economic situation. During his visit to the People's Republic in June 1998, President Clinton praised the PRC's self-restraint: 'China has steadfastly shouldered its responsibilities to the region and the world in this latest financial crisis, helping to prevent another cycle of dangerous devaluation' (*The Washington Post*, 29 June 1998: A12). On this opportunity to do unforeseen damage (to a scenario similar to the late 1920s and early 1930s global depression), the PRC instead tried to stabilise the situation. In fact, the PRC has been desperately trying to enter international economic regimes and institutions since the 1970s, i.e., World Bank, IMF, APEC, and is desirous to get into the WTO. The contemporary PRC unlike the PRC of Mao is not a system destabiliser; it has desirous to make the system stable when and where its interests are at stake. It has as much at stake to keep the system stable as the United States. I will now attempt to evaluate why China's economic development is desirable to the 'West'.

---

[55] Is the PRC a cultural or a racial threat? This is obviously beyond the scope of this book. But it must be remembered the legacy of European colonialism is still very much evident around the entire world, including China. English and other European languages are dominant throughout the world. Chinese is only spoken mainly in PRC, and small pockets of overseas Chinese communities. European languages on the other hand dominate a vast geographical area of the world. Is China a racial threat? Maybe, considering it has the largest population in the world – but this is too simple an explanation – a la India. The Chinese are predominantly based in PRC and its surrounding peripheries – it has no colonies, and probably does not intend to have colonies, whereas the 'white' race is strategically located all over the world.

The PRC's economic development is desirable to the West to preclude the dangers of an overly weak and internally unstable PRC that could damage the wider region. Washington believes that nurturing Beijing into an economic partner that supports and co-operates with the United States and the international system would be more profitable than to isolate it. Contenders, however, argue that economic engagement helps build the basis for increased PRC political and military power that might eventually be employed in ways detrimental to U.S. interests. This dilemma is epitomised by the Loral Inc. satellite controversy. Although the Loral Inc satellite project was entirely civilian, the civilian technology could easily be transferred into the military arena, in which case the U.S. firm would have provided the PRC with the technical information that improved the reliability of rocket-powered launch vehicles. Financially, it costs several hundred million U.S. dollars to launch a satellite on a U.S. rocket. The PRC offered to do it for up to $25 to $85 million per launch. The problem with the PRC's rockets was that they had a poor performance record. By offering their technical assistance to the PRC's rocket programme, the U.S. firms sought to provide them with access to launch vehicles that were both cheap and reliable. Indirectly, Lorel Inc. had provided the PRC with the technology to improve the civilian counterpart of the intercontinental ballistic missiles. Roy coldly warned, 'in maximising their profit today, these Silicon Valley firms have enhanced China's ability to destroy them in a nuclear strike tomorrow' (1998: 235).

The PRC hard-liners, on the other hand, believe that apart from bringing considerable economic benefits, the economic engagement with the United States and Western countries entails the PRC losing some of its sovereign autonomy to decide its economic welfare and independence and thus ultimately puts the PRC's economic pattern under the control of foreigners. To the hard-liners, engagement has meant accepting dependence on America and other countries with which the PRC's relations are often less than friendly for the supplies and market access for the PRC to maintain its economic development. The hard-liners contend that these countries have and can threaten the use of economic sanctions to shape the PRC's policies. Thence, Beijing has had its financial, legal and other systems subjected to the scrutiny of investigators from U.S. or U.S. supported organisations, who then dictate reforms that the Chinese are required to implement to be eligible for participation in some international economic arrangements (Jing-dong Yuan, 1997). For example, the threat of sanctions because of the PRC's human rights record, property rights, copyright laws, using prisoners as cheap labour, and the contentious wrangling over the conditions for entry into the World Trade Organisation (WTO).

However, if the PRC rulers refused to liberalise their economy and behaved in an autarchic fashion, the impressive economic performance of China would certainly peter out (M. Cox in K. Booth, 1998). Without economic and political liberalisation, the Chinese cannot hope to enjoy the same level of educational and cultural development as Americans, Europeans, or other East Asians. They would instead be viewed as a pariah state, and a state that supports the few rogue states –

which are poor and generally disliked by the rich capitalist countries.

Given that liberal democracies rarely if ever go to war with one another, an effort needs to be made to establish the perception and behaviour of the Chinese people towards the rest of the world, especially towards the United States. At the same time, we need an approach that recognises the needs of America and what it stands for. In the words of Robert Zoellick, former under-secretary of state and deputy chief of staff under the Bush administration, 'We need the wisdom of realpolitik, wedded to the goals of American exceptionalist tradition. . . . If two of the largest economies fail to get along, the effects are likely to be damaging both to one another and to the rest of the world' (1996/97: 15).

The PRC's economic interdependence was not just about economics. Although Deng's reforms, after 1978, were designed only to modernise Chinese agriculture, industry, national defence and technology, they indirectly transformed the way in which Chinese work and think.

The policies of decollectivising of Chinese agriculture, for example, by allowing farmers to control their own land and to dispose of their agricultural surplus in ways they thought fit, permitted the better-off farmers to accumulate land, and hire and fire labour. The second part of the reform was to change the way in which industry was managed. The main objective here was to 'shift to emphasis away from production for production's sake to help shift production more geared for the market' (M. Cox, 1998b: 229). In the third part of the reform, Deng opened China's economic doors to the world market and foreign direct investment. This involved the creation of 'special economic zones' in the eastern coastal provinces (investment is increasingly directed at the interior and western part of China). It legalised foreign direct investment (the greater part of which was to come from Taiwan and the 'overseas' Chinese diaspora). The fourth part of Deng's reform was military modernisation.

Professor Michael Cox notes that 'the implications of these various alterations in China's economic relationship to the capitalist world should not be underestimated' (1998b: 229). In the past, communist China regarded economic association with the capitalist world as unnecessary and ideologically threatening. Economic modernisation brought the country closer to complete integration into the world economy. It began essentially a process of re-developing the sense of 'Trust' amongst Chinese, that was devastated by Mao's tyrannical and brutal rule. It also changed aspects of Chinese society. What has changed has been the scope for individual activities that lie outside the purview of central government control. Chinese urban and rural inhabitants are increasingly having a larger control over their daily lives.[56]

Due to the more 'responsible' reform plans, the PRC's annual per capita income has increased significantly. Famine and other manmade disasters that often ravaged the PRC under Mao's draconian policies are less frequent (certainly in the

---

[56] My observations in China, and my experiences with 'overseas' societies in East Asia (Taiwan, Vietnam, Singapore, Malaysia, Indonesia and Hong Kong), the UK, and North America (U.S. and Canada).

case of famine, the Chinese communists appear to have managed that issue). As the Chinese experienced these 'responsible' economic reforms, the majority of them began to enjoy the benefits.[57]

Different statistics tell different stories about China's living standards. In 1999, the annual per capita income of China stood at between $779 and $3100, depending on how the figures are calculated. Though this hardly makes China a rich country, nevertheless, the statistics are impressive. This economic change has not only been reflected in the material gains itself – it has substantially affected the societal and political behaviour of many Chinese people. In China as in European societies in the 19th century and early 20th century 'economic growth . . . is never limited to the economic sphere of life; it extends also to the social and political' (N. Rosenberg and L.E. Birdzell, 1986). Former U.S. Secretary of Commerce Ron Brown captures this strategy and explained that a commercially based China diplomacy was more sensible and more profitable than harping on human rights. He said:

> Rather than confronting China over human rights, it was better for the United States to compete with other countries and win contracts in China to sell, for example, a power plant that would bring light to the 100 million Chinese who were currently without electric power . . . they could then read at night or watch television and absorb Western ideas and ideals. Withholding trade benefits as a means to try to pressure China over sensitive domestic issues, such as human rights and Tibet, would only reinforce China's suspicion of the West, and rebound to the disadvantage of American companies seeking to do business in the fastest growing economy in the world.[58]

A 'Democratic Peace'?

From the advantages of economic interaction and exchange, can the ideal of liberal democracy become embedded into Chinese society? In the following pages, I analyse the propositions developed in the PRC. The strategies applied by the late Deng Xaio Ping and the current regime of Jiang Zemin appear to indicate that the PRC wants to move out of the dangerous Hobbesian power games of Mao. Despite

---

[57] Obviously, the gap between the have and the have little has increased. This is true in every sense but there were always destitute people in China, whether they are on the increase is debatable. Certainly many in China before the 1978 reforms were in a destitute position in the first place. The living standard during the Mao era had been for most people been below subsistence level. The fact is the general living standard of the ordinary Chinese people, rural and urban has improved. Under Mao's reign, the state got richer whilst the ordinary people got poorer. Since they were poorer, they were seen as more equal.

[58] Ron Brown cited in Gary Klintworth and Murray Mclean (1996) 'China and the United States: Neither Friends nor Enemies' in Stuart Harris and Gary Klintworth (1995) (Eds.) *China as a Great Power: Myths, Realities and Challenges in the Asia-Pacific Region* (Longman: Melbourne), p. 78.

the 'mistaken' American missiles attack on the PRC's embassy in Belgrade in spring 1999, the PRC's Vice-President Hu Jintao stated:

> The Chinese are people who uphold justice and love peace. We are willing, together with the people of other countries across the world, to support each other and strengthen cooperation, and work in concerted efforts for mankind's great cause of peace and development.[59]

Likewise, the Clinton doctrine of engagement and enlargement of democratic peace and prosperity was designed to give the international system a 'breath-of-fresh-air'. This is not to deny that Clinton's view does not face determined opponents. Interest groups inside both the United States and PRC plan precisely to head along the path set forth by Huntington's *Clash of Civilisations* (see also Berstein and Munro, 1997; P. Buchanan, 1998; B. Gertz, 1999). Indeed, the military-industrial-complex in both the United States and PRC are highly interested in preserving the jobs and national military prestige of the armed forces and its related industries – to sustain their influential position inside the decision-making.

What are the options for the United States and its allies to expand the zone of democratic peace and competitive prosperity into the PRC? What are the prospects for Chinese progress into the zone of democratic peace and competitive prosperity? Would including the PRC in the club serve the United States as an extra spoke for expanding democracy and prosperity? Does the U.S. need the PRC as spoke in the hub in the first place? Do other powers really want the PRC to belong to this group? Moreover, do the Chinese want to belong to this group?

Ideally, China under the U.S. hub, as another partner – equivalent to the EU – would increase the chances of expanding the zones of democratic peace and prosperity. It would evolve into a new meaning to world politics. As explained earlier, neo-realists believe 'rising power and an already dominant one are not natural allies' (*Far Eastern Economic Review*, 17 June 1999: 18). On the other hand, as explained in chapter five, if multipolarity is out of the question, and rationally the PRC cannot transform itself into a hegemonic challenger against the United States, what are the alternatives?

One alternative is that the PRC may follow a method of improving education and making the people more affluent – What one might term the 'Japanisation' of China – thus, providing it with a systemic root to organically grow into the international order without risking strategic (open) conflict with the United States and/or other western countries. Using knowledge and economic and technological warriors, instead of using military might. In this sense, it is not territory or possession of geography that matter, it is ideas and the transmitting of ideas and the transformation of other people's perception that matter.[60] Although

---

[59] China's Vice-President Hu Jintao's television speech on U.S.-led NATO attack on Chinese embassy in Belgrade on 9th May 1999, *Beijing Review*, 24 May 1999, p. 7.
[60] The author would like to thank Dr. Randall Germain, formerly of the Department of Politics, University of Newcastle, for his time in discussing this matter.

the Western countries are currently the main supplier and the dominant source of transmitting ideas, the weaknesses of 'Western' culture, especially its encouragement of hedonistic lifestyle, could be opened up and manipulated. However, could China take advantage of this opportunity? These serious questions need deep structural societal evaluation.

Extrapolating from the teaching of Western democracy and philosophy, Western teachers have great expectations that the Chinese, on the expectation that Chinese economic progress can reach similar levels to the Taiwanese, Koreans, and Japanese, could become pluralist democratic capitalists. Many Chinese 'students', do *not* ' . . . dispute the great virtues of democratic institutions . . . *however*, democracy is justified by the human needs that it serves' (J. Gray, 1998: 149). The problem with the United States' expectation of democracy happening in the PRC is that it is measured by a single yardstick – the holding of free and open elections (see Steve Smith, 1999). While democratisation may be one element of reform, it is not the only one, especially in countries lacking the most rudimentary institutions of governance and a society as complex and multi-ethnic as China.

Critics of the American strategy of enlargement and engagement argue that the U.S. is more:

> . . . confident than ever that liberal institutions and ideology are the source of global peace and prosperity . . . driven by a deep-seated impulse to serve as the 'light of the world', preaching its beliefs to the rest of the planet . . . the presumption that states with democratic political systems rarely, if ever, go to war against each other . . . Making the spread of democracy the central principle of American grand strategy represents a step towards convergence between the oft contradictory impetus and national ideals (Roy, 1998: 233).

In addition, critics maintain that when outsiders apply their standards to China and try to introduce new systems quickly or forcefully, what occurs is never quite what was planned. Critics argue that authoritarian rule in China has lasted since the early dynasties of Chinese civilisation, and there has been a long history of violence and suppression, of conformity and enforced collectivised living, of ruler worship and obedience. To introduce democracy could mean opening a Pandora's box.

Chinese decision-makers and some scholars believe that it would be 'unwise' to follow and develop 'Western' style form of governance, and argue that the move towards a pluralistic democracy would bring about uncertainty and instability. Worse, Chinese communists view the U.S. post-Cold War policy as a 'new hegemonism and power politics' that seeks to impose Western values of democracy, Western versions of human rights, and capitalism throughout the world.

Despite the rhetoric, China remains in an embryonic stage of pluralistic democratic government. One of the greatest dangers embracing premature democratic development is aggressive nationalism. Although a '[p]opular movement which toppled the regime could succeed in establishing a democratic government, historically, revolutionary transformations have rarely produced this result. It is far more likely that whatever regime emerged out of such process would be nationalistic and aggressive rather than democratic and progressive' (W.J. Murphy, 1994: 70). Furthermore, the roots of democracy 'might still fail with economic reform' (P.L. Berger, 1986). The scars of Tiananmen have not healed, and will probably not heal. There is no indication that the communists will give up their hold on power without a struggle. Michael Cox opines that: 'There is little doubting the fact that if Beijing was faced with a major threat to its authority, it would not hesitate to use force' (M. Cox, 1998b: 233).

To many Chinese, both in the PRC and overseas, the overriding slogan today is 'make money, not politics'. Attempts to go outside the political system to try to change it can end in death and destruction. A former U.S. ambassador to China, James Lilley asserted: 'the primary concern of the Chinese will be to grow strong, prosperous, and respected in Asia and elsewhere. Their fears will be chaos, fragmentation, and foreign intervention. Democracy will be important but secondary' (J. Lilley, 1998: 20).

The Chinese view of democracy is, however, more as a means than an end. To many Chinese that I have come across in China and those living overseas, democracy is seen more as a measure to tackle government corruption, economic inefficiency and making it more transparent and accountable, than a principled form of self-government. They believe that democracy is good for the long-term, but in the short-term they remain prudent at its development, especially the lack of structure and institutions to maintain democratic stability.[61] To understand the prudence of towards democracy, I will now investigate the historical development of democratic stability and toleration of differences in society.

Historic Development Settings for Democracy

In the 'West' and most developed countries, history has shown that political reform has taken essentially three processes: (1) The establishment of norms governing

---

[61] This myopic approach is even evidenced by the overseas Chinese reluctance towards democracy in other East Asian countries – such as Malaysia, where the Chinese populace accounts for one-third of the population and is alleged to control a large part of the economy. Despite their economic affluence and economic power, they are discriminated against (note also the Jewish people in Europe before World War II) – because they do not have political power and most foolishly many of them do not perceive political power, or a democratic pluralistic system, as a way to help them – the weakness in them having economic power without political power is that the Malays can easily change the law with regard to money control and wealth control – i.e., affirmative action and positive discrimination (see also chapter two). This is the old paradigmatic battle between economic power and political power, with regards to what is more influential, or both on an equal basis or running side by side as liberals would argue. In the case of most developing states, empirical evidence has shown that political power overrides economic power. Whereas in most developed states, both economic and political powers go side by side, for Marxists and economists (and many overseas Chinese) economic power influences political action.

elite politics; (2) the restructuring of basic institutions governing relations among parts of the state, such as the division of power among the government's different branches; and (3) the strengthening of the institutions of political participation. China is in an embryonic stage of developing norms for elite politics, institutions and tolerant political participation.

The challenge to political reform facing post-Deng China is fundamentally different to the stages of democratic development in Western industrial democracies. In the West, the constitutional framework and political institutions conducive to the development of an industrial market economy had been established before economic takeoff. The clear division of power among different parts of the state increased the security of property and enabled the enforcement of contract. Moreover, the West's economic climb proceeded slowly, allowing its political systems time to make institutional adjustments. This is not true for China. Unlike the West, China faced the challenge of restructuring its political institutions and modernising its economy simultaneously. Minxin observed that whilst 'it took the United States 47 years to double its per capita income, it took China only 9; in fact, China has quadrupled its per capita income in the past 18 years. It took the United States 50 years to reduce the share of the labour force engaged in agriculture from 70 percent to 50 percent; China accomplished the same change in 17 years' (Minxin Pei, 1998: 74). However, behind the success lie massive socio-economic dislocation, corruption, a rapid shift in values and beliefs, and mounting pressures on the political system to tackle new social economic problems.[62] What

---

[62] There are major problems in China's internal structure. First, the draconian law of the one child in the early 1980s, with economic aims but not societal or family consideration is beginning to have an unbalance gender effects on the population demography. That truculent policy has produced a society of an artificial generation – where vocabulary terms, such as brother, sister, uncle, and auntie may soon become uncommon in everyday usage. It is an unnatural process, and the unnatural consequences will rip and bring new meaning and direction to the Chinese population, its society and its family.

Second, as China sheds its dinosaur industries for innovative and productive industries and enterprises, the lay-off of state owned industries has created mass unemployment, both urban and rural. The abandonment of state collective benefits for workers and farmers and rural unemployment imposes high cost. (See Philip Segal (1999, 3 June) 'Chinese Layoff Putting Millions on the Streets', *International Herald Tribune*, www.iht.com/IHT/Today/thu/fpage/chicon.2.html. As the rural people believe that cities are wealthier than rural areas and because of the glittering lights, masses from the countryside have shifted into cities. The exoduses of people from the rural areas have created major problems for cities and urban areas, as these areas are unable to cope with the masses. The government has introduced a system of 'passports' to keep rural people from flooding into cities. (The author would like to thank Dr. Barry Gills for pointing this out.) In the liberalisation transition, the urban workers in the state industry are also being downsized, creating labour surplus.

Third, the rapid infrastructural development has created dangerously low quality infrastructure. China, because of its rapid economic development has gone for quantity rather than quality. (In my stay in China, I frequently heard of bridges collapsing and houses collapsing. Roads and pavements, although newly built, already show signs of potholes. In

mechanisms and institutions are needed to cushion the rapid shift? These tensions could pose major problems; without the necessary institutions and regimes the political system in the PRC could be overwhelmed.

Another challenging aspect of political reform in post-Deng China is the restructuring of relations between the state and society and the establishment of institutions of democratic participation. Progress in democratic reform, with the exception of village elections, has been lagging. However, the relations between the government and its people have changed dramatically.[63]

Finally, one of the most fundamental and perhaps desperate forms of government in Mao's PRC was the brutal cycle of power struggles. In these struggles or dynastic conversions, individual and whole groups were either being amalgamated or annihilated. Historically, Chinese power struggles have been vicious. Throughout most of Chinese dynastic political struggles, and also during the Mao era, the struggle for political survival was characterised by ferocity and intrigue. During the Mao era, party leaders even to the highest levels of power in the communist echelon paid a heavy price for being defeated in power struggles.[64] Deng Xiao Ping, who himself suffered from these power struggles, sought to ensure a minimum level of personal security for the ruling elite so that defeat

---

addition, electric cables are dangerously placed. The safety and hygiene standards are poor.)

Fourth, the need for modernity and industrialisation during the Mao and post-Mao era has left many areas in China facing ecological problems, the deforestation and the desertification of areas in Inner Mongolia, the rapid expansion of environmental pollution in cities, the degradation of the ecosystem for the sake of modernisation, and its people artificially tampered with. These issues will involve huge repercussions and repair costs in the future.

Fifth, with economic success, there has been an increase in the power and resources of the prosperous provinces. Guangdong, Fujian, Zheijiang, Shanghai, Shangdong and Jiangsu, for example, have demanded economic autonomy from Beijing. These provinces feel that they should not bear the burden of financing other provinces. With Marxism no longer serving its purpose as a legitimising ideology, the political authorities have turned more towards nationalism to maintaining political authority. Finally, there are demands by minority groups for independence in Xizang (Tibet) and Xinjiang.

[63] The CCP's decline is a leading source of tension in rural areas. (China must have other parties to represent their interests or the interests of the farmers will not be identifiable with the CCP and the urban areas.) CCP's decay in the villages is one source where other internal and external forces must take advantage. It was in the rural areas that the CCP had the greatest support against the KMT and the Japanese. 'In the long run, the CCP's lack of rural support will make it difficult for it to manage democratic reform', and rule the country. If the CCP lose the support of the countryside, the cities are all but lost. If the CCP resists democratic reform and pluralistic system of power sharing, in the long-term there is a real danger of the rural areas rejecting the rules of the towns and cities. Moreover, China as a single political entity is very likely to disintegrate.

[64] In the author's opinion, China and the Chinese people should remind themselves constantly of the ghost of Mao in their transition to democracy and beyond. Just as Oliver Cromwell's ghost is present in the writing of the American constitution and their practice of democracy (see R. Kaplan, 1998, for this view).

would be less dire. In the document 'Some Principles on the Party's Internal Politics' initiated in February 1980, he sought to reduce the pain resulting from the fall of grace. Elite politics in Deng's era had become 'kinder and gentler' (Minxin Pei, 1998: 70). As a sign of setting an example to other 'old' commanders of the long march, Deng himself retired and in turn other Long March cadres also followed his advice.[65]

Conclusion

In conclusion, China, for all the good things said about it, remains a police state controlled by 'a self-perpetuating communist dictatorship, a regime for which lawless coercion remains very much a fundamental tool of politics' (A. Waldron, 1998: 40). It is a regime that continues to abuse human rights – the most prolific being the one child policy,[66] and the crackdown on political/religious dissidents. China despite being 'more interdependent' with its neighbours continues to periodically deploy military strength as a sign of symbolic power and as an instrument to get its way when diplomatic measures fail. There is no evidence that the PRC will not be tempted to use naked force in the future to get its way.

Although China is emerging as a regional dominant power, it is not likely to become a global one for a long time. China recognises the limitation of its political influence and its military capabilities. Since the end of the Mao era and the unsuccessful military campaign against Vietnam in spring 1979, China has moderated or given up on the emphasis of class struggle and military might as a resort to gain pre-eminence (with the exception of Taiwan), and it has given priority to economic development and shrewd diplomatic manoeuvres. Since the adoption of the four modernisation reform programmes and opening up policies, relations between China and the world have significantly improved.

The shape of China's economics is the beginning of a shift away from the attitude of the collective, away from the central state having to provide the basic needs of the people to a neo-individualistic and more orientated to the smaller unit within the family rather than the traditional larger family or clan. Property rights and the legal system are being developed or rediscovered to uphold these rights – Chinese society and people are shifting away from their egalitarian Marxist principles. Believers of Marxist ideology will feel disgusted at the laissez-faire

---

[65] Two of Deng's successors, Zhao Ziyang and Hu Yaobang, fell in power struggles, but the effects of their falls were cushioned. Their personal security and material privileges were protected. Nearly all the losers were eased out of their posts to lessen the impact on the regime's stability. None of the power struggles led to massive internal purges like those under Mao. Rather, the victors co-opted most of the followers of the defeated leaders.

[66] This policy is rarely reported, whilst the 'so-called' human rights issue on political dissidents, although still highly important, is over emphasised by the media and U.S. government. In some cases, there are views that the West remains supportive of the draconian one-child policy.

approach of development. However, as the breadth and scale of change is undermining the very core of the communist dream,[67] the egalitarian way set by Mao and comrades of the Long March is rapidly being painted over.

Without structural changes – i.e., without the proper political system and structure to accommodate the rising economic affluence of its people – the PRC cannot hope to prosper on equal terms with other affluent East Asian states let alone western countries. Without a transparent political system, China's internal struggles will more likely end up in conflict between rival groups of the bourgeois, proletariat, military, and between rural and urban.

It is not a question of whether China remains a one party state or moves towards a more pluralistic political state. What is important is that its government is fair, transparent and accountable to its people, with checks and balances so as not to allow the tyrannical despotism so often seen throughout Chinese history, evident by the draconian rule of Mao, to re-emerge.

Despite China's notable progress in restoring elite norms, establishing legal institutions, and maintaining a new social contract, its leaders have strongly resisted democratic reform. This resistance stems from their fear for China as well as for their own positions, and from knowledge of the party's weakness. Chinese leaders are acutely aware of the present system's fragility. The power and roles of the different parts of the state remain poorly defined and political institutions designed to resolve conflicts remain inadequate or non-existent. Judging from the Soviet experience, the anxiety of the PRC is not unjustified. Gorbachev's political reform strategy was flawed because he opened up politics to democratic participation, before he could implement it, let alone consolidate the constitutional reforms that would establish the institutions to govern democratic participation. Opening up the political process to mass democratic participation is viewed by Chinese leaders as a recipe for chaos. This is even more true in the cases of African states and the breaking up of the Yugoslavian republic, where premature democracy could end up in bloodshed and ethnic cleansing and geopolitical fragmentation. Premature democracy and liberalisation of ideas and religion in China could very easily lead to a similar scenario.

Although there remains a rump of hard-line communist forces in the ranks of the Chinese communist party, the overwhelming majority of Chinese favour some form of compromise with Western ideas, exchanges and open market capitalism. This will not only benefit China as a whole, but will also benefit the international community, as China is seen by the West as becoming more 'responsible' for its actions in the international system.

A hegemonic ambition similar to the scale of the United States is beyond China at present. China's geographic position is limited, and the cultural and image

---

[67] For example, the sons and daughters and grandchildren of most communist cadres are increasingly educated in Western societies and the United States in particular, many of them are more concerned to better their economic position rather than pursuing or continuing the egalitarian/communist ideals of their forefathers. Even the son of President Jiang Zemin was educated in Harvard.

of the 'yellow' skin people are only limited to East Asia — any attempt to expand beyond that region would bring unwanted fear in other countries.[68] The aims to expand its navy can only be limited to the Western Pacific Ocean, going beyond that will bring unease in the U.S., Russia, Japan, India, and Europe. If China decides to become militarily hegemonic without a strong economic base and an educated and affluent people, its collapse would be even more disastrous than the one experienced by the Soviet Union. China needs to play the power game extremely carefully. Regionally, other powers, such as India, Russia, Japan, East Asian republics, and Central Asian republics warily watch China. Historically, none of the powers are 'benign' to the Chinese. Many of them have operated as friends of convenience, rather than natural allies.

The strategic benefits of links between China and America are enormous; China needs America as much as America needs China. According to Brzezinski, 'China should consider America a natural ally for historical as well as political reasons . . . without a Sino-American strategic accommodation as the eastern anchor of America's involvement in Eurasia, America will lack a geostrategy for mainland Asia, which will deprive America of a geostrategy for Eurasia as well' (1997b: 61).

The United States has claimed its interests and values are in parallel with the values and interest of the global society. China needs to learn this important lesson. Universalism and cosmopolitanism is nothing new to Chinese strategy in the centuries past, it is an effective strategy to assimilate friends and others into the central ideology and societal behaviour. Hegemonic globalisation should not be viewed as an entrapment of China, but it is an opportunity for China to exert itself without the fear and dangers of being seen as being overturned by the U.S. and the 'West'. Chinese or 'Eastern' morals and philosophy stand to benefit from entering into the hegemonic globalisation, in view that '[t]he West can teach the East how to get a living, but the East must eventually be asked to show the West how to live'.[69] For China to return to an isolationist stance would mean that rather than controlling the impact or taking the helm of globalisation, China would be pushed by globalisation (or more appropriately modernisation). Rather than being driven, China can become the main driving force!

---

[68] For example, even in the UK where a small Chinese community resides, there are elements in among local inhabitants that feel that the Chinese are set to 'take over the place' with their economic power.
[69] Tehyi Hsieh (1948) *Chinese Epigrams Inside Out and Proverbs*, p. 588, cited in Bernard Stonehouse (1987) *Philips' Illustrated Atlas of the World*, p. 71.

Chapter 9

The European Union:[1] The 'Grand Plan' or Just 'Hanging Together'?

If a free society cannot help the many who are poor, it cannot save the few who are rich.
John F. Kennedy.

Introduction

This chapter is divided into four sections. Section one will give a brief analysis of the history of European integration and American strategy. It investigates the main framework for the relationship and U.S. dominance (especially in NATO), and interrogates the common interests and tensions in and between U.S.-EU relations.

The second section examines the U.S.-EU relationship following the collapse of the Soviet Union. With the Soviet Union no longer in existence and with no perceivable threat to immediate European security, what is the credibility of the U.S.-Western European security framework? Can the traditional idea of the transatlantic alliance still hold? Or are the EU and the U.S. on the threshold of becoming diverging hegemonic blocks, a development that holds the potentiality of an EU challenge to U.S. hegemony? The section assesses, with theory and empirical evidence of whether the EU is a challenger or a system supporter. It traces the attempts of Western European states for preponderance and questions how the changing scenario of the post-Cold War era has affected U.S.-EU relations.

As developed in section one, the third section of this chapter examines the role of NATO in U.S.-Western European security relations. That section argues that NATO, more so than any other international organisation within Europe, gives the U.S. direct influence over the military structure of Western Europe, in the sense that NATO allies continue to operate as spokes within the American wheel. In addition, the section examines the strategy behind NATO expansion and the strategy necessary for that expansion without provoking Russia into Cold War

---

[1] As of writing this book (1999), the EU comprises of Austria (1995), Belgium (1957), Denmark (1973), Finland (1995), France (1957), Germany (1957), Greece (1981), Ireland (1973), Italy (1957), Luxembourg (1957), the Netherlands (1957), Portugal (1986), Spain (1986), Sweden (1995), and the United Kingdom (1973). Those that are likely or able to join in the future, include such as Poland, the Czech Republic, Hungary, Slovenia, and Turkey. Those able, but at present unwilling to join are Switzerland and Norway.

hostility (see also chapter seven on Russia).

The fourth section elaborates on the argument developed in the previous three sections. It analyses how the U.S. and the EU (and others) are initiating (into something of a joint condominium) an agenda to promote the expansion of the 'zone of peace and prosperity'. This set of agenda, thus, invalidates the argument that the EU and the U.S. are going their separate ways. The section shows how they are, in fact, consolidating a bloc to enhance the influence of democracy, liberal free trade policies, promoting 'their' version of human rights and intervening directly into other sovereign states to enhance and uphold this belief. However, this last set of affairs raises serious issues of international law, especially concerning national sovereignty, and questions the 'profitability' (as well as the motives and interests) of military intervention as a means to maximise power and the feasibility of ideals 'expanding democratic peace and prosperity'.

The conclusion of this chapter draws together the arguments developed; it highlights that despite the undeniable tensions in the relationship between the EU and the U.S., the EU remains a supporter of, rather than a competitor to U.S. hegemony.

Section I: U.S. Strategy and European Integration

The desire for and the evolution of European integration, in many respects, stems from the European tragedy of the two world wars and the Cold War that followed. The 'madness' of Hitler (to rejuvenate German power over the continent of Europe) not only ended in utter defeat, it also hammered the final nail in the coffin of other European empires around the world. The end of World War II unleashed a 'new' dawn in world politics. Europe was no longer to be the *foci* of world politics. Instead, it found itself becoming 'provincial' outposts of the United States and the Soviet Union (Hudson, 1968). The divided Europe became a 'stalemate battleground' between communism and capitalism. Eastern Europe followed (or was forced to follow) a centralised Soviet style system dominated by Moscow, whilst Western Europe remained capitalist and was attracted into the orbit of the United States.

With much of Europe and East Asia devastated by World War II, the communist appeals of promises of egalitarianism, community, and freedom from bourgeois class exploitation were highly captivating to the masses. With the appeals of proletarian revolution, the U.S. administration feared that, having beaten three enemies (Nazi Germany, fascist Italy, and Japan), and neutralising two imperial powers (the British and the French), it would be caught off-guard in its victories by the appeals of communism.

The fear of the spread of communism into the vacuum left by the demise of the European empires, prompted the U.S. to make every effort to 'lock' the Western European and East Asian states into what was left of the liberal capitalist world order (T.H. Etzold and J.L. Gaddis, 1978; G. Kennan, 1947; F.G Burwell and I.H. Daalder, 1999). It initiated various economic and political programmes, i.e., the Marshall Plan,[2] to 'rescue' or 'restore' capitalist confidence in the devastated countries. It aimed to 're-invent' and 'rejuvenate' capitalism, by allowing countries in Western Europe and East Asia to 'free-ride' on its security and economic policies, to minimise the appeals of communism. In Europe, the U.S. reassured Europeans (especially France) that to keep West Germany down, it was necessary for them to 'lock' West Germany into a system with them. The U.S. saw that by giving West Germany a sense of being part of a greater community and 'rejoining' that community, the avoidance of the post-World War I scenario would undermine a renaissance of German revanchism and stop West Germany falling into communist influence (T. Judt, 1996).

In addition to these goals, the onset of U.S. policy towards Western Europe was to rely on it to have a coherent agenda and strategy against the perceived threat from the communist movement. Initially, the U.S. believed that Britain, an unbeaten power in World War II, would lead Western Europe, under, perhaps, a joint condominium, with the U.S. to battle against communist forces. Britain however, for historical and imperial reasons had other (greater) agendas (such as the Dominions and Commonwealth) for reconsideration. As such, Britain still viewed itself as one of the three superpowers in the international arena. To act merely as a regional ally or as America's military wing in Europe was not on the agenda for the British policy-makers (G. Lundestad, 1994).

British unwillingness to follow Washington's tactics prompted the U.S. to look elsewhere for support. Washington came to realise that France was more interested in leading European integration. Thereafter, Washington was to rely on France to take the lead in European integration. In 1950, Robert Schuman took the initiative in forming the European Coal and Steel Community (ECSC).[3] The ECSC treaty ensured that France and Germany (Western) co-operated to form an alliance that would make it more difficult for these two countries to go to war with each other. The U.S. welcomed the proposal by stating that it was 'the basis for establishing an entirely new relationship between France and Germany and open a new outlook for Europe'.[4] With Germany and France content in forming such a union, the smaller countries surrounding them were only too willing to follow the

---

[2] 'The Marshall Plan was approved by Congress because it implicitly mandated cooperation among the European powers and the sharing of sensitive national economic data as a precondition for receiving aid. The Plan was thus able to virtually eliminate economic nationalism on the continent, creating an atmosphere of openness and trust among previously competitive European states', Catherine McArdle Kelleher (1998) 'Western Europe: challenges of the post-Cold War era', in Ken Booth (Ed.) (1998) *Statecraft and Security: The Cold and Beyond* (Cambridge: Cambridge University Press), p. 181.

[3] The heavy industries of the two countries were to be locked with each other – iron and coal were thought of as the main engines for war. By locking these industries with each other, both France and Germany reassured each other.

[4] U.S. Department of State, Bulletin, 29 May 1950, 828., cited in Geir Lundestad (1998) *"Empire" by Integration: The United States and European Integration, 1945-1997* (Oxford: Oxford University Press), p. 7.

plan, as it would mean peace for them too – not having to worry about possible routes for invasion by either power.

In these measures, three distinctive coherent and inter-related interests were visible for U.S. to assigning the countries in Western Europe for integration. The first interest for the U.S. in Western European integration was to develop a coherent defence structure that would be co-ordinated under U.S. military structure to 'defend' Western Europe against possible Soviet invasion. The strategy for the U.S. was to create a military outpost in its campaign against communism. NATO was the organisation to entwine Western European insecurity under U.S. security umbrella (M. Hudson, 1968; D. Smith, 1989). Dan Smith commented, 'The commitment to NATO made the U.S. the political and strategic leader in Western Europe' (1989: 78). The second interest for an integrated Western Europe was the commercial and economic stakes involved for American businesses and corporations. Commercially, an integrated economic structure in Western Europe would make it 'easier' for American business to operate without having to deal with numerous hindrances of individual national standards and regulations (K.V. der Pijl, 1984). Thirdly, there was a belief in the U.S. that Western European states could form a governing system similar to the American federal system[5] (see G. Lundestad, 1998).

Although America wanted these ideals – be it strategic, commercial and federal democratic governance – the U.S. did not seek to impose them forcefully on these countries. Jean Monnet, one of the founders of European integration, argued that the American insistence 'is the first time in history that a great power, instead of basing its policy on ruling by dividing, has consistently and resolutely backed the creation of a large community uniting people previously apart' (F. Duchene, 1994: 386). Even when France withdrew from the NATO alliance in 1966, although losing a vital member in that alliance, the U.S. did not draw up plans to invade that country to uphold the alliance.[6] The American strategy in this sense was, according to Geir Lundestad, 'unlike' traditional great powers (1998: 154).

Yet, while the United States supported and tolerated an integrated Western

---

[5] The United States had initially started with 13 republics. Therefore, the United States anticipated that the western European states would also be moulded into a similar system of governance as the United States. Since many western European countries already have similar views of democracy and checks and balances of governance, liberalism, and free trade – the United States' view was not utopian. Geir Lundestad (1998) *"Empire" by Integration: The United States and European Integration, 1945-1997* (Oxford: Oxford University Press).

[6] Note, however, that in the case of the countries in Latin America, any uprising or tendency to lean towards socialism/communism or moving away from the U.S-led orbit system caused direct intervention. For more details see Noam Chomsky (1985) *Turning the Tide: U.S. Intervention in Central America and the Struggle for Peace* (Boston: South End Press); Tom J. Farer (1988) *The Grand Strategy of the United States in Latin America* (Oxford: Transaction Books); William I. Robinson (1996) *Promoting Polyarchy: Globalisation, U.S. Intervention and Hegemony* (Cambridge: Cambridge University Press).

Europe, this was not to be an independent Europe, in the sense of a 'third force',[7] that would challenge U.S. supremacy.[8] The integration of Europe had to be taken into an Atlantic framework as well. Though President Nixon and Henry Kissinger blurred this by arguing for a multipolar system with five areas/regions: the U.S., USSR, EU, Japan and China, this was to operate or resemble European politics in the nineteenth century under the multipolar Concert of Europe. As President Nixon put it in 1971:

> As we look ahead 5 years, 10 years, perhaps it is 15 . . . we see five great economic powers . . . these are the five that will determine the economic future and, because economic power will be the key to other kinds of power, the future of the world in other ways in the last third of this century . . . we face a situation where four other potential economic powers have the capacity [to] challenge us on every front.[9]

However, the 'American' strategy on Western European integration was always to be within the wider global framework, working as a spoke around the American hub (J. Joffe, 1995; 1997; F.G. Burwell and I. Daalder, 1999). Through this framework, the United States would presumably be able to protect its leading role and enlarge and globalise/Americanise the international system (M. Hudson, 1968).

The question that needs careful examination is that with the communist challenge to capitalism no longer in existence, and given that historically, the real power position after World War II was *not* a shift from capitalism to communism (Huntington, 1967: 927-8), in fact, the *real* shift in the international system was that from European domination of the world to American preponderance, would the emerging world order drift into rivalry between the United States and European Union states? Alternatively, how far and how long does the European powers accept that the U.S. should remain the primary player in world affairs? Is the intention of European integration aimed at 'reclaiming' past glories? With European historical record clearly marked over the past five hundred years (see Barraclough, 1978/87; P. Kennedy, 1989; J.M. Roberts, 1976/92; A.G. Frank and B.K. Gills, 1993), serious analysis needs to be open-minded to reveal the intention of European integration. The section below will inquire into these contentious issues.

---

[7] Contrast G. John Ikenberry (1989) 'Rethinking the Origin of American Hegemony', *Political Science Quarterly*, Vol. 104, No. 3, pp. 375-400, where he argues that 'the United States wanted to encourage an independent – a third force – and not to establish an American sphere of influence' in Europe, p. 390.
[8] See also Geir Lundestad (1998) *"Empire" by Integration: The United States and European Integration, 1945-1997* (Oxford: Oxford University Press). Lundestad argues that 'Washington never supported a really independent "third force" in Western Europe. Western Europe was definitely meant to belong within the American "empire"' p. 154.
[9] Richard Nixon (1971, 6 June) 'Remarks to Midwestern News Media Executives Attending a Briefing on Domestic Policy in Kansas City, Missouri', *Public Papers of the Presidents*, pp. 806-7.

Section II: Post-Cold War Relations Between the EU and the USA

In its formation, the EU[10] has achieved a combination of several layers of action and influence. It is sub-national, national, intergovernmental, transnational, and supranational. At the supranational level, the EU is a complex set of institutions that has the potential to provide a powerful voice for member states. At the same time, at the inter-national and national levels, its member states are adjusting their internal differences and initiating a 'powerful framework' under which they can bargain with other countries or groups of countries.

Many scholars have identified this 'power framework' as unlike any other 'federation' of the past. The EU, they claim, is seen as a 'civilian power', a 'new kind of power' (K. Aldred and M. Smith, 1999: 134) that does not have a military command structure that is (often) used to impose rules on members or on others.[11] According to Susan Strange, in this 'realignment' of power structures in international affairs, certainly in the developed and democratic areas of the world, civilian and economic power has increasingly become more influential and has had a more consistent impact on every day events than the traditionally 'hard' powers of military and diplomatic relations (Susan Strange, 1988; 1991). This realignment of power structure has, thus, equipped the European Union countries to adapt and to apply a less coercive stance to achieve objectives in non-hard power politics.

However, the extent to which this 'new' power, especially economic power, can override the traditional military and political power regimes remains contentious and suspect. Certainly, as outlined in chapter two, the operation of economic relations would not be smooth, without a firm and stable military and political framework. In addition, the extent that civilian/economic power can influence events that require traditional military power is still very limited and may even be ineffective. With these recognised weaknesses, the following pages will analyse the measures taken by the EU to overcome this problem.

In 1991, former European Union President Jacques Delors stated:

> ... in the last resort, security means the ability to defend oneself by force of arms. If the community is to contribute to the new world order, it must accept that this presupposes participation, where necessary, in forces which are given the task of ensuring respect for international law, when all other attempts to create a basis of understanding and co-operation between nations have failed (quoted in K. Aldred and M. Smith, 1999: 138).

Delors was arguing, in effect, that in order to play a credible and effective international role, the EU should become more, rather than less, like a traditional superpower, despite the ending of the Cold War (K. Aldred and M. Smith,1999: 138).

---

[10] The systemic process of European integration is well documented elsewhere, it is beyond this book to look into it in detail here.

[11] The EU as of writing this book (1999) is so far militarily disunited, each member continues to have sovereign control over its armed forces.

In its attempts to overcome military weaknesses, analysts have raised the dilemma that as the EU engages on the development of a viable military structure and with the desires to act as an 'international player' in international arenas, there are 'real dangers' that the EU may be set to 'challenge' U.S. pre-eminence. The following section examines the theoretical and empirical suggestions of the EU's rise to 'challenge' U.S. supremacy. It will examine counter-arguments claiming that the EU is far from ready or even involved in a strategy that is evident of challenging U.S. supremacy.

The EU as a Challenger

Before the end of the Cold War, Samuel Huntington argued that the most probable challenge to U.S. hegemony would come from the European Union. He asserted that if the European Union became politically cohesive:

> ... it would have the population, resources, economic wealth, technology and actual and potential military strength to be the pre-eminent power of the 21st Century. Japan, the United States, and the Soviet Union have specialised respectively in investment, consumption, and arms. Europe balances all three ... It is also possible to conceive of a European ideological appeal comparable to the American one. Throughout the world, people line up at the doors of American consulates seeking immigration visas. In Brussels, countries line up at the door of the Community seeking admission. A federation of democratic, wealthy, socially diverse, mixed economy societies would be a powerful force on the world scene. If the next century is not the American century it is most likely to be the European century (1988/89: 93).

Following this Huntington analysis, and given consideration that the EU is to become an area that almost operates under a single currency, is the 21st Century to be another European century? If such is the case, is rivalry inevitable between the United States and its EU allies? What are the evidences for the EU becoming the 'pre-eminent' power in the 21st Century? I have outlined six points which I believe are fundamental to support the book that the EU may become a potential rival to U.S. hegemonic position.

- First, statistically on paper, the EU, with 15 of the most industrialised states in the world, has an aggregate gross domestic product of approximately $8950 billion, against the United States' $8848.4 billion,[12] (see Appendix 1A, 3A-D). The launch of the Euro on 1 January 1999 (to rival the U.S. dollar) and set to operate as the sole currency within the Eurozone from 2001 has at last become

---

[12] *The Economist*, 'The World in 1999', however, the imbalance in the EU's rich (Denmark and Luxembourg: $35,000) and poorer (Greece and Portugal: $11,000) countries gives the EU's average GDP per head of about $24,633, whilst the United States is about $32,495.

a reality. Until this development, the post-1945 international economic system, the dollar has not known a rival international currency.
- Second, the EU's population of 372 million substantially exceeds that of the United States of 272 million. It is a vibrant and highly educated population on technological and educational/research levels. On the basis of knowledge and technological advances, the differences between the EU and U.S. are inconclusive.
- Third, diplomatically, the EU probably has more connections (bearing in mind that the 15 countries all have embassies in most countries around the world – thus, making their collective diplomatic leverage far greater than the United States) than that of the United States.[13] Moreover, because of the age of European imperialism, virtually all (with probably the exception of Luxembourg, Greece, Ireland, and the Scandinavian countries) European Union countries have vested interests or links with their former colonies or dependencies. For example, Britain via the Commonwealth holds together an impressive 53 countries around the world (the organisation has an estimated population of 1.7 billion, making it the second largest (political) international organisation in the world after the United Nations). France also has similar influence in its former colonies, especially in Africa, Southeast Asia, South America, and the Pacific. Germany and Austria have deep interest and influence in Central and Eastern Europe, the Middle East, and Central Asia. Spain and Portugal have a direct heritage link with Central and South America, and even into the southern states of the U.S. The Latin connection has been displayed by the EU's increased interest in negotiating greater co-operation with the Mercosur countries (K. Aldred and M. Smith, 1999: 158-60) (which automatically fuses with or challenges the American backyard). Aldred and Smith observed that the Union has a 'mission' of 'taking up a role in promoting and helping consolidate democracy in Latin America and in promoting social justice and human rights' (1999: 159). This, Aldred and Smith argues, is an implicit criticism of the U.S. for not having been sufficiently proactive itself in helping in the region, and, thus, 'effectively abdicating a measure of leadership responsibility' (1999: 159).[14] Another dispute involving EU resistance to U.S. activities in Latin America was the Helms-Burton Act with regard to Cuba. Finally, others, such as, Belgium, the Netherlands, and Denmark have post-imperialist power influences in various parts of the world – such as in Africa, the Caribbean, Southeast Asia, and the North Atlantic. Anthony Smith observed that as the EU seek to assert a stronger collective identity, 'it is more likely that the challenge to U.S. position will take place *vis-à-vis* the developing world' (1992: 75-6).

---

[13] Quantity however does not necessarily reflect in quality, especially ones that are backed up by coercion.
[14] For good presentation of EU Commission thinking, see the report The European Union and Latin America: the Present Situation and Prospects for Closer Partnership 1996-2000, CABIII/164/95-EN. European Union website – www.europa.eu.int.

- Fourth, in addition to its diplomatic, cultural, and economic projections, the EU currently has two member states, Britain and France, both of whom have permanent membership in the United Nations Security Council. This automatically gives the EU control of 2/5th of the UN Security Council veto power. Britain and France are also nuclear powers. Militarily, the EU, if it decided to integrate defence affairs would (eventually) be a formidable force (see Appendix 1A).
- Fifth, according to liberals and some neo-Gramscians, as the world becomes 'less anarchic' because of greater interdependence, at least in the developed countries, countries are increasingly operating under the regime of 'soft power' (Joseph Nye, 1990). The EU is predominately a civil power. As military forces are diminished in operation and not necessarily the best or viable option to implement peaceful interactions, soft power has been increasingly seen as a vital mechanism to achieve and influence political events and economic outcomes (S. Strange, 1988). Under these circumstances, soft power is an ideal tool to impose EU views in world affairs, especially international regimes and institutions (R. Keohane and J. Nye, 1977; S. Krasner, 1983). This new source of diplomacy would ideally suit the EU power projection.
- Finally, for reasons of cultural prestige, a transition from American hegemony to European hegemony would be less of a drastic cultural transition being from 'west' to 'west' rather than 'west' to 'east'– at least not as humiliating or threatening as it would be if say China, Japan and/or Russia were to take over the mantle of global leadership. Since Europe is the original home of the majority of Americans, America shares many principles in common with most EU countries, for example their values, partaking of the same religions, the idea of pluralistic democratic governance, human rights, and most importantly race (these issues are elaborated in more detail below). On these accounts, the European Union would be ideally placed to re-emerge as hegemonic in the international system, without endangering fundamental U.S. principles and values.

Under such circumstances, U.S. neo-realists argue for cautionary approaches to the likelihood of a challenge from the EU. First, U.S. neo-realists have contended that as the EU becomes more integrated economically and politically, it will pose a direct threat to the United States. They argue that since the EU, as in the case of a rising power, wants its 'place in the sun' or more accurately *wants* to regain its place in the sun again, it inevitably has to override the current hegemonic power, the U.S. They point out that the economic rivalry between the two sides would inevitably lead the EU and U.S. apart (J. Mearsheimer, 1990). They will compete against each other for the sake of their own interests – thus, bringing the international system into a 'balance of power' and a return to 'normalcy' (C. Layne, 1993; 1997). Henry Kissinger argues that, 'in the years ahead, all the traditional Atlantic relationships will change. Europe will not feel the previous need for American protection and will pursue its economic self-interest much more aggressively' (1994: 821). Other commentators have argued that trade conflicts between the major capitalist powers are spilling over into the spheres of politics and security. Echoing these claims, William Pfaff, argued that '[w]hile most West Europeans would only with the greatest reluctance enter into conflict with the United States, issues of industrial domination and strategic sovereignty and survival will compel them to do so' (1998/99: 5).

Second, neo-realists argue that since the EU faces no real formidable external enemy (with communism buried and the Soviet Union defunct) there is no longer any imperative cause for Europe to be under U.S. security framework. In such circumstances and since most European states are not yet fully 'burden sharing', and often very critical of American actions, the United States should withdraw its commitments (e.g. from the NATO alliance) and allow the Europeans to get on with their own business.

Third, neo-realists argue that because many EU countries have a history of imperialism, it would be naïve to anticipate that the EU would become largely pacifistic in the international arena. Neo-realists assert that because international politics is about the distribution of power, it is highly unlikely that the EU would simply allow neighbouring countries to 'catch-up' to a similar level of economic development without reciprocal return. Neo-realists and 'outsiders' have deep reservations about deeper European integration. They question the EU intentions where member states constantly recall of past glories and supremacy. Neo-realists and critics of European power raise two simple questions (analogies): First, do wolves become vegetarians overnight? Second, 'once the European states hunted alone, does the integration of European states mean that they intend to hunt together?'

Fourth, neo-realists emphasise that the economic policies (either intentionally or otherwise) applied by the U.S. before World War II had the indirect effect of bringing about Europe's downfall. With a more vibrant Europe emerging and its interests not connected to those of the U.S., neo-realists claim that it is only inevitable that Europe would challenge the U.S. position. Evidence of this includes the formation of a single European currency and tendencies towards a common political and security union.

Why the EU is Not a Challenger

This section analyses why the EU to date, either by intention or capability, is not challenging U.S. centrality. The suggestions of EU challenge remains non-conclusive. Even if the EU does decide to go down the road of matching America in the global arena, what are the criteria needed for it to be taken seriously as a serious challenger? I have outlined nine points that suggest why the EU is far from ready to challenge the U.S. for the global hegemonic position.

- First, the EU would have to have a combined European military force (it is happening), but they would have to have a military force that is comparable to the United States. However, what would that mean? What would happen to NATO? Would the emergence of the EU as a single entity within the WEU substitute NATO? The emergence of a unified EU defence force would probably mean the EU having to spend hundreds of billions of pounds (or Euros) on command, control, and other sophisticated armoury. They would have to revolutionise the whole force structure of the EU. Is that realistic? Can they do that? Are they going to the electorate and say that? Most unlikely. It is a non-starter. The EU is already spending comparably about the same amount of GDP as the U.S. on defence (see Appendix 1A), to add the burden of upgrading and developing further advances to the military would be enormous.
- Another serious and fundamental problem is national security. Even national economic policies are often kept secret amongst members. What is the likelihood that national security secrets, for example, of Germany will be given to France or Britain, or Britain to France, Spain or anyone else? Very unlikely. National sovereignty is most acute when it comes to national security and national industrial security. Although a constitutional framework (i.e., the creation of a unitary state) would allow for this, however that is speculation and it would be very unlikely. How far would the EU go down the road of 'federation' in terms of centralised power for these 'secrets' to be transparent to partners?
- Since the collapse of the Bretton Woods system of the fixed gold exchange standard, and the liberalisation of finance by the United States (discussed in chapter four) – the, so-called, 'Anglo-Saxon' model in international economics and financial affairs has become even more predominant. Instead of challenging the liberalisation and globalisation of finance and trade, many European countries have followed the U.S. to liberalise their economic infrastructure and trade practices.
- The EU has more to gain from a co-operative strategy than a competitive strategy with the U.S. The European Union, it must be remembered, is an area that is both democratic and prosperous – it is one, along with Japan and the U.S., of three major areas within the zone of democratic peace and prosperity. The EU and the U.S. are vital to each other's central prosperity. It is inconceivable that the European Union or the United States should decide to wage a hegemonic war with one another. For the EU and the U.S. to wage a hegemonic 'cold war' with each other would prove to be disastrous for both. The two spheres are engaged in a more sophisticated political manoeuvre that goes beyond the activity of power politics and traditional domination. The historical reasons for them to co-operate are very clear. Before World War I, prosperous and democratic countries failed to co-operate with each other. This failure became even more evident before the Second World War. Their failure to co-operate and their resort to self-interest led directly to the rise of extremism (e.g., the rise of communism in Russia and fascism/Nazism in Italy,

Spain, and Germany). If current economic prosperity are not maintained between the prosperous and democratic countries, and if co-operation falters, the lessons of the rise of extremism are obvious.
- The neo-realists have misread the scripts of the grand strategy of the United States. The United States has (as argued in the previous chapters) played and is playing its game very carefully indeed. It is well aware of the consequences of the balance of power. Consequently, neo-realists have placed 'too high a value on the balance of power instead of the maximisation of power' (M. Hind, 1996: 6-7; C. McArdle Kelleher in K. Booth, 1998: 182). They have misapprehended the nature of power being played in the emerging world order.
- As outlined in the previous chapters, and touched on in the previous two points, the United States recognises that it is not in its interest to see the European Union aligning with Russia, the PRC, Japan, and/or any other individual state or group as economic or military counter-balancer. European Union countries and/or Japan also realise that there is less benefit to be gained in returning to the balance of power scenario. The EU is developing closer relations with the United States, perhaps even closer than at the time of the Cold War, for example its co-operation with the United States concerning the Iraq, Bosnia, and Kosovo crises. The neo-realists and the promoters of balance of power have misapprehended the current international scenario by arguing that each region has its own (presumably exclusive) sphere of influence. Instead in an era of democracy and prosperity, it is the democratic and prosperous countries that are allying with each other even more closely and they are preparing to expand yet further. I contend that the EU is not a threat, but a reinforcing power and is in fact assisting U.S. hegemony.
- From an 'outsiders' perspective, the major engine driving the EU's continuing attempts to become more 'federal' is a desire to achieve a more prominent role in world affairs. It follows that many Euro-technocrats should want to unify European political, military and diplomatic affairs, so that this may offer the EU a larger voice in international affairs. However, many 'outsiders' believe that this strategy might lead to the consolidation of the 'European civilisation' and the segregation of itself from other civilisations to the South and East. This 'fortress' image of the EU hinders the EU from playing a global role.
- Reinforcing the 'outsider' perspective is the 'insider' perspective. It is often argued that a unified European Union would offer the European Union people greater opportunity to compete in the world. The perception created by Eurocrats is that '[t]o be "European" today means to be nice, gentle, and civilised' (M. Mann, 1993: 126). Yet, there is evidence that Europeans remain racially xenophobic. Many far right groups and parties exist, for instance the Freedom Party of Austria, the Vlaam Blok in Belgium, far right parties in Germany, France, Italy, Spain, Denmark, Sweden, and United Kingdom. They feel unease and are even 'fearful' of incorporating fellow Eastern Europeans into the Union, and this is even before non-white/non-Christian communities can be accepted. The 'race' issues remain serious problems for the European

Union. Although there is no evidence of European Union technocrats being 'racists', and they would probably vehemently attack racist remarks, the domestic politics of many of EU members tells a different story. For example the pro-Nazi Freedom party of Austria attracted the votes of 32% of Austrians, and Le Pen's nationalist party gained systematically more than 10% of the French electorate in local, parliamentary and presidential elections since 1989. Although policy-makers attempt on paper to gloss over 'racism', the 'normal' reality of the grass-root populace may show a different picture. It is not colourful.

On these principles, non-Europeans and even Eastern Europeans will not trust the EU's intentions – the legacy of European colonialism makes it difficult for many developing countries to swallow the fact that the Europeans can be a 'bringer of good' and not planning a cunning plot to re-colonise and oppress them, again. Many victims of colonisation readily remember that 'the leopard does not change its spots'. The EU may say it is a benign power. The intentions are however contestable, for instance the new forms of control are economic influence, resource allocation, and keeping resources to themselves, and/or destroying them deliberately, i.e., the CAP to keep third world imports out.

- Yet, despite the previous two points, the EU is uncertain of its direction and what its agenda really is. It is not engaged in a 'we' and 'them' scenario. The direction of EU is all contested and debated, and the EU is not a unified voice. It has no coherent capabilities (yet) to challenge U.S. centrality. A unified European challenge to U.S. hegemony is not (yet) realistic. There are potentials (same as China) but not yet actuality. In ideological terms, they are perhaps least likely to challenge U.S. position and ideals. In fact, the EU has often acted, according to Susan Strange, more like a 'loyal opposition' to American power. According to Strange, 'it is in our interest that the U.S. does not make mistakes, because the interests are so intertwined that someone has to be objective about what they are doing, because they aren't. It has to be us.'[15]

Having established that the EU is not a challenger to U.S. pre-eminence, the following section examines the need for U.S.-EU relationship. This relationship, especially during the Cold War, was based around a common threat, communism, and to uphold U.S.-EU relations was the security framework built around NATO. With the communist threat no longer feasible, what are the realities of U.S.-EU common relations?

Section III: U.S.-EU-NATO and Russia

It must be noted that 11 out of the 15 members of the EU are NATO members (see Appendix 9A). This gives the U.S. an obligation to defend them. In the U.S.

---

[15] The author is indebted to Dr. B. Gills for pointing this out.

perspective, the maintenance of NATO in Europe has many important strategic goals. First, the United States has a deep interest in maintaining and enlarging NATO to avoid a redivision of Europe into blocs, with the West on one side, Russia and its sphere of influence on the other, and even the possibility of Muslim states aligning with one side or another. Dan Smith observed,

> At the heart of it lies a simple strategic fact: the security policies of European NATO governments are predicated on the continuing U.S. military commitment to NATO and Europe. It is a system of dependent partnership, sought by the Western European governments at its inception, for which they were prepared to make concessions on sovereignty and policy. It was built on their political and economic weakness at the time of NATO foundation, and has survived all their accretions of economic and political strength since. Whatever else has changed, the USA's strategic hegemony has been barely affected (1989: 4-5).

Second, the concern for the instability in the Russia Federation and former Soviet republics (for example the failed coup of August 1991, as well as the Yeltsin-Duma stand-off which followed in Autumn 1993, and the on-going volatile political situation in Russia) are indications that U.S. forces need to remain on the European continent as a guarantee to European security.[16] The delicate situation in that region has made decision-makers in European capitals and Washington apprehensive of a U.S. withdrawal (see also chapter seven on Russia).

Third, the United States' commitment in Europe is seen not only to enhance or sustain its power position; to smaller European countries, keeping U.S. forces in Europe is seen as a security 'mechanism' for keeping French and German ambitions in check, and as a guarantee against potentially erratic military ambitions re-emerging on the continent.

Finally, NATO is an alliance (unlike the EU) that includes Turkey, and not allowing it to move into the Islamic camp, or not allowing Turkish ambitions to forming a Trans-Turkic nation stretching from Turkey to Turkmenistan in Central Asia. NATO has vested interests in keeping Turkey from the temptation of initiating an Islamic alliance or a 'Trans-Turkey' federation in Central Asia. The cases of Bosnia and Kosovo, where the NATO stance supported the weaker Muslim minorities in those regions after diplomatically playing down suggestions of NATO being an organisation that would eventually be used against the Muslim countries in North Africa and the Middle East.

Besides these points, the alliance also provides important advantages for the United States in shaping the post-Cold War system. Brzezinski argues that 'any expansion in the scope of Europe becomes automatically an expansion in the scope of direct U.S. influence' (1997: 59). The Pentagon presented this rationale for NATO expansion in the *Report to the Congress on Enlargement of the North*

---

[16] Institute for National Strategic Studies (1997) *Strategic Assessment, 1997: Flashpoints and Force Structure* (Washington, D.C: National Defense University).

Atlantic Treaty Organisation: Rationale, Benefits, Costs, and Implications.[17] This document argued that the enlargement of NATO is not military, but political. The second reason for NATO expansion was that it aimed to avoid excessive reduction of the armed forces in the post-Cold War environment. Thirdly, the U.S. Defense Department stated that a wider Europe and an enlarged NATO will serve the short-term and longer-term interests of U.S. policy with 'NATO . . . serving as the bedrock of Europe's security integration and the linchpin of its security partnership with the United States' (The White House, 1999, 22 March). To the American decision-makers, a larger Europe will expand the range of American influence without simultaneously creating a Europe so politically integrated that it could challenge the United States on matters of geopolitical importance, particularly in the Middle East.

Yet, the NATO enlargement has required a high degree of political and diplomatic skill, which may have unnecessarily complicated NATO-Russia relations (see chapter seven). Although it antagonised Russia, the NATO expansion was, according to the Pentagon, necessary because it would be unwise to delay NATO enlargement until the EU expands:

> . . . if we accept a point of view on intra-European security, the delay 'would unnecessarily postpone measures that are worthwhile and possible today, and it would diminish America's voice in current efforts to build the security of the Euro-Atlantic region'.[18]

Ambassador Vershbow bluntly stated, 'NATO must continue to enlarge and project stability still further'.[19]

On the other hand, Russia 'views NATO's projected eastward expansion as something unacceptable because such expansion threatens its national security'.[20]

---

[17] U.S. Department of Defense. *Report to the Congress on Enlargement of the North Atlantic Treaty Organisation: Rationale, Benefits, Costs and Implications*. Washington D.C., 24 February 1997. This Report was issued at the same time as that of the State Department report: U.S. Department. *Report to the Congress on Enlargement of the North Atlantic Treaty Organisation: Rationale, Benefits, Costs and Implications*. Washington D.C., 24 February 1997.

[18] U.S. Department of Defense (1997) *Report to the Congress on Enlargement of the North Atlantic Treaty Organisation*, p. 31.

[19] 'Collective defense will remain the Alliance's fundamental task, but we hope the 1999 edition [of the Strategic Concept] will make clear that NATO is not just about defending territory, but defending the common interests of its members. We think the alliance should be the "instrument of choice" for defending those common interests, whenever there is a consensus to act.' U.S. Ambassador to NATO Alexander Vershbow, Speech at the NATO Defense College, 9 November 1998, in Julianne Smith and Martin Butcher (Eds.) (January 1999) 'The New Strategic Concept', *A Risk Reduction Strategy for NATO*, Research Reports, Basic Publications, http://www.basicint.org/natorr1.html. The New Strategic Concept, obtained on 17 August 1999.

[20] National Security Concept of the Russian Federation, *Novosti Review*, 9 January 1998, p. 2: obtained from http://www.ria-novosti.com/products/dr/1998/01/09-02-1.htm.

The most difficult diplomatic task in NATO expansion was to cajole Russia into acquiescence. NATO's expansion priority was to minimise Russia's sentiments over feeling that it is being outflanked and isolated.

In cajoling the Russians into believing they had a part to play in the NATO-Russia Founding Act[21] and the Permanent Joint Council, America and NATO allies were able to expand the alliance. However, the agreement does not provide the Russian Federation any role in the North Atlantic Council, despite the Partnership for Peace with Russia, or NATO decision-making[22] and certainly does not give Russia a veto on NATO actions. To soften Russian concerns, the International Monetary Fund and World Bank grants and structural loans to Russia were relaxed and made more easily accessible to Russia. This technique was used just before NATO actions against the Serbs in the Yugoslav crisis in spring 1999. Billions of extra IMF dollars were rushed to Russia, to keep Russia's opposition to NATO's action in Kosovo to a minimum.

However, this type of strategy can only raise great concern regarding the strategy of the U.S. and its NATO allies. As discussed in the Russian chapter, for how long can the prosperous countries continue to support Russia, without tackling the heart of the problem – i.e., the establishment of a stable, prosperous and democratic Russia that has similar ideals to the western countries? The western countries continue to be wary of Russian armament, and the feeding of IMF and World Bank funds to Russia that only go to the rich and powerful is not going to alleviate the problems of the common Russian people. Without Russian ideals similar to the countries in the zones of peace and prosperity, how long can NATO and America keep telling the Russians that NATO is not a threat? To feed Russia with billion of dollars that does not change its civil society and develop a strong democratic base is not only a lost opportunity for the prosperous and democratic countries, but would help the Russian military establishment and actions in Chechnya, without helping its people.

Section IV: Joint Condominium?

In this final section of the chapter, I will draw out the implications of the above three sections for EU/U.S. relations. This entails an examination of the strategies and relations that have developed between the EU and the U.S./NATO in their attempts to become more cohesive of a 'joint condominium' in their approach to international political, economic, and security affairs. As argued earlier, scholars and politicians have become increasingly concerned about how to reconcile divergences in the U.S. and EU perspectives of political/economic affairs. As

---

[21] The White House Fact Sheet (15 May 1997) NATO-Russia Founding Act http://www.nato.int/usa/policy/d970515a.html.
[22] Resolution of Ratification to Treaty Document No. 105-36, Protocols to the North Atlantic Treaty of 1949 on the Accession of Poland, Hungary and the Czech Republic, 30 April 1998.

argued earlier, many scholars fear that unless the divergences are overcome, the two areas could find themselves developing on separate tracks, and that would create new barriers to trade and eventually division on security issues.

Here, I argue that relations between governments of democracies, with checks and balances, and beliefs in liberal toleration, the level differences will remain relatively minor.[23] There is no doubt of the continuous bickering, but that is natural for liberal democracy. Capitalism and democracy encourages rivalry and competition. Without these bickerings and competition, we might as well live under authoritarian, totalitarian, or fundamentalistic regimes. Unfortunately, the popular press has often exaggerated the bickering into nationalist conflicts, seldom concerning itself with the positive issues of U.S.-EU relations and economic interests. Nevertheless, these positive issues are more important than the negative. Furthermore, we must remember that it is not fundamental principles and values that are being contested; it is the division of market share and the amount of profits to be made. Henry Nau argues:

> I am not talking about war, but an intense economic and industrial competition that the United States will not necessarily win – neither side is likely to 'win'– whose political consequences will bring an end to the American-dominated international system that has existed since the close of the Cold War.[24]

Concerning security issues, there are no significant difficulties in defining the nature of EU and U.S. relations. As argued in the previous chapters, the U.S. government and its elite do not intend to see the emergence of a hostile power or a hostile regional coalition in the EU. It has been stated plainly that its aim is, 'Preventing the emergence of hostile regional coalitions or hegemons',[25] either in Western Europe or elsewhere. Former U.S. National Security Advisor Zbigniew Brzezinski has argued a proposed U.S. policy:

> To put it in a terminology that hearkens back to the more brutal age of ancient empires, the three imperatives of imperial geostrategy are to prevent collusion and maintain security dependence among the vassals, to keep the tributaries pliant and protected, and to keep the barbarians from coming together (1997: 40).

On the other hand, since the end of the Cold War, the U.S. has argued that the European alliance should constitute a distinctive pillar. For example, it has encouraged the European Union's efforts on a Common Foreign Security Policy (CFSP) and West European Union (WEU) to become more cohesive (D.C. Gompert and F.S. Larrabee, 1998), to the point where the EU should be

---

[23] *The Washington Post* (1998, 27 May) 'Disputes Among Allies', in the *International Herald Tribune*, obtained from http://www.iht.com/iht/today/wed/ed/edtrade.html.
[24] Interview with Henry Nau, 16 July 1998.
[25] William S. Cohen, Secretary of Defense, (1999). *Annual Report to the President and the Congress*' obtained from http://www.dtic.mil/execsec/adr1999.html.

responsible for its own 'backyard'. Yet, the central interest of U.S. strategy is to avoid the erosion of NATO's central role in the European security theatre. Former Secretary of State Warren Christopher stated that it was in the interest of the United States

> ... to help build an integrated, peaceful, and democratic Europe that works in harmony with the United States. If that can be achieved, for the first time in history the tranquillity of Europe will not be endangered by hostile rivalries and threats of armed conflict across fortified borders. ... The heart of U.S-European policy is the strengthening of NATO (1998: 547).

So what is the intention of the United States? On the one hand, it wishes to see a more integrated Europe that can become an 'equal' pillar in power sharing, yet on the other hand, elements in the U.S. are wary of the prospect of a hostile integrated Europe forming a rival to American interests.

From these conflicting interests, the analysis, here, is to examine the nature of the alliance and the nature of that pillar. Assuming that the United States wants the EU to become an equal partner with it, the central question that needs to be answered is: does the European Union have the capability and will to act as an equal pillar?

The United States may argue that it wants Europe to share its burden as an equal pillar. However, the term 'equal' in regard to the United States and the EU is suspect. European economic strength (as argued above) could be an equal to that of the U.S., however, its military capabilities are far from being 'equal' (given the multiple command of national forces). In addition, the United States often expects the Western Europeans to 'provide moral and practical support to United States' global policy: in the event of a major regional conflict, the U.S. will look to its close Western European allies for a collective, multilateral effort' (D. Garcia, 1999). Yet, when Europe decides to act unilaterally, the U.S. insists that, 'since European and American objectives were identical, European autonomy was either unnecessary or dangerous' (H. Kissinger, 1994: 823), and the U.S. warned that if Western Europe did not assist the U.S., Washington would act unilaterally (P. Tyler, *The New York Times*, 1992, 8 March: 1, 14).

Unsurprisingly, Europeans complain that the U.S. finds it difficult to share power. To the U.S. this would mean multilateralism, thence limiting its capacity and power. The United States may suggest that it is a pillar of equals, but to Europeans, that partnership is always going to be under U.S. preponderance. Dan Smith (1989: 95) observed:

> For if the U.S. wishes to defend Western Europe against perceived threats, it is not simply out of altruism. It is above all defending its interests in Western Europe. Its regional role is part of its world role. Thus, in the end, the burden-sharing argument is not about getting Western Europeans to pay for their own defence, but about having them contribute to the costs of the USA continuing to be a superpower.

From the European (particularly French) perspective, the United States would prefer to have the European Union as a subject rather than a partner in the power sharing posture (for counter argument, see D.C. Gompert and F.S. Larrabee, 1998). Many European allies have come to the view that the U.S. may use NATO and its European allies as a tool for global engrandisement (D. Smith, 1989: 39). For instance, some EU member states believe that the United States' idea of 'responsibility sharing' is not only burden sharing but also alliance support, foreign aid, peacekeeping and anti-proliferation measures. Wallace and Zeilonka regard such policies by the U.S. as 'an ongoing and direct leadership role for the United States in European security affairs' while demanding that 'the responsibility and financial burden of defending the democracies of Europe . . . be more equitably shared' (1998: 71). Again Wallace and Zeilonka argue that, '[t]he United States calls for greater collective European action but insists on American approval before any joint European initiative, especially in security matters' (1998: 76). Moreover, U.S.-EU relations have often shifted from geopolitical concerns to geoeconomic approaches, this is especially true in the case for the United States, where it has used its military commitment policy in Europe as a bargaining tool in difficult economic negotiation situations.

Bearing this in mind, it is unsurprising that Europeans, especially France, have wanted to stem U.S. hegemonism. At the Amsterdam summit in 1997, for example, France and Germany, supported by Spain, Italy, Belgium, Luxembourg and Greece put forward an agenda to merge the EU and the WEU because they believed such a merger would give the EU more leverage against U.S. blackmail power in its geopolitical and geoeconomic negotiations. Britain, being a traditional Atlanticist power, rejected it because it would open a gap in the transatlantic relations with the United States and the position of NATO. Neutral countries, such as Ireland, unsure of the nature of a merger and of whether it would mean losing their neutrality position, followed British stance in rejecting such an outcome.

American hawks believe that the merger of the EU and the WEU without U.S. participation may eventually pose a threat to the United States militarily. Washington is particularly concerned that the exclusion of the United States from military alliances in Europe such as the Franco-German Corp would mean a possible counter-balance to U.S. hegemony. U.S. hawks have thus called for a wider and weaker European Union (EU), whilst diplomatically the U.S. administration insists on 'avoiding the renationalisation of European security policies' (W. Cohen, 1999).

To alleviate potential disagreements, at the Edinburgh meeting of the North Atlantic Assembly on 13 November 1998, UK Prime Minister Tony Blair announced:

> Europe needs a genuine military operational capability – not least forces able to react quickly and work together effectively – and genuine political will. Without these, we will always be talking about an empty shell.[26]

---

[26] Speech by UK Prime Minister Tony Blair to the North Atlantic Assembly, International

The UK, instead of being antagonistic to other EU policies of deepening was proposing the formation of a European defence force. The British plan was to allow neutral EU members to opt out of mutual defence forces, whilst clearing the way for those that want tighter co-operation on defence issues to proceed. The U.S. reaction to this proposal was quite different to its reaction to the French/German proposal to merge the EU and the WEU. To the U.S, it would give America a stronger voice in EU defence policy, especially via NATO. U.S. Secretary of State Albright expressed this clearly when she told NATO ministers in December 1998 that the U.S. and the EU should work together to:

> ... develop a European Security and Defense Identity, or ESDI, within the Alliance, which the United States has strongly endorsed. We enthusiastically support any such measures that enhance European capabilities. The United States welcomes a more capable European partner, with modern, flexible military forces capable of putting out fires in Europe's own back yard and working through the Alliance to defend our common interests. The key to a successful initiative is to focus on practical military capabilities. Any initiative must avoid pre-empting Alliance decision-making by de-linking ESDI from NATO, avoid duplicating existing efforts, and avoid discriminating against non-EU members (quoted in J. Smith and M. Butcher, 1999, January).

To the U.S., the role for the EDSI would be to act as a support for U.S. initiatives, or on occasions where the U.S. wished action to be taken, but not to participate itself. To France, fearing that it might be out-manoeuvred by Anglo-American strategy, and even have to bear the brunt of American 'adventurism', such a prospect has become anathema.

However, there is ample evidence of closer co-operation between the EU and the U.S. on security issues. For example, in the aftermath of the Bosnian crisis and the Kosovo crisis, the EU and the U.S. set themselves a clearer and more cohesive agenda for the challenges that they assume they may face in the emerging world order. They have formulated a new alliance posture to sustain the areas of peace and prosperity, and enlarge and engage into the areas surrounding it. At the EU-U.S. summit in June 1999, the European Union and the United States affirmed:

> [the] commitment to a full and equal partnership ... Together we [the EU and U.S.] are a powerful force to meet the challenges we face: fragility in regions important to both of us, new transnational threats to our common security, and the complexity of ensuring that democracy and free markets improve tangibly the lives of people in a rapidly globalising world.[27]

Conference Centre, Edinburgh, 13 November 1998, quoted in Julianne Smith and Martin Butcher (Eds.) (January 1999) 'Document on European Security and Defense Identity (ESDI)' *A Risk Reduction Strategy for NATO*, Research Reports, BASIC Publications. http://www.basicint.org/natorr6.h...urity and Defense Identity (ESDI), obtained on 17 August 1999.

[27] The United States Mission to the European Union, Brussels, Belgium. 'U.S.-EU Summit

In that summit the EU and U.S. aimed to:

- strengthen further [U.S-EU] . . . joint capacity to prevent or deal with regional crisis;
- work to extend the benefits of peace, stability, and democracy;
- expand the range of . . . joint initiatives to combat transnational threats that are of direct concern to our citizens;
- promote prosperity, development, and free-market economies in a rapidly changing world;
- improve [the] . . . ability to develop early warning of potential disputes between us and more effective ways to handle these differences, and
- bolster the essential human dimension of our partnership, and strengthen the bonds between our people and societies.[28]

This type of agenda raises a serious final question: is the United States and the EU supported by most other OECD members on the creation of joint condominium to govern the world or are they at the onset to creating the scenario of the West versus the Rest?

The origins of these intentions were proposed in 1995, but were only becoming explicit in 1997. Initially, the U.S. and the EU had laid out an ambitious and comprehensive agenda for providing a framework for promoting peace and prosperity across the north Atlantic area. That framework was entitled the New Transatlantic Agenda (NTA).[29] Although the NTA aimed to reduce economic barriers, supporting and promoting multilateral trading systems, and to promote co-operation between the U.S. and EU on fighting crime and narcotics, and improving health and the environment, the most interesting and controversial proposal was the initiation of a U.S.-EU alliance for co-operation in tackling global challenges.[30]

It is interesting and certainly gives hints that the NTA may, in fact, be used as a mechanism to separate the 'core Western civilisation' from the rest. Is the Huntington thesis (1993b; 1996) being interpreted into the New Transatlantic Agenda? As argued earlier, hawks in the west have found it harder to define the direction of their policies. The hawks argue that since the allies face no formidable external enemy (with Russia being too weak, the Muslim states of the Middle East and North Africa too divided, and China too far away), their common interest was no longer there, thus, it would mean them having to define their own interests. Such a scenario, they stressed, would be of no benefit to 'Western Civilisation'. To gel and sustain the 'Western Civilisation', there needs to be an enemy, and if there is no enemy – an enemy needs to be created (S. Huntington, 1993b; 1996).

Declaration', obtained from http://www.useu.be/summit/declar0699.html.
[28] Ibid.
[29] The Alliance's Strategic Concept, agreed by the Heads of State and Government participating in the meeting of the North Atlantic Council in Rome on 7-8 November 1991, Paragraph 16, available on the web: http://www.nato.int/docu/comm/c911107a.htm.
[30] The New Transatlantic Agenda: Update (1997, 4 February) Bureau of European and Canadian Affairs, U.S. Department of State, Washington D.C. obtained from http://www.state.gov/www/regions/eur/eu/transatagnd.html.

Thence, the maxim is to focus on the enemy, however defined: and subsume your own disunity.

However, unlike Huntington's idea of segregation and consolidation (building walls to keep the barbarians out), the New Transatlantic Agenda sets out to 'expand U.S.-EU cooperation on promoting peace and democracy, expanding trade, addressing global challenges and building bridges . . .'.[31] The NTA has, thus, been a tool for the U.S. in its hegemonic globalisation quest.

That quest has been reinforced by the New Strategic Concept,[32] which would not only safeguard the freedom and security of its members as in the traditional NATO guidelines, but it emphasised:

> . . . risks and instability around the Euro-Atlantic area and regional crisis at the periphery of the Alliance, from economic, political and social difficulties to ethnic rivalries, territorial disputes, abuse of human rights and dissolution of states that can lead to local and regional instability.[33]

The New Concept aims not only to minimise the instability or threat to the EU-NATO area, but it has argued that the EU and the NATO must take steps to prevent countries in the zone of turmoil from creeping into the core (see M. Singer and A. Wildavsky, 1993). Following the events in Bosnia and before the war in Kosovo, U.S. Ambassador to NATO Alexander Vershbow remarked to the NATO Defence College:

> A serious threat to stability in the Euro-Atlantic area demands that NATO demonstrate the highest degree of cohesion and transatlantic solidarity. When confronted with instability and external armed forces, political will is not enough if Allied military forces are not there to back it up. Threats to the Alliance are most likely to emanate from outside NATO territory. This bears out the strategic rationale for enlargement – increasing the secure space in Europe and extending stability still

---

[31] U.S. Department of State, Bureau of European and Canadian Affairs, Washington D.C., 4 February 1997 'The New Transatlantic Agenda: Update.', obtained from http://www.state.gov/www/regions/eur/eu/transatagnd.html.

[32] The 1999 NATO Washington Summit, as well as accepting three new member states (Czech Republic, Hungary, and Poland) into the organisation, reaffirmed the New Strategic Concept.
The New Strategic Concept aims:
– to provide an indispensable foundation of security in Europe, based on the growth of democratic institutions and commitments to the peaceful resolutions of disputes.
– to serve in accordance with Article IV as a transatlantic forum for Allied consultations.
– to deter and defend against any threat of aggression against the territory of any NATO member states.
– to preserve the military balance within Europe.
See also Julianne Smith and Martin Butcher (Eds.) (January 1999) 'The New Strategic Concept' in A Risk Reduction Strategy for NATO (BASIC Publications), obtained from http://www.basicint.org/natorr1.html.

[33] Ibid.

bears out the strategic rationale for enlargement – increasing the secure space in Europe and extending stability still further beyond NATO borders. While a UN Security Council Resolution is often desirable basis for military intervention, NATO can and will act without such a resolution if there is a consensus among its members.

- NATO must prepare, both politically and militarily, to act out of area. Most crises will not likely occur on NATO territory; NATO must be equipped to go to the crisis.
- NATO must continue to be the vanguard of our efforts to promote Western values of freedom, democracy, human rights, the rule of law across the continent.
- NATO must remain the cornerstone of Allies' efforts to ensure security in the Euro-Atlantic area. The OSCE, EU, and UN will all have active roles to play, but they will be hard-pressed to act effectively in the security field without NATO'.[34]

The policy commitment to 'act out of area' and prepare 'without UN resolution' is most evident in U.S./EU/NATO action in Kosovo during spring 1999. In his 1999 annual report to the U.S. president and U.S. congress, U.S. Secretary of Defense William Cohen states:

> U.S. defense efforts in Europe are aimed at achieving a peaceful, stable region where an enlarged NATO, through U.S. leadership, remains the pre-eminent security organisation for promoting stability and security . . . [The U.S.] seeks to move the alliance away from a static forward defense posture toward more capable and mobile reaction forces that can project power, including crisis management operations.

This expansion of NATO's role to humanitarian intervention was endorsed by Kofi Annan, the UN Secretary General:

> State sovereignty, in its most basic sense, is being redefined by the forces of globalisation and international cooperation . . . The state is now widely understood to be the servant of its people, and not vice versa. At the same time individual sovereignty – and by this I mean the human rights and fundamental freedoms of each and every individual as enshrined in our Charter – has been enhanced by a renewed consciousness of the right of every individual to control his or her own destiny (quoted in F. Ching, 1999, 21 October: 40).

The issue of legal authority for such humanitarian intervention goes to the heart of global security in the next century. The impression given by U.S. officials is that,

---

[34] 'Collective defense will remain the Alliance's fundamental task, but we hope the 1999 edition [of the Strategic Concept] will make clear that NATO is not just about defending territory, but defending the common interests of its members. We think the alliance should be the "instrument of choice" for defending those common interests, whenever there is a consensus to act.' U.S. Ambassador to NATO Alexander Vershbow, Speech at the NATO Defense College, 9 November 1998, in Julianne Smith and Martin Butcher (Eds.) (January 1999) 'The New Strategic Concept', *A Risk Reduction Strategy for NATO*, Research Reports, Basic Publications, http://www.basicint.org/natorr1.html. The New Strategic Concept, obtained on 17 August 1999.

if the UN Security Council failed to endorse an effective act of humanitarian intervention, it can and should be ignored – a doctrine that was not endorsed during the Cold War. In this respect, it seems that the United States is seeking to free itself from UN authority in pursuit of its interests, by using NATO to replace the UN as the legitimate military organisation. Mr. Versbow made this shift in NATO commitments and objectives quite explicit:

> Our shared values – freedom, democracy, the rule of law, respect of human rights – are themselves every bit as much worth defending as is our territory. And second, that sometimes force can only be stopped by force. This is where the role of NATO comes in. NATO is no longer geared toward the threat of a massive ground-force invasion of Western Europe ... [NATO] needed to meet the full spectrum of threats that continue to exist in the new security environment ... [NATO's] mission was to stop the scourge of ethnic cleansing and to make clear that genocide, and the politics of hatred and conquest are not acceptable to the modern world.[35]

Although 'righteous' in policy, politics is simply never seen as black and white, the projection of power re-alignment raised serious issues concerning international law of sovereignty and non-intervention. The UN Charter Article 18 states:

> No State or group of States has the right to intervene, directly or indirectly, for any reason whatever, in the internal or external affairs of any other State. The foregoing principle prohibits not only armed force but also any other form of interference or attempted threat against the personality of the State or against its political, economic and cultural elements (cited in T.J. Farer, 1988: 26).

NATO members may regard it as an enlightened humanitarian policy to tackle the problems of human rights abuses; others have expressed it as a new form of colonialism. This concourse between the EU and the U.S. has left many in North Africa, the Middle East, Central Asia, Russia and others, feeling that such measures are deliberately designed and has caused great concern. Certainly, following the events in Kosovo, many countries, such as Russia, China, and others have complained about the U.S-EU-NATO actions concerning the position of national sovereignty.

Although the NATO alliance serves as a structure for stability and peace, the utilisation of force by this organisation, where other means would be 'appropriate' remains contentious. The utilisation of military power in the Yugoslav crises, for example, remains debatable as to its effectiveness in an area where other power resources and capabilities may have been more effective (that is to help that area and people live in peace and prosperity rather than to feed the military organisations (NATO and others)). Instead of relying on guns and bombs,

---

[35] Speech delivered by Ambassador Alexander Vershbow, U.S. Permanent Representative. 'Shared values as much worth defending as territory', Marshall Center Graduation Ceremony, Germany, 30 July 1999, obtained from
http://www.nato.int/usa/ambassador/s990730a.htm.

it would certainly achieve its 'humanitarian' objectives *more* effectively by organically ingrowing into the areas by economic, political, cultural, and other soft power methods, than to rely solely on military means.

Metaphorically speaking, the U.S. and EU with NATO can use military power to smash the 'rock', but by smashing the rock, many small pieces will be shattered. Moreover, sometimes those shattered pieces have fallen into such extremism that it may be impossible to recruit these countries to the zone of peace and prosperity as the primary objective. On the other hand, by using the soft power means, the U.S. and EU can gain their objective *more* effectively by influencing the alternating of institutions via groups and parties to change regimes, without having to rebuild the 'shattered' pieces. In addition, as a result of the intensification of the crisis/war in Kosovo, many refugees have tried to seek refuge in EU and other Western countries, where their welcome in these countries have been 'mixed'. Portrayal of the ethnic 'Albanians' as near criminals are very different to the pictures that were 'created' by the media during the beginning of the campaign. This raises the real intention of the EU and NATO, after the bombardment. NATO defence procurements may have benefited from the conflict, however it leaves a serious question on the real intent of the conflict and the interests that are involved in creating images of conflicts.

For the U.S. and EU nations, the utilisation of militarily means in affairs that could be settled by 'soft power' is a *waste* of resources and a *wrong* strategy. From this perspective, the Kosovo intervention in 1999 was premature and a miscalculated strategy carried out against a small power. The U.S., NATO, and EU chose the wrong options. The Yugoslav republic might have made concessions to the countries of NATO alliance had it had a better opportunity for economic growth. The military offensive helped to germinate unease at the United States and NATO's desire to intervene 'anywhere' or in its near borders without fully recognising the complexities of internal history and social struggles of these countries.

In addition, the strategic implication of the U.S.-EU-NATO Kosovo intervention, by NATO's circumvention of the UN Security Council, 'makes a mockery' of the legitimacy of the UN agreement on respect for sovereignty and non-interference in the internal affairs of other states (S. Chesterman and M. Byers, 1999: 27-30). According to Chesterman and Byers, '[a]s result of the conflict the UN has become increasingly marginalised . . . the veto is effectively dead. We have lost the normative safety-valve, which, by denying legitimacy to an untold number of interventions' (1999: 30). Not only are the major powers, such as China and Russia, concerned about the U.S. abusing its hegemonic position, but so are many other multi-ethnic states around the world. These countries are wary at the prospect that the United States and allies may send military assistance to insurgent groups hoping for independence. In their perception, the United States is the only country capable of deploying mass military forces over great distances, and Washington's willingness to intervene in Kosovo (without considering the international legality) because of 'humanitarian' principles, rather than calculated geostrategic interests, leaves open some serious questions for these countries. With restive minority populations of their own, Beijing, Moscow, and New Delhi now share a common interest in undermining the precedent for intervention set in Kosovo.

Conclusion

The western European landscape has, perhaps, witnessed the most bloodshed in modern history (discounting the conflicts in East Asia and Russia). The integration of Western Europe promises to forestall future wars between the major western European powers — notably between France, Britain, and Germany. The plans of Jean Monnet and Robert Schumann to today's proponents of the EU was/is clear: 'if Europe is to recover the relative importance in the world it possessed around 1900, it must avoid wars among its members, harmonise economic practices, and evolve common policies, including foreign and defence policies' (P. Kennedy, 1993: 257). The association of western European powers had an interest in rebuilding itself from the ashes.

Although with different interests, the United States wanted Western Europe to be relatively economically stable and prosperous so as not to fall prey to communist ideology, and to serve as a luxurious market for U.S. goods and services. The aim in Western Europe, on the other hand, was to rejuvenate its own position in world politics, and not to simply serve American interests. However, since Western Europe cannot regain its imperial glories, without raising serious implications for the rest of the world, there is a perception that it may aim to 'isolate' itself from the rest of the world — in the feeling that it had found a 'utopia' in co-operation, where centuries of conflict have failed, in an area that has finally succeeded in founding 'an area of prosperity and democratic peace' without a bloody power struggle.

In this process, the European Union faces two fundamental dilemmas. First, Europe, through its 'fortress', can go it alone. Alternatively, it can share condominium with the American ambition of hegemonic globalisation. Which of these alternatives it chooses, will depend on how effectively each will be to tackle the EU's paramount concerns — to reduce unemployment and public debt; to stimulate economic growth and prosperity without increasing taxes; to maintain social services and pensions; and to stimulate economic prosperity for peripheral areas, to prevent them from sliding into turmoil.

Under the guise of hegemonic globalisation, the logic is for the EU to expand. It is not only in the interest of the U.S., but the EU also has vested interests in promoting stability and democracy to the countries in Eastern Europe. Douglas Johnston has argued '[t]hese places may be strategic backwaters, but the longer the world's wealthy suburbs ignore its deteriorating "slums", the more the slum dwellers themselves will be tempted to look for other neighbourhoods' (D. Johnston, 1996: 28). It is up to the EU, whether its interests lay in the promotion, extension, and consolidation of democracy and liberal free trade to these countries, or to have interests that feed on instability and possibly violence.

For the United States, the central interest and puzzle during the Cold War was to contain and stem the rise of communism, in that the U.S. developed a series of networks and alliances and succeeded. Western Europe (with the EU integration and NATO) was perhaps the most important piece, besides of course the North American continent and the U.S., in the U.S. grand plan for global hegemony and the battle with communism. However, many U.S. persons believed that the establishment of these organisations was not out of self-interest, but to 'help' Europe from falling into the Soviet sphere, thus, many argued that Western Europe 'enjoyed' a 'free-ride' on U.S. defence commitments. The benefits for the U.S. to setting the defence alliance in Western Europe were, however, fundamentally to keep Western European states under the paternal wing of Washington. To the U.S, the European allies were(are) a geopolitical bridgehead in Eurasia, and vital in America strategy for global preponderance. Even without a Soviet threat, Europe remains vital to American security and economic interests. In the U.S. search for global preponderance, Europe will always be a leading political, economic and strategic interest in U.S. policies.

However, America's goal of continuing to prevent European ambitions from getting out of line with U.S. interests could cause uneasiness in European decision-making. The extent of this uneasiness has, however, not materialised into tangible variables that may suggest that the EU is setting up itself to challenge the U.S. on global and systemic issues. There are three main reasons which stems and gels the nature of U.S.-EU relations, their politics and ideology. First, the EU and the U.S. share many common values and principles. Their differences are in interests rather than their relative positions in the structure or on the 'reconstruction' of the international system. The establishment of common objectives – liberal economic order (with numerous economic and trading institutions), the non-proliferation of weapons of mass destruction, defence and protection of human rights and democracy – are readily shared by both sides.

The second reason is that both Western Europe and the U.S. are firmly 'anchored' in the zone of democratic peace and prosperity. The Western European desire for democratic peace and prosperity is obvious, whilst the U.S. reinforces these desires because there are greater benefits for the U.S. to be gained than having to see a Europe that is at war with itself (which would probably require U.S. blood to resolve). In this way, the EU development of democracy and liberal trade has suited the U.S. search for hegemonic globalisation, in the sense that the EU acts as an important partner and outpost, which helps the U.S. to influence, consolidate, and expand the ideals of free trade and democracy.

The third reason for the structural solidarity in U.S. and Western Europe relations has been the embedded U.S. interest in the maintenance of the NATO military alliance. This alliance has served both Europe and America in their respective interests. For the U.S., it is, as pointed out in section one, part of the jigsaw puzzle that enables the U.S. to remain the dominant power in international affairs. For the Western Europeans, it inter-links and entwines the national security interests of member states so as not to 'threaten' one another.

With these common interests and the desire to promote 'democratic peace' and 'prosperity', it would appear that the U.S. and EU are initiating condominium to govern the international system. Their view of the promotion of 'universal' human rights and 'humanitarian' intervention has provoked contentious debates over value and belief systems.

In the strategy to promoting the 'zone of democratic peace and prosperity' the expansion of NATO is part of the U.S. strategy to pave the way for this ideal and to maximise U.S. power. However, and especially the military intervention in Yugoslavia, Russia, China, and other powers resistant to U.S. power maximisation, view the U.S.-EU and NATO expansion and actions in Yugoslavia as hegemonic arrogance that attempts to undermine the international structure as determined by the UN. This type of approach leaves open the real intention of the agenda for the 'promotion of democratic peace and prosperity' and the underlying Westphalian international system of sovereign states.

Chapter 10

U.S.-Japan Relations: 'The Anchor in the East'

Introduction

The north Pacific is a region that is vigorously contested by four of the world's five great powers, the United States, Russia, China, and Japan.[1] It is no exaggeration to suggest that the stability of the international system in the early twenty-first century will be principally determined by these powers. The position of Japan and the United States in this quadrangle is unique. For Japan, the alliance with the United States is an 'axis of Japan's foreign policy' (*Diplomatic Bluebook*, 1998: 18). For the United States, the bilateral 'security alliance with Japan is the linchpin of its security policy in Asia and is key to many U.S. global objectives' (W.S. Cohen, 1999).

From this perspective, the objective of this chapter is to explore the historical developments in U.S.-Japan relations, and to understand what that relationship entails in the post-Cold War system. Thence this chapter is divided into two sections. The first section is subdivided into five parts. The first part looks at the historical background of the U.S.-Japanese security alliance after 1945 and explores the 'compromised sovereignty' of Japan *vis-à-vis* the United States.

The second part interrogates the debate over the so-called Japanese economic rise and the problems that evolved from that rise. The objective is to understand the tension in the relationship and to inquire into the strategies initiated by the U.S. and Japan to resolve the 'problem' especially following the collapse of the communist threat.

The third part examines why, in resolving the 'problem', Japan has been left in a state of restructuring. Part four confirms why Japan was never a systemic challenger to U.S. hegemony. Part five reinforces the last two inquiries. It explains why the U.S. strategy of 'engagement and enlargement', also known as hegemonic globalisation, has had such effects on Japanese society and East Asia.

Section two is subdivided into four parts. The first part analyses the extent of the changing security regime in the post-Cold War system; it examines the challenges and opportunities of the U.S.-Japan security relations. Thenceforth, the second part examines the Japanese intentions of working under the U.S.-led economic system, and analyses the extent of Japanese economic power being utilised to support that economic system. Part three analyses the extent of Japanese

---

[1] The other great power/region being the European Union.

'soft' power being a promoter of liberal democratic values. Whilst part four outlines why Japan remains locked by its historical background and attempts at playing a greater international role (especially on political and military issue) continues to be viewed with suspicion by its neighbours.

The conclusion attempts to draw on the analysis developed previously; it attempts to locate the strengths and weaknesses of U.S.-Japan relationship from the perspective of hegemonic globalisation.

Section I: The 'Making' of Post-1945 Japan: 'Compromised Sovereignty'[2]

After Japan's unconditional surrender came into effect on 2 September 1945, Japan was placed under U.S./Allied control through the Supreme Commander for the Allied Powers (SCAP). General Douglas MacArthur was placed at the helm of power in Japan, and effectively ruled as generalissimo from 2 September 1945 to 28 April 1952. Initially, the SCAP was instructed to enforce and ensure that Japan would become a peaceful nation; it was charged to establish a pluralistic democratic self-government, where the Japanese military elite would be eradicated and not creep back into the realm of decision-making in Japanese politics. The directive was to 'eradicate the Japanese social structures that had fuelled the country's expansionist tendencies' (D.A. Lake, 1999: 173). The promotion of free speech, individual liberties, and a free press was established. These measures were embodied in the Initial Post-Surrender Policy (document SWNCC 150/4/A). Finally, a 'Peace Constitution' was introduced on 3 May 1947, with Article 9 reading as follows:

> Aspiring sincerely to an international peace based on justice and order, the Japanese people forever renounce war as a sovereign right of the nation, and the threat or use of force as a means of settling international disputes.
> In order to accomplish the aim of the preceding paragraph, land, sea, and air forces, as well as other war potential, will never be maintained. The right of belligerency of the state will not be recognised (cited in Tatsuo Akaneya, 1998: 14).[3]

However, in less than five years the pattern of Japanese military renunciation shifted as strategic pressure from the United States intervened to re-organise the military framework of Japan.

In defending a possible contradiction with Article 9, the Ashida Amendment (named after Hitoshi Ashida former diplomat, and Chairman of the Special Committee of the Imperial Diet (Hitoshi Ashida later became PM in 1948), subtly re-interpreted Article 9. Ashida argued that 'while Article 9 provides

---

[2] The author acknowledges Barry Gills for this sub-title.
[3] See also Bureau of East Asian and Pacific Affairs, U.S. Department of State *Background Notes: Japan, March 1999*', obtained from
http://www.state.gov/www/background_notes/japan_0399_bgn.html on 22 April 1999.

Japan's renunciation of war and the threat or use of force as a means of settling international disputes in the first paragraph, and Japan's commitment not to possess armed forces for the purpose in the second paragraph, the article did not say anything about Japan's right of self-defence and possession of armed forces specifically to that end' (cited in Tatsuo Akaneya, 1998: 15). Moreover, the United Nations Charter, Article 51 (which states that every sovereign state has an inherent right to self-defence) was used to defend that policy. The Ashida Amendment opened the way for Japanese rearmament, which it did in any case, as General MacArthur ordered the establishment of a 75,000 man Police Reserve Force to maintain internal order in Japan as U.S. occupying forces moved to the Korean peninsula to 'defend' South Korea. In 1952, the Police Reserve Force evolved into the Japanese National Safety Forces, and by 1954, following negotiations with the United States under the Mutual Defence Agreement, it became the Japanese Self-Defence Force, comprising of ground, air and naval forces.

Unlike the reconstruction of the state and society envisaged in Germany (west), the United States perceived that it would be advisable to leave the Japanese pre-war bureaucracy (including the emperor) intact rather than destroying it. Instead of purging the conservative and elite forces that were the structural backbone of Japanese society during World War II, vigorous purges were set forth against leftists and labour unions (which were suspected as being communist insurgents). The United States allowed conservative Japanese to focus on economic reconstruction, aided these techno-nationalists even more by opening its own market to Japanese exports, and facilitated technology transfers (C. Hurst III, 1997: 70). According to Shigeto Tsuru, '[t]he U.S. was determined to restore Japan's pre-war position as the "workshop of Asia" and to preserve her economy as far as possible from socialist encroachment' (1993: 38). In that relationship:

> ... the Japanese elite settled for growing rich under American hegemony. America would manage the world security and provide a global currency. America would run the GATT, the IMF, the World Bank. The American market would be open to all comers, while Japan would be left alone to build an international machine behind barriers that kept out foreigners, their investments, and the products. America would get unrestricted access to military bases in Japan while Japan would be part of the global nuclear network, although both countries would pretend otherwise. Japan would pay lip service in the United Nations and other international forums to American foreign policy goals. But Japan would not be asked and would not seek to play hegemonic functions (R. T. Murphy, 1996: 175).

Thus, Tokyo was supposed 'to make money and share [with] us [the] wealth when Washington comes calling . . .[and] the U.S. is supposed to defend Japan and Japanese interests'.[4] However, even before the collapse of the Soviet Union, serious strategic and economic questions began to emerge in both Tokyo and

---

[4] *The Japan Times* (1999, 19 July) 'Japan's defense dependency', by Doug Bandow, p. 21. (emphasis added).

Washington on the reliability of the bilateral relationship.[5] In the following section, I will analyse the tensions that emanated in Japan-U.S. relations following Japan's economic success and the collapse of the 'common' threat of communism.

The Emerging Economic Power and the Emerging Tensions

It must be emphasised that from the start, the U.S. and Japan security treaty (was)is never between one of equals. Very often the role (was)is on the basis that 'Washington makes the decisions; Tokyo carries them out' (*The Japan Times*, 1999, 19 July, p. 21). No matter how the relationship was set to be, the long term viability of this arrangement inevitably raises serious challenges as to how long the relationship may remain on such bases. Four points stand out.

- Japan has become the world's second largest economic power (see Appendix 3A to 3D). It can easily defend itself if desired.
- The Soviet Union and the communist systemic challenge have collapsed. As such, Japan may now feel that it neither needs a shield nor faces any threats from which it needs to be shielded.
- For the United States, the massive yearly surplus of Japan's current account relative to the United States (for example, see *The Economist Intelligence Report – The United States of America, 1999*), and the inability of U.S. and Japanese governments and officials to resolve that matter threatened to alter the political relationship.
- In February 1990, Washington demanded that Japan 'change' its business practices and act more decisively to cut its current account surplus or else the Mutual Security Treaty was open for reconsideration (see M. Cox, 1995).

From the United States' perspective, if Japan did not amend its mercantilistic economic practices, it was projected that the Japanese rate of growth and its large surplus would eventually surpass the United States as the number one economic power in the world, and soon U.S. political power in the world as well! (E. Vogel, 1979; C. Prestowitz, JR., 1988; P. Kennedy, 1989). These fears opened a host of scholarly and non-scholarly work from both sides of the Pacific since the mid-1970s, voicing the case for a re-definition of the U.S.-Japan relationship. Some of the exchanges were so vitriolic that, according to David Asher, 'it is easy to forget that the two countries were allies at all' (1997: 348).

Amongst the most pronounced was the American debate based around the assumption of the endless onslaught of Japanese industries into the U.S. market without the United States' industries significantly denting into the Japanese

---

[5] For more details on the Japan-U.S. bilateral relationship, including the Yoshida Doctrine (1951) and the Treaty on of Mutual Cooperation and Security (1960), see M.S. Gallicchio (1988), Shigeto Tsuru (1993), and R. Drifte (1996), (2000).

market. Many American companies demanded that the United States government increase protectionist measures or demand Japan change its trade practices. Other companies however simply moved their production to lower-cost environments.[6]

It was emphasised that Japanese business was so successful that Japanese capitalism was prescribed as the prototype of world capitalism in the twenty-first century (R.N. Rosescrance, 1986). Japanese style management and production techniques, along with Japanese culture, language, and any other thing that was connected with 'Japaneseness' were imitated, just as the Japanese had imitated 'Western' technological approaches previously. Reinhard Drifte writes, '"[l]earning from Japan" has in many countries become a motto to overcome industrial decline and to cope with Japanese competition' (1996: 108). Kenneth Waltz shows that: '[i]n any competitive system the winners are imitated by the losers, or they continue to lose' (1999: 695). On these points, some Japanese began to show signs of arrogance. In America, Western Europe, and other parts of the world, in concealed deliberation and open mien,[7] the Japanese economic successes were screened with nationalistic resentments. A way was needed to outflank and undermine this Japanese success and arrogance (this is discussed in more detail below).

In other reports, the Japanese government was denoted to be behind the operation of national industries and finance, in order to develop national champions directed against U.S. corporations. American political scientists and economists complained of the mercantilistic nature of Japanese government/bureaucratic-business practice (see, for example, C. Johnson, 1982; P. Krugman, 1994/97/98, 3rd edit; 1999) in undermining liberal capitalism and ultimately U.S.-Japan relations. American analysts identified six key categories of Japan business practice and 'culture', which were viewed as incompatible with the America way of business and life.

Firstly, Krugman (1999) argues that close ties between government and industry enabled the latter to be protected unfairly in free competition. It was apprehended that throughout the 1950s to the 1970s, the Japanese government, in

---

[6] This latter strategy indirectly, although not entering the Japanese market, hastened the pace of globalisation into other parts of the world, that would have serious consequences for Japanese businesses in the 1990s.

[7] Even before the Japanese reached comparable developmental and economic level as 'Western countries', many western scholars have viewed Japanese politics and its economic 'catch up' with the West with fascination, and to certain degrees in nationalist factions in European-American mentality been difficult to accept [see for example Endymion Wilkinson (1980) *Japan versus the West: image and reality* (London: Penguin)]. In the period of European and American colonisation, Japan was not only able to identify and fend off the so-called European traders and missionaries as forerunners of military conquest and imperialism, but was the first non-white nation to decisively defeat another 'white' power, in the Japan-Russian War 1904-5, in modern warfare techniques. That victory pushed Japan into becoming the first non-European Great Power in modern history. It was also a psychological victory for many non-white people under European dominance, and it brought an end to the myth of the invincibility of European powers.

the guise of the Ministry of International Trade and Industry (MITI) and the quieter, but perhaps even more influential Ministry of Finance 'played a strong role in directing the economy' (P. Krugman, 1999: 63). Geoffrey Hawthorn pictures the Japanese style of capitalism as:

> ... [a]t the start, there was mugi-fumi, 'treading on wheat nurseries', strengthening young plants by massaging their roots. Thus stimulated, firms were promised yamagoya, 'mountain shelters'; if they over-reached themselves and had difficulties, there would be relief. No-one forced anyone to do anything, and where there were laws, as there eventually were on prices, these were almost always 'undrawn swords' whose mere existence made the guidance cut better (in K. Booth, 1998: 211).

The second feature is the long-term relationships among banks and firms, where the firms (Keiretsu) would ally themselves around a main bank (K.V. Wolferen, 1989; G. Hook and M. Weiner, 1992). Reciprocally, both would own large quantities of each other's shares. The banks were the main source of funds, thus making the selling of shares to outside stockholders rare and unnecessary.

Third, analysts (e.g. K.V. Wolferen, 1989) denote that Japanese business practice and societal behaviour were(are) set on the basis of whom you know rather than what you know. In this practice, class, race and education were(are) important to moving up the social ladder.[8]

Fourth, American scholars (e.g., C. Johnson, 1982) argued that there was a tendency for corporations to have their employees on a lifetime of employment. It was often expected that employees would align themselves to the company, as a citizen would align himself or herself to the nation, and the company would protect that employee as a state would its citizens.

Fifth, it was affirmed that Japanese society tended to place a higher emphasis on production over consumption (T. Murphy, 1996). Japanese people were portrayed as thrifty and a saving-only society.

Finally, the Japanese characteristic was seen as consensual and supported a hierarchical order for economic development rather than being 'creative' or 'individualistic' (W.J. Holstein, 1990).

In these operations and 'catch up' *vis-à-vis* the 'West', the Japan practices were viewed as something 'totally alien' and 'winning the game of international economic competition by playing according to a different set of rules' (M. Mastanduno, 1998: 2). It was even pronounced that Japan had become so successful that it was jeered that '[t]he Cold War is over and Japan has won'

---

[8] The point is that Japanese distinguish very sharply between the in-group and out-group. A gaijin (foreigner) living in Japan can never be in the in-group, and is never fully accepted, so there is no social ladder for them to move up. Gaijins are a permanent out-group. Perhaps the key issue concerns Koreans and other Asian people living in Japan, in some cases for several generations and racially indistinguishable from most Japanese, but who are still discriminated against both officially and informally. The author thanks Rod Hague and Michael Cox for these points.

(quoted in W. Horsley and R. Buckley, 1990: 238), referring of course to the economic success of the country (by free-riding on 'benign' U.S. policies). This perspective led Akaha and Langdon to suggest that, '[a] good part of the U.S. decline . . . has been attributed to the expansion of the Japanese economy' (1993: 5). This perception became so bad that many nationalist Americans and labour union leaders became convinced that 'the Japanese had concocted some evil plot to buy up and control the American economy' (cited in S. Strange, 1998: 47). The media reinforced and exaggerated the extent of Japanese buying power into 'traditional' American businesses, such as the auto-industry, super semiconductor industries, electronics and computer industries. In one amplified example, Pearl Harbour was referred to and U.S. nationalists portrayed the situation by suggesting that: 'they [the Japanese] don't need to invade the place, they already own it!' These sentiments were quickly transferred into popular belief that Japan (rather than the Soviet Union) was the number one threat to the United States. David Asher spelled it out: '[d]espite their admiration for Japan's accomplishments as a developmental capitalist economy, they identified growing Japanese economic power as a threat to the American way of life no less in need of containment than Soviet communism' (1998: 345). Racist remarks even went as far as suggesting a 'yellow peril' replacing the spectre of the 'red peril' overshadowing 'Western' civilisation, and that war between the U.S. and Japan would be a likely outcome (G. Friedman and M. Lebard, 1991). On geostrategic matters, Japan was also criticised by the United States for being mute during the 1991 Gulf War, and for not giving generous aid to the democratising process in Russia.

With these attacks and reconsideration by the Americans on the relationship, the Japanese in return began to challenge the United States on some of these issues. In the Japanese view, if the United States wanted to reduce the economic deficit, the United States' businesses should become more like Japanese (see H. McRae, 1994). In one Japanese view, although admiring in general the American ideals, some Americans were perceived as being 'lazy', consumer-based, 'selfish', a society awash with firearms, quarrelsome, discourteous, and litigious (see, for example, Shintaro Ishihara, 1989/91). Second, the U.S., according to many Japanese, was a society that worships the disparities in the distribution of wealth and ignores the mass underclass. Third, in response to the lack of enthusiasm towards Russia, Tatsuo Akaneya bluntly stated, 'as if all of a sudden the former common enemy had become a close friend of the West' (1998: 4; see also K. Sasae, 1994).

Under these circumstances and tensions, the next section investigates the validity of the arguments and explains why this was not what the U.S.-Japan relationship was really based upon.

The 'Collapse' of the Japanese Challenge

One thing that Paul Kennedy's 'outstretch' idea got right was not the 'over-stretch' of the United States, but two of its nearest 'rivals' in the dimension of economics and geopolitics: Japan in geo-economics and the Soviet Union in geopolitics. Both of these powers rather than the United States, had, 'over-stretched' their limits of military capabilities and economic capabilities. For the Soviet Union, it was the stalemate in Afghanistan and the inability of the Soviet economy to support that costly endeavour that punished the Soviet system (M. Cox, 1995; see chapter seven on Russia). For the Japanese, it was economic overstretch, which was aggravated by the strong yen, that forced many Japanese companies to move overseas, thus, leaving Japan 'kudoka' (empty).[9] Furthermore, the blind greed of some on a spectacularly over-priced real-estate market in the major cities eventually led to the bursting of the Japanese economic bubble (R.T. Murphy, 1996; S. Strange, 1998). As mentioned earlier, during the 1980s, the Japanese economy was said to be on the brink of becoming the next global economic hegemon. It was sailing high in confidence; Japanese citizens and companies brought up assets and property across the world, and there seemed to be no limits. Yet, within a few years, '[the] Japanese economy has fallen into a permanent slower-growth pattern. [Japan's economic weight is] declining' (K.W. Tong, 1996-7: 114, emphasis added).

How was the United States able to reverse a trend that had been assumed was on the brink of bankruptcy and decline? Why had so many analysts hastily concluded that the United States had already declined? Alternatively, were they using the right set of concepts to understand U.S. power, the international organisations and institutions, and its relationship with the other major powers?

This book has argued that the United States was in a period of reconfiguration and not decline (see chapter three). The U.S. focus was not on the European powers, nor on Japan, the real enemy was the ideological threat coming from the Soviet Union and communist insurgents around the world (M. Cox, 1995: 21). The U.S. geopolitical game with the Soviet Union was zero-sum. That threat had to be contained and, where possible, had to be vanquished. Although, the 'advantages given' to Japan and European partners was noticed (as the above analysts have pointed out), the critique of Japanese economic practice was, however, kept to a minimal, so as not to 'rock the boat' amongst allies. Japan was fully aware of this relationship.

This, however, did not mean that the 'advantages given' were without strings. The objective of the U.S. implementation of its 'benevolent' economic and security system was always based on an ensnaring strategy that the partners would operate under an U.S.-centric system. At times, the United States' weakness[es] were exaggerated to give the sense of vulnerability that, if the allies were to avoid

---

[9] Yochanan Schachmurore (1999) 'A Puzzle Resolved: Japan's High Currency Value and Trade Surplus', *The American Economist*, vol. 43, no. 1, (spring), p. 49. However, Japan has tried to maintain most of its most sophisticated technology processes, and research and development in Japan, while production abroad required less skilled labour.

communism or the collapse of the capitalist system, the allies had to support that system – or at least give leeway for the 'well-being' of the United States, otherwise by tormenting on the weakness of the U.S., the capitalist system would collapse and, thus, would probably mean their own collapse also. The strengths and the variables were always in America's favour.

Why Japan is Not a Challenger

Thus, the position of Japan as a challenger to U.S. centrality does *not* have credibility without facing serious strategic obstacles (see D.P. Rapkin, 1990: 191-212; B.K. Gills in S. Gill, 1993: 186-212). The most obvious hindrance is Japan's weakness on the security regime, although the Japanese military *has* become the third highest in terms of military expenditure and *has* an inflatable military infrastructure, if it desires to develop it (see Appendix 1A). The consequences of such action would, however, bring great uneasiness to its neighbours and the United States. Military assertiveness is beyond Japan. It is difficult to see the Koreans and/or other East Asian nations sitting idly by whilst Japan is militarily assertive, or to having to rely on Japanese military protection or/and as the guardian of their trade routes. In that, it and other countries continue to rely on the United States 'goodwill' to guard the trade routes – the bloodline, especially for a sea-faring nation, of national well-being – of industry and commerce.

Second, unlike the United States, Japan does not (even if it tried) have that magnetic pull effect on other countries and people. Japan is principally an insular and homogeneous society, although, there is evidence of some cosmopolitanism in the large cities. Japan, however, remains largely restrictive to foreigners acquiring Japanese citizenship. There are even criticisms of embedded racism in that society, for example Koreans who have lived there for generations, yet are still treated as aliens and second class citizens[10] (see also R. Drifte, 1996: 130). In addition, the Japanese media tend to associate crime and criminal activities with foreigners. Even scholars, such as Takashi Inoguchi, assert that, 'many Japanese are relatively defenseless against the more assertive and aggressive behaviour of many foreigners' (Takashi Inoguchi, 1999: 167). This is not only a weakness for any country which might seek to acquire global superpower or regional leadership status, but also raises a very serious psychological reflective question concerning the brutality inflicted on others by the Japanese people during its history of piracy, conquest and imperialism. In the words of David Rapkin: 'when it comes to universalisable norms, values, and ordering principles that might serve as the foundation of future world order, Japan is seldom thought to be a likely source' (D.P. Rapkin, 1990: 199).

---

[10] *The Japan Times* (1999, 28 July) 'Seoul again urges Japan [*to consider*] voting rights [*for Korean minorities in Japan*]', p. 2, emphasis added.

Third, according to the Trilateral Commission, Japan's population is ageing at an uneven rate, and faster than any other industrialised country; the baby-boomers of the 1950s and 1960s are soon becoming the pensioners; the total fertility rate (birth per woman) is 1.4, which is among the lowest in the world. By 2010 to 2015, the Trilateral Commission estimates, a quarter of the population will be sixty-five years of age or older, and every two Japanese in the working population (those fifteen to sixty-four) will have to support one person of sixty-years or older (B. Emmot, Koji Watanabe, and P. Wolfowitz, 1997: 30).

Fourth, even before it attempts to be a regional hegemon, let alone global hegemon, Japan would face numerous obstacles from regional powers, such as China, the two Koreas, and Russia. For example, in the Chinese perspective, the 'question of where Japan is heading has aroused grave concern', a Japanese century or 'a Pacific era with Japan as the centre is unacceptable' (Wan Guong, 1989: 30). This is even before it encounters the United States for global pre-eminence. The idea of Japanese challenge was popular in the 1980s and early 1990s, but their analysis was based on a wrong set of assumptions and they did not truly comprehend the nature of American power. The Japanese position has left Ethan Kapstein arguing that 'Japan's contemporary challenge is hardly the achievement of regional hegemony, but rather the maintenance of its status as a relatively prosperous and secure nation-state' (E. Kapstein and M. Mastanduno, 1999: 477). With so many difficult and conflicting dilemmas, it is unlikely that Japan should wish to 'balance' the United States or engage in any strategy that may be seen to 'prepare' itself for global hegemony without facing serious problems.

Finally, how can a country that has had a 'free-ride' for so long and so successfully, wish to change and assume hegemonic burdens? American critics argue that Japan's behaviour during the Gulf War in 1990-1991, the crises surrounding China-Taiwan (in 1996 and 1999), and the East Asian economic crisis of 1997-1999 are just a few examples of issues that Japan either does not, or is not equipped, or is not willing to tackle. For the Japanese to show direction and leadership in these situations would most likely mean an about face in Japanese society, i.e., to manage crises, and act with 'benign responsibility' in the world-system (R. Drifte, 1996; 2000). This would mean a total overhaul of the Japanese domestic attitude towards global issues and global responsibility. It would also mean a redefinition of Japanese defence policy and foreign relations.

Even with these obstacles, many commentators did perceive that Japan was to become the contender for the hegemonic throne in the twenty-first century. However, by the late 1990s, Ernest Preeg asserts, 'the widespread pessimism of only two or three years ago about being surpassed by Japan is greatly muted' (in B. Roberts, 1996: 147). The shift in emphasis by the U.S. on economics has created 'leaner and meaner American competitors' (M. Mastanduno, 1998). What was then seen as unstoppable, was by the 1990s seriously malfunctioning. Michael Mastanduno observed that, 'U.S. officials no longer fear that the Japanese style of capitalism may be unstoppable; they are more concerned to assure that the Japanese economy remains unsinkable' (1998: 4-5). Mastanduno has even urged the United States 'to devise the equivalent of a Marshall Plan to rescue Japan from itself' (1998: 5).

The 'Re-designing' of Japan, Again

Under these circumstances, in the 1990s, many Japanese suspect that the Americans were behind an 'evil plot that handicapped their banks and economy' (S. Strange, 1998: 47). According to R. Taggart Murphy, '[t]he recession . . . was placed squarely on the United States. . . . Both the MOF (Ministry of Finance) bureaucrats and executives at Japanese security houses fumed about how the Americans were "undermining" the Japanese market' (1996: 156). For some Japanese the economic circumstances represented, 'the second defeat in the Pacific War' (Y. Funabashi, 1999: 28). These statements leave interesting evaluations, but are we again in danger of entering another cycle whereby the analogies of the previous United States-Japan debate are being replayed all over again, except on a reverse side of the coin? Because this book has contested that debate and questioned the viability of the variables and methods being used, there is a danger that these evaluations may get it wrong again. For this reason, it is, thus, of interest here to examine and understand the U.S. strategy for global preponderance, rather than fall into that category.

As emphasised in chapter four, the break-up of the fixed exchange rate of the Bretton Woods system was viewed by many scholars as 'destined' to go protectionist (for example Gilpin, 1981). It was a view that perceived that capitalist states would increase the trade barriers and develop regional trading blocs, thus severely constraining international finance and trade. As argued in chapter four, the break-up of the fixed exchange system did not serve or initiate this purpose. Instead, the aim by the U.S. was focused on the enhancement of 'free trade' for its corporations to operate more freely across international borders. The intention was to increase 'free-trade' and 'liberal' competition to large and small corporations. Under the Bretton Woods system, the European and Japanese corporations and businesses were protected by their governments and the 'fixed' exchange rate system. Although, the Bretton Woods system served to stabilise international trade and the movement of finance, it did not serve U.S. corporate or financial interests relative to their European and Japanese partners (who optimised that system with protective measure for their financial and corporate sectors). The impact of the break-up of the Bretton Woods fixed exchange rate system, however, did not have an immediate effect on Japanese and Europe corporations in the 1970s and 1980s, but as the U.S. corporations endured in the 'free' competitive market, that lesson was to be vital for their battle against Japanese firms in the 1990s. As U.S. corporations lobbied the U.S. government on the unfair practices of Japanese and European companies, the U.S. in turn pressured Japanese and European governments to 'liberalise' their trading practices (see the U.S. House of Representatives, Committee on Ways and Means, 1997).

The late 1970s and 1980s was a period of paradigmatic struggle between the policies of strategic trade and the liberalisation of trade. The battle revolved around the question of whether and for how long the European and Japanese practice of 'strategic trade policies' by subsidising their 'uncompetitive' national corporate champions and eating into the 'unprotected' national champions of the U.S. was to continue. The manoeuvres by the U.S. to 'open up' and 'liberalise' trade practices in the 1980s and 1990s was met unsurprisingly with hostile Japanese and European resistance. However, the fortune of U.S. negotiation changed following the collapse of the communist challenge. The U.S. was able to intensify its negotiation pressure on European and Japanese government to 'deregulate' their business practices without fearing them to slip into the communist camp.

The new U.S. negotiation tactics revolved around two main strategies. First, from the U.S. perspective, either the world economy was to be free for competition, or it would return to protectionism and that would mean the self-professed scenario of 'beggar-thy-neighbour', which no 'sensible' capitalist country would really want. Second, if Japan and European countries did not liberalise their trading practices, the security treaties with them would be under reconsideration or/and abandoned. In both these modes, either the allies were to operate according to the U.S. regime of 'free' trade and 'liberal' market or else the U.S. was to tighten its market and the security alliance would be reconsidered.

These new measures raised serious dilemmas for Japan. If it allowed its market to be opened and liberalised, many uncompetitive companies would suffer and consequently would bring higher unemployment. On the other hand, if it did not open and liberalise its market and comply with U.S. demands, it would risk U.S. protectionist reprisals, which would also mean serious economic problems for Japan. In addition, it would also risk U.S. defence withdrawal, thence meaning that Japan may have to develop its own defence structure. Under such circumstance, this strategy would almost certainly alarm its neighbours, and spiral the region into an arms race. The position for Japan was not good whether it opened up and liberalised or remained stubborn to its strategic trade practices. The U.S. negotiation strategy caught Japan in a no win scenario.

In 'pushing' the Japanese to open and deregulate economic practices, the U.S. has inadvertently (or intentionally) brought about a reconstruction of Japanese internal politics, again. The history of the U.S. directly or inadvertently restructuring Japanese internal political affairs is identifiable in three phases. The first image was after Commodore Perry and the 'black-ships' entering Tokyo Bay in July 1853 demanding diplomatic and trade relations. The Perry visits had enormous consequences in Japan: they showed that the 'Tokugawas were not strong enough to resist foreign demands and began a train of events which was to lead to the fall of the Tokugawa shogunate' (D. Townson, 1994/5: 653). The second image occurred during the U.S. occupation of Japan from 1945 to 1952, which created a Japanese political system that would make power less concentrated in the hands of politicians and military forces. Japanese national power was largely centred in the national bureaucracies, the old corporate firms and their families. Although not what many Americans had intended, but as mentioned earlier, the fear of communism meant that the bureaucratic oligarchy image would suffice. The third phase, as outlined above, to refine the Japanese power structure, can be traced to President Nixon's abandonment of the fixed exchange rate system and President Ronald Reagan's push to make Japan more deregulated and open to U.S. competition, especially in the financial structure – allegedly the most global and non-national economic realms. The Structural Impediment Initiative (SII) talks during the 1980s, especially following the Plaza Agreement of September 1985, 'was conceived to make Japan more like America' (G. C. Hurst III, 1997: 72). Diplomatically of course, '[t]he point we need to make to our Japanese friends is that their country is being asked to change and bring under mutual rules only those practices that palpably impinge on others in a globally interdependent age – what John Stuart Mill would have called "other-regarding" behaviour – not to overturn their entire heritage'.[11]

Behind the smoke screen, however, the damage had already been done. The technique was to apply politics to change economic circumstances, which would in turn change the political discourse of Japan. In Ethan Kapstein's analysis, the liberalisation of financial regimes was '. . ."the result of deliberate political decision", in which the United States instigated liberalisation by substantially deregulating its own domestic marketplace and then seeking market openings overseas' (in E. Kapstein and M. Mastanduno, 1999: 474). Rather than creating a 'borderless' world of finance, 'the United States insisted on the creation of a new international regulatory structure based on the concept of "home country control" of financial institutions, culminating in the 1988 Basle Accord on bank capital adequacy (the Basle Accord sets a single international capital adequacy standard for all major banking institutions)' (E. Kapstein and M. Mastanduno, 1999: 474). The U.S. Federal Reserve Board has in this respect developed into a body that 'governs' and regulates international finance (P. Hirst and G. Thompson, 1998 2nd edit.). In effect, what the commentators are suggesting is that the fundamental force that drives the global economy is the United States. The term global economy 'is, in effect, the global advance of an American style market economy. It is in the midst of this process, moreover, that the United States has succeeded in re-establishing its economic pre-eminence' (Saeki Keishi, 1998: 9-10).

In this globalisation guise, the United States has insisted that it is the dynamics of global capitalism (see T. Friedman, 1999), rather than U.S. pressure,[12]

---

[11] Ivan P. Hall (1992) 'Samurai legacies, American illusions', *National Interest*, (summer) p. 16, in Reinhard Drifte (1996) *Japan's Foreign Policy in the 1990s: From Economic Superpower to What Power?* (London: Macmillan), p. vi.

[12] It is interesting to recall a parallel with E.H. Carr (1939, 1946 2nd edit., 1956) *The Twenty Years Crisis, 1919-1939* (London: Harper and Row), when analysing Britain in the nineteenth century. Carr wrote: 'British nineteenth-century statesmen, having discovered that free trade promoted British prosperity, were sincerely convinced that, in doing so, it also promoted the prosperity of the world . . . British predominance in world trade was at the

that is now forcing Japan to attempt to revitalise its economy by adopting a deregulated and open system, politically and economically. The (former) Japanese Prime Minister Obuchi responded to this globalising pressure by stating: '[b]asically I do support restructuring . . . [although] on a third way'.[13] However, the Japanese Economic Council, an advisory affiliate to the Economic Planning Agency, delivered its report, *Ideal Socioeconomy and Policies for Economic Rebirth* in July 1999, admittedly stated that the 1990s recession is not cyclical but structural in nature, and hence recognises that sustainable GDP growth 'can only be achieved by transforming Japan into a more competitive and individualistic society' (cited in *The Economist Intelligence Unit, Country report Japan, 1999, 3rd Quarter*, pp. 18-19). The report calls for 'an end to the lifetime employment system, eliminating mandatory retirement rules, forming a common market with South Korea and perhaps with other Asian countries, and tolerating greater disparities in income and wealth' (ibid., pp. 18-19). Analytically, Japan is, for the third time in its diplomatic history with the U.S., being transformed into another image that suits the United States.

In these circumstances the questions that need to be answered are: 'was Japan punished by the forces of hegemonic globalisation, or was Japan too complacent to the forces of hegemonic globalisation?' Alternatively, did Japan already know the consequence of resistance, and take advantage of it for as long as possible. The scenario in the 1990s is that, whilst the United States has enjoyed economic prosperity relative to other core regions, Japan has suffered from recession since the early 1990s. Japan is not only struggling; Japan is perhaps caught in a paradigmatic battle of whether to continue the state reliance strategy for its industries or to leave it to the 'market' forces. It is even suggested that Japan is 'in the middle of a fundamental transformation on the scale of the Meiji Restoration' (Tatsuo Akaneya, 1998: 30). The very systems that guaranteed Japanese economic success during the Cold War period are now regarded as obstacles, hampering progress in a new environment and in need of fundamental restructuring. Takamitsu Sawa suggests, '[w]e need urgently to clean up our markets, making them free, transparent, and fair. . . . It includes deregulation, disclosure of information, strengthening of regulatory oversight, and decentralisation of government authority' (Takamitsu Sawa, 1999: 182).

It must be noted, however, that there is a danger in the temptation to infer that the American style economic system is fair, while the Japanese economic

---

time so overwhelming that there was a certain undeniable harmony between British interests and the interests of the world. British prosperity flowed over into other countries, and a British economic collapse would have meant world-wide ruin. British free traders could and did argue that protectionist countries were not only egotistically damaging the prosperity of the world as a whole, but were stupidly damaging their own, so that their behaviour was both immoral and muddle headed', p. 81. Is this a parallel with U.S. post-Cold War strategy?

[13] Japanese PM Keizo Obuchi in the *Far Eastern Economic Review* (1999, 2 December) 'We've Got to Grow', by Chester Dawson and Nayan Chanda, p. 10.

system is unfair. Second, is the pitfall that assumes that the Japanese bureaucratic and political conservatives are wrong because they are trying to preserve an opaque and unfair economy; and that the United States is correct because it aims to reform that system. Third, and perhaps most contentious is that the media and academia in Anglo-American societies give the impression that 'collective' societies are inferior to 'individualistic' societies.

These are serious contradictory conditions, whereby both are at political extremes. Without unmasking the internal U.S. framework and the layers beneath that complex society, imitating or aspiring to the American ideal as superior to others is, however, indecisive and can have serious implications. There is little doubt that the U.S. society believes in the invisible hand and its business thrives on this principle. However, beneath the invisible hand also lies a very powerful iron fist (with the largest intelligence and counter-intelligence security service and armed forces in the world) that aims to make sure the invisible hand is protected (see chapter two). Second, the United States has often tried to portray itself in the world as the defender of individualism and free competition, and it wants the world to believe that these are the very foundations of the American dream. This, again, is simplified. A significant area that the U.S. often leaves out from its ideals is in actuality the real forces that sustain and hold that society together. These include a very strong religious following and an almost 'police' state regulation on individual freedom. What it regards as individual liberty can easily be measured as a regulation of that freedom – freedom that is regulated, rather than being liberated. Behind this regulation is a massive secret service force which tries to uphold (although it can be argued that these forces are undermining) these ideals of liberty and freedom. Fourth, the U.S. is a country where wealth is created at an astronomical rate, yet, for a country so 'rich' and powerful, the distribution of wealth is dismal, leaving the rich to become despotic above the masses. Fifth, it is a society that preaches equal opportunities for all, but again that opportunity is regulated. The poor and the underprivileged are trapped in a time and environmental dimension of economic and educational poverty. In this deception, the under-class are preached the right of individual liberty, because it is taught that in and through this right – individual liberty – an individual may set out to achieve what is in their desire to achieve. Indeed, many people have become very successful in pursuing this dream. However, most people that have succeeded have had very strong foundations. People without collective support, either through family or association, or by fortune, going out into the U.S. framework, the rags to riches scenario is almost impossible to achieve.

Contrary to individualism, American politicians and community leaders constantly preach in favour of strong community ethics, family values, morality, and religious values. On the other hand, many U.S. administrations constantly preach to the international community on how America had achieved its success largely because of the belief in individual freedom and free market competition. Yet, domestically the administrations aimed to revive traditional family values, conservative ethics, and Christian morality (see for example, E.W. Lefever, 1999).

In these contrary conditions, unless revealed, the layers beneath the principles of American strategy may be missed. These contrary conditions may prove fatal for those imitating or aspiring to the American ideal.

The exposing of the Japanese system was a serious 'gamble' that the American administrations, especially Clinton's economic policies, undertook. It has been emphasised that the arm-twisting trade negotiations did very little to adjust the trade imbalances. However, what Clinton wanted was to demand from Japan that which is almost politically impossible for any Japanese prime minister, to concede economic sovereignty to the United States (M. Cox, 1995: 90). The implication of this is, as yet, undecided. Intrinsically though, the initiation of the hegemonic economic globalisation is already corroding the sub and superstructure of Japanese social, economic and cultural behaviour. Hypothetically, had the Japanese not given way to the U.S. demands, it would not only have meant the total collapse of the Japanese economic system, but very possibly leading to collapse of the foundation of the world trading system (M. Cox, 1995: 90). The Japanese economic/financial gurus and cartels have, as yet, decided not to respond. Without exaggerating the implications, the Clinton administration executed a dangerous manoeuvre to enhance hegemonic position of the United States.

Section II

In this section, I will analyse the security relations of the U.S. and Japan, and try to understand the nature of U.S.-Japan security arrangements following these events. The section is divided into four parts. The first examines the nature and changing security regime of the U.S. and Japan in the emerging international order, and analyses the possibilities of Japanese emergence of becoming a military 'great power'. The second and third part raises the extent to which Japan is really following and supporting the U.S. hegemonic globalisation. Part four questions the Japanese reluctance to come to terms with its historic past, it looks at why this remains a tension between not only with Japan's neighbours but also with the United States.

The Changing Security Regime

In 1993, Kenneth Waltz stated:

> Countries have always competed for wealth and security, and the competition has often led to conflict. Why should the future be different from the past? Given the expectation of conflict, and the necessity of taking care of one's interests, one may wonder how a state with the economic capability of a great power can refrain from arming itself with the weapons that have served so well as the great deterrent ... For a country to choose not to become a great power is a structural anomaly. For that reason, the choice is a difficult one to sustain. Sooner or later the international status

of countries has risen in step with their material resources. Countries with great economic power have become great powers, whether or not reluctantly. (1993: 64-6).

Brzezinski says that,

> It is unlikely that Japan's current position – on the one hand, as a globally respected economic powerhouse and, on the other hand, as a geopolitical extension of American power – will remain acceptable to the new generation of Japanese . . . For reasons of both history and self-esteem, Japan is a country not entirely satisfied with the global status quo . . . It feels, with some justification, that it is entitled to formal recognition as a world power . . . (1997: 174).

Does this mean that Japan should become a military great power due to its economic successes? Historically, countries became great powers for various reasons. Japan, although its economic position can easily make it become a great power if it desires, has yet to do so in this current period. There are seven possible scenarios whereby Japan may opt to decide for a more militarily prominent position:

- The U.S. decides that its role as hegemon no longer gives it sufficient benefits, and decides to withdraw its forces from Japan to such an extent that it no longer defends the vital security interests of Japan.
- The U.S. or Japan no longer see each other as reliable partners. A shift in the alliance would emerge, and a readjustment of the balance of power in East Asia would emerge.
- If and when U.S. military supremacy and the mechanisms of international organisations and institutions are no longer able to stem the recurrence of the cycle of the balance of power. Japan would feel militarily vulnerable, and calls for the development of nuclear military capabilities and conventional forces to protect its national interests would increase.
- Alternatively, Japan decides to develop conventional and nuclear capabilities by stealth. Such a scenario would raise considerable hostility in the U.S., East Asia, and beyond.
- A major power shift towards China or Russia, and these countries becoming militarily assertive. Without a U.S. balancer, Japan would most likely consider the development of sophisticated weapons system to check Chinese or Russian military assertiveness.
- North Korea develops nuclear weapons and the delivery system capable of reaching Japan. Although the security alliance with the U.S. would not change, there would, however, be a serious internal debate for a deterrence system against possible North Korean aggression.
- Taiwan (by stealth) develops a nuclear deterrent and a system capable of deterring PRC aggression in event of declaring itself 'independent' from Beijing (see *The Japan Times*, 30 July 1999: 4). The PRC might shift its

strategic relations with Russia, whereby an axis would exist between the two powers (see chapter eight on China).

These are possible scenarios for Japanese 'reconsideration' and could potentially lead to the divergence of U.S.-Japan relations. The emergence of these scenarios was especially visible in the aftermath of the end of the Cold War, with pressure from both the U.S. and Japan to 'cut-down' on defence procurements. Other powers, including allies, demanded that U.S. forces be withdrawn from the region, they ask 'what is the purpose of military forces when there is no threat present?' The Philippines, for example, demanded that U.S. forces leave that country.

In Japan, U.S. military was placed into question when the Liberal Democratic Party (LDP), which had been a crucial supporter of the security alliance with the United States since the mid-1950s, lost its majority in 1993. A coalition of smaller parties, headed by the Social Democratic Party (SDP) (formerly known as the Japanese Socialist Party) formed the new government. The SDP argued that since the United States had connected trade issues with the security alliance in its trade negotiation and threatened to withdraw its forces if Japan did not comply, it was therefore only appropriate that if the U.S. had desired to end the relationship, then U.S. forces should leave and let trade negotiation be on a more 'equal' footing. An interim draft report made by the Advisory Group on Defence, for example argued that, although the alliance with the United States remains important, the United Nations peacekeeping operations and 'multilateral security cooperation' *should take priority*.[14] Ochiro Ozawa[15] expressed that '[w]e [Japan] must consider the central role of the United Nations . . . in reinforcing world efforts to build a new order' (in D. Lai, ed. 1997: 37). Tadashi Aruga argued '[i]f the Japan-U.S. security arrangements are to continue to function smoothly, the Japanese will have to face up to the ambiguous nature of their pacifism. Although the number of issues on the global agenda that are apt to be resolved by force is fewer than ever, power politics remains one aspect of international politics' (1996: 40). Because of trade disputes sentiments, Washington saw this as an indication that Japan was setting its course to drift away from the security alliance.

Strategists in both Japan and the United States attacked both the U.S. government and the new Japanese government as rash and naïve in their understanding of 'geopolitical' structure and operation of 'world' affairs. The then Assistant U.S. Defense Secretary Joseph Nye used the dictum 'security is like oxygen' (J.S. Nye, Jr. 1995: 91), to describe the potential dangers of hasty mishandling of a potentially dangerous scenario not only for the United States and

---

[14] The Advisory Group submitted the report to Prime Minister Murayama in August 1996. The report is known as the 'Higuchi Report' after the name of the chairman of the Advisory Group, Kotaro Higuchi, president of Asahi beer company. Tatsuo Akaneya (1998) *The Japanese-U.S. Alliance: A New Definition*, p. 6.
[15] Ichiro Ozawa is the president of the New Frontier Party of Japan. Before he formed and became president of this party in 1993, he was a principal thinker of the Liberal Democratic Party.

Japan, but also for East Asia and the world. Nye urged the U.S. government to consider the role of Japan in its long-range international strategy, rather than pinpointing it on short-term relative economic gain. Nye emphasised that the shift of the global balance of power toward Asia meant Japan's strategic importance was increasing, not decreasing. In reinforcing Nye's view, the Aspen Strategy Group Report, recommended that Japan's power had to be 'harnessed' to America's advantage, just as the Japanese had so sophisticatedly utilised U.S. power to their advantage (K. Dam, J. Deutch, J.S. Nye, Jr. 1993). Tactically, the Aspen group recommended that, '[i]f the United States is to preserve its latitude for influencing events on a global scale, it must ensure that the strategic choices that Japan makes will be those that most closely match U.S. interests. The challenge . . . is to forge a strategy toward Japan that will secure U.S. interests well into the next century' (ibid., 1993: 30). Further, the alliance with Japan, according to Brzezinski, would be critical, for example, to managing the integration of China into the international system as an emerging major power (Z. Brzezinski, 1997). This persuasion appeared to have lowered the Clinton administration's aggressive trade stance towards Japan, and placed more emphasis on security issues. Thus the security alliance with Japan was reported as not only important for that country, but:

> If the American presence in Asia were removed, the security of Asia would be imperilled, with consequences for Asia and America alike. Our ability to affect the course of events would be constrained, our markets and our interests would be jeopardised . . . Our security alliance with Japan is the linchpin of the United States security policy in Asia.[16]

On the other hand, in another Pentagon East Asian Strategy Report in 1995, the U.S. administration indicated that it had not de-emphasised economic interests in favour of security, but it aimed to 'promote simultaneously and with vigour both U.S. economic and security interests' (M.M. Mochiszuki, 1997: 14). In fact, by tightening the security relationship, Washington had more room to be assertive towards Japan on trade issues without pushing Japan away politically.

However, what seemed to be a triumphant strategy almost led to a public relations disaster. The rape of a schoolgirl by U.S. servicemen in Okinawa, where relationships between the local inhabitants and the U.S. servicemen were already strained,[17] early in September 1995, posed a 'most difficult political challenge to the alliance' (M.M. Mochiszuki, 1997: 14). Japanese popular support for the

---

[16] U.S. Department of Defense, Office of International Security Affairs (1995, February) *United States Security Strategy for the East Asia-Pacific Region* (Washington D.C.: Department of Defense), pp. 9-10. For an example of criticism of this document, see Chalmers Johnson and E.B. Keehn (1995) 'The Pentagon's Ossified Strategy' *Foreign Affairs*, (July/August), pp. 103-14.

[17] Prior to the schoolgirl rape incident, a 24-year-old Okinawan woman was hammered to death by a U.S. soldier. The newspapers pigeonholed it as a 'love triangle gone wrong', writing that the woman had been divorced – as if that had anything to do with it. See Yoichi Funabashi (1999) *Alliance Adrift*, pp. 296-324.

security alliance dropped sharply. The Okinawans demanded that U.S. forces on Okinawa be withdrawn.

In an effort to defuse a politically injurious situation, the U.S. and Japanese governments created a Special Action Committee to find a way of 'reducing the intrusion of U.S. forces' facilities and personnel on the Okinawan people'.[18] However, the misgivings did not die out. The Okinawan governor, Masahide Ota, who had already been committed to the demand for the withdrawal of U.S. forces from the island, stiffened up his campaign and suggested that since Japan provided 70 percent of the costs[19] of overall maintenance of the forces, Japan should have some right to promote the good behaviour of the servicemen and direct jurisdiction over them, or else the servicemen should leave. In the end, the 'high' politics of the U.S. and Japanese governments forced Ota to agree on continued stationing of U.S. troops on that island, whether he liked it or not (see Yoichi Funabashi, 1999: 318-20). Chalmers Johnson reportedly stated in 1996 that 'Okinawa itself is like a rape victim turned out on the street by her pimp, with the United States being the rapist and the Japanese government in the role of the pimp'.[20] Incidentally, President Clinton's decision not to attend the APEC summit in Osaka in November 1995 (following the Okinawan rape incident) ostensibly because of the budget battle in Washington, proved to be a blessing in disguise.

An event that, perhaps, saved public disillusion towards the hostilities against the U.S. forces in Japan was the 'provocative' behaviour of the Taiwan President by advocating the 'two China' policy. The PRC without delay set its de jure claim on Taiwan by firing missiles, and eventually staging military exercises in spring 1996 around the island. This mini-crisis and unfolding events in North Korea (see B.K. Gills and S. Qadir, 1995) provided a good context to remind the Japanese and Americans of the strategic importance of the security alliance.

Since then, the Japanese, especially under PM Hashimoto (1996-1998), have worked hard to provide a firmer alliance structure for Japanese and U.S. military co-operation, and to establish measures to 'promote the consolidation, realignment and reduction of U.S. facilities and areas in Okinawa' (*Diplomatic Bluebook*, 1998: 13). In April 1996, two reports were issued to enhance the political, security, and economic interests between Japan and the United States.[21]

---

[18] 'Public Affairs Plan: Special Action Committee on Okinawa (SACO)', briefing memorandum, U.S. Forces in Japan, December 1995, in Mike M. Mochiszuki (Ed) (1997) *Toward A True Alliance: Restructuring U.S.-Japan Security Relations*, p. 15.

[19] Joseph S. Nye, Jr (1995) 'The Case for Deep Engagement' *Foreign Affairs*, vol. 74, no.4, (July/August), stated: 'it is cheaper to base the forces in Asia than in the United States. Japan pays nearly all the yen based cost of the 46,000 American forces, or nearly 70 percent of the troops' overall costs', p. 98.

[20] Glen Davis (14 October 1996) 'Scholar Says U.S. Policy Raping Okinawa' United Press International, cited in David Asher (1997) 'A U.S.-Japan Alliance for the Next Century', *Orbis*, vol. 41, no. 3, (summer), p. 361.

[21] They were the 'Message from Prime Minister Hashimoto and President Clinton to the People of Japan and the United States', and the 'Japan-U.S. Joint Declaration on Security.'

In September 1997, the Japanese and U.S. government reaffirmed 'Guidelines for Japan-U.S. Defence Cooperation' based on the Japan-U.S. Joint Declaration on Security. In 1998, the U.S. Department of Defense issued The East Asia Strategy Report, it emphasised:

> There is no more important bilateral relationship than the one we have with Japan. It is fundamental to both our Pacific security policy and our global strategic objectives. Our security relationship with Japan is the linchpin of United States security policy in Asia. It is seen not just by the United States and Japan but throughout the region as a major factor for securing stability in Asia.[22]

However, the security declarations have created uneasiness in the PRC and Russia, especially its emphasis on the 'possibility of the development of a Theatre Missile Defence (TMD) to be installed around Japan' (*Diplomatic Bluebook*, 1998: 57). The issue on the development of such a system has raised serious doubt in Chinese reaction and behaviour in the region (see the chapters on China and Russia). Furthermore, the NATO action in Kosovo in 1999 has created serious strategic and security questions for the PRC and Russia (see also the chapter on the EU).

Even Japan, the anchor for U.S. grand strategy in East Asia, feels unease about the U.S.-NATO actions. Ichiro Ozawa had predicted in 1997 that: 'If America tires of bearing its burden in international society, acts only with its own interests in mind, and thereby weakens the United Nations, Japan's present foreign policy will no longer be applicable and will have to be revamped' (Ichiro Ozawa in D. Lai, 1997: 39). Given Tokyo's emphasis on UN principles and its pursuit of a permanent UN Security Council seat (for details see R. Drifte, 2000), the Japanese feel undercut by the Kosovo affair. It remains unclear whether the interventions will push Tokyo closer to Washington or whether Japan will distance itself from what it perceived as a domineering power that is attempting to redefine the United Nations' clause on national sovereignty. Many Japanese are also concerned that U.S. interventionism may dictate that Japan participate in military operations outside the present Japanese defence guidelines.

Given the unease, especially the U.S.'s handling of Japanese economic guidelines linking it directly with the security alliance, and violating international agreement on sovereignty in the Kosovo conflict, it is contentious as to whether Japan can still feel that it can sit by and be dictated to by the United States, or alternatively distance itself from U.S. position? The only way to understand this is to look at the strategy played by the Japanese in the international system, and ask whether Japan is a system supporter or a system challenger.

Japan, after 1945, did strive to be a great power and it worked strenuously to (re)-establish an honourable position in the world. However, unlike its previous military ambitions before World War II (i.e., to establish a 'Greater Asia Co-

---

[22] Bureau of East Asian and Pacific Affairs (1998, 28 April) 'U.S.-Japan Relations' http://www.state.gov/www/regions/eap/.

prosperity Sphere'), Japan was constrained both by its constitution and its people, and by external forces, that compelled its military forces not to pose a menace to its neighbours. Japan, thus, whole-heartedly concentrated on (re)developing its economic prowess, whilst leaving the military aspect to the Americans, in the sense that there was an hegemonic 'division of labour' in East Asia between the U.S. and Japan. The constraints on Japan becoming a 'military' great power have been outlined and reinforced by security ties (or grip) with/by U.S. military pre-eminence. The following passages will analyse the extent of Japan being a supporter of that system.

Is Japan a (U.S.) Economic System Supporter?

The first aim here is to look at the economic contribution that Japan has played in sustaining its position and reinforcing that of the United States' goal of enhancing 'hegemonic globalisation' in the emerging world order. The second aim is to focus on Japanese democracy promotion and the extent to which Japan wants to promote those ideals.

Former Japanese Prime Minister Miyazawa (1991-1993) stated: 'The outlook for the world going into the twenty-first century will largely depend on whether or not Japan and the United States . . . are able to provide co-ordinated leadership under shared vision' (cited in Z. Brzezinski, 1997: 180).

According to *The Economist's The World in 2000 Report*, Japan accounts for 60 percent of Asia's regional output. One would suspect that Japan would play a major role in the global economy. Yet, it hosts less than 1 percent of the world's total investment (compared with 30 percent for the United States), and '[o]nly 6 percent of Japanese agree that all barriers and regulations should be eliminated. *Even in* China, a socialist country, twice as many respondents (13 percent) favoured free trade' (*The Japan Times*, 9 July 1999: 21). In these circumstances, critics argue that the Asian economic crises of 1997-1999 were perfect opportunities for Japan to show that it does shoulder responsibilities.

Critics argue that with its huge economic prowess Japan would at least provide some support to alleviate the distress of its East Asian neighbours. Yet. 'Japan acted like a deer caught in a car's headlights, seemingly incapable of action' (in E. Kapstein and M. Mastanduno, 1999: 475). This is, however, unfair to suggest that Japan did not consider rescuing the countries in the crisis (see P. Gowan, 1999: 103-24). Japan did try to deliver a solution by initiating an Asian Monetary Fund (AMF) in the early stages of the crisis. This was, however, quashed by the United States for fearing that the potential AMF would replace the IMF and World Bank as 'stabiliser' of 'last-resort' in the region which would mean the U.S. losing significant influence and power in and over the countries affected by the economic and financial crises. Japan was instead accused by the United States, and even some ASEAN countries, of being unwilling to solve the problem.[23] Recall a former Japanese trade negotiator's complaint: 'We are always being told, "you should take on more responsibilities" . . . If we try to raise our voice, we face the comment that "you are trying to dominate." If we are silent, we face the criticism that "you are too silent"' (cited in J. Chace, 1992: 99). What can Japan do?

IMF and World Bank funds were, thus, allocated to solve the crisis. With IMF and World Bank policies, the position of hegemonic globalisation has taken a stronger hold in the 'regulated markets' of many Asian economies (P. Gowan, 1999). The World Bank and IMF (1998) issued that for East Asian countries to recover, they had to deregulate and make their economic practices transparent. Many East Asians, such as the Malaysian Prime Minister Mahathir, viewed such practices as a 'conspiracy on behalf' of the United States and international financiers to weaken Asia's economic development. Yet, such a perspective is controversial given the United States strategy of maintaining its preponderant position in the region, and its strategy of engagement and enlargement of the zone of peace and prosperity. Had the crisis deepened and the countries (such as Thailand, Korea, and others) not been able to resolve their financial problems quickly, social unrest and political instability were very near on the horizon, as happened in Indonesia for example. Social unrest and political instability would not only challenge the foundations of decades of economic development in these countries, but potentially had the contagion effect of reaching other developed countries and ultimately the U.S. as well. Consequently, the 'U.S. officials have viewed the Asian financial crisis . . . not as an opportunity to weaken economic competitors but as a potential threat to the security and stability of the region and to the global economy' (M. Mastanduno, 1998: 12). This, however, may be regarded by Malaysian PM Mahathir and Gowan (1999) as a diplomatic smoke screen to change the political system in these countries.

Initially, the East Asian countries were reluctant to implement the IMF and World Bank programmes (IMF Staff Papers, 1999). The policy recommendations were to convince East Asia to deregulate or suffer the full force of capital mobility and globalisation. The countries were told that either they were to follow the advice of the United States-led institutions, or they were to be locked into an economic trap. The message was clear: 'conform or suffer' (Waltz, 1999: 694). The policy recommendations have had mixed results. Although South Korea and Thailand can be said to have 'conformed' and may have 'come out' of the crisis and are growing again, Malaysia, which never conformed to the U.S. pressure, has also managed to recover. Indonesia, on the hand, has lost a President and may be on the brink of civil war, partially because of conforming to the 'rules'.

Despite the weakness in the 'end-game' of Japanese economic power execution in the economic crisis. Japan has been a major contributor to the IMF

---

[23] Malaysian Prime Minister Mahathir Bin Mohamad, for example, bemoaned the red tape involved in securing funds from Japan's U$30 billion plan for Asia's recovery. He is reported to have said, 'By the time Malaysia eventually gets to see the money, the crisis will be over', *Far Eastern Economic Review*, 28 January 1999, p. 30.

and World Bank, and is a member of the G7(8). It has an ODA programme, which is engaged in the promotion of economic development for lesser-developed countries. As the U.S. and Japan are members of the WTO, OECD, the World Bank, the IMF, and regionally APEC, the U.S. State Department reports that Japan and the United States have a shared interest and responsibility for promoting global growth, open markets, and a world trading system (U.S. Bureau of East Asian and Pacific Affairs, 28 April 1998). As America acts as the hub for most industrialised countries, Reinhard Drifte states that Japan too 'can be compared to that [position] to many Asian nations . . . [and] increasingly the NIEs form their own hubs and spoke to the less developed Asian countries, as is demonstrated by Korean, Taiwanese and Thai development in Vietnam, the Philippines, mainland China and so on' (1996: 141, emphasis added).

Is Japan a 'Liberal Democratic' Promoter?

Even before the collapse of the Soviet Union, analysts have commented that Japan defined itself as a culture holding the principles of liberalism, democracy, and peace. Nevertheless, the 'principles' have been criticised as being 'superficial principles (tutemae)'. It is claimed that, '[t]he fundamental objective (honne) was powering all our strength into economic growth' (K.B. Pyle, 1992: 122). The critics of Japanese democracy point to the 'superficiality of Japan's cultural borrowing from the West and the shallowness of many Japanese persons' comprehension of Western values and motivations' (K.W. Tong, 1996-7: 108). Second, they argue that 'Japan needs to assume a role in the international community appropriate to its status as a democratic country' (T. Aruga, 1996: 41). Third, if such is the benefit for Japan as a trading nation why have the Japanese bureaucracy and governments been unwilling to implement a freely liberal trading regime which, in any case, would have benefited Japanese business even more? Fourth, if there is a convergence in Japanese and American political philosophy, why is there such scepticism from both sides?

Each of the above questions will be looked at separately. However, firstly, it should be noted that neither the United States nor Western Europe should claim to have a monopoly of democracy, peace, and prosperity. To argue that democracy can take form only in Western civilisation is false. Even the Trilateral Commission asserts: 'We should perhaps remind ourselves that democracy – defined as government of the people, by the people, and for the people – is of relatively recent origin and is still developing' (B. Emmott et al, 1997: 40). The development of universal suffrage in most of Western Europe did not occur after the 1930s and 1940s; in Britain in 1928, and in Switzerland in 1971. The United States did not break out of its slavery system until after a civil war (1861-1865) and universal suffrage in the U.S. did not occur until 1920. However, the massive disenfranchisement of black citizens in the South, for federal as well as state and local elections, was not reversed until the court and legislature actions that culminated in the Voting Rights Act in 1965 (I. Mclean, 1996: 484). On these very simple grounds, the 'West' has not experienced democracy or universal suffrage any longer than most countries. Many countries around the world did not gain their independence until after World War II. Given such a short period of readjustment from colonial rule, and the [re]-development of their countries, the development of democracy and other institutions that can help enable a checks and balance system to stem the concentration of power in the hands of powerful individuals and groups, although not perfect, have been developing.

However, is Japan a democracy? Japan is an 'unusual' democracy but it is still a democracy. First, Japan shares 'the same basic political principle' (Y. Nagatomi, 1988: 241) as the United States. Second, 'Japan aspires for a free and open order both domestically and in international society'. Third, 'Japan's economic prosperity is inseparably bound up with a free and open world economic order' (Y. Nagatomi, 1988: 241-2). The Japanese *Diplomatic Bluebook*, 1986, defined the Japanese position in the international environment as 'being a member of free democratic nations sharing common political ideals' (quoted in B. Emmott et al, 1997: 36). They argue that it was(is) imperative for Japan in co-operation with the U.S. and EU to 'contribute positively to the development of an international economic system based upon the principles of freedom and mutual respect, and it must be prepared to share the cash necessary in making such contributions' (Y. Nagatomi, 1998: 52).

Japanese techniques are more orientated to business promotion. Japanese investments have been harnessed (indirectly) to the development of middle classes in East Asian countries (see chapter eight). This is soft power (see Drifte, 1996), the power to ingrain messages and images with economic wealth is significant in Japanese power. Although it may not be issued under trade investment agreements between governments, the movement of ideas and wealth does create images and perceptions on the material wealth of foreigners in these countries. The messages sent are seen clearly, that 'if you want to be rich and successful, you must become like us'. Whether this can directly lead to pluralistic democracy is debatable, but the evidence from South Korea and Taiwan does indicate that economic development in East Asia does enhance the development of pluralistic democratic system. The tendency to create polyarchy (W. Robinson, 1996) which, being educated and affluent, would eventually demand more open pluralistic political participation, policy-making and the rule of law.

On this account, Japan's 'soft' power strategy has accommodated and helped U.S. interests on the promotion of economic prosperity and enhanced the organic position of democracy in less developed and less democratic countries. Thus, as Akaha and Langdon insist, it is not that Japan is not in support of the U.S. hegemonic system, it is 'disbursing its economic aid (ODA) to countries considered of strategic importance to the United States' (1993: 8). If the pooling of capital in the IMF and World Bank would account for the maintenance of the U.S. hegemonic system – then Japan has been responsible for that maintenance since it became a net contributor. In the *Ideal Socioeconomy and Policies for Economic*

Rebirth, the Japanese Economic Council proposed to 'help create a framework to make organisations like the IMF better able to deal with currency crisis' (in *The Economist Intelligence Unit, Country Report: Japan, 1999, 3rd Quarter*, pp.18-19). On the maintenance of U.S. power projection in East Asia, Japan supported the maintenance of about 70 percent of the cost of the U.S. forces in Japan. It was reported that in 1991 the Japanese government offered to pay the Philippines an equivalent of $1 billion in economic aid if the latter would agree to retain American bases on its soil (K. Aldred and M.A. Smith, 1999: 88).

Because Japan's constitution restricts Japan from sending military personnel abroad, Japan is caught between an economically superpower status and a politically restricted constitution. Until recently, the only means it has had to support the United States is to supply it with monies, for example in the UN efforts to dislodge Saddam Hussein from Kuwait, Japan donated $13 billion for UN military efforts.

In its efforts to enhance the UN's credibility and to become a permanent member of the Security Council, Japan has contributed generously. Japan has become the second largest contributor to the United Nations, accounting for about 20% of the UN annual budget. Japan views this as an effort to enhance human rights, humanitarian development, and promoting democracy (*Diplomatic Bluebook*, 1998: 41). Regionally, ASEAN has been an increasingly important component in Tokyo's foreign policy, with ASEAN countries even calling on Japan to represent their interests in the G7/8 meeting. In its relations with South Korea, Japan is proposing to '[s]trengthen co-operation with South Korea as the first step to creating an Asian free-trade zone.... Use APEC to develop economic interaction in Asia and lead the thrust for regional economic integration' (in *The Economist Intelligence Unit, Country Report: Japan, 1999, 3rd Quarter*, pp.18-19). In its relations with China, Japan is the largest investor in that country and China receives the highest contribution of any country of Japanese Overseas Development Aid (ODA) (R. Drifte, 1996: 111).

If such is the case, why does the United States appear to have misunderstood Japan's economic and political intentions? Secondly, if the Clinton administration has an agenda for the promotion of the enlargement and engagement policies of democratic peace and prosperity across the world, why has it been critical of the Japanese on issues that would, in any event, promote these very ideals? For example, the Japanese emergency packages for the East Asian financial crisis.

The answer probably lies in that – and this has been the emphasis throughout this book – certain members of the Clinton administration and sections of the U.S. public have ideals of engagement and enlargement. These interests are, however, not free from the impingement of certain interests that are both narrow and short-term. This leaves the U.S. in a dilemma between a traditional nationalist relative gain/relative loss, protectionist argument on the one hand, and the strategy of sustaining allied support for its grand strategy of enlargement via hegemonic globalisation on the other. The grand strategy is the ideal, the vision. However,

America is not an altruistic state. Once relative losses set in, the U.S. Congress and other nationalistic interest groups very quickly change their position, blaming others for its failures; or complaining that others are not taking a fair share of the responsibilities, to the reciprocal benefit of the U.S.; or it may deliberately isolate itself; and/or disband that internationalised system altogether.

Unfinished Business

It would seem, from the analysis above, that Japan does have a supporting role in enhancing U.S. hegemonic globalisation. Yet, one despairing phenomenon that has puzzled many has been its inability to come to terms with its 'cruel' and 'genocidal' behaviour before and during the Second World War. The Japanese government remains adamant in not fully condemning the actions of the Japanese imperial government before and during World War II. Some Japanese have even defended Japan's colonial and wartime record.[24] Professor Reinhard Drifte shows how even the Japanese government has demanded 'changing Victory over Japan Day to Victory in the Pacific Day' (R. Drifte, 1996: 168). In other cases, the Japanese population is portrayed as the victim of its own military as much as of foreign states (J. Agnew and S. Corbridge, 1995: 150; T.U. Berger, 1993: 119-50; R. Drifte, 1996). John Naisbitt has lambasted that '[i]t is not a Japan that can say "no" – it is a Japan that can't say "I'm sorry" . . . The whole enterprise leaves one judging Japan as a country that has no moral compass or backbone, no real sense of who it is or what it has done' (1996: 31). U.S. State Department official Kurt Tong described it as follows: 'it seems that Japan still cannot decide whether its conduct during World War II was somehow uniquely wrong or whether it was just caught up in evil circumstances' (1996-7: 108).

This circumstantial issue raises a serious dilemma for the Japanese. For example, how can Japan pursue a moralist international role in the promotion of democracy and liberalisation, and attempt to become a permanent member of the UN Security Council, when its government and sections of its populace refuse to question their past crimes against humanity? Japan may try and has tried to buy votes in the poorer countries with its ODA and investment in these countries. However, human dignity in many East Asian countries makes it questionable as to whether money can be used to buy the Japanese out of their past atrocities. For Japan to buy its way out of its crimes would rub salt in the wound. What many East Asians and Europeans (i.e., Britain) simply demand is an official condemnation, by the Japanese Head of State, of the Japanese atrocities of the past and an official apology for those misdeeds. If Japan realistically aims to become an influential power in East Asia and the wider world, a recognition of its past would

---

[24] The governor of Tokyo, Shintaro Ishihara has frequently called the Nanjing massacre a lie. Howard W. French (22 January 2000) 'The Rape of Nanking Swirls Again in Japan', New York Times Services in The International Herald Tribune obtained from http://www.iht/com/iht/today/sat/fpage/tokyo.2.html.

elevate Japan into a more benign position in its quest for permanent membership of the UN Security Council. Without this acceptance, any closer alignment with either the EU or other East Asian nations, i.e., in the WTO against U.S. dominance would always be hit by this thorn. In such case, the United States enjoys not only military and economic dominance, but also from Japanese pride to recognise its wrongs of its past.

Acceptance of its responsibility before and during the Second World War is, perhaps, one of the biggest thorns that Japan can remove. Japan has desires to become a permanent member of the UN Security Council. Japanese funding accounts for 20 percent of the UN organisation's funding (*Diplomatic Bluebook*, 1998: 41), and the Japanese Ministry of Foreign Affairs has indicated that: 'If the United Nations simply engages in repetitious debate and proves incapable of reforming itself to adapt to the changing times, the credibility of the organisation in the eyes of the international community could be severely undermined' (*Diplomatic Bluebook*, 1998: 41). Japan may have a case, but that is rhetorical. In its quest for the UN Security Council seat, no Asian nation has yet supported the Japanese cause (R. Drifte, 2000: 153). It is not only that these nations have vivid memories of Japanese atrocities, but also it is the Japanese perception that the Japanese invasion was an unfortunate phase in their history, and is best to be forgotten.[25]

Japan can play a significant role in maintaining and advancing international peace and prosperity. A state apology to the countries on which it inflicted pain and suffering before and during World War II would not only gain the region's confidence, but would offer the Japanese opportunities for greater respect rather than to be perceived with hidden hatred. Japan under the U.S. guise of hegemonic globalisation has mixed its responses.

Conclusion

The Japanese relationship with the United States, since the 'black ships' of Commodore Perry entering Tokyo bay in 1853 to the emerging world order, can be summarised as being periods of:

---

[25] On the other hand, many Japanese have emphasised great remorse at their forefathers' actions. Ichiro Ozawa for example states: 'Our Asian neighbours continue to feel distrust and alarm about Japan, as a result of World War II. We need to develop the trust of our neighbours if we are to place greater emphasis on our political ties in the region. "History" is not an issue we can avoid . . . We must reflect soberly on our history, examine it in good faith, and apply its lessons to our principles and behaviour, our present actions, and our future plans. We cannot deny the part of aggression has played in our history in Asia . . . If Japan is to represent the interests of the Asia-Pacific region in the international arena and act as mediator in disputes, it must first earn the trust of the people of the region . . .' in David Lai (Ed.) (1997) *Global Perspectives: International Relations, U.S. Foreign Policy, and the View from Abroad*, p. 39, pp. 43-44.

- 'opening-up' (end of Tokugawa),
- 're-organising' (Meiji restoration),
- systemic 'challenger' (1920s to 1945),
- 'compromise sovereignty' (1945 -),
- so called 'economic challenge' (1970s to 1990s)
- 'opening-up' (1990s)
- 're-organising' and 'compromised' to hegemonic globalisation.

In response to the 'opening-up', Japan reorganised its perspective of outsiders especially toward 'Westerners', and was determined to 'catch-up' with the West technologically. In the process of that early catch-up, Japan too was caught in the imperialist ambitions. That ambition led to Japan becoming the system challenger in the 1920s to 1945. From 1945 to the end of the Cold War, Japan was a subordinate and compromised its sovereignty to being a supporter of U.S. geopolitical system. In supporting that system, Japan benefited significantly from the economic structure of that system. However, that benefit was seen by the U.S. of Japan taking 'too much' advantage of America endeavours. The breaking up of the Bretton Woods system and the assertion by the Reagan and Clinton administrations was deliberately targeted at Japan as being an unfair and a 'selfish' trading partner, whose only aim was just to maximise its economic prowess without considering U.S. relational loses. In such relationship, bickerings would only intensify. The Clinton administration called for a reconsideration of the relationship, and threatened to withdraw from the security treaty. In responding to U.S. criticism and the sea change in Japan politics in 1993, Japan issued that if that was the U.S. attitude then maybe the security treaty should be changed. U.S. and Japanese strategists, however, quickly dampened the potential fire destroying the relationship. The Nye Report reinforced U.S. commitment to Japan and East Asia. However, the damage was already done as the Japanese economic bubble burst in the early 1990s. As the U.S. freed itself from the fixed exchange rate system and intensified its economic activities, Japanese businesses found it more difficult to compete with U.S. corporations. Under recession and U.S. pressure to reform to a more liberal internal market, Japan is transforming itself 'again' to accommodate to U.S. liberal hegemonic order.

Chapter 11

U.S. Grand Strategy in the Emerging World Order: 'The Sun and Its Planets'[1]

> Our task is not to fix the blame of the past, but to fix the course for the future.
> John F. Kennedy
>
> Politics is no longer a question of who gets what, where and when, but of the term in which the world is to be understood.
> D. Miller, 1987/1997: 358.

In the 'geopolitics' of international relations, the U.S. has managed to stay close to the EU, Japan, China, and Russia, whilst these powers have, for reasons of historical, geographical, and/or racial tensions, been quite reluctant and mistrustful of each other. These realities have been advantageous to the United States. The U.S. is aware that, if the United States misses this opportunity or happens to misunderstand the circumstance that the United States is faced with, the consequences will evolve and open a 'new chapter' in human civilisation (National War College, 1998-9). In the setting process of U.S. strategy, the United States has been keen to make sure that other powers do not align with each other so as to challenge U.S. supremacy (D. Cheney, 1992; 1993; W. Cohen, 1997; 1999) and its aim to hegemonically globalise the world.

This book has advocated that the global system in the zone of peace and prosperity – that is the areas of North America, Western Europe and part of East

---

[1] Noam Chomsky used a solar system analogy to analyse on the relations that the United States had with its southern neighbours. In that analogy, the sun was being described as the United States and the planets being the countries in Central and South America. In my argument, this same rule can be said to apply to the international system, where powers like the EU, Japan, the countries in the OECD, and others are revolving around America, but also have their own system i.e., satellites in the planetary movement. Thus, it will mean each having the sphere of influence, but with liberal and democratic characteristics which are similar to the United States. The main source of pull however remain to be the United States. So in the system of sun, planets, satellites (moons) and asteroids and other bodies. With this analogy, the game of the classical balance of power is unnecessary. This system is unlike insitutionalists who rely heavily on regimes and organisations to gel the world from falling apart. In this system, it becomes unnecessary because each power operates in the same manner as others, they have similar interests and similar goals.

Asia – during the Cold War and after was/is never balanced by the traditional balance of forces. It was and is instead conformed into a U.S.-led economic and security network. That network is presently reaching out and penetrating into areas once outside its sphere of interest. In the centre of that network is America, where it is able to control the speed and direction of the components of the international political/economic system (A. Valladao, 1996: T. Friedman, 1999). These variables are, in turn, deciding the nature and relations with the EU, Japan and other powers such as, China, Russia, as they become more encompassed with the countries in the zone of peace and competitive prosperity.

Scholars of the democratic peace (on democratic peace see M. Doyle, 1983a, 1983b; B. Russett, 1993; M. Brown et al, 1997; L. Diamond et al, 1997, 1999; H. Nau, 1998), which involves more variables than simple political democracy, argue that although fierce economic competition is rampant between the U.S., EU and Japan, the nature of the competition does not call into question the 'vital' national interest – such as the territorial survival of the nation-state – of these countries. According to Henry Nau, 'it is difficult to perceive in the immediate structure of international relations or the policies implemented by and between them an indication that America, the EU or Japanese should go to war with each other over trade disputes'.[2] In fact, the question that America should attack Japan or Europe to make them comply with American demands does not even come into the minds of decision-makers, let alone being contemplated. Nau declares, 'today Europe, Japan and America may threaten each other with economic warfare when negotiations stall, this is, however, where it ends, because everyone knows the deadly consequences of destroying the global trading system'.[3]

Behind this fear, lays the twin-headed monster of power politics and neo-mercantilistic practices, which may resurface and cause unforeseen damages (Kindleberger, 1973; Gilpin, 1981). *Fortunately*, the current international system and the domestic contradictory forces have not reached such a serious dilemma. For the countries in the zone of peace and prosperity, the welfare and benefits to be gained from trading and co-operating with each, far outweigh the advantages of them not trading or co-operating with each other and the international community. By trading and co-operating, these states are not just becoming more prosperous, but they are also increasingly becoming compliant to international trading rules and regulations. Even countries that do not share the same economic principles as those of the United States (such as Russia, China, India, and others) and may even pose a direct threat to the American-led economic system, are themselves reluctant to become disengaged with the U.S.-led system or to entertain breaking away from the system. They are aware of the disadvantages of not incorporating with the international trading standards and regulations. Even China, for example, often described as an authoritarian state, one which may pose as the most potential challenger to the U.S.-led system, and one that has been described as most likely

---

[2] Interview with Henry Nau, 10 July 1998, Washington, D.C.; see also J.M Scott (ed) (1999) *After the End*, p. 16.
[3] Henry Nau, ibid.

to want to destabilise the system and replace it with its own, does not contemplate this, because even it knows that for it to develop, it has to be part of the system and yields to those norms and regulations. That is why, when it is negotiating trade with the United States, China is extremely careful not to breach trade laws and regulations set out by the United States and its partners. China will not only risk losing its largest market and the abundance of high technology, but its economic prosperity would grind to a halt if China does not take measures to liberalise its trading practices and liberalise its internal political structure. Likewise, with the United States when it deals with China. The United States knows that it has most of the trump cards when dealing over trade issues with China, however, the United States also knows that it cannot push the Chinese too far, so as to push China back to the seclusive ways of Maoism. That is why the United States has been prepared to accept the $60 billion[4] trade deficit with China. By maximising the exposure of materialism and liberal ideas into the Chinese populace, thus, indirectly building a vibrant middle class structure is the way in which many U.S. analysts seek to 'organically' replace the communist regime (see Brzezinski, 1997). The United States hopes that this can eventually change the political and economic structure in China without causing too much political instability both inside and outside China (see chapter eight).

In this scenario, geopolitics amongst the major powers has, for the time being, been submerged by the need for economic growth and development. If this proposition on the postponement of geopolitics amongst the major powers in the post-Cold War is to hold, there is a real opportunity for the first time in human history where a power (the United States) with its followers (the OECD) may encompass others outside the zone of peace and prosperity to actually amalgamate them closer into the system. The White House 1996 document, *A National Security Strategy of Engagement and Enlargement*, implied this and outlined that 'the more that democracy and political and economic liberalisation take hold in the world, . . . the safer our nation is likely to be and the more our people are likely to prosper'.[5] The earnest challenge, for the United States and others in the zone of democratic peace and prosperity notwithstanding, is to convince the countries outside the zone of peace and prosperity that it is in their benefit to be part of the system,[6] rather than to rotate around the old wary contemplation that this is just another plot by the rich to exploit the poor, or the West's re-attempting to colonise the rest (The White House, 1999).

If the logic of the advance of liberal democracy and international economic liberalisation is the intention of the United States, then Bill Clinton was clearly

---

[4] See A. Friedman and Jonathan Gage (1999, Feb'1) 'A Proposal to Monitor World Finance System', *International Herald Tribune*. www.iht.com/IHT/Today/Mon/Fpage/davos.html.
[5] The White House (February 1996) *'A National Security Strategy of Engagement and Enlargement.'* (www.fas/org/spp/military/docops/national/1996stra.htm) p. 7.
[6] Bimal Ghosh (1998, 17 November) 'Stop Demonising Globalisation, and Learn to Manage It.' *International Herald Tribune*, www.iht.com/IHT/TODAY/TUE/ED/edghogh.html.

misunderstood when accused by pundits of lacking that 'vision thing'.[7] His goal may reach far beyond the patterns of realpolitics as how the commentators may have understood it. Before taking office in 1993, he asserted that it is 'a world where freedom, not tyranny, is on the march, the cynical calculus of power politics simply does not compute. It is ill-suited to a new era' (cited in J. Mearsheimer, 1994/5: 5). Clearly, this type of vision has not been witnessed since the days of Woodrow Wilson. However, you may recall that within 20 years of Wilson's idealism, the world was again up in arms. There are many reasons for genesis of WWII, to blame it directly on Wilson's idealism is unfair. War was then glorified by at least four of the seven major powers.[8] In the post-Cold War era, mankind, especially in the developed countries of Western Europe, Japan and North America, has increasingly become fearful of his/her past. Perhaps the nightmares of the past and the apocalyptic nuclear holocaust can remind him/her of the horrors and sufferings of war. This is, however, not to say that we should all surrender when faced with authoritarian threats that challenge our livelihood and liberty such as those posed by Saddam Hussein. On the contrary, it is an argument that stresses the importance of the changes that have developed in the industrial democratic societies over the past fifty years, where a consensus has been reached on the desirability of peace and prosperity. War between them is of no benefit to either victor or loser. This is not an ideal, but the reality that needs to be addressed and advanced. Immanuel Kant developed an early notion of perpetual peace amongst republic states where he argued:

---

[7] In the *Foreign Policy* journal 1997-98 (Winter), several commentaries from the respective regions or countries gave their opinions on the performance of President Clinton's foreign policy. Moises Naim (1997-98) 'Clinton's Foreign Policy: A Victim of Globalisation?', pp. 35-45, stated that President Clinton is 'unlikely to be remembered for his foreign policy'; Christopher Bertram (1997-98) 'A View from Europe (1)', pp.45-7, writes Clinton's foreign policy 'if it exists at all, is difficult to decipher'; Jorge I. Dominguez (1997-98) 'A View from Latin America', pp. 48-51, exclaims, 'I long for Bush's "vision"!'; Yoichi Funabashi (1997-98) 'A View from Asia (1)', pp. 51-4, points to a 'notable lack of the "vision thing"'; Jacques Attali (1997-98) 'A View from Europe (2)', pp. 54-7, notes Clinton as 'lacking a long-term vision, his administration seeks to impose its fancied solutions on an ad hoc basis'. Fawaz A. Gerges (1997-98) 'A View from the Middle East', pp. 57-62, laments 'more than any other recent president, Clinton appears to conduct foreign policy on an ad hoc basis, often gearing it toward satisfying domestic constituencies'. Rupert Pennant-Rea (1997-98) 'A View from Europe (3)', pp. 62-4, observes that 'it is surely fair to be disappointed by Clinton's foreign policy record: relentlessly tactical and never in the case of strategy'; Yegar Gaidar (1997-98) 'A View from Russia', pp. 64-6, concludes that 'one of the chief distinguishing characters of President Clinton's foreign policy has been his unwillingness to make clear choices or to provide a coherent vision'. Nayan Chanda (1997-98) 'A View from Asia (2)', pp. 66-9, observes that in Asia 'the indirection that has marked Clinton's policy toward the region only confirmed the initial apprehension of 1992'.

[8] Germany, Japan, Italy, and Russia propagated the importance of militarism. Whilst France and Britain were too exhausted by WWI, the people of the United States did not share the vision of their leader, President Woodrow Wilson.

> ... the republican constitution ... [gives favourable prospect for perpetual peace] ... [The reason is this]. If ... the consent of the citizens is required to determine whether there shall be war or not, nothing is more natural than that they should weigh the matter well. ... For in decreeing war ... they must fight themselves; they must hand over the costs of the war out of their own property ... [But] in a constitution which is not republican, the plunging into war is the least serious thing in the world. For the ruler is not a citizen, but the owner of the state, and does not lose a whit by the war. ... He can decide therefore on war for ... as if it were a kind of pleasure party (I. Kant, 1795, Perpetual Peace, translated by M.C. Smith, 1903: 122-3, emphasis added).

In following aspects of the Kantian philosophy, the Clinton administration has demonstrated that it is '... in our interest that democracy be at once the foundation and the purpose of the international structure'.[9] The White House document continues by outlining that,

> Promoting democracy does more than foster our ideals. It advances our interests because we know that the larger the pool of democracies, the better off we, and the entire community of nations, will be. Democracies create free markets that offer economic opportunity, make for more reliable trading partners and are far less likely to wage war on one another.[10]

The White House document indicated that what was necessary was for the developed and democratic countries to *persuade* countries outside that zone, that they too can be part of the zone of peace and prosperity, on the condition that if they play the game by the rules of democracy and liberalism, and they too can become rich and peaceful. However, the document emphasised that this is 'particularly in countries of strategic importance to us'.[11]

So, whilst it aims to enlarge the community of democracies and capitalism, the U.S. administration is also highly selective of its target. This brings tensions inside the U.S. policy-making, especially with regards to what can be gained from the promotion of liberal democracy and free trade to countries that are not of strategic importance to it. In addition, the question that has perplexed the U.S. since the renewal-decline debate, 'is the U.S. to gain relatively or absolutely and even lose from the promotion of liberal democracy and free trade'? As outlined in chapter two, politics is power, and power is politics, the struggle for power and politics is continuously contested. Despite the arguments put forth by democratic peace scholars, it is not easy to deny that power relations and its relative gain or loss is not important. In some form or another, power is apparent in all parts of society whether domestic or international, it would be foolish to deny that it does not operate. However, this is beside the point. The point here is to understand

---

[9] The White House (February 1996) *'A National Security Strategy of Engagement and Enlargement.'* p. 6.
[10] Ibid., pp. 6-7.
[11] Ibid., p. 7.

what type and at what level power is being struggled for and for what purpose.

In traditional power politics, the preponderance of military power, with a strong economic base, often prevails over other competing power configurations.[12] Moreover, in the post-Cold War system, despite having significantly more power resources and capabilities than that of its 'competitors', and contrary to the advocation of the democratic peace theories, Michael Cox observes that 'the object of the game [for the United States] now was not to prevent the spread of an alien ideology, but rather to maintain and where possible increase market share' (1995: 21-2, emphasise added; see also M. Borrus et al, 1992). Cox argues that this has not made it any less competitive. For if the United States succeeded in 'winning' the economic battle, 'it would mean domestic prosperity and continued influence abroad. Failure to do so could easily lead to decline internationally and rising social tensions at home. The stakes in the post-communist era were every bit as high as they had been during the Cold War itself' (M. Cox, 1995: 22). Robert Gilpin wrote in 1981 that '[i]n the modern era, nations have most frequently had more to gain through economic efficiency, co-operation, and an international division of labour than through war, imperialism, and exclusive economic sphere' (1981: 200). However, he stressed, 'the growth of economic interdependence and the prospect of mutual gain have not eliminated competition and mutual distrust among nations. Trade has not always proved to be a force for peace' (Gilpin, 1981: 200). He maintains that '[e]conomic nationalism has never been far below the surface, [i.e. Japan and U.S. over trade imbalances and trade disputes], and in this century the breakdown of the international economy in response to nationalism has been a contributing factor to conflict' (Gilpin, 1981: 220, emphasise added). On the other hand, why does the United States (because of its preponderant military power) not just warn other powers that it does not want to have to compete economically with them, and that they should pay their tributes to the political/military hegemon, or at least pay their fair share of the military burden that the hegemon has to bear in maintaining the stability of the anarchic international system within which they all operate and prosper?[13] The obvious diplomatic answer would be that that United States does not wish to be perceived as a malign power, nor does it want to be perceived as being hegemonic (R. Kagan, 1998; E. Petterson, 1998).

Despite this diplomatic smoke-screen, the Pentagon's *Defense Planning Guidance for Fiscal Years 1994-1999* indicated that it was in the United States national interest '[to discourage large industrial nations] from challenging our leadership or seeking to overturn the established political and economic order'.[14]

---

[12] Niccolo Machiavelli advised that 'For gold alone will not produce good soldiers, but good soldiers will always produce gold'. Luigi Ricci, trans. (1950) *The Prince and the Discourses* (New York: Modern Library), p. 310.

[13] See Leslie H. Gelb (1992) 'They're Kidding', *New York Times*, 9 March, p. A15; William Plaff (1992) 'Does the United States Want to Lead Through Intimidation?' *Los Angeles Times*, 11 March 1992, p. B7.

[14] 'Excerpts From Pentagon Plan: "Prevent the Re-emergence of a New Rival"', *New York*

Although the document was later rephrased (only because it was leaked to the press), the United States Government remains adamant in its position, for it does not want to be challenged by any other power for its predominant position in any way. Former Secretary of Defense Dick Cheney wrote in 1993 in the *Defense Strategy for the 1990s: The Regional Defense Strategy* reminds the world that, '*it is our* (the United States') *goal* to preclude any hostile power from dominating a region critical to our interests ... These regions include Europe, East Asia, the Middle East/Persian Gulf, and Latin America.' He goes on to say: ' ... the United States must show the leadership necessary to encourage sustained cooperation among major democratic powers'.[15] Also, in that document, it was identified that Germany and Japan, rather than China or Russia, are the most potential candidates to challenge the United States supremacy.

Such is the concern of the United States on the emergence of new great powers challenging the position of the United States, the strategies adopted by the late Bush and early Clinton administration of the early 1990s by adopting aggressive economic pressure on East Asia states and Western European states were exactly aimed at preventing them from being serious challengers. President Clinton has argued that for the United States to be competitive it had to rethink the relationship between government and business (see J. Bergner, 1991; L. Tyson, 1992; L. Thurow, 1992). Clinton argued that 'U.S. business had not received the support needed or deserved ... in a cut-throat world economy where governments in other countries were actively promoting business' (cited in M. Cox, 1995: 24-6). In fact, the Clinton political economy, 'rested upon an assumption that the United States had to be at the heart of a regionalised world economy' (M. Cox, 1995: 24). Whereby,

> ... it would ensure continued U.S. leadership of the world economic system; it would prevent any move by these regions towards self-sufficiency; and it would facilitate the movement towards a more open world economy upon which future U.S. prosperity and influence depended – one idea central to this was globalisation (M. Cox, 1995: 24).

The talk of premature decline of America power in the 1970s to the early 1990s has led Washington in adopting the preventive strategy vindicated by Robert Gilpin, where he had indicated that '[t]he most attractive response to a society's decline is to eliminate the source of the problem. By launching a preventive war, the declining power destroys or weakens a rising challenger ...' (R. Gilpin, 1981: 191; see also E. Luttwak, 1967 for preventative strategy against possible emergence of 'dangerous' rivals). Thus, short of launching military pre-emptive strikes, the financial crisis of East Asia 1997-1999 can be argued to have its genesis in the American trade policies in the late 1980s to early 1990s (for this argument see

---

Times, 8 March 1992, p. A14 (emphasis added).
[15] Dick Cheney (former Secretary of Defense) (January 1993) *Defense Strategy for the 1990s: The Regional Defense Strategy*, U.S. Department of Defense.

P. Gowan, 1999). Two strategic scenarios were possible for the U.S. to apply a tougher stance against these countries. The first is with the disappearance of the Soviet Union, these countries were no longer viewed as geo-strategically significant as they once were. Second, is that these countries have become so 'engaged' and 'locked' into the U.S.-led system that for them to withdraw would mean their economic stagnation. In addition, if they did not change their political practices and remained authoritarian they would constantly be attacked diplomatically for abuses on human rights and 'unfair' trading practices. Thus the U.S. has been able to take advantage of these situations to forward America's insistence on the advancement of liberal democracy and liberal economics, without fearing implications of possible backlash on its policies.

It is still speculation as to whether East Asia states (collectively) will counter the American strategy by returning to some form of corporate economic nationalism, or to co-operate with each other as to 'balance' the United States. The second problem for the U.S. applying this strategy is how to identify what is a 'developed' state (even though some NIE economic development level are comparable to economically developed liberal democracies), and how to identify what the necessary conditions are for political maturity for liberal democracy. In this sense, it is not only economic engagement and economic development, but it also involves nurturing and harnessing ideas of liberal democracy and tolerance into the populace of these regimes. Yet, the strategy deployed by the United States before and during the East Asian economic crisis (1997-99) gives indications that the United States is prepared to safeguard its position, even if it means the destructive restructuring of others (M. Mastanduno, 1998; this was elaborated in the Japan chapter) in compliance with American 'desires'.

An overriding question remains, however, even if democracies and countries that believe in similar 'liberal' economic principles 'are far less likely to go to war with each other . . . [and] are more likely to promote open markets and free trade, and to pursue policies that lead to sustained economic development' (Christopher, 1995: 15). Why is the United States so concerned over its alleged relative economic decline with countries that share its values and principles? What is the United States attempting to achieve, when it portrays itself by trying to apply a strategy of global primacy (leadership) via the policies of deep engagement and enlargement into new areas of zones of prosperity and peace, and yet still appear to compete in a condition '[of] cold war, geostrategic mentality where security and economic issues [still] predominate?' (R. Travis in J. Scott, 1998: 263, emphasis added). Why are U.S. decision-makers constantly concerned about the relative gain of others, even when they are liberal democratic and believe in the same values? Why is relative power or relative economic gain so important despite the fact that other states (EU and Japan) are close or virtually integrated into the American hegemonic system of the 'zone of peace and prosperity'? Is it, as Jeffrey Garten (1992) puts it, '[a] Cold Peace', where allies of the cold war begin to struggle for supremacy? Or, is it as Lester Thurow (1992) outlined the beginning of a 'head to head' battle between the leading industrialised countries in an effort to gain market share and access?

In observing this, Robert Jervis questioned, '[i]f statesmen expect peace among the developed countries, what are the competitive reasons for seeking primacy?' (1993: 53). The question of gaining relative power and its importance was answered by the Dr. Jekyll and Mr. Hyde nature of Samuel Huntington (1993), where he reminds us that 'politics is power' and the struggle for that power is the foremost amongst powers and individuals, whether in peace or war. This has been the thorn of political economy that has haunted scholars since Adam Smith, who have sought to dislodge the 'realist' mentality of statesmen and business people. Although Smith's philosophy, as outlined in chapter two, argued that the absolute gain is derived from every party co-operating. The philosophy is to argue that by co-operating every party gets their sufficient share of the 'cake'. In realist and business psychology however, it is not because co-operation will benefit the parties, but the most important factor is who gains more compared to the states that co-operated. In evaluation, the problem of relative gain and relative loss may not be solvable, and one that may not hold any answers and may not be possible to answer.

The logic from here is to reconcile the two conflicting theories, one based on democratic peace and absolute gain, and the other being that of relative gain and loss. This problem can only be understood by addressing the policies adopted and applied by the U.S. government.

Aspects of U.S. Foreign Policy Preferences in the Post-Cold War Era

In an attempt to pinpoint U.S. behaviour, Richard Haass has analysed five policy preferences that could be identified since William Clinton came to power in 1993: Wilsonianism, economism, realism, humanitarianism, and minimalism. Haass argues that, it is not that any preference is mutually exclusive of another, the real issue is to 'determine how much weight to give any one over the other four' (1995: 46). In addition to these ends, Haass also identified three approaches that are categorised as 'means' to be implemented to the ends. These are unilateralism, neo-internationalism, and U.S. leadership. Although these may appear to be independent of each other, each has a tendency to reinforce the other. According to Haass, '[t]he Clinton administration, in its words and deeds, has at one point or another (and on occasion the same) time reflected the full range of both means and ends' (1995: 52). What emerges, then, is an administration that embraces large elements of minimalism, Wilsonianism, and economism alongside doses of realism and humanitarianism. What this means is that the U.S. will attempt to ascertain what potential threats and gains are present. It will initiate its own agenda, but that agenda will depend on whom or what that policy is intended to be implemented against. In this constantly evolving nature of international affairs, Luttwak (1998) argues for the American foreign policy to be capable of adapting to these dynamic changing conditions, the application of a multiple strategy to the multiple dimension of international affairs (this was elaborated in chapter one).

The obvious danger with such policy strategy, however, is that it has the tendency of inconsistency and may confuse ally powers and give adversaries wrong signals. In addition, as the struggle for policy preferences to be implemented increases, the divisions among policy-makers in Washington may also increase (as it is happening with the policy over China). Therewithal, there is no coherent U.S. foreign policy in the post-Cold War era. What is visible is the combination of directions that the White House, the Departments of State, the Treasury and Defense, and the two Houses of Congress have tried to enshrine into a new doctrine for the post-Cold War era (see J. Scott, 1998). Critics, however, identify this as a weakness and have accused the United States decision-making apparatus as having no real direction in its implementation of grand strategy. The critics argue that 'victory' over the Soviet Union 'has bequeathed to American foreign policy makers an uncertain legacy; with no material rival, the nation's purpose and role in the global system is no longer self-evident' (A. McGrew, 1994: 201). This book has conveyed that this is not the case (see chapters one and five). The American global strategy has founding principles and it is an evolving set of process(es); and that process was set forth long before the Second World War – it is a strategy that seeks both relative gain and increasing the absolute gain for all.

Similar to Haass' analysis, I have identified two tendencies in U.S. strategy through words and deeds since the collapse of the Soviet Union in 1991, to reconcile the classic problem of relative gain and loss. These are unilateral assertion and multilateral consensus. Yet, even in this, there exists common denominators between the policies of unilateralism and multilateralism, and continuity from the era of George Bush senior. First, both believe in the preservation of U.S. strategic interests has been vital and the prevention of an emergence of strategic challengers (D. Cheney, 1992; 1993; W. Cohen, 1997, 1999). Second, both argue that the United States did not become primus inter pares in the international system in the long and tedious task of real politicking and then having to be challenged again or to be dislodged by another power or group of powers. Third, they are in agreement to preserve, as long as possible or even indefinitely, the international order under U.S. hegemony. Fourth, both argue that without U.S. leadership, aggressive powers will arise and challenge the zones of peace and prosperity, and the advancement of democracy will be weakened. Fifth, both agree that *if* the United States withdraws from the international system, its friends, such as Japan and Germany, will be forced to re-arm themselves, which may eventually harm the United States.

Although both theories have been invariably incorporated into the U.S. decision-making in the post-Cold War, their tune and context have diverged as the United States has to decide whether to become unilaterally assertive, especially its self-proclaimed leadership role or the maintenance of security stability in Europe, Asia and the Middle East, or to behave multilaterally on occasions where it wants to be portrayed as hegemonically benign, in that it wants to be seen as acting in concert with others in achieving some form of consensus, such as international trade forums. On other occasions, it even asked or left regional powers to take the leading role, such as the initial U.S. policy with the EU on Bosnia.

However, unlike multilateralists, unilateralists are opposed to abandoning any national sovereignty to international organisations, such as the United Nations. Unilateralists are highly sceptical of collective security and the ability of multinational institutions like the UN to play an effective role in international security. Unless, of course, the UN were to act directly under the commands of the United States. It should be noted that unilateralists have different approaches to those of isolationists. Whereas isolationists advocate the abandonment of the American-led alliance systems, and revoke American commitments or abandon international institutions and take care of America first, unilateralists place strong emphasis on maintaining strong bilateral ties with key actors and see U.S.-led alliance systems as crucial for maintaining a stable order in important regions and preventing the emergence of new hegemons in those regions. On the other hand, multilateralists would argue that the nature of the world has become highly integrated with the interdependence of nations, markets and environment, unilateral acts by the U.S., they argue, would have multilateral effects as well (see R. Keohane and J. Nye, 1989). Thus, multilateralists emphasise that to gain relatively, as well as absolutely, the U.S. has to incorporate other powers' variables into its strategy. Unilateralists, however, perceive that this is weakening U.S. manoeuvrability by entangling itself to multilateralist arrangements.

In words and deeds, the unilateralist theory is often associated with the Pentagon and sections of the Congress. Generally, unilateralists perceive world politics in terms of powers' rise and decline. Thence, a relative rise or decline in power variables is extremely important, since power has the ability to influence and force others to comply with the hegemon's wishes. Although this is recognised by the White House, State Department, Treasury and sections of the Congress, they would much prefer to act and speak diplomatically than to lambast 'unworthy allies' who have a tendency to free-ride the American-led system and then complain about American hegemonism. In circumstances where the United States has acted unilaterally, it has always defined to the international community that it did so for the benefit of the international community, for example the invasion of Haiti to restore 'rightful legitimate ruler' Aristide to power; the almost military confrontation with China over the Taiwan issue in 1996; the unilateral (with Britain) surgical air strikes against Iraq and the Bosnian Serbs; and the surgical cruise missile retaliatory attacks against Taliban terrorists in Afghanistan and The Sudan in August 1998. In these events, with the exception of Taiwan and the cruise missile attack against the Taliban rebels, the United States has tried to get international consent for its actions. However, where its interests are directly threatened, as in the case of the Taliban attacks on its embassies in summer 1998, the United States was quick to resort to unilateral action. In the case of Taiwan, although the United States does *not* have 'serious obligation' to defend Taiwan, it was quick to send its forces to tell the Chinese that it means business, and any attempt by China to retake the island through force would be severely punished.

The 'Neo-Gramscian' Strategy of Hegemonic Globalisation

Whether by unilateralism or multilateralism, the United States' central formula to maintain and enhance its unipolar position has involved a hybrid of realpolitic and the manoeuvring of position by U.S. elites into favourable positions in international institutions, regimes and agencies, and in some cases even into the national domestic politics of other national bureaucracies and government offices.[16] Behind the success of U.S. policies has been the U.S. adoption of neo-Gramscian strategy of the 'war of positioning', or 'the victory of its positioning' in the international system of bureaucrats who are favourable to U.S. ideology. This power manifestation has enabled the U.S. to, one way or another, influence decision-making by applying various methods of apparent openness as well as clandestine agreements. The sources that the United States have often used during and after the Cold War mainly involved the CIA, U.S. sponsored agencies (such as the National Endowment for Democracy (NED), and the Trilateral Commission, RAND, Carnegie, broadcasting networks such as Radio Free Asia and Radio Free Europe, and 'private' media networks such as CNN and CNBC); political manoeuvres in international regimes and institutions or related agencies by positioning men/women in vital posts of international organisations and institutions during and after the cold war whose ideology were orientated towards U.S. ideals, i.e., the Organisation of American States Resolution 1080, which pledge democracies in the Western Hemisphere to act jointly in the case of an interruption of democratic process in a member state (R. Travis in J. Scott, ed. 1998: 255; see also J. Nye, 1990; S. Gill, 1990; H. Nau, 1990; T.V. Paul and J. Hall, 1999). Increasingly, the deployment of transnational class groups, i.e., mainly professional and business elites, although in some cases inadvertent and innocent, has intensified (R. Cox, 1981; S. Strange, 1990; 1991; S. Gill, 1990; 1993; Robinson, 1996).

The influences and capabilities of U.S. power in the theatre of international politics/security/economics are so overwhelming that 'rising' powers are faced with a serious dilemma of actually trying not to upset the United States too much. Instead, many states are beginning to face the jibing prospect that 'if you can't beat them you might as well join them', or else be faced with the unenviable consequences of underdevelopment or even worse. This is illustrated by Vietnam, North Korea, Cuba, Iran, and other 'renegade' states as compared to countries that are oriented to liberal democratic capitalism. The rush to modernise with the race to globalise have led countries, especially China and Vietnam, to abandon their fundamental ideology, Communism. In fact, this rush to modernise has led these states into being 'more' laissez faire than most liberal democratic developed countries. The rush to develop in many parts of China, for example, has considerable resemblance to the American rush to the 'West', where the search for

---

[16] Examples of U.S. installed governments around the world or at least highly sympathetic to the United States – South Korea, Haiti, Israel, Taiwan, Philippines.

riches and fortune often overrode social welfare. Most of the areas under development have very little regulatory rules or norms. For the Chinese, with capitalism running rampant (for this see K. Polanyi, 1957), favouring the strong and powerful, and central government thousands of miles away, lawlessness often abounds as officials are easily bribed. Either by design or accident, it is in this power scenario that 'grass-root' and 'low intensity' (Gills et al, 1993) movements may actually work in conjunction with the U.S. to sustain the U.S. position as well as enhancing their own. Under this circumstance, the U.S. is not only trying to convert them or just to bring them into the capitalist democratic union, the U.S. is enhancing, further, its power position.

However, this scenario is, by no means, that simple. Steve Smith (1999) questions the assumption that free markets or capitalism equals democracy on historical records and in practices. Smith outlines that there are major difficulties in pursuing these two goals simultaneously. First, the specific issues involved in the opening up of markets may be destabilising for democracy (especially young democracies), making it more difficult to consolidate or export democracy, and may push democracy in an unintended direction. Second, to ignore these contradictory aspects and just to assume the set equation is not only problematic but would have profound consequences. This problem was identified by Alexis de Tocqueville, where in his 'Author's Introduction' to *Democracy in America*, Tocqueville showed how democracy evolved in the West, not through the kind of moral fiat that the Western media is trying to impose throughout the world, but as an organic outgrowth of development. Tocqueville illustrated how European societies had reached a level of complexity and sophistication at which the aristocracy, so as not to overburden itself, had to confer a measure of equality upon other citizens and allocate some responsibility to them: 'a structured division of the population into peacefully competing interest groups was necessary if both tyranny and anarchy were to be averted' (in R. Kaplan, 1997: 60). Kaplan, following the argument of Alexis de Tocqueville, shows how states that have weak internal organs of regimes, whether in the institution of law and order or/and 'inadequate' educational level, often do not make good liberal democracies. They are usually, soon after elections, ravaged by setbacks, corruption and political bickering by groups (i.e., in large areas of Africa, the former Yugoslav republics, and the former republics of the Soviet Union, like Armenia and Azerbaijan where democracy has been tried). Because of the inadequacies of internal organs of regime, institutions and the lack of a consolidated civil society, this has led to problems of tribalism, religious intolerance, ethnic cleansing and even genocide, all in the name of democracy, self-determination, and popular nationalism. In other words, in a society that has not reached the appropriate level of development as Toqueville described, 'a multi-party system merely hardens and institutionalises established ethnic and regional divisions' (in R. Kaplan, 1997: 60).

As such, the U.S. movement of hegemonic globalisation faces potential drawbacks in internal policy and external instability. However, these setbacks are not the 'new enemies' that hinder U.S. hegemonic globalisation. The real battle involves the task of intensification of the already evolving dynamics of globalisation and to expand liberal democratic values into authoritarian regimes. To set and expand liberal democracy to underdeveloped states and 'change' authoritarian regimes around the world, the U.S. priority is to have patience and time for it to nurture properly. *If* the U.S. is compelled to rush into the process of liberal democracy because of pressure, especially from the media, to attack authoritarianism, without recognising the grass-root development of democracy, then the stability of democracy in countries that are targeted may not have sufficient know-how to operate on the level or standard of a modern liberal democracy, thus, it would mean a drawback to democracy rather than its advancement.

Conclusion

In conclusion, the end of the Cold War has left the U.S. in a most fortunate position. It is not entangled in any serious disagreement with any one major power. Two (Japan and the EU) of the four leading powers are allies and are 'locked' in the U.S.-led system in what has been called 'the zone of the democratic peace and prosperity'. With regard to the other two great powers (China and Russia), they are 'constructively engaged' with the U.S. rather than collaborating with each other to 'challenge' or even 'contain' the U.S.-led system.

The success of this was generated by the United States' search for greatness since its independence from the United Kingdom, that search became evident prior to the Cold War. In its 'grand design' during and after World War II, the United States' implemented various hybrids of realpolitic, which were used against allies, visible rivals and potential rivals, that is now bearing fruits in the immediate international system. One of the strategic interests that had had a major impact and set pace for influence and legalisation of American moral values, other than containing rivals in the international system, was the manoeuvring of position by U.S. elites into favourable positions in the U.S.-led international institutions, regimes and agencies. In some cases, even into the national domestic politics of other national bureaucracies and government offices as well[17] (see Appendix 1B).

In the post-Cold War era, without communist hindrance to the advancement of the democratic peace and free trade, the U.S. grand strategy for global dominance is increasing even further. The U.S. strategy is 'freer' in its manoeuvres and has been able to apply a multiple set of policies to change and adapt to the multiple changing conditions and circumstances of international political and economic affairs. A widespread tactic has been Clinton's strategy of 'enlargement and engagement'. Whether directly or indirectly, the U.S. has attempted to gather countries into the zone of peace and competitive prosperity (The White House,

---

[17] Examples of U.S. 'installed' governments around the world – Bosnia, Chile, Grenada, Haiti, Israel, Kuwait, Philippines, South Korea, Taiwan, and others.

1996; 1997; 1999). To others that do not wish to become 'engaged', the U.S. has simply isolated them, which also means isolation from the international system as well. In the third strategy, such as applied to China, the U.S. has played a combination of carrot and stick to influence decision-making. These policies may seem inconsistent, but that is the nature of U.S. policy that aims to preserve the U.S. preponderant position in the international system. To make sense of it via claims of consistency or parsimonious theory and to mechanise in boxes is to impair our understanding of 'real' U.S. policy.

Via this strategic philosophy, the U.S. has influenced and will influence the rising powers, (Japan, the EU, China, Russia, India, and Turkish states) even more. In fact, the fear of being left out has made these powers into something rather like subordinate units of U.S. power. Most countries that act as subordinates to the United States are often in a better position, at least economically than those who are not subordinated. For example, the economic success of East Asia and Latin America countries compared to the satellites of the former Soviet Union or the countries in the Middle East or Africa, that have resisted throughout most of the Cold War, supports this perspective.

Behind this 'success' has been the United States military, foreign affairs (scholars and practitioners), economic (financial and corporate), the U.S. media corporations and other apparatus to apply a multiple strategy of alliance configuration to gel the multiple interests of others into that of the United States. The strategy is for the major and minor states, non-states actors, etc., to need the U.S. more than they need each other. On the global level, the United States is the leading nation and leading promoter of the G7/8, the OECD, the IMF, the World Bank, and the WTO. On regional arrangements, the United States is member and leading advocate of NAFTA, AFTA, NATO, and APEC, and the North Atlantic Cooperation Council. In all these international regimes and institutions, the United States is the main power, where major decisions are eventuated and accepted to be universalised, only with U.S. approval. The United States also has bilateral agreements with many countries across the globe, i.e., Canada, Israel, Egypt, Saudi Arabia, South Korea, Japan, Singapore, Taiwan, South Africa, Chile, and many others on areas of mutual economic and military interest (see Appendix 1A). In some of these states, the reliance on the bilateral agreement with the United States also means their very own survival, i.e., Kuwait, Israel, South Korea, Taiwan, Canada, and Mexico. No one power on earth has such an extensive range of complex associations and alliances than the U.S.; the U.S. diplomatic ties, connection and influence is such that no other great power in the history of human civilisation can hope or perceive of conjuring.

PART IV

CONCLUSION

Conclusion

Hegemonic Globalisation: 'The Highest Stage of Capitalism'?

I have tried, in this book, to understand, conceptualise, and re-analyse the nature of theory and practice in international relations and its 'reality'. I found that, instead of being confined to the rigidity of formal theory, a multiple combination of concepts may be required to capture the nuances of international 'reality'. From this standpoint, formal 'theories' of IR may not have been adequate (or were, perhaps, in some even manipulated or distorted by scholars) for understanding the nature of contemporary change in international affairs. It is noteworthy, however, that some theories do offer some form of guidance to decision-makers. In some cases, it should at least offer them a partial understanding of contemporary events, based upon past events (R. Cox and T. Sinclair, 1996: 144-73). What I have proposed is the 'alternating' of theories to solve conditions of reality and to condition how reality is to be perceived. How these theories are applied depends on the objective circumstances faced by the actor. It is the actors that make history, and scholars are there to learn, analyse and evaluate the perils and pitfalls of the decision-makers' political action. No theory has ever been capable of providing (an entirely) complete picture for 'The Prince', and it is probably never possible, given the infinite variables involved.

In my evaluation of these difficulties and confusions, I have discovered that most theories are often inter-linked and overlap with one another, and in some cases may even offer contradictory concepts and terms (i.e., hegemony and balance of power within the neo-realist paradigm) within the theory itself. This is curious, and may not end here. However, what is most important in this study is not how we, academics view the world, but rather how practitioners, themselves, view the world, and especially how they practice their 'art of politics'.

I have followed this framework of analysis because large aspects of the dominant theories ('realism', 'liberalism', and Marxism) of international relations, due to their dogmatic rigidity, have failed to see the significance of the transformation of power in contemporary world affairs. This is especially so, concerning the United States' power position in international affairs. Amongst the failures was the declinist argument (which cuts across the theoretical spectrum, from Marxism, Liberalism, and Realism), which underestimated and misunderstood U.S. power centrality in world affairs.

In this book, I re-analysed the concepts of power, hegemony, and balance of power in light of contemporary international relations. These concepts were necessary because of the nature of the study, which was to explore the nature and development of U.S. power, from the Cold War to the contemporary period of so called 'globalisation'.

A second failure of the dominant theories was their inability to contemplate or predict the systemic collapse of communism. According to these theories, again ranging across the theoretical and political spectrum, (i.e., from Wallerstein to Modelski to Gilpin on the cycle of great powers), the Soviet Union 'should have' reacted with some 'preventive measure', or even vindicated a 'hegemonic war' to prevent its own decline. Not only did no 'hegemonic war' occur, the Soviet Union did not even try effectively to prevent its own demise. The three dominant theories were ineffective in providing an explanation. From the explanation provided by these theories, the 'rationality' of Gorbachev's actions to allow the disintegration of the Soviet Empire just did not make sense. Even U.S. decision-makers misunderstood this behaviour. President Bush, himself, was reluctant to allow the demise of the Soviet Union. This caution was one of the major foreign policy issues that gained President Clinton the initiative, by allowing him to argue that, since the Soviet Union had been the communist 'enemy' for nearly half a century, why allow it to continue to survive?

The third major failure, and relating to point one, was the (general) American overestimation of Japanese power and the ability of Japan to actually 'challenge' and 'replace' U.S. centrality. This never happened. Instead, Japan was caught up in a decade of stagnation.

If these major issues could not be recognised by flagship theories in the discipline, what is there left of the discipline capable of analysing changing power relations? In 1984, Richard Ashley warned of the 'orrery of errors' in the discipline which had made 'ahistorical and depoliticised the understanding of politics' (in Keohane, 1986: 256). From such warnings, and the abysmal failures, it is only fair to point out that the discipline of international relations seems to be plagued by spiralling errors that continuously accumulate. This accumulation of errors reproduces itself through the academic practice of analysis, which is often ideological and prejudiced. In support of this view, Vasquez states, 'they [he was largely targeting neo-realists] fail to see because their theories do not allow them to do so' (1998: 296, emphasis added). This has not only 'blinded' 'experts', but what is worse is that the 'experts' continue to feed students with false perceptions of reality.

What is at stake here is not simply abstract, but goes to the heart of the discipline. As Michael Cox (1998) stresses, international relations scholarship, and academia in general, have made it even more difficult for students to come to terms with 'reality' and change in the global picture. This book is not only an attempt to offer hints to rejuvenate the discipline, but to ask scholars to reconsider their theoretical methodology and how the discipline is taught.

What has further disappointed and astounded since these failures has been the emergence of scholarship that seems to emphasise that if America does not create an enemy eventually (because of the death of the Soviet Union), America will lose its pivotal position. Some scholars and analysts have suggested that for the United States not to lose its direction, a strategy of 'balance of power' should be utilised. In fact, they are so obsessed with that theory that Waltz explicitly claims that, 'if there is any distinctively political theory of international politics, balance-of-power is it' (1979: 117). Waltz argues that '[t]he self-help system stimulates states to behave in ways that tend towards balance of power' (1979: 118). This is not only *not* the case, but shows how deeply affected the discipline is by the 'misperception' of theories to explain 'reality'. In fact, the flagship of current IR, neo-realism, has abandoned one of the core values of analysing history. History is to study *what is*, instead neo-realists, neo-liberals, and some Marxists have made it their virtue (and sadly fatal error) of studying *what ought to be*. This book has tried to demonstrate that 'reality' cannot be comprehended, let alone well understood, without firm empirical evidence. To 'explain' in terms of 'ought' assumptions, without fully understanding empirical reality, simply adds more confusion and myth to the situation. In addition, history is not pre-determined, meaning that the theories of balance of power, and the theories of the rise and fall of great powers, may not be viable to understand the nature of U.S. policies and contemporary liberal capitalism. Baylis and Smith points this out on the dynamics of international affairs: 'the Westphalian order was a historical phenomenon. . . . Sovereign statehood is not a timeless, natural condition. Politics operated without this organising principle prior to the seventeenth century, and there is no reason why world history could not once again carry on without a system of sovereign states' (1997: 21).

The Complexity of U.S. Centrality

In adapting concepts for the analytical framework, this study has shown how the historical development of the rise of U.S. power and its ambitions are multidimensional and multi-layered, which does not follow any simple theory *per se*. The formidable complexity of U.S power ranges from military power to economic strength, to political manoeuvres against enemies and allies (inside and outside international regimes and institutions), to the strategies of the creation of alliance structures amongst democratic liberal economies and others. This is not easy to understand from the perspective of any one theory. In fact, to apply a single theory would probably only ascertain one aspect of U.S. power. The complexity of U.S. power may not be understood completely, however, my book has shown that a possible way is by utilising a combination of concepts which may offer a clearer picture of U.S. global strategy.

What were the concepts from the three theories that validate the behaviour of the United States in post-1945? The first, perhaps stems from the 'Marxist-Gramscian' analysis of international affairs, i.e., that of the 'international transnational class', and the 'war of position' that is involved in this group. These two concepts are valid because of the commonality between (western) Europe and

North America in remaining the pivotal centres of world capitalism.[1] This capitalistic corporate 'class' had shared beliefs and values, and common enemies – the communists and the nationalistic insurgents of the colonised countries (compare H. Kissinger, 1994, especially Ch. 24). For them to survive was not to 'out-do' each other (as seen in the two world wars), but to foster a common (military, political, economic, and ideological) front against the rise of international communism and the 'nationalist' demands from colonised countries for independence. This commonality made them wary that if they did not find a common agenda, their ability to lead and remain prosperous in world affairs would be in jeopardy. Fearing these combinations of challenges emerging after World II, the United States, with the support of its capitalist allies, designed and built international regimes and institutions to 'regulate' international behaviour with rules and standards that were capitalistic and orientated to sustaining Western led and essentially U.S. supremacy. With allied support, the United States had few problems in incorporating these capitalists together, in the common purpose to counter possible Soviet aggression, world communism, and nationalistic resurgence in third world countries.

The second concept that has validity in explaining contemporary affairs emerges from hegemonic stability theory (largely a liberal-realist combination to explain the strategies available to the declining hegemon, i.e., the United States). Similar to the 'transnational class' concept, hegemonic stability theory shows how the role of the single dominant power in establishing and maintaining the norms and rules of a liberal economic order is essential to that order. The theory illustrated how the United States was able to 'restructure the western economies according to its preferences after World War II because of its market size and its control over hard currency and [resources]' (E.B. Kapstein and M. Mastanduno, 1999: 469, emphasis added). However, this theory (concept) suffers from its pessimism about the United States' ability to adapt to a changing environment. It, thus, argues that when the hegemonic state suffers relative decline, 'the liberal order is greatly weakened' (R. Gilpin, 1987: 72). However, this was not the case. The United States' durability and ability to adapt and change is what validates the United States as the primus inter pares of world powers – in fact the central power.

From historical evidence and in light of the above two concepts, the 'hegemonic' designs of the U.S. were in their infancy and the U.S. had limited manoeuvrability and expansion during the Cold War, when it was countered

---

[1] On 14 April 1929, Luigi Pirandello declared: 'Americanism is swamping us. I think that a new beacon of civilisation has been lit over there . . . The money that runs through the world is American (?!), and behind the money (?!) runs the way of life and the culture' (in A. Gramsci, 1971/1998: 316). Gramsci wrote, ' . . . we are not dealing with a new type of civilisation. This is shown by the fact that nothing has been changed in the character of and the relationships between fundamental groups. What we are dealing with is an organic extension and an intensification of European civilisation, which has simply acquired a new coating in the American climate' (1971/1998: 318).

especially by the Soviet Union and its affiliates. Now that U.S. ideas no longer face serious challenges to their expansion, the American 'liberal order' is expanding and moving in all directions. In fact, '[i]t is this role-based context, coupled with its capacity to project military power more widely and effectively than any other country, and its still being one of the world's most significant economies, that the United States can be called the most complete global power' (K. Aldred and M.A. Martin, 1999: 169).

From this setting, two essential questions can be raised: First, has 'globalisation', with U.S. hegemony, managed to cut into the core of international relation's theory of balance of power? It would appear so, as Mastanduno contends, '[t]he behaviour of the United States and the other major powers does not conform to the predictions of balance of power theory' (1997: 59; 72). Again Mastanduno, '. . .the longer unipolarity persists, the more imperative it will become to reconsider the logic of balancing behaviour and to reassess the historical evidence that presumably supports that theory' (1997: 86). So, if the great powers are not balancing each other, what does this mean for balance of power theory on the 'grand scale'? If one accepts this argument, then why should scholars continue to trap themselves in dogmatic precepts? Certainly, the longer we progress from the end of the Cold War, the more it becomes visible how powerful the United States global hegemony really is. Historical 'patterns' of recurrence of balance of power have not happened and may not necessarily happen. The class conflicts predicted by Marxist theory have subsided by the 'capitalist' re-inventing itself in the 'third wave' of promoting prosperity for the masses.

Second, does American democratic promotion and capitalist expansionism mean 'globalisation', or alternatively, is it the nature of American capitalism, which means liberal capitalism incorporated into American policies? Certainly, the pursuit of U.S. policies of 'free trade' and 'democratic promotion' as against the neo-mercantilist course flirted with in the early 1990s has meant that the U.S. has managed to create a situation, whereby the interest of world capitalism was also the interest of the United States. In this manner, an expansion of 'globalisation' was also an expansion of American power. Thence, any challenge or counter against globalisation was also a direct challenge to the U.S. policies and the allies that are associated with that promotion.

Indeed, what is the evidence of serious efforts to counter U.S. power? Firstly, the EU may emerge as potential challenger, and given the historical record of Europe in the last five hundred years, there is every possibility that it will do so again, but on a different face. Secondly, the introduction of the single currency within the EU could be analysed as a challenge to the dollar's domination in international finance. Yet, as long as the U.S. and the EU remain democratic liberal economies and operate under similar rules, the EU and the U.S. would remain very close allies, and may even 'manage' the world in a form of condominium (with perhaps also Japan and other OECD countries). It is just not conceivable to see the two setting apart, if faced with 'real' challenges coming from China, Russia, or others. They share too many common interests and perhaps a common 'European' or 'Western' civilisation, as Gramsci indicated (see footnote 1, pp. 277-8).

The talk of the Chinese challenge in the emerging world order is not 'realistic' either. China just does not have the military capability or (military) technological sophistication, economic and financial power, alliance structure amongst the major powers, and most importantly, it is not 'trusted' by other major powers to allow it to successfully sustain a challenge. In fact, China has, since the demise of the Soviet Union, become more 'Westphalian' in its emphasis on state sovereignty, whilst the United States has become more interventionist, and perhaps even set to redefine national sovereignty for purposes of so-called humanitarian intervention. The fundamental differences on this issue are enough to open many controversies in U.S-Sino relations in the emerging world order. On the other hand, to whom can China be a challenge to? It is a country with over one billion people, with most of these concentrated along the east coast. Given the vulnerability of its population, a hegemonic war with the United States would be disastrous for the Chinese people. A conflict with the United States would almost inevitably involve other great powers, and it is very unlikely, because of history, race, and ideology, that the EU or Japan would side with China against the United States. As for an alliance with Russia, this is still premature, and from the past historical experiences of these two countries, an alliance between them would only occur in very extreme circumstances, eloping from a series of miscalculations by the U.S. and western strategy for China and Russia to come together. Both countries in the immediate international order 'need' the United States and the 'west' more than they need each other, for economic prosperity and accumulation of power.

In regard to Russia, there is very little evidence that Russia can re-emerge in the form of the former Soviet Union without causing great uneasiness in the U.S., EU, China, Japan, and others. In the immediate term, Russia will restructure itself rather than venture into 'constructing' the direction of world politics. Unless the United States misreads the inter-relationships completely, there need not be any serious warming of relations between China and Russia (to insulate them from U.S. pressure). The likelihood of the United States allowing this to happen appears to be minimal.

Japan was dubbed by many scholars in the 1980s as not only being a potential challenger to U.S. 'hegemony' but also as a possible replacement to it. This argument was clearly wrong. Any evidence that Japan may emerge as 'hegemon' in world affairs is as remote as the United States giving up on its position. Second, had Japan managed to become hegemonic, the reactions from China, the EU, Russia, and other surrounding powers would not be benign, given the historical diplomatic and military relations with these countries. It is more likely that Japan would much prefer to sustain its position and prosperity than to destabilise that situation. In this way, Japan will remain behind the scenes supporting U.S. power and its manoeuvres for hegemonic globalisation. Third, Japan does not have a sufficient internal market (as an importing nation) to shape the behaviour of leading trading partners. Repeatedly, the United States has successfully threatened to close the U.S. market for Japanese goods. As Kapstein emphasises, '[s]o long as the United States remains the world's biggest market for traded goods and services, it will have substantial leverage over its commercial partners' (in E.B. Kapstein and M. Mastanduno, 1999: 476). Finally, instead of being dismantled because of the collapse of the Soviet threat, the U.S.-Japan security relationship remains vital for both Japanese security and U.S. interests in East Asia. Far from challenging the United States, Japan has worked with the United States for its national security and economic prosperity, and promotes the ideals of liberal democracy and capitalism.

Another problem that may undermine the U.S. global hegemonic position is American domestic politics. As there is really no 'real' international threat to the United States, Americans may feel it unnecessary to place too much interest in international affairs, and thence revert to 'isolationism'. This has not happened, and is unlikely to happen.

Finally, and perhaps the most difficult scenario, how far does the United States' power increase before there is a 'crack'? This remains, as yet, an academic debate about what the 'sub-merged' forces of counter-hegemony may do. One thing that *is* clear from this politics is that the more American power increases the more subtle it has to become to persuade others that it is not all powerful. Otherwise, and recalling Lord Acton's famous statement: 'Power corrupts, absolute power corrupts absolutely.' The danger to abuse unchecked power is all too real.

From all these challenges to the United States-led world order, an interesting question remains: what would happen to world politics without American exceptionalism? Is American exceptionalism due to its 'fortune'? This, as we know from Machiavelli, is only half the case, for 'fortune governs half our actions [which] . . . leaves [half to] our power to control' (1977: 67, emphasis added). '[A] prince who depends entirely on Fortune comes to grief immediately she changes. I believe further that a prince will be fortunate who adjusts his behaviour to the temper of the times, and on the other hand will be unfortunate when his behaviour is not well attuned to the times' (Machiavelli, 1977: 68). So it becomes admissible from this Machiavellian perspective to ask: what kind of power would consciously pursue policies that are likely to provide them with greater costs than benefits? Given ordinary rationality, it is very unlikely that the United States would deliberately pursue policies that are of no benefit to itself. Given this being the (assumed) case, what type of policies would American leaders implement if it meant the United States losing its exceptionalism? The United States would lose its exceptionalism, if it chooses to, or is forced to revert to the balance of power by the politicking of other powers in very unusual circumstances.

However, this has not happened. The exceptionality of U.S. power centrality can be identified by the fact that the U.S., alone, is placing itself as the 'Sun' around which other powers, such as the EU, China, Japan, Russia, India, and others, revolve. In this strategic manoeuvre, the United States has not involved itself in 'balancing' or fallen into seeking a separate 'great power' sphere. U.S.

decision-makers recognise, and also propagandise, that without U.S. exceptionalism, that is, by separating the U.S. from international affairs and involvement at the strategic level, the international (state) system would become extremely volatile, and would probably return to a balance of power system. Political analysts, such as Huntington, Kissinger, Waltz, and others, who have inclined towards the notion that each power should have their own sphere of influence and that the United States should not interfere in these spheres, have misread the nature of contemporary U.S. policies for maintaining and expanding U.S. power. Their arguments are reasonable, only if we are to believe that the international system should return to some form of balance of power or some cycle of transition in the international system.[2] This is not the case. In fact, the United States has become so confident of its power that Americans can boast that 'it is futile to compete with American power, either in size of forces or in technological capabilities' (W. Kristoland and R. Kagan, 1996: 26). Kapstein claims that '[f]rom economics to security to culture, it has been impossible for countries to hide from the long arm of the United States, or to pursue with any success strategies that are at odds with its preferences and interests' (in E.B. Kapstein and M. Mastanduno, 1999: 465).

Perhaps the most important channels of power to influence this, and how other powers perceive the U.S., is through international institutions such as NATO, UN, IMF, World Bank, WTO, OECD, and the G-8. Layne and Schwartz declare, 'as long as the US can use its superpower capabilities to manipulate, regulate, and calibrate regional politics in Europe and East Asia, it can continue to prevent international politics from relapsing into normal patterns' (1993: 9). In support of this 'Pax Americana' position, the U.S. seeks establishment of international alliances and international institutions to back-up and reinforce its power position (G.J. Ikenberry, 1998). With so much power, and support from its allies, regimes and institutions, the United States is setting forth to globalise the entire planet around the U.S.-led system. On the other hand, Mearsheimer makes claim that 'realists' do not believe that institutions are an important cause of peace. In fact, he argues that, 'institutions have minimal influence on state behaviour, and, thus, hold little promise for promoting stability in the post-Cold War world' (1994/5: 7). If this is the case, why are the major powers, with the exception of China, continuing to be members in the key U.S-led institutions – i.e., the G7(8), the OECD, WTO, WB, and IMF – these institutions remain pivotal for the direction of the leading countries in international affairs. The disappearance of the Soviet-led institutions has meant that there are no rivals to American institutions in economic or security fields. In fact, these U.S.-led institutions have increased in importance, not less.

---

[2] The study in this book does not envisage a 'concert of power' (Kupchan and Kupchan, 1994, 1995; Rosescrance, 1992) governing the international system, however alluring such a path may be. The concert of power has not managed the peace well in the past and it is unlikely that it will do so in the future. What this book has shown is that instead of a concert of power, the international system is under the central influence of the United States as the main power above all other powers.

Both China and Russia are in the APEC, both show willingness to join the WTO, with Russia demanding a seat in the G7/8, and China (so far) deprived of being a member of the WTO, but seeking to join. Mearsheimer and others have misread the nature of not just the importance of international institutions, but probably the inter-relationship between the great powers as well, which is manifest in their continual reliance on these key institutions.

It might well be through these regimes and institutions that the United States can hope to rely to reassure others that it is not attempting an imperium over them, or that the world should operate under 'anarchy' or 'self-help'. It is a system that calls for 'all' to join in, including allies and non-allies, so that the welfare of the system is also their welfare. It is in this new global power scenario that these powers are in actuality working in conjunction with the U.S. to sustain the U.S. position as well as enhancing their own. Thus, in this power scenario, the liberal democratic capitalist countries are setting the international moral norm for all. At the heart of this manifestation is the 'American culture', where people in developed and underdeveloped countries are buying that 'bit' of the American dream, whether it be the idea of materialistic wealth or hedonistic lifestyle, but more importantly the idea of liberty and individual freedom (T. Friedman, 1998).

Thus, the economic and technological inter-connection and 'stickiness' of international communication and trade have made it extremely difficult for countries to be isolated. The main drive behind this is not just the United States, but the willingness of others to advance their own economic development and material wealth. The development of global capitalism, and the 'engine' of world creativity, now lie within people's willingness to buy into this 'life style'. Global capitalism and these countries' own economic development now go side by side. Developing countries are simply 'pulled' in, or have the urge to join with these 'successful' economies. It is not just about liberal capitalism or rival capitalism, however. The goals of the United States go beyond one form of capitalism per se. The advancement of global development requires different forms and economic models. Even the United States was not historically always 'laissez-faire' in its foreign economic policies.

In this circumstance, globalisation, 'is not the straightforward process of homogenisation . . . globalisation has by no means brought an end to cultural diversity. . . [G]lobalisation has contributed to a proliferation of national, ethnic, and religious revivalist movements' (J. Baylis and S. Smith, 1997: 18). However, there have always been conflicts in the past between peoples. To blame conflict today totally on 'globalisation' is unfair. Colonisation, civil wars, and wars against colonisation in the past are just some of the conflicts that appear to have been dismissed by contemporary scholars when assessing the present 'fragmentation' of world politics.

Nor is it simply about America's 'universal mission' of creating a 'single global market'. On the contrary, the goal is wealth creation and the advancement of the welfare of the people. It is never possible for any system to be perfect or free from contention. Perfection of human society may not be possible, but it is humanity in the quest for learning by trial and error, and to analyse, evaluate, and to improve that matters. Machiavelli advised,

> ... a prince should read history and reflect on the actions of great men. He can see how they carried themselves during their wars, and study what made them win, what made them lose, so that he can imitate their success and avoid their defeats. Above all, he should do as great men have done before him, and take as a model for his conduct some great historical figure who achieved the highest praise and glory by constantly holding before himself the deeds and achievement of a predecessor (1977: 41-2).

Those scholars (e.g., A.G. Frank, 1979; selective authors in J. Frieden and D. Lake, 1991 2nd edit.; J. Gray, 1998) that have developed theories that say countries ought not 'imitate' Western practices and should develop their own have also misread the politics of the present era. Obviously, people should be allowed to have their own choice and select what is suitable for them. Yet in a highly competitive world, this cannot entirely be the case even if that people or country desire to be 'isolated'. Many countries that have been isolated have been driven into stagnation because of the rapidity of change in technology and wealth creation, thence making themselves into 'cases' to be studied because of their 'backwardness' (F. Braudel, 1987). Because 'Western' culture has established the level of being 'civilised' and 'advanced' around the level of economic, technological, and educational development, what these scholars have proposed is somewhat misguided. To say that developing countries ought not to mimic is fine, but the consequences for them to be treated as 'unequal' because of their economic weakness and inadequacies in terms of 'modern' society is just not realistic. Machiavelli said, 'if he has good weapons, he will never lack good friends' (1977: 50). For '. . . the masses are always impressed by the superficial appearance of things, and by the outcome of an enterprise . . .' (1977: 49). Some talk of 'uniqueness' of culture and pride in differences (not to mention 'resistance to globalisation'). Although this is highly sensitive, the lens of 'justice' is very often seen in terms of equality in power. This is always evident when '. . . nothing is so weak and unstable as a reputation for power not founded on strength of one's own' (Machiavelli, 1977: 40).

Thenceforth, 'hegemonic globalisation' is not simply about economic interdependence, but most importantly it is the belief in and commitment to shared values, which are not necessarily 'Western' or 'American', but those of human dignity and the aspiration for a more 'just' system of governance within and without international relations. The rapid development of technology and the intensification and speed of communication reinforces these values. It also helps open dialogue between different groups and people, as well as opening tension and conflict if groups do not believe in toleration of different values. Globalisation is not seen simply as a harmonisation of interests, but the development to resolve past and future tensions and conflict. The conditions of harmonisation of interests between all groups, as argued throughout the book, will never be the true position when power is contested. Nonetheless, the identification of differences and particularly not allowing zealots to manipulate past grievances would require great responsibility and statecraft. Groups that act irrespective of the potential tensions that may boil over and spill into conflict should have the responsibility to recognise the dangers involved when advocating their 'differences'. This is particularly the case for (Western-global) media groups, most of whom seem to be ideologically dogmatic or ignorant of locals' needs, concerns, and historical roots of the peoples about whom they are reporting. In its ideological-normative judgement, the (Western-global) media has created more problems than it has solved. The media should show more regard and recognise that it is not neutral or 'value free' when making (hasty) ethical judgements. Their confinement in their own ideological dogma creates more dangers of conflict than it appears. Too often the media obfuscates nuances and numerous important factors in local history, and distorts events to suit what it wants to see. Given this problem, how can we understand what is 'objectivity', rather than propaganda, and how the media 'creates' unfolding events? A good starting point is to re-affirm that history is not simply a struggle between good and evil, where the West is by definition *Good*. To make such assumption is the highest self-congratulatory illusion and produces a crusade of the worst type.

Marx forecast the development of capitalism stretching to every corner of the world. Globalisation in the post-colonial era has seen the intensification and the proliferation of national and ethnic awareness. Some scholars see it as a challenge to the Westphalian system; though even this is not necessarily the case. The intensification and fluidity of information flow and awareness emancipates more and more groups. The development of much awareness engenders a certain harmonisation, but also brings out tensions and conflicts. These conflicts or tensions must be resolved by greater awareness.

Indeed, hegemonic globalisation may well be the 'highest stage of capitalism'. Unlike the stage of capitalism that Lenin contemplated, the geopolitical reality since the end of the cold war and especially following Clinton's second term is not that there will be a 'clash of capitalists' or imperialists. Rather, hegemonic globalisation is a unique phase of capitalism, which scholars have identified in the 'zone of democratic peace and prosperity'. Kapstein argues that it is '[the] overwhelming set of American generated economic forces (the word 'globalisation' is really a contemporary euphemism for American economic dominance) that they must adapt to if they wish to modernise and liberalise their economies . . . States that wish to counter this order and go their own way in economic policy will likely find the costs of doing so exceedingly high' (E.B. Kapstein and M. Mastanduno, 1999: 468).

Conclusion

No single state in the world (historically) has effectively dominated the world, although the United States is perhaps currently the closest to being labelled in this way. It has, however, been carefully discreet, so as not to be labelled as such. Yet, in the multidimensional nature of power, resources, and capabilities, the United States' position remains the most truly persuasive of the term 'hegemonic'. The U.S. is careful not to simply 'impose' its will on the international community, especially towards allies and other major powers. It recognises that to do so would inevitably lead to resentment from them, and the U.S. itself would eventually fall into the trap of being isolated. The United States is not immune to retaliation, especially on financial and commercial issues. Instead, the United States, since the end of the Cold War, has been active in promoting what it believes to be 'universal' goals – that is the promotion of economic well being and prosperity. It is engaged in 'promoting' and 'enlarging' the zone of economic liberalism and carefully selected political enlargement. In the 'art of politics', American leaders want to be perceived as not wishing to be seen as bullying. U.S. leaders have been careful not to appear to be dominant, and careful to discern the concerns of others.

The U.S. has sought (and even 'created') legitimacy for its actions, but more importantly, it is the U.S.'s avoidance of a scenario where major powers may align against it that is the key. The U.S. in the post-Cold War era has been skilful in its foreign policy in gaining advantage without antagonising other states and/or frightening them into a united front. The politics of the United States since its independence (from another 'hegemon', Great Britain) has placed it in the prime position, the hub that effectively benchmarks the international activities of others. It is the main guardian, enforcer, and 'legislator' of international law, or as Clinton would have it, 'the night-watchman' of international relations. However, the U.S. is not totally dominant (tyrannically), and it has compromised its position and role, especially with its allies in Western Europe and East Asia, chiefly to preserve good relations with them. These allies are an essential underpinning of the U.S. power position globally.

Although some Americans would find that this detracts from American 'grander' plans, 'there is probably no real alternative if the overall goal of U.S. policy is to maintain the country's pivotal position' (K. Aldred and M.A. Smith, 1999: 173). If the United States were to appear too dominant, other states would most likely align with each other to 'balance' U.S. power. This has not happened because the United States does not seek world domination by traditional military means. However, the U.S. military presence in Western Europe, East Asia, the Middle East, and the major oceans in the world demonstrates that it is only the United States that can play such a global role. If we look at Russia, Japan, the EU, and China, none of these powers really has such a comparable military force. Second, the development and the agreement of major powers for the continuation of U.S.-led international regimes and institutions is essential to the maintenance of the stability of the international order, thus also maintaining the power position of the United States – it being the most important player.

The doctrine of economic engagement and democratic enlargement may be seen as the U.S. drive for 'liberal-democratic capitalism', but the U.S. is not alone in this, allies and their related institutions play a significant role in promoting this as well. Thus, the drive for 'hegemonic globalisation' is not just an American project, but the development of a larger compromise of the leading world powers. The hegemonic globalisation does not even require the United States to be too actively or directly involved in persuading countries to align with the 'zone of democratic peace'. U.S. allies and related institutions also play their parts in this promotion. Because of the lack of a viable alternative route to prosperity and economic development for 'material' and economic prestige, many developing countries have found the models for material well-being of developed countries attractive for their own development. However, to define the international community as a separation of 'core' and 'periphery' is too simple an explanation. This segregation gives the impression that only the 'core' countries are capable of development and the others not. In addition, it also gives a false image of polarisation of the rich core and poor periphery. This is not the whole truth and is, therefore, unconvincing. Developing countries are striving for economic prosperity. This is due to the increasing global economic interdependence and awareness of the need for people's welfare. This awareness of economic prosperity and political dignity means that it has become increasing more difficult for any country to remain isolated or to choose an autarchic economic development model. To be successful is not to be isolated. Success requires engagement and involvement in the international community. The idea that by exposing developing countries to globalisation they will only be exploited is misguided.

In summary, the international system that the United States has promoted since the end of the Second World War will continue to expand and engage into areas that were once inaccessible – because of the 'Cold War' with the Soviet Union and allies, and because many 'Third World' countries distrusted the nature of U.S. and Western policies. That dilemma has changed. The victory over communism has pushed the United States into a new platform, whereby the United States and its allies have been keen to stress the advancement of 'democracy', 'freedom', and 'free trade' to the rest of the world. Those that have tried to diverge, challenge, or obstruct (as in the case of the Soviet Union and allies) are left stagnated, isolated, and underdeveloped. I conclude with a remark made by Thomas Paine, '[The American Revolution] was not made for America alone, but for mankind'. Paine might be right, as the 'American Revolution' is today reaching into virtually all aspects of human life.

Appendices

APPENDIX 1A

A Comparison of Capabilities Amongst the Five Leading Powers in the World in 2000

	USA	EU	CHINA	RUSSIA	JAPAN
GDP (US$bn)*	$9,333.0bn	$8,796.8bn	$1,001.0bn	$205.3bn	$3,913.3bn
GDP (US$bn)**	$8,500.0bn	-	$703bn	$1,100.bn	$3,800.0bn
GDP per head (US$)*	$33,946	$23,370	$790	$1,410	$30,720
GDP per head (US$)**	$31,100	-	$3,700	$6,600	$23,700
Population*	274.9m	376.4m	1,266.5m	145.7m	127.4m
Population **	273.1m	-	1,244.m	146.3m	126.5m
GDP growth*	2.7%	3.0%	7%	1%	0%
GDP growth**	3.9%	-	7.8%	-4.6%	-2.6%
Inflation*	2.6%	1.9%	2.5%	38%	0.1%
Inflation**	1.5%	-	0.8%	27.8%	0.7
% share of World GDP ($30,700.7bn).*	30.4%	28.65%	3.26%	0.67%	12.75%
Defence expend. (US$bn)**	$265.89bn	$173.1bn	$36.7bn	$53.9bn	$36.99bn
Defence expend. US$ per capita**	$982	$455	$30	$368	$293
Defence expend. as % of GDP**	3.2%	2.1%	5.3%	5.2%	1%
Armed forces (000)**	1,401.6	1,922.2	2,820.0	1,159.	242.6
% of population under arms**	0.51%	0.51%	0.22%	0.8%	0.19%
Estimated Reserves (000)**	1,796.7	3,927.4	1,200.	2,400.	48.6
Paramilitary (000)**	89.	513.4	1,000.	543.	12.
Troops deployed overseas**	200,000+ see Appendix, 1B	100,000+	20+ UN peace-keeping	e30,000 see Appendix Russia, 7D	45 UN peace-keeping
Principle Surface Combatants**	130+	177+	53+	35+	55+
Carriers**	12+	6	0	1+	0
Submarines**	76+	88	71	70+	16
SSBN**	18+	7	1	21	0
ICBM**	701+	?	15-20	756+	0
SLBM**	464+	112?	12	592+	0
Long-range bombers**	315+	?	0	74	0
Combat aircraft**	5,000+	3,253+	3,520+	1,800+	337+

SSBN = ballistic-missile submarine nuclear-fuelled
ICBM = intercontinental ballistic missile
SLBM = sea-launched cruise missile

Source: * The World in 2000. *The Economist.*
** International Institute for Strategic Studies, *The Military Balance 1999/2000*, London.

APPENDIX 1B

U.S. Troops Deployed Overseas

European Command includes the Mediterranean 6th Fleet	
Belgium	1,360
Germany	75,665
Greece	435
Italy	11,300
Mediterranean	14,000
Netherlands	785
Norway	83
Portugal	1,038
Spain	2,433
Turkey	3,029
UK	11,496
Total	118,595

Pacific Command includes Pacific Fleet (3rd Fleet and 7th Fleet)	
Alaska	16,207
Australia	35
Diego Garcia	900
Guam	6,690
Hawaii	46,005
Japan	39,930
Singapore	140
South Korea	35,920
Total	145,827

Central Command includes 5th Fleet: 2,070	
Kuwait	1,259
Qatar	52
Saudi Arabia	444+4,150 on short-term duty
Total	1,755+4,150 on short-term duty

APPENDIX 1B (continued)

Southern Command	
Honduras	56
Panama	6,230
Total	6,286

Atlantic Command includes the Atlantic Fleet (2nd and 6th Fleet)	
Bermuda	800
Cuba (Guantanamo)	1,640
Iceland	2,510
Portugal	960
UK	150
Total	6,060

UN and Peacekeeping	
Bosnia	8,427 + 228 civil police
Croatia	704 + 36 civil police
Egypt	917
FYROM	502
Georgia	4 Observers
Haiti	47 civil police
Hungary	4,900
Western Sahara	15 Observers
Total	15,450 + 311 civil police + 19 Observers

Source: International Institute for Strategic Studies, *The Military Balance 1997/98*, London.

APPENDIX 2A

Arms Trade (Value of Arms Deliveries 1996)

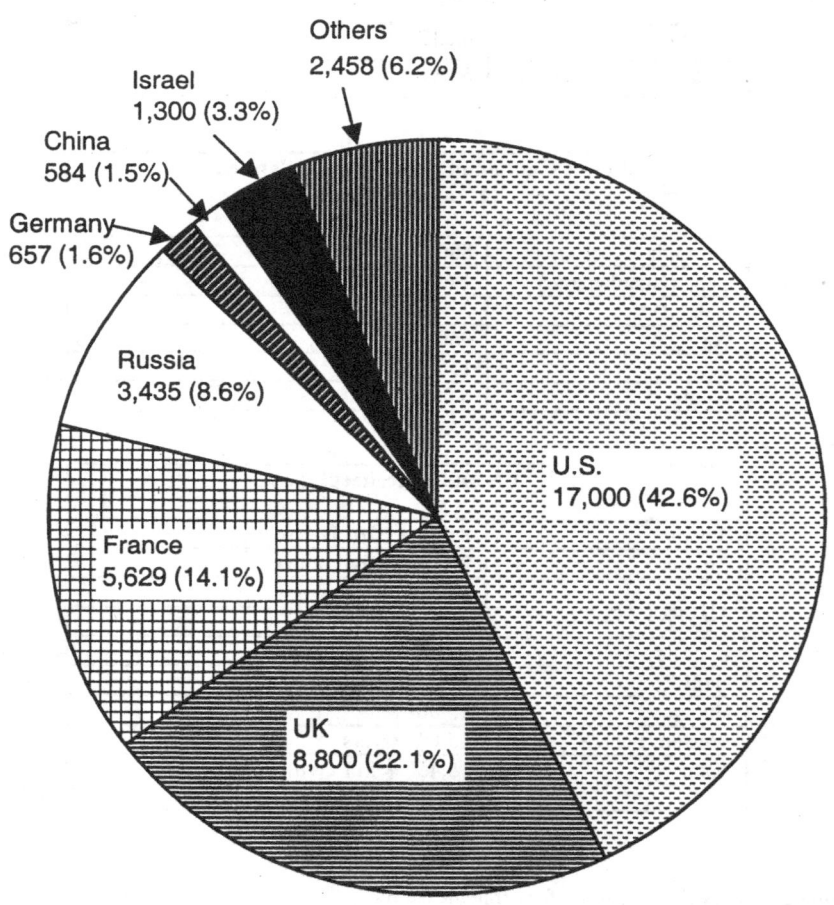

Note: (1995 $US m)

Source: International Institute for Strategic Studies, *The Military Balance 1997/98*, London.

APPENDIX 2B

Arms Trade (Value of Arms Deliveries 1996)

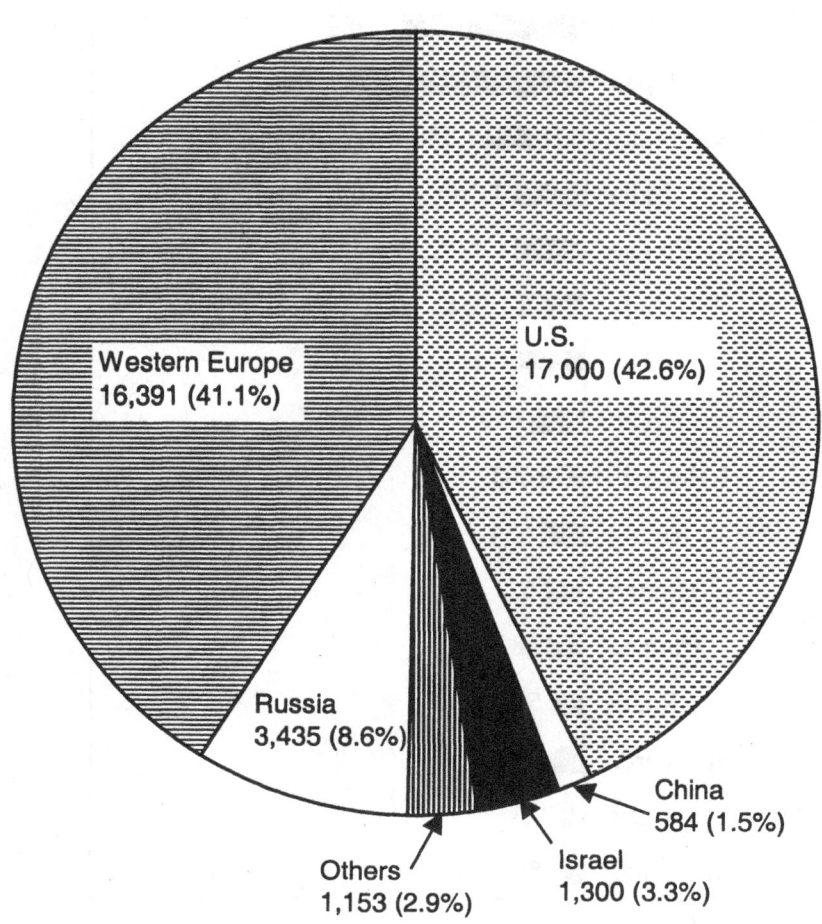

Note: (1995 $US m).

Source: International Institute for Strategic Studies, *The Military Balance 1997/98*, London.

APPENDIX 3A

**Purchasing Power Parity (PPP)
Exchange Rate GNP ($U.S. bn) in 1996**

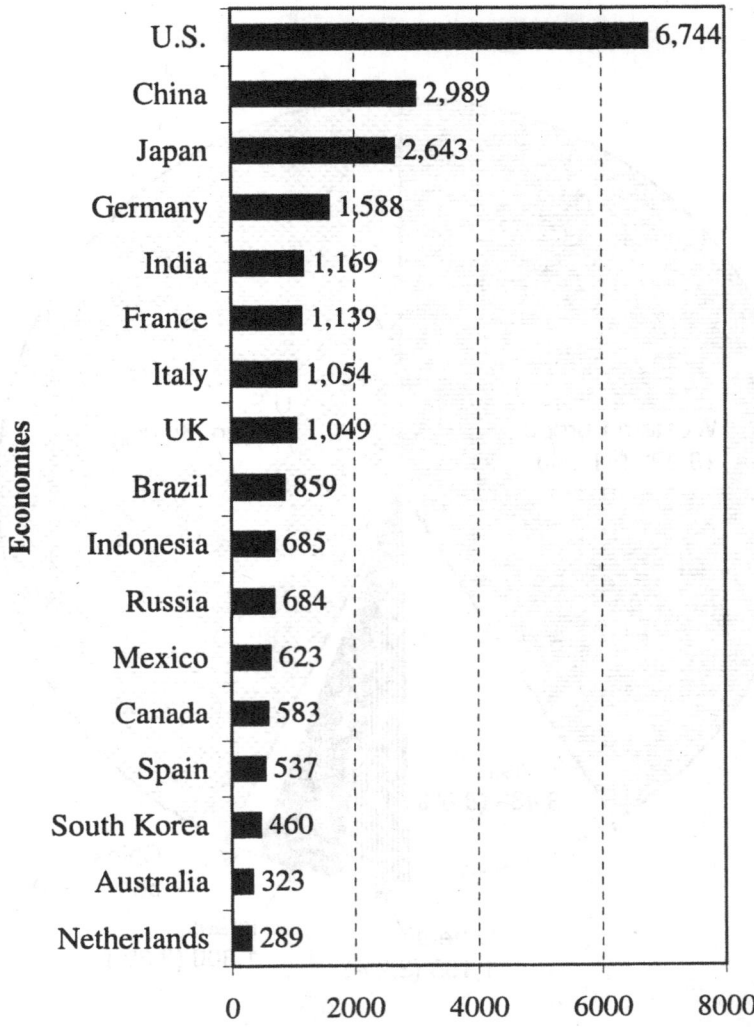

Source: World Bank, *World Development Report 1996*.

APPENDIX 3B

Market Exchange Rate GNP ($U.S. bn) in 1996

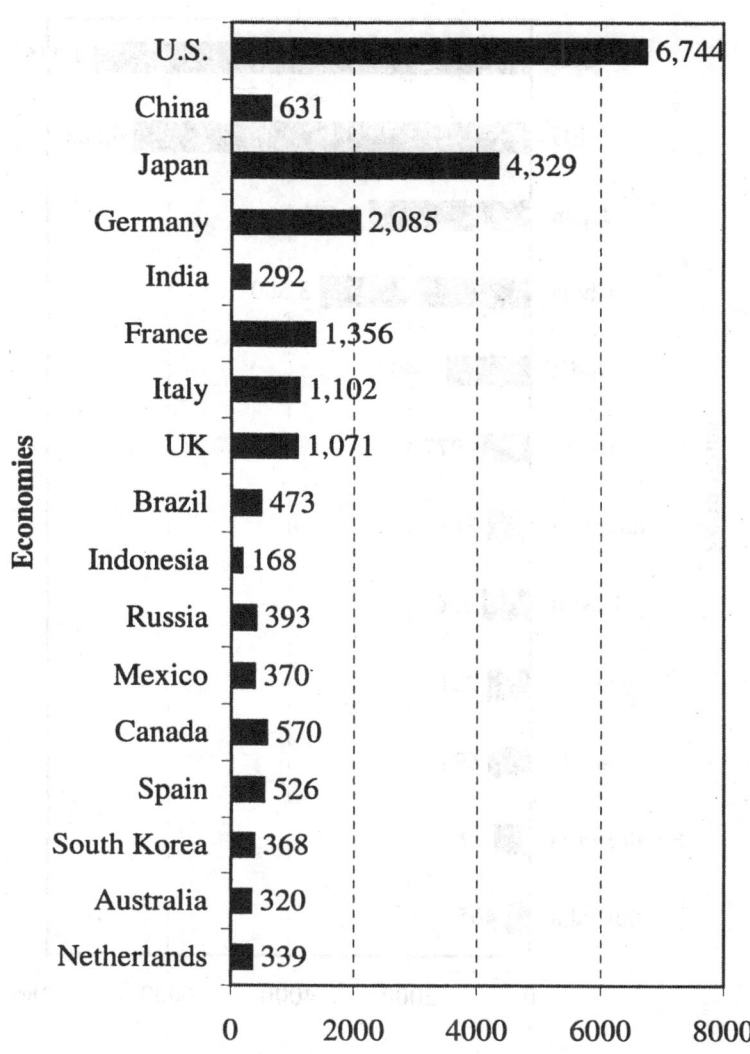

Source: World Bank, *World Development Report 1996*.

APPENDIX 3C

GDP ($U.S. bn) in 1999

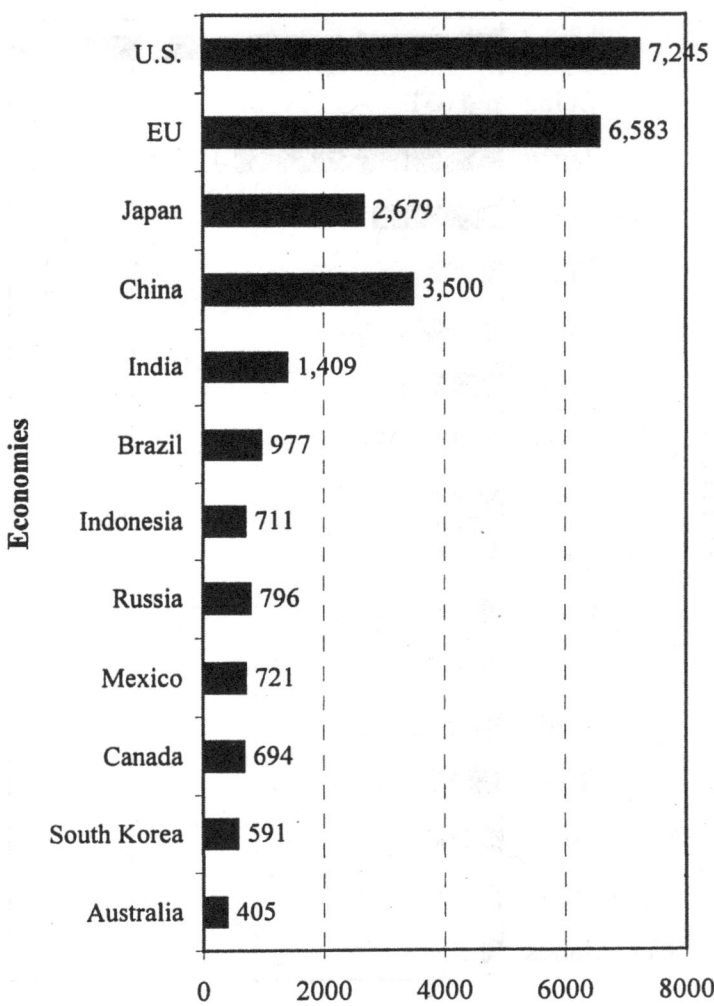

Source: Rand McNally, *World Facts and Maps 1999*.

APPENDIX 3D

GDP ($U.S. bn) in 1999

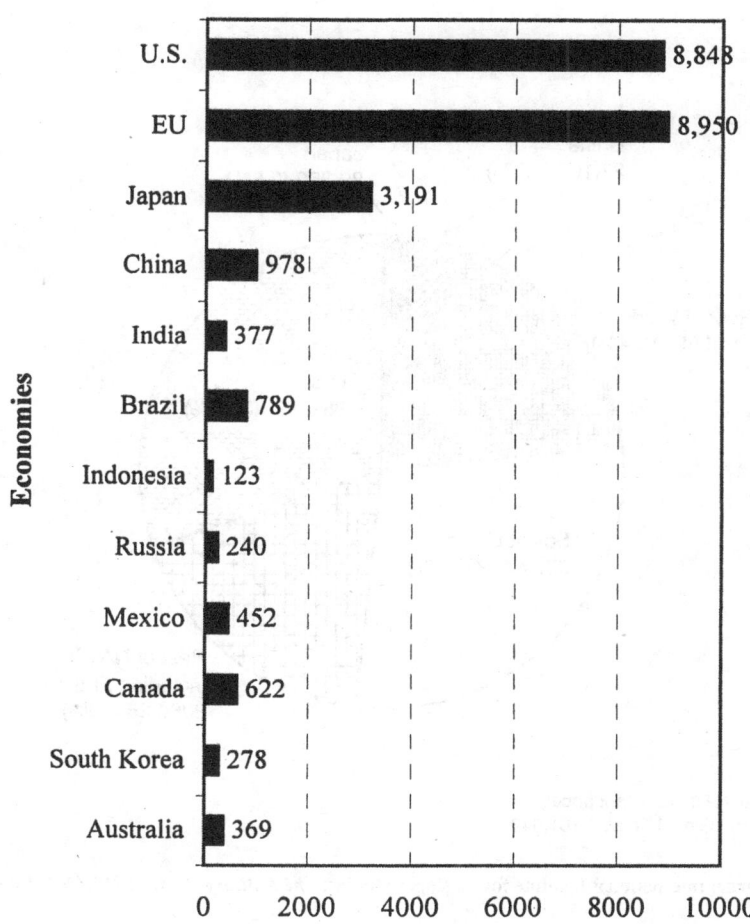

Source: *The Economist, The World in 1999.*

APPENDIX 4A

World Defence Expenditure, 1985 by Proportion ($U.S. m) (percentage)

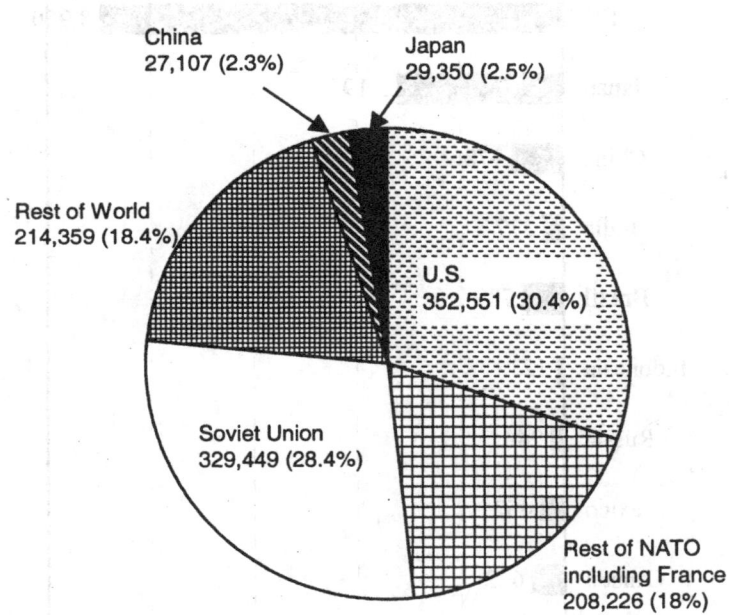

Note: (1995 constant prices)
Note ii: Global Total: 1,161,042

Source: International Institute for Strategic Studies, *The Military Balance 1997/98*, London.

APPENDIX 4B

World Defence Expenditure, 1996 by Proportion ($U.S. m) (percentage)

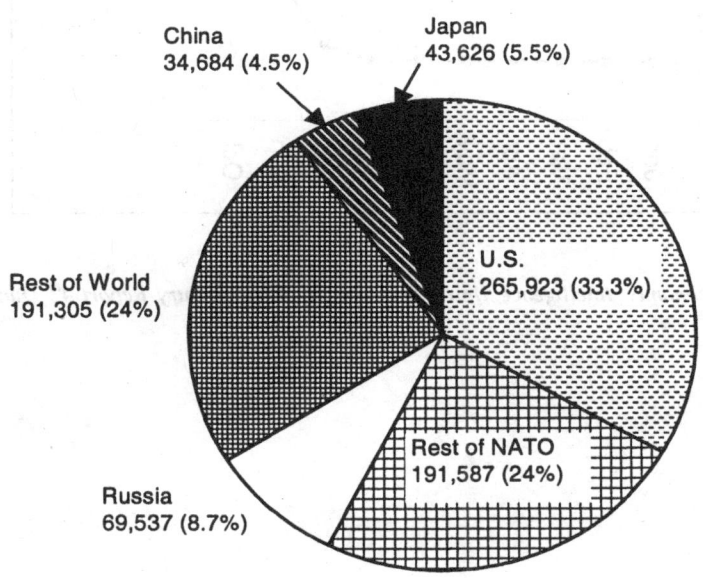

Note: (1995 constant prices)
Note ii: Global Total: 796,572
Note iii: The Czech Republic, Hungary, and Poland became full NATO members in 1999.

Source: International Institute for Strategic Studies, *The Military Balance 1997/98*, London.

APPENDIX Russia, 7A

Exchange Rate, 1998 (Rb:US$)

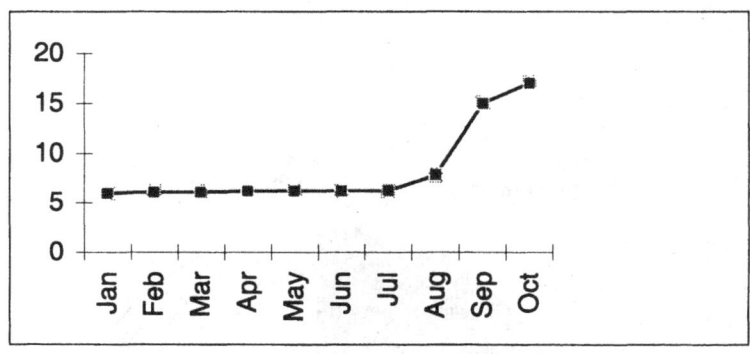

Source: *The Economist Intelligence Unit 1998. Russia. EIU Country Report 4th Quarter 1998*, p. 33.

APPENDIX Russia, 7B

Inflation Trends (% Change) and Unemployment Rate

	Consumer Prices		Industrial Input Prices			
	Month on month	Year on year	Month on month	Year on year	Unemployment (m)	Unemployment rate (%; ILO definition)
1997						
Jan	2.3	19.7	1.1	23.1	7.3	10.1
Feb	1.5	18.1	1.6	21.7	7.5	10.3
Mar	1.4	16.7	1.3	20.2	7.6	10.5
Apr	1.0	15.3	0.8	18.3	7.8	10.7
May	0.9	14.5	0.5	17.5	7.9	10.9
Jun	1.1	14.5	0.9	16.6	7.9	10.9
Jul	0.9	14.7	0.2	15.5	7.9	10.9
Aug	-0.1	14.9	0.5	13.8	7.9	10.9
Sep	-0.3	14.2	0.1	11.9	8.0	11.0
Oct	0.2	13.0	0.2	9.1	8.1	11.1
Nov	0.6	11.5	0.2	8.4	8.2	11.2
Dec	1.0	11.0	-0.1	7.4	8.2	11.3
1998						
Jan	1.5	10.5	0.9	7.1	8.2	11.3
Feb	0.9	9.4	0.6	6.0	8.3	11.4
Mar	0.6	8.5	-0.1	4.5	8.3	11.4
Apr	0.4	8.0	0.1	3.7	8.4	11.6
May	0.5	7.5	-0.9	2.4	8.4	11.5
Jun	0.1	6.4	0.1	1.6	8.4	11.5
Jul	0.2	5.6	-0.8	0.5	8.4	11.5
Aug	3.7	9.7	-1.2	-1.2	8.4	11.5
Sep	38.4	52.2	7.5	6.2	8.5	11.5
Oct	4.5	58.8	5.9	12.1	8.5	11.6

Source: Russian Economic Trends, *The Economist Intelligence Unit 1998. Russia. EIU Country Report 4th Quarter 1998*, pp. 29-30.

APPENDIX Russia, 7C

External Sovereign Debt (Mid-1998)

($ Bn)	
Eurobonds	16.0
International Organisations	25.4
IMF	19.7
World Bank	5.7
Inherited from the USSR	70.3
London Club	26.1
Paris Club	40.2
Not restructured	4.0
Other	29.3
Total	141.0

Sources: *Fitch-IBCA; EIU; United Financial Group.*

APPENDIX Russia, 7D

Ethnic Russians Outside Europe

	Titular Nationality (percent)	Russian (percent)	Total Population (thousands)
Russia	–	82	149,300
Belarus	78	13	10,370
Ukraine	73	22	51,821
Moldavia	65	13	4,455
Armenia	93	2	3,481
Azerbaijan	83	6	7,573
Georgia	70	6	5,634
Turkmenistan	73	10	3,914
Uzbekistan	71	8	22,127
Tajikistan	65	4	5,836
Kyrgyzstan	52	22	4,625
Kazakhstan	42	37	17,156
Lithuania	80	9	3,819
Estonia	62	30	1,608
Latvia	52	34	2,735

Source: Institute for National Strategic Studies *Strategic Assessment 1997: Flashpoints and Force Structure* (Washington D.C.: National Defense University), p. 17.

APPENDIX Russia, 7E

Russian Forces Abroad

Armenia	3,100
Georgia	5,000
Moldova	2,600
Tajikistan	8,200
Ukraine	1,500
Africa	100
Cuba	800
Syria	150
Vietnam	700

Source: International Institute for Strategic Studies, *The Military Balance 1999/2000*, London, p. 117.

APPENDIX 9A

Membership of European Security Organisations

	OSCE	PFP	EAPC	WEU	EU	NATO
Belgium	X	X	X	X	X	X
Denmark	X	X	X	X	X	X
France	X	X	X	X	X	X
Germany	X	X	X	X	X	X
Greece	X	X	X	X	X	X
Italy	X	X	X	X	X	X
Luxembourg	X	X	X	X	X	X
Netherlands	X	X	X	X	X	X
Portugal	X	X	X	X	X	X
Spain	X	X	X	X	X	X
UK	X	X	X	X	X	X
Iceland	X	X	X	A		X
Norway	X	X	X	A		X
Turkey	X	X	X	A		X
Ireland	X			O	X	
Austria	X	X	X	O	X	
Finland	X	X	X	O	X	
Sweden	X	X	X	O	X	
Bulgaria	X	X	X	AP		
Czech Republic	X	X	X	A		X
Estonia	X	X	X	AP		
Hungary	X	X	X	A		X
Latvia	X	X	X	AP		
Lithuania	X	X	X	AP		
Poland	X	X	X	A		X
Romania	X	X	X	AP		
Slovakia	X	X	X	AP		
Slovenia	X	X	X	AP		
Canada	X	X	X			X
U.S.	X	X	X			X
Albania	X	X	X			
Armenia	X	X	X			
Azerbaijan	X	X	X			
Belarus	X	X	X			
FYROM	X	X	X			
Georgia	X	X	X			
Georgia	X	X	X			
Kazakhstan	X	X	X			
Kyrgyz tan	X	X	X			
Moldova	X	X	X			
Russia	X	X	X			
Turkmenistan	X	X	X			
Ukraine	X	X	X			
Uzbekistan	X	X	X			
Malta	X					
Tajikistan	X	X	X			
Andorra	X					
Bosnia-Herzegovina	X					
Croatia	X					
Cyprus	X					
Holy See	X					
Liechtenstein	X					
Monaco	X					
San Marino	X					
Switzerland	X	X				
FRY	S					

Key

OSCE = Organisation for Security and Co-operation in Europe
PFP = Partnership for Peace
EAPC = Euro-Atlantic Partnership Council
WEU = Western European Union
EU = European Union
NATO = North Atlantic Treaty Organisation
X = Member
O = Observer
A = Associate Member
AP = Associate Partner
S = Membership suspended

Source: International Institute for Strategic Studies, *The Military Balance* 1999/2000, London.

Bibliography

Archives and Government Documents

U.S. Government Documents

Bureau of East Asian and Pacific Affairs

_____(1998, 28 April) *U.S.-Japan Relations* (U.S. Department of State, Washington, D.C.), http://www.state.gov/www/regions/eap/.
_____(1998, October) *Background Notes: China* (U.S. Department of State, Washington, D.C.) http://www.state.gov/www/background_notes/china_1098_bgn.html.
_____(1999, March) *Background Notes: Japan* (U.S. Department of State, Washington, D.C.), http://www.state.gov/www/background_notes/japan_0399_bgn.html.

Bureau of European and Canadian Affairs

_____(1997, 4 February) *The New Transatlantic Agenda: Update* (U.S. Department of State: Washington, D.C.) http://www.state.gov/www/regions/eur/eu/transatagnd.hmtl.
_____(1997, 23 June) *U.S. Relations With Russia* (U.S. Department of State: Washington, D.C.) http://www.state.gov/www/regions/nis/fs-us_russian_970623.hmtl.
_____(1998, 30 April) *G-7/G-8 Summits: History and Purpose* (U.S. Department of State, Washington, D.C.) http://www.state.gov/www/regions/eur/.
Kornblum, John C. (Assistant Secretary of State for European and Canadian Affairs) (8 October 1996) *A Tour Through the New Atlantic Community* http://www.state.gov/www/regions/eur/10-8korn.html.
The United States Mission to the European Union. (1999, 21 June) 'Joint U.S.-EU Statement on "Early Warning" Mechanism' http://www.useu.be.summit/earlwarn0699.html.
_____(1999, 21 June) 'U.S.-EU Transatlantic Economic Partnership Steering Group Report' http://www.useu.be.summit/teprep0699.html.
_____(1999, 21 June) 'Joint U.S.-EU Statement on "Early Warning" Mechanism' http://www.useu.be.summit/earlwarn0699.html.
_____(1999, 21 June) 'U.S.-EU Summit Declaration' http://www.useu.be.summit/declar0699.html.

The White House

_____(1996, February) *'A National Security Strategy of Engagement and Enlargement'* http://www.fas.org/spp/military/docops/national/1996stra.html.
_____(1997, May) *'A National Security Strategy for A New Century'* http://www.whitehouse.gov/wh/eop/nsc/strategy/.
_____(1997, 13 December) *Statement by Secretary Rubin and Ambassador Barshefsky Regarding the Successful Conclusion of WTO Financial Services Negotiations.* (Office of the Press Secretary, Washington, D.C.).

_____(1998, 17 June) *'Press Briefing by National Security Advisor Sandy Berger, Treasury Secretary Robert Rubin and Director of the National Economic Council Gene Sperling'*, (Office of the Press Secretary, Washington, D.C.).
_____(1999, 19 January) *President Clinton: 1999 State of the Union Meeting the Challenges of the 21st Century* http://www2.whitehouse.gov/wh/work/01199.html.
_____(1999, 22 January) *President Clinton and Vice President Gore: Keeping America Secure for the 21st Century* http://www2.whitehouse.gov/wh/work/012299.html.
_____(1999, 26 February) *President Clinton and Vice President Gore: American Leadership for Peace, Prosperity and Freedom in the 21st Century* http://www2.whitehouse.gov/wh/work/022699.html.
_____(1999, 22 March) *President Clinton: Promoting Peace and Security for Americans and Europeans* http://www2.whitehouse.gov/wh/work/032299.html.
_____(1999, 7 April) *President Clinton: World Leader for Peace and Security* http://www2.whitehouse.gov/wh/work/040799b.html.
Weekly Compilation of Presidential Documents (1998, 26 January), Vol. 34, No. 4, pp. 85-126. Government Printing Office: Washington D.C.
_____(1998, 16 February), Vol. 34, No. 7, pp. 227-61. Government Printing Office: Washington D.C.
_____(1998, 30 March), Vol. 34, No. 13, pp. 479-523. Government Printing Office: Washington D.C.
_____(1998, 20 April), Vol. 34, No. 16, pp. 635-69. Government Printing Office: Washington D.C.
_____(1998, 11 May), Vol. 34, No. 19, pp. 755-836. Government Printing Office: Washington D.C.
_____(1998, 25 May), Vol. 34, No. 21, pp. 883-   956, Government Printing Office: Washington D.C.

U.S. Department of Defense

Cheney, Dick ((former) Secretary of Defense) (1992, February) *Annual Report to the President and the Congress* (U.S. Government Printing Office: Washington, D.C.).
_____(1993, January) *Defense Strategy for the 1990s: The Regional Defense Strategy* (U.S. Government Printing Office: Washington D.C.).
Cohen, William S. (Secretary of Defense) (12 February 1997). *Cohen Testimony on FY 1998 Defense Budget* http://www.usis.usemb.se/speeches/Cohen.defbug.html.
_____(1999) Annual Report to the President and the Congress. http://www.dtic.mil/execsec/adr1999.html.
U.S. Department of Defense. (24 Feb, 1997) *Report to the Congress on Enlargement of the North Atlantic Treaty Organisation: Rationale, Benefits, Costs and Implications*. Washington, D.C.
White, John P. (Deputy Secretary of Defense) (24 June 1997) *Transforming the NATO Alliance for the 21st Century* http://www.usis.usemb.se/speeches/jpwhite/nato.html.
Wisner, Frank (U.S. Under Secretary of Defense for Policy), Press Conference, U.S. Embassy, Tokyo, 2 August 1993, USIS Wireless File, p. 169, 4 August 1993.

U.S. House of Representatives

Committee on Ways and Means U.S. House of Representatives: *Overview and Compilation of U.S. Trade Statutes* (1997 edition), 25 June 1997 (U.S. Government Printing Office: Washington, D.C.).

Hamilton, Lee (1993) *U.S. Foreign Policy in the Post-Cold War Era: Report and Recommendations* (Committee on Foreign Affairs, U.S. House of Representatives: U.S. Government Press Office, Washington D.C.).

U.S. State Department

Albright, Madeleine K. (Secretary of State) (29 May 1997). *Sec State Albright Speech at Inaugural Meeting of EAPC*
http://www.usis.usemb.se/speeches/albright/speech.hmtl.
_____(29 May 1997) *Basic Document of the Euro-Atlantic Partnership Council*
http://www.usis.usemb.se/speeches/albright/basic.hmtl.

State Department report. (24 Feb. 1997) *Report to the Congress on Enlargement of the North Atlantic Treaty Organisation: Rationale, Benefits, Costs and Implications*. Washington, D.C.

Steinberg, James B. (Director of Policy Planning U.S. Department of State) (24 January 1996) *Policy and .Principles: The Clinton Administration's Approach* (New York: Foreign Policy Association).

Talbott, Strobe (Deputy Secretary of State) (12 September 1995) *American Eagle or Ostrich: American Engagement in the post-Cold War World* (Milwaukee Town Hall Meeting, Pabst Theatre, Milwaukee, Wisconsin).

Other Official Sources

Ministry of Foreign Affairs, Japan

_____Diplomatic Bluebook, 1998. Japan's Diplomacy towards the 21st Century – New Developments and New Challenges Facing the International Community. (Tokyo).
_____Diplomatic Bluebook, 1999. Japan's Diplomacy with Leadership Toward the New Century. (Tokyo). Distributed on
http://www.mofa.go.jp/policy/other/bluebook/1999.html.

NATO

_____(1997, 15 May) NATO-Russia Founding Act,
http://www.nato.int/usa/policy/d970515a.html.
_____(1999) The New Atlantic Community
http://www.nato.int/usa/info/atlantic_community.html.
_____(1999, 20 July) Defense Secretary Cohen Testifies on Lessons of Kosovo, Security Issues Digest No. 138, http://usa/grmbl.com/s19990720f.html.
_____(1999, 30 July) 'Shared values as much worth defending as territory', Speech delivered by Ambassador Alexander Vershbow, U.S. Permanent Representative at the Marshall Center Graduation Ceremony, Germany,
http://www.nato.int/usa/ambassador/s990730a.html.

_____ (1999, 8 November) 'The U.S.-Russia Partnership – Russia: Ten Years After', Speech delivered by Ambassador Alexander Vershbow, U.S. Permanent Representative, http://www.nato.int/usa/ambassador/s991108a.html.

_____ (1999, 17 December) Next Steps on European Security and Defense: a U.S. View', remarks by Ambassador Alexander Vershbow, U.S. Permanent Representative http://www.nato.int/usa/ambassador/s991217a.html.

Books

Agnew, John (1998) *Geopolitics: Re-visioning World Politics* (London: Routledge).
Agnew, John and Stuart Corbridge (1995) *Mastering Space: Hegemony, territory and international political economy* (London: Routledge).
Akaha, T. and F. Langdon (Eds.) (1993) *Japan in the Posthegemonic World* (London: Lynne Reinner).
Akaneya, Tatsuo (1998) *The Japanese-U.S. Alliance: A New Definition* (London: The Royal Institute of International Affairs, Discussion Paper 76).
Aldred, K. and M.A. Smith (1999) *Superpowers in the Post-Cold War Era* (London: Macmillan Press).
Alker, H.R. (1996) *Rediscoveries and Reformulations: Humanistic Methodologies for International Studies* (Cambridge: Cambridge University Press).
Allison, G. and G. Treverton (Eds.) (1992) *Rethinking America's Security: Beyond Cold War to New World Order* (London: W.W. Norton).
Ambrose, S.E. and D.G. Brinkley (1971, 1997 8th edit.) *Rise to Globalism: American Foreign Policy Since 1938* (London: Penguin Books).
Amin, Samir (1997) *Capitalism in the Age of Globalisation: The Management of Contemporary Society* (New York: St. Martins).
Amin, S., G. Arrighi, A.G. Frank and I. Wallerstein (1982) *Dynamics of Global Crisis* (London: Macmillan).
(1990) *Transforming the Revolution: Social Movements and the World System* (New York: Monthly Review Press).
Anderson, J., C. Brook and A. Cochrane (Eds.) (1995) *A Global World? Re-ordering Political Space* (Oxford: Oxford University Press).
Anderson, Jeffrey (1999) *German Unification and the Union of Europe* (Cambridge: Cambridge University Press).
Anderson, Peter J. (1996) *The Global Politics of Power, Justice and Death* (London: Routledge).
Armacost, Michael H. (1996) *Friends or Rivals: The Insider's Account of U.S.-Japan Relations* (New York: Columbia University Press).
Aron, Raymond (1967) (Translated by Richard Howard and Annette Baker Fox) *Peace and War: A Theory of International Relations* (New York: Fredrick A. Praeger).
Avery, G. and F. Cameron (1998) *The Enlargement of the European Union* (Sheffield: Sheffield Academic Press).
Axford, Barrie (1995) *The Global System: Economics, Politics and Culture* (Cambridge: Polity Press).
Axtmann, Roland (Ed.) (1998) *Globalisation and Europe: Theoretical and Empirical Investigations* (London: Pinter).
Bacon, Francis (1601) *The Essays* (World's Greatest Classic Books. Electronically Enhanced Text, World Library).

_____ (1944, revised edit.) (With introduction by James E. Creighton) *Advancement of Learning and Novum Organum* (New York: Wiley Books).

Bagby, Meredith (1998) *Annual Report of the United States of America, 1998* (New York: McGraw-Hill).

Baldwin, David A. (Ed.) (1993) *Neorealism and Neoliberalism: The Contemporary Debate* (New York: Columbia University Press).

Barnes, Barry (1988) *The Nature of Power* (Cambridge: Policy Press).

Barraclough, Geoffrey (Ed.) (1978, 1987 rev. edit.) *The Times Atlas of World History* (London: Guild Publishing).

Barston, R.P. (1988) *Modern Diplomacy* (London: Longman).

Baylis, J. and S. Smith (Eds.) (1997) *The Globalisation of World Politics* (Oxford: Oxford University Press).

Bell, C. (1989) *The Reagan Paradox: US Foreign Policy in the 1980s* (New Brunswick, New Jersey: Rutger University Press).

Beloff, M. (1967) *The Balance of Power* (London: Allen & Unwin).

Berger, Peter (1986) *The Capitalist Revolution* (New York: Basic Books).

Berger, P. and T. Luckmann (1966/1979 Peregrine Books) *The Social Construction of Reality* (Harmondsworth, Middlesex: Penguin).

Bergsten, C. Fred (1988) *America in the World Economy: A strategy for the 1990s* (Washington, DC: Institute for International Economics).

Bergsten, C. Fred and M. Noland (1993) *Reconcilable Differences? United States-Japan Economic Conflict* (Washington, DC: Institute for International Economics).

Bernstein, Peter L. (1998) *Against the Gods: The Remarkable Story of Risk* (New York: John Wiley & Sons, Inc).

Berstein, Richard and Ross H. Munro (1997a) *The Coming Conflict with China* (New York: Knopf).

Binnendijk, H. and R.N. Montaperto (Eds.) (1998) *Strategic Trends in China* (Washington D.C.: National Defense University).

Blair, Alasdair (1999) *The European Union since 1945* (London: Longman).

Booth, Ken (Ed.) (1998) *Statecraft and Security: The Cold War and Beyond* (Cambridge: Cambridge University Press).

Boyer, M. (1993) *International Cooperation and Public Goods: Opportunities for the Western Alliance* (Baltimore: Johns Hopkins University Press).

Boyer, R. and D. Drache (Eds.) (1996) *States Against Markets: The Limits of Globalisation* (London: Routledge).

Braudel, Fernand (1987) (1993, translated by Richard Mayne) *A History of Civilisations* (London: Penguin Books).

Brecher, Michael (1993) *Crisis in World Politics: Theory and Reality* (Oxford: Pergamon Press).

Bridges, Brian (1993) *Japan: Hesitant Superpower* (UK: Research Institute for the Study of Conflict and Terrorism).

Brilmayer, Lea (1994) *American Hegemony: Political Morality in a One-Superpower World* (London: Yale University Press).

Brogan, Hugh (1985) (1990 Penguin edition) *The Penguin History of the United States of America* (London: Penguin).

Brown, M.E., S.M. Lynn-Jones and S.E. Miller (Eds.) (1997, 2nd edit.) *Debating the Democratic Peace* (London: The MIT Press).

Brown, M.E., O.W. Cote, S.M. Lynn-Jones, and S.E. Miller (Eds.) (1997) *America's Strategic Choices* (London: The MIT Press).

Brzezinski, Zbigniew (1993) *Out of Control: Global Turmoil on the Eve of the 21st Century* (New York: A Robert Stewart Book).

_____(1997a) *The Grand Chessboard: American Primacy and Geostrategic Imperatives* (New York: Basic Books).

Buchanan, Patrick J. (1998) *The Great Betrayal: How American Sovereignty and Social Justice Are Being Sacrificed to the Gods of the Global Economy* (Boston: Little, Brown & Co.).

Bull, Hedley (1977) (1995, 2nd edit.) (Foreword by Stanley Hoffman) *The Anarchical Society: A Study of Order in World Politics* (London: Macmillan).

Burman, S. (1991) *America in the Modern World: The Transcendence of United States Hegemony* (Hemel Hempstead, Hertfordshire: Harvester Wheatsheaf).

Burwell, Frances G. and Ivo H. Daalder (Eds.) (1999) *The United States and Europe in the Global Arena* (New York: St. Martin's Press).

Butterfield, Herbert and Martin Wight (Eds.) (1966) *Diplomatic Investigations: Essays in the Theory of International Politics* (London: Allen & Unwin).

Buzan, Barry (1991, 2nd edit.) *People, States and Fear: An Agenda for International Security Studies in the Post-Cold War Era* (London: Harvester Wheatsheaf).

Cafruny, Alan 'A Gramscian Concept of Declining Hegemony: Stages of US Power and the Evolution of International Relations', in D. Rapkin (1990) (ed.), *World Leadership and Hegemony*, pp. 97-118.

Calleo, David P. (1976) *Money and the Coming of World Order* (New York: New York University Press).

_____(1982) *The Imperious Economy* (London: Harvard University Press).

_____(1987) *Beyond American Hegemony: The Future of the Western Alliance* (New York: Basic Books).

_____(1993) 'Good Housekeeping and the US Global Role' in R. Morgan, J. Lorentzen, A. Leander and S. Guzzini *New Diplomacy in the Post-Cold War* (London: Macmillan).

Calvocoressi, Peter R. (1968) (1991, 6th edit.) *World Politics Since 1945* (London: Longman).

_____ (1991) *Resilient Europe: A Study of the Years 1870-2000* (London: Longman).

Camilleri, J.A. and J. Falk (1994) *The End of Sovereignty? The Politics of a Shrinking and Fragmenting World* (Aldershot: Edward Elgar).

Carr, Edward H. (1939: Macmillan) (1946: St. Martin) (1964 edit.) *The Twenty Years' Crisis, 1919-1939: An Introduction to the Study of International Relations* (London: Harper & Row).

_____(1961) *What is History?* (London: Macmillan).

Casti, John L. (1989) *Paradigms Lost: Images of Man in the Mirror of Science* (London: Abacus).

Catley, Bob (1996) *Globalising Australian Capitalism* (Cambridge: Cambridge University Press).

Cerny, Phil G. (1993) *Finance and World Politics: Markets, Regimes and States in the Post-Hegemonic Era.* (Aldershot: Edward Elgar).

Chace, James (1992) *The Consequence of the Peace: The New Internationalism and American Foreign Policy* (Oxford: Oxford University Press).

Chan, Steve (1990) *East Asian Dynamism: Growth, Order, and Security in the Pacific Region* (Oxford: Westview Press).

Chase-Dunn, Christopher 'The Limits of Hegemony: Capitalism and Global State Formation,' in David P. Rapkin (ed.) (1990) *World Leadership and Hegemony* (London: Lynne Rienner), pp. 213-40.
_____(1998: Updated Edition) *Global Formation: Structures of the World-Economy* (Oxford: Rowman & Littlefield Publishers).
Christopher, Warren (1998) *In the Stream of History* (Stanford, California: Stanford University Press).
Clarke, Ian (1997) *Globalisation and Fragmentation: International Relations in the Twentieth Century* (Oxford: Oxford University Press).
Claude, I. (1986) *American Approaches to World Affairs* (London: University Press of America).
Clemens, C. and W.E. Paterson (1998) *The Kohl Chancellorship* (London: Frank Cass).
Cohen, Robin (1997) *Global Diasporas: An Introduction* (London: UCL Press).
Cohen, Stephen D. (1988, 3rd edit.) *The Making of United States International Economic Policy* (New York: New York).
Cottingham, John (Ed.) (1996) *Western Philosophy: An Anthology* (London: Blackwell).
Cox, Michael (1995) *US Foreign Policy after the Cold War: Superpower Without a Mission* (London: Pinter).
_____(Ed.) (1998a) *Rethinking the Soviet Collapse: Sovietology, the death of communism and the new Russia* (London: Pinter).
_____(1998b) 'New China: new Cold War?' in Ken Booth (ed.) (1998) *Statecraft and Security: The Cold War and Beyond* (Cambridge: Cambridge University Press), pp. 224-46.
_____(Ed.) (1999) *The Eighty Years Crisis: International Crisis, 1919-1999* (Cambridge University Press).
_____(Ed.) (2000a) *E. H. Carr: A Critical Appraisal* (London: Macmillan).
_____(Ed.) (2000b) *American Democracy Promotion* (London: Macmillan).
_____(Ed.) (2000c) *The Interregnum: Controversies in World Politics, 1989-1999* (Cambridge: Cambridge University Press).
Cox, Robert W. (1987) *Production, Power, and World Order* (New York: Columbia University Press).
_____(Ed.) (1997) *The New Realism: Perspectives on Multilateralism and World Order* (New York: United Nations University Press).
Cox, R.W. and T.J. Sinclair (1996) *Approaches to World Order* (Cambridge: Cambridge University Press).
Cox, Ronald W. and Skidmore-Hess, D. (1999) *U.S. Politics and the Global Economy: Corporate Power, Conservative Shift* (London: Boulder).
Craig, G.A. and A.L. George (1983) (1990, 2nd edit.) *Force and Statecraft: Diplomatic Problems of Our Time* (London: Oxford University Press).
Crawford, C. (1986) *Balance of Power: International Politics as the ultimate global game* (Redmond, Washington: Microsoft Press).
Croft, S., J. Redmond, G.W. Rees, and M. Webber (1999) (Forwarded by Han Van Den Broek) *The Enlargement of Europe* (Manchester: Manchester University Press).
Cronin, Richard P. (1992) *Japan, the United States, and prospects for the Asia-Pacific century, three scenarios for the future* (Singapore: Institute of Southeast Asian Studies).
Curtis, Gerald L. (Ed.) 1993) *Japan's Foreign Policy: After the Cold War, Coping with Change* (London: An East Gate Book).

_____ (Ed.) (1994) *The United States, Japan, and Asia* (London: W.W. Norton and Company).
Dalby, S. (1990) *Creating the Second Cold War: The Discourse of Politics* (London: Pinter).
Dark, K.R. (1998) *The Waves of Time: Long-term change and International Relations* (London: Pinter).
Denton, Geoffrey (1999) *A New Transatlantic Partnership* (London: Federal Trust for TEPSA).
Der Derian, James (Ed.) (1995) *International Theory: Critical Investigation* (New York: New York University Press).
der Pijl, Kees van (1984) *The Making of an Atlantic Ruling Class* (London: Verso).
_____ (1998) *Transnational Class and International Relations* (London: Routledge).
Diamond, L. and M.F. Plattner (Eds.) (1993) *The Global Resurgence of Democracy* (Baltimore: The Johns Hopkins University Press).
Diamond, L., M.F. Plattner, Y-H. Chu and H-M. Tien (Eds.) (1997) *Consolidating the Third Wave Democracies: Themes and Perspectives* (London: The Johns Hopkins University Press).
Diamond, Larry (1999) *Developing Democracy: Toward Consolidation* (London: The Johns Hopkins University Press).
Donelan, Michael (Ed.) (1978) *The Reason of States: A Study in International Political Theory* (London: George Allen & Unwin).
Doran, Charles (1971) *The Politics of Assimilation: Hegemony and its Aftermath* (Baltimore: Johns Hopkins University Press).
Dore, Donald (1997) *Japan, Internationalism and the United Nations* (New York: Routledge).
Dornan, Jr. James E. (Ed.) (1978) (Intro. by Frank Barnett) *United States National Security Policy in the Decade Ahead* (London: Macdonald and Jane's).
Doyle, Michael W. (1997) *Ways of War and Peace* (London: W.W. Norton).
Drexler, K. Eric (1990) (1996) (foreworded by Marvin Minsky) *Engines of Creation: The Coming Era of Nano-technology* (London: Fourth Estate).
Drifte, Reinhard (1990) *Japan's Foreign Policy* (New York: Royal Institute of International Affairs).
_____ (1996) *Japan's Foreign Policy in the 1990s: From Economic Superpower to What Power?* (Oxford: St Anthony's College).
_____ (2000) *Japan's Quest for a Permanent Security Council Seat: A Matter of Pride or Justice?* (London: Macmillan Press).
Dryer, H.C. (1989) *The Study of International Relations: The State of the Art* (Basingstoke: Macmillan).
Duchene, Francois (1994) *Jean Monnet: The First Statesman of Interdependence* (New York: Norton)
Ebrey, Patricia Buckley (1996) *The Cambridge Illustrated History: China* (Cambridge: Cambridge University Press).
Elvin, Mark (1973) *The Pattern of the Chinese Past* (Stanford: Stanford University Press).
Emmott, Bill (1989) *The Sun also Sets: Why Japan will not be Number One* (London: Simon & Schuster).
Emmott, B., K. Watanabe and P. Wolfowitz (1997) *Managing the International System Over the Next Ten Years* (New York, Paris and Tokyo: The Trilateral Commission).
Etzold, T.H. and J.L. Gaddis (Eds.) (1978) *Containment: Documents on American Policy and Strategy, 1945-1950* (New York: Columbia University Press).

Evans, Graham and Jeffrey Newnham (1992) *The Dictionary of World Politics* (London: Harvester Wheatsheaf).
_____(1998) *The Penguin Dictionary of International Relations* (London: Penguin Books).
Farer, Tom J. (1988) *The Grand Strategy of the United States in Latin America* (Oxford: Transaction Books).
Featherstone, K. and R.H. Ginsberg (1993) (1996, 2nd edit.) *The United States and the European Union in the 1990s: Power in Transition* (London: Macmillan).
Feldstein, M. (1988) *The United States in the World Economy* (London: The University of Chicago Press).
Ferrill, Arthur (1991) 'The Grand Strategy of the Roman Empire' in Paul Kennedy (1991) *Grand Strategies in War and Peace* (London: Yale University Press), pp. 71-85.
Feyerabend, Paul (1975) (1978, Verso edit.) *Against Method: Outline of an anarchistic theory of knowledge* (London: Verso).
Fontana, Benedetto (1993) *Hegemony and Power: On the Relation between Gramsci and Machiavelli* (London: University of Minnesota Press).
A Foreign Affairs Reader (1996) *The Clash of Civilizations? The Debate* (New York: Foreign Affairs).
_____(1998a) *Democracy* (New York: Foreign Affairs).
_____(1998b) *Is Global Capitalism Working?* (New York: Foreign Affairs).
_____(1998c) *The Rise of China* (New York: Foreign Affairs).
_____(1998d) *A New Europe?* (New York: Foreign Affairs).
Frank, Andre Gunder (1998) *ReOrient: Global Economy in the Asian Age* (London: University of California Press).
Frank, A.G. and B.K. Gills (Eds.) (1993) *The World System: Five hundred years or five thousand?* (London: Routledge).
Freeman, Jr. Chas. W. (1994; revised edit. 1997) *The Diplomat's Dictionary* (Washington, D.C.: United States Institute of Peace Press).
_____(1997) *Arts of Power: Statecraft and Diplomacy* (Washington, D.C.: United States Institute of Peace Press).
Frieden, J.A. and D.A. Lake (Eds.) (1991, 2nd edit.) *International Political Economy: Perspectives on Global Power and Wealth* (London: Unwin Hyman).
Friedman, George and Meredith Lebard (1991) *The Coming War with Japan* (New York: St. Martin Press).
Friedman, Thomas (1999) *The Lexus and the Olive Tree* (London: HarperCollins).
Fry, E.H., S.T. Taylor and R.S. Wood (1994) *America the Vincible: US Foreign Policy for the Twenty-First Century* (Englewood Cliffs: Prentice Hall).
Fukuyama, Francis (1992) *The End of History and the Last Man* (London: Penguin Books).
_____(1995) *Trust: The Social Virtues and the Creation of Prosperity* (London: Penguin Books).
Funabashi, Yoichi (Ed.) (1994) *Japan's International Agenda* (London: New York University Press).
_____ (1999) *Alliance Adrift* (New York: Council on Foreign Relations Press).
Gallicchio, Marc S. (1988) *The Cold War Begins in Asia: American East Asian Policy and the Fall of the Japanese Empire* (New York: Columbia University Press).
Gallie, W.B. (1978) *Philosophers of Peace and War* (Cambridge: Cambridge University Press).
Gamble, A., D. Marsh and T. Tant (Eds.) (1999) *Marxism and Social Science* (London: . Macmillan).

Garten, Jeffrey E. (1992) *A Cold Peace: America, Japan, Germany and the struggle for Supremacy* (New York: Times Books).

Gates, Jeff (1998) *The Ownership Solution: Toward a Shared Capitalism for the Twenty First Century* (London: Penguin Books).

Gates, Robert M. (1996) *From the Shadows* (New York: Simon & Schuster).

Geller, D.S. and J.D. Singer (1998) *Nations at War: Scientific Study of International Conflict* (Cambridge: Cambridge University Press).

Gerth, H.H., and C.W. Mills (1948) (1985) (Translated, edited and with introduction) *From Max Weber: Essays in Sociology* (London: Routledge & Kegan Paul).

Gertz, Bill (1999) *Betrayal: How the Clinton Administration undermined American Security* (Washington, D.C.: Regnery Publishers).

Gibbon, Edward (1896-98) *The History of the Decline and Fall of the Roman Empire*, 7 Vols. (London: Methuen and Co.)

Gill, Stephen (1990) *American Hegemony and the Trilateral Commission* (Cambridge: Cambridge University Press).

_____(Ed.) (1993) *Gramsci, Historical Materialism and International Relations* (Cambridge: Cambridge University Press).

_____(Ed.) (1997) *Globalisation, Democratisation and Multilateralism* (London: Macmillan).

Gill, Stephen and David Law (1988) *The Global Political Economy: Perspectives, Problems and Policies* (London: Harvester Wheatsheaf).

Gills, Barry K. 'The hegemonic transition in East Asia: a historical perspective' in Stephen Gill (ed.) (1993) *Gramsci, Historical Materialism and International Relations* (Cambridge: Cambridge University Press).

_____(ed.) (2000) *Globalisation and the Politics of Resistance* (London: Macmillan).

Gills, B.K., J. Rocamora and R. Wilson (1993) *Low Intensity Democracy: Political Power in the New World Order* (London: Pluto Press).

Gills, B.K. and Shahid Qadir (Eds.) (1995) *Regimes in Crisis: The Post-Soviet Era and the Implications for Development* (London: Zed Books).

Gilpin, Robert (1975) *US Power and the Multinational Corporation: The Political Economy of Direct Foreign Investment* (New York: Basic Books).

_____(1981) *War and Change in the International System* (Cambridge: Cambridge University Press).

_____(1987) *The Political Economy of International Relations* (Princeton, New Jersey: Princeton University Press).

_____(1994) 'The Cycle of Great Powers: Has it Finally Been Broken?' in Geir Lundestad (ed.) *The Fall of Great Powers: Peace, Stability, and Legitimacy* (Oxford: Oxford University Press), pp. 313-30.

GlaeBner, Gert-Joachim (Ed.) (1996) *Germany After Unification, Coming to terms with the recent past* (Amsterdam: Ropodi).

Goldstein, J. (1988) *Long Cycles: Prosperity and War in the Modern Age* (New Haven, Con.: Yale University Press).

Gompert, David C. (1998) *Right Makes Might: Freedom and Power in the Information Age* (Washington D.C: National Defense University, McNair Paper 59).

Gompert, D.C. and F.S. Larrabee (Eds.) (1998) *America and Europe: A partnership for a new era* (Cambridge: Cambridge University Press).

Good, D.S.G. and G. Segal (Eds.) (1994) *China Deconstructs: Politics, trade and regionalism* (London: Routledge).

Goody, Jack (1996) *The East in the West* (Cambridge: Cambridge University Press).

Gowan, Peter (1999) *The Global Gamble: Washington's Faustian Bid for World Dominance* (London: Verso).
Gracian, Balthasar (1637) translated by Joseph Jacob (1993) *The Art of Worldly Wisdom* (London: Shambhala).
Gramsci, Antonio (1971, reprinted 1998) edited and translated by Quintin Hoare and G.N. Smith *Selections from the Prison Notebooks* (London: Lawrence and Wispart).
Gray, John (1998a) *False Dawn: The Delusions of Global Capitalism* (London: Granta Books).
Green, R. and Joost Elffers (1998) *The 48 Laws of Power* (London: Profile Books).
Greenville, J.A.S. (1976) (1984, 6th Impression) *Europe Reshaped, 1848-1878* (Glasgow: Fontana/Collins).
Groom, A.J.R. and M. Light (Eds.) (1994) *Contemporary International Relations: A Guide to Theory* (London: Pinter).
Grove, Eric (Ed.) (1991) *Global Security: North American, European and Japanese Interdependence in the 1990s* (London: Brassey's).
Guanzi (translated by Allyn Ricket, 1985) *The Guanzi* (Princeton, NJ: Princeton University Press).
Guzzini, Stefano (1992) *The Continuing Story of a Death Foretold: Realism in International Relations/International Political Economy* (Badia Fiesolana, San Domenico: European University Institute).
_____(1998) *Realism in International Relations and International Political Economy: The Continuing Story of a Death Foretold* (London: Routledge).
Haass, Richard N. (1997) *The Reluctant Sheriff: The United States After the Cold War* (New York: Council on Foreign Relations).
Hall, J.A., and G. John Ikenberry (1989) *The State* (Milton Keynes: Open University Press).
Halliday, Fred (1994) *Rethinking International Relations* (London: Macmillan).
Hammond, Grant T. (1998) *Global Security Beyond the Millennium: American and Russian Perspectives* (New York: St Martin's Press).
Harris, S., and G. Klintworth (Eds.) (1995) *China as a Great Power: Myths, Realities and Challenges in the Asia-Pacific Region* (New York: St. Martin's Press).
Heifetz, R.A. (1994) *Leadership Without an Easy Answers* (London: Harvard University Press).
Herod, A., G.O. Tuathail and S.M. Roberts (1998) *An Unruly World? Globalisation, Governance and Geography* (London: Routledge).
Herzog, Roman (1999) *Preventing the Clash of Civilisations: A Peace Strategy for the Twenty-First Century* (New York: St. Martin's Press).
Higgs, Robert (Ed.) (1990) (Foreworded by William A. Niskanen) *Arms, Politics, and the Economy: Historical and Contemporary Perspectives* (London: Holmes & Meier).
Hippler, J. (1994) *Pax Americana? Hegemony or Decline* (London: Pluto Press).
Hirst, P. and G. Thompson (1996, 1999 2nd edit.) *Globalisation in Question: The International Economy and the Possibilities of Governance* (Cambridge: Polity Press).
Hobbes, Thomas (1651) (reprinted in 1976) *Leviathan* (London: Everyman).
Hobsbawm, Eric J. (1968) (1990) *Industry and Empire* (London: Penguin).
Holstein, J. William (1990) *The Japanese Power Game: What It Means for America* (New York: Charles Scribner's Sons).
Holsti, K.J. (1985) *The Dividing Discipline: Hegemony and Diversity in International Theory* (London: Allen & Unwin).

Holsti, O.R., R.M. Siverson and A.L. George (Eds.) (1980) *Change in the International System* (Boulder, Colorado: Westview Press).
Holsti, O.R. and J.N. Rosenau (1984) *American Leadership in World Affairs* (London: George Allen and Unwin Ltd).
Holton, Robert J. (1998) *Globalisation and the Nation-State* (London: Macmillan).
Hook, G.D. and M.A. Weiner (1992) *The Internationalisation of Japan* (London: Routledge).
Hopkins, T.K., I. Wallerstein, et al (1996) *The Age of Transition: Trajectory of the World-System 1945-2025* (London: Zed Books).
Horsman, M., and A. Marshall (1994) *After the Nation-State: Citizens, Tribalism and the New World Order* (London: Harper Collins Publishers).
Howe, Christopher (Ed.) (1996) *China and Japan: History, Trends, and Prospects* (Oxford: Clarendon Press).
Howorth, Jolyon and Anand Menon (Eds.) (1997) *The European Union and National Defence Policy* (London: Routledge).
Hudson, G.F. (1931) *Europe and China: A Survey of their Relations from the Earliest Times to 1800* (London: Edward Arnold).
Hudson, Michael (1968) *Super Imperialism: The Economic Strategy of American Empire* (New York: Holt, Rinehart and Winston).
Huntington, Samuel P. (1968) *Political Order in Changing Societies* (London: Yale University Press).
_____(1991) *The Third Wave: Democratisation in the Late 20th Century* (London: University of Oklahoma Press).
_____(1996) *The Clash of Civilizations and the Remaking of World Order* (New York: Simon and Schuster).
Hyland, William G. (1999) *Clinton's World: Remaking American Foreign Policy* (London: Praeger).
Inoguchi, Takashi and D.I. Okimoto (Eds.) (1988) *The Political Economy of Japan, Vol. 2: The Changing International Context* (Stanford: Stanford University Press).
Institute for National Strategic Studies (1995) *Strategic Assessment 1995: U.S. Security Challenges in Transition* (Washington D.C.: National Defense University).
_____(1997) *Strategic Assessment 1997: Flashpoints and Force Structure* (Washington D.C.: National Defense University).
International Institute for Strategic Studies (1997/98) *The Military Balance 1997/98* (London: IISS).
_____(1999/2000) *The Military Balance 1999/2000* (London: IISS).
Jiang Zemin (1996) 'Let Us Work Together for a Better World'. The UN at 50: Statements by World Leaders (New York: United Nations) reprinted in David Lai (1997) (ed.) *Global Perspectives: International Relations, U.S. Foreign Policy, and the View from Abroad* (London: Lynne Rienner Publishers).
Jervis, Robert (1994) 'What Do We Want to Deter and How Do We Deter It?' in L.B. Ederington and M.J. Mazar (eds.) *Turning Point: The Gulf War and U.S. Military Strategy* (Boulder, Colo: Westview Press).
Jervis, Robert and Jack Snyder (1991) *Dominoes and Bandwagons: Strategic Beliefs and Great Power Competition in the Eurasian Rimland* (Oxford: Oxford University Press).
Joffe, Josef (1998) *The Future of the Great Powers* (London: Phoenix).
Johnson, Alexis U. et al (1990) *The United States and Japan: Comparative Leadership for Peace and Global Prosperity* (London: University Press of America).

Johnson, Chalmers (1982) *MITI and the Japanese Miracle* (Stanford: Stanford University Press).
Johnson, Robert H. (1994) *Improbable Dangers: U.S. Conceptions of Threat in the Cold War and After* (New York: St. Martin's Press).
Johnston, Alastair Iain (1998) *Cultural Realism: Strategic Culture and Grand Strategy in Chinese History* (Princeton, NJ: Princeton University Press).
Johnston, Douglas (1996) *Foreign Policy into the 21st Century: The U.S. Leadership Challenge* (Washington, D.C.: The Center for Strategic and International Studies)
Judt, Tony (1996) *A Grand Illusion? An Essay on Europe* (London: Penguin).
Kant, Immanuel (selected and translated by Watson, John (1901) *The Philosophy of Kant* (Glasgow: James Maclehose and Sons).
_____(Translated by W. Hastie, B.D. with introduction by Edwin D. Mead, 1914) *Eternal Peace: and Other International Essays* (Boston: The World Peace Foundation).
_____(1795, translated by M. Campbell Smith, 1903) *Perpetual Peace, A Philosophical Essay* (London: Swan Sonnenschein & Co.).
_____(1983, translated and introduction by Ted Humphrey) *Perpetual Peace and other essays on Politics, History, and Morals* (Indianapolis: Hackett Publishing).
Kapstein, E.B. and M. Mastanduno (Eds.) (1999) *Unipolar Politics: Realism and State Strategies After the Cold War* (New York: Columbia University Press).
Kapur, Harish (1990) *Distant Neighbours: China and Europe* (London: Pinter Publishers).
Kirkpatrick, E.M. (ed.) (1983/85/86 edit.) *Chambers 20th Century Dictionary* (Edinburgh: Chambers).
Kassim, Hussein and Anand Menon (Eds.) (1996) *The European Union and National Industrial Policy* (London: Routledge).
Kennedy, Paul (1988/1989, Fontana edit.) *The Rise and Fall of the Great Powers: Economic Change and Military Conflict from 1500 to 2000* (London: Fontana Press).
_____(Ed.) (1991) *Grand Strategies in War and Peace* (London: Yale University Press).
_____(1993) *Preparing for the Twenty-First Century* (London: HarperCollins).
Kenwood, A.G. and A.L. Lougheed (1971/1992, 3rd edit.) *The Growth of the International Economy, 1820-1990: An Introductory Text* (London: Routledge).
Keohane, Robert O. (1980) "The Theory of Hegemonic Stability and Change in International Economic Regimes, 1967-1977," in Holsti, O.R., et al (Eds.) *Change in the International System* (Boulder, Colorado: Westview Press).
_____(1983) 'The demand for international regimes', in Stephen Krasner (Ed.) *International Regimes* (London: Cornell University).
_____(1984) *After Hegemony: Cooperation and Discord in the World Political Economy* (Princeton, NJ: Princeton University Press).
_____(Ed.) (1986) *Neorealism and Its Critics* (New York: Columbia University Press).
_____(1989) *International Institutions and State Power: Essays in International Relations Theory* (London: Westview Press).
Keohane, R.O. and J.S. Nye (1977/1989 2nd edit.) *Power and Interdependence: World Politics in Transition* (New York: Longman).
Kester, Anne Y., et al (1995) *Following the Money: U.S. Finance in the World Economy* (Washington, D.C.: National Academy Press).
Khalilzad, Zalmay M. (1995) *From Containment to Global Leadership: America and the World After the Cold War* (Santa Monica: RAND).
Kindleberger, Charles P. (1970) *Power and Money: The Economics of International Politics and the Politics of International Economics* (London: Basic Books).

_____(1973) *The World in Depression 1929-1939* (Los Angeles: University of California Press).
_____(1976) 'Systems of International Economic Order' in Calleo, D.P. *Money and the Coming of World Order* (New York: New York University Press).
_____(1981) *International Money: A Collection of Essays* (London: Allen & Unwin).
_____(1984) *The International Economic Order: Essays on Financial Crisis and International Public Goods* (London: Harvester Wheatsheaf).
Kiernan, V.G. (1978) *America: The New Imperialism, From White Settlement to World Hegemony* (London: Zed Press).
Kissinger, Henry (1974) *American Foreign Policy* (New York: Norton).
_____(1979) *The White House Years* (Boston: Little, Brown).
_____(1994) *Diplomacy* (London: Simon & Schuster).
Kofman, E. and G. Young (Eds.) (1996) *Globalization: Theory and Practice* (London: Pinter).
Kolko, J. and G. Kolko (1972) *The Limits of Power: The World and United States' Foreign Policy* (London: Harper & Row Publishers).
Krasner, Stephen. D. (Ed.) (1983) *International Regimes* (London: Cornell University Press).
Krauthammer, Charles (1992) 'The Unipolar Moment' in G. Allison, and G. Treverton (Eds.) *Rethinking America's Security: Beyond Cold War to New World Order* (London: W.W. Norton).
Krugman, Paul (1990/1998, 3rd edit.) *The Age of Diminished Expectations* (London: MIT Press).
_____(1999) *The Return of Depression Economics* (London: Penguin Books).
Kuhn, Thomas S. (1962/1970/1996, 3rd edit.) *The Structure of Scientific Revolutions* (London: The University of Chicago Press).
Laclau, E. and C. Mouffe (1994) *Hegemony and Socialist Strategy: Towards a Radical Democratic Politics* (London: Verso).
Lai, David (Ed.) (1997) *Global Perspectives: International Relations, U.S. Foreign Policy, and the View from Abroad* (London: Lynne Rienner).
Laitin, D.D. (1986) *Hegemony and Culture: Politics and Religious Change among the Yoruba* (London: The University of Chicago Press).
Lakatos, I. and A. Musgrave (Eds.) (1970) *Criticism and the Growth of Knowledge* (Cambridge: Cambridge University Press).
Lake, David A. (1999) *Entangling Relations: American Foreign Policy in Its Century* (Princeton, N.J.: Princeton University Press).
Lenin, V.I. (reprinted in 1939) *Imperialism: The Highest Stage of Capitalism* (New York: International Publishers).
Levin, N.D., Lorell, M. and A. Alexander (1993) *The Wary Warriors: Future Directions in Japanese Security Policies* (Santa Monica, CA. RAND).
Lieber, Robert (Ed.) (1997) *Eagle Adrift: American Foreign Policy at the End of the Century* (London: Longman).
List, Friedrich (1922, translated by Sampson S. Lloyd, with an Introduction by J. Shield Nicholson) *The National System of Political Economy* (London: Longman, Green and Co).
Liu, Shugin (1993) 'China's Reform and Opening Up and Foreign Policy', *Foreign Affairs Journal* (Beijing), Vol. 28, June, p. 4, cited in Stuart Harris and Gary Klintworth (1995) (Eds.) *China as a Great Power: Myths, Realities and Challenges in the Asia-Pacific Region* (Longman: Melbourne), p. 8.

Lu Xun (1983) 'The True Story of Ah Q' in Lu Xun et al *Masterpiece of Modern Chinese Fiction, 1919-1939* (Beijing: Foreign Language Press).
Lundestad, Geir (Ed.) (1994) *The Fall of Great Powers: Peace, Stability, and Legitimacy* (Oxford: Oxford University Press)
_____(1998) *"Empire" by Integration: The United States and European Integration, 1945-1997* (Oxford: Oxford University Press).
Luttwak, Edward N. (1976) *The Grand Strategy of the Roman Empire: From the 1st Century AD. to the 3rd* (Baltimore: The Johns Hopkins University Press).
Machiavelli, Niccolo (1992, 2nd edit., translated and edited by Robert M. Adams) *The Prince* (London: W.W. Norton).
_____(1983 edit.) *The Discourses* (London: Penguin).
Mclean, Iain (1996) *Oxford Concise Dictionary of Politics* (Oxford: Oxford University Press).
McClelland, David C. (1961) *The Achieving Society* (London: The Free Press).
McCormick, Thomas J. (1989/95, 2nd edit.) *America's Half-Century: United States Foreign Policy in the Cold War and After* (London: The Johns Hopkins University Press).
McCormick, Thomas M. (1998) 'Interest Groups and the Media in Post-Cold War U.S. Foreign Policy', in James Scott (1998) (Ed.) *After the End: Making U.S. Foreign Policy in the Post-Cold War World* (London: Duke University Press), pp. 170-198.
McFarland, A.S. (1969) *Power and Leadership in Pluralist Systems* (Stanford, California: Stanford University Press).
McRae, H. (1994) *The World in 2020: Power, Culture and Prosperity: A Vision of the Future* (London: Harper Collins Publishers).
McGrew, Anthony (Ed.) (1994) *Empire: The United States in the Twentieth Century* (London: Hodder & Stoughton)
Mann, James (1999) *About Face: A History of America's Curious Relationship with China, from Nixon to Clinton* (New York: Alfred A. Knopf).
Mann, Michael (1986) *The Sources of Social Power, vol. 1, A history of power from the beginning to AD. 1760* (Cambridge: Cambridge University Press).
_____(1993) *The Sources of Social Power, vol. 2, The rise of classes and nation-states, 1760-1914* (Cambridge University Press).
Marsh, D. and G. Stoker (Eds.) 1995) *Theory and Methods in Political Science* (London: Macmillan).
Miller, David (Ed.) (1987/1997) *The Blackwell Encyclopædia of Political Thought* (Oxford: Blackwell Publishers).
Miyamoto Musashi (1974, translated by Victor Harris), *A Book of Five Rings* (New York: The Overlook Press).
_____(1993, translated by Thomas Cleary) *The Book of Five Rings* (London: Shambhala).
Mochizuki, Mike M. (Ed.) (1997) *Toward A True Alliance: Restructuring U.S.-Japan Security Relations* (Washington, D.C: Brookings Institute Press).
Modelski, George (1987a) *Long Cycles and World Politics* (Seattle: Washington University Press).
_____(Ed.) (1987b) *Exploring Long Cycles* (London: Lynne Pinters).
Modelski, G. and S. Modelski (1988) *Documenting Global Leadership* (London: University of Washington Press).
Morgan, R., Lorentzen, A. Leander, and S. Guzzini (1993) *New Diplomacy in the Post-Cold War World: Essays for Susan Strange* (London: Macmillan).
Morgan, Patrick (1983) *Deterrence: A Conceptual Analysis* (Beverly Hills: Sage).

Morgenthau, Hans J. (1948/93, revised by Kenneth W. Thompson) *Politics Among Nations: The Struggle for Power and Peace, Brief Edition* (New York: McGraw-Hill)
_____(1952) *American Foreign Policy: A Critical Examination* (London: Methuen & Co.).
_____ 'Political Power: A Realist Theory of International Politics,' in John A. Vasquez (1990, 2nd edit.) *Classics of International Relations* (Englewood Cliffs, N.J.: Prentice Hall).
Morse, R.A. and Shigenobu Yoshida (Eds.) (1985) *Blind Partners: American and Japanese Responses to an Unknown Future* (London: University Press of America).
Muravchik, Joshua (1991) *Exporting Democracy: Fulfilling America's Destiny* (Washington, D.C.: The AEI Press).
_____(1996) *The Imperative of American Leadership: A Challenge to Neo-Isolationism* (Washington, D.C.: The AEI Press).
Murphy, Craig N. (1994) *International Organisation and Industrial Change: Global Governance since 1850* (Cambridge: Polity Press).
Murphy, Taggart R. (1996) *The Real Price of Japanese Money* (London: Weidenfeld and Nicolson).
Nagatomi, Yuichiro (ed.) (1988) *To Evolve the Global Society* (Tokyo: Foundation for advanced information and research).
Naisbitt, John (1996) *Megatrends Asia: The Eight Asian Megatrends that are Changing the World* (London: Nicholas Brealey Pub.).
Nathan, J.A. and J.K. Oliver (1983) (1994, 3rd edit.) *Foreign Policy Making and the American Political System* (London: The Johns Hopkins University Press).
Nau, Henry (1990) *Myth of America's Decline: Leading the World Economy into the 1990s* (Oxford: Oxford University Press).
Niebuhr, R. (1936) *Moral Man and Immoral Society* (New York: Scribners).
Norris, Christopher (1982, 1991 revised edit.) *Deconstruction: Theory and Practice* (London: Routledge).
Novak, Michael (1982/91) *The Spirit of Capitalism* (London: The IEA Health and Welfare Unit).
Nye, Joseph (1990) *Bound to Lead: The Changing Nature of American Power* (New York: Basic Books).
Nye, J., K. Biedenkopf and M. Shina (1991) *Global Cooperation After the Cold War: A Reassessment of Trilateralism* (New York: The Trilateral Commission).
Olson, William Clinton (Ed.), 1960/91, 8th edit.) *The Theory and Practice of International Relations* (Englewood Cliffs, NJ: Prentice Hall).
Ostry, Sylvia (1997) *The Post-Cold War: Trading System: Who's on First?* (London: The University of Chicago Press).
Oye, K., R. Rothchild, and R. Lieber (1979) *Eagle Entangled: US foreign policy in a complex world* (New York: Longman).
Paine, Thomas (1792) *The Rights of Man* (World's Greatest Classic Books, Electronically Enhanced Text, World Library CD-ROM).
Palan, R.P. and B.K. Gills (Eds.) (1994) *Transcending the State-Global Divide: A Neostructuralist Agenda in International Relations* (London: Lynne Rienner Publishers).
Palmowski, Jan (1997) *Dictionary of Twentieth Century World History* (Oxford: Oxford University Press).
Parkes, Stuart (1997) *Understanding Contemporary Germany* (London: Routledge).

Patterson, Rubin (1997) *Foreign Aid After the Cold War: The Dynamics of Multipolar Competition* (Trenton, NJ: Africa World Press).
Paul, T.V. and John A. Hall (1999) *International Order and the Future of World Politics* (Cambridge: Cambridge University Press).
Pearce, David W. (Ed.) (1988/92, 4th edit.) *Macmillan Dictionary of Modern Economics* (London: Macmillan).
Pearsall, Judy (Ed.) (1998) *The New Oxford Dictionary of English* (Oxford: Clarendon).
Plato (1992 edit, translated by A.D. Lindsay) *The Republic* (London: Everyman).
Polanyi, Karl (1944/1957) *The Great Transformation: The political and economic origin of out time* (Boston: Beacon Press).
Popper, Karl R. (1945/66, 5th edit., reprinted 1999) *The Open Society and Its Enemies: Vol. 1, The Spell of Plato* (London: Routledge & Kegan Paul).
_____(1945/66, 5th edit., reprinted 1999) *The Open Society and Its Enemies: Vol. 2, The High Tide of Prophecy: Hegel, Marx, and the Aftermath* (London: Routledge & Kegan Paul).
_____(1957) *The Poverty of Historicism* (London: Routledge & Kegan Paul).
Poulantzas, Nico (1978/80 translated by Patrick Camiller) *State, Power, Socialism* (London: Verso).
Preston, P.W. (1998) *Pacific Asia in the Global System: An Introduction* (Oxford: Blackwell).
Prestowitz, Jr. Clyde V. (1988) *Trading Places: How We Allowed Japan to Take the Lead* (New York: Basic Books).
Prestowitz, Jr. C.V., R.A. Morse and A. Tonelson (1991) *Powernomics: Economics and Strategy After the Cold War* (Lanham, Maryland: Madison Books).
Pyle, Kenneth B. (1992) *The Japanese Question: Power and Purpose in a New Era* (Washington, D.C: The AEI Press).
Quested, R.K.I. (1984) *Sino-Russian Relations: A Short History* (London: George Allen & Unwin).
Rand McNally (1999 edit.) *World Facts and Maps: concise international review* (USA, Rand McNally).
Rapkin, David P. (Ed.) (1990) *World Leadership and Hegemony* (London: Lynne Rienner).
Rawls, John (1993) *Political Liberalism* (New York: Columbia University Press).
Reich, Robert B. (1991) *The Work of Nations: Preparing ourselves for 21st Century Capitalism* (London: Simon & Schuster Ltd).
Rissen-Kappen, Thomas (1995) *Cooperation Among Democracies: The European Influence on U.S. Foreign Policy* (Princeton, NJ: Princeton University Press).
Ritzer, George (1998) *The McDonaldisation Thesis* (London: Sage Publications).
Roberts, Brad (Ed) (1995) *Order and Disorder after the Cold War* (London: MIT Press).
_____(1996) *New Forces in the World Economy* (Cambridge: MIT Press).
Roberts, J.M. (1992) *The Penguin History of the World* (London: Penguin Press).
Roberts, Richard (1998) *Inside International Finance* (London: Orion Business Books).
Robertson, Patrick (Ed.) (1992) (Foreword by Margaret Thatcher). *Reshaping Europe in the Twenty-First Century* (London: Macmillan).
Robertson, R. (1992) *Globalisation: Social Theory and Global Culture* (London: Sage Publications).
Robinson, William I. (1996) *Promoting Polyarchy: Globalisation, U.S. intervention, and Hegemony* (Cambridge: Cambridge University Press).
Rosecrance, Richard (1976) *America as an Ordinary Country* (Ithaca: Cornell University Press).

_____(1986) *The Rise of the Trading State: Commerce and Conquest in the Modern World* (New York: BasicBooks).
Rosenberg, N. and L.E. Birdzell (1986) *How the West Grew Rich: The Economic Transformation of the Industrial World* (London: I.B. Tauris & Co.).
Ross, Robert S. (Ed.) (1993) *China, The United States, and The Soviet Union: Tripolarity and Policy-Making in the Cold War* (London: M.E. Sharpe).
Rousseau, Jean-Jacque (translated by Christopher Betts, 1994) *The Social Contract* (Oxford: Oxford University Press).
Rowland, B.M. (Ed.) (1976) *Balance of Power or Hegemony: The Interwar Monetary System* (New York: New York University Press).
Rueter, T. (1994) *The United States in the World Political Economy* (London: McGraw-Hill).
Ruggie, John G. (1996) *Winning the Peace: America and World Order in the New Era* (New York: Columbia University Press).
Rupert, Mark (1995) *Producing Hegemony: The politics of mass production and American global power* (Cambridge: Cambridge University Press).
Russett, Bruce (1993) *Grasping the Democratic Peace: Principles for a Post-Cold War World* (Princeton, New Jersey: Princeton University Press).
Sanderson, S.K. (Ed.) (1995) *Civilisations and World Systems: Studying World-Historical Change* (London: Altamira Press).
Sasae, Kenichiro (1994, December) *Rethinking Japan-U.S. Relations* (London: Adelphi Paper No. 292).
Schell, Orville (1994) *Mandate to Heaven, A new generation of entrepreneurs, dissidents, bohemians and technocrats lays claim to China's future* (London: A Little, Brown Book).
Schmergel, G. (1991) *US foreign policy in the 1990s* (London: Macmillan).
Schraeder, P.J. (Ed.) (1992) *Intervention into the 1990s: US Foreign Policy in the Third World* (London: Lynne Rienner).
Scott, James M. (Ed.) (1998) *After the End: Making U.S. Foreign Policy in the Post-Cold War World* (London: Duke University Press).
Screpanti, E. and S. Zamagni (1993) (Translated by David Field) *An Outline of the History of Economic Thought* (Oxford: Clarendon Press).
Searle, John R. (1995) *The Construction of Social Reality* (London: Penguin).
Shambaugh, David (Ed.) (1995) *Greater China: The Next Superpower?* (Oxford: Oxford University Press).
The Book of Lord Shang (1974 edit. translated from the Chinese with introduction and notes by J.J.L. Duyvendak) *The Book of Lord Shang* (San Francisco: Chinese Materials Center).
_____(reprinted 1998) *The Book of Lord Shang* (Ware, Herts, UK: Wordsworth).
Shintaro Ishihara (1991) (translated by Frank Baldwin) (foreword by Ezra F. Vogel) *The Japan That Can Say NO* (London: Simon & Schuster).
Shoup, L.H. and W. Minter (1977) *Imperial Brain Trust: The Council on Foreign Relations and the United States Foreign Policy* (New York and London: Monthly Review Press).
Singer, M. and A. Wildavsky (1993) *The Real World Order: Zones of Peace/Zones of Turmoil* (Chatham, New Jersey: Chatham House Publishers).
Smith, Dan (1989) *Pressure: How America Runs NATO* (London: Bloombury).
Snow, D.M. (1995) *The Shape of the Future: The Post-Cold War World* (London: M.E. Sharpe).

Snow, Donald and Eugene Brown (1996) *The Contours of Power* (New York: St. Martin Press).
Soros, George (1998) *The Crisis of Global Capitalism: Open Society Endangered* (New York: Public Affairs).
Spengler, Oswald (1991) (with new introduction by H.S. Hughes) *The Decline of the West* (Oxford: Oxford University Press).
Spykman, Nicholas John (1942, reprinted 1970) *America's Strategy in World Politics: The United States and the Balance of Power* (New York: Harcourt Brace).
Stauffer, R.B. (1982) *Losing Hegemony* (Transnational Corporations Research Project, University of Sydney).
Steel, Ronald (1967) *Pax Americana* (London: Hamish Hamilton).
_____(1995) *Temptations of a Superpower* (London: Harvard University Press).
Steiner, Zara (1994) 'The Fall of Great Britain: Peace, Stability, and Legitimacy', in Geir Lundestad (Ed.) (1994) *The Fall of Great Powers: Peace, Stability, and Legitimacy* (Oxford: Oxford University Press), pp. 47-79.
Stent, Angela E. (1999) *Russia and Germany Reborn, Unification, the Soviet Collapse and the New Europe* (Princeton, NJ: Princeton University Press).
Stonehouse, Bernard (Ed.) (1987) *Philips' Illustrated Atlas of the World* (London: Gild Publishing)
Stopford, J. and S. Strange, with Henley, J.S. (1991) *Rival States, Rival Firms: Competition for World Market Shares* (Cambridge: Cambridge University Press).
Strange, Susan (1982) 'Still an Extraordinary Power: American Role in a Global Monetary System', in Raymond Lombra and Willar Witte (eds.), *Political Economy of International and Domestic Monetary Relations* (Ames: Iowa State University Press).
_____(1986) *Casino Capitalism* (Oxford: Blackwell).
_____(1988) *States and Markets* (London: Pinter).
_____(1990) 'The Name of the Game', in Rizopoulos, N. X. (Ed.) *Sea-Changes: American Foreign Policy in a World Transformed* (New York: Council on Foreign Relations).
_____(1991) 'The future of the American Empire', in Little, R. and Smith, M. *Perspectives on World Politics* (London: Routledge).
_____(1996) *The Retreat of the State: The Diffusion of Power in the World Economy* (Cambridge: Cambridge University Press).
_____(1998) *Mad Money* (Manchester: Manchester University Press).
Stubbs, R. and G.R.D. Underhill (Eds.) (1994) *Political Economy and the Changing Global Order* (London: Macmillan).
Sun Tzu (1994 edit., translated by Ralph D. Sawyer) *The Art of War* (Oxford: Westview Press).
_____(1998 edit., translated by Yuan Shibing) *The Art of War* (Ware, Hert, UK: Wordsworth).
Taylor, A.J.P. (1960) *The Struggle for Mastery in Europe 1848-1918* (London: Claredon).
Taylor, Peter J. (1996) *The Way the Modern World Works: World Hegemony to World Impasse* (Chichester: John Wiley & Sons).
Tarnas, Richard (1991) *The Passion of the Western Mind: Understanding the ideas that have shaped our world view* (London: Pimlico).
Thompson, E.P. (1978) *The Poverty of Theory and other essays* (London: Merlin Press).
Thompson, Kenneth W. (1980) *Masters of International Thought* (London: Louisiana State University Press).

_____ (1994) *Fathers of International Theory: The Legacy of Political Theory* (London: Louisiana State University Press).
Thucydides (1993, edited and translated by Paul Woodruff) *On Justice, Power, and Human Nature: The Essence of Thucydides' History of the Peloponnesian War* (Cambridge Hackett Publishing).
_____ (1997, translated by Richard Crawley) *The History of the Peloponnesian War* (Ware, Hert, UK: Wordsworth).
Thurow, Lester (1992) *Head to Head: The coming economic battle among Japan, Europe, and America* (New York: William Morrow and Co.).
Tocqueville, Alexis De (1994, with an introduction by Alan Ryan) *Democracy in America* (London: Everyman).
Townson, Duncan (1994) *Dictionary of Modern World History, 1789-1945* (London: Penguin).
Tsuru, Shigeto (1993) *Japan's capitalism: creative defeat and beyond* (Cambridge: Cambridge University Press).
Tuo-Kofi Gadzey, A. (1994) *The Political Economy of Power: Hegemony and Economic Liberalism* (London: Macmillan).
Tyson, Laura D' Andrea (1992) *Who's Bashing Whom: Trade Conflict in High Technology Industries* (New York: Institute for International Economics).
Valladao, Afredo G.A. (1993/96, translated by John Howe) *The Twenty-First Century Will Be American* (London: Verso).
Vasquez, John A. (Ed.) (1986/90, 2nd edit.) *Classics of International Relations* (Englewood, NJ: Prentice Hall).
_____ (1998) *The Power of Power Politics: From Classical Realism to Neotraditionalism* (Cambridge: Cambridge University Press).
Vogel, Ezra F. (1979) *Japan as Number One* (New York: Harper and Row).
Wallerstein, Immanuel (1974) *The Modern World System: Capitalist Agriculture and the Origins of the European World-Economy in the Sixteenth Century* (New York: Academic Press).
_____ (1980a) *The Capitalist World-Economy* (London: Cambridge University).
_____ (1980b) *The Modern World System II: Mercantilism and the Consolidation of the European World Economy, 1600-1750* (New York: Academic Press).
_____ (1984) *The Politics of the World Economy: The States, the Movements and the Civilisations, Essays* (London: Cambridge University Press).
Walt, Stephen M. (1987) *The Origins of Alliances* (London: Cornell University Press).
Walter, Andrew (1993) *World Power and World Money: The Role of Hegemony and International Monetary Order* (London: Harvester Wheatsheaf).
Waltz, Kenneth N. (1959) *Man, the State, and War: A Theoretical Analysis* (New York: Columbia University Press).
_____ (1979) *Theory of International Politics* (London: McGraw-Hill).
Waters, Malcolm (1995) *Globalization* (London: Routledge).
Wayman, F.W. et al (Eds.) (1994) *Reconstructing Realpolitik* (U.S.A.: The University of Michigan Press).
Webber, M. (1996) *The International Politics of Russia and the Successor States* (Manchester: Manchester University Press).
Webster, Charles (1951) *The Foreign Policy of Palmerston* (London: G. Bell & Sons).
Wendt, Alexander (1999) *Social Theory of International Politics* (Cambridge: Cambridge University Press).

Westlake, Martin (Ed.) (1998) *The European Union beyond Amsterdam, New Concepts of European Integration* (London: Routledge).
Wheeler, N.J. and K. Booth (1992) 'The Security Dilemma', in J. Baylis and N.J. Reneger (eds.) *Dilemmas in World Politics: International Issues in a Changing World* (Oxford: Oxford University Press).
Whitcomb, Roger S. (1998) *The American Approach to Foreign Affairs: An Uncertain Tradition* (London: Praeger).
Wight, Martin (1978) *Power Politics* (Leicester, Leicester University Press).
Wilkins, Burleigh Taylor (1978) *Has History Any Meaning? A Critique of Popper's Philosophy of History* (Hassocks, Sussex: The Harvester Press).
Wilkinson, Endymion (1983/90, revised edit.) *Japan versus the West, Image and Reality* (London: Penguin).
Wilson, Dick (1996) *China: The Big Tiger* (London: Little, Brown and Company).
Wolfer, Arnold (1962) *Discord and Collaboration* (Baltimore: Johns Hopkins University Press).
Wolferen, Karel van (1989) *The Enigma of Japanese Power: People and Politics in a Stateless Nation* (London: Macmillan).
Yahuda, Michael (1996) *The International Politics of the Asia-Pacific, 1945-1995* (London: Routledge).
Yarbrough, B. and R. Yarbrough (1992) *Cooperation and Governance in International Trade: The Strategic Organisational Approach* (Princeton, NJ: Princeton University Press).
Yen Mah, Adeline (1997) *Falling Leaves Return to Their Roots, The true story of an unwanted Chinese daughter* (London: Penguin Books).

Journal Articles

Achcar, Gilbert (1998) 'The Strategic Triad: The United States, Russia and China', *New Left Review*, No. 228, March/April, pp. 91-126.
Agawa Naoyuki (1999) 'Japan as the Fifty-first State', *Japan Echo*, (December), pp. 12-18.
Ahnlid, A. (1996) 'Comparing GATT and GATS: regime creation under and after hegemony', *Review of International Political Economy*, Vol. 3, No. 1, Spring, pp. 65-94.
Aho, Michael C. (1993) 'America and the Pacific century: trade conflict or cooperation?' *International Affairs*, Vol. 69, No. 1, pp. 19-37.
Aho, M.C. and B. Stokes (1990/91) 'The Year the World Economy Turned', *Foreign Affairs*, Vol. 70, No. 1, pp. 160-78.
Akaha, Tsuneo (1989) 'Japan's Security Policy After US Hegemony', *Millennium: Journal of International Studies* Vol. 18, No. 3, pp. 435-54.
_____ (1995) 'Japan's security agenda in the post-cold war era', *The Pacific Review*, Vol. 8, No. 1, pp. 45-76.
Akiyama, Masahiro (1998) 'Japan's Security Policy Toward the 21st Century', *RUSI Journal*, April, pp. 5-9.
Albo, G. and A. Zuege (1999) 'European Capitalism Today: Between the Euro and the Third Way', *Monthly Review*, Vol. 51, No. 3 (July/August), pp. 100-19.
Anderson, Jennifer (1997) 'The Limits of Sino-Russian Strategic Partnership', *Adelphi Papers* 315 (December).

Albright, Madeleine (1998) 'The Testing of American Foreign Policy', *Foreign Affairs*, Vol. 77, No. 6, pp. 50-64.
Andreatta, Filippo (1999, June) 'The Politics of Symmetry: European Integration and Transatlantic Relations', *NATO 1997-1999 Fellowship Report*, University of Bologna.
Arase, David (1995) 'A Militarised Japan?' *The Journal of Strategic Studies*, Vol. 18, No. 3, pp. 84-103.
Aruga, Tadashi (1996) 'Japan-U.S. Relations: In Search of a New Paradigm', *Japan Review of International Affairs*, Vol. 10, No. 1, (winter), pp. 35-54.
Asher, David L. (1997) 'A U.S.-Japan Alliance for the Next Century' *Orbis*, Vol. 41, No. 3 (summer), pp. 343-73.
Ashwin, Sarah (1998) 'Endless Patience: Explaining Soviet and Post-Soviet Social Society' *Communist and Post-Communist Studies*, Vol. 31, No. 2 (June), pp. 187-95.
Aslund, Anders (1999) Russia's Collapse. *Foreign Affairs*, vol. 78, no. 5, (Sept-Oct), pp. 64-77.
Baker, H.H. and E.L. Frost (1992) 'Rescuing the U.S-Japan Alliance', *Foreign Affairs*, Vol. 71, No. 2, (spring), pp. 97-113.
Baldwin, D.A. (1971) 'Money and Power', *The Journal of Politics*, Vol. 33, pp. 578-614.
_____(1979) 'Power Analysis and World Politics: New Trends versus Old Tendencies', *World Politics*, Vol. 31, No. 2, pp. 161-94.
Barber, Benjamin (1998) 'Democracy at Risk: American Culture in a Global Culture', *World Policy Journal*, (summer), pp. 29-41.
Bell, Carol (1990/91) 'Why Russia Should Join NATO: From Containment to Concert', *The National Interest*, winter, pp. 37-47.
Bello, Walden, (1997) 'The Balance of Power Doomsday Machine', *AMPO Japan-Asia Quarterly Review*, Vol. 27, No. 2, pp. 12-28.
_____(1998/99) 'The Asian Economic Implosion: Cause, dynamics, prospects', *Race and Class*, Vol. 40, No. 2/3, October-March, pp.133-44.
Berger, John (1998/99) 'Against the great defeat of the world', *Race and Class*, Vol. 40, No. 2/3, October-March, pp. 1-4.
Berger, Samuel R. (2000) 'A Foreign Policy for the Global Age', *Foreign Affairs*, Vol. 79, No. 6, pp. 22-39.
Berger, Thomas U. (1993) 'From Sword to Chrysanthemum: Japan's Culture of Anti-militarism', *International Security*, Vol. 17, No. 4, pp. 119-50.
Bergsten, C. Fred (1996a) 'APEC in 1996 and Beyond: The Subic Summit', *Institute for International Economic*, Working paper 96-1 http://www.206.65.84.109/9612.html.
_____(1996b) 'Competitive Liberalisation and Global Free Trade: A Vision for the Early 21st Century', *Institute for International Economic*, Working paper 96-15 http://www.206.65.84.109/9615.html.
_____(1997) 'Open Regionalism', *Institute for International Economic*, Working paper 97-3 http://www.206.65.84.109/97-3.html.
Berkowitz, Bruce D. (1998) 'Handicapping the George Kennan Sweepstakers', *Orbis*, Vol. 42, No. 3, (summer), pp. 465-73.
Berstein, Richard and Ross H. Munro (1997) 'The Coming Conflict with America', *Foreign Affairs*, Vol. 76, No. 2, (March-April), pp. 18-32.
Bevacqua, Ron (1998) 'Whither the Japanese model? The Asian economic crisis and the continuation of Cold War politics in the Pacific Rim', *Review of International Political Economy*, Vol. 5, No. 3, (autumn), pp. 410-23.

Bhagwati, Jagdish (1989) 'U.S. Trade Policy at Crossroads', *The World Economy*, Vol. 12, No. 4, pp. 439-79.
Bobrow, Davis B. (1999) 'Hegemony management: the U.S. in the Asia-Pacific', *The Pacific Review*, Vol. 12, No. 2, pp. 173-97.
Bowen, J. R., (1996) 'The myth of global ethnic conflict', *Journal of Democracy*, Vol. 7, No. 4, (October), pp. 3-14.
Bowen, Wyn (2000) 'Missile Defense: Shield against rogues', *The World Today*, January, pp. 5-6.
Bracken, Paul (1997) 'The New American Challenge', *World Policy Journal*, (summer), pp. 10-18.
Broad, R. and J. Cavanagh (1999) 'The Death of the Washington Consensus?' *World Policy Journal*, (fall), pp. 79-88.
Brzezinski, Zbigniew (1989/90) 'Post-Communist Nationalism', *Foreign Affairs*, Vol. 68, No. 5 (winter), pp. 1-25.
_____(1991) 'Selective Global Commitment', *Foreign Affairs*, Vol. 70, No. 4 (spring), pp. 1-20.
_____(1997b) 'A Geostrategy for Eurasia' *Foreign Affairs*, 76, 5, Sept-Oct. pp. 50-64.
_____(1998) 'Will China Democratise? Disruption without Disintegration', *Journal of Democracy* Vol. 9, No. 1 (January), pp. 4-5.
Buchanan, Patrick (1998) 'Our China Problem', *The American Enterprise*, July/August, p. 31.
Burnham, P. (1992) 'Re-evaluating the Washington Loan Agreement: a revisionist view of the limits of post-war American power' *Review of International Studies*, Vol.18, pp. 241-59.
Burstein, Daniel and Keijzer Arne De (1998) 'The "Chinese Threat" Is Overblown', *The American Enterprise*, July/August, pp. 44-8 and 56.
Calleo, David. P. (1998) 'A New Era of Overstretch? American Policy in Europe and Asia', *World Policy Journal*, Vol. 15, No. 1 (spring), pp. 11-26.
Carpenter, Ted Gallen (1998) 'Roiling Asia: U.S. Coziness with China Upsets the Neighbours' *Foreign Affairs*, Vol. 77, No. 6 (November/December), pp. 2-6.
Castro, Renato De (1994) 'US Grand Strategy in Post-Cold War Asia-Pacific', *Contemporary Southeast Asia*, Vol. 16, No. 3 (December), pp. 342-53.
Catley, Bob (1997) 'Hegemonic America: The Benign Superpower?' *Contemporary Southeast Asia*, Vol. 18, No. 4 (March), pp. 377-99.
_____(1999) 'Hegemonic America: The Arrogance of Power', *Contemporary Southeast Asia*, Vol. 21, No. 2 (August), pp. 157-75.
Cederman, Lars-Erick (1994) 'Emergent Polarity: Analysing State-Formation and Power Politics', *International Studies Association*, Vol. 38, pp. 501-33.
Cerny, P.G. (1989) 'Political Entropy and American Decline' *Millennium: Journal of International Studies*, Vol. 18, No. 1, pp. 47-63.
Chace, James (1997a) 'The Dilemmas of the City upon a Hill', *World Policy Journal*, (spring), pp. 105-7.
_____(1997b) 'An Empty Hegemony', *World Policy Journal*, (summer), pp. 97-8
_____(1997c) 'Between Chaos and Order', *World Policy Journal*, (fall), pp. 97-8.
Chan, Gerald (1998) 'Toward an International Relations Theory with Chinese Characteristics?' *Issue and Studies*, Vol. 34, No. 6 (June), pp. 1-28.
Chan, Stanley (1997) 'The American Military Capability Gap', *Orbis* (summer), pp. 385-400.

Chang Ya-chun (1998) 'Beijing's Maritime Rivalry with the United States and Japan: The Search for Institutionalised Mechanisms of Competition', *Issues and Studies*, Vol. 34, No. 6 (June), pp. 56-79.

Chen, Jie, Yang Zhong and Jan William Hillard (1997) 'The Level and Sources of Popular Support for China's Current Political Regime', *Communist and Post-Communist Studies*, Vol. 30, No. 1 (March), pp. 45-64.

Chesterman, C. and M. Byers (1999) 'Has U.S. Power Destroyed the UN?' *RUSI*, August, pp. 27-30.

Christensen, Thomas J. (1996) 'Chinese Realpolitik', *Foreign Affairs*, Vol. 75, No. 5, pp. 37-52.

Christensen, Thomas J. and Snider, Jack (1997) 'Progressive Research on Degenerate Alliances', *American Political Science Review*, Vol. 91, No. 4 (December), pp. 919-26.

Christopher, Warren (1995) 'America's Leadership, America's Opportunity', *Foreign Policy*, No. 98 (spring), pp. 6-27.

Clarke, J. (1995/96) 'Leaders and Followers', *Foreign Policy*, No. 101 (winter), pp. 37-51.

Cohen, Stephen D. (1998) 'Limits of Friendship: Why the United States and the European Union have been unable to devise a common trade strategy toward Japan', *The International Trade Journal*, Vol. 12, No. 2 (summer), pp. 193-225.

Cooper, R.N. (1972/73) 'Trade Policy Is Foreign Policy', *Foreign Policy*, Vol. 9 (winter), pp. 18-36.

Cowhey, P.F., and Long, E. (1983) 'Testing theories of regime change: hegemonic decline or surplus capacity?' *International Organisation*, Vol. 37, No. 2 (spring), pp. 157-88.

Cox, Michael (1994) 'The necessary partnership? The Clinton presidency and post-Soviet Russia', *International Affairs*, Vol. 70, No. 4, pp. 635-58.

_____(1998c) 'Rebel Without a Cause? Radical Theorists and the World System After the Cold War', *New Political Economy*, Vol. 3, No. 3, pp. 445-59.

Cox, Robert W. (1981) 'Social Forces, States and World Orders: Beyond International Relations Theory', *Millennium: Journal of International Studies*, Vol. 10, No. 2, pp. 126-55.

_____(1983) 'Gramsci, Hegemony and International Relations: An Essay in .Method', *Millennium: Journal of International Studies*, Vol. 12, No. 2, pp. 162-75.

_____(1996) 'Civilisations in World Political Economy', *New Political Economy*, Vol. 1, No. 2, pp.141-56.

Crawford, B. (1994) 'The New Security Dilemma under International Economic Interdependence', *Millennium: Journal of International Studies*, Vol. 23, No. 1 (spring), pp. 25-55.

Crone, Donald (1993) 'Does Hegemony Matter? The Reorganisation of the Pacific Political Economy', *World Politics*, Vol. 45 (July), pp. 501-25.

Cummings, B. (1984) 'The Origins of Development of the Northeast Asian Political Economy: Industrial Sector, Product Cycles and Political Consequences', *International Organisation*, Vol. 38, No. 3 (winter), pp. 1-39.

Dam, K., Deutch, J., Nye, J.S. Jr. and D.M. Rowe (1993) 'Harnessing Japan: A U.S. Strategy for Managing Japan's Rise as a Global Power', *The Washington Quarterly*, (spring), pp. 29-42.

Danner, Mark (1997) 'Marooned in the Cold War: America, the Alliance, and the Quest for a Vanished World', *World Policy Journal* (fall), pp. 1-23.

Daquilla, Teofilo C. (1999) 'Japan-Asia Economic Relations: Trade, Investment, and the Economic Crisis', *East Asia: An International Quarterly*, Vol. 17, No. 3 (autumn), pp. 88-115.

De Castro, R. (1994) 'US Grand Strategy in Post-Cold War Asia Pacific', *Contemporary Southeast Asia*, Vol. 16, No. 3 (December), pp. 342-53.

Deudney, D. and G.J. Ikenberry (1994) 'After the Long War', *Foreign Policy*, No. 94 (spring), pp. 21-35.

Diamond, Larry (1996) 'Beyond the Unipolar Moment: Why the United States Must Remain Engaged', *Orbis*, Vol. 40, No. 3 (summer), pp. 405-13.

Dibb, P., Hale, D.D., and P. Prince (1998) 'The Strategic Implications of Asia's Economic Crisis', *Survival*, Vol. 40, No. 2 (summer), pp. 5-26.

Dietz, Mary G. (1986) 'Trapping the Prince: Machiavelli and the Politics of Deception', *American Political Science Review*, Vol. 80, No. 3, September, pp. 777-99.

Dole, Bob (1995) 'Shaping America's Global Future', *Foreign Policy*, Vol. 98 (spring), pp. 29-43.

Doyle, Michael W. (1983a) 'Kant, Liberal Legacies, and Foreign Affairs, part 1', *Philosophy and Public Affairs*, Vol. 12, No. 3 (summer), pp. 205-35.

_____ (1983b) 'Kant, Liberal Legacies, and Foreign Affairs, part 2', *Philosophy and Public Affairs*, Vol. 12, No. 4 (fall), pp. 323-53.

Emmerson, Donald K. (1998) 'Americanising Asia?' *Foreign Affairs*, Vol. 77, No. 3 (May/June), pp. 46-56.

Evans, Graham (1997) 'The Vision Thing: In Search of the Clinton Doctrine', *The World Today* (August-September), pp. 213-16.

Forde, Steven (1995) 'International Realism and the Science of Politics: Thucydides, Machiavelli, and Neorealism', *International Studies Quarterly*, Vol. 39, pp. 141-60.

Funabashi, Yoichi (1998) 'Tokyo's Depression Diplomacy', *Foreign Affairs*, Vol. 77, No 6 (November/December), pp. 26-36.

Gaddis, John Lewis (1998) 'History, Grand Strategy and NATO Enlargement', *Survival*, Vol. 40, No. 1 (spring), pp. 145-51.

Garson, R. (1990) 'The rise and rise of American exceptionalism', *Review of International Studies*, Vol. 16, pp. 173-9.

Gergen, David (1991/92) 'America's Missed Opportunities', *Foreign Affairs*, Vol. 71, No. 1 (winter), pp. 1-19.

Gill, Stephen (1986) 'American Hegemony: Its Limits and Prospects in the Reagan Era', *Millennium: Journal of International Studies*, Vol. 15, No. 3 (winter), pp. 311-36.

_____ (1992) 'Economic Globalisation and the Internationalisation of Authority: Limits and Contradictions', *Geoforum* (Special Issue: Regulating the Global Economy and Environment), Vol. 23, No. 3 (August), pp. 269-83.

Gills, Barry K., and Dong-Sook Gills (1999) 'South Korea and Globalization: The Rise of Globalism?', *Asian Perspective*, Vol. 23, No. 4, pp. 199-228.

Gills, Barry K. (2000) 'The crisis of postwar East Asian Capitalism: American power, democracy and the vicissitudes of globalization', *Review of International Studies*, Vol. 26, pp. 381-403.

Gilpin, Robert (1984) 'The Richness of the Tradition of Political Realism', *International Organisation*, Vol. 38, pp. 287-304.

Goldgeier, J.M. and M. McFaul (1992) 'A tale of two worlds: core and periphery in the post-cold war era', *International Organisation*, Vol. 46, No. 2 (spring) pp. 467-91.

Goldman, Marshall (1997) 'The Pitfalls of Russian Privatisation', *Challenge*, Vol. 40 (May-June), pp. 35-49.
Gowa, J. (1989) 'Rational Hegemons, Excludable Goods, and Small Groups: an Epitaph for Hegemonic Stability Theory?' *World Politics*, Vol. 41, No. 3, pp. 307-24.
Gray, Colin S. (1996) 'The Continued Primacy of Geography', *Orbis*, Vol. 40, No. 2 (spring), pp. 247-59.
Gray, John (1998b) 'Global Utopias and Clashing Civilisations: Misunderstanding the Present', *International Affairs*, Vol. 74, No. 1, p. 151.
Gregg, Donald P. (1997) 'The Case for Continued U.S. Engagement', *Orbis* (summer), pp. 375-84.
Gregor, A James (1998) 'Fascism and the New Russian Nationalism', *Communist and Post-Communist Studies*, Vol. 31, No. 1, pp. 1-15.
Grieco, Joseph M. (1988) 'Anarchy and the limits of cooperation: a realist critique of the newest liberal institutionalism', *International Organisation*, Vol. 42, No. 3 (summer), pp. 485-507.
Grunberg, I. (1990) 'Exploring the "Myth" of hegemonic stability', *International Organisation*, Vol. 44, No. 4 (autumn), pp.431-77.
Guehenno, Jean-Marie (1998-99) 'The Impact of Globalisation on Strategy', *Survival*, Vol. 40, No. 4 (winter), pp. 5-19.
Haass, Richard N. (1995) 'Paradigm Lost', *Foreign Affairs*, Vol. 74, No. 1, pp. 43-58.
_____ (1997) 'Fatal Distraction: Bill Clinton's Foreign Policy', *Foreign Policy*, No. 108 (fall), pp. 112-23.
Haggard, Stephan (1988) 'The institutional foundation of hegemony: explaining the Reciprocal Trade Agreements Act of 1934', *International Organisation*, Vol. 42, No. 1 (winter), pp. 91-119.
_____ (1998) 'Models and Crisis: turbulence in Asian economies', *Review of International Political Economy*, Vol. 5, No. 3 (autumn), pp. 381-92.
Hakamada Shigeki (1998) 'Yeltsin's Sacking of His Cabinet and Visit of Japan', *Japan Echo*, Vol. 25, No. 4 (August), pp. 23-6.
Halliday, F. (1990) 'The Ends of Cold War', *New Left Review*, 180 (March/April), pp. 5-23.
Hasenclever, A., Mayer, P. and Rittberger, V. (1996) 'Reflection, Evaluation, Integration: Interests, Power, Knowledge: The Study of International Regimes', *Mershon International Studies Review*, Vol. 40, pp. 177-228.
Hassner, Pierre (1996/97) 'Huntington's Clash of Civilisation: 1. Morally Objectionable, Politically Dangerous', *The National Interest*, No. 46 (winter), pp. 63-9.
Hendrickson, David C. (1997/98) 'In Our Own Image: The Source of American Conduct in World Affairs', *The National Interest*, No. 50 (winter), pp. 9-21.
Hillen, John (1997) 'America's Alliance Anxieties: Superpowers Don't Do Windows', *Orbis*, Vol. 41, No. 2 (spring), pp. 241-57.
Hirschfield, Thomas J. (1999) 'Assessing China's Military Potential', *East Asia, An International Quarterly*, Vol. 17, No. 1 (spring), pp. 95-107.
Hirst, Paul (1998) 'The eighty years' crisis, 1919-1999: Power', *Review of International Studies*, Vol. 24 (December), pp. 133-48.
Holbrooke, Richard (1991/92) 'Japan and the United States: Ending the Unequal Partnership', *Foreign Affairs*, Vol. 70, No. 4 (fall), pp. 41-57.
Hoogvelt, Ankie (1995) 'Review Essay: Japan and the World', *Review of International Political Economy*, Vol. 2, No. 4, pp. 719-27.
Horner, Charles (1996/97) 'The Third Side of the Triangle: The China-Japan Dimension', *The National Interest*, No. 46 (winter), pp. 23-31.

Horng, Der-Chin (1998) 'The EU's New China Policy: The Dimension of Trade Relations', *Issues and Studies*, Vol. 34, No. 7 (July), pp. 85-115.
Hughes, Christopher W. (1996) 'Japan's subregional security and defence linkage with ASEANs, South Korea and China in the 1990s', *The Pacific Review*, Vol. 9, No. 2, pp. 229-50.
Huntington, Samuel P. (1988/89) 'The U.S. – Decline or Renewal?' *Foreign Affairs*, Vol. 67, No. 2, pp.76-96.
_____(1993a) 'Why International Primacy Matters?' *International Security*, Vol. 17, No. 4 (spring), pp. 68-83.
_____(1993b) 'The Clash of Civilizations?' *Foreign Affairs*, Vol. 72, No. 3 (summer), pp. 22-49.
_____(1996) 'The West Unique, Not Universal', *Foreign Affairs*, Vol. 75, No. 6 (November-December), pp. 28-46.
_____(1997b) 'The Erosion of American National Interest', *Foreign Affairs*, Vol. 76, No. 5 (September-October), pp. 28-49.
Hwei-ling Huo (1992) 'Pattern of Behaviour in China's Foreign Policy: The Gulf War Crisis and Beyond', *Asian Survey*, Vol. 32, No. 3 (March), pp. 268-9.
Hurrell, A. (1992) 'Latin America in the New World Order: a regional bloc of the Americas?' *International Affairs*, Vol. 68, No. 1, pp. 121-39.
Hurst III, Cameron G. (1997) 'The U.S.-Japanese Alliance at Risk', *Orbis* (winter), pp. 69-76.
Ikenberry, G. John (1989) 'Rethinking the Origins of American Hegemony', *Political Science Quarterly*, Vol. 104, No. 3, pp. 375-400.
_____(1996) 'The Myth of Post-Cold War Chaos', *Foreign Affairs*, Vol. 75, No. 3 (May-June), pp. 79-91.
Ikenberry, G.J., and C.A. Kupchan, (1990) 'Socialisation and hegemonic power', *International Organisation*, Vol. 44, No. 3 (summer), pp. 283-315.
Ikle, Fred C. (1996) 'The Second Coming of the Nuclear Age', *Foreign Affairs*, Jan/Feb. pp. 126-27.
Iokibe Makoto (1998) 'Tough America, Kindly Japan', *Japan Echo*, (December), pp. 19-24.
Ishiyama, John T. and Matthew Velten (1998) 'Presidential Power and Democratic Development in Post-Communist Politics', *Communist and Post-Communist Studies*, Vol. 31, No. 3 (September), pp. 217-33.
Itoh, Mayumi (1995) 'Expanding Japan's Role in the United Nations', *The Pacific Review*, Vol. 8, No. 2, pp. 283-302.
James, Alan (1989) 'The realism of Realism: the state and the study of International Relations', *Review of International Studies*, pp. 215-29.
Jervis, Robert (1993) 'International Primacy: Is the Game Worth the Candle?' *International Security*, Vol. 17, No. 4 (spring), pp. 52-67.
Jing-dong Yuan (1997) 'Sanctions, Domestic Politics, and U.S. China Policy', *Issues and Studies*, Vol. 3, No. 10 (October), pp. 90-123.
Joffe, Josef (1995) '"Bismarck" or "Britain"? Toward an American Grand Strategy after Bipolarity', *International Security*, Vol. 19, No. 4 (spring), pp. 94-117.
_____(1997) 'How America Does It', *Foreign Affairs*, Vol. 76, No. 5 (September-October), pp. 13-27.
Johnson, C. and E.B. Keehn (1995) 'The Pentagon's Ossified Strategy' *Foreign Affairs*, Vol. 74, No. 4 (July-August), pp. 103-14.

Johnson, Chalmer (1999, 6 June) 'American Intelligence Services Lose Credibility Over East Asian Security Problem', *JPRI*, Vol. 6, No. 6, obtained from http://jpri.org/public/crit6.6.html.

Johnstone, Christopher B. (1998) 'Japan's China Policy: Implications for U.S.-Japan Relations', *Asian Survey*, Vol. 38, No. 2, November, pp. 1067-85.

Kagan, Robert (1998) 'The Benevolent Empire', *Foreign Policy*, summer, pp. 24-35.

Kaldor, M. (1990) 'After the Cold War', *New Left Review*, 180 (March-April), pp. 25-37.

Kamp, Karl-Heinz (1998) 'NATO Entrapped: Debating the Next Enlargement Round', *Survival*, Vol. 40, No. 3 (autumn), pp. 170-86.

Kaplan, Robert D. (1997) 'Was Democracy Just a Moment?' *The Atlantic Monthly*, December.

Kapstein, Ethan (1998/99) 'A Global Third Way: Social Justice and the World Economy', *World Policy Journal*, Vol. 15, No. 4 (winter), pp. 23-35.

Katzenstein, P.J. and Nobuo Okawara (1993) 'Japan's National Security: Structures, Norms, and Policies', *International Security*, Vol. 17, No. 4, pp. 84-118.

Kaufman, D. and P. Siegelbaum (1996) 'Privatisation and Corruption in Transition Economies', *Journal of International Affairs*, Vol. 50 (Winter), pp. 419-48.

Kazumasa Iwata (1999) 'The Japanese Big Bang and the Financial Crisis', *Japan Review of International Affairs*, vol. 13, no. 1 (spring), pp. 55-73.

'X' (George F. Kennan) (1947) 'The Sources of Soviet Conduct', *Foreign Affairs*, Vol. 25 (July), pp. 566-82.

Kennan, George F. (1995) 'On American Principles', *Foreign Affairs*, Vol. 74, No. 2 (March/April), pp. 116-26.

Keohane, Robert O. (1982) 'The demand for international regimes', *International Organisation*, Vol. 36, No. 2 (spring), pp. 325-55.

Kimura Hiroshi (1998) 'Talks with Russia: Learning from the Mistakes of the Past', *Japan Echo*, Vol. 25, No. 4 (August), pp. 27-30.

Kindleberger, C.P. (1981) 'Dominance and Leadership in the International Economy', *International Studies Quarterly*, Vol. 25, No. 2, pp. 242-54.

Kissinger, Henry A. (1968) 'The White Revolutionary: Reflections on Bismarck', *Daedalus* (summer), pp. 888-924.

Kitfield, James (1996, 26 October) 'A World of Woes', *National Journal*, pp. 2274-9.

_____ (1999, 13 March) 'Stars and Stripes on the Silk Road', *National Journal*, pp. 676-8.

Klein, B.S. (1988) 'Hegemony and strategic culture: American power projection and alliance defence politics', *Review of International Studies*, Vol. 14, pp. 133-48.

Kotkin, Joel (1998) 'A Chinese Century?' *The American Enterprise*, July/August, pp. 26-32.

Krauthammer, Charles. (1990/91) 'The Unipolar Moment', *Foreign Affairs*, Vol. 70, No. 1, pp. 23-33.

Kristol, W. and R. Kagan (1996) 'Toward a Neo-Reaganite Foreign Policy', *Foreign Affairs*, Vol. 75, No. 4 (July/August), pp. 18-32.

Kristof, Nicholas D. (1998) 'Japan 2: The Problem of Memory', *Foreign Affairs*, Vol. 77, No. 6 (November/December), pp. 37-49.

Krugman, Paul (1998) 'America the Boastful', *Foreign Affairs*, Vol. 77, No. 3 (May/June), pp. 32-45.

Ku, Samuel C.Y. (1998) 'Taiwan's Diplomatic Manoeuvres in the Asia-Pacific: A Perspective of Complex Interdependence', *Issues and Studies*, Vol. 34, No. 6 (June), pp. 80-97.

Kupchan, Charles A. and Clifford A. Kupchan (1991) 'Concerts, Collective Security, and the Future of Europe', *International Security*, Vol. 16, No. 1 (summer), pp. 114-61.

Kurth, James (1996) 'America's Grand Strategy: A Pattern of History', *The National Interest*, No. 43, (spring), pp. 3-18.
_____(1997) 'The Adolescent Empire: America and the Imperial Idea', *The National Interest*, No. 48 (summer), pp. 3-15.
Lake, David A. (1988) 'The State and American Trade Strategy in the Pre-hegemonic era', *International Organisation*, Vol. 42, No. 1 (winter), pp. 33-58.
_____(1993) 'Leadership, Hegemony, and the International Economy: Naked Emperor or Tattered Monarch with Potential?' *International Studies Quarterly*, Vol. 37, No. 4, pp. 459-89.
Laqueur (1992/93) 'Russian Nationalism', *Foreign Affairs*, Vol. 71, No. 5, pp. 103-16.
Layne, Christopher (1993) 'The Unipolar Illusion: Why New Great Powers Will Rise', *International Security*, Vol. 17, No. 4 (spring), pp. 5-51.
_____(1996) 'Less is More: Minimal Realism in East Asia', *The National Interest*, No. 43 (spring), pp. 64-77.
_____(1997a) 'From Preponderance to Offshore Balancing: America's Future Grand Strategy', *International Security*, Vol. 22, No. 1 (summer), pp. 86-124.
_____(1997b) 'A House of Cards: American Strategy toward China', *World Policy Journal* (fall), pp. 77-95.
_____(1998) 'Rethinking American Grand Strategy: Hegemony or Balance in the Twenty-First Century?' *World Policy Journal* (summer), pp. 8-28.
Layne, C. and B. Schwartz (1993) 'American Hegemony – Without an Enemy', *Foreign Policy*, No. 92, pp. 5-23.
Lebow, Richard Ned (1994) 'The Long Peace, the End of the Cold War, and the Failure of Realism', *International Organisation*, Vol. 48, No. 2 (spring), pp. 249-77.
Lee, Hochul (1998) 'Global Liberalisation and Domestic Accommodation: The Case of the Chinese Socialist Market Economy', *Issue and Studies*, Vol. 34, No. 6 (June), pp. 117-34.
Lehmann, J.P. and S. Thomsen (1993) 'Review articles: Washington thinking on trade' *International Affairs*, Vol. 69, No. 3, pp. 527-45.
Lemke, D. and S. Werner (1996) 'Power Parity, Commitment to Change, and War', *International Studies Quarterly*, Vol. 40, pp. 235-60.
Leifer, Michael (1995) 'Chinese Economic Reform and Security Policy: The South China Sea Connection', *Survival*, Vol. 37, No. 2 (summer), pp. 44-59.
Liberman, Peter (1996) 'Trading with the Enemy: Security and Relative Economic Gains', *International Security*, Vol. 21, No. 1 (summer), pp. 147-75.
Libicki, Martin (1996) 'The Emerging Primacy of Information' *Orbis*, Vol. 40, No. 2 (Spring), pp. 261-75.
Lilley, James R. (1998) 'Is China Becoming Democratic?' *The American Enterprise*, July/August, p. 20.
Lincoln, Edward J. (1998) 'Japan's Financial Mess', *Foreign Affairs*, Vol. 77, No. 3, May/June, pp. 57-66.
Lind, Michael (1996) 'Pax Atlantica: The Case for Euramerica', *World Policy Journal*, Vol. 13, No. 1 (spring), pp. 1-7.
Lipschutz, R. (1992) 'Reconstructing World Politics: The Emergence of Global Civil Society', *Millennium: Journal of International Studies*, Vol. 21, No. 3, pp. 389-420.
Lowenhardt, John et al (1998) Special Issue: 'Party Politics in Post-Communist Russia', *Journal of Communist Studies and Transition Politics*, Vol. 14, No. 1 & 2, (March/June), pp. 1-265.

Lukin, Alexander (1999) 'Russia's Image of China and Russian-Chinese Relations', *East Asia: An International Quarterly*, Vol. 17, No. 1 (spring), pp. 5-39.
Luttwak, Edward N. (1998) 'Why We Need an Incoherent Foreign Policy', *The Washington Quarterly*, Vol. 21, No. 1 (winter), pp. 21-31.
Mack, Andrew (1992) 'Security Cooperation in Northeast Asia: Problems and Prospects', *Journal of Northeast Asian Studies* (summer), pp. 21-34.
Malcolm, N. (1995) 'The Case Against "Europe"', *Foreign Affairs*, Vol. 74, No. 2.
Mann, Michael (1993) 'Nation-States in Europe and Other Continents: Diversifying, Developing, Not Dying', *Daedulus* (summer), pp. 115-40.
Maoz, Zeev (1997) 'The Controversy over the Democratic Peace: Rearguard Action or Cracks in the Wall?' *International Security*, Vol. 22, No. 1, (summer), pp. 162-98.
Martinez, Armando B. (1999) 'The New World Order and What We make of It', *World Policy Journal*, fall, pp. 69-78.
Masefield, T. (1989) 'Co-prosperity and co-security: managing the developed world', *International Affairs*, Vol. 65, No. 1, pp. 1-13.
Mastanduno, Michael (1997) 'Preserving the Unipolar Moment: Realist Theories and the U.S. Grand Strategy after the Cold War', *International Security*, Vol. 21, No. 4 (spring), pp. 49-88.
May, C. (1996) 'Strange Fruit: Susan Strange's Theory of Structural Power in the International Political Economy', *Global Society*, Vol. 10, No. 2, pp. 167-89.
Maynes, Charles William (1993) 'A Workable Clinton Doctrine.' *Foreign Policy*, Vol. 93 (winter), pp. 3-20.
_____(1997) '"Principled" Hegemony', *World Policy Journal* (fall), pp. 31-6.
_____(1998) 'The Perils of (and for) an Imperial America', *Foreign Policy* (summer), pp. 36-48.
Mearsheimer, John J. (1990) 'Back to the Future: Instability in Europe after the Cold War' *International Security*, Vol. 15, No. 1 (summer), pp. 5-56.
_____(1994/95) 'The False Promise of International Institutions', *International Security*, Vol. 19, No. 3 (winter), pp. 5-49.
Miasnikov, Vladimir (1998) 'Russia and China: Prospects for Partnership in the Asia-Pacific Region in the 21st Century', *Far Eastern Affairs*, No. 6, p. 8.
Mikoyan, Sergo A. (1998) 'Russia, the U.S. and Regional Conflict in Eurasia', *Survival*, Vol. 40, No. 3 (autumn), pp. 112-26.
Miller, L.B. (1990) 'American foreign policy: beyond containment?' *International Affairs*, Vol. 66, No. 2, pp. 313-24.
Milner, H. and Snyder, J. (1988) 'Lost Hegemony?' *International Organisation*, Vol. 42, No. 4, pp. 749-50.
Minxin Pie (1998) 'Is China Democratising?' *Foreign Affairs*, Vol. 77, No. 1 (Jan/Feb), pp. 68-82.
Mochizuki, M. and M. O'Hanlon (1998) 'A Liberal Vision for the U.S.-Japan Alliance', *Survival*, Vol. 40, No. 2 (summer), pp. 127-34.
Mosher, Steven W. (1998) 'Are the Chinese Ready for Liberty and Self-Government?' *The American Enterprise*, July/August, pp. 50-3.
Murphy, William J. (1994) 'Power Transition in Northeast Asia: U.S.-China Security Perceptions and the Challenges of Systemic Adjustment and Stability', *Journal of Northeast Asia Studies*, Vol. 8, No. 4 (winter), pp. 62-84.
Naim, Moises et al. (1997/98) 'Clinton's Foreign Policy: A Victim of Globalisation?' *Foreign Policy*, (winter), pp. 34-69.

Nathan, A.J. (1996) 'China's Goals in the Taiwan Strait', *The China Journal*, No. 36, (July), pp. 87-93.
Nariai Osamu (1998/99) 'Restructuring in a Deflating Japanese Economy', *Japan Echo* Vol. 25, No. 4 (August), pp. 36-9.
Nesadurai, Helen E.S. (1996) 'APEC: A tool for U.S. regional domination?' *The Pacific Review*, vol. 9, no. 1, pp. 31-57.
Neufield, Mark (1996) 'The State In/Of International Relations Theory', *Mershon International Studies Review*, Vol. 40, pp. 262-5.
Nicholson, Michael (1998) 'Realism and utopianism revisited', *Review of International Studies*, Vol. 24 (December), pp. 65-82.
Nye, Jr. Joseph S. (1988) 'Understating U.S. Strength', *Foreign Policy*, Vol. 72 (fall), pp.105-29.
_____(1992) 'What New World Order?' *Foreign Affairs*, Vol. 71, No. 2, (spring), pp. 83-96.
_____(1995) 'The Case for Deep Engagement', *Foreign Affair*, Vol. 74, No. 4, (July/August), pp. 90-102.
_____(1999) 'Redefining the National Interest', *Foreign Affairs*, Vol. 78, No. 4, (July/August), pp. 22-35.
O'Brien, P.K. and G.A. Pigman (1992) 'Free Trade, British Hegemony and International Economic Order in the Nineteenth Century', *Review of International Studies*, Vol. 18, pp. 89-113.
Panitch, L. (1994) 'Globalisation and the State', in Ralph Miliband and Leo Panitch (eds.) *The Socialist Register* (London: Merlin Press), pp. 60-93.
Payne, A. (1994) 'US hegemony and the reconfiguration of the Caribbean', *Review of International Studies*, Vol. 20, pp. 149-68.
Pfaff, William (1990/91) 'Redefining World Power', *Foreign Affairs*, Vol. 70, No. 1, pp. 34-48.
_____(1998/99) 'The Coming Clash of Europe and America', *World Policy Journal*, Vol. 15, No. 4 (winter), pp. 1-9.
Pipes, Richard (1997) 'Is Russia Still an Enemy?' *Foreign Affairs*, Vol. 76, No. 5, (September/October), pp. 65-78.
Piven, F.F. (1995) 'Globalizing Capitalism and the Rise of Identity Politics', Leo Panitch (ed.) *The Socialist Register*, London: Merlin Press, pp. 102-16.
Porter, Norman (1970) 'Bismarck's Imperialism 1862-1890', *Past and Present*, No. 48, August.
Powell, Robert (1991) 'Absolute and Relative Gains in International Theory' *American Political Science Review*, Vol. 85, No. 4, (December), pp. 1303-20.
Preston, Peter W. (1998) 'Reading the Asian Crisis: History, Culture and Institutional Truths', *Contemporary Southeast Asia*, Vol. 20, No. 3, (December), pp. 242-60.
Prueher, Joseph W. (1998) 'Asia-Pacific Security: The U.S. Pacific Command Perspective', *RUSI Journal*, (April), pp. 10-14.
Radu, Michael (1997) 'Agenda 2000: Why Eastern and Central Europe Look West', *Orbis*, (winter), pp. 39-57.
Richard, D. (1993) 'A Chaotic Model of Power Concentration in the International System', *International Studies Quarterly*, Vol. 37 (March), pp. 55-72.
Rieff, David (1996) 'Whose Isolationism, Whose Isolationism?' *World Policy Journal*, Vol. 13, No. 2, (summer), pp. 1-11.
Robinson, William I. (1996) 'Globalisation: nine theses on our epoch', *Race and Class*, Vol. 38, No. 2, pp. 13-31.

Rodman, K. (1995) 'Sanctions at bay? Hegemonic decline, multinational corporations, and US economic sanctions since the pipeline case', *International Organisation*, Vol. 49, No. 1 (winter), pp. 105-37.

Rosescrance, Richard (1992) 'A New Concert of Powers', *Foreign Affairs*, Vol. 71, No. 2 (spring), pp. 64-82.

Rothkopf, David (1997) 'In Praise of Cultural Imperialism?' *Foreign Policy*, (summer), pp. 38-53.

Roy, Denny (1994) 'Hegemon on the Horizon?: China's Threat to East Asian Security', *International Security*, Vol. 19, No. 1 (summer), pp. 149-68.

_____(1998) 'Current Sino-U.S. Relations in Strategic Perspective', *Contemporary Southeast Asia*, Vol. 20, No. 3, (December), pp. 225-40.

Rubenstein, R.E. and J. Crocker (1994) 'Challenging Huntington', *Foreign Policy*, Vol. 96 (fall), pp. 113-28.

Rubinstein, Alvin Z. (1991) 'New World Order or Hollow Victory?' *Foreign Affairs*, Vol. 70, No. 4 (fall), pp. 53-65.

_____(1996) 'The New Moralists on a Road to Hell', *Orbis*, Vol. 40, No. 2 (spring), pp. 277-95.

_____(1997) 'America's Stake in Russia Today', *Orbis*, Vol. 41, No. 1 (winter), p. 35.

Rupert, Mark (1997) 'Globalisation and American Common Sense: Struggling to Make Sense of a Post Hegemonic World', *New Political Economy*, Vol. 2, No. 1, pp. 105-16.

Russett, Bruce (1985) 'The Mysterious Case of Vanishing Hegemony; or, Is Mark Twain Really Dead?' *International Organisation*, Vol. 39, No. 2 (spring), pp. 207-31.

Sachs, Jeffrey and Wing Thye Woo (1994) 'Reform in China and Russia: structural factors in the economic reforms of China, Eastern Europe, and the Former Soviet Union', *Economic Policy* (April), pp. 101-45.

Saeki Keishi (1999) 'Beyond Anti-Americanism', *Japan Echo* (December), pp. 8-11.

Sakakibara, Eisuke (1995) 'The End of Progessivism: A Search for New Goals', *Foreign Affairs*, Vol. 74, No. 5, (September/October), pp. 8-14.

Santis, Hugh De (1998/99) 'Mutualism', *World Policy Journal*, Vol. 15, No. 4 (winter), pp. 41-52.

Scalapino, Robert A. (1999) 'The United States and Asia in 1998: Summitry and Crisis', *Asian Survey*, Vol. 39, No. 1, January/February, pp. 1-11.

Scherrer, Christoph (1995) 'The Commitment to a Liberal World Market Order as a Hegemonic Practice: The Case of the USA', *Journal of World-Systems Research*, Vol. 1, No. 4, csf.colorado.edu/wsystems/journals.

Schlesinger, Stephen (1998/99) 'The End of Idealism: Foreign Policy in the Clinton Years', *World Policy Journal*, Vol. 15, No. 4 (winter), pp. 36-40.

Schroeder, Paul (1994) 'Historical Reality vs. Neo-realist Theory', *International Security*, Vol. 19, No. 1 (summer), pp. 108-48.

Schwartz, Benjamin (1997) 'Permanent Interests, Endless Threats: Cold War Continuities and NATO Enlargement', *World Policy Journal* (winter), pp. 24-30.

Schweller, Randall (1997) 'New Realist Research on Alliances: Refining, Not Refuting Waltz's Balancing Proposition', *American Political Science Review* Vol. 91, No. 4, (December), pp. 927-35.

Segal, Gerald (1996) 'East Asia and the "constrainment" of China', *International Security*, Vol. 20, No. 4 (spring), pp. 108-12.

Shackmurove, Yochanan (1999) 'A Puzzle Resolved: Japan's High Currency Value and Trade Surplus', *The American Economist*, Vol. 43, No. 1 (spring), pp. 47-51.

Shambaugh, David (1992) 'China's Security in the Post-Cold War Era', *Survival*, Vol. 34, No. 2 (summer), pp. 88-106.
Sharp, J.P. (1996) 'Hegemony, popular culture and geopolitics: the Reader's Digest and the construction of danger', *Political Geography*, Vol. 15, No. 6/7, pp. 557-70.
Shin'ichi Kitaoka (1999) 'The Constitutional Debate in Japan: Cutting the Gordian Knot', *Japan Review of International Affairs*, Vol. 13, No. 3, (fall), pp. 191-205.
Shiraishi Takashi (1998/99) 'The Currency Crisis and the End of Asia's Old Politico-Economic Set-up', *Japan Echo*, Vol. 25, No. 4 (August), pp. 31-5.
Shlapentokh, Vladimir (1998) '"Old", "New" and "Post" Liberal Attitudes Towards the West: From Love to Hate', *Communist and Post-Communist Studies*, Vol. 31, No. 3, pp. 199-216.
Smith, Anthony (1992) 'National Identity and the Idea of European Unity', *International Affairs*, Vol. 68, No. 1, pp. 55-76.
Smith, J. and M. Butcher (Eds.) (Jan. 1999) 'A Risk Reduction Strategy for NATO', *BASIC Publications*, obtained from http://www.basicint.org/natorr.html.
Smith, M., and Woolcock, S. (1994) 'Learning to co-operate: the Clinton administration and the European Union' *International Affairs*, Vol. 70, No. 3, pp. 459-79.
Smith, Martin A. and Graham Timmins (1999) 'The European Union and NATO Enlargement Debates in Comparative Perspective: A Case of Incremental Linkage?' *West European Politics*, Vol. 22, No. 3 (July), p. 25.
Snidal, Duncan (1985) 'The limits of hegemonic stability theory', *International Organisation*, Vol. 39, No. 4 (autumn), pp. 579-614.
_____(1991) 'Relative Gains and the Pattern of International Cooperation', *American Political Science Review*, Vol. 85, No. 3 (September), pp. 701-26.
Sorensen, George (1998) 'IR theory after the Cold War', *Review of International Studies*, Vol. 24 (December), pp. 83-100.
Soros, George (1998/99) 'Capitalism's Last Chance?' *Foreign Policy* (winter), pp. 55-66.
Staar, Richard F. (1996) 'Beyond the Unipolar Moment: Moscow's Plans to Restore Its Power', *Orbis*, Vol. 40, No. 3 (summer), pp. 375-89.
Starobin, Paul (1999, 13 March) 'The New Great Game' *National Journal*, pp. 666-75.
Stein, A.A. (1984) 'The Hegemon's dilemma: Great Britain, the United States, and international economic order' *International Organisation*, Vol. 38, No. 2 (spring), pp. 355-86.
Stiles, K.W. (1995) 'The ambivalent hegemon: explaining the "lost decade" in multilateral trade talks, 1948-1958', *Review of International Political Economy* (winter), pp. 1-26.
Stone, Peter H. (1999, 13 March) 'Caspian Wells Common in for K Street', *National Journal*, pp. 680-5.
Strange, S. (1985) 'Protectionism and world politics', *International Organisation*, Vol. 39, No. 2, pp. 234-59.
_____(1987) 'The persistent myth of lost hegemony', *International Organisation* Vol. 41, No. 4, pp. 551-74.
_____(1988) 'The persistent myth of lost hegemony: reply to Milner and Snyder', *International Organisation*, Vol. 42, No. 4, pp. 751-2.
_____(1990) 'Finance, information, and power', *Review of International Studies*, Vol. 16, No. 3, pp. 259-74.
_____(1992) 'States, firms and diplomacy', *International Affairs*, Vol. 68, No. 1, pp.1-15.
_____(1994) 'Wake up, Krasner! The world has changed', *Review of International Political Economy*, Vol. 1, No. 2 (summer), pp. 210-19.

_____(1995) 'The Defective State', *Daedalus*, Vol. 124, No. 2 (spring), pp. 55-74.
Suzuki, Motoshi (1994) 'Economic Interdependence, Relative Gains, and International Cooperation: The Case of Monetary Policy Coordination', *International Studies Quarterly*, Vol. 38, pp. 475-89.
Tabb, William K. (1999) 'The End of the Japanese Postwar System', *Monthly Review*, Vol. 51, No. 3 (July/August), pp. 71-80.
Takamitsu Sawa (1999) 'End of the Road for Japanese-Style Capitalism', *Japan Review of International Affairs*, Vol. 13, No. 3 (fall), pp. 172-90.
Takashi Inoguchi (1999) 'Globalisation and Japan's Foreign Policy', *Japan Review of International Affairs*, Vol. 13, No. 3 (fall), pp. 157-71.
Talbott, Strobe (1997) 'Globalisation and Diplomacy: A Practitioner's Perspective', *Foreign Policy* (fall), pp. 69-83.
Tanaka, Akihiko (1999) 'Issues for Japan's East Asian Diplomacy', *Japan Review of International Affairs*, Vol. 13, No. 1, summer, pp. 3-16.
Tanzi, Vito (1998) 'Corruption around the World: Causes, Consequences, Scope, and Cures', *IMF Staff Papers*, Vol. 45, No. 4 (December).
Taylor, Peter J. (1996a) 'What's modern about the modern world-system? Introducing ordinary modernity through world hegemony' *Review of International Political Economy*, Vol. 3, No. 2, (summer), pp. 260-86.
Thayer, Bradley A. (1995) 'The Causes of Nuclear Proliferation and the Utility of the Nuclear non-proliferation Regime', *Security Studies*, Vol. 4, No. 3 (spring), p. 503.
Tong, Kurt W. (1996-97) 'Revolutionising America's Japan Policy', *Foreign Policy* (winter), pp. 107-24.
Tooze, R. (1990) 'Understanding the Global Political Economy: Applying Gramsci' *Millennium: Journal of International Studies*. Vol. 19, No. 2, pp. 273-80.
Tsepkalo, Valery V. (1998) 'The Remaking of Eurasia', *Foreign Affairs*, Vol. 77, No. 2, (March/April), pp. 107-26.
Tucker, Nancy Bernkopf (1998) 'China-Taiwan: U.S. Debates and Policy Choices', *Survival*, Vol. 40, No. 4 (winter), pp. 150-67.
Van Ness, Peter. (1996) 'Competing Hegemons', *The China Journal*, No. 36, (July), pp. 125-8.
Vasquez, John A. (1997) 'The Realist Paradigm and Degenerative versus Progressive Research Programs: An Appraisal of Neotraditional Research on Waltz's Balancing Proposition', *American Political Science Review*, Vol. 91, No. 4, (December), pp. 899-912.
Ullman, Richard (1999) 'The U.S. and the World: An Interview with George Kennan', *New York Book Review*, 12 August, http://www.nybooks.com/nyrev/wwwfeatdisplay.cgi?19990812?
Uriu, Robert (1999) 'Japan in 1998: Nowhere to Go but Up?' *Asian Survey*, Vol. 34, No. 1, January/February, pp. 114-24.
Wade, Robert (1998/99) 'The Coming Fight over Capital Flows', *Foreign Policy* (winter), pp. 41-54.
Waldron, Arthur (1997) 'Eight Steps toward a New China Policy', *Orbis* (winter), pp. 77-82.
_____(1998) 'Why China Could Be Dangerous', *The American Enterprise*, July/August, pp. 40-3.
Walker, Martin (1996) 'The New American Hegemony', *World Policy Journal*, Vol. 13, No. 2 (summer), pp. 13-21.

_____(1997) 'Present at the Solution: Madeleine Albright's Ambitious Foreign Policy', *World Policy Journal*, Vol. 14, No. 1 (spring), pp. 1-10.
Wallace, W. and Jan Zeilonka (1998) 'Misunderstanding Europe', *Foreign Affairs* November/December, Vol. 77, No. 6, p. 71.
Wallerstein, Immanuel (1974b) 'The Rise and Future Demise of the World Capitalist System: Concepts for Comparative Analysis', *Comparative Studies in Society and History*, Vol. 16, pp. 387-415.
Waltz, Kenneth N. (1991) 'America as a Model for the World? A Foreign Policy Perspective', *PS: Political Science and Politics*, December, p. 669.
_____(1993) 'The Emerging Structure of International Politics', *International Security*, Vol. 18, No. 2, (fall), pp. 44-79.
_____(1997) 'Evaluating Theories', *American Political Science Review*, Vol. 91, No. 4, (December), pp. 913-17.
_____(1999) 'Globalisation and Governance', *PS*, December, pp. 693-700.
Wan Guong (1989) 'China's Foreign Policy Goals', *Harvard International Review*, Vol. 11, No. 2 (spring).
Wang Gungwu (1996/97) 'Huntington's Clash of Civilisations: 2. A Machiavelli for Our Times', *The National Interest*, No. 46 (winter), pp. 69-73.
Wang, Jianwei and Zhimin Lin (1992) 'Chinese Perceptions in the Post Cold-War Era: Three Images of the United States', *Asian Survey*, Vol. 32, No. 10 (October), pp. 908-11 and 917.
Wasefield, T. (1989) 'Co-prosperity and co-security: Managing the developed world', *International Affairs*, 1 (winter), pp. 1-13.
Webb, M.C., and S.D. Krasner (1989) 'Hegemonic Stability Theory: an Empirical Assessment', *Review of International Studies*, Vol. 15, pp. 183-98.
Weede, Erich (1995) 'Future Hegemonic Rivalry between China and the West?' *Journal of World-Systems Research*, Vol. 1, No. 14, csf.colorado.edu/wsystems/journals.
Weidenfeld, Werner (1998/99) 'A Demanding Agenda for the New Europe', *World Policy Journal*, Vol. 15, No. 4 (winter), pp. 53-7.
Weiss, L. (1997) 'Globalisation and the Myth of the Powerless State', *New Left Review*, No. 225 (September-October), pp. 3-27.
Wendt, Alexander E. (1987) 'The Agent-Structure Problem in International Relations Theory', *International Organisation*, Vol. 41, No. 3 (summer), pp. 335-70.
Worsley, P. (1980) 'One world or three? A critique of the world-system theory of Immanual Wallerstein', in Ralph Miliband and John Saville (Eds.) *The Socialist Register* (London: The Merlin Press), pp. 298-338.
Xu, G. (1998) 'Anti-U.S. Sentiments in China, 1989-1996: Sources, Development and Impact', *Issues and Studies*, Vol. 34, No. 1 (January), pp. 79-99.
Yang, Jiawen (1998) 'Some Current Issues in U.S.-China Trade Relations', *Issues and Studies*, Vol. 34, No. 7 (July), pp. 62-84.
Yarbrough, B., and R. Yarbrough (1987) 'Cooperation in the liberation of international trade: after hegemony, what?' *International Organisation*, Vol. 41, No. 1 (winter), pp. 1-26.
Yavlinsky, Gregory (1998) 'Russia's Phony Capitalism', *Foreign Affairs*, Vol. 77, No. 3 (May/June), pp. 67-79.
Yesson, Erik (1999) 'NATO and Russia in Kosovo', *RUSI*, August, pp. 20-6.
Yost, David S. (1998) 'The New NATO and Collective Security', *Survival*, Vol. 40, No. 2 (summer), pp. 135-60.

Zhao, Suisheng (1992) 'Beijing's Perception of the International System and Foreign Policy Adjustment in the Post-Cold War World', *Journal of Northeast Asian Studies*, Vol. 11, No. 3 (Fall), pp. 70-4.

Zinsmeister, Karl (1998) 'Why China Doesn't Scare Me', *The American Enterprise*, July/August, p. 5.

Zizek, Slavoj (1997) 'Multiculturalism, Or, the Cultural Logic of Multinational Capitalism', *New Left Review*, No. 225 (September-October), pp. 28-51.

Zoellick, Robert B. (1996/97) 'China: What Engagement Should Mean', *The National Interest*, No. 46 (winter), pp. 13-22.

Zuckerman, Mortimer B. (1998) 'A Second American Century', *Foreign Affairs*, Vol. 77 (May-June), pp. 18-31.

Newspapers, Magazines and Internet Sources

Beijing Review

_____(1996, 21-27 October) 'U.S. China Policy: Containment or Engagement?' pp. 6-7, by Wang Jisi.

_____(1996, 21-27 October) 'Jiang on Sino-U.S. Relations', pp. 8-9.

_____(1996, 21-27 October) 'Sino-U.S. Relations: An Overview', pp. 9-11, by Jin Canrong.

_____(1996, 21-27 October) 'Why Against China?' p.11, by Shi Yinhong.

_____(1996, 21-27 October) 'U.S. Media: Behind the Demonization of China', p. 12, by Li Xiguang.

_____(1996, 21-27 October) 'China Say "No" to the United States', p. 13, by Si Cheng.

_____(1996, 21-27 October) 'Milestones of Sino-U.S. Relations', p. 14.

_____(1996, 21-27 October) 'Chinese Foreign Ministry News Briefing' p. 15.

_____(1997, 28 April-4 May) 'U.S. to Deal with Rise of non-Western Powers', p. 7.

_____(1997, 5-11 May) 'Jiang's Russian Visit a Significant Event: Rogachev', pp. 7-8.

_____(1997, 5-11 May) 'Sino-Russia Partnership Marching Into 21st Century', pp. 9-12, by Xia Yishan.

_____(1997, 5-11 May) 'U.S.-Russian Strategic Balance Fragile' pp. 12-13, by Shen Dingli.

_____(1997, 12-18 May) 'China, Russia Hail Relations', pp. 4-5.

_____(1997, 12-18 May) 'WTO Entry Policy Reiterated', p. 6.

_____(1997, 12-18 May) 'Joint Statement by the People Republic of China and the Russian Federation on the Multipolarisation of the World and the Establishment of A New International Order', pp. 7-8.

_____(1997, 12-18 May) 'Jiang: Peace and Stability Ensure a Just, Better World', pp. 9-11.

_____(1997, 10-16 November) 'Jiang Kicks Off Visit to U.S.', pp. 4-5.

_____(1997, 10-16 November) 'Key Events in Sino-U.S. Relations', pp. 5-7.

_____(1997, 10-16 November) 'Jiang Zemin: The Core of China's Leadership', pp. 8-9.

_____(1997, 10-16 November) 'Remarks by U.S. President in Address on China and the National Interest', pp. 12-16.

_____(1997, 17-23 November) 'Sino-U.S. Joint Statement', pp. 7-9.

_____(1997, 17-23 November) 'Clinton Hosts State Banquet for Chinese President', p.10.

_____(1997, 17-23 November) 'Chinese, U.S. Presidents Hold Press Conference', p. 11.

_____(1997, 17-23 November) 'Jiang Expounds Principles Guiding Sino-U.S. Relations', p. 12.
_____(1997, 17-23 November) '"Russia"' Asia Diplomacy', p. 13, by Tang Jiniu.
_____(1997, 17-23 November) 'Foreign Ministry News Briefing', p. 14.
_____(1999, 11-17 January) '''98 International Situation in Review', pp. 6-7, by Zhang Dezhen and Xu Hongzhi.
_____(1999, 7 June) 'Who Whips up Anti-American Feeling?' *Beijing Review*, p. 12, by Luo Tongsong.
_____(1999, 14 June) 'New Acts – A Historical Retrogression', *Beijing Review*, pp. 12-14, by Xu Zhixian and Yang Bojiang.
_____(1999, 19 July) 'EU and Latin America Strengthen Ties', p. 10, by Xiao Li.
_____(1999, 23 August) 'International Security Environment Goes Through Changes', pp. 10-11, by Lu Zhongwei.

China Daily

_____(2000, 14 January) 'U.S. arms control pull-back threaten world peace', by Chen Yali.

The Economist Intelligence Unit

Japan, Country Report 4th quarter 1998.
Japan, Country Report 3rd quarter 1999.
Russia, Country Report 4th quarter 1998.
United States of America, Country Report 4th quarter 1998.
United States of America, Country Report 3rd quarter 1999.

The Economist

_____(1993, 13 February) 'In Search of Clarity', pp. 45-6.
_____(1993, 26 June) 'The New Cold War', p. 91.
_____(1994, 1 October) 'Beyond Bretton Woods', pp. 27-31.
_____(1995, 7 October) 'Japan's Unspoken Fears', pp. 93-4.
_____(1996, 10 May) 'Uncle Sam and the World', p. 58.
_____(1996, 21 September) 'Leadership by Stealth', pp. 17-18.
_____(1998, 24 December) 'America, Asia and Europe', p. 33.
_____(1999, 2 January) 'Europe's adventure finally begins', pp. 15, 19-24.
_____(1999, 5 June) 'France: The grand illusion', Special Issue.
_____(1999, 31 July) 'The New Geopolitics: Who are we, who are they?' Special Issue.
_____(1999, 25 September) 'A Survey of the World Economy: The Navigators'. Special Issue.
_____(1999, 23 October) 'America's world', p. 15.

Far Eastern Economic Review

_____(1997, 6 February) 'Collision Course', pp. 39-40.
_____(1997, 1 May) 'The Coming Battle', pp. 36-9.
_____(1997, 26 June) 'Not to Our Liking: China is Opposing the updated U.S.-Japan Security Treaty', pp. 26-7.

_____(1998, 1 October) 'Asian Indigestion', pp. 10-12, by Henry Sender.
_____(1999, 8 April) 'Behind the Lines', pp. 18-20.
_____(1999, 10 June) 'China's Gentler Face', p. 29.
_____(1999, 17 June) 'Uneasy Together', pp. 10-12.
_____(1999, 17 June) 'Brave New World', pp. 13-14, by Susan V. Lawrence.
_____(1999, 17 June) 'Selective Targeting', p. 14, by Lorien Holland.
_____(1999, 12 August) 'Flying the Flag', pp. 18-19, by Chester Dawson.
_____(1999, 21 October) 'UN: Sovereignty or Rights?' p. 40, by Frank Ching.
_____(1999, 2 December) 'Slowly, Slowly', pp. 9-10, 12, by C. Dawson and N. Chanda.
_____(1999, 2 December) 'The IMF Didn't Fail', p. 28, by Rudi Dornbusch.
_____(1999, 2 December) 'Fortress America?' p. 34, by Frank Ching.
_____(1999, 2 December) 'East-West Divide', pp. 40-1.

The Financial Times

_____(1998, 31 Oct-1 Nov) 'Brussels files suit over aviation deals with U.S.', p. 1, by M. Smith and M. Suzman.
_____(1998, 31 Oct-1 Nov) 'A Russian sphinx', p.11, by John Thornhill.
_____(1998, 31 Oct-1Nov) 'G7 backs plan to help vulnerable economies', pp. 1, 2, 10.
_____(1999, 23-24 January) 'How Project Super Bowl won the day', p. 2, by H. Dixon and A. Nicoll.
_____(1999, 2 March) 'Russia's debt', p. 17.
_____(1999, 15 March) 'Make-or-break talks to resume in Paris', p. 2.
_____(1999, 15 March) 'G7 still wary despite Russian hopes on IMF', p. 2.
_____(1999, 15 March) 'Bonn spurs debate over EU security', p. 2, by Peter Norman.
_____(1999, 15 March) "Fine tuning' for EU farm reform deal', p. 2, by Peter Norman.
_____(1999, 15 March) 'Santer under pressure to act on report', p. 2, by Emma Tucker.
_____(1999, 16 March) 'Fraud report slams EU executive', pp. 1-2, 23, by E. Tucker, M. Smith, and P. Norman.
_____(1999, 20-21 March) 'Earthquake in Europe', p. 10, by Quentin Peel.
_____(1999, 22 March) 'A new agenda for Europe', p. 17.
_____(1999, 10-11 April) 'One hundred days of the Euro', p. 10.
_____(1999, 10-11 April) 'European rate cut wins plaudit but doubt remain on growth prospect', p. 3, by Tony Barber.
_____(1999, 10-11 April) 'Barshefsky upbeat on China trade talks', p. 4, by S. Fidler and N. Dunn.
_____(1999, 10-11 April) 'Zhu faces resistance to plan for WTO entry', p. 4, by James Harding.
_____(1999, 12 April) 'Currency star whose brightness has failed to dazzle', p. 6, by Alan Beattie.
_____(1999, 12 April) 'Crisis in the making', p. 19, by John Plender.
_____(1999, 12 April) 'A new cold war in the making', p. 3, by John Lloyd.
_____(1999, 13 April) 'A bigger European big', p. 21.
_____(1999, 14 April) 'Handling Russia', p. 19.
_____(1999, 14 April) 'Nato's "gradual" military strategy questioned', p. 2, by A. Nicholl and S. Fidler.
_____(1999, 29 April) 'Yet more dollars', p. 26, by Samuel Brittan.
_____(1999, 30 April) 'Union finds renewed unity of purpose', p. 3, by Peter Norman.
_____(1999, 30 April) 'Balkan mission', p. 19.

_____(1999, 1-2 May) Yeltsin eases U.S.-Russian tensions', p. 2.
_____(1999, 1-2 May) 'U.S. challenges French Airbus subsidies', p. 4.
_____(1999, 12 May) 'China seeks US concessions', p. 1.
_____(1999, 12 May) 'EU to offer payments to settle beef dispute', p. 6, by Paul Abrahams.
_____(1999, 12 May) 'U.S. and Europe to seek trade "warning system"', p. 6, by Mark Suzman.
_____(1999, 12 May) 'Point of no return', p. 25.
_____(1999, 19 May) 'Diverging Europe'.
_____(1999, 25 May) 'The rebirth of confidence', p. 19, by Haig Simonian.
_____(1999, 25 May) 'EU democracy', p. 19.
_____(1999, 25 May) 'Nato plan to unite Serbs against Milosevic', p. 2.
_____(1999, 25 May) 'Fighting talk is lost on Russians', p. 2, by John Lloyd.
_____(1999, 7 June) 'Nato peace in his time', p. 23.
_____(1999, 8 June) 'G8 nations near deal on Kosovo peace plan', pp. 1-2.
_____(1999, 9 June) 'Policies for New Europe', p. 27.
_____(1999, 9 June) 'Crisis of Identity', p. 26, by Martin Wolf.
_____(1999, 9 June) 'Resolution allows UN to return to centre stage', p. 2.
_____(1999, 11 June) 'U.S., Russia discuss shape of contingent', p. 2, by John Thornhill.
_____(1999, 11 June) 'Taming the big bear', p. 20, by Philip Stephens.
_____(1999, 11 June) 'The perils of peace', p. 21, by David Buchan.
_____(1999, 12 June) 'China condemns U.S.-Japan pact', by James Kynge.
_____(1999, 15 June) 'A blow to consensus', p. 23, by Robert Peston.
_____(1999, 15 June) 'Where angels fear to tread', p. 23.
_____(1999, 15 June) 'Few reasons to be cheerful', p. 23, by Peter Norman.
_____(1999, 15 June) 'U.S., Russia to meet over dispute', p. 4.
_____(1999, 17 June) 'The cold peace', p. 24, by Quentin Peel.
_____(1999, 17 June) 'Black Sea route still open to Moscow', p. 2, by Charles Clover.
_____(1999, 17 June) 'France backs defence criteria', p. 2.
_____(1999, 22 June) 'Europe escapes grip of U.S. tightening', p. 41, by Michael Peel.
_____(1999, 23 June) 'Jaw-jaw', p. 23.
_____(1999, 24 June) 'Uncle Sam shares secrets of success', p. 14, by Kevin Brown.
_____(1999, 28 June) 'Europe's farmers stand in way of Mercosur deal', p. 6.
_____(1999, 28 June) 'Euro plays walk-on part in historic drama', p. 37, by Alan Beattie.
_____(1999, 28 June) 'Under the volcano', p. 23.
_____(1999, 1 July) 'The lingering question', p. 25, by Alexander Nicholl.
_____(1999, 7 July) 'Citizens' confidence in EU declines', p. 2, by Neil Buckley.
_____(1999, 9 July) 'Short memories, long odds', p. 15, by John Thornhill.
_____(1999, 12 July) 'Great expectations', p. 17, by Peter Norman.
_____(1999, 12 July) 'Two cheers for Mr. Prodi', p. 17.
_____(1999, 13 July) 'Euro slides closer to dollar', p. 1.
_____(1999, 13 July) 'U.S. to apply sanctions over EU meat ban', p. 6.
_____(1999, 14 July) 'Euro-zone forecast to benefit from improve world outlook', p. 3, by Tony Barber.
_____(1999, 14 July) 'Much ado about little', p. 17, by Tony Barber.
_____(1999, 17-18 July) 'The truce that lied', p. 10, by Niall Ferguson.
_____(1999, 20 July) 'Euro Defence', p. 19.
_____(1999, 20 July) 'Why NATO's war machine may drop the pilot', p. 14, by Alexander Nicholl.

_____(1999, 21 July) 'Making Europe Work', p. 16, by Martin Wolf.
_____(1999, 23 July) 'No meeting of minds', p. 19, by Guy de Jonquieres.
_____(1999, 24 July) 'EU agriculture policy under fire in U.S.', p. 7, by Nancy Dunne.
_____(1999, 27 July) 'A tethered superpower', p. 19, by David Buchan.
_____(1999, 29 July) 'Turning back the clock', p. 25, by Robert Graham.
_____(1999, 26 August) 'Yeltsin and Jiang attack U.S. hegemony', p. 4, by Charles Clover.

Fortune

_____(1998, 28 September) 'Why the Global Storm Will Zap the U.S. Economy', pp. 22-3, by Jim Rohwer.
_____(1998, 28 September) 'China: The Real Economic Wild Card', pp. 62-6, by Jim Rohwer.
_____(1998, 28 September) 'Can the U.S. Economy Hold Up?' pp. 49-54, by Justin Fox.
_____(1998, 26 October) 'Should Alan Greenspan be the World's Banker?' pp. 22-3, by Justin Fox.

Hong Kong Standard

_____(1999, 27 August) 'Jiang Signs Pact on Security' http://online.hkstandard.com/today/default.asp?pagetype=ach5.
_____(1999, 27 August) 'Five Nations find One Voice' http://online.hkstandard.com/today/default.asp?pagetype=aop5.

The International Herald Tribune

_____(1997, 24 April) 'Russia and China Agree: Washington Is Too Bossy' http://www.iht.com/iht/today/thu/fpage/moscow.html, by Lee Hockstader.
_____(1997, 20 June) 'Denver Spotlight: The U.S. Boom and Yeltsin: Down but Never Out, Russian Rebounds' from the *Washington Post Service* http://www.iht.com/iht/today/fri/fpage/yeltsin.html, by David Hoffman.
_____(1997, 20 June) 'Denver Spotlight: The U.S. Boom and Yeltsin: At Summit, Gloating, but No Lecturing' from the *New York Times Service* http://www.iht.com/iht/today/fri/fpage/g7.html, by David E. Singer.
_____(1997, 21 June) 'U.S. and Japan Paper Over Dispute: Russia's Status, In but Not Quite' http://www.iht.com/iht/today/sat/fpage/club.html, by Peter Baker.
_____(1997, 24 June) 'Is There a Viable "Third Way" for Global Capitalism?' http://www.iht.com/iht/today/tue/fpage/third.html, by S. Pearlstein and P. Blustein.
_____(1997, 2 July) 'A New Order Takes Its Place in Hong Kong', http://www.iht.com/iht/today/wed/fpage.hong.html, by Velisarious Kattoulas.
_____(1997, 2 July) 'Clinton Putting Wager on Beijing', in *The Washington Post* http://www.iht.com/iht/today/wed/fpage/policy.html, by Thomas W. Lippman.
_____(1997, 3 July) 'Not All in Asia Back U.S. View on Civil Rights' *New York Times Services* http://www.iht.com/iht/today/thu/fpage/react.html, by Andrew Pollack.
_____(1997, 10 July) 'NATO Embraces Ukraine as Partner' http://www.iht.com/iht/today/thu/fpage/nato.html, by John Vinocur.

Bibliography

_____(1997, 11 July) Growing Pains at a New NATO'
http://www.iht.com/iht/today/fri/fpage/nato.html, by William Drozdiak.
_____(1997, 27 October) 'Risk and Opportunity for Both Sides: America Pays in Technology in Vast Market', from the *Washington Post Service* in http://www.iht.com/iht/today/mon/fpage/chicon.html, by Paul Blustein.
_____(1997, 27 October) 'Jiang Begins Historic U.S. Visit: Albright Warns that He'll Get an Earful of Noisy Democracy'
http://www.iht.com/iht/today/mon/fpage/china.html, by Brian Knowlton.
_____(1997, 28 October) 'In Deng's Footsteps, Jiang Treads His Own Path'
http://www.iht.com/iht/today/tue/fpage/beijing.html, by Steven Mufson.
_____(1997, 29 October) 'Clouds Over Jiang Visit'
http://www.iht.com/iht/today/wed/fpage/jiang.html, by Brian Knowlton.
_____(1997, 29 October) 'Business Leads Diplomacy in Relations with Beijing'
http://www.iht.com/iht/today/wed.fpage.china.html, by David E. Sanger.
_____(1997, 30 October) 'On Bosnia, Clinton Edges Towards Longer Mission', from the *New York Times Service* http://www.iht.com/iht/today/fpage/bosnia.html, by Steven Erlanger.
_____(1997, 30 October) 'China and U.S. Reach Nuclear Deal'
http://www.iht.com/iht/today/thu/fpage/summit.html, by Brian Knowlton.
_____(1997, 31 October) 'U.S.-China Summit on a Tightrope: There's Plenty of Process, But Not Much Progress', from the *New York Times Services* in http://www.iht.com/iht/today/fri/fpage/assess.html, by R.W. Apple, Jr.
_____(1997, 31 October) 'U.S.-China Summit on a Tightrope: In a Rare Sight, 2 Leaders Spar in Public Over Rights', from *The Washington Post Service* http://www.iht.com/iht/today/fri/fpage/debate.html, by John Harris.
_____(1997, 31 October) 'Jiang Vows More Democracy: He defends "Open Society" to Congressional Leaders' http://www.iht.com/iht/today/fri/fpage/jiang.html, by Brian Knowlton.
_____(1997, 24 November) 'Beijing Plays Key Role as East Asians Improve Ties'
http://www.iht.com/iht/today/mon/fpage/pacif.html, by Michael Richardson.
_____(1997, 26 November) 'APEC Puts On a Brave Face As Asian Market Tremble'
http://www.iht.com/iht/today/wed.fpage.apec.html, by Brian Knowlton.
_____(1997, 27 November) 'American Foreign Policy Stumbles in the Middle East'
http://www.iht.com/iht/today/thu/ed/edpfaff.html, by William Pfaff.
_____(1997, 28 November) 'What Sort of Friend Is a Resentful France?'
http://www.iht.com/iht/today/fri/ed/cohen.html, by Richard Cohen.
_____(1998, 11 January) 'IMF is on the Right Tracks, even with Adjustments'
http://www.iht.com/iht/today.wed/ed/edcam.html, by Michael Camdessus.
_____(1998, 3 April) 'Europe Can Be Part of the Solution for East Asia'
http://www.iht.com/iht/today/fri/ed/edbuck.html, by R. Buckley, and W. Horsley.
_____(1998, 3 April) 'China to Propose Tariff Cuts in WTO Bid'
http://www.iht.com/iht/today/fri/fin/asem.html, by Barry James.
_____(1998, 3 April) 'For Chinese, Economic and Political Progress Go Together'
http://www.iht.com/iht/today/fri/ed/edjames.html, by James Moorhouse.
_____(1998, 3 April) 'China's New "Self-Defense" Tool: U.S. Bonds'
http://www.iht.com/iht/today/fri/fin/chibond.html, by Gerald Segal.
_____(1998, 3 April) 'Pessimism in Japan Hits Asian Markets'
http://www.iht.com/iht/today/fri.fpage.yen.html, by Sheryl WuDunn.

_____(1998, 10 April) 'An Inside Look at U.S. Foreign Policy Indecision' http://www.iht.com/iht/today/fri/ed/edhoag.html, by Jim Hoagland.
_____(1998, 20 April) 'Megabank Musical Chairs: How a Few Will Soon Dominate World Finance', from the *Washington Post Service* http://www.iht.com/iht/today/today/mon/fin/mega.html, by S. Pearlstein and P. Pae.
_____(1998, 6 May) 'East Asia Needs Transparency and Financial Oversight' http://www.iht.com/iht/today/wed/ed/edrich.html, by Richard Hu.
_____(1998, 6 May) 'Clinton, Scolding Congress, Pleads for Leadership on Global Stage', http://www.iht.com/iht/today/wed/fpage/prexy.html, by Brian Knowlton.
_____(1998, 6 May) 'Japan Is a Friend' http://www.iht.com/iht/today/wed/ed/edjapan.html
_____(1998, 9 May) 'Debating the IMF's Role in a Tumultuous New World' http://www.iht.com/iht/today/sat/ed/edhoag.html, by Jim Hoagland.
_____(1998, 13 May) 'A World of Global Capital Markets Pushes Integration' http://www.iht.com/iht/today/wed/ed/edpaul.html, by Paul Volcker.
_____(1998, 20 May) 'A Globalisation Summit' http://www.iht.com/iht/today/wed.ed/edsewell.html, by J.W. Sewell, and M.H. McDowell.
_____(1998, 27 May) 'Disputes Among Allies' http://www.iht.com/iht/today/wed/ed/edtrade.html
_____(1998, 6 November) 'Trilateral Instead of Unilateral' http://www.iht.com/iht/today/fri/ed/edlamb.html, by Otto Graf Lambsdorff.
_____(1998, 6 November) 'Democracy is a Cultural Hothouse' http://www.iht.com/iht/today/fri/ed/edflora.html, by Flora Lewis.
_____(1998, 7 November) 'Coming to Grips with a World in Transition' http://www.iht.com/iht/today/sat/ed/edshear.html, by Derek N. Shearer.
_____(1998, 11 November) 'Asian Crisis Felt in U.S. Heartland' http://www.iht.com/iht/today/wed/fin/factory.html, by Tim Smart.
_____(1998, 13 November) 'Unexpected Praise for Multinationals', http://www.iht.com/iht/today/fri/fin/think.html, by Reginald Dale.
_____(1998, 14 November) 'Divided and Distracted, APEC Prepares to Meet' http://www.iht.com/iht/today/sat/fpage/apec.html, by Michael Richardson.
_____(1998, 14 November) 'Clinton Gains New Freedom in Dealing with Saddam' http://www.iht.com/iht/today/sat/fpage/diplo.html, by Joseph Fitchett.
_____(1998, 16 November) 'APEC Cuts Vague Deal on Tariff Reductions' http://www.iht.com/iht/today/mon/fpage/apec.html, by Michael Richardson.
_____(1998, 17 November) 'Stop Demonising Globalisation, and Learn to Manage It' http://www.iht.com/iht/today/tue/ed/edghogh.html, by Bimal Ghosh.
_____(1998, 17 November) 'Three Asia-Pacific Challenges' http://www.iht.com/iht/today/tue/ed/edtim.html, by Timothy Ong.
_____(1998, 17 November) 'Western Foolishness' http://www.iht.com/iht/today/tue/ed/edger.html, by Gerald Segal.
_____(1998, 18 November) 'Gore Opens APEC Rift with Praise of Reform' http://www.iht.com/iht/today/wed/fpage/pacif.html, by Michael Richardson.
_____(1998, November 19) 'U.S. Strategy to Buy Time for World Economy' http://www.iht.com/iht/today/thu/fpage.html, by David E. Sanger.
_____(1998, 20 November) 'The U.S.-Japan Alliance Needs Urgent Repair' http://www.iht.com/iht/today/fri/ed/edplate.html, by Tom Plate.

Bibliography 349

_____(1998, 20 November) 'Economic Turmoil Means Lower Expectations for APEC' http://www.iht.com/iht/today/fri/fin.html, by Michael Richardson.

_____(1998, 20 November) 'Japan, Not China, Is America's Chief Partner in Northeast Asia' http://www.iht.com/iht/today/fri/ed/edseg.html, by Gerald Segal.

_____(1998, 17 December) 'Answering Asian Critics, Japan Unveils New Loans' http://www.iht.com/iht/today/thu/fpage/pacif.html, by Michael Richardson.

_____(1999, 11 January) 'In Europe, Japan Seeks an Economic Counterweight' http://www.iht.com/iht/today/mon/ed/edpfaff.html, by William Pfaff.

_____(1999, 15 January) 'China Holds a Weak Hand, but U.S. Won't Raise Stakes' http://www.iht.com/iht/today/fri/ed/edmir.html, by Jonathan Mirsky.

_____(1999, 16 January) 'A Self-Confident Europe is America's Best Partner' http://www.iht.com/iht/today/sat/ed/edmoisi.html, by Dominique Moisi.

_____(1999, 19 January) 'Globalisation: A Century's Perspective' http://www.iht.com/today/tue/fin/think.html, by Reginald Dale.

_____(1999, 22 January) 'Asians Warn of Trade Wars' http://www.iht/today/fri/fin/taipei.html, by Thomas Crampton.

_____(1999, 22 January) 'U.S. Plan Threaten Moscow Arms Pact: Clinton Decision on Missile Defense Could Doom Start-2, Russians Say', from the *Washington Post Service* http://www.iht.com/iht/today/fri/fpage/miss.html, by David Hoffman.

_____(1999, 23 January) 'U.S. and EU on the Brink of Trade War: Dispute Over Imports of Bananas Worsens', http://www.iht.com/iht/today/sat/fin/trade.html

_____(1999, 23 January) 'Russia Rejects Any Changes in ABM Treaty' in the *Washington Post Service* http://www.iht.com/iht/today/sat/in/moscow.html, by Daniel Williams.

_____(1999, 30 January) 'Global Financial Reform: A Clash of Perception' http://www.iht.com/iht/today/sat/fpage/davos.html, by J. Gage, and A. Friedman.

_____(1999, 1 February) 'A Proposal to Monitor World Finance System' http://www.iht.com/iht/today/mon/fpage/davos.html, by Alan Friedman, and J. Gage.

_____(1999, 1 February) 'The Global Economy Needs New Rules and Institutions' http://www.iht.com/iht/today/mon/ed/edghosh.html, by Bimal Ghosh.

_____(1999, 1 February) 'No Dissent, if You Please' http://www.iht.com/iht/today/mon/fpage/alps.html, by Anne Swardson.

_____(1999, 4 February) 'A Yankee Currency for Argentina?' http://www.iht.com/iht/today/thu/fin/peso.html, by Anthony Faiola.

_____(1999, 4 February) 'U.S. Talks of "Crisis" in Japan Trade' http://www.iht.com/iht/today/thu/fin/trade.html, by Alan Friedman.

_____(1999, 4 February) 'The Trans-Atlantic Partnership Needs Tending' http://www.iht.com/iht/today/thu/edflora.html, by Flora Lewis.

_____(1999, 9 February) 'U.S. Trade Leadership on the Mend' http://www.iht.com/iht/today/tue/fin/think.2.html, by Reginald Dale.

_____(1999, 11 February) 'Missiles Facing Taiwan Challenges U.S. Goal', from the *Washington Post Service* http://www.iht.com/iht/today/thu/fpage/taiwan.2.html, by John Pomfret.

_____(1999, 16 February) 'After the Cold War, U.S. Foreign Policy Is Out of Control' http://www.iht.com/iht/today/tue/ed/edpfaff.html by William Pfaff.

_____(1999, 24 February) 'Or America and Europe Could Gang Up on Japan' http://www.iht.com/iht/today/wed/ed/edlevine.html, by Robert A. Levine.

_____ (1999, 8 March) 'Russia Matters, So "Strategic Patience" Isn't Enough', from *The Washington Post* http://www.iht.com/iht/today/mon/ed/edfred.html, by Fred Hiatt.

_____ (1999, 2 April) 'NATO Has to Prevail, Introducing Ground Troops if Necessary' from *Newsweek* http://www.iht.com/iht/today/fri/ed/edkiss.2.html, by Henry Kissinger.

_____ (1999, 2 April) 'U.S.-China Tensions Are Bad News for the Economies of Asia' http://www.iht.com/iht/today/fri/ed/ed/eddupont.2.html, by Alan Dupont.

_____ (1999, 2 April) 'Bailing Out Moscow' from *The Washington Post* http://www.iht.com/iht/today/fri/ed/edrussia.2.html

_____ (1999, 13 April) 'Why the Generation of 1968 Chose to Go to War' from *Newsweek* http://www.iht.com/iht/today/tue/ed/edblair.2.html, by Tony Blair.

_____ (1999, 13 April) 'Yugoslavia Seeks Union with Russia and Belarus' from *The Washington Post Service* http://www.iht.com/iht/today/tue/fpage/union.2.html, by Michael Dobbs.

_____ (1999, 14 April) 'U.S. and Russia "Narrow Differences" on a Common Approach to Kosovo', from the *Washington Post Service* http://www.iht.com/iht/today/wed/in/diplo.2.html, by William Drozdiak.

_____ (1999, 14 April) 'For Asians, Battle for Kosovo Is Distant' http://www.iht.com/iht/today/wed/fpage/react.2.html, by J. Vinocur, and M. Richardson.

_____ (1999, 16 April) 'World Bank Has New Loan for Russia' http://www.iht.com/iht/today/fri/fin/ruble.2.html.

_____ (1999, 16 April) 'Balkan Conflict Erodes U.S.-EU Trust' http://www.iht.com/iht/today/fri/fin/think.2.html, by Reginald Dale.

_____ (1999, 22 April) 'Stronger U.S.-Japanese Ties Can Bolster Asian Stability' http://www.iht.com/iht/today/thu/ed/ednishi.html, by Masashi Nishihara.

_____ (1999, 8 May) 'China's Softer NATO Line' from the *Washington Post Service* http://www.iht.com/iht/today/sat/in/react.2.html, by John Pomfret.

_____ (1999, 10 May) 'For a Trade Deal to Open the WTO Door to China' http://www.iht.com/iht/today/mon/ed/edbar.2.html, by Charlene Barshefsky.

_____ (1999, 10 May) 'For the Alliance, Suspect Friends' http://www.iht.com/iht/today/mon/fpage/assess.2.html, by John Vinocur.

_____ (1999, 13 May) 'The Democracy Club' from the *Washington Post Service* http://www.iht.com/iht/today/thu/ed/eddemoc.2.html.

_____ (1999, 15-16 May) 'U.S. More Optimistic China Will Reopen WTO Talks', from the *Washington Post Service*, p. 9, by Paul Blustein.

_____ (1999, 15-16 May) 'Insecure China is Stoking Xenophobic Nationalism', by David Shambaugh.

_____ (1999, 17 May) 'Impeachment Is Off, but Yeltsin's Troubles Worsen' pp. 1, 7, by Celestine Bohlen.

_____ (1999, 17 May) 'Zhu's Tears Over Embassy Bombing Whet the Interest of China-Watchers', p. 4, by Seth Faison.

_____ (1999, 17 May) 'U.S. Finds "Pervasive" China Spying', by W. Pincus and V. Loeb.

_____ (1999, 18 May) 'Bombing Highlights China's Weakness', from the *Washington Post Service*, by John Pomfret.

_____ (1999, 18 May) 'It's Official: All of the World Is Entitled to Democracy', by Nancy Rubin.

_____ (1999, 19 May) 'Adjusting Our Vision of China' from *The New York Times*, by Thomas L. Friedman, p. 6.

_____(1999, 19 May) 'Clinton Refuses to Rule out Ground Troops in Yugoslavia', from the *New York Times Services*, by Kathrine Q. Seelye, pp. 1, 4.
_____(1999, 19 May) 'Globally, Air War Gives U.S. the Name of a Bully' from the *Washington Post Service*, by Anthony Faiola, pp. 1, 5.
_____(1999, 1 June) 'Congress Accused on Nuclear Security' from the *Washington Post Service* for http://www.iht.com/iht/today/tue/in/spy.2.html, by Helen Dewar.
_____(1999, 2 June) ' America must show Russia the Way on Disarmament', from the *Washington Post Service* http://www.iht.com/iht/today/wed/ed/edkrepon.2.html, by Michael Krepon.
_____(1999, 3 June) 'Squabbling Traders Can Be Dangerous' http://www.iht.com/iht/today/wed/ed/edroy.2.html, by Roy Denman.
_____(1999, 3 June) 'Chinese Layoffs Putting Millions on the Streets' http://www.iht.com/iht/today/thu/fpage/chicon.2.html, by Philip Segal.
_____(1999, 5 June) 'A Disappearing World of Western Military Supremacy', from *The Washington Post* http://www.iht.com/iht/today/sat/ed/edpaul.2.html, by Paul Bracken.
_____(1999, 5 June) 'Bush Backs Clinton on China Trade' http://www.iht.com/iht/today/sat/fpage/pacif.2.html, from *Reuters News*.
_____(1999, 10 June) 'Stop Dozing and Give Us a Globalisation Summit' http://www.iht.com/iht/today/thu/ed/edsewell.2.html, by J.W. Sewell and M.H.C. McDowell.
_____(1999, 12 June) 'China Maps Changes In Defense Strategy' from *The Washington Post Service* http://www.iht.com/iht/today/sat/fpage/beijing.2.html, by John Pomfret.
_____(1999, 18 June) 'Watch for VIP Casualties of the Chinese Embassy Bombing', by Tom Plate.
_____(1999, 16 July) 'In the Balkans, a Hard New Challenge for Europe' http://www.iht.com/iht/today/fri/ed/edflora.2.html, by Flora Lewis.
_____(1999, 16 July) 'Europe: Toward a New Economic Culture for Culture Creation' http://www.iht.com/iht/today/fri/ed/edscaglia.2.html, by Silvio Scaglia.
_____(1999, 19 July) 'High Time for Realism in U.S.-Chinese Relations', from *The Washington Post* http://www.iht.com/iht/today/mon/ed/edhoag.html, by Jim Hoagland.
_____(1999, 20 July) 'Beware of Pre-emptive Aggression' http://www.iht.com/iht/today/tue/ed/edclark.html, by Gregory Clark.
_____(1999, 31 July) 'Yeltsin Calls For Warning of NATO Ties' http://www.iht.com/iht/today/sat/fpage/yeltsin.2.html, from *Reuters News*.
_____(1999, 4 August) 'If America's Wealth Bubble Bursts' from the *Los Angeles Times Service* http://www.iht.com/iht/today/wed/ed/edkevin.2.html, by Kevin Phillips.
_____(1999, 6 August) 'Memo to the Pentagon: The Costly Cold War is Over', from the *Los Angeles Times Service* http://www.iht.com/iht/today/fri/ed/edkorb.2.html, by Lawrence Korb.
_____(1999, 9 August) 'Tone Down This Rhetoric About the "Indispensable Nation"' from *The Washington Post* http://www.iht.com/iht/today/mon/ed/edgeneva.2.html, by Geneva Overholser.
_____(1999, 10 August) 'Look Who's Snooping on Europe', from the *Los Angeles Times Service* http://www.iht.com/iht/today/tue/ed/edsimon.2.html, by Simon Davies.
_____(1999, 12 August) 'The European Union Needs to Change Its Spots', http://www.iht.com/iht/today/thu/ed/edmilada.html, by Milada Anna Vachudova.

_____(1999, 16 September) 'Japanese Find Plenty Wrong With Once-Successful System' http://www.iht.com/iht/today/thu/fpage/wrong.2.html, by Don Kirk.
_____(1999, 3 December) 'U.S. Seeks to Convince Allies on Missile Shield' http://www.iht.com/iht/today/fri/fpage/nato.2.html, by William Drozdiak.
_____(1999, 18 December) 'Defense Dreams That Create Mistrust Among Allies', from *The Washington Post* http://www.iht.com/iht/today/sat/ed/edjulie.2.html, by Jim Hoagland.
_____(2000, 15 January) 'Russia Acts To Toughen Its Security Framework', from the *Washington Post Service* http://www.iht.com/iht/today/sat/fpage/policy.2.html, by David Hoffman.
_____(2000, 17 January) 'The New Capitalism Is About Turning Culture Into Commerce' from the *Los Angeles Times* http://www.iht.com/iht/today/mon/ed/edrifkin.2.html, by Jeremy Rifkin.
_____(2000, 18 January) 'Globalisation Debate Getting Focused' http://www.iht.com/iht/today/tue/fin/think.2.html, by Reginald Dale.
_____(2000, 18 January) 'New Twist From Clinton: Now It's One China, Two Policies' http://www.iht.com/iht/today/tue/ed/edkagan.html, by Robert Kagan.
_____(2000, 19 January) 'Japan Advised to Open Up to the World' http://www.iht.com/iht/today/wed/fpage/tokyo.2.html.
_____(2000, 19 January) 'As an Alternative to the EU, Britain Should Join NAFTA' http://www.iht.com/iht/today/wed/ed/edroger.2.html, by Roger Helmer.
_____(2000, 19 January) 'Defining New Goals for Diplomacy of the 21st Century' http://www.iht.com/iht/today/wed/ed/ed/ramesh.2.html, by Ramesh Thaker and Steve Lee.
_____(2000, 20 January) 'U.S.-Japan Talks Fail' http://www.iht.com/iht/today/thu/fin/mas.2.html.
_____(2000, 20 January) 'Missile Fails in Setback For U.S. Defense', from the *New York Times Service* http://www.iht.com/iht/today/thu/fpage/shield.2.html, by Elizabeth Becker.
_____(2000, 20 January) 'U.S. Unfazed by Russia Plan', from *Reuters News* http://www.iht.com/iht/today/thu/in/russia.2.html.
_____(2000, 20 January) 'Strong U.S. Economy Helps All but the Poorest', from the *New York Times Service* http://www.iht.com/iht/today/wed/fpage/fed.2.html, by Richard W. Stevenson.
_____(2000, 20 January) 'Steps for Asia-Pacific Security' http://www.iht.com/iht/today/thu/ed/edtony.html, by Tony Tan.
_____(2000, 21 January) 'Is the New Strongman in Moscow a Nationalist or an Imperialist?' http://www.iht.com/iht/today/fri/ed/edmax.2.html, by Max Jakobson.
_____(2000, 21 January) 'In Russia's Future, Hard Work Instead of Tempest', from *The Washington Post* http://www.iht.com/iht/today/fri/ed/edmasha.2.html, by Masha Lipman.
_____(2000, 21 January) 'Foreign Policy? Blame Both Congress and the White House' http://www.iht.com/iht/today/fri/ed/edstan.2.html, by Stanley R. Sloan.
_____(2000, 21 January) 'In Japan, a Nation of Conformists Is Urged to Break Out of the Mould', from the *Washington Post Service*. http://www.iht.com/iht/today/fri/in/tokyo.2.html, by Doug Struck.
_____(2000, 22 January) 'G-7 Talks: An Us-Versus-Them Event' from the *New York Times Service* http://www.iht.com/iht/today/sat/fpage/seven.2.html, by Stephanie Strom.

_____(2000, 22 January) 'The Coming Trade Battle Between Japan and the U.S.' from the *Los Angeles Times* http://www.iht.com/iht/today/sat/ed/edplate.2.html, by Tom Plate.
_____(2000, 22 January) 'The "Rape of Nanking" Swirls Again in Japan', from the *New York Times Service* http://www.iht.com/iht/today/sat/fpage/tokyo.2.html, by Howard W. French.

The Irish Times

_____(1999, 12 April) 'NATO has to explain its motives and aims' http://www.ireland.com/newspaper/opinion/1999/0412/opt2.html.

The Japan Times

_____(1999, 3 July) 'Stealth democracy sneaks up on the world', from the *Los Angeles Times*, p. 18, by Zephirin Diabre.
_____(1999, 3 July) 'Dealing with China, Russia: More nuance, less naivete' from the *International Herald Tribune*, p. 18, by William Pfaff.
_____(1999, 5 July) 'U.S. feels Kosovo repercussions in Asia', p. 21, by B. Kennedy and P. Giarra.
_____(1999, 7 July) 'Crisis manual details aid to U.S. troops', pp. 1-2.
_____(1999, 7 July) 'Toward a debate on national security', p. 20.
_____(1999, 8 July) 'A visit to the dark side of the 'Buy American' campaign', from *The Washington Post*, p.19, by Dana Frank.
_____(1999, 9 July) 'Asian ambition, self-confidence barely dented by the crisis', p. 21, by Brad Glosserman.
_____(1999, 10 July) 'Tokyo, Beijing move forward', pp. 1, 3.
_____(1999, 10 July) 'Obuchi, Zhu shake hands on WTO pact', pp. 1, 12.
_____(1999, 10 July) 'Chinese paper prints stark reminder of war', p.3.
_____(1999, 13 July) 'Taiwan scraps "one China" policy', p. 1.
_____(1999, 13 July) 'Break deadlock on base issues', p. 18, by Keizo Nabeshima.
_____(1999, 14 July) 'U.S. restates "one-China" policy despite Taiwan move to reject it', p. 4.
_____(1999, 16 July) 'China's fury raises real threat of force', from *Reuters*, p. 21, by Benjamin Kang Lim.
_____(1999, 16 July) 'U.S. scrambles to gauge impact of Lee's bombshell', from *Reuters*, p. 21, by Christopher Wilson.
_____(1999, 17 July) 'Europe dissents from U.S. on gene-altered food', from the *Los Angeles Times*, p. 6.
_____(1999, 17 July) 'Money rules U.S. politics', from the *International Herald Tribune*, p. 20, by William Pfaff.
_____(1999, 17 July) 'Cross-strait relations at risk', p. 21, by Ralph Cossa.
_____(1999, 17 July) 'How globalisation can undercut security', p. 21, by Edward Neilan.
_____(1999, 19 July) 'The key to Japan's future', p. 20, by Hajime Karatsu.
_____(1999, 19 July) 'Japan's defense dependency', p. 21, by Doug Bandow.
_____(1999, 20 July) 'Jiang refuses to rule out use of force over Taiwan', pp. 1, 4.
_____(1999, 22 July) 'Two Chinas, but only one solution', from *The Washington Post*, p. 19, by David Shambaugh.
_____(1999, 23 July) 'Flag, anthem march on', pp. 1, 3.

_____(1999, 23 July) 'True leadership in the 21st century', p. 20.
_____(1999, 24 July) 'U.S. flirts with post-Cold War hysteria', from the *Los Angeles Times*, p. 21, by Tom Plate.
_____(1999, 24 July) 'The Pendulum swings again', p. 21, by Gregory Clark.
_____(1999, 25 July) 'China accuses U.S. Congress of acting to support Taiwan', p. 4.
_____(1999, 26 July) 'U.S., Russia urged to reduce warheads', pp. 1-2.
_____(1999, 26 July) 'China warns U.S. not to back Taiwan', p. 1.
_____(1999, 26 July) 'Date set for pact on defense cooperation details', p.1.
_____(1999, 27 July) 'Asia-based forum expresses concern for Korean security', p.1.
_____(1999, 27 July) 'Albright, Ivanov hope hotline will help restore ties', p. 1.
_____(1999, 27 July) 'A force that will make or break us', p. 16.
_____(1999, 27 July) 'Japan's role in peacekeeping', p. 16, by Keizo Nabeshima.
_____(1999, 28 July) 'Pyongyang missile posturing an extreme concern: report', pp.1, 2.
_____(1999, 28 July) 'Japan, Seoul, U.S. warn North Korea against missile test', pp. 1, 4.
_____(1999, 28 July) 'Komura, Albright try to ease Taiwan tension', pp. 1, 4.
_____(1999, 28 July) 'China agrees to join nuclear-arms free zone', p. 1.
_____(1999, 28 July) 'No ABM pact impasse: Moscow', p. 1.
_____(1999, 28 July) 'Asia undermining global security: Akashi', p. 2.
_____(1999, 28 July) Seoul again urges Japan voting rights', p. 2.
_____(1999, 28 July) 'A message for Mr. Cohen', p. 21, by Ronald Morse.
_____(1999, 29 July) 'U.S. to share tracking data if Pyongyang launches missiles', pp.1, 3.
_____(1999, 29 July) 'Russia, U.S. agree to begin negotiations on START III', p. 1.
_____(1999, 29 July) 'U.S. House set to cut foreign aid', p.13.
_____(1999, 29 July) 'U.S. "new economy" now looks like an old-fashion bubble', p. 19, by Brad Glosserman.
_____(1999, 29 July) 'NATO pushing Russia down path of Weimar Germany', from the *Los Angeles Times*, p. 19, by Helga Graham.
_____(1999, 30 July) 'Taiwan denies recent missile, A-bomb development program', p. 4.
_____(1999, 31 July) 'Asian instability may force Japan's nuclear hand', p. 2, by Eric Johnston.
_____(1999, 1 August) 'A Survival strategy for Japan', p. 21, by Ichiro Ozawa.
_____(1999, 2 August) 'Welcome to the grave new world of terror', from *The Washington Post*, p. 19, by William Cohen.
_____(1999, 2 August) 'Taiwan tires of the status quo', p. 19, by Robert A. Manning.
_____(1999, 3 August) 'Mending relations with Russia', p. 16.
_____(1999, 5 August) 'Woe to the U.S. if the bubble bursts', from the *Los Angeles Times*, p. 19, by Kevin Philips.
_____(1999, 5 August) 'Taipei's policies sow distrust rather than real solutions', from the *Los Angeles Times*, p. 19, by Brent Scowcroft.
_____(1999, 6 August) 'Japan, South Korea hold first-ever joint naval drill', pp.1, 3, by Toshi Maeda.
_____(1999, 11 August) 'Looking back at the cultural Cold War', from the *International Herald Tribune*, p. 19, by William Pfaff.
_____(1999, 14 August) 'Growing scrutiny of Japan's defense policy', p. 21, by Brad Glosserman.
_____(1999, 15 August) 'U.S. Taiwan policy is courting disaster', p. 21, by Gregory Clark.
_____(1999, 15 August) 'End the "one China" fiction', p. 21, by Alexander K. Young.

_____(1999, 17 August) 'Europe's new defense burden', from the *Los Angeles Times*, p. 18, by Robert E. Hunter.
_____(1999, 21 August) 'Asian recovery challenges U.S. economy', p. 11.
_____(1999, 26 August) 'Kyrgyz meet urges "multipolar world"', pp. 1, 6.
_____(1999, 27 August) 'Cash is keyword in Sino-Russian ties', from *The Strait Times*, p. 21, by Michael Walker.
_____(1999, 27 August) 'A China-Taiwan showdown would pit size against sophistication', p. 21, by Martin Sieff.
_____(1999, 28 August) 'Japan's new strategic shift', from the *Los Angeles Times*, p. 19, by Jim Mann.
_____(1999, 30 August) 'Who can withstand "McDonaldization"?', p. 17, by Becky Boykin.

The Los Angeles Times

_____(1992, 11 March) 'Does the United States Want to Lead Through Intimidation?' p. B7, by William Pfaff.
_____(1998, 12 July) 'New Grand Strategy Uses Lofty and Material Desires', Opinion Section M2, by G. John Ikenberry.
_____(1999, 1 June) 'China's Military Power Lags U.S. Despite Spy Fears' http://www.latimes.com/home/news/politics/chinaspy/lat_china990601.html, by Maggie Farley.
_____(1999, 22 August) 'Fewer Nations are Making War' http://www.latimes.com/home/news/opinion/t000074880.html, by E.J. Wilson III, and R. Gurr.

The New York Times

_____(1992, 8 March) 'U.S. Strategy Plans Calls for Insuring no Rivals. Develop: A One-Superpower world', pp. A1, A14, by Patrick E. Tyler.
_____(1992, 9 March) 'They're Kidding', p. A15, by Leslie H. Gelb.
_____(1992, 24 May) 'Pentagon Drops Goal of Blocking New Superpowers', pp. A2, A14., by Patrick E. Tyler.
_____(1995, 25 October) 'Meagre Progress as China Leader and Clinton Meet', by Alison Mitchell.
_____(1999, 18 May) 'Fury in China: Distrust of U.S. Goals Still Deep', by Erik Eckholm.
_____(1999, 25 May) 'Text of House Committee Report' http://www.nytimes.com/library/world/asia/052699china-spy-report.html.
_____(1999, 1 August) 'Empty Isles Are Signs Japan's Sun Might Dim', http://www.nytimes.com/library/world/asia/080199japan-decline.html, by Nicholas D. Kristof.
_____(1999, 23 August) 'Three Rules for a Superpower to Live By' http://www.nytimes.com/yr/mo/day/oped/23harr.html, by Owen Harries.
_____(1999, 25 August) 'Nimble Security Juggler: Sandy Berger, the Strategist and Politician' http://www.nytimes.com/library/politics/082599berger-profile.html, by R.W. Apple Jr.

Newsweek

_____(1999, 28 June) 'Getting Serious?' pp. 30-2, by Richard Ernsberger Jr.
_____(2000, 21 January) 'U.S. and Them: A Target Too Good to Resist', pp. 20-9, by Michael Elliott.

Telegraph/Sunday Telegraph

_____(1999, 11 April) 'Why Nato is splitting up', p. 31, by Edward Luttwak.

The Times/Sunday Times

_____(1999, 11 April) 'Enter the Bear', pp. 13-18.

The Sydney Morning Herald

_____(1998, 31 December) 'E-Day Eye: Support from Asia will be key barometer of currency's future' http://www.smh.com.au/news/9812/31/world/world4.html, by Mark Magnier.
_____(1999, 6 January) 'Love for Euro not as deep as markets suggest' http://www.smh.com.au/news/9901/06/business/business3.html, by Geoff Kitney.

The Wall Street Journal

_____(1988, 12 May) 'America's "Decline": Illusion and Reality', p. 22, by Charles Wolf.
_____(1998, 26 October) 'Asia's Puzzle' http://interactive.wsj.com/public.../articles/sb90915607474354500.htm, by G. Pierre Goad.

The Washington Post

_____(1992, 10 April) 'The Anti-Superpower Fallacy', p. A27.
_____(1998, 12 June) 'What Stalled Russian Reform', p. A27, by Leon Aron.
_____(1998, 12 June) 'Self-abasement Of Foreign Policy', p. A27, by Charles Krauthammer.
_____(1998, 17 June) 'The World's Economic Curse', p. A27, by Robert J. Samuelson.
_____(1998, 23 June) 'If Not U.S. Hegemony, Then What?' p. A17, by Robert Kagan.
_____(1998, 25 June) 'Endangering Russia', p. A23, by Robert Novak.
_____(1998, 25 June) 'The Proliferation of Nations' p. A23, by George F. Will.
_____(1998, 8 July) 'Cyberwar: A New Weapon Awaits a Set of Rules', pp. A1, A10, by Bradley Graham.
_____(1999, 1 June) 'China: U.S. Nuclear Secrets "Easily Found" on the Internet', p. 10, by Michael Laris.
_____(1999, 2 June) 'It's Time to Rethink a Muddled China Policy', by Fred Hiatt.
_____(1999, 5 June) 'Chinese Embrace Evolution', p. A1.
_____(1999, 11 June) 'China Rethinks Security After NATO Attack', p. A16.
_____(1999, 12 June) 'Russia Laments Lost Post', p. A1, by David Hoffman.

Academic Manuscripts, Dissertations and Unpublished Papers

Davis, M. (1994) *The Cultural Project of Neoliberalism in Chile: Hegemony or Cultural Imperialism?* (paper presented to The International Studies Association 35th Annual Conference, Washington, DC. for the Panel: 'Revisiting Cultural Imperialism' 1 April).

der Pijl, Kees Van (1999) *America Over Europe. Atlantic Unity and Rivalry From Gorbachev to Kosovo* (paper presented at the British International Studies Association 24th Annual Conference, Manchester, 20-22 December).

Duong, Thanh (1996) *The International Political Economy of U.S. Hegemony after the Cold War: A Synthesis of U.S. Hegemony and International Balance of Power*, MA dissertation, University of Newcastle, Newcastle-upon-Tyne.

Garcia, David (1999) *The Relations Between the European Union and the U.S.: The Implementation problem of the New Transatlantic Agenda First Objective of the Action Plan*, 1997-1999 NATO Fellowship.

Ikenberry, G. John (1997) *Liberal Hegemony: The Logic and Future of America's Post-war Order* (paper prepared for a conference on 'International Order in the 21st Century'. McGill University, Montreal, Canada, 16-18 May.

Mastanduno, Michael (1998) *Models, Markets and Power: Reflections on Asia-Pacific Political Economy at the End of the 1990s* (paper prepared at the International Conference on 'Global Visions Towards the Next Millennium: Modern Civilisation and Beyond', The Graduate Institute of Peace Studies, Kyung Hee University).

Nye, Jr. Joseph S. (1990b) *American Strategy after the Cold War* (Seoul: The Fourth Series of the Inchon Memorial Lecture, Korea University).

Pigman, G.A. (1992) *Hegemony and Free Trade Policy: Britain 1846-1914 and U.S.A. 1944-1990* (PhD thesis, University of Oxford).

Ralph, Jason G. (1999) *'High Stakes' and 'low intensity democracy/liberalism'. Understanding America's Policy of Promoting Democracy*, (paper presented at the British International Studies Association 24th Annual Conference, Manchester, 20-22 December).

Smith, Steve (1999) *U.S. Democracy Promotion: Theoretical Reflections.* (paper presented at the British International Studies Association 24th Annual Conference, Manchester, 20-22 December).

Wienner, J. (1994) *Making Rules for Agriculture in the Uruguay Round of the GATT: A Study in International Leadership* (PhD thesis, University of Kent at Canterbury).

Interviews and Informal Conversations

The author conducted interviews with the following:

Erik Peterson (Director), The Center for Strategic and International Studies (CSIS).
Henry Nau, The George Washington University.
G. John Ikenberry (Director at the Brookings Institute), University of Pennsylvania.
Hans Binnendijk (Director), National Defense University,. Washington, D.C.

During my research in the USA, I was fortunate to discuss in formal and informal conversations with junior staff and internees (whose names I will keep anonymous) from the U.S. White House, the U.S. Treasury Department, the U.S. State Department, the Pentagon, the U.S. Justice Department, and various other U.S. Senators' and Congressmen internees; internees in the IMF and the World Bank.

In my research in China, I was fortunate to talk to various people from nearly all walks of life, from the villagers to the city dwellers, the office managers to the public officials (I have reserved their names in strict confidence).

Finally, I have had many informal conversations and debates with Chinese in the PRC (and including those in America, Britain, Hong Kong, Indonesia, Malaysia, Singapore, Taiwan, and Vietnam), Americans, Bengalis, Brazilians, British, Canadians, Estonian, French, Germans, Greeks, Indians, Iranians, Italians, Japanese, Kazakhs, Koreans (South), Mexicans, Nigerians, Pakistanis, Portuguese, Russians, Spanish, Turks, Vietnamese, Zimbabweans, friends, colleagues and associates about the nature of 'world politics'.

Index

Afghanistan 76, 81, 120, 170, 179, 235, 267
Agnew, J. 80, 254
Akaha, T. 5, 34, 234, 252
Akaneya, Tatsuo 229-30, 234, 241, 245
Albright, M. 14, 46, 143, 219
Aldred, K. 35, 42, 129, 131, 134, 140, 205, 207, 253, 279, 286
Amin, S. 106-107
Annan, Kofi 222
Anti-Ballistic Missile treaty (ABM treaty) 147-8, 151, 174
Arrighi, G. 74
Aruga, Tadashi 245, 251
Asean Free Trade Area (AFTA) 124, 271
Asher, David 231, 234
Ashida, Hitoshi 229-30
Ashwin S. 133-4
Asia Pacific Economic Cooperation (APEC) 86, 100, 124, 188, 247, 251, 253, 271, 283
Aslund, A. 135
Association of South East Asia Nations (ASEAN) 7, 171, 250, 253
Atlantic Council 86, 116, 215, 220

Baker, James 83
Balance of power, 4-5, 10, 12, 32, 66, 89-92, 94-7, 99-101, 103-9, 111, 120, 123-5, 175-6, 178, 182, 208, 211, 244, 246, 257, 275, 277, 279, 281-2
Baldwin, D. 23, 27
Bank of International Settlements (BIS) 73, 86
Barraclough, G. 63, 161, 204
the Basle Accord 240
Baylis, J. 6, 19, 26, 40-41, 52, 277, 283
Bennett, P. 21-2
Berger, P.L. 28, 194
Berger, Samuel 7-8
Bergner, J. 263
Bhagwati, J. 83
Binnendijk, H. 97-9, 101, 185-7
Bismarck, Otto von 5, 123-4,

Blair, Tony 218
Booth, K. 110, 142, 151, 170-1, 189, 202, 211, 233
Bosnia(n) 32, 97, 142, 211, 213, 219, 221, 267, 270
Braudel, F. 161, 284
Bretton Woods 11, 19, 64, 71-2, 74, 79, 82, 88, 210, 238, 256
Britain 5, 9, 44, 58, 62-3, 66, 72, 78, 99, 101, 124, 160, 178, 187, 190, 199, 202, 207-8, 210, 218, 225, 240, 251, 254, 260, 267, 286
British hegemony 64, 66, 120
Brogan, H. 14, 71, 89
Brown, M. 91, 115, 175, 258
Brown, Ron 191
Brzezinski, Z. 6, 65, 72, 98-9, 110, 112, 115, 120-2, 132-3, 142, 148, 151-3, 156, 164, 176, 199, 213, 216, 244, 246, 249, 259
Buchanan, P. 7, 172, 192
Bull, H. 10, 107, 147
Bush, George 7, 9, 93, 190, 260, 263, 266, 276
business civilisation 59, 84

Cafruny, A. 79
Calleo, D. 64, 66, 82,
Calvocoressi, P. 164, 166
capitalism 3, 24, 77, 79, 106, 111, 130, 132-3, 135-6, 148, 165-6, 168, 170, 177-9, 193, 198, 201-2, 204, 216, 232-3, 237-40, 261, 268-9, 275-87
capitalist(s) *see* capitalism
Carr, E.H. 8, 20-1, 31-2, 42-5, 113, 240
Central Intelligence Agency (CIA) 135, 143, 180, 182, 242, 268
Cerny, P. 5, 77
Chace, J. 5, 169, 250
Chan, S. 71
Chase-Dunn, C. 67, 175
Chechnya 142, 145, 185, 215
Cheney, D. 9, 151, 257, 263, 266

359

China 4, 10, 12, 32, 44, 59, 63, 65, 67, 75-6, 81, 89, 93-7, 101-2, 108-9, 113, 115-17, 121-6, 135, 143, 145-8, 153, 158-99, 204, 208, 212, 220, 223-4, 227-8, 237, 244-9, 251-3, 257-9, 263, 266-8, 270-1, 279-83, 286
   'Greater China' 183
   'open door' policy 163
   People's Republic of China (PRC) 22, 80, 158-99, 211, 244, 247-8
   Republic of China (Taiwan) 32, 80, 97, 122, 124, 148, 160, 169, 173-4, 180-1, 184-7, 190, 193, 197, 237, 244, 247, 251-2, 267, 270-1
   Tiananmen Square massacre 159, 170, 177
Ching, Frank 222
Chomsky, Noam 140, 203, 257
Christopher, Warren 9, 85, 112, 121, 154, 217, 264
Churchill, Winston 96, 98, 166-7
civil society 59, 86, 107, 109, 119-20, 215, 269
Clash of Civilisations 12-13, 110, 158, 172, 192
Clinton, William. 7, 9, 85-6, 97, 126, 146, 149, 186, 188, 192, 243, 246-7, 253, 256, 259-61, 263, 265, 270, 276, 285-6
   Clinton Doctrine 192
Cohen, W. 121, 146-7, 180, 183, 216, 218, 222, 228, 257, 266
Cold War 4-5, 7, 9-10, 19, 27, 40, 65, 67, 71-3, 81, 85, 89, 92-3, 96, 101, 110-11, 120, 123, 129-31, 139, 144, 149-51, 153-4, 156, 158-60, 168-72, 176, 180, 183, 193, 200-1, 205-6, 210-14, 216, 223, 226, 238, 241, 245, 256, 258-60, 262, 264-6, 268, 270-1, 276, 278-9, 282, 285-7
Concert of Europe 66, 204
consensus 9, 11, 59, 67, 74, 84, 88, 98, 214, 222, 260, 266
Corbridge, S. 80, 254
Council of Mutual Economic Assistance (CMEA) 134
counter-intelligence services *see* CIA
Cox, M. 7-8, 11, 18, 22, 26, 42, 82, 85-6, 144, 147-8, 150, 162, 164, 170, 173-4, 189-90, 194, 231, 233, 235, 243, 262-3, 276
Cox, R. 5, 21, 27, 51, 59-61, 268, 275
Cuba 97, 123-4, 165, 207, 268

debt crisis 77
Delors, Jacques 93, 205
democracy promotion 9, 85, 249
democratic peace 85, 99, 107, 109, 115, 117, 126, 146-7, 154-5, 191-2, 196, 201, 210, 225-7, 253, 258-9, 261-2, 265, 270, 285, 287
Deng Xiao Ping 190-2, 196-7
der Pijl, K.V. 6, 86, 203
Desert Storm 173, 181
Diamond, L. 115, 258
Doyle, M.W. 3, 10, 21, 23, 40-1, 45, 51, 90, 103-5, 258
Drifte, R. 19, 31, 34, 46, 60, 231-2, 236-7, 240, 248, 251-5
Duchene, F. 203
Dyer, H.C. 26

East Asian economic crisis 137, 237, 264
Elffers, J. 34-5, 98, 110, 129, 158
Emmot, B. 237, 251-2
engagement and enlargement 9, 12, 96, 105, 115, 121, 148, 192, 228, 250, 253, 259, 261, 264
European Union (EU) 7-8, 12, 19, 22, 59, 67, 73, 78, 85, 87, 93-5, 97, 100, 102, 113, 115-18, 122-4, 145-6, 154-6, 158-9, 175, 192, 200-27, 248, 252, 255, 257-8, 264, 267, 270-1, 279-81, 286
   Common Agricultural Policy (CAP) 212
   European Coal and Steel Community (ECSC) 202
   Joint Condominium 201-2, 215, 220
   Western European Union (WEU) 100, 210, 216, 218-9

Farer, T.J. 203, 223
financial crisis 81, 133, 188, 250, 253, 263
Fordism 84
Foucault, M. 19, 52

France 9, 44, 58, 66, 72, 76, 93, 123-4, 144-6, 178, 200, 202-3, 207-8, 210-11, 218-19 225, 260
Frank, A.G. 67, 74, 134, 161, 172, 175, 204, 284
Freeman, C.W. 17, 24, 34-7, 43, 46, 75, 112-13, 119
Frieden, J.A. 77, 284
Friedman, F. 92
Friedman, T. 4, 96, 240, 258
Fukayama, F. 10
Funabashi, Yoichi 238, 246-7, 260

Gaddis, J.L. 144, 165, 201
Gallicchio, M.S. 231
Garcia, D. 217
Garten, J. 7, 264
General Agreement on Tariffs and Trade (GATT) *see* WTO
geopolitics 6, 75, 93, 144, 154, 165, 171, 184, 198, 235, 257, 259
Germany 4, 8-9, 66, 72, 74, 78, 85, 87, 90, 94, 98-102, 120, 123-4, 139-40, 144-6, 160, 178, 187, 200-2, 207, 210-11, 218, 223, 225,230, 260, 263, 266
  Prussia 66, 149
Gertz, B. 171-3, 192
Gill, S. 6, 61, 74, 84, 86, 236, 268
Gills, B.K. 6, 8, 21, 44, 46, 54, 67, 86, 107, 134, 166, 175, 195, 204, 212, 229, 236, 247, 269
Gilpin, R. 10, 34, 37, 47-8, 57, 64-5, 72, 77-8, 87, 91-2, 94, 109, 122, 154, 175, 179, 187, 238, 258, 262-3, 276, 278
Globalisation 5-8, 10-13, 22, 36-7, 67, 88, 106-7, 109, 111, 115, 120, 126, 160, 188, 199, 203, 210, 221-2, 225-9, 232, 243, 249-50, 254-6, 259-60, 263, 268, 270, 275-87
Gold exchange standard 77, 210
Goldstein, J. 10
Gompert D.C. 216, 218
Gorbachev, Mikhail 81, 129-30, 142, 198, 276
Gowan, P. 8, 31-2, 80, 83, 249-50, 264
Gramsci, A. 5, 53, 59, 61, 278, 280
  Gramscian 38, 53, 59-62, 71, 78, 84, 277

neo-Gramscian 53, 57, 59, 62, 64, 203, 268
war of position 56, 60, 268
Gray, John 158, 193, 284
Greene, R. 34-5, 98, 110, 129, 158
Groom, A.J.R. 21-3, 27
Group of 3 (G3) 86
Group of 7/8 (G7/8) 7, 86, 124, 130, 156, 251, 253, 271, 282-3
The *Guanzi* 24, 32-4, 41

Haass, Richard 32, 265-6
Hapsburg empire 63
Harris, Stuart 161, 166, 182-4, 191
Hegemony 4-6, 8, 10-11, 13-14, 50, 57-67, 71-2, 74, 77-9, 82, 84-8, 89-92, 94, 97, 103-7, 120, 122, 125, 146, 200-1, 203-4, 206, 208, 211-13, 218, 226, 228, 230, 237, 266, 270, 275-87
  challenge 8, 10-12, 19, 22, 65, 76, 79, 83, 86-8, 91, 95, 97, 108-9, 121-3, 158-60, 172, 174, 178-80, 183, 187, 192, 195-6, 200, 202, 204, 206-9, 212, 214, 219-21, 226, 228, 231, 234-7, 239, 245, 248, 250, 256-9, 263, 266, 270, 276, 278-81, 285, 287
  counter-hegemony 86, 91, 93, 107, 109, 264, 281
  cycle of hegemony 10
  decline 19, 31, 71, 75-8, 80, 82, 84-5, 87, 159, 172, 175, 189, 196, 235, 261-4, 267
  declinist-renewal debate 19, 75, 87, 176
  free-riding 65, 74, 93, 234
  global hegemony 5, 14, 22, 66, 85, 87, 125, 226, 237, 257, 268, 270, 279
  great power(s) 4-5, 7-8, 10, 12, 19, 49, 57, 62-3, 67, 71, 73, 75, 77-8, 86-7, 89-95, 99-101, 108-15, 118-26, 140, 147, 154, 159, 161, 166, 171, 173, 175, 183-4, 187, 191, 203, 228, 232, 243-4, 248-9, 263, 270, 272, 276-83
  hegemonic war 4, 8, 11, 87, 175, 179-80, 210, 276, 280
  hegemonic stability theory (HST) 64-6, 72, 278
  leadership 57, 62, 67, 72, 75, 100, 122, 207-8, 218, 222, 237, 249, 263-7

Herzog, Roman 158, 172
Higgot, R. 22
Hind, M. 211
Hippler, J. 85
Hirst, P. 6, 240
Hitler, A. 96, 168, 201
Hobbes, T. 112,
    Hobbesian 100, 104, 178, 191
Hobsbawm, E. 7
Holstein, W.J. 233
Hu Jintao 192
Hudson, M. 3, 5, 72, 74, 201, 203-4
human rights 85, 97, 121, 141-2, 154, 162, 173-4, 189, 191, 193, 197, 201, 207-8, 221-3, 226-7, 253, 264
Huntington, S. 5, 12-13, 78, 91, 94-5, 110, 123, 172, 192, 204, 206, 220-1, 265, 282
Hurst III, C. 230, 240
Hussein, Saddam 253, 260

The *I Ching* 20, 41
Ikenberry, G.J. 18, 23-4, 72, 107, 125, 204, 282
imperial 3-5, 51, 72, 80, 86-7, 89, 101, 103, 124, 161-3, 167, 170, 177-9, 183, 201-2, 207, 209, 216, 225, 232, 236, 254, 256, 262, 285
    imperialism see imperial
    imperialist see imperial
    neo-imperialism 155
India 93-4, 102, 113, 122, 147, 168, 171, 188, 199, 258, 271, 281
Indonesia(n) 45, 93, 113, 190
intelligence services *see* CIA
International Monetary Fund (IMF) 9, 72-4, 86, 95, 100, 124, 136, 140, 152, 155, 188, 215, 230, 249-53, 271, 282
Iran 76, 81, 93, 97, 120, 123, 268
    Revolution 81
Iraq 8, 32, 81, 85, 97, 106, 122-4, 143, 151, 174, 211, 267
Islam 20, 63, 81, 113, 161, 172, 213
    Islamic fundamentalism 76, 81, 120, 123, 146, 213
Israel 79, 97, 124, 155, 268, 270-1
    Yom Kippur War 79

Japan 4-5, 7-9, 11-12, 19, 22, 44, 46-7, 59, 67, 72-6, 78-80, 83, 85-7, 90, 93-5, 98, 102, 108-9, 113, 115-18, 122-5, 147-8, 151, 158-9, 162-4, 167, 170-2, 174-5, 178, 184, 186-7, 192-3, 196, 199, 201, 204, 206, 208, 210, 228-58, 260, 262-4, 266, 270-1, 276, 279-81, 286
    Commodore Perry 255
    Diplomatic Bluebook 228, 247-8, 252-3, 255
    'Greater Asia Co-prosperity Sphere' 248
    Liberal Democratic Party (LDP) 245
    militarisation 80
    Ministry of Finance 233, 238
    Ministry of International Trade and Industry (MITI) 233
    Okinawa 246-7
    Overseas Development Aid (ODA) 253-4
    Peace Constitution 229
    recession 83, 238, 241, 256
    U.S.-Japan security alliance 86, 228, 239, 244-5
Jervis, R. 4, 89, 265
Jiang Zemin 174, 191, 198
Joffe, J 5, 96, 98, 121, 123-4, 204
Johnson, Chalmer 180, 232-3, 246-7
Johnson, Lyndon 169
Johnston, D. 134, 171
Judt, T. 202

Kant, Immanuel 3, 17, 103-6, 260-1
    Kantian 9, 50, 104-6, 145, 261
Kaplan, R. 196, 269
Kapstein, E. 19, 41, 237, 240, 249, 278, 281-2, 285
Kautilya 41
Kennan, G. 13, 72-3, 110-11, 144, 165, 201
Kennedy, John F. 9, 169, 172, 200, 257
Kennedy, P. 45, 78, 80, 87, 91, 94, 110, 175, 179, 204, 225, 231, 235
Keohane, R. 23, 27, 34, 41, 49, 57-9, 64, 72-3, 78, 208, 267, 276
Khalizad, Z.M. 100
Khrushchev, N. 168
Kindleberger, C. 57, 64-5, 72, 77, 258

Kissinger, H. 4, 34-5, 47, 51, 76, 89, 91, 93, 95, 112, 123, 158, 169, 172, 175, 204, 208, 217, 278, 282
Klintworth, Gary 161, 166, 184, 191
Kohl, H. 47
Kolko, G. 5, 72, 74
Kolko, J. 5, 72, 74
Korea 95, 148, 165-7, 193, 236-7, 250-2
  North 123-4, 147, 184, 186, 244, 247, 268
  South 80, 124, 155, 165, 186, 230, 241, 250, 252-3, 268, 270-1
Kosovo 107, 133, 138, 142-3, 211, 213, 215, 219, 221-5, 248
Krasner, S. 64, 72-3, 113, 208
Krauthammer, C. 4, 80, 89
Krugman, P. 232-3
Kuhn, T. 18, 21, 25-7
Kurth, J. 94, 100-101

Lai, D. 245, 248, 255
Lake, D.A. 77, 229, 284
Langdon, F. 5, 34, 234, 252
Lao Tzu 40, 43, 47-8, 53-4
Larrabee, F.S. 216, 218
Lawson, Fred 79
Layne, C. 4, 85, 89, 92-5, 100, 171, 178, 208, 282
League of Nations 73, 103
Lefever, E. 89, 91, 242
Liberal(ism) 6, 8, 10, 13-14, 23, 25, 27-30, 40, 47-9, 58, 60, 64-5, 71-2, 77-8, 82, 84, 90, 100, 103-9, 112, 114, 129-30, 132-3, 136-9, 143, 146, 148, 152-3, 155-6, 160, 175, 189-90, 193-4, 196, 198, 201, 203, 208, 216, 226, 232, 238-9, 245, 251, 256-7, 259, 261, 264, 275, 277-9, 283, 285-6
  laissez faire 43, 47, 132-3, 177, 198, 269
  liberal democracy 11, 61, 74, 101, 105, 107, 109, 115, 159-61, 178, 187, 190, 192, 216, 229, 251, 259, 261, 264, 269, 281, 283, 286
  neo-classical 28, 42, 47-8
  neo-liberalism 28, 30, 47, 57, 64, 138, 277
Libya 97, 124
Light, M. 21-2, 27

Lilley, J. 194
long cycle 62-3
Lundestad, Geir 154, 175, 187, 202-3
Lugar, R. 149
Luttwak, E. 263, 265

MacArthur, D. 229-30
McGrew, A. 266
Machiavelli, N. 11, 27, 31-2, 35, 41, 46, 49, 113, 262, 281, 284
Mackinder, H. 72, 120
  rim-heartland theory 72, 120
McRae, H. 110
Mahatir Mohammed 83, 93
Mann, M. 37, 39, 211
Mao Zedong 43, 51, 162, 164-5, 167-70, 177, 184, 188, 190-2, 196-8
Marsh, D. 24-5
Marshall Plan 73, 154, 156, 202, 223, 238
Marxism 23, 25, 28-30, 40, 50-1, 54-5, 71, 78, 84, 90, 103, 105-8, 131, 168, 196, 198, 275, 277, 279
  bourgeois(ie) 3, 51, 53, 106, 167, 169, 177, 167, 201
  class 11, 44-5, 51-4, 84, 86, 106-7, 109, 134, 161-2, 168, 197, 201, 233-4, 236, 242, 252
  Communist Manifesto 3, 50, 53, 106
  division of labour 84, 249
  Engels, Friedrich 3, 50, 53, 106, 167
  Marx, Karl 3, 18, 22, 24, 50, 52-3, 106, 167-8, 285
  neo-Marxism 30
  proletariat 51-3, 106, 167-8, 198
Mastanduno, M. 8, 233, 237, 240, 249-50, 264, 278-9, 281-2, 285
Mearsheimer, J. 89, 260, 282-3
Mercantilism 47, 50, 231-2, 258
  mercantilist *see* mercantilism
  neo-mercantilism 65, 77, 279
Mercosur 207
Metternich 47
Mexico 7, 77, 271
  debt crisis 77
Mikoyan, S.A. 141-2, 148-50, 153-5
Miller, D. 257
Minxin Pei 195, 197
Miyamoto Musashi 28, 36
Mochizuki, M. 246

Modelski, G. 10, 62-3, 276
Mongol empire 4, 63, 89
  Mongolia 168-9, 187, 196
Monnet, J. 203, 225
Morgenthau, H. 34, 37, 40, 163
Munro, R.H. 172, 192
Muravchik, J. 4, 25, 80, 89
Murphy, R. Taggart 230, 233, 235, 238
Murphy W.J. 179, 194

Nagatomi, Y. 252
Naisbitt, John 254
Napoleon 58, 63, 101, 103, 157-8
National Endowment for Democracy (NED) 268
nationalism 51, 77, 140-1, 154-5, 157, 166, 171, 193, 196, 202, 262, 264-5, 269
Nau, H. 5, 10, 97, 99, 112, 216, 258, 268
The Netherlands 62-3, 200, 207
New International Economic Order 79
New Strategic Concept 214, 221-2
New Transatlantic Agenda (NTA) 220-1
New World Order 4, 9, 85, 93, 175, 205
Nicholson, M. 21-2
Nixon, Richard 76-7, 79-80, 169-70, 204, 240
Non-Aligned Movement 93
Norris, C. 19
North American Free Trade Area (NAFTA) 7, 100, 124, 271
North Atlantic Treaty Organisation (NATO) 9-10, 65, 73-5, 86, 100, 116, 120, 124, 133, 138, 141-7, 149, 151, 154-6, 173, 180-1, 184, 192, 200-3, 209-10, 212-15, 217-19, 221-4, 226-7, 248, 271, 282
NSC-68 165
Nye, J. 5, 34, 53, 60, 63-4, 66, 72, 74, 79-80, 87, 112, 122, 181-2, 208, 245-7, 256, 267-8

Obuchi, Keizo 241
Oksenberg, M. 166
Organisation for Economic Cooperation and Development (OECD) 9, 74, 86, 124, 126, 220, 251, 257, 259, 271, 279, 282

Organisation for Security Cooperation in Europe (OSCE) 100, 145, 147, 222
Organisation of Petroleum Exporting Countries (OPEC) 77, 79-80
Ottoman empire 63, 102, 124
Oye, K. 77
Ozawa, Ochiro 245, 248, 255

Paine, Thomas 287
Pakistan 113, 122
Pentagon 9, 24, 85, 121, 246, 262, 267
Perry, W. 145
Perot, R. 7
Pfaff, William 209
Pipes, R. 142, 152
Polanyi, K. 31, 134, 269
Popper, K. 22, 27, 30, 33
Portugal 62-3, 200, 206-7
Poulantzas, N. 50, 52-3
Power 3-8, 11-13, 19, 22-3, 25-8, 31-67, 72-3, 75, 78-9, 83, 85-109, 111-13, 118-21, 125-6, 130-1, 135-8, 140, 142-5, 148-9, 151-6, 159-61, 163, 166, 169-73, 175-6, 178-9, 185-9, 191-2, 194-9, 201-12, 215-9, 225, 227, 239-40, 246, 248-9, 252-3, 257-72, 275-87
  authority 6-7, 17, 34, 44-5, 194, 196, 223, 241
  cultural 35, 37, 59, 61-2, 84, 95, 113, 119, 124, 158, 173, 188, 190, 199, 208, 223-4, 243, 251
  economic 7, 10, 35, 37, 39, 44-5, 49, 52, 56, 76, 78, 82, 85, 89-90, 92-5, 98, 100-1, 103, 106, 108-9, 171, 194, 199, 204-5, 228-9, 231, 234, 234-5, 237, 244, 250, 277-8, 280, 282
  hard power 44, 61
  influence 31, 45, 60, 64-5, 73, 79-81, 83-5, 88, 94-5, 98, 101, 114, 125, 163, 166-8, 183, 194, 197, 200-2, 205, 207-8, 211-14, 227, 255, 267, 282
  knowledge 38-9, 48, 52-3, 119
  legitimacy 43-5, 74, 88, 105, 125, 187, 224
  military 4, 8, 35, 37-9, 42-5, 47-8, 52, 79, 89-90, 92, 94, 97-100, 108-9, 140, 148, 162, 174, 180-4, 205, 224, 262, 277, 279
  perception 34-7, 53, 159, 190, 193

Index

political 37, 39, 44-5, 48, 52, 91-2, 98, 101, 107, 205, 231, 261, 265, 267, 275
power politics 8-10, 47, 81, 91, 100, 111-12, 114, 125, 194, 205, 210, 245, 258, 260, 262
relational 11-12, 37-9, 112, 114
religion 51, 56
security 39, 48-9, 264, 267-8
soft power 53, 60-1, 84, 208, 224, 229, 252
structural 39
technology 38, 259, 280, 282-4
will 35, 39, 43, 56
world 59, 62, 71, 78, 84, 89-90, 92-3, 95, 103, 244, 278, 287
Primakov, Yevgeny 131, 133, 138-9, 141
Pyle, K.B. 251

Rapkin, D.P. 236
Reagan, Ronald 14, 77, 81-2, 240, 256
Realism 10, 25, 27-30, 32-3, 40-47, 50-1, 90, 108, 112-13, 153, 265, 275, 277
  first image 42-5
  neo-realism 10, 28, 30, 42, 78, 104, 171, 173, 175-6, 178-9, 192, 208-9, 211, 275-7
  realist 10, 23, 28, 32-3, 40-43, 45, 47, 49-51, 55-6, 71, 74, 78-82, 98, 103-4, 106, 110-11, 145, 150, 166, 170, 176, 178, 265, 276, 278, 282
  second image 45-7
  realpolitic 170, 260, 268, 270
regimes 5-6, 9, 40, 49-50, 60-1, 64, 72-4, 78, 86, 97, 107, 109, 123-5, 129, 132, 136, 184, 188, 196, 205, 208, 216, 224, 228, 236, 239-40, 243, 251, 257, 264, 268-71, 277-8, 282-3, 286
Reich, R. 7
Roberts, B. 237
Roberts J.M. 63, 204
Robinson, W. 11, 74, 86, 252, 268
Rome 4, 44, 89, 124
Roosevelt, F.D. 89, 163, 167
Rosecrance, R. 77
Rothkopf, D. 12
Roy, Denny 164, 186, 189, 193
Rubin, Robert 24
Ruggie, J. 4, 73, 89
Ruhe, Volker 145-6

Rupert, M. 84
Rusk, Dean 164
Russett, B. 5, 61, 91, 115, 258
Russia *see* USSR

Saeki Keishi 240
Sawa, Takamitsu 241
Schumann, R. 225
Schwartz, B. 85, 282
Scott, J. 4, 90, 96-7, 119, 159, 258, 264, 266, 268
Serbia 32, 97, 122, 142-4, 151
Shambaugh, D. 93, 173, 175
Shigeto Tsuru 230
Singer, M. 94, 221
Smith, Adam 24, 48-9, 265
Smith, Dan 203, 213, 217-18
Smith, M. 35, 42, 129, 131, 134, 140, 205-7, 279, 286
Smith, Steve. 7, 11, 19, 26, 40-1, 47, 52, 193, 269, 283, 277
Soros, G 130, 133, 136-7
sovereignty 49, 91, 160, 167, 169, 174, 184, 189, 201, 209-10, 213, 222-4, 228-9, 243, 248, 256, 267
Soviet Union *see* USSR
Spykman N.J. 72, 99, 120
Staar, R. 142, 153
Stalin, J. 82, 164, 167-8
Steel, R. 4-5, 72, 125
Stoker, G. 24-5
Strange, S. 5-6, 17, 21, 34, 36-9, 41, 59, 82, 84, 205, 208, 212, 234-5, 238, 268
Strategic Arms Limitation Talks (SALT) 76
the Structural Impediment Initiative (SII) 240
Sun Tzu 36, 41
Sun Yat-Sen 23

Takashi Inoguchi 236
Talbot, Strobe 149-50
Tanzi, Vito 135
Taylorism 74, 84
Theatre Missile Defense (TMD) 248
Thompson, E.P. 27
Thompson, G. 6, 240
Thucycides 41, 58, 63
Thurow, L. 7, 92, 263-4

Tocqueville, Alexis de 269
Tong, K.W. 235, 251, 254
Townson, D. 239
Trade Act Section 301 83
transnational class 6, 11, 57, 84, 86, 268, 277-8
Trilateral Commission 74, 86, 237, 251, 268
Turkey 213
Tyler, P. 9, 85, 121, 217
Tyson, L. 7, 266

Union of Soviet Socialist Republics (USSR) 11, 51, 72-6, 82, 86, 88, 107, 131, 150, 159, 165-6, 168, 204
   Russia 9-10, 12, 22, 44, 59, 63, 66-7, 85, 93-7, 101, 108-9, 113-15, 120, 122-6, 129-59, 166-7, 169, 171-3, 175, 177-8, 185-6, 199-200, 208, 210-15, 221, 223, 225, 227-8, 234-5, 237, 244-5, 248, 257-8, 260, 263, 270-1, 279-81, 283, 286
   collapse 8, 11-12, 42, 51, 71, 75, 81, 87, 107, 111, 121, 125, 129, 141, 170, 199-200, 228, 230-1, 239, 251, 276, 281
   corruption 135-40, 156
   Orthodox Church 136
   Partnership for Peace (PfP) 141, 143, 155
   Soviet Union 3, 5, 8, 10, 14, 18, 42, 51, 55, 65-6, 71, 74-6, 81-2, 85, 87, 90, 129, 131, 139, 141, 157-8, 160, 164-73, 179-80, 199-201, 206, 209, 230-1, 234-5, 251, 264, 266, 269, 271, 276, 279-80, 287
Unipolar 4-5, 9, 89-93, 268, 282
UK *see* Britain
United Nations (UN) 9, 73-4, 143, 145, 163, 167, 174, 182, 185, 208, 222-4, 227, 248, 253-5, 267, 282
   UN Charter Article 18 223

Vadney, T.E. 166
Valladao, A. 4, 88-9, 258
Vasquez, J.A. 21-2, 24, 41, 47, 276
Vershbow, Alexander 214, 221
Vietnam 19, 71, 75-6, 81, 94-5, 135, 139-40, 162, 165-6, 169-70, 183-4, 190, 197, 251, 268
Vogel, E. 231

Wall Street 24, 136
Wallace, William 218
Wallerstein, I. 10, 59, 74, 78, 175, 179, 276
Walt, S. 96, 105, 122, 147
Waltz, K. 4, 10, 21-3, 25, 33, 42-3, 45, 89, 91, 95, 107, 175, 232, 243, 250, 277, 282
Warsaw Pact 8, 66, 169
Watanabe, Koji 237
Weede, E. 131
Weinner, J. 67
Wendt, A. 26-7, 31, 36, 40, 114, 119-20
Western European Union (WEU) *see* European Union (EU)
Whitcomb, R. 119
Wight, M. 8, 10, 20, 58, 64, 66, 90, 103-4
Wildavsky, A. 94, 221
Wilson, Woodrow 103, 145, 260, 265
Wolferen, K.V. 233
Wolfers, A. 23
Wolfowitz, P. 237
World Bank (WB) 72-4, 95, 100, 124, 130, 140, 143, 152, 182, 188, 215, 230, 249-52, 271, 282
World Trade Organisation (WTO) 9, 72, 83, 86, 100, 124, 174, 188-9, 230, 251, 255, 271, 282-3

Yavlinsky, G. 131, 133, 136-7, 141, 143,
Yeltsin, Boris 93, 130-1, 137-9, 213

Zeilonka, Jan 218
Zhou Enlai 51, 158
Zoellick, R.E 170, 190
zone of peace and prosperity 85, 122, 126, 156-7, 201, 210, 224, 226-7, 250, 257-9, 261, 264, 270
Zyuganov, G. 131